College Reading
and Study Skills

College Reading
and Study Skills

Kathleen T. McWhorter
Niagara County Community College

Eighth Edition

Longman

New York San Francisco Boston
London Toronto Sydney Tokyo Singapore Madrid
Mexico City Munich Paris Cape Town Hong Kong Montreal

Senior Acquisitions Editor: Steven Rigolosi
Developmental Editor: Leslie Taggart
Marketing Manager: Melanie Goulet
Supplements Editor: Donna Campion
Full Service Production Manager: Denise Phillip
Project Coordination, Text Design, and Electronic Page Makeup:
    Thompson Steele, Inc.
Cover Design Manager: John Callahan
Cover Designer: Kay Petronio
Photo Researcher: PhotoSearch, Inc.
Senior Manufacturing Buyer: Dennis Para
Printer and Binder: Courier Corp.
Cover Printer: Phoenix Color Corp.

For permission to use copyrighted material, grateful acknowledgment is made to the copyright holders on pp. 449–456, which are hereby made part of this copyright page.

Library of Congress Cataloging-in-Publication Data

McWhorter, Kathleen T.
    College reading and study skills / Kathleen T. McWhorter.--8th ed.
      p. cm.
    Includes bibliographical references and index.
    ISBN 0-321-04956-X
    1. Reading (Higher education) 2. Study skills. I. Title.

  LB2395.3 .M386 2001
  428.4'071'l--dc21   00-029641

Please visit our website at http://www.awlonline.com/mcwhorter

ISBN 0-321-04956-X

4 5 6 7 8 9 10—CRK—03 02

For Thomas, Brette, Terrence,
Quinne, and Zayne

BRIEF CONTENTS

CONTENTS

CHAPTER 4 TAKING NOTES IN CLASS 64

PART TWO Reading Textbooks and Assignments 83

CHAPTER 5 ACTIVE READING STRATEGIES 83

CHAPTER 6 UNDERSTANDING PARAGRAPHS 107

CHAPTER 7 FOLLOWING THOUGHT PATTERNS 134

CHAPTER 8 READING GRAPHICS AND TECHNICAL WRITING 167

PART **SEVEN** Thematic Readings 375

PREFACE

Beginning college students require a foundation in reading and study skills that will enable them to handle college-level work. *College Reading and Study Skills,* Eighth Edition, presents the basic techniques for college success, including time management, analysis of learning style, active reading, and note taking. The text offers strategies for strengthening literal and critical comprehension, improving vocabulary skills, and developing reading flexibility. Students also discover methods for reading and learning from textbook assignments and for taking exams. The reading and study skills I have chosen to present are those most vital to students' success in college. Each unit teaches skills that are immediately usable—all have clear and direct application to students' course work.

More than 30 years of teaching reading and study courses in two- and four-year colleges have demonstrated to me the need for a text that covers both reading and study skills and provides for both instruction and application. This book was written to meet those needs.

Reading and study skills are inseparable. A student must develop skill in each area in order to handle college work successfully. With this goal in mind, I have tried to provide complete coverage of both skills throughout and to show their relationship and interdependency. In doing so, my emphasis has been on direct instruction. My central aim is to teach reading and study through a how-to approach.

Because I believe that critical thinking and reading skills are essential to college success, these skills are emphasized in the text. I introduce students to critical thinking skills by explaining Bloom's hierarchy of cognitive skills early and then showing their academic application throughout the text. *College Reading and Study Skills* offers direct skill instruction on critical reading and includes key topics such as making inferences, asking critical questions, and analyzing arguments.

CONTENT OVERVIEW

The units of the text are interchangeable, which enables the instructor to adapt the material to a variety of instructional sequences.

Success Workshops Appearing both at the beginning and the end of the text, the Success Workshops use a fun, lively, and accessible format to provide students with skills that will directly and immediately contribute to their college success. Topics include acclimation to the college environment, textbook parts and learning aids, academic image, class participation, concentration, collaborative learning, stress management, oral presentations, and learning with computers.

Part One: Building a Foundation for College Success This section provides an introduction to the college experience and presents skills, habits, and attitudes that contribute to college success. Topics include time management and goal setting, learning style, teaching style, active learning, levels of thinking, and the demands and expectations of college. Chapter 3 in this section establishes the theoretical framework of the text by discussing the learning and memory processes and the principles on which many of the skills presented throughout the text are based. Because lecture note taking is integral to college success, it is included in this section, as well.

Part Two: Reading Textbooks and Assignments This section focuses on the development of reading skills for textbook usage. Topics include monitoring concentration, prereading and predicting, defining purposes for reading, and comprehension assessment. Paragraph structure is explained and recognition of thought patterns introduced. Strategies for reading graphics and technical material are presented. Reading electronic sources, including how to adapt reading strategies for online sources, is discussed in depth. Critical thinking and reading skills are emphasized. Students are guided in making inferences, asking critical questions, and analyzing arguments.

Part Three: Developing Your Vocabulary This section teaches students how to expand their vocabulary and use references sources, including the dictionary and the thesaurus. Students are shown methods of learning specialized vocabulary and discover systems for vocabulary learning. Vocabulary skills include contextual aids and structural analysis.

Part Four: Studying Textbooks These chapters teach skills that enable students to learn from text: how to highlight and mark a textbook; how to organize a system of study for various academic disciplines; and how to organize information using outlining, summarizing, and mapping. Methods of learning through writing—paraphrasing, self-testing, and keeping a learning journal—are described.

Part Five: Studying for Exams The purpose of this section is to help students prepare for and take exams. Organizing for study and review, identifying what to study, and review methods are emphasized. Students learn specific strategies for taking objective tests, standardized tests, and essay exams, as well as for controlling test anxiety.

Part Six: Reading Flexibility Rate improvement is the focus of this section. Students learn to adjust their rate to suit their purpose, desired level of comprehension, and the nature of the material they are reading. Specifically, students learn methods for skimming and scanning.

Part Seven: Thematic Readings This section contains 15 readings, grouped according to five themes: body adornment (sociology/cultural anthropology), men's and women's communication (communication), endangered and extinct species (biology), computers and privacy (business/computer technology), and multicultural identity (humanities/literature). These readings, which represent readings that may be assigned in academic courses, provide students with an opportunity to apply skills taught throughout the text. Two activities at the end of each theme, Making Connections and World Wide Web Activity, encourage students to synthesize ideas and develop Internet search skills.

SPECIAL FEATURES

The following features enhance the text's effectiveness and directly contribute to students' success:

- **Visual Appeal**   The text recognizes that many students are visual learners and presents material visually using maps, charts, tables, and diagrams.
- **Learning Style**   The text emphasizes individual student learning style and encourages students to adapt their reading and study techniques to suit their learning characteristics, as well as the characteristics of the learning task.
- **Skill Application**   Students learn to problem-solve and explore applications through case studies of academic situations included at the end of each chapter. Students also apply chapter skills when completing the "Collaborative Learning" exercise included at the end of each chapter.
- **Metacognition**   Students are encouraged to establish their concentration, activate prior knowledge, define their purposes, and select appropriate reading strategies prior to reading. They are also shown how to strengthen their comprehension, monitor that comprehension, select what to learn, and organize information. They learn to assess the effectiveness of their learning, revise and modify their learning strategies as needed, and apply and integrate course content.
- **Writing to Learn**   The text emphasizes writing as a means of learning. Writing-to-learn strategies include paraphrasing, self-testing, outlining, summarizing, mapping, and keeping a learning journal.
- **Realistic Reading Assignments**   Exercises often include excerpts from a wide range of college texts, providing realistic examples of college textbook reading.
- **Thematic Readings**   Fifteen readings, grouped according to five themes, are contained in Part Seven. These readings provide realistic materials on which to apply skills taught in the text. They also provide students with an essential link between in-chapter practice exercises and independent application of new techniques in their own textbooks, and valuable practice in synthesizing and evaluating ideas. For instructors who wish to use a complete textbook chapter, a free supplement is available. For more details, see the description of *The Longman Textbook Reader,* below.
- **Reading as a Process**   This text emphasizes reading as a cognitive process. Applying the findings from the research areas of metacognition and prose structure analysis, students are encouraged to approach reading as an active mental process of selecting, processing, and organizing information to be learned.
- **Chapter Summaries**   The chapter summaries use an interactive question-answer format that encourages students to become more active learners.

NEW TO THE EIGHTH EDITION

The eighth edition of this text includes changes and additions that reflect the changing student population. It also takes into account current emphases and directions in research on adult learning processes, as well as research on how reading online differs from reading more traditional print materials. The primary purposes of the revision are to emphasize the growing importance of reading and evaluating electronic sources, to increase the accessibility of the text, and to make it more interactive. Specific changes include the following.

- **Success Workshops** The book opens and concludes with a set of success workshops. Using a fun, lively, and accessible format, these workshops provide students with immediately usable skills that will help them begin their semester successfully. These workshops—many of which include a visual element—provide a positive, nonthreatening introduction to the book. Topics include high-interest topics such as concentration, stress management, academic image, and class participation.

- **New Chapter on Reading Electronic Sources** This new chapter recognizes that students need to learn how to locate, read, and evaluate electronic sources. The features of a Web site are discussed, and the differences between reading electronic and print sources are emphasized. Students are shown how to develop new ways of thinking and reading when using electronic sources.

- **Chapter Focus and Purpose Questions** Each chapter opens with a question that models the question students commonly ask before beginning an assigned chapter: Why should I learn this? Following each question are several answers that establish the importance and relevance of the skills taught in the chapter.

- **Learning Experiments/Learning Principles** Each chapter begins with an interactive learning experiment designed to engage the student immediately in an activity that demonstrates a principle of learning that will help students learn the chapter content. The student begins the chapter by doing, not simply by beginning to read. For example, Chapter 5, "Active Reading Strategies," begins by asking students to draw the face of a one-dollar bill. Most students quickly discover their recall is poor. The learning principle of *intent to remember* is then introduced and related to textbook learning. Students discover that in order to learn textbook material they must establish an intent to remember, and they are encouraged to use the skills presented in the chapter to do so.

- **Thematic Readings** Part Seven of the book contains 15 readings, grouped according to five themes: body adornment, men's and women's communication, endangered and extinct species, computers and privacy, and multicultural identity. The first reading in each thematic group is a textbook excerpt. The other two readings in each group represent a wide variety of sources, including Internet sources, from which instructors from across the disciplines might draw supplementary readings. Each thematic unit is intended to simulate actual reading assignments that students might receive in academic courses. Throughout earlier portions of the book, students are referred to one or more of the thematic readings to complete an in-chapter assignment designed to apply chapter skills.

  Each thematic group concludes with "Making Connection" questions that encourage students to synthesize ideas and sources and evaluate them. A "World Wide Web Activity" is also provided that directs students to use search engines and locate and evaluate Internet sources pertinent to the theme.

THE TEACHING AND LEARNING PACKAGE

Book-Specific Ancillary Materials

- **Assessment Package/Test Bank**   An assessment package/test bank accompanies the text. It contains both content-based chapter quizzes and newly developed self-scoring mastery tests that enable students to apply skills taught in each chapter. The ten-item multiple choice quizzes provide a measure of students' knowledge of chapter content, and the mastery tests provide an assessment of students' ability to apply concepts, principles, and techniques taught in the chapter. The mastery tests simulate actual academic situations, assignments, and course materials and are designed to be self-scoring, if the instructor so desires. 0-321-04958-6

- **Instructor's Manual**   An instructor's manual gives the instructor a detailed description of the text and offers specific suggestions for classroom use. It includes a complete answer key, strategies for approaching individual chapters, a set of overhead projection materials, and suggestions for integrating the many available Longman ancillaries (including electronic ancillaries) into the classroom. 0-321-04959-4

- **Manual for Adjunct Faculty**   To assist adjunct faculty in teaching developmental courses, a *Manual for Adjunct Faculty to Accompany McWhorter Texts* is also available; it offers instructors additional strategies and techniques for teaching reading and study skills. 0-673-97667-X

- **PowerPoint Slides** A series of PowerPoint slides for each chapter can be downloaded free from the Instructor Resource section of the McWhorter Web site at **http://www.awlonline.com/mcwhorter.**

- **McWhorter Web Site**   A dedicated Web site to accompany the McWhorter reading and study skills series is available to instructors and students. This Web site includes study tips, electronically scored quizzes and tests, Internet activities and links, a bulletin board, a chat room, and more. Please visit the site at **http://www.awlonline.com/mcwhorter.**

THE LONGMAN DEVELOPMENTAL READING PACKAGE

In addition to the book-specific supplements discussed above, a series of other skills-based supplements is available for both instructors and students. All of these supplements are available either free or at greatly reduced prices.

For Additional Reading and Reference

- **The Dictionary Deal**   Two dictionaries can be shrinkwrapped with this text at a nominal fee. *The New American Webster Handy College Dictionary* Third Edition is a paperback reference text with more than 100,000 entries. *Merriam Webster's Collegiate Dictionary,* tenth edition is a hardback reference with a citation file of more than 14.5 million examples of English words drawn from actual use. For information on how to take advantage of the Dictionary Deal, contact your local Addison Wesley Longman sales consultant.

- **Penguin Quality Paperback Titles** A series of Penguin paperbacks is available at a significant discount when shrinkwrapped with this title. Some titles available are: Toni Morrison's *Beloved*, Julia Alvarez's *How the Garcia Girls Lost Their Accents*, Mark Twain's *Huckleberry Finn*, *Narrative of the Life of Frederick Douglass*, Harriet Beecher Stowe's *Uncle Tom's Cabin*, Dr. Martin Luther King, Jr.'s *Why We Can't Wait*, and plays by Shakespeare, Miller, and Albee. For a complete list of titles or more information, please contact your Addison Wesley Longman sales consultant.

- **The Longman Textbook Reader** This supplement, for use in developmental reading courses, offers five complete chapters from AWL textbooks: computer science, biology, psychology, communications, and business. Each chapter includes additional comprehension quizzes, critical thinking questions, and group activities. Available free upon adoption when packaged with *College Reading and Study Skills*.

- *The Pocket Reader,* **First Edition, and** *The Brief Pocket Reader,* **First Edition** These inexpensive volumes contain 80 or 50 brief readings respectively (1–3 pages each) on a variety of themes: writers on writing, nature, women and men, customs and habits, politics, rights and obligations, and coming of age. Also included is an alternate rhetorical table of contents. *The Pocket Reader:* 0-321-07668-0. *The Brief Pocket Reader:* 0-321-07699-9

- *Newsweek* **Alliance** Instructors may choose to shrinkwrap a 12-week subscription to *Newsweek* with any Longman text. The price of the subscription is 57 cents per issue (a total of $6.84 for the subscription). Available with the subscription is a free "Interactive Guide to *Newsweek*"—a workbook for students who are using the text. In addition, *Newsweek* provides a wide variety of instructor supplements free to teachers, including maps, Skills Builders, and weekly quizzes. Contact your local Addison Wesley Longman sales consultant for information on how to order *Newsweek* with your texts.

Electronic and Online Offerings

- **Longman Reading Road Trip Multimedia Software, Version 2.0** This innovative and exciting multimedia reading software is available either in CD-ROM format (0-321-07900-0) or as a site license. The package takes students on a tour of 15 cities and landmarks throughout the United States. Each of the 15 modules corresponds to a reading or study skill (for example, finding the main idea, understanding patterns of organization, and thinking critically). All modules contain a tour of the location, instruction and tutorial, exercises, interactive feedback, and mastery tests. This second release includes a more streamlined and flexible navigation, along with hundreds of new readings, exercises, and tests.

- *Researching Online,* **Third Edition** A perfect companion for a new age, this indispensable new supplement helps students navigate the Internet. Adapted from *Teaching Online,* the instructor's Internet guide, *Researching Online* speaks directly to students, giving them detailed, step-by-step instructions for performing electronic searches. Available free when shrinkwrapped with this text. 0-321-05802-X

- **The Longman English Pages Web Site** Both students and instructors can visit our free content-rich Web site for additional reading selections and writing exercises. From the Longman English pages, visitors can conduct a simulated Web search, learn how to write a resume and cover letter, or try their hand at poetry writing. Stop by and visit us at **http://www.awlonline .com/englishpages**.

* **The Longman Electronic Newsletter**   Twice a month during the spring and fall, instructors who have subscribed receive a free copy of the Longman Basic Skills Newsletter in their e-mailbox. Written by experienced classroom instructors, the newsletter offers teaching tips, classroom activities, book reviews, and more. To subscribe, visit the Longman Basic Skills Web Site at **http://www.awlonline.com/basicskills**, or send an e-mail to **Basic Skills@awl.com**.

For Instructors

* **Electronic Test Bank for Reading**   Available in December 2000, this electronic test bank offers more than 3,000 questions in all areas of reading, including vocabulary, main idea, supporting details, patterns of organization, language, critical thinking, analytical reasoning, inference, point of view, visual aids, and textbook reading. With this easy-to-use CD-ROM, instructors simply choose questions from the electronic test bank, then print out the completed test for distribution. 0-321-08179-X

* **CLAST Test Package, Fourth Edition**   These two 40-item objective tests evaluate students' readiness for the CLAST exams. Strategies for teaching CLAST preparedness are included. Free with any Longman English title. Reproducible sheets: 0-321-01950-4; Computerized IBM version: 0-321-01982-2; Computerized Mac version: 0-321-01983-0

* **TASP Test Package, Third Edition**   These 12 practice pre-tests and post-tests assess the same reading and writing skills covered in the TASP examination. Free with any Longman English title. Reproducible sheets: 0-321-01959-8; Computerized IBM version: 0-321-01985-7; Computerized Mac version: 0-321-01984-9

* *Teaching Online: Internet Research, Conversation, and Composition,* **Second Edition**   Ideal for instructors who have never surfed the Net, this easy-to-follow guide offers basic definitions, numerous examples, and step-by-step information about finding and using Internet sources. Free to adopters. 0-321-01957-1

* *Reading Critically: Texts, Charts, and Graphs,* Second Edition   For instructors who would like to emphasize critical thinking in their courses, this brief book (65 pages) provides additional critical thinking material to supplement coverage in the text. Free to instructors. 0-673-97365-4

ACKNOWLEDGMENTS

In preparing this edition, I appreciate the excellent ideas, suggestions, and advice provided by my reviewers:

Sheila Allen, Hartford Community College
Christine Arieta, Landmark College
Larry Browning, Baylor University
Rosann M. Cook, Purdue University, Calumet
Marvin Epstein, Montgomery County Community College
Blanche Feero, Naugatuck Valley Community–Technical College

Gwendolyn Gray, Eastern Kentucky University
Linda M. Gubbe, University of Toledo
Phyllis Guthrie, Tarleton State University
Carol Hochman, California University of Pennsylvania
Ron Kyhos, U.S. Naval Academy
Kathy L. Martin, Lewis and Clark State College
Dorothy Minkoff, The College of New Jersey
Jandy Sharpe, Patrick Henry Community College
Sharon Smallwood, Saint Petersburg Junior College
Laura B. Soldner, Northern Michigan University
Joann Walker, Central Missouri State University
Suzanne Weisar, San Jacinto College
Barbara Willig, Miami-Dade Community College

I am particularly indebted to Leslie Taggart, my developmental editor, for her creative energy and valuable advice and guidance throughout the project and to Steven Rigolosi, Senior Acquisitions Editor, for his active role in and enthusiastic support of the revision.

Kathleen T. McWhorter

STUDENT REVIEW PANEL

"Why can't all the textbooks be like this?"
—*Janaina Kfuri, student reviewer*

We are proud to introduce our Student Review Panel. We asked student reviewers to help us make *College Reading and Study Skills* an even more complete resource for your college success. Each reviewer read a portion of the manuscript and suggested ways that we could improve this book. We are grateful for their many suggestions, which we incorporated into this, our eighth edition.

After a couple of stops and starts, **Janaina Kfuri** is finishing up basic course requirements and moving into education courses that will enable her to teach elementary school. Janaina loves working with children. She explains, "There are good people and there are bad people, but kids are just kids." To avoid becoming discouraged in college, she suggests, "Keep thinking about your goals, about finishing college. . . . You don't want to be stuck with just any job." What Janaina likes best about our textbook are the learning experiments and exercises that require students to reflect upon their own ways of thinking and learning, which she believes "keeps your attention, makes it more fun, and actually makes you want to do it."

John Kerby
Tarleton State College

Janaina Kfuri
*Miami-Dade
Community College*

"[Chapter 9: 'Reading Electronic Sources'] is a good basic chapter to give students the resources to use the Internet," according to student reviewer **John Kerby.** John received his first computer as a high school graduation present and took to the technology so enthusiastically that he soon found himself working in the computer lab at college, helping others. Currently a senior and a participant in the Army ROTC program, John hopes to serve with the Army Signal Corps in the telecommunications and satellite communications areas after graduation. Eventually, he wants to use his computer and communications experience in combination with his degree in agriculture to develop high-tech equipment for increasing food production and quality.

Mindy Davis
Tarleton State College

"I like to play. I'm kind of a big kid," says **Mindy Davis**, explaining her goal to become a kindergarten teacher. The fact that her mother taught kindergarten, and that most of her relatives are teachers, is a strong influence as well. Her own experience with overcoming dyslexia, which made learning to read difficult, and with living with arthritis, which has caused her daily joint pain since starting high school, motivates Mindy's interest in working with children who are challenged by obstacles to their learning. She believes that her optimistic outlook, developed through her own experiences will inspire others—"The things that give you problems, they're the things that make you strive harder, make you stronger, and make you succeed."

"As hard as college may sometimes seem, face it as a challenge because life is a kind of training and you are learning each day," suggests **Anelise Pires**, a transfer student whose home is Brazil. Less than a year ago, Anelise came to the United States to pursue a degree in marketing, and, eventually, a masters degree in business administration. Following her own advice, she has learned English, developed a circle of supportive friends, and focused her energy on her goals. She plans to become involved in international business or possibly in marketing personal fitness products, which she believes have great potential here and in Brazil. Anelise reviewed the Reading Electronic Sources chapter for us and found the information on evaluating sources on the Internet most helpful.

Anelise Pires
*Central Missouri
State University*

Paul Howie
*Central Missouri
State University*

Paul Howie wants a career that involves working with people, but, for now, he is keeping his options open to a range of possibilities including teaching physical education, sports psychology, or the ministry. Paul describes his biggest challenge as time management—dividing his time between his studies and playing catcher for his college baseball team, one of the top twenty Division 2 teams in the country. He explains, "[As a member of a team,] I have a greater responsibility to take care of myself and my grades. I have to discipline myself to always be doing something constructive." Paul found that the "Learning Strategies Questionnaire" in Chapter 2 helped him address material from his other courses according to his own learning style. His advice, simply put: "Read as much as you can."

Kim Amos and her family are looking forward to Kim becoming the first person in the family to graduate from college. She attends school full-time and works afternoons in order to pay her own expenses. Kim plans to take a

Kim Amos
*Ann Arundel
Community College*

paralegal course after finishing her associates degree. Eventually, she would like to pursue a law degree. Kim used the seventh edition of *College Reading and Study Skills* in her first semester at college and found the skills she learned helpful as she adjusted to the reading and study demands of her other courses. We asked her to review the new Success Workshops section located at the end of this revised edition and Kim gave it high marks for its potential benefit to beginning students— especially the information about staying healthy and relaxed.

David Sierra
*Miami-Dade
Community College*

David Sierra will also be the first person in his family to graduate from college, and his family is behind him 100 percent. After reviewing some of the reading selections for us, David congratulated us for including topics that are fresh, current, and interesting to students. David's goal is to become a forensic specialist working in a crime lab. He explains that it is important to him that his work be challenging and varied from day to day. David took a wrong turn in high school and had to take courses at night school while continuing regular high school courses during the day in order to graduate. His advice: "I didn't think I was going to make it. . . . You have to want something. You have to stop and think 'I'm going to do it. It has to be done, because I'm not going to work [a minimum-wage job] for the rest of my life.' "

Yuvette Murray
University of Toledo

To be self-motivated, to achieve the goals you set for yourself, **Yuvette Murray** suggests, "Envision yourself doing what you want to do in life." She envisions herself attending medical school and becoming an anesthesiologist. To keep her vision alive, Yuvette spends time in hospitals "shadowing," or watching, professionals at work. Yuvette believes in building in good habits now that will help her desired role in the future. She explains, "When I pick up a book to do my math, when I pick up a book to look at microbiology, I know that my goal is to help others, and they are depending on me to do it the right way." Need we mention that Yuvette has a straight A average? Her closing thought—"You are not judged by what you start. You are judged by what you finish."

SUCCESS
Workshops

Polish Your Academic Image

Get the Most Out of Your Textbooks

Participate in Class

Learn Everything You Can in the First Week

Strengthen Your Concentration

LEARN EVERYTHING YOU CAN IN THE FIRST WEEK

Your first week of classes and your first week on campus are some of the most important days you will ever spend.

Discovering . . .
What Your Courses Require

When you accept a new job, your manager spends time explaining your job and its responsibilities. These first few days are important because you learn what is expected and what you must do to earn your paycheck. Similarly, the first few days of a college course are equally important. You learn what your instructor expects and what you must do to earn a grade and receive credit for the course. Much of this information is often contained in a course syllabus—a handout distributed on the first day or in the first week of class. Look and listen for the answers to the following questions.

Course objectives: What are you expected to learn in the course? (Pay particular attention to these; exams measure your ability to achieve these objectives.)

Course organization: How is the course structured? What portions will be lecture, conferences, discussion, small group work, and so forth?

Exams, quizzes, and assignments: When are exams scheduled and what assignments are due? (Record dates for each in a pocket calendar.) What are the penalties for late assignments? Are make-up exams offered?

Grading system: How will your grade be determined? How much does each test and assignment count?

Class participation and attendance: What are your instructor's policies regarding attendance? Is class participation part of your grade?

Office hours: Where is your instructor's office and what hours is he or she available?

Be sure to ask your instructor if any of the above information is not provided during the first week of class.

Analyzing . . .
Your Course Syllabi

Examine the syllabus for each of your courses. Identify the course objectives and course organization. Highlight or underline the schedule for assignments, quizzes, and exams. Then immediately transfer these dates into your pocket calendar. After your first week of classes, go through your pocket calendar, noting the due dates for the next month. Begin now to plan how you will schedule your time to meet your due dates.

Learning . . .
How Your Campus Is Organized

College is a completely new environment. There is a wealth of programs, services, clubs, and activities available. During your first week you need to learn as much as you can about the college programs and services and their physical locations. Here's how to find information quickly:

▲ Read the college catalog and check the college's Web site.

▲ Read the student newspaper.

▲ Attend student orientation sessions.

▲ Get a map of the college and take your own tour.

▲ Get to know students in your classes and share information.

▲ Take a guided tour of the library or attend a library orientation workshop.

Test Yourself!

Campus Resources and Rules

Discover what you already know and what you need to know about your college by answering the following questions.

1. List at least five student activities (clubs, teams, etc.) sponsored by the college.

2. How would you request that a transcript be sent to an employer?

3. Does the college allow you to take courses on a pass/fail or satisfactory/unsatisfactory basis instead of receiving a letter grade? When and how may you elect to take this type of grade?

4. Where is the Student Health Office located?

5. What is the last day that you can withdraw from a course this semester?

6. Where would you go to change from one major to another?

7. What is meant by grade point average or quality point average and how is it computed?

8. Where on campus are computers available for student use?

9. Where would you refer a friend who needs help with a drug or alcohol problem?

10. What are the library's hours?

GET THE MOST OUT OF YOUR TEXTBOOKS

Have you ever wondered?

Question: How do textbooks differ from other information sources, such as dictionaries, reference books, and most nonfiction books?

Answer: Textbooks contain numerous features to help you learn. Most are not just page after page of print. They contain charts, tables, diagrams, and photographs, each of which is designed to help you learn.

Question: Who writes college textbooks?

Answer: Textbooks are almost always written by college teachers. (Check the title page of your textbooks; you will see the author's name and the name of his or her college or university.) College teachers know what you are likely to need help understanding. They know when you need, for example, a diagram to help you visualize a concept. Consequently, when they write textbooks, they build features into each chapter.

Analyzing . . .
The Features of Your Textbooks

Using a textbook for one of your other courses, check which of the following features it contains. Place a checkmark in front of each item that you find (not all texts will have all features). Then decide how you can use each feature to help you learn.

Feature	Value
❑ Chapter Objectives	_____
❑ Chapter Outline	_____
❑ Marginal Definitions of Key Vocabulary	_____
❑ Problems or Exercises	_____
❑ Discussion Questions	_____
❑ Review Questions	_____
❑ List of Key Terminology	_____
❑ Chapter Summary	_____
❑ Suggested Readings	_____
❑ Glossary	_____
❑ Appendix	_____

Getting an Overview . . .
The Preface or "To the Student"

The Preface is the introduction to the book; it describes its organization and use.

▲ Read the Preface or "To the Student" in one of your other textbooks.

▲ Write a list of information you learned about your textbook from reading the Preface or "To the Student." Look for the answers to these questions:
   How is the book organized?
   What topic does the book cover?
   What makes the book unique?
   What learning features are included?

▲ Of all the information in the Preface or "To the Student," what strikes you as most interesting? Why?

Textbooks have features designed to help you learn.

Examining an Outline . . .
The Table of Contents

The Preface or "To the Student" usually gives a summary of the book's organization and content. The Table of Contents provides you with a more detailed outline of the book's topics. The chapter titles are the main divisions of the book, and the titles within each chapter give the smaller subdivisions of the topics.

▲ Look at the Table of Contents of one of your textbooks for another course. Choose one chapter that you will have to read soon.

▲ Examine the titles and subtitles for that one chapter. What is the main topic of the chapter? What are the major divisions of that main topic?

▲ Think about what you already know about this topic, from talking to other people, watching the news, reading, or listening to the radio.

▲ What do you expect to learn from reading this chapter?

POLISH YOUR ACADEMIC IMAGE

Why?

Imagine that you are a teacher meeting a class of students for the first time. Look at the students in the photos below from the **teacher's point of view.** Next to each photo, write your first impressions of how each student will approach his or her course work. For example:

▲ Who do you think will participate in class?

▲ Who will turn in careful, neatly organized work?

▲ Who will be early, on time, or late for class?

▲ Who will come to your office to ask questions when they don't understand an assignment? Who will you never see there?

▲ Who will tell you the dog ate their homework?

Be prepared to discuss your reasoning.

Discovering . . .
How Do You Rate Your Academic Image?

	Always	Sometimes	Never
1. I ask and answer questions in class.	❑	❑	❑
2. I make eye contact with my instructor during class.	❑	❑	❑
3. I speak to my instructors when I see them on campus.	❑	❑	❑
4. I turn in neat, carefully done assignments.	❑	❑	❑
5. I make myself known to instructors by speaking to them before or after class.	❑	❑	❑
6. I attend all classes and explain any necessary lengthy absences to my instructors.	❑	❑	❑
7. I avoid talking with classmates while the instructor is talking.	❑	❑	❑
8. I come to class before the instructor and stay until class is dismissed.	❑	❑	❑
9. I try to stay alert and interested, and show that I am alert and interested.	❑	❑	❑
10. I sit in class with other students who demonstrate a positive academic image.	❑	❑	❑

If you answered "Sometimes" or "Never" to more than one or two questions, your academic image should be improved.

Think about It!

When you meet someone new, how do you figure out what they are like? You can't read their minds to know what they are thinking, so, normally, you try to understand others by the way they act—their behavior. It's the same for your instructors.

How can your instructor tell that you are interested in the course material? She can watch for behaviors that usually go along with interest—asking questions when you want to know more or don't understand something, answering questions that the instructor poses, paying attention to what she says, and taking notes. She can also see if you ever visit her office for help or if you seem to need extra help.

Suppose you were introduced to a new person, but she only glanced at you and mumbled a quick "hi" while continuing her conversation with someone else. You might think that she didn't want to get to know you or that she was rude. If you talk to your classmates instead of paying attention to your instructor, she will likely make the same judgment about you.

On the other hand, if you meet someone who looks you in the eye, repeats your name, shakes your hand, and spends a few minutes talking with you, you'll have quite a different impression. Which classroom behaviors from the questionnaire above are similar to this example?

You can also tell a lot about people from the pride they take in their work. If you took your car to a mechanic to fix the brakes, and the brakes worked again but made a terrible screeching noise, what judgment would you make about the mechanic's pride of work? What is a similar situation in college classes that can affect your academic image?

Think about it.

Changing . . .
Planning a More Successful Academic Image

For each response of "Sometimes" or "Never" you gave in the questionnaire above, write a new statement about how you can change your everyday behavior in class and on campus to improve your academic image. What will help your instructors think of you as a serious, hard-working, responsible student? (Remember what things look like from the front of the room!)

1. I will _____

    _____

2. I will _____

    _____

3. I will _____

    _____

4. I will _____

    _____

5. I will _____

    _____

6. I will _____

    _____

7. I will _____

    _____

Reflecting . . .
Every Week or Two, Check Again

▲ Am I communicating with my instructors?
  • Do I talk to instructors before or after class?
  • Do I take advantage of my instructor's office hours?
  • Have I explained any problems to my instructor?

▲ Am I participating in my classes?
  • Am I making eye contact with my instructor?
  • Do I ask and answer questions in class?
  • Do I show my interest and motivation in class?

▲ Am I turning in good work?
  • Are the assignments I submit neat and complete?
  • Do I always write my name, date, course, and section numbers on my assignments?
  • Do I type or word process all my papers?

▲ Am I projecting a successful academic image?

Interest

Motivation

Attention

Good work

Energy

PARTICIPATE iN CLASS

Why?

▲ You will learn more in class if you are actively involved rather than merely observing the other students interacting with the instructor.

▲ You will find it easier to concentrate and stay interested in the class if you participate.

▲ Many instructors include class participation as part of your grade.

Brainstorming . . .
What Are Your Options?

What are the different ways students can participate in class? List three to five activities.

1. _____

2. _____

3. _____

4. _____

5. _____

Discovering . . .
How Involved Are You?

	Yes	No	Sometimes
1. As I read assigned material, I record my ideas, impressions, and reactions in the margin in preparation for class.	❑	❑	❑
2. I ask questions in class.	❑	❑	❑
3. I answer questions asked by the instructor.	❑	❑	❑
4. I comment on ideas expressed by other students.	❑	❑	❑
5. Before class begins, I skim through the reading assignment to refresh my memory.	❑	❑	❑

Reflecting . . .
What Stops You?

Below are two columns. In the left column are reasons students sometimes give for not participating in class. Talk the problem over with a few classmates, and then write a piece of advice in the right column for the student.

My Problem Is . . .	Our Advice to You Is . . .
I'm afraid I don't know very much about this subject.	_____
I'm afraid I will not be able to say what I really mean.	_____
I wonder if the other students will laugh at my ideas.	_____
I'm not sure I should say anything if the instructor hasn't asked a specific question.	_____
I'm not as smart as the students who are usually participating in class.	_____

Eight Tips for Participating in Class

1. *Say something early.* Even if you are reluctant to speak before a group, try to say something early in the discussion; the longer you wait, the more difficult it becomes. Also, the longer you wait, the greater the chance that someone else will say what you were planning to say.

2. *Make your comments brief.* Make your comments brief and to the point. If your instructor feels you should say more, he or she will probably ask you to explain or elaborate further.

3. *Speak to the group.* Try to avoid getting involved in direct exchanges or disagreements with other class members. Always speak to the group, not to individuals, and be sure that your comments are related to issues of interest to the entire class.

4. *Prepare your listeners.* When you feel it is appropriate to introduce a new idea, clue your listeners that you are changing topics or introducing a new idea. You might say something like "On a related question . . ." or "Another point to consider is . . . ."

5. *Jot down ideas.* When you think of comments or ideas that you want to make during the discussion, jot them down. Then, when you get a chance to speak, you will have your notes to refer to. Notes help you organize and present your ideas in a clear and organized fashion.

6. *Be fair.* Keep an open mind. Leave personal dislikes, attitudes toward other members of the group, and your own biases and prejudices aside.

7. *Organize your remarks.* First, connect what you plan to say with what has already been said. Then state your ideas as clearly as possible. Next, develop or explain your idea.

8. *Watch for reactions.* Watch both your instructor and the other students as you speak. Their responses will show whether they understand you or need further information, whether they agree or disagree, and whether they are interested. Based on their responses, you can then decide whether you made your point effectively or whether you need to explain or defend your argument more carefully.

STRENGTHEN YOUR CONCENTRATION

Why?

Strengthening your concentration is important. No matter how intelligent you are, or what skills and talents you possess, if you can't keep your mind on the task at hand, studying will be difficult and frustrating. But it doesn't have to be.

What Is Wrong with This Picture?

Why is this student having trouble concentrating? List as many reasons as you can think of below.

_____

_____

_____

_____

_____

_____

Have You Ever Made Comments Like These?

"I just can't seem to concentrate!"

"I've got so much reading to do; I'll never be able to catch up!"

"I try to study, but nothing happens."

"I waste a lot of time just trying to get started."

If you have, consider the following suggestions for improving your study surroundings and focusing your attention.

Learning . . .
Improve Your Surroundings

Make sure you create a workable study environment.

▲ Choose a place with minimum distractions.

▲ Establish a study area with a table or desk that is yours alone for study.

▲ Control noise levels. Determine how much background noise, if any, you require and choose a place best suited to you.

▲ Eliminate distracting clutter. Get rid of photos, stacks of bills, mementos, and so forth.

▲ Have necessary supplies at your fingertips: for example, dictionaries, pens, calculator, calendar, clock.

Changing . . .
Plan a Better Study Area

Put a check mark next to each suggestion above that you could use to improve your surroundings. Plan how you will improve each area, assigning one task to do on each of the next three days. (Change the days of the week if you need to.)

On Monday, I will _____

_____

_____.

On Tuesday, I will _____

_____

_____.

On Wednesday, I will _____

_____

_____.

Learning . . .
Focus Your Attention

Once your study area is set up, use these ideas to focus your attention.

▲ Establish goals and time limits for each assignment. Deadlines will keep you motivated and create a sense of urgency in which you are less likely to daydream or become distracted.

▲ Reward yourself. Use rewards such as phoning a friend or ordering a pizza when you complete an evening of study.

▲ Use writing to keep mentally and physically active. Highlighting, outlining, or note taking will force you to keep your mind on the material you are reading.

▲ Vary your activities. Alternate between writing, reading, reviewing, and solving math problems.

▲ Keep a distractions list. As distracting thoughts enter your mind, jot them on a notepad. You may, for example, think of your mother's upcoming birthday as you're reading psychology. Writing it down will help you remember it and will eliminate the distraction.

Changing . . .
Plan Ways to Focus Your Attention

How many of the ideas above would help you focus your attention while studying? Make a plan here for trying out each idea for a week to see which you find most helpful.

This week, I will _____

_____

_____ .

In week 2, I will _____

_____

_____ .

In week 3, I will _____

_____

_____ .

In week 4, I will _____

_____

_____ .

In week 5, I will _____

_____

_____ .

Reflecting . . .
What Worked, and What Didn't?

In order to learn from what you do, you need to keep track of what worked and what did not. Of the various ideas you have tried, which were the most helpful? Which weren't as helpful? For the ideas that didn't seem to work as well, can you think of different ways to put them into action that might work better for you? Keep experimenting until you think you have made full use of all the suggestions.

Remember . . .
Focus

Figure out how to make your study area work for you.

Organize your assignments to vary your activities.

Concentrate on one task at a time.

Use writing to stay actively engaged in study.

Set goals and time limits for each assignment.

CHAPTER 1

Setting Goals and Managing Your Time

Why Learn to Set Goals and Manage Your Time?

▲ **Setting goals can keep you on track, motivate you to work, and help you measure your progress.**

▲ **Managing your time allows you to get your course work done and still have time for a social life.**

▲ **Managing your time allows you to make steady progress on long-term projects instead of being surprised at the last minute by rapidly approaching due dates.**

Learning Experiment

Form two groups, Group 1 and Group 2. Each group should follow the directions given below for their group.

Directions for Group 1

Study the photograph on the next page for one minute at the beginning of class and one minute at the end of class. The group should focus on the details of the photograph.

Directions for Group 2

Study the following photograph for two consecutive minutes at the beginning of class.

Both Groups

The members of each group should meet, separate from the other group. The group should write down as many details from the photograph as they can remember. Group members may want to do this partly in the form of a diagram or sketch of the photograph, so they can indicate the placement of the various details.

Each group then appoints someone to speak for them. The speakers from each group will tell the whole class what their group remembered about the photograph. Then the class compares each group's details with the actual photograph to find out how much was remembered.

The Results

Which group remembered more details, more accurately? Why? Most classes find that the group who studied two separate minutes (Group 1) recalled more items than those who studied for one two-minute block of time. Group 1 also had a goal in mind as they studied, whereas Group 2 did not.

Learning Principle (What This Means to You)

Several short periods of study are more effective than one large block of study. Having a goal (purpose) for studying also improves recall. This chapter will show you how to set goals and how to plan and manage your time. As you create a semester or weekly study plan, be sure to spread out your study; include three or four short periods of study and review for each of your courses.

ESTABLISHING YOUR GOALS AND PRIORITIES

One of the first steps in getting organized and succeeding in college is to set your priorities—to decide what is and what is not important to you. For most college students, finding enough time to do everything they *should* do and everything they *want* to do is nearly impossible. They face a series of conflicts over the use of their time and are forced to choose among a variety of activities. Here are a few examples:

Want to:		**Should do:**
1. Watch late movie	*vs.*	get good night's sleep
2. Go to hockey game	*vs.*	work on term paper
3. Go out with friends	*vs.*	finish psychology reading assignment

These day-to-day choices can be frustrating and can use up valuable time as you weigh the alternatives and make decisions. Often, these choices can be narrowed down to wanting to take part in an enjoyable activity even though you know you should be studying, reading, or writing a paper. At other times, there may be a conflict between two things you need to do, one for your studies and another for something else important in your life.

One of the best ways to handle these frequent conflicts is to identify your goals. Ask yourself, "What is most important to me? What activities can I afford to give up? What is least important to me when I am pressured for time?" For many students, studying is their first priority. For others with family responsibilities, caring for a child is their first priority, and attending college is next in importance.

How to Discover What Is Important

1. Make a list of the ten most joyous moments in your life. A phrase or single sentence of description is all that is needed.
2. Ask yourself, "What do most or all these moments have in common?"
3. Try to write answers to the above question by describing why the moments were important to you—what you got out of them. (Sample answers: helping others, competing or winning, creating something worthwhile, proving your self-worth, connecting with nature, and so forth.)
4. Your answers should provide a starting point for defining life goals.

Defining Goals

In defining your goals be specific and detailed. Use the following suggestions:

- Your goals should be positive (what you want) rather than negative (what you want to avoid). Don't say "I won't ever have to worry about credit card balances and bill collectors." Instead, say "I will have enough money to live comfortably."
- Your goals should be realistic. Unless you have strong evidence to believe you can do so, don't say you want to win an Olympic gold medal in swimming. Instead, say you want to become a strong, competitive swimmer.
- Your goals should be achievable. Don't say you want to earn a million dollars a year; most people don't. Set more achievable, specific goals, such as "I want to buy my own house by the time I am thirty."

- Your goal should be worth what it takes to achieve it. Becoming an astronaut or a brain surgeon takes years of training. Are you willing to spend that amount of time?
- Your goal should include a time frame. The goal "to earn a bachelor's degree in accounting," should include a date, for example.
- Don't hesitate to change your goals as your life changes. The birth of a child or the loss of a loved one may cause you to refocus your life.

You will find that clearly establishing and following your goals eliminates much worry and guilt. Instead, you'll know what is important and feel that you are on target, working steadily toward the goals you have established.

EXERCISE 1

DIRECTIONS   Write a list of five to ten goals.

_____

_____

_____

_____

_____

How a College Education Contributes to Your Goals

College can help you achieve many of your life goals. College can provide you with the self-awareness, self-confidence, knowledge, skills, practice facilities, degrees, friendships, business contacts, and so forth that can help you achieve your life goals.

Try to make the connection between college and life goals clear and explicit. College demands hard work and a stick-with-it attitude. You will be more motivated to work hard if you can see directly how that hard work will pay off in helping you fulfill your life goals.

EXERCISE 2

DIRECTIONS   For each of your life goals, explain how attending college will help you achieve that goal.

_____

_____

_____

_____

_____

ANALYZING YOUR TIME COMMITMENTS

Once you've established your priorities, the next step is to analyze your time commitments. They should reflect your priorities. For example, if playing on the volleyball team has high priority, then you must reserve time for practice and games. You can reserve enough time to study for an exam in psychology, do library research, and read biology assignments. To do this, though, you must determine how much time is available and then decide how you will use it.

	Hours per Day	Hours per Week
Sleep	_____	_____
Breakfast	_____	_____
Lunch	_____	_____
Dinner	_____	_____
Part- or full-time job	_____	_____
Time spent in class	_____	_____
Transportation time	_____	_____
Personal care (dressing, shaving, etc.)	_____	_____
Household/family responsibilities (cooking, dinner, driving mother to work, etc.)	_____	_____
Sports	_____	_____
Other priorities	_____	_____
Total committed time per week		_____

Figure 1.1
Weekly Time Commitments

Let's begin by making some rough estimates. That way, you'll see where your time goes each week. Fill in the chart shown in Figure 1.1, making reasonable estimates. After you've completed the chart, total your hours per week and write the answer in the space marked "Total committed time per week." Next, fill in that total below and complete the subtraction.

$$168 \text{ hours in one week}$$
$$- \ \underline{\hspace{2cm}} \text{ total committed time}$$
$$\underline{\hspace{2cm}} \text{ hours available}$$

Are you surprised to see how many hours per week you have left? Now answer this question: Do you have enough time available for reading and studying? As a rule of thumb, most instructors expect you to spend two hours studying for every hour spent in class. Complete the following multiplication.

Hours spent in class _____ hours $\times$ 2 = Study hours needed _____ hours

Do you have this much time available each week? If your answer to the question is no, then you are overcommitted. If you are overcommitted, ask yourself the following question: Can I drop any activity or do it in less time? Can I reduce the number of hours I work, or can another family member split some time-consuming responsibilities with me? If you are unable to reduce your committed time, talk with your advisor about taking fewer courses.

If you are overcommitted or feel you want to use your time more efficiently, now is the time to develop a weekly schedule that will help you use your available time more effectively. You are probably concerned at this point, however, that your time analysis did not take into account social and leisure activities. That omission was deliberate up to this point.

Although leisure time is essential to everyone's well-being, it should not take precedence over college work. Most students who develop and follow a time schedule for accomplishing their course work are able to devote reasonable amounts of time to leisure and social activities. They also find time to become involved with campus groups and activities—an important aspect of college life.

	Monday	Tuesday	Wednesday	Thursday	Friday	Saturday	Sunday
7:00							
8:00							
9:00	History	Psychology	History	Psychology	History		
10:00				Transportation			
11:00	Math		Math		Math		Church
12:00	Lunch	Lunch	English	Lunch	English	Lunch	Lunch
1:00			Lunch		Lunch		
2:00	Chemistry	Chemistry	Chemistry		Chemistry		
3:00	Transportation	Lab	Transportation		Transportation		
4:00							
5:00	Dinner	Transportation / Dinner	Dinner	Dinner	Dinner	Dinner	Dinner
6:00							
7:00	Work		Work		Work		Call Parents
8:00							
9:00							
10:00							
11:00							

Transportation Time

Figure 1.2
Sample Term Plan

BUILDING A TERM PLAN

A term plan lists all your unchanging commitments. These may include class hours, transportation to and from school and work, family commitments, religious obligations, part-time job hours (if they are the same each week), sleep, meals, and sports. A sample term plan is shown in Figure 1.2. You should prepare this plan only once a semester. Then make enough photocopies of this plan for each week in the semester or term. You'll use your term plan to build weekly time schedules.

	Monday	Tuesday	Wednesday	Thursday	Friday	Saturday	Sunday
7:00	Wake up				→		
8:00	English class	Englis clas	E		→	transpor-tation	transpor-tation
9:00	English class	↓			→	work	work
10:00	computer class	Study	computer class		transpor-tation		
11:00	↓				work		
12:00	transpor-tamtion	↓					
1:00	Lunch	TS clas					
2:00	Homework	↓					
3:00		transpor-tation					
4:00		Lunch					
5:00					transpor-tamtion	transpor	transpor-tation
6:00							
7:00	take a bath	Homework			Dinner		
8:00	Dinner	take a bath			Watch TV	transpor-tation	
9:00	go to sleep	go to sleep					
10:00					go to sleep	go to sleep	
11:00							

Figure 1.3
Term Plan

EXERCISE 3   ■ **DIRECTIONS**   Using the form shown in Figure 1.3, build your own term plan.

BUILDING YOUR WEEKLY SCHEDULE

A weekly schedule is a plan of when and what you will study. It includes specific times for studying particular subjects as well as specific times for writing papers, conducting library research, and completing homework assignments for each course.

	Monday	Tuesday	Wednesday	Thursday	Friday	Saturday	Sunday
7:00							
8:00							
			Transportation Time				
9:00							
	History Class	Psychology Class	History Class	Psychology Class	History Class		
10:00	review History notes; read assignment	study	review History notes; read assignment	Transportation	review History notes	type Chemistry Lab report	revise English paper
11:00	Math Class	Psychology	Math Class	study Psychology	Math Class	(other typing)	Church
12:00	Lunch	Lunch	English Composition	Lunch	English Composition	Lunch	Lunch
1:00	Math homework	review lab procedures	class	Math homework	class	draft English paper	Review History assignment
2:00			Lunch	read Chemistry	Lunch	read Psychology chapter	Math homework
	Chemistry Class		Chemistry class		Chemistry class		
3:00	Transportation	Chemistry Lab			Transportation		read and
4:00						review Psychology notes	study Chemistry
5:00	Dinner	Transportation Dinner	Dinner	Dinner	Dinner	Dinner	Dinner
6:00	WORK	Write lab report; start reading new chemistry chapter; type English Composition	WORK	read English assignment	WORK		Call Parents
7:00							
8:00				revise returned Composition			plan next week's Schedule
9:00							
10:00							
11:00							

Figure 1.4
Example of a Weekly Time Schedule

At the beginning of each week, decide what you need to accomplish that week. Consider upcoming quizzes, exams, and papers. A schedule will eliminate the need to make frustrating last-minute choices between "should" and "want to" activities. The sample weekly time schedule in Figure 1.4 was developed by a first-year student. Read it carefully, noticing how the student reserved times for studying each of her courses.

Your Own Weekly Schedule

Now that you have seen a sample weekly schedule, you can begin to build your own. Fill in the blank schedule shown in Figure 1.4, using the following suggestions.

1. *Before the week begins, assess the upcoming week's workload.* Reserve a specific time for this activity. Sunday evening works well for many students. Check your assignment notebook or calendar for upcoming quizzes, exams, papers, and assignments.
2. *Write in any appointments, such as with the doctor or dentist or for a haircut.* Add in new commitments such as baby-sitting your niece on Saturday afternoon or helping a friend repair his car.
3. *Estimate the amount of time you will need for each course.* Add extra time if you have an important exam or if the amount of reading is particularly heavy.
4. *Plan ahead.* If there's a paper due next week that requires library research, allow time this week to begin your research.
5. *Block out reasonable amounts of time, especially on weekends, for having fun and relaxing.* For example, mark off the time when your favorite television show is on or allocate time for going to see a movie.
6. *Study difficult subjects first.* It's tempting to get easy things and short assignments out of the way first, but don't give in to this approach. When you start studying, your mind is fresh and alert and you are at your peak of concentration. This is when you are best equipped to handle difficult subjects. Thinking through complicated problems or studying complex ideas requires maximum brain power, and you have the most at the beginning of a study session.
7. *Leave the routine and more mechanical tasks for later in the evening.* Activities such as recopying papers or alphabetizing a bibliography for a research paper do not require a high degree of concentration and can be left until you are tired.
8. *Schedule study for a particular course close to the time when you attend class.* Plan to study the evening before the class meets or soon after the class meeting. If a class meets on Tuesday morning, plan to study Monday evening or Tuesday afternoon or evening.
9. *Build into your schedule a short break before you begin studying each new subject.* Your mind needs time to refocus—to switch from one set of facts, problems, and issues to another.
10. *Short breaks should also be included when you are working on just one assignment for a long period of time.* A 10-minute break after 50 to 60 minutes of study is reasonable.
11. *When reading or studying a particular subject, try to schedule two or three short, separate blocks of time for that course rather than one long, continuous block.*
12. *Schedule study sessions at times when you know you are usually alert and feel like studying.* Do not schedule a study time early on Saturday morning if you are a person who does not really wake up until noon on weekends, and try not to schedule study time late in the evening if you are usually tired by that time.
13. *Plan to study at times when your physical surroundings are quiet.* If the dinner hour is a rushed and confusing time, don't attempt to study then if there are alternative times available.
14. *Set aside a specific time each week for developing next week's plan and reviewing your prior week's performance.*

	Monday	Tuesday	Wednesday	Thursday	Friday	Saturday	Sunday
7:00							
8:00							
9:00							
10:00							
11:00							
12:00							
1:00							
2:00							
3:00							
4:00							
5:00							
6:00							
7:00							
8:00							
9:00							
10:00							
11:00							

Figure 1.5
Weekly Time Schedule

EXERCISE 4

DIRECTIONS Using the form given in Figure 1.5 or a photocopy of the term plan you wrote in Exercise 3, write a plan for next week.

Using your weekly schedule will be a challenge because it will mean saying no in a number of different situations. When friends call or stop by and ask you to join them at a time when you planned to study, you will have to refuse, but you could let them know when you will be free and offer to join them then. When a friend or family member asks you to do a favor—such as driving her or him somewhere—you will have to refuse, but you can suggest some alternative times when you will be free. You will find that your friends and family will accept your restraints and may even respect you for being conscientious. Don't you respect someone who gets a great deal done and is successful in whatever he or she attempts?

Electronic Time Management

 Many computer programs are equipped with an electronic calendar that enables you to keep track of important tests and quizzes, paper due dates, and appointments, as well as to plan study time. If you do not have an electronic calendar, you can create a weekly calendar like the one in Figure 1.4 by using the commands you would use to create a table. Each week, then, you can easily adjust the calendar to suit upcoming study demands.

TIME-SAVING TIPS FOR STUDENTS WITH BUSY SCHEDULES

Here are a few suggestions that will help you to make the best use of your time. If you are an older student with family responsibilities who is returning to college, or if you are trying both to work and to attend college, you will find these suggestions particularly valuable.

1. *Use the telephone.* When you need information or must make an appointment, phone rather than visit the office. To find out whether a book you've requested at the library has come in, for example, phone the circulation desk.
2. *Use a word processor to write papers.* Computers are time savers. They enable you to make changes in papers easily and quickly without retyping or recopying your work. Watch for the word processor icon throughout the book to direct you to other suggestions for using computers to your advantage when you study. Also, read the Success Workshop on page 422, "Use Computers as a Learning Tool."
3. *Set priorities.* There may be days or weeks when you cannot get every assignment done. Many students work until they are exhausted and leave remaining assignments unfinished. A better approach is to decide what is most important to complete immediately and which assignments could, if necessary, be completed later.
4. *Use spare moments.* Think of all the time you spend waiting. You wait for a class to begin, for a ride, for a friend to call, for a pizza to arrive. Instead of wasting this time, you could use it to review a set of lecture notes, work on review questions at the end of a chapter, or review a chemistry lab setup. Always carry with you something you can work on in spare moments.
5. *Learn to combine activities.* Most people think it's impossible to do two things at once, but busy students soon learn that it's possible to combine some daily chores with routine class assignments. Some students, for example, are able to go to a laundry and, while there, outline a history chapter or work on routine assignments. Others review formulas for math or science courses or review vocabulary cards for language courses while walking to classes.
6. *Use lists to keep yourself organized and to save time.* A daily "to do" list is helpful in keeping track of what daily living/household tasks and errands, as well as course assignments, need to be done. As you think of things to be done, jot them down. Then look over the list each morning and try to find the best way to get everything done. You may find, for instance, that you can stop at the post office on the way to the bookstore, thus saving yourself a trip.
7. *Don't be afraid to admit you're trying to do too much.* If you find your life is becoming too hectic or unmanageable, or if you are facing pressures you

can't handle, consider dropping a course. Don't be too concerned that this will put you behind schedule for graduation. More than half of all college students take longer than the traditional time expected to earn their degrees. Besides, you may be able to pick up the course later during a summer session or carry a heavier load another semester.

FIGHTING THE TENDENCY TO PROCRASTINATE

Have you ever felt that you should work on an assignment, and even wanted to get it out of the way, but could not get started? If so, you may have been a victim of procrastination—putting off tasks that need to be done. Although you know you should review your biology notes this evening, for instance, you procrastinate and do something else instead. Tedious, difficult, or uninteresting tasks are often those that we put off doing. It is often these very tasks, however, that are essential to success in college courses. The following suggestions can help you overcome or control a tendency to procrastinate and put you on track for success.

Give Yourself Five Minutes to Start

If you are having difficulty beginning a task, say to yourself that you will work on it for just five minutes. Often, once you start working, motivation and interest build and you will want to continue working.

Divide the Task into Manageable Parts

Complicated tasks are often difficult to start because they are long and seem unmanageable. Before beginning such tasks, spend a few minutes organizing and planning. Divide each task into parts, and then devise an approach strategy. In other words, list what needs to be done and in what order. In devising an approach strategy for a one-hour biology exam on the topic of cells, one student wrote the following list of subtopics to review.

Cells

atoms and molecules	cell organization
organic molecules	cell functioning
cell theory	cell division

She then decided in what order she would study these topics, which study strategy she would use, and how much time she would devote to each.

Clear Your Desk

Move everything from your desk except materials for the task at hand. With nothing else in front of you, you are more likely to start working and less likely to be distracted from your task while working.

Regardless of What You Do, Start!

If you are having difficulty getting started, do something other than sit and stare, regardless of how trivial it may seem. If you are having trouble writing a paper from rough draft notes, for example, start by recopying the notes. Suddenly you'll find yourself rearranging and rephrasing them, and you'll be well on your way toward writing a draft.

Recognize When You Need More Information

Sometimes procrastination is a signal that you lack skills or information. You may be avoiding a task because you're not sure how to do it. You may not really understand why a certain procedure is used to solve a particular type of math problem, for example, so you feel reluctant to do math homework. Similarly, selecting a topic for a term paper may be difficult if you aren't certain of its purpose or expected length. Overcome such stumbling blocks by discussing them with classmates or with your professor.

Think Positively

As you begin a task, send yourself positive messages such as "I'll be able to stick with this" and "It will feel great to have this job done." Avoid negatives such as "This is so boring" and "I can't wait to finish."

Recognize Escape Routes

Some students escape work by claiming they don't have enough time to get everything done. Close analysis of their use of time often reveals that they are wasting valuable time by following one or more escape routes. One such route is needlessly spending time away from your desk: returning library books, going out to pick up take-out food, dropping off laundry, and so on. Another escape route is to overdo routine tasks: meticulously cleaning your room, pressing clothing, or polishing the car. Doing things by hand also consumes time: copying a friend's notes rather than photocopying them or balancing your checkbook by hand rather than using a calculator. Analyze your time carefully to detect and avoid any escape routes such as these.

Avoid "The Great Escape"—Television

For some students, television poses the greatest threat to keeping to their study-time schedule, and certainly it is often the cause of procrastination. If a TV set is on, it is tempting to watch whatever is showing. To overcome this temptation, turn it on and off at specific times for particular programs you want to see. Don't leave it on between programs you intend to watch; if you do, you'll probably continue watching.

 **EXERCISE 5**

DIRECTIONS   Read each situation described, and then answer the questions that follow. Discuss your responses with another student or write your answers in the spaces provided.

   1. In analyzing his amount of committed time, George Andrews filled in a weekly chart, in hours, as follows:

Sleep	56
Breakfast, lunch, dinner (total)	14
Job	35
Time in classes	23
Transportation	10
Personal care	15
Household/family	20
Total	173

George is overcommitted; his total commitments add up to more hours than there are in a week (168). He has to have at least a part-time job in order to pay for school. He is enrolled in science lab technology, so he must spend a lot of class hours in lab. He estimates that he needs 30 hours per week to maintain a high B average this semester. If he schedules this amount of time, he will have virtually no time for leisure and recreation. Look at his chart again. What could he do? What are his choices? Try to find as many alternatives as you can.

_____

_____

2. Susan is a serious student but is having difficulty with her accounting course. She has decided to spend all day Sunday studying accounting. She plans to lock herself in her room and not come out until she has reviewed four chapters. What is wrong with her approach? What study plan would be more effective?

_____

_____

3. Mark realizes that he has three assignments that must be completed in one evening. The assignments are to revise an English composition, to read and highlight ten pages in his anatomy and physiology text, and to recopy a home-work assignment for sociology. He decides to get the sociology assignment out of the way first, to do the English composition next (because English is one of his favorite subjects), and then to read the anatomy and physiology text. Evaluate Mark's plan of study.

_____

_____

4. You are taking a course in music appreciation, and your instructor often asks you to listen to a certain part of a concert on FM radio or to watch a particular program on television. You cannot predict when these assignments will be given or at what time you will need to complete them. What could you do to include them in your weekly study schedule?

_____

_____

5. Sam Smith is registered for the following courses, which meet at the times indicated.

Business Management 109	T-Th 12–1:30 P.M.
English 101	M-W-F 11 A.M.–12 Noon
Math 201	T-Th 9–10:30 A.M.
Biology 131	Class M-W-F, 2–3 P.M.; Lab W, 3–5 P.M.
Psychology 101	M-W-F, 9–10 A.M.

The workload for each course is as follows:

English	One 250-word essay per week
Math	A homework assignment for each class, which takes approximately one hour to complete; a quiz each Thursday
Biology	Preparation for weekly lab; one chapter to read per week; a one-hour exam every three weeks
Business Management	Two chapters assigned each week; midterm and final exams; one term paper due at the end of the semester
Psychology	One chapter to read per week; one library reading assignment per week; four major exams throughout the semester

Because Sam has a part-time job, he has the following times available for study.

Between his classes

Evenings: Tuesday, Wednesday

Afternoons: Monday, Thursday, and Friday

Weekends: Saturday morning, all day and evening Sunday

What study schedule would you recommend for Sam? Indicate the times he should study each subject and what tasks he should work on. Use a blank time schedule (Figure 1.5) to plan a schedule for Sam.

LEARNING *Collaboratively*

DIRECTIONS   Working with another student in your class, exchange and critique the term plans and weekly schedules you wrote in this chapter. Answer the following questions.

1. Where do you see potential problems in the schedule presented?
2. Is enough study time included?
3. Are study times scheduled appropriately? (See suggestions 1–14, p. 23.)
4. Are there "empty hours" that could be used more efficiently?

Applying YOUR LEARNING

DIRECTIONS   Working in pairs, analyze this situation and discuss answers to the questions that follow.

Sarah decided she didn't need a time schedule because every day is the same for her. She gets up, makes breakfast, gets her children ready for school, and puts them on the bus. Then she goes to two classes, has lunch, goes to another class, and comes home to study for an hour until her children return. She spends the rest of the afternoon and evening with her husband and children. Recently, Sarah's grades have begun to fall. One of her instructors told her he felt she should spend more time preparing for class.

1. How could making a time schedule help Sarah? What might she learn?
2. Make some suggestions about how Sarah can get more study time.
3. What kinds of changes would she need to make?
4. What important decisions does Sarah need to make?

SELF-TEST SUMMARY

1. Why should I set goals?

Establishing your goals will eliminate many day-to-day choices, eliminate conflicts, and keep you focused. Begin by establishing your priorities and following them to achieve your academic goals. Next, compare the time you have allotted to various commitments with the priorities you have assigned to those activities. Finally, build a term plan that you will adjust weekly.

2. What is a term plan?

A term plan is a time schedule that lists all your fixed time commitments, including your classes, transportation time, part-time job hours, sleep, meals, sports, and family commitments. This is your basic time schedule for the semester. From it you can build your weekly schedules more easily.

3. What is the value of a weekly time schedule?

A weekly time schedule helps you to plan your study time in advance and avoid last-minute choices of how to use your time best. It is your commitment on paper to how you intend to do what is necessary to accomplish your goals for the week.

4. What can a student on a busy schedule do to save time?

Many students who have heavy family and work responsibilities need to find ways to make the most of their time. They can do this by setting their priorities, organizing their time with lists, using the telephone as a time-saving tool, learning to combine activities, and using their spare moments for study tasks.

5. How can students overcome the urge to procrastinate?

Procrastination can knock even the best students off the success track. To help yourself deal with difficult, tedious, and uninteresting tasks, clear your work area of anything that will distract you, break the task up into manageable parts, get into the task immediately, avoid thinking negatively about it, avoid typical escape routes such as television, and be aware when you need more information and get it.

Take a Road Trip to Mount Rushmore!

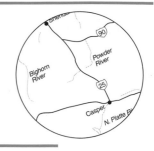

If your instructor has asked you to use the Reading Road Trip CD-ROM, be sure to visit the Memorization and Concentration module for multimedia tutorials, exercises, and tests, as well as additional coverage of time management.

2

Learning Style and Learning Strategies

Why Analyze Your Learning Style?

▲ **You will understand your strengths and weaknesses as a learner and how to choose study methods accordingly.**

▲ **You will realize why you learn more easily from some instructors than others.**

▲ **You will discover what kinds of learning and thinking are expected in college.**

Learning Experiment

Step 1

Study the photograph on the next page for one minute.

Step 2

Draw a sketch of the person speaking in the photograph.

Step 3

Write two or three sentences describing the speaker in the photograph.

Step 4

Compare your drawing and descriptions with those of your classmates by quickly passing them around the room.

The Results

No doubt, some sketches were much better than others. Some were detailed, accurate likenesses; others may have resembled stick figures. Likewise, some students wrote detailed descriptive sentences; others did not. You can conclude that some students have stronger artistic ability than others. Some students have stronger verbal abilities than others. Which students do you expect will do well in an art class? Who will do better on essay exams? Who might consider a career in graphic design? Who should not?

Learning Principle (What This Means to You)

You have strengths and weaknesses as a learner; you should capitalize on your strengths and strive to overcome your weaknesses. In this chapter you will learn to identify strengths and weaknesses and choose study methods accordingly. You will also discover that instructors have unique teaching styles and discover how to adapt to them. Finally, you will learn what kinds of learning and thinking instructors expect of you.

ANALYZING YOUR LEARNING STYLE

Have you noticed that some types of tasks are easier to learn than others? Have you also discovered that some study methods work better than others? Have you ever found that a study method that works well for a classmate does not work as well for you? These differences can be explained by what is known as *learning style.* Just as you have a unique personality, you also have a unique learning style. People differ in how they learn and in the methods and strategies they use to learn. Your learning style can, in part, explain why some courses are easier than others and why you learn better from one instructor than another. Learning style can also explain why certain assignments are difficult and other learning tasks are easy.

To begin to understand learning style, think of everyday tasks and activities that you have learned to do easily and well. Think of others that are always troublesome. For example, is reading maps easy or difficult? Is drawing or sketching easy or difficult? Can you assemble items easily? Are tasks that require physical coordination (such as racquetball) difficult? Can you easily remember the lyrics to popular songs? Just as some everyday tasks are easy and others difficult, so are some academic tasks easy and others more challenging.

The following questionnaire will help you analyze how you learn and enable you to learn more efficiently. Complete the following Learning Style Questionnaire before continuing.

Learning Style Questionnaire

Directions: Each item presents two choices. Select the alternative that best describes you. In cases where neither choice suits you, select the one that is closer to your preference. Write the letter of your choice in the blank to the left of each item.

Part One

_____   1. I would prefer to follow a set of
      a. oral directions.
      (b.) written directions.

_____   2. I would prefer to
      a. attend a lecture given by a famous psychologist.
      (b.) read an article written by the psychologist.

_____   3. When I am introduced to someone, it is easier for me to remember the person's
      a. name.
      (b.) face.

_____   4. I find it easier to learn new information using
      a. language (words).
      (b.) images (pictures).

_____   5. I prefer classes in which the instructor
      a. lectures and answers questions.
      (b.) uses films and videos.

_____ 6. To follow current events, I prefer to
a. listen to the news on the radio.
b. read the newspaper.

_____ 7. To learn how to operate a fax machine, I would prefer to
a. listen to a friend's explanation.
b. watch a demonstration.

Part Two

_____ 8. I prefer to
a. work with facts and details.
b. construct theories and ideas.

_____ 9. I would prefer a job that involved
a. following specific instructions.
b. reading, writing, and analyzing.

_____ 10. I prefer to
a. solve math problems using a formula.
b. discover why the formula works.

_____ 11. I would prefer to write a term paper explaining
a. how a process works.
b. a theory.

_____ 12. I prefer tasks that require me to
a. follow careful, detailed instructions.
b. use reasoning and critical analysis.

_____ 13. For a criminal justice course, I would prefer to
a. discover how and when a law can be used.
b. learn how and why it became law.

_____ 14. To learn more about the operation of a high-speed computer
printer, I would prefer to
a. work with several types of printers.
b. understand the principles on which it operates

Part Three

_____ 15. To solve a math problem, I would prefer to
a. draw or visualize the problem.
b. study a sample problem and use it as a model.

_____ 16. To remember something best, I
a. create a mental picture.
b. write it down.

_____ 17. Assembling a bicycle from a diagram would be
a. easy.
b. challenging.

_____ 18. I prefer classes in which I
a. handle equipment or work with models.
b. participate in a class discussion.

_____ 19. To understand and remember how a machine works, I would
   a. draw a diagram.
   b. write notes.

_____ 20. I enjoy
   a. drawing or working with my hands.
   b. speaking, writing, and listening.

_____ 21. If I were trying to locate an office on an unfamiliar university campus, I would prefer
   a. a map.
   b. a set of written directions.

Part Four

_____ 22. For a grade in biology lab, I would prefer to
   a. work with a lab partner.
   b. work alone.

_____ 23. When faced with a difficult personal problem, I prefer to
   a. discuss it with others.
   b. resolve it myself.

_____ 24. Many instructors could improve their classes by
   a. including more discussion and group activities.
   b. allowing students to work on their own more frequently.

_____ 25. When listening to a lecturer or speaker, I respond more to
   a. the person presenting the ideas.
   b. the ideas themselves.

_____ 26. When on a team project, I prefer to
   a. work with several team members.
   b. divide up tasks and complete those assigned to me.

_____ 27. I prefer to shop and do errands
   a. with friends.
   b. by myself.

_____ 28. A job in a busy office is
   a. more appealing than working alone.
   b. less appealing than working alone.

Part Five

_____ 29. To make decisions, I rely on
   a. my experiences and gut feelings.
   b. facts and objective data.

_____ 30. To complete a task, I
   a. can use whatever is available to get the job done.
   b. must have everything I need at hand.

_____ 31. I prefer to express my ideas and feelings through
   a. music, song, or poetry.
   b. direct, concise language.

_____ 32. I prefer instructors who
      a. allow students to be guided by their own interests.
      b. make their expectations clear and explicit.

_____ 33. I tend to
      a. challenge and question what I hear and read.
      b. accept what I hear and read.

_____ 34. I prefer
      a. essay exams.
      b. objective exams.

_____ 35. In completing an assignment, I prefer to
      a. figure out my own approach.
      b. be told exactly what to do.

To score your questionnaire, record the total number of times you selected choice a and the total number of times you selected choice b for each part of the questionnaire. Record your totals in the scoring grid provided.

Scoring Grid Parts	Total # of Choice a	Total # of Choice b
Part One	0	7
	Auditory	Visual
Part Two	7	0
	Applied	Conceptual
Part Three	4	3
	Spatial	Verbal
Part Four	6	2
	Social	Independent
Part Five	4	3
	Creative	Pragmatic

Now circle your higher score for each part of the questionnaire. The word below the score you circled indicates an aspect of your learning style. Scores in a particular row that are close to one another, such as a 3 and a 4, suggest that you do not exhibit a strong, clear preference for either aspect. Scores that are farther apart, such as a 1 and a 6, suggest a stronger preference for the higher score. The next section explains how to interpret your scores and describes these aspects.

Interpreting Your Scores

The questionnaire was divided into five parts; each part identifies one aspect of your learning style. These five aspects are explained below.

Part One: Auditory or Visual Learners

This score indicates the sensory mode you prefer when processing information. Auditory learners tend to learn more effectively through listening, whereas visual learners process information by seeing it in print or other visual modes, including films, pictures, or diagrams. If you have a higher score on auditory than visual, you tend to be an auditory learner. That is, you tend to learn more easily by hearing than by reading. A higher score in visual suggests strengths with visual modes of learning.

Part Two: Applied or Conceptual Learners

This score describes the types of learning tasks and learning situations you prefer and find easiest to handle. If you are an applied learner, you prefer tasks that involve real objects and situations. Practical, real-life learning situations are ideal for you. If you are a conceptual learner, you prefer to work with language and ideas; practical applications are not necessary for understanding.

Part Three: Spatial or Verbal Learners

This score reveals your ability to work with spatial relationships. Spatial learners are able to visualize, or mentally see, how things work or how they are positioned in space. Their strengths may include drawing, assembling things, or repairing. Verbal learners lack skills in positioning things in space. Instead, they tend to rely on verbal or language skills.

Part Four: Social or Independent Learners

This score reveals your preferred level of interaction with other people in the learning process. If you are a social learner, you prefer to work with others—both peers and instructors—closely and directly. You tend to be people-oriented and to enjoy personal interaction. If you are an independent learner, you prefer to work and study alone. You tend to be self-directed or self-motivated and often are goal-oriented.

Part Five: Creative or Pragmatic Learners

This score describes the approach you prefer to take toward learning tasks. Creative learners are imaginative and innovative. They prefer to learn through discovery or experimentation. They are comfortable taking risks and following hunches. Pragmatic learners are practical, logical, and systematic. They seek order and are comfortable following rules.

EXERCISE 1

DIRECTIONS   Write a paragraph describing yourself as a learner. Include aspects of your learning style and give examples from everyday experience that confirm your profile. Explain any results of the Learning Style Questionnaire with which you disagree.

Developing an Action Plan for Learning

Now that you know more about *how* you learn, you are ready to develop an action plan for learning what you read. Suppose you discovered that you are an auditory learner. You still have to read your assignments, which is a visual task. However, to learn the assignment you should translate the material into an auditory form. For example, you could repeat aloud, using your own words, information that you want to remember, or you could tape-record key information and play it back. If you also are a social learner, you could work with a classmate, testing each other out loud.

Figure 2.1 lists each aspect of learning style and offers suggestions for how to learn from a reading assignment. To use the figure:

1. Circle the five aspects of your learning style for which you received higher scores. Disregard the others.
2. Read through the suggestions that apply to you.
3. Place a check mark in front of those suggestions you think will work for you. Choose at least one from each category.
4. List the suggestions you chose in the following Action Plan for Learning box.

Action Plan for Learning

Learning Strategy 1._____

_____

Learning Strategy 2._____

_____

Learning Strategy 3._____

_____

Learning Strategy 4._____

_____

Learning Strategy 5._____

_____

Learning Strategy 6._____

_____

Now that you have listed suggestions to help you learn what you read, the next step is to experiment with these techniques, one at a time. (You may need to refer to the chapters listed in parentheses in Figure 2.1 to learn or review how a certain technique works.) Use one technique for a while, then move to the next. Continue using the techniques that seem to work; work on revising or modifying those that do not. Do not hesitate to experiment with other techniques listed in the figure; you may find other techniques that work well for you.

Developing Strategies to Overcome Limitations

You should also work on developing the weaker aspects of your learning style. Your learning style is not fixed or unchanging. You can improve areas in which you scored lower. Although you may be weak in auditory learning, for example,

Auditory	**Visual**
1. Tape review notes. 2. Discuss/study with friends. 3. Talk aloud when studying. 4. Tape lectures.	1. Use mapping (see Chapter 14). 2. Use visualization. 3. Use CD-ROMS if available. 4. View videos when available. 5. Draw diagrams, charts, and maps.
Applied	**Conceptual**
1. Associate ideas with their application. 2. Take courses with a lab or practicum. 3. Think of practical situations to which learning applies. 4. Use case studies, examples, and applications to cue your learning.	1. Use outlining. 2. Focus on thought patterns (see Chapter 7). 3. Organize materials into rules and examples.
Spatial	**Verbal**
1. Draw diagrams; make charts and sketches. 2. Use outlining. 3. Use visualization. 4. Use mapping (see Chapter 14).	1. Record steps, processes, and procedures in words. 2. Write summaries. 3. Translate diagrams and drawings into language. 4. Write your interpretations next to textbook drawings, maps, and graphics.
Social	**Independent**
1. Interact with the instructor. 2. Find a study partner. 3. Form a study group. 4. Take courses involving class discussion. 5. Work with a tutor.	1. Use computer-assisted instructions if available. 2. Enroll in courses using a traditional lecture-exam format. 3. Consider independent study courses. 4. Purchase review books and study guides, if available.
Creative	**Pragmatic**
1. Take courses that involve exploration, experimentation, or discussion. 2. Use annotation to record impressions and reactions. 3. Ask questions about chapter content and answer them.	1. Write lists of steps, processes, and procedures. 2. Write summaries and outlines. 3. Use a structured study environment. 4. Focus on problem-solving and logical sequence.

Figure 2.1
Learning Strategies for Various Learning Styles

many of your professors will lecture and expect you to take notes. If you work on improving your listening and note-taking skills, you can learn to handle lectures effectively. Make a conscious effort to work on improving areas of weakness as well as taking advantage of your strengths.

Several Words of Caution

Ideally, through activities in this section and the use of the questionnaire, you have discovered more about yourself as a learner. However, several words of caution are in order.

1. The questionnaire is a quick and easy way to discover your learning style. Other more formal and more accurate measures of learning style are available.

These include *Kolb's Learning Style Inventory* and the *Myers–Briggs Type Indicator.* These tests may be available through your college's counseling, testing, or academic skills centers.

2. There are many more aspects of learning style than those identified through the questionnaire in this chapter. To learn more about other factors affecting learning, see one or more of the tests listed above.

3. Learning style is *not* a fixed, unchanging quality. Just as personalities can change and develop, so can learning style change and develop through exposure, instruction, or practice. For example, as you attend more college lectures, your skill as an auditory learner may be strengthened.

4. You probably will not be clearly strong or weak in each aspect. Some students, for example, can learn equally well spatially and verbally. If your scores on one or more parts of the questionnaire were quite close, then you may have strengths in both areas.

5. When most students discover the features of their learning style, they recognize themselves. A frequent comment is "Yep, that's me." However, if for some reason you feel the description of yourself as a learner is incorrect, then do not make changes in your learning strategies on the basis of the outcome. Instead, discuss your style with your instructor or consider taking one of the tests listed in point 1.

UNDERSTANDING YOUR INSTRUCTORS' TEACHING STYLES

Just as each student has his or her own learning style, so does each instructor have his or her own teaching style. Some instructors, for example, have a teaching style that promotes social interaction among students. An instructor may organize small group activities, encourage class participation, or require students to work in pairs or teams to complete a specific task. Other instructors offer little or no opportunity for social interaction, in a lecture class for example.

Some instructors are very applied; they teach by example. Others are more conceptual; they focus on presenting ideas, rules, theories, and so forth. In fact, the same five categories of learning style identified on page 37 can be applied to teaching style as well.

To an extent, of course, the subject matter also dictates how the instructor teaches. A biology instructor, for instance, has a large body of factual information to present and may feel he or she has little time to schedule group interaction.

Comparing Learning and Teaching Style

Once you are aware of your learning style and consider the instructor's teaching style, you can begin to understand why you can learn better from one instructor than another and why you feel more comfortable in certain instructors' classes than others. When aspects of your learning style match aspects of your instructor's teaching style, you are on the same wavelength, so to speak: The instructor is teaching the way you learn. On the other hand, when your learning style does not correspond to an instructor's teaching style, you may not be as comfortable, and learning will be more of a challenge. You may have to work harder in that class by taking extra steps to reorganize or reformat the material into a form better suited to your learning style. The following section presents each of the five categories of learning–teaching styles and suggests how you might make changes in how you study to accommodate each.

Auditory–Visual

If your instructor announces essential course information (such as paper assignments, class projects, or descriptions of upcoming exams) orally and you are a visual learner, you should be sure to record as much information as possible in your notes. If your instructor relies on lectures to present new material not included in your textbook, taking complete lecture notes is especially important. If your instructor uses numerous visual aids and you tend to be an auditory learner, consider tape-recording summaries of these visual aids.

Applied–Conceptual

If your instructor seldom uses examples, models, or case studies and you are an applied learner, you need to think of your own examples to make the course material real and memorable to you. Leave space in your class notes to add examples. Add them during class if they come to mind; if not, take time as you review your notes to add examples. If your instructor uses numerous demonstrations and examples and you are a conceptual learner, you may need to leave space in your class notes to write in rules or generalizations that state what the examples are intended to prove.

Spatial–Verbal

If you are a spatial learner and your instructor has a verbal teaching style (he or she lectures and writes notes on the board), then you will need to draw diagrams, charts, and pictures to learn the material. On the other hand, if you are a verbal learner and your instructor is spatial (she frequently uses diagrams, flowcharts, and so forth), then you may need to translate the diagrams and flowcharts into words in order to learn them easily.

Social–Independent

If your instructor organizes numerous in-class group activities and you tend to be an independent learner, then you will need to spend time alone after class reviewing the class activity, making notes, and perhaps even repeating the activity by yourself to make it more meaningful. If your instructor seldom structures in-class group activities and you tend to be a social learner, try to arrange to study regularly with a classmate or create or join a study group.

Creative–Pragmatic

Suppose your instructor is very systematic and organized in his or her lectures, and, as a creative learner, you prefer to discover ideas through experimentation and free-flowing discussion. In this case, you should consider creating a column in your class notes to record your responses and creative thoughts or reserve the bottom quarter of each page for such annotations. If your instructor is creative and tends to use a loose or free-flowing class format, and you tend to be a pragmatic learner, you may need to rewrite and restructure class notes. If he or she fails to give you specific guidelines for completing activities or assignments, you should talk with your instructor or ask for more information.

EXERCISE 2

DIRECTIONS Analyze your instructors' teaching styles by completing the following chart for the courses you are taking this semester. List as many teaching characteristics as you can, but do not try to cover every aspect of learning–teaching style.

Course	Instructor's Name	Teaching Style Characteristics
1. _____		
2. _____		
3. _____		
4. _____		
5. _____		
6. _____		

EXERCISE 3

DIRECTIONS After you have completed the chart in Exercise 2, select one of your instructors whose teaching style does not match your learning style. Write a paragraph describing the differences in your styles. Explain how you will change your study methods to make up for these differences.

MEETING YOUR INSTRUCTORS' EXPECTATIONS

Learning in college is different from high school or on-the-job training. Now that you have a profile of yourself as a learner, it is time to discover what kinds of learning is expected of you. Whether you have just completed high school or are returning to college with work experiences or family responsibilities, you will face new demands and expectations in college. The following sections describe your instructors' expectations.

Take Responsibility for Your Own Learning

In college, learning is mainly up to you. Instructors function as guides. They define and explain what is to be learned, but they expect you to do the learning. Weekly class time is far shorter than in high school. Often there isn't enough time in class for instructors to provide drills, practices, and reviews of factual course content. Instead, college class time is used primarily to introduce content that is to be learned and to discuss ideas. Instructors expect you to learn the material and to be prepared to discuss it in class. *When, where,* and *how* you learn are your decisions. Be sure to take into account the five aspects of your learning style as you make these decisions.

Focus on Concepts

Each course you take will require that you learn a great many facts, statistics, dates, definitions, formulas, rules, and principles. It is easy to become convinced that learning these is sufficient and to become a robot learner—memorizing facts from texts and lectures and then recalling them on exams and quizzes.

Actually, factual information is only a starting point, a base from which to approach the real content of a course. Most college instructors expect you to go beyond facts to analysis—to consider what the collection of facts and details *means*. Many students, however, "can't see the forest for the trees"; they get caught up in specifics and fail to grasp the larger, more important concepts. To avoid this pitfall, be sure to keep the following questions in mind as you read and study.

- Why do I need to know this?

- Why is this important?

- What principle or trend does this illustrate?

- How can I use this information?

- How does this fit in with other course content?

Focus on Ideas, Not "Right Answers"

Through previous schooling, many students have come to expect their answers to be either right or wrong. They assume that learning is limited to memorizing a collection of facts and that their mastery of the course is measured by the number of "right answers" they have learned. Accordingly, they are lost when faced with an essay question such as:

> Defend or criticize the arguments that are offered in favor of capital punishment. Refer to any readings that you have completed.

There is no one right answer to this question. You can either defend the arguments or criticize them. The instructor who asks this question expects you to think and to provide a reasoned, logical, consistent response that draws on information you have acquired through your reading. Here are a few more examples of questions for which there are no single correct answers.

> Do animals think?

> Would you be willing to reduce your standard of living by 15 percent if the United States could thereby eliminate poverty? Defend your response.

> Imagine a society in which everyone has exactly the same income. You are the manager of an industrial plant. What plans, policies, or programs would you implement to motivate your employees to work?

Evaluate New Ideas

Throughout college you will continually meet new ideas; you will agree with some and disagree with others. Don't make the mistake of accepting or rejecting a new idea, however, until you have really explored it and have considered its assumptions and implications. Ask questions such as:

- What evidence is available in support of this idea?

- What opposing evidence is available?

- How is my personal experience related to this idea?

- What additional information do I need in order to make a decision?

Explore Ideas Using a Journal

As you begin college, you will encounter many new ideas and meet many new people, both classmates and instructors, from whom you will discover new approaches and conventions—new ways of looking at and doing things. You will also begin to explore many academic fields that you did not study in high school. It is easy to feel overwhelmed by it all. Sometimes you need to sort out ideas and your reactions to them. Many students find it helpful to keep a journal. A journal is an informal record of your thoughts, ideas, impressions, and reactions. Most students use a spiral-bound notebook, but because a journal is written for you, not your instructor, it may take any form you select and may contain whatever you choose. Some students record impressions and feelings; others record new ideas they want to explore. Writing about your ideas will focus them and clarify your response to them. Journal entries, by the way, are an excellent source of ideas when you have to choose a topic about which to write a paper.

Because learning is a major focus of college, and because you will be reading about new learning strategies throughout this book, consider including in your journal a record of each learning strategy you tried and how it worked. You will find it helpful to review your journal; often, doing so will suggest which strategies seem to work for each of your courses. A learning journal is discussed in more detail in Chapter 15, page 309.

DEVELOPING ACTIVE LEARNING STRATEGIES

Your instructors also expect you to become an active learner, illustrated by the following situation. A first-year student who had always thought of himself as a B student was getting low Cs and Ds in his business course. The instructor gave weekly quizzes; each was a practical problem to solve. Every week the student memorized his lecture notes and carefully reread the assigned chapter in his textbook. When he spoke with his instructor about his low grades, the instructor told him that his study methods were not effective and that he needed to become more active and involved with the subject matter. Memorizing and rereading are passive approaches. The instructor suggested that he try instead to think about content, ask questions, anticipate practical uses, solve potential problems, and draw connections between ideas.

Active versus Passive Learning

How did you learn to ride a bike, play racquetball, or change a tire? In each case you learned by doing, by active participation. College learning requires similar active involvement and participation. Active learning is expected in most college courses and can often make the difference between barely average grades and top grades. Figure 2.2 lists common college learning situations and contrasts the responses of active and passive learners. The examples in Figure 2.2 show that passive learners do not carry the learning process far enough. They do not go beyond what instructors tell them to do. They fail to think about, organize, and react to course content.

	Passive Learners	Active Learners
Class lectures	Write down what the instructor says	Decide what is important to write down
Textbook assignments	Read	Read, think, ask questions, try to connect ideas
Studying	Reread	Consider learning style, make outlines and study sheets, predict exam questions, look for trends and patterns
Writing class assignments	Only follow the professor's instructions	Try to discover the significance of the assignment, look for the principles and concepts it illustrates
Writing term papers	Do only what is expected to get a good grade	Try to expand their knowledge and experience with a topic and connect it to the course objective or content

Figure 2.2
Characteristics of Passive and Active Learners

Active Learning Strategies

When you study, you should be thinking about and reacting to the material in front of you. This is how you make it happen:

1. Ask questions about what you are reading. You will find that this helps to focus your attention and improve your concentration.
2. Consider the purpose behind assignments. Why might a sociology assignment require you to spend an hour at the monkey house of the local zoo, for example?
3. Try to see how each assignment fits with the rest of the course. For instance, why does a section called "Amortization" belong in a business mathematics textbook chapter entitled "Business and Consumer Loans"?
4. Relate what you are learning to what you already know from the course and from your background knowledge and personal experience. Connect a law in physics with how your car brakes work, for example.
5. Think of examples or situations in which you can apply the information.

Throughout the remainder of this text, you will learn many strategies for becoming an active learner. Active learning also involves active reading. In Chapter 5 you will learn specific strategies for becoming an active reader.

EXERCISE 4

DIRECTIONS   Review each of the following learning situations. Answer each question by suggesting active learning approaches.

1. Having a graded exam returned to you by your history professor. How could you use this as a learning device?

   _____

2. Being assigned "Letter from Birmingham Jail" by Martin Luther King, Jr., for your English composition class. What questions would you try to answer as you read?

   _____

3. Completing a biology lab. How would you prepare for it?

   _____

4. Being assigned by your sociology instructor to read an article in *Newsweek* on crime in major U.S. cities. How would you record important ideas?

THINKING CRITICALLY

In college, your instructors expect you to learn actively, and they also expect you to think critically. A first step in becoming a critical thinker is to become familiar with the types of thinking that college instructors demand. Figure 2.3 lists the levels of thinking in order of increasing complexity. Based on a progression of thinking skills developed by Benjamin Bloom, it is widely used by educators in many academic disciplines.

The *knowledge* level of thinking is basically memorization; this is something you've been doing for years. The *comprehension* level is also familiar. If you are able to explain how to convert fractions to decimals, then you are thinking at the comprehension level. At the *application* level, you apply to a new situation information that you have memorized and understood. When you use your knowledge of punctuation to place commas correctly in a sentence, you are functioning at the application level. The *analysis* level involves examining what you have learned and studying relationships. When you explain how a microscope works, you are analyzing its operation. The *synthesis* level requires you to put ideas together to form something new. When you write a paper by drawing on a variety of sources, you are synthesizing them. *Evaluation* involves making judgments. When you decide what is effective and what is ineffective in a classmate's presentation in a public speaking class, you are evaluating the presentation.

Using Levels of Thinking

The last three levels—analysis, synthesis, and evaluation—involve critical thinking. Some exam questions require you to think at knowledge, comprehen-

Level	Examples
Knowledge: recalling information, repeating information with no changes	Recalling dates, memorizing definitions for a history exam
Comprehension: understanding ideas, using rules and following directions	Explaining a mathematical law, knowing how the human ear functions, explaining a definition in psychology
Application: applying knowledge to a new situation	Using knowledge of formulas to solve a new physics problem
Analysis: seeing relationships, breaking information into parts, analyzing how things work	Comparing two poems by the same author
Synthesis: putting ideas and information together in a unique way, creating something new	Designing a new computer program
Evaluation: making judgments, assessing the value or worth of information	Evaluating the effectiveness of an argument opposing the death penalty

Figure 2.3
Levels of Thinking

sion, and application levels. Many objective exams (multiple-choice, true–false) include items that focus on these levels. Essay exams, however, as well as some multiple-choice questions, require thinking at the three higher levels. Participating in class discussions, writing papers, making speeches, and artistic expression (music, painting, and the like) all require analysis, synthesis, and/or evaluation. In later chapters, you'll learn more about these levels of thinking when preparing for and taking exams (see Chapters 16 and 17), and writing research papers (see Appendix).

Applying Levels of Thinking

Reading and Levels of Thinking

As you read, be sure to think at each level. Here is a list of questions to help you read and think at each level.

Level of Thinking	Question
Knowledge	What information do I need to learn?
Comprehension	What are the main points and how are they supported?
Application	How can I use this information?
Analysis	How is this material organized? How are the ideas related? How are the data presented in graphs, tables, and charts related? What trends do they reveal?
Synthesis	How does this information fit with other sources (class lectures, other readings, your prior knowledge)?
Evaluation	Is this information accurate, reliable, and valuable? Does the author prove his or her points?

EXERCISE 5

DIRECTIONS   Identify the level or levels of thinking that each of the following tasks demands.

1. Retelling a favorite family story to your nieces and nephews
   _____

2. Using the principles of time management discussed in Chapter 1 to develop a weekly study plan _____

3. Learning the names of the U.S. presidents since World War II
   _____

4. Reorganizing your lecture notes by topic _____

5. Writing a letter to the editor of your hometown newspaper praising a recently passed city ordinance that restricts new toxic waste disposal sites
   _____

6. Writing a term paper that requires library research
   _____

7. Using prereading techniques when reading your speech communication textbook _____

8. Listening to speeches by two candidates who are running for mayor and then deciding which one gets your vote _____

9. Watching several hours of TV programming to determine the amount of time given to commercials, to public service announcements, to regular programs, and to news _____

10. Writing an article for the campus newspaper explaining why on-campus parking is inadequate _____

EXERCISE 6

DIRECTIONS   Read "Dimensions of Nonverbal Communication" and answer the questions that follow.

Dimensions of Nonverbal Communication

In recent years, research has reemphasized the important role of physical, or non-verbal, behaviors in effective oral communication. Basically, three generalizations about nonverbal communication should occupy your attention when you are a speaker:

1. *Speakers reveal and reflect their emotional states through their nonverbal behaviors.* Your listeners read your feelings toward yourself, your topic, and your audience from your facial expressions. Consider the contrast between a speaker who walks to the front of the room briskly, head held high, and one who shuffles, head bowed and arms hanging limply. Communications scholar Dale G. Leathers summarized a good deal of research into nonverbal communication processes: "Feelings and emotions are more accurately exchanged by nonverbal than verbal mean. . . . The nonverbal portion of communication conveys meanings and intentions that are relatively free from deception, distortion, and confusion."

2. *The speaker's nonverbal cues enrich or elaborate the message that comes through words.* A solemn face can reinforce the dignity of a funeral eulogy. The words, "Either do this or do that," can be illustrated with appropriate arm-and-hand gestures. Taking a few steps to one side tells an audience that you are moving from one argument to another. A smile enhances a lighter moment in your speech.

3. *Nonverbal messages form a reciprocal interaction between speaker and listener.* Listeners frown, smile, shift nervously in their seats, and engage in many types of nonverbal behavior. . . . There are four areas of nonverbal communication that concern every speaker: (a) *proxemics,* (b) *movement and stance,* (c) *facial expressions,* and (d) *gestures.*

—Gronbeck et al., *Principles of Speech Communication,* pp. 217–218

1. Knowledge: What are the three generalizations?
2. Comprehension: Explain how a speaker can reveal his or her emotional state.
3. Application: Give an example (not used in the excerpt) of how a speaker can reveal his or her emotional state.
4. Analysis: If nonverbal communication is free from deception, is it possible to tell a lie using body language?
5. Synthesis: To what extent is this information consistent with what I already know about nonverbal messages?
6. Evaluation: How is this information useful and important to me in a public speaking class?

EXERCISE 7

DIRECTIONS   Read "Body Adornment," in Part Seven, pp. 376–378. Then write two questions that require thinking at each of the levels we have discussed (a total of twelve questions).

LEARNING *Collaboratively*

DIRECTIONS   Working in groups of two or three, prepare a "Need to Know" list for new freshmen on your campus. Include information you have discovered so far about learning and studying in college. Groups should compare and compile lists and may wish to prepare a handout for next semester's class, post information on the campus Web site, or submit the final list to the college newspaper for publication or to the director of student orientation for use with incoming students.

Applying YOUR LEARNING

DIRECTIONS   Form groups of three or four students and analyze the following situation. Discuss answers to the questions that appear after it.

A history professor has just returned graded midterm exams to her class. One student looks at the grade on the first page, flips through the remaining pages while commenting to a friend that the exam was "too picky," and files it in her notebook. A second student reviews his exam for grading errors and notices one error. Immediately, he raises his hand and asks for an adjustment in his grade. The instructor seems annoyed and tells the student she will not use class time to dispute individual grades. A third student reviews her exam bluebook to identify a pattern of error; on the cover of the bluebook, she notes topics and areas in which she is weak.

1. Compare the three students' responses to the situation.
2. What does each student's response reveal about his or her approach to learning?
3. Analyze the student's response to the instructor's error in grading. What alternatives might have been more appropriate?
4. At what level(s) of thinking was each of the three students functioning?

SELF-TEST SUMMARY

1. **Why is it useful to analyze your learning style?**

Analyzing your learning style can help you to understand why you may learn better from one instructor than another and why some courses are easier for you than others. Building an awareness of how you learn best and what your limitations are can help you understand how to study more effectively and become a more efficient learner.

2. **Why is it important to analyze your instructors' teaching styles?**

You may need to make changes in how you learn to suit each instructor's teaching style.

3. **What do instructors expect of college students?**

In college, students are expected to set their own operating rules, take responsibility for their own learning, and focus on and evaluate ideas and concepts.

4. **What does "becoming an active learner" mean?**

Active learning is essential to success in college. To become a more effective learner, you should get actively involved with reading assignments, lectures, and class activities by (a) asking questions about class presentations and reading assignments, and (b) looking for the purpose behind learning the information presented.

5. **What levels of thinking are expected of college students?**

College instructors expect their students to read and think critically. There are six levels of thinking: knowledge, comprehension, application, analysis, synthesis, and evaluation. Analysis, synthesis, and evaluation define critical thinking. Many classroom activities, such as exams, papers, and discussions, require reading and thinking at these levels.

3

Understanding How Learning and Memory Work

Why Learn about How Learning and Memory Work?

▲ **You will discover how to learn more efficiently.**

▲ **Learning is your primary job while in college; the more you know about it, the more confident and comfortable you will become.**

Learning Experiment

Step 1

Suppose you wanted to become a better swimmer. What would you do? List some ideas here:

_____

_____

_____

Step 2

Now read the following paragraph that explains the physics of swimming.

For every action, there's an equal and opposite reaction. Swimmers move *forward* by pushing *back* against the water (instead of pushing *up* and *out* as many do). The greater the resistance of the water, the greater the forward thrust. And since still water provides greater resistance than water that's already moving backward, the old straight-arm pull isn't the most efficient way to swim. The most effective stroke, instead, is one that's curved so that you're always pushing against a column of "new" or still water. Resistance in the right places is a swimmer's friend. In the wrong places, though, it's an enemy, and it's known as a drag. In order to move through water most efficiently, your body must pose as little resistance (drag) as possible. This is called streamlining. To streamline your body, keep it generally horizontal along the central axis (your spine) so that all your energy is used for propelling your body *directly forward,* and none is wasted by moving it vertically, to the side, or even backward.

—Katz, *Swimming for Total Fitness: A Progressive Aerobic Program,* p. 99

Step 3

Would the above paragraph help you become a better swimmer? Why or why not?

The Results

You probably agreed that the paragraph would be useful. Why? By understanding how the process works, you might be able to make changes in how you stroke, position your body, and move through the water.

Learning Principle (What This Means to You)

By reading about the dynamics of swimming, you received an overview of the process. **If you understand how a process works, you will be able to put it to use more easily.** In this chapter you will learn how memory works and become familiar with the principles that make learning easier. After you have completed this chapter you will be better prepared to learn from lectures and textbooks.

FORGETTING

Have you ever wondered why you can't remember what you have just read? Have you noticed students in your classes who seem to remember everything? Do you wonder how they do it? The answer is not that these other students are brighter than you are or that they have studied twice as long as you have. It is that they have learned *how* to learn and to remember; they have developed techniques for effective learning.

Forgetting, which is defined as the loss of information stored in memory, is a normal, everyday occurrence. It happens because other information interferes with or prevents your recall of the desired information. Psychologists have extensively studied the rate at which forgetting takes place. For most people, forgetting occurs very rapidly right after learning and then levels off over time. Figure 3.1 on the next page illustrates just how fast forgetting normally occurs and how much information is lost. The figure depicts what is known as the *retention curve,* and it shows how much you are able to remember over time.

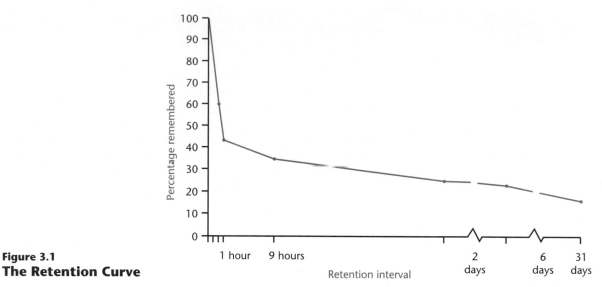

Figure 3.1
The Retention Curve

The retention curve is important to you as a learner. Basically, it suggests that unless you are one of the lucky few who remember almost everything they hear or read, you will forget a large portion of the information you learn unless you do something to prevent it. For instance, the graph shows that your recall of learned information drops to below 50 percent within an hour and to about 25 percent within two days.

Fortunately, certain techniques can prevent or slow down forgetting. These techniques are the focus of the remainder of this book. Throughout the book, you will learn techniques that will enable you to identify what to learn (pick out what is important) and to learn it in the most effective way. Each technique is intended to help you remember more and to slow down your rate of forgetting. For instance, in Chapter 4 you will learn how taking notes during class lectures can help you learn and remember what the lecture is about. In Chapter 15 you will learn a system for reading to learn and remember more.

Before we go on to present these specific techniques, however, you should understand something about the learning and memory process and why forgetting occurs. Once you know how learning occurs, you will be able to see why and how the techniques suggested throughout this book are effective. Each reading and study technique is based on the learning and memory process and is designed to help you learn in the most efficient way.

EXERCISE 1

DIRECTIONS   Apply what you have learned about the rate of forgetting to each of the following study situations. Refer to Figure 3.1.

1. How much information from a textbook chapter can you expect to recall two days after you read it?

   _____ 30 %. _____

2. How much information in a lecture last week can you expect to remember this week if you do not take any notes on the lecture?

   _____ 20%. _____

3. What do you think your level of recall would be if you took notes on a particular lecture but did not review your notes for two weeks?

   _____

4. Why would it be necessary to take notes on a film shown in class if you had to write a reaction paper on it that evening?

   because you can remember

HOW PEOPLE LEARN AND REMEMBER

Three stages are involved in the memory process: encoding, storage, and retrieval. First, information enters the brain from a variety of sources. This process is known as *encoding*. In reading and study situations, information is entered primarily through reading or listening. This information lingers briefly in what is known as *sensory storage* and is then either *stored* or discarded. Momentary or brief storage is called *short-term memory*. Next, information in short-term memory is either forgotten or transferred into more lasting storage called *long-term memory*. Anything that is to be remembered for more than a few seconds must be stored in long-term memory. To place information in long-term memory, one must learn it in some way. Finally, information can be brought back, or remembered, through a process known as *retrieval*. Figure 3.2 is a visual model of the learning and memory processes. Refer to it frequently as you read the sections that explain each stage.

How Encoding Works

Every waking moment, your mind is bombarded with a variety of impressions of what is going on around you. Your five senses—hearing, sight, touch, taste, and smell—provide information about your surroundings. Think for a moment of all the signals your brain receives at a given moment. If you are reading, your eyes transmit not only the visual patterns of the words, but also information about the size and color of the print. You may hear a door slamming, a clock ticking, a dog barking. Your sense of smell may detect perfume or cigarette smoke; your sense of touch or feeling may signal that a pen you are using to underline will soon run out of ink or that the room is chilly. When you listen to a classroom lecture, you are constantly receiving stimuli—from the professor, from the lecture hall, from students around you. All these environmental stimuli are transmitted to your brain for very brief sensory storage and interpretation.

How easily we interpret new information depends, in part, on its familiarity and on whether it fits with an existing schema. A *schema* is an organized set of general knowledge that is stored in long-term memory. Think of a

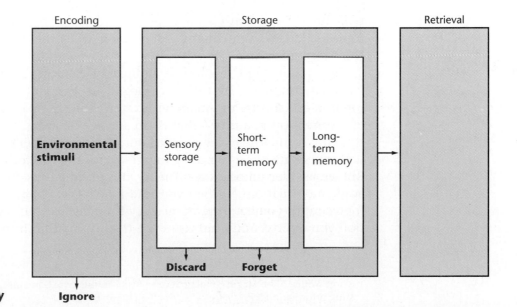

Figure 3.2
A Model of Memory

schema as a pattern, blueprint, or structure. When we encounter new information, we try to make it fit with existing information. Sometimes this strategy works. You realize, for example, that a new sport, such as racquetball, is similar to one you already know, such as tennis. At other times, no existing schema is available to help us understand a new idea or concept. In this case, encoding is more difficult.

How Sensory Storage Works

Information received from the sense organs is transmitted through the nervous system to the brain, which accepts and interprets it. The information stays briefly in the nervous system while the brain interprets it; this lingering is known as *sensory storage.*

How does your mind handle the barrage of information conveyed by your senses? Thanks to what is known as *selective attention,* your brain automatically sorts out the more important signals from the trivial ones. Trivial signals, such as insignificant noises around you, are ignored or discarded. Through skills of concentration and attention, you can train yourself to ignore other, more distracting signals, such as a dog barking or people talking in the background.

Although your sensory storage accepts all information, data are kept there only briefly, usually less than a few seconds. Then the information either fades or decays or is replaced with incoming new stimuli. The function of sensory storage, then, is to retain information long enough for you to selectively attend to it and send it to your short-term memory.

How Short-Term Memory Works

Short-term memory holds the information that was sent from your sensory storage system. It is used to store information you wish to retain for only a few seconds. A telephone number, for example, is stored in your short-term memory until you dial it. A lecturer's words are retained until you can record them in your notes. Most researchers agree that short-term memory lasts much less than a minute—perhaps 20 seconds or less. Information can be maintained longer if you practice or rehearse the information (repeating a phone number, for example). When you are introduced to someone, then, you will not be able to remember the person's name unless you repeat or rehearse it at the time of the introduction. New incoming information will otherwise force it out of your short-term memory.

Your short-term memory is limited in capacity as well as in time span. Research conducted by the psychologist George Miller suggests that we have room in our short-term memories to store from five to nine bits (pieces or sets) of information at a time—that is, an average of seven. If you try to store more than this, earlier items are bumped out. The size of each bit, however, is not limited to a single item. You can group items together to form a longer bit or piece. Known as the Number Seven Theory, this finding is useful in both daily life and academic situations.* When you read a textbook chapter or listen to a lecture, for example, your short-term memory is unable to retain each piece of information you receive. You must rearrange the information into groups or sets—ideas

---

*George Miller, "The Magic Number Seven plus or minus two: Some limits on our capacity for processing information," *Psychological Review,* 63 (1956): 81–97.

or topics. To retain information beyond the limitations of short-term memory, you must transfer it to long-term memory for more lasting storage.

DIRECTIONS   Use your knowledge of the memory process to answer the following questions.

1. Observe and analyze the area in which you are sitting. What sensory impressions (sights, sounds, touch sensations) have you been ignoring as a result of selective attention?

   _____

2. Can you remember what you ate for lunch three weeks ago? If not, why not?

   _____

3. Use your knowledge of the Number Seven Theory to explain why dashes are placed in your Social Security number after the third and fifth numbers and after the area code and the first three digits of your phone number.

   _____

4. Explain why two people are able to carry on a deep conversation at a crowded, noisy party.

   _____

5. Explain why someone who looks up a phone number and then walks into another room to dial it may forget the number.

   _____

Learning: The Transfer from Short- to Long-Term Memory

To retain information beyond the brief moment you acquire it, you must transfer it to long-term memory for permanent storage. There are several ways to store information in long-term memory: rote learning, elaborative rehearsal, and recoding.

Rote Learning

Rote learning involves repeating information in the form in which you acquired it in sensory storage. Learning the spelling of a word, memorizing the exact definition of a word, and repeating a formula until you can remember it are examples. Material learned through this means is often learned in a fixed order. Rote learning usually doesn't work well for storing large quantities of information. If you learn by rote, you are operating at the knowledge level of thinking (see Chapter 2, p. 46).

Elaborative Rehearsal

Rehearsal involves much more than simple repetition or practice. Elaborative rehearsal is a thinking process. It involves connecting new material with material already learned, asking questions, and making associations. It is a process of making the information meaningful and fitting it into an established category or relating it to existing memory stores. This form of rehearsal is discussed in more detail later. When you use elaboration, you are functioning at the comprehension and application levels of thinking (see p. 46).

Recoding

Recoding is a process of rearranging, rephrasing, changing, or grouping information so that it becomes more meaningful and easier to recall. Expressing ideas in your own words and outlining a reading assignment are forms of recoding. Taking notes in lectures is also a form of recoding, as is writing a term paper that summarizes several reference sources. When you recode, you are using higher levels of thinking—analysis and synthesis (see p. 46).

Rehearsal and recoding are the underlying principles on which many learning strategies presented later in this book are based. Chapter 13, for example, discusses textbook highlighting and marking. Highlighting is a form of rehearsal. In deciding which information to highlight, you review the information and sort the important from the unimportant. When you make notes in the margins of books, you recode the information by classifying, organizing, labeling, or summarizing it.

 **EXERCISE 3**

DIRECTIONS   Decide whether each of the following activities primarily involves rote learning, elaborative rehearsal, or recoding.

1. Learning a formula in economics for computing the rate of inflation

   _____

2. Relating to your personal experience the ideas and feelings expressed in a poem read in your English literature class

   _____

3. Making a chart that compares three political action groups

   _____

4. Learning metric equivalents for U.S. units of volume and weight

   _____

5. Drawing a diagram that shows the processes by which the Constitution can be amended

   _____

EXERCISE 4

DIRECTIONS   Use your knowledge of the memory process to answer the following questions.

1. Two groups of students read a textbook chapter. One group highlighted key ideas on each page; the second group paraphrased and recorded the important ideas from each page. Explain why the second group received higher scores than the first group on a test based on the chapter.

   _____

2. On many campuses, weekly recitations or discussions are scheduled for small groups to review material presented in large lecture classes. What learning function do these recitation sections perform?

   _____

3. After lecturing on the causes of domestic violence, a sociology instructor showed her class a videotape of an incident of domestic violence. What learning function(s) did the film perform? How would the tape help students remember the lecture?

_____

4. A text that contains photographs is often easier to learn from than one without them. What learning function do the pictures perform?

_____

How Long-Term Memory Works

Long-term memory is a relatively permanent store of information. Unlike short-term memory, long-term memory is nearly unlimited in both span (length) and capacity (size). It contains hundreds of thousands of facts, details, impressions, and experiences that you have accumulated throughout your life.

Once information is stored in your long-term memory, you recall it through a process known as _retrieval_. Academic tasks that require you to retrieve knowledge include math or science problems, quizzes and exams, and papers. Retrieval is tied to storage. The manner in which information is stored in your memory affects its availability and how easily you can retrieve it. For example, suppose you have studied a topic but find that on an exam you are unable to remember much about it. There are several possible explanations: (1) You never completely learned (stored) the information in the first place, (2) you did not study (store) the information in the right way, (3) you are not asking the right questions or using the right means to retrieve it, or (4) you have forgotten it. Later in this chapter, you will learn principles that will enable you to store information effectively.

 **EXERCISE 5**

DIRECTIONS Decide whether each of the following activities involves encoding, storage, and/or retrieval.

1. Taking an essay exam _____

2. Listening to a lecture _____

3. Taking notes on a film shown in class _____

4. Solving a homework problem in mathematics _____

5. Balancing a ledger in accounting _____

EXERCISE 6

DIRECTIONS Use your knowledge of how memory works to explain each of the following situations.

1. A student spends more time than anyone else in her class preparing for the midterm exam, yet she cannot remember important definitions and concepts at the time of the exam. Offer several possible explanations of her problem.

_____

2. Try to recall the sixth digit of your Social Security number without repeating the first five. What does this show about how you learned your number?

    _____

3. A computer science instructor begins a class session by handing out a quiz. One student is surprised and says he did not know there would be a quiz. All the other students recall the instructor announcing the quiz the week before. The student has never been absent or late for class. Why does he not know about the quiz?

    _____

4. A business instructor plans to lecture on the process of analyzing job stress. Before class she draws a diagram of this process on the chalkboard. During the lecture she refers to it frequently. Why did the instructor draw the diagram?

    _____

5. A student is studying a difficult chapter in biology. Her roommate asks her a question, but she does not answer. The roommate assumes she is being ignored and storms out of the room. What is the cause of this misunderstanding?

    _____

6. Suppose you are reading a section of your history text. You come across an unfamiliar word and look up its meaning. Once you have looked up the word, you find that you must reread the section. Why?

    _____

7. A political science instructor is discussing an essay on world terrorism. He begins the discussion by asking his students to recall recent terrorist acts and how they were resolved. How is the instructor helping his students learn the content of the essay?

    _____

8. A sociology instructor asks her students to read and write a summary of a journal article she has placed on reserve in the library. How is she helping her students learn the material?

    _____

EXERCISE 7

Academic
Application

DIRECTIONS   Identify your most difficult course. Consider the material you are required to learn for the next major test. Spend some time organizing textbook and lecture material that you are sure will be on the next test. Make a study plan that uses at least four of the techniques described in this chapter. Show your work to a class-mate. You and she or he should then offer each other suggestions to make studying more effective.

IMPROVING ENCODING, STORAGE, AND RETRIEVAL

Now that you have a notion of how memory works, you are ready to learn strategies that will both enhance your memory processes and retard forgetting.

Strategies for Improving Encoding

The following suggestions will help you to improve encoding, the process of taking in information.

Exclude Competing Stimuli

Deliberately exclude everything that does not relate to what you want to encode. For instance, if you are reading, do not sit where there are other competing visual stimuli, such as television.

Use Various Sensory Modes

Use as many senses as possible to take in information. When listening to a lecture, for example, pay attention to visual clues the lecturer provides as well as to what he or she says.

Carefully and Specifically Define Your Purpose

As you filter incoming information, know clearly and specifically what types of information you need. If you are reading reference material for a research paper, you may need to pay attention to facts and statistics. If you are reading material to prepare for a class discussion, however, you might focus on controversial issues.

Use Prereading

Since encoding involves accepting an incoming message, it is helpful to anticipate both the content and structure of that message. Prereading, which is discussed in Chapter 5, provides this preliminary information.

Strategies for Improving Storage

Use the following suggestions to improve how efficiently you store information.

Use Immediate Review

After working on a chapter for several hours (with frequent breaks) it is tempting, when you finish, to close the book and move on to something else. To quit, however, without taking five to ten minutes to review what you have read is a serious mistake. Since you have already invested several hours of time and effort, it is worthwhile to spend a few more minutes insuring that investment. *Reviewing immediately* following reading is an effective way of storing information and facilitating retrieval. Review of your notes immediately following a lecture is also effective. To review a chapter you have just read, reread each chapter heading and then reread the summary.

Use Periodic Review

Periodic review means returning to and quickly reviewing previously learned material on a regular basis. Suppose you have learned the material in the first three chapters of your criminology text during the first two weeks of the course. Unless you review that material, you are likely to forget it and have to relearn it by the time your final exam is given. You might establish a periodic review schedule in which you quickly review these chapters every three weeks or so.

Use Mnemonic Devices

Mnemonics are memory tricks, or aids, that you can devise to help you remember information. Mnemonics include rhymes, anagrams, words, nonsense words, sentences, and mental pictures that aid in the recall of facts. Do you remember this rhyme? "Thirty days hath September, / April, June, and November. / All the rest have thirty-one / except February, alone, / which has twenty-eight days clear / and twenty-nine in each leap year." The rhyme is an example of a mnemonic device. It is a quick and easy way of remembering the number of days in each month of the year. You may have learned to recall the colors of the rainbow by remembering the name *Roy G. Biv;* each letter in this name stands for one of the colors that make up the spectrum: *Red, Orange, Yellow, Green, Blue, Indigo, Violet.* Mnemonic devices are useful when you are trying to learn information that has no organization of its own. You will find them useful in reviewing texts and lecture notes as you prepare for exams.

Use Numerous Sensory Channels to Store Information

Many students regard reading and studying as only a visual means of taking in information. You can learn better, however, if you use sight, sound, and touch, as well. If you can incorporate writing, listening, drawing or diagramming, and recitation or discussion into your study habits, storage will be more effective.

Organize Information

Remembering a large number of individual facts or pieces of information is often a difficult, frustrating task. Organize or reduce information into groups or chunks. Instead of overloading your memory with numerous individual facts, learn organized, meaningful sets of information that are stored as one chunk.

To organize information, keep the following suggestions in mind:

- Discover how the material you are studying is connected. Search for some organizing principle.
- Look for similarities and differences.
- Look for sequences and for obvious divisions or breaking points within the sequences.

Use Elaboration

Mere repetition of material is seldom an effective storage strategy. Studying a chapter by rereading it, for instance, would not be effective. Instead you must think about, or *elaborate,* upon the material—ask questions, make associations and inferences, think of practical applications, and create mental images.

Connect New Learning with Previous Learning

Isolated, unrelated pieces of information are difficult to store and also difficult to retrieve. If, however, you can link new learning to already stored information, it will be easier to store and retrieve since you have an established memory slot in which to hold it. For example, an economics student associated the factors influencing the supply and demand curves with practical instances from his family's retail florist business.

EXERCISE 8

DIRECTIONS   Decide how you could organize or recode each of the following types of information for most effective storage.

1. The causes of homelessness
2. The problems of teen pregnancy
3. The importance of free trade
4. The results of environmental pollution

EXERCISE 9

DIRECTIONS   Discuss techniques that might improve storage of the following tasks.

1. Learning the process of amending the Constitution for an American government course
2. Learning the factors that influence market price for an economics course
3. Learning different forms of mental illness for a psychology course
4. Learning to recognize and distinguish the different types of figurative language for a literature course

Strategies for Improving Retrieval

Your ability to retrieve information is the true test of how accurately and completely you have stored it. The following strategies will improve your ability to retrieve information.

Use Visualization

As you read, study, and learn a body of information, try to visualize, or create a mental picture of it. Your picture or image should be sufficiently detailed to include as much related information as possible. A student of anatomy and physiology found visualizations an effective way to learn the parts of the skeletal system. She would first draw it on paper and then visualize, or mentally draw, the system.

Visualization, a type of imaginal coding, makes retrieval easier because the information is stored in one unified piece, and, if you can recall any part of the mental picture, you will be able to retrieve the whole picture.

Develop Retrieval Clues

Think of your memory as having slots or compartments in which information is stored. If you can name or label what is in the slot, you will know where to look to find information that fits that slot. Think of memory slots as similar to the way kitchen cupboards are often organized, with specific items in specific places. If you need a knife to cut a pizza, you look in the silverware and utensils drawer. Similarly, if you have a memory slot labeled "environmental problems" in which you store information related to pollution, its problems, causes, and solutions, you can retrieve information on air pollution by calling the appropriate retrieval clue. Developing retrieval clues involves selecting a word or phrase that summarizes or categorizes several pieces of information. For example, you might use the phrase "motivation theories" to organize information for a psychology course on instinct, drive, cognitive, arousal, and opponent-process theories and the major proponents of each.

Simulate Retrieval Tasks

Practice retrieving learned information by simulating test conditions. If you are studying for a math exam, prepare by solving problems. If you know your exam in a law enforcement course will consist of three essay questions, then prepare by anticipating possible essay questions and drafting an answer to each. The form and process of practice, then, must be patterned after and modeled upon the event for which you are preparing.

Overlearn

It is tempting to stop studying as soon as you feel you have learned a given body of information. However, to ensure complete, thorough learning, it is best to conduct a few more reviews. When you learned to drive a car, you did not stop practicing parallel parking after the first time you accomplished it correctly. Similarly, for a botany course you should not stop reviewing the process of photosynthesis and its place within the carbon cycle at the moment you feel you have mastered it. Instead, use additional review to make the material stick and to prevent interference from subsequent learning.

Use Context

It is easier to recall information when you are in the same setting (context) in which it was learned. Consider reviewing your notes in the lecture hall in which you took them. Also, study if possible in the room in which you will take the exam.

EXERCISE 10

DIRECTIONS   What strategies would you use to learn (encode, store, and retrieve) each of the following types of information most efficiently?

1. The process of cell division for a biology course
2. Important terms from an introductory sociology course
3. The different types of white collar crimes and their cost to society for a criminology course
4. A comparison of the different kinds of psychoactive drugs for a health course

LEARNING Collaboratively

DIRECTIONS   Form pairs with another student. If possible, choose a student who is taking or has taken one of the same courses you are taking or is taking a course in the same field (science, mathematics, business, and so on). Together, prepare a list of strategies for improving storage and retrieval, and give examples from the course or field of study you share. Include storage and retrieval strategies that would be helpful to other students taking the course. Make your strategy list available to other class members who may take the course. Select two strategies and begin using them immediately.

Applying YOUR LEARNING

Carlos is having difficulty with his human anatomy and physiology course. He feels overwhelmed by the volume of facts and details, as well as the new terminology he must learn. His next assigned chapter is "The Skeletal System." It first discusses functions and types of bones and then describes all the bones in the human skeletal system, including the skull, vertebral column, pelvis (hip), and extremities (arms, legs, feet, and hands). Carlos says that he understands the material as he reads it but cannot remember it later. His instructor gives weekly quizzes as well as hour-long exams.

1. Explain why Carlos understands information as he reads it but cannot recall it later.
2. What can Carlos do to correct his lack of recall?
3. What learning principles would help Carlos learn the skeletal system?

SELF-TEST SUMMARY

1. What is forgetting and how does it occur?

Forgetting is the loss of information stored in memory. It occurs when other information interferes and prevents you from recalling the information you want. Forgetting occurs very rapidly, but certain techniques can prevent forgetting or slow down its normally rapid rate.

2. How do we learn and remember?

Three stages are involved in the memory process: encoding, storage, and retrieval. Encoding is the process through which information enters your brain through your senses. This information lingers briefly in sensory storage, where it is interpreted. Next the information is either stored briefly in short-term memory or discarded and forgotten. Then you must either transfer information into the more lasting long-term memory or allow it to be forgotten. Transferring facts from short-term to long-term memory involves rote learning, elaborative rehearsal, and recoding.

3. What can be done to improve encoding, storage, and retrieval?

Encoding: Exclude competing stimuli, use various sensory modes, carefully and specifically define your purpose, use prereading.

Storage: Use immediate and periodic review, use mnemonic devices, use numerous sensory channels, organize information, use elaboration, connect new learning with previous learning.

Retrieval: Use visualizations, develop retrieval clues, simulate rehearsal tasks, overlearn, use context.

Take a Road Trip to
Mount Rushmore!

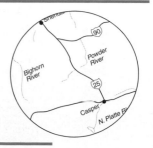

If your instructor has asked you to use the Reading Road Trip CD-ROM, be sure to visit the Memorization and Concentration module for multimedia tutorials, exercises, and tests.

Taking Notes in Class

Why Take Notes from Lectures?

▲ **Taking notes keeps your mind on the lecture.**

▲ **Taking notes helps you decide what is important.**

▲ **Taking notes will help you recall the lecture.**

▲ **Your notes will be a valuable study tool.**

Learning Experiment

Step 1

Ask a friend to (or your instructor may choose to) read each of the following paragraphs aloud. (Each paragraph may be read aloud twice.) While paragraph 1 is being read to you, just listen. While and after paragraph 2 is being read to you, write a set of notes that contain its most important ideas.

Paragraph 1

Did you know that use of empty space is a form of communication? How humans use space can communicate as loudly as words and phrases. How close or how far away you stand from another person communicates a message. Research by Edward Hall identifies four types of distance, each of which defines the relationship you establish with others. The first, intimate distance, is not considered appropriate in public (except in crowded places, such as elevators). Family members and spouses may use the intimate distance. Personal distance is the space around you that no one invades unless invited, such as to shake hands. Social distance is the distance at which you operate in daily living—sitting in classrooms, attending a play, shopping, and so forth. The fourth type, public distance, is used when you are not involved with the other person.

Paragraph 2

Communication occurs with words and gestures, but did you know it also occurs through sense of smell? Odor can communicate at least four types of messages. First, odor can signal attraction. Animal species give off scents to attract members of the opposite sex. Humans use fragrances to make themselves more appealing or attractive. Smell also communicates information about tastes. The smell of popcorn popping stimulates the appetite. If you smell a chicken roasting you can anticipate its taste. A third type of smell communication is through memory. A smell can help you recall an event months or even years ago, especially if the event is an emotional one. Finally, smell can communicate by creating an identity or image for a person or product. For example, a woman may only wear one brand of perfume. Or a brand of shaving cream may have a distinct fragrance, which allows users to recognize it.

Step 2

Wait 24 hours, or until the next class session, then, *without* reading either paragraph or looking at your notes, answer the following questions.

Paragraph 1

1. Name the four types of distances discussed in the paragraph.

Paragraph 2

1. Name the four messages that smell can communicate.

Check your answers on p. 440.

The Results

You probably got more information correct for paragraph 2 than you did for paragraph 1. Why? Because you listened to paragraph 2 and then you wrote. In doing this, you used three sensory modes: hearing (listening), touching (writing), and seeing (reading). For paragraph 1, you used only one sensory mode: hearing.

Learning Principle (What This Means to You)

You have five senses—five ways of taking in information from the world around you: sight, touch, smell, sound, and taste. **The more senses you use to learn something, the easier it will be to learn.** When you listen to a college lecture, you are using only one sensory mode. If you take notes on the lecture as you listen, you are using your sense of touch as well as your sense of hearing. When you reread the notes after you have written them, you are employing a third sensory mode—sight. In this chapter you will learn how to take notes effectively, how to edit them, and how to develop a system to study them.

SHARPENING YOUR LISTENING SKILLS

The first step in taking good lecture notes is to sharpen your listening skills. The average adult spends 31 percent of each waking hour listening. By comparison, 7 percent is spent on writing, 11 percent on reading, and 21 percent on speaking. Listening, then, is an essential communication skill. During college lectures, listening is especially important: It is your primary means of acquiring information.

Have you ever found yourself not listening to a professor who was lecturing? Her voice was loud and clear, so you certainly could hear her, but you weren't paying attention—you tuned her out. This situation illustrates the distinction between hearing and listening. Hearing is a passive, biological process in which sound waves are received by the ear. Listening, however, is an intellectual activity that involves the processing and interpretation of incoming information. Listening must be intentional, purposeful, and deliberate. You must plan to listen, have a reason for listening, and carefully focus your attention. Use the following suggestions to sharpen your listening skills.

1. Approach listening as a process similar to reading.

When you read, you not only recognize words but also understand, connect, and evaluate ideas. Similarly, listening is not simply a process of hearing words. It is a comprehension process in which you grasp ideas, assess their importance, and connect them to other ideas. All the reading comprehension skills you will develop in Part Three of this text are useful for listening as well. Focus on identifying main ideas, and on evaluating the importance and connection of details in relation to the main idea. Be alert for transitions—speakers tend to use them more frequently than writers. Also, try to identify patterns of thought to improve both comprehension and recall.

2. Focus on content, not delivery.

It is easy to become so annoyed, upset, charmed, or engaged with the lecturer as an individual that you fail to comprehend the message he or she is conveying. Force yourself to focus on the content of the lecture and disregard the personal style and characteristics of the lecturer.

3. Focus on ideas as well as facts.

If you concentrate on recording and remembering separate, unconnected facts, you are doomed to failure. Remember, your short-term memory is extremely limited in span and capacity, so while you are focusing on certain facts, it is inevitable that you will ignore some and forget others. Instead, listen for ideas, significant trends, and patterns, as well as facts.

4. Listen carefully to the speaker's opening comments.

As your mind refocuses from prior tasks and problems, it is easy to miss the speaker's opening remarks. However, these are among the most important. Here the speaker may establish connections with prior lectures, identify his or her purpose, or describe the lecture's content or organization.

5. Attempt to understand the lecturer's purpose.

If the lecturer's purpose is not stated explicitly, try to reason it out. Is it to present facts, raise and discuss questions, demonstrate a trend or pattern, or present a technique or procedure?

6. Fill the gap between rate of speech and rate of thinking.

Has your mind ever wandered back and forth during a lecture? Although you may be interested in what the speaker is saying, do you seem to have time to think about other things while listening? This is natural, because the rate of speech is much slower than the speed of thought. The average rate of speech is around 125 words per minute, whereas the rate at which you can process ideas is over 500 words per minute. To listen most effectively, use this gap to think about lecture content. Anticipate what is to follow, think of situations in which the information might be applied, pose questions, or make the information fit your prior knowledge and experience.

7. Approach listening as a challenging mental task.

We all know concentration and attention are necessary for reading, yet many of us treat listening as something that should occur without effort. Perhaps because of the constant barrage of spoken words we are bombarded with through radio, television, and conversation, we assume that listening occurs automatically. Lectures, however, are a concentrated form of oral communication that require you to put higher-level attention and thinking skills into gear.

PREPARING FOR A LECTURE CLASS

Before you attend a lecture class, you should become familiar with the main topic of the lecture and be aware of important subtopics and related subjects.

Understanding the lecture and taking notes will be easier if you have some idea what the lecture is about. If your instructor assigns a textbook chapter that is related to the lecture, try to read the assignment before attending. If you are unable to read the entire chapter before class, at least preread the chapter to become familiar with the topics it covers. (You will learn about prereading in Chapter 5.) If no reading assignment is given in advance, check your course outline to determine the topic of the lecture. Then preread the sections of your text that are about the topic.

Once you arrive at a lecture class, get organized before it begins. Take your coat off and have your notebook, pen, and textbook chapter (if needed) ready to use. While waiting for class to begin, try to recall the content of the previous lecture: Think of three or four key points that were presented. Check your notes, if necessary. This process will activate your thought processes, focus your attention on course content, and make it easier for you to begin taking notes right away.

HOW TO TAKE LECTURE NOTES

A good set of lecture notes must accomplish three things. First, and most important, your notes must serve as a record or summary of the lecture's main points.

Second, they must include enough details and examples so that you can recall the information several weeks later. Third, your notes must in some way show the relative importance of ideas presented and the organization of the lecture.

Record Main Ideas

The main ideas of a lecture are the points the instructor emphasizes and elaborates. They are the major ideas that the details, explanations, examples, and general discussion support. Instructors frequently give clues to what is important in a lecture. The following are a few ways in which speakers show what is important.

Change in Voice

Some lecturers change the tone or pitch of their voices in order to emphasize major points. A speaker's voice may get louder or softer or higher or lower as he or she presents important ideas.

Change in Rate of Speech

Speakers may slow down as they discuss important concepts. Sometimes a speaker goes so slowly that he or she seems to be dictating information. If a speaker giving a definition pauses slightly after each word or phrase, this is a signal that the definition is important and you should write it down.

Listing and Numbering Points

A lecturer may directly state that there are "three important causes" or "four significant effects" or "five possible situations" as he or she begins discussing a particular topic. These expressions are clues to the material's importance. Frequently, a speaker further identifies or emphasizes the separate, particular facts or ideas that make up the "three causes" or "four effects" with words such as *first, second,* and *finally,* or *one effect, a second effect, another effect,* and *a final effect.*

Writing on the Chalkboard

Some lecturers write key words or outlines of major ideas on the chalkboard as they speak. Not all important ideas are recorded on the chalkboard, but you can be sure that when an instructor does take the time to write a word or phrase on the chalkboard, it is important.

Use of Audiovisuals

Some instructors emphasize important ideas, clarify relationships, or diagram processes or procedures by using audiovisual aids. Commonly used are overhead projectors that project on a screen previously prepared material or information the instructor draws or writes. Also, an instructor may use movies, filmstrips, videotapes, or photographs to emphasize or describe important ideas and concepts.

Direct Announcement

Occasionally, an instructor will announce straightforwardly that a concept or idea is especially important. He or she may begin by saying, "Particularly important to remember as you study is . . ." or "One important fact that you must keep in mind is . . . ." The instructor may even hint that such information would make a good exam question. Be sure to mark hints like these in your notes. Emphasize these items with an asterisk or write *Exam?* in the margin.

Nonverbal Clues

Many speakers give as many nonverbal as verbal clues to what is important. Some lecturers walk toward their audience as they make a major point. Others use hand gestures, pound the table, or pace back and forth as they present key ideas. Each speaker is different, but most speakers use some nonverbal means of emphasizing important points.

EXERCISE 1

Academic Application

DIRECTIONS   Select one of your instructors and analyze his or her lecture style. Attend one lecture, and, as you take notes, try to be particularly aware of how he or she lets you know what is important. After the lecture, try to analyze your instructor using the following questions.

1. Did the instructor's voice change? When? How?

   _____

2. Did the rate of speaking vary? When?

   _____

3. Did the instructor list or number important points?

   _____

4. Did the instructor use the chalkboard?

   _____

5. Did he or she directly state what was important?

   _____

6. What nonverbal clues did the instructor give?

   _____

Record Details and Examples

A difficult part of taking notes is deciding how much detail to include with the main ideas. Obviously, you cannot write down everything; lecturers speak at the rate of about 125 words per minute. Even if you could take shorthand, it would be nearly impossible to record everything the lecturer says. As a result, you have to be selective and record only particularly important details. As a rule of thumb, record a brief phrase that summarizes each major supporting detail. Try to write down a phrase for each detail that directly explains or clarifies a major point.

If an instructor gives you several examples of a particular law, situation, or problem, be sure to write down, in summary form, at least one example. Record more than one if you have time. Although at the time of the lecture it may seem that you completely understand what is being discussed, you will find that a few weeks later you really do need the example to boost your recall.

Record the Organization of the Lecture

As you write down the main ideas and important details of a lecture, try to organize or arrange your notes so that you can easily see how the lecture is organized. By recording the organization of the lecture, you will be able to determine the relative importance of ideas, and you will know what to pay the most attention to as you study and review for an exam.

A simple way to show a lecture's organization is to use indentation. Retain a regular margin on your paper. Start your notes on the most important of the topics at the left margin. For less important main ideas, indent your notes slightly. For major details, indent slightly more. Indent even more for examples and other details. The rule of thumb to follow is this: The less important the idea, the more it should be indented. Your notes might be organized like the sample that follows.

        Major topic
            Main idea
                detail
                detail
                    example
            Main idea
                detail
                detail
                detail
        Major topic
            Main idea
                detail
                    example

Note that this sample looks like an outline but is missing the Roman numerals (I, II, III), capital letters (A, B, C), and Arabic numerals (1, 2, 3) that are usually contained in an outline. Also note, however, that this system of note taking accomplishes the same major goal as an outline—it separates important infor-

Pattern	Note-Taking Tips
Comparison–contrast	Record similarities, differences, and basis of comparison; use two columns or make a chart.
Cause–effect	Distinguish causes from effects; use diagrams.
Sequence or order	Record dates; focus on order and sequence; use a time line for historical events; draw diagrams; record in order of importance; outline events or steps in a process.
Problem–solution	Record parameters of the problem; focus on the nature of the problem; record the process of arriving at a solution.
Classification	Use outline form; list characteristics and distinguishing features.
Definition	Record the general category or class; then list distinguishing characteristics; include several examples.
Listing	Record in list or outline form; record the order of presentation.

Figure 4.1
Using Patterns in Lecture Note Taking

mation from less important information. This indentation system, like an outline, shows at a glance how important a particular fact or idea is. If the organization of a lecture is obvious, you may wish to use a number or letter system in addition to indenting.

Lectures are often organized using patterns: definition, time sequence, comparison–contrast, cause–effect, problem–solution, or enumeration. Figure 4.1 lists tips for "customizing" your note taking to each of these patterns. An entire lecture may be organized using one pattern; a history lecture, for example, may use the time sequence pattern throughout. More often, however, several patterns will be evident at various points in a lecture. A psychology professor, for instance, may discuss definitions of motivation and compare and contrast different motivational theories. (Refer to Chapter 7 for a review of organizational patterns and the directional words that signal them.)

The notes in Figure 4.2 (below) and Figure 4.3 (page 72) show that effective lecture notes should record main ideas, important details, and examples and that they should reflect the lecture's organization. Both sets of notes were taken on the same lecture. One set of notes is thorough and effective; the other is lengthy and does not focus on key ideas. Read and evaluate each set of notes.

Make Note Taking Easier

If you record main ideas, details, and examples using the indentation system to show the lecture's organization, you will take adequate notes. However, there are some tips you can follow to make note taking easier, to make your notes more complete, and to make study and review easier.

A. Social Stratification Soc. 106
 Defs 9/16
  Soc. Start. —hierarchy of ranks that exist in society
  Status —criteria to find positions in soc.
   2 types
    1. ascribed status—handed down; inherited
     ex.: titles, race, wealth, ethnic background
    2. achieved status—things you control
     ex.: education, jobs
B. Social Mobility
 Def. —how indiv. moves in hierarchy
  —amt. of movement depends on society
 2 Types
  1. caste—ex.: India—no mobility—you inherit class + status
  2. open—large amt. of achieved status—great mobility—ex.: USA.

Figure 4.2
Notes Showing Lecture Organization

Social Stratification

Social stratification—defined as the ranks that exist in society—the position that any person has—ascribed status—it is handed down—
example: titles. A second kind is achieved—it is the kind you decide for yourself.
Social stratification is important in understanding societies. How a person moves up and down + changes his social status is called mobility. Some societies have a lot of mobility. Others don't have any—example is India.
There are 2 kinds of movement.
1. Caste system is when everybody is assigned a class and they must stay there without any chance to change.
2. Open—people can move from one to another. This is true in the United States.

Figure 4.3
Less Effective, Unfocused Lecture Notes

Use Ink

Pencil tends to smear and is harder to read.

Use a Standard-Sized Notebook and Paper

Paper smaller than 8½ by 11 inches doesn't allow you to write as much on a page, and it is more difficult to see the overall organization of a lecture if you have to flip through a lot of pages.

Keep a Separate Notebook or Section for Each Course

You need to have your notes for each course together so that you can review them easily.

Date Your Notes

For easy reference later, be sure to date your notes. Your instructor might announce that an exam will cover everything presented after, for example, October 5. If your notes are not dated, you will not know where to begin to study.

Leave Blank Spaces

To make your notes more readable and to make it easier to see the organization of ideas, leave plenty of blank space. If you know you missed a detail or definition, leave additional blank space. You can fill it in later by checking with a friend or referring to your text.

Mark Assignments

Occasionally an instructor will announce an assignment or test date in the middle of a lecture. Of course you will jot it down, but be sure to mark "Assignment" or "Test Date" in the margin so that you can find it easily and transfer it to your assignment notebook.

Mark Ideas that Are Unclear

If an instructor presents a fact or idea that is unclear, put a question mark in the margin. Later, ask your instructor or another student about this idea.

Sit in the Front of the Classroom

Especially in large lecture halls, it is to your advantage to sit near the front. In the front you will be able to see and hear the instructor easily—you can maintain eye contact and observe his or her facial expressions and nonverbal clues. If you sit in the back, you may become bored, and it is easy to be distracted by all the people in front of you. Because of the people seated between you and the instructor, a feeling of distance is created. You may feel that the instructor is not really talking to you.

Don't Plan to Recopy Your Notes

Some students take each day's notes in a hasty, careless way and then recopy them in the evening. These students feel that recopying helps them review the information. Actually, recopying often becomes a mechanical process that takes a lot of time but very little thought. Time spent recopying can be better spent reviewing the notes in a manner that will be suggested later in this chapter. If, however, you are reorganizing and expanding upon your notes and not just copying them, then rewriting can be useful.

Recognize that Tape-Recording Lectures Is Time-Consuming

As a maximum effort to get complete and accurate notes, some students tape-record very detailed or complicated lectures. After the lecture, they play back the tape and edit their notes, starting and stopping the tape as needed. This is a time-consuming technique, but some students find it a helpful way to build their confidence, improve their note-taking techniques, and assure themselves that their notes are complete. If you decide to tape-record, do so sparingly. Unless your notes are incomplete, listening to a recording requires a great deal of time and often yields little gain. *If you plan to tape-record, be sure to ask your instructor for permission to do so.*

Use Abbreviations

To save time, try to use abbreviations instead of writing out long or frequently used words. If you are taking a course in psychology, you do not want to write out *p-s-y-c-h-o-l-o-g-y* each time the word is used. It would be much faster to use the abbreviation *psy*. Try to develop abbreviations that are appropriate for the subject areas you are studying. The abbreviations shown in Figure 4.4 on the next page, devised by a student in business management, will give you an idea of the possibilities. Note that both common and specialized words are abbreviated.

As you develop your own set of abbreviations, be sure to begin gradually. It is easy to overuse abbreviations and end up with notes that are almost meaningless.

Academic Application

EXERCISE 2

DIRECTIONS Select one set of lecture notes from a class you recently attended. Reread your notes and look for words or phrases you could have abbreviated. Write some of these words and their abbreviations in the spaces provided on the next page.

Word	Abbreviation
_____	_____
_____	_____
_____	_____
_____	_____
_____	_____
_____	_____
_____	_____
_____	_____

Create a Code System

Devise a system by which you record or mark specific types of information in specific ways. For example, number the items in a list, write "ex" next to each example, or put question marks next to ideas you don't understand. (A system for marking textbooks is given in Figure 13.1, p. 280.)

Make the Most of Your Learning Style

Use your knowledge of your learning style preferences to guide your note taking. By adapting your note-taking strategies to take advantage of your learning style, you will also make study and review easier. Figure 4.5 on the facing page offers some suggestions for tailoring your note taking to your learning style.

Overcoming Common Note-Taking Problems

Instructors present lectures differently, use various lecture styles, and organize their subjects in different ways. Therefore, students often have difficulty taking notes in one or more courses. Figure 4.6 identifies common problems associated with lecture note taking and offers possible solutions.

Figure 4.4
Abbreviations for Use in Note Taking

Common words	Abbreviation	Specialized words	Abbreviation
and	+	organization	org.
with	w/	management	man.
compare		data bank	D.B.
comparison	comp.	structure	str.
importance	imp't	evaluation	eval.
advantage	adv	management	
introduction	intro	by objective	MBO
continued	con't	management	
		information system	MIS
		organizational	
		development	OD
		communication	
		simulations	comm/sim

Learning Characteristics	Note-Taking Strategy
Auditory	Take advantage of your advantage! Take thorough and complete notes.
Visual	Work on note-taking skills; practice by tape-recording a lecture; analyze and revise your notes.
Applied	Think of applications (record as annotations). Write questions in the margin about applications.
Conceptual	Discover relationships among ideas. Watch for patterns.
Spatial	Add diagrams and maps, as appropriate, during editing (see p. 76).
Nonspatial	Record lecture's diagrams and drawings—but translate into language during editing (see p. 76).
Social	Review and edit notes with a classmate. Compare notes with others.
Independent	Choose seating in close contact with the instructor; avoid distracting groups of students.
Creative	Annotate your notes, recording impressions, reactions, spinoff ideas, and related ideas.
Pragmatic	Reorganize your notes during editing. Pay attention to the lecturer's organization.

Figure 4.5
Adapting Note Taking to Your Learning Style

Problem	Solution
"My mind wanders and I get bored."	Sit in the front of the room. Be certain to preview assignments. Think about questions you expect to be answered in the lecture.
"The instructor talks too fast."	Develop a shorthand system; use abbreviations. Leave blanks and fill them in later.
"The lecturer rambles."	Preview correlating text assignments to determine organizing principles. Reorganize your notes after the lecture.
"Some ideas don't seem to fit anywhere."	Record them in the margin or in parentheses within your notes, and think about them later during editing.
"Everything seems important." "Nothing seems important."	You have not identified key concepts and may lack necessary background knowledge (see Chapter 5)—you do not understand the topic. Preview related text assignments.
"I can't spell all the new technical terms."	Write them phonetically: the way they sound. Fill in correct spellings during editing.
"The instructor uses terms without defining them."	Write the terms as they are used; leave space to record definitions later, when you can consult the text glossary or a dictionary.
"The instructor reads directly from the text."	Mark passages in the text; write the instructor's comments in the margin. Record page references in your notes.

Figure 4.6
Common Note-Taking Problems

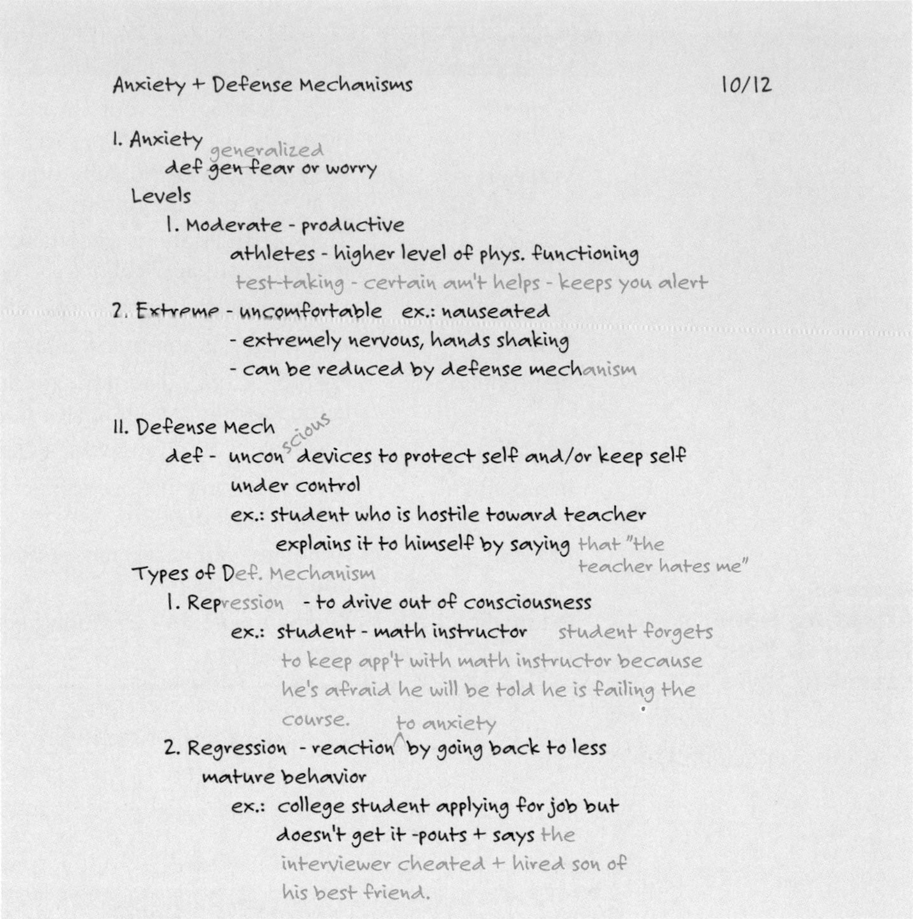
Anxiety + Defense Mechanisms 10/12

I. Anxiety
def ~~gen~~ generalized fear or worry
Levels
1. Moderate - productive
athletes - higher level of phys. functioning
test-taking - certain am't helps - keeps you alert
2. Extreme - uncomfortable ex.: nauseated
- extremely nervous, hands shaking
- can be reduced by defense mechanism

II. Defense Mech
def - unconscious devices to protect self and/or keep self under control
ex.: student who is hostile toward teacher explains it to himself by saying that "the teacher hates me"
Types of Def. Mechanism
1. Repression - to drive out of consciousness
ex.: student - math instructor student forgets to keep app't with math instructor because he's afraid he will be told he is failing the course.
2. Regression - reaction to anxiety by going back to less mature behavior
ex.: college student applying for job but doesn't get it - pouts + says the interviewer cheated + hired son of his best friend.

Figure 4.7
Edited Lecture Notes

HOW TO EDIT YOUR NOTES

After you have taken a set of lecture notes, do not assume that they are accurate and complete. Most students find that they missed some information and were unable to record as many details or examples as they would have liked. Even very experienced note takers face these problems. Fortunately, the solution is simple. Don't plan on taking a final and complete set of notes during the lecture. Instead, record just enough during the lecture to help you remember a main idea, detail, or example. Leave plenty of blank space; then, if possible, sit down immediately after the lecture and review your notes. Fill in the missing information. Expand, or flesh out, any details or examples that are not fully explained. This process is called *editing.* It is essentially a process of correcting, revising, and adding to your notes to make them complete and more accurate. Editing notes for a one-hour lecture should take no more than five or ten minutes.

If you are unable to edit your notes immediately after a lecture, it is critical that you edit them that evening. The more time between note taking and editing, the less effective editing becomes. Also, the greater the time lapse, the more facts and examples you will be unable to recall and fill in.

The sample set of lecture notes in Figure 4.7 has been edited. The notes taken during the lecture are in black; the additions and changes made during editing are in color. Read the notes, noticing the types of information added during editing.

Editing is also a time for you to think about the notes you've taken—to move beyond the literal knowledge and comprehension levels of thought to the levels that involve critical thinking.

Applying Levels of Thinking

Editing Notes and Levels of Thinking

As you edit your notes, keep the following questions in mind.

Level of Thinking	Question
Application	How can I use this information?
Analysis	How do these notes fit with other lectures? With the textbook assignment?
Synthesis	What does this all mean? How can I summarize it?
Evaluation	How useful is this information? Was it clear and well presented? What additional information do I need? What don't I fully understand?

Do not hesitate to add marginal notes, jot down questions, add reactions, draw arrows to show relationships, and bracket sections that seem confusing.

Using a Computer to Organize Your Notes

Consider using a word processor to edit and reorganize your notes. The computer makes it easy to rearrange ideas in a way that makes sense to you or that parallels how they are presented in the textbook chapter. The process of entering your notes into the computer can function as review—a time when you think about, consolidate, or expand on ideas presented in the lecture.

Tips for Keeping a Computerized Notebook

Here are a few tips for keeping computerized lecture notes:

1. Create a separate file for each of your courses.
2. Transfer your notes onto the computer as soon as possible after each class while the lecture is still fresh in your mind.
3. As you transfer, edit and reorganize your notes, using the suggestions given above.
4. Develop a system in which you designate major topics, key points, definitions, and examples by using different typefaces (bold, capitals, italics) or symbols (asterisks, bullets).
5. Save your work frequently onto a disk so you have a record of your notes in case your hard drive fails.
6. Print a copy of your notes and take them to class, because you may want to refer to them during the next lecture.

Integrating Text and Lecture Notes

A continual problem students wrestle with is how to integrate lecture and textbook notes. The computer offers an ideal solution to the integration of textual and lecture notes. The cut-and-paste option enables you to move pieces (sections) of your notes to any desired place in the document. Thus, you can easily integrate text and lecture notes on each major topic.

HOW TO STUDY YOUR NOTES

Taking and editing lecture notes is only part of what must be done to learn from your instructor's lectures. You also have to learn and review the notes in order to do well on an exam. To study lecture notes, try to apply the same principles that you use in learning material in your textbooks:

1. Do not try to learn your notes by reading them over and over. Rereading is not an efficient review technique because it takes too much time relative to the amount you learn.
2. As in reading textbook assignments, identify what is important. You must sort out what you will learn and study from all the rest of the information you have written in your notes.
3. Have a way of checking yourself—of deciding whether you have learned the necessary information.

To study lecture notes, you can use a system called the *recall clue system.*

The Recall Clue System

The recall clue system helps make the review and study of lecture notes easier and more effective. To use the recall clue system, follow these steps:

1. Leave a 2-inch margin at the left side of each page of notes.
2. Write nothing in the margin while you are taking notes.
3. After you have edited your notes, fill in the left margin with words and phrases that briefly summarize the notes.

The recall clues should be words that will trigger your memory and help you recall the complete information in your notes. These clues function as memory tags. They help you retrieve from your memory any information that is labeled with these tags. Figure 4.8 shows a sample of notes in which the recall clue system has been used. When you are taking an exam, the recall clue from your notes will work automatically to help you remember necessary information.

A variation on the recall clue system that students have found effective is to write questions rather than summary words and phrases in the margin (see Figure 4.9 on page 80). The questions trigger your memory and enable you to recall the information that answers your question. The use of questions enables you to test yourself, simulating an exam situation.

Using the Recall Clue System

To study your notes using the recall clue system, cover up the notes with a sheet of paper, exposing only the recall clues in the left margin. Next, read the first recall clue and try to remember the information in the portion of the notes beside it. Then slide the paper down and check that portion to see whether you remembered all the important facts. If you remembered only part of the information, cover up that portion of your notes and again check your recall. Continue checking until you are satisfied that you can remember all the important facts. Then move on to the next recall clue on the page, following the same testing–checking procedure.

To get into the habit of using the recall clue system, mark off with a ruler a 2-inch column on the next several blank pages in each of your notebooks. Then, when you open your notebook at the beginning of the class, you will be reminded to use the system.

Numerical Properties of Atoms   Chem 109
                                                      2/9

                    I. Prop. related to Temperature + Heat

melting point   A. Melting Point
                - when particles in a solid move fast
                  enough to overcome forces holding them
                  together - temp at which this happens =
                  melting point.

freezing point   - Freezing Pt. -temp at which forces
                  attracting particles to one another hold
                  particles together.

heat of fusion   - Heat of Fusion -amt. of heat req'd. to
                  melt one gram of any substance
                  at its melting pt.

boiling point   B. Boiling Point
                - Point at which molecules of a liquid
                  begin to escape as gas.

heat of vap.   - Heat of vaporization -amt. of heat req'd.
                  to change one gram of liquid to a gas
                  at its boiling pt.

Condensation pt.   - Condensation Pt. - point at which gas,
                  cooling, changes back to liquid.

spec. heat   C. Specific Heat
                    ex. beach -sand hot, water cold- why?
                    Sand + H_2O have different spec. heat
                def. -am't. of heat needed to raise temp.
                of a spec. mass of substance by a
                certain am't.

formula for S.h.   formula - S.h. = heat in cals.
                    mass in grams x temp. diff. in °C
$$S.h. = \frac{cal}{g \times °C}$$

Figure 4.8
Lecture Notes with Recall Clues Added

EXERCISE 3

DIRECTIONS Read the sample set of notes in Figure 4.10 on page 81. Fill in the recall clues or formulate questions that would help you study and learn the notes.

EXERCISE 4

DIRECTIONS For each course you are taking this semester, use the recall clue system for at least one week. Use the recall clues to review your notes several times. At the end of the week, evaluate how well the system works for you.

1. What advantages does it have?

_____
_____

2. Did it help you remember facts and ideas?

_____
_____

3. Are there any disadvantages?

_____

Marketing 104
10/8

Role of Advertising

What is Advertising?	Advertising —Widely used in our economy. —Promotes competition; encourages open system. definition—presentation of a product/service to broad segment of the population.

What are its
Characteristics?
	Characteristics
	1. non-personal—uses media
	   rather than person-to-person
	   contact.
	2. paid for by seller
	3. intended to influence the
	   consumer.

What is the Ultimate Objective?	Objectives Ultimate objective—to sell product or service

What are the
Immediate Objectives?
	Immediate objectives
	1. to inform—make consumer
	   aware
	   ex. new product available
	2. to persuade—stress value,
	   advantages of product
	   ex. results of market research
	3. to reinforce—happens after
	   1 and 2
	   —consumers need to be
	   reminded about prod./service—
	   even if they use it.
	   —often done through slogans
	   and jingles.

Figure 4.9
Lecture Notes with Recall Questions Added

LEARNING Collaboratively

DIRECTIONS   Working in pairs, bring two sets of lecture notes to class. The first set should be notes taken *before* this chapter on note taking was assigned. The second should be a set of notes taken after this chapter was assigned and should contain editing and recall clues. Assess each other's progress, and suggest areas for further improvement.

I. Psychoanalytic theory—created by Sigmund Freud
   A. free association—major diagnostic techniques in psychoanalysis; patient reports whatever comes to mind/holds nothing back.
   B. repression—psych. process of driving ideas out of consciousness.
   C. suppression—conscious of an idea, but won't tell anyone about it.
   D. trauma—particularly disturbing event; most psych. disturbances traceable to a trauma.
   E. interp. of dreams—dreams—fantasies that person believes to be true/have profound influence on personality devlpmt.
   F. Id—power system of personality providing energy.
      1. pleasure principle—all unpleasant events should be avoided.
         a. primary process—normal logic does not operate. ex. bizarre dreams, hallucinations
   G. Ego—strategist of personality/concerned w/what a person CAN do.
      1. reality principle—distinction between real + unreal rather than dist. between pleasure + pain. Satisfies id in a realistic manner.
         a. secondary process—rational, logical, critical.
   H. Superego—"good versus bad," rewards and punishments.
      1. conscience—critical, punitive aspect of superego.

Figure 4.10
Sample Lecture Notes

Applying YOUR LEARNING

Jan is taking an American government course in which class lectures are very important. She has trouble following the lecture and knowing what is important because her instructor does not follow the textbook and often digresses from the topic. The instructor lectures at a fast pace, so Jan feels she is missing important information.

1. What advice would you give Jan for taking lecture notes?
2. How should she study and review her notes?
3. What thought patterns could she expect to find in an American government course?
4. Should Jan tape-record the lectures?
5. Would rewriting or editing her notes be helpful? If so, what changes should she make?

SELF-TEST SUMMARY

1. Why should you improve your lecture note taking?

Because many college instructors expect you to remember and apply the facts and ideas in their class lectures, it is necessary to take good lecture notes, edit them properly, and develop a system for studying them effectively.

2. What are the characteristics of effective lecture notes?

Effective lecture notes should accomplish three things. First, good notes should summarize the main points of the lecture. Well-taken lecture notes are a valuable aid to study. Second, lecture notes should include enough details and examples so that you can recall and completely understand the information several weeks later. Third, the notes should show the relative importance of ideas and reflect the organization of the lecture.

3. How can you improve your listening skills?

Taking good lecture notes depends on good listening skills. To make your listening more intentional, purposeful, and deliberate, you should apply good reading skills to listening: Focus on content and ideas, not on the speaker's style or on facts alone; pay attention to opening statements; look for the speaker's purpose; and prevent your mind from wandering by focusing your concentration, attention, and thinking skills.

4. Why should you edit your lecture notes?

After taking a set of lecture notes, it is necessary to correct, revise, fill in missing or additional information, and expand your notes. This editing process results in clearer, more accurate notes.

5. How should you study your lecture notes?

The recall clue system is a way of making study and review easier and more effective. During note taking, leave blank a 2-inch margin at the left of each page of notes. Later, as you reread your notes, write in the margin words and phrases that briefly summarize the notes. These phrases, or recall clues, trigger your memory and help you recall information in the notes.

Take a Road Trip to
Seattle!

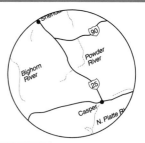

If your instructor has asked you to use the Reading Road Trip CD-ROM, be sure to visit the Note Taking and Textbook Highlighting module for multimedia tutorials, exercises, and tests.

CHAPTER 5

Active Reading Strategies

Why Become an Active Reader?

▲ Active reading stimulates your thinking.

▲ Active reading helps you get interested and stay involved with what you read.

▲ It makes reading easier by providing you with a mental outline of the material.

▲ Active reading increases your recall.

Learning Experiment

Step 1

In the space provided draw the face of a one-dollar bill.

Step 2

Find a one-dollar bill and compare your drawing with it. Notice the features you did not include.

The Result

Although hundreds of one-dollar bills have passed through your hands over the years, you probably did not recall very many features. Why? You did not recall these features because you did not plan to remember them. (No doubt you would have done better if the experiment directed you to study the face of a one-dollar bill for several minutes, and then put it away and draw it.)

Learning Principle (What This Means to You)

We all remember what we intend to remember. If you do not decide what you should remember before reading a textbook chapter, your recall is likely to be poor. On the other hand, if you decide what you need to know before you start, your recall will be much higher. This chapter will demonstrate several techniques that will help you decide what to learn in a textbook chapter. Specifically, you will learn to preread before reading, to discover what you already know about the topic, and to define your purposes for reading. You will also learn to monitor and strengthen your comprehension as you read.

PREREADING AND PREDICTING

Do you check for traffic before crossing a street? Do you check the depth of a pool before diving in? What do you do to an article or chapter before you read it, before you "jump in"? In this section, you will become acquainted with the technique of prereading—a useful way of checking any written material before you read it. Just as most people check traffic before crossing a street or water depth before diving, to be an efficient reader you should check printed materials before reading to become generally familiar with the overall content and organization.

Before reading, you should make predictions about the material. You might make predictions, or educated guesses, about how difficult or interesting the material will be, what topics will be discussed, or how the author will approach the subject. You might also anticipate how the material will be organized—how it progresses from one idea to another.

How to Preread

Your overall purposes in prereading are to identify the most important ideas in the material and note their organization. You look only at specific parts and skip over the rest. The portions to look at in prereading a textbook chapter are described in the following paragraphs. Later you will learn how to adapt this procedure to other types of material.

1. Read the title and subtitle.

The title provides the overall topic of the article or chapter; the subtitle suggests the specific focus, aspect, or approach toward the overall topic.

2. Read the introduction or first paragraph.

The introduction, or first paragraph if there is no introduction, serves as a lead-in to the chapter. It gives you an idea of where the material starts and where it is going.

3. Read each major heading.

The headings function as labels or topic statements for what is contained in the sections that follow them. In other words, a heading announces the major topic of each section.

4. Read the first sentence under each heading.

The first sentence frequently tells you what the passage is about or states the central thought. You should be aware, however, that in some types of material and in certain styles of writing, the first sentence does not function as a central thought. Instead, the opening sentence may function as a transition or lead-in statement, or it may be designed to catch your interest. If the first sentence seems unimportant, read the last sentence; often this sentence states or restates the central thought.

5. Note any typographical and graphical aids.

Italic (slanted) type is used to emphasize important terms and definitions by distinguishing them from the rest of the passage. Note any material that is numbered 1, 2, 3, lettered a, b, c, or presented in list form. Graphs, charts, pictures, and tables are other means of emphasis and usually signal something that is important in the chapter. Be sure to read the captions for pictures and the legends on graphs, charts, and tables. Note words in italics or bold print—usually a definition follows.

6. Read the last paragraph or summary.

The summary or last paragraph gives a condensed view of the chapter and helps you identify key ideas. Often the summary outlines the key points in the chapter.

7. Read quickly any end-of-article or end-of-chapter material.

This might include references, study questions, vocabulary lists, or biographical information about the author. These materials will be useful later as you read and study the article or chapter, and it is important, as part of your prereading, to note whether such materials are included. If there are study questions, it is useful to read them through quickly, because they will indicate what is important in the chapter. If a vocabulary list is included, rapidly skim through it to identify terms you will need to learn as you read.

Demonstration of Prereading

The textbook chapter excerpt seen in Figure 5.1 has been included to demonstrate what it is like to preread. This excerpt is taken from an introductory text, *Psychology,* by Wade and Tavris. To illustrate how prereading is done, these pages have been specially marked. Everything that you should look at or read has been shaded. Preread this excerpt now, reading only the shaded portions of each page.

SOME SOURCES OF STRESS

Stressors do not lead directly to illness. But are some stressors more likely than others to affect the immune system and thus lead eventually to poor health? To find out, some psychologists study the significant events that disrupt our lives; some count the irritating nuisances; and others emphasize continuing pressures in the environment.

BEREAVEMENT AND LOSS   One of the most powerful stressors in anyone's life is the loss of a loved one or a close relationship, especially through divorce or the death of a spouse. In the two years following bereavement, widowed people are more susceptible to illness and physical ailments, and their mortality rate is higher than expected. Divorce also often takes a long-term health toll: Divorced adults have higher rates of heart disease, pneumonia, and other diseases than comparable adults who are not divorced (Jacobson, 1983).

Bereaved and divorced people may be vulnerable to illness in part because, feeling unhappy, they don't sleep well, they stop eating properly, and they consume more drugs and cigarettes. In addition, broken attachments affect us at a basic cellular level; attachment is a biological need of the species. Bereavement, and the emotional loneliness it creates, produces cardiovascular changes, a lowered number of white blood cells, and other abnormal responses of the immune system (Laudenslager, 1988; Stroebe et al., 1996). The quality of the attachment is as important as its presence or absence. Unhappily married individuals show the same decline in immune function as unhappy divorced people (Kiecolt-Glaser et al., 1993).

HASSLES, NOISE, AND CROWDS   Everyday hassles are hazardous to health primarily for people who tend to be highly anxious and quick to overreact (Kohn, Lafreniere, & Gurevich, 1991). Every little thing, to them, feels like the last straw. For most people, however, hassles are short-term (*acute*) nuisances that may be annoying but that don't have any long-term risks, unless they turn into chronic (*recurring or constant*) stressors.

One unhealthy chronic stressor is loud noise, which impairs the ability to think and work, even when people believe they have adjusted to it. Children in noisy schools, such as those near airports, tend to have higher blood pressure and other elevated physiological responses, be more distractible, have poorer long-term memory, and have more difficulty with puzzles, reading, and math than do children in quieter schools (Cohen et al., 1980; Evans, Hygge, & Bullinger, 1995). In adults, noise contributes to cardiovascular problems, irritability, fatigue, and aggressiveness, probably because of overstimulation of the autonomic nervous system (Staples, 1996). The noise that is most stressful to people, however, is noise they cannot control. The rock song that you choose to listen to at jackhammer loudness may be pleasurable to you but intolerable—stressful—to anyone who does not share your musical taste.

Another chronic stressor is crowding, which, like noise, becomes most stressful when it curtails your sense of freedom and control. Crowds are detrimental to health and intellectual performance not when you *are* crowded but when you *feel* crowded or trapped. Thus people who work without interruptions in a densely packed room feel less crowded and are less stressed than those who work with fewer people but lots of interruptions (Taylor, 1995). Chronic residential crowding— whether in prisons, dorms, or households—is also associated with psychological distress, but this link occurs primarily when people feel they are having too many interactions that are unwanted, intrusive, and inescapable (Evans, Lepore, & Schroeder, 1996).

Figure 5.1
Prereading

> **CONTINUING PROBLEMS**   People at the lower end of the socioeconomic ladder have worse health and higher mortality rates for almost every disease and medical condition than those on the upper rungs (Adler et al., 1994). One obvious reason is that poor people cannot afford good medical care, healthy food, and preventive examinations. But another has to do with the continuous stressors they live with: higher crime rates, fewer community services, dilapidated housing, fewer recreational facilities, and greater exposure to environmental hazards (Taylor, Repetti, & Seeman, 1997).
>
> In summary, the stressors we have discussed are related to health, yet they are not the whole story. Some people show impaired immune function as a result of bereavement, living with uncontrollable noise, and uncontrollable job tensions; yet many individuals show no immune changes at all (Manuck et al., 1991). Some show heightened blood pressure and heart rate when faced with an exam or other challenge, but others do not (Uchino et al., 1995). Something else, as we will see next, is going on between the stressful event and a person's physical response to it.

Figure 5.1
(Continued)

 EXERCISE 1

DIRECTIONS   Answer each of the following questions after you have preread the reading titled "Some Sources of Stress" in Figure 5.1 above. Do *not* read the entire selection. Mark T after statements that are true and F after those that are false. Do not look back in the reading to locate the answers. When you finish, check your answers in the answer key and write your score in the space indicated.

1. Some stressors seem to affect the immune system.   _____

2. The loss of a loved one is one of the most powerful stressors.   _____

3. Crowds are usually not a source of stress.   _____

4. Stressors affect everyone in the same way   _____

5. Socioeconomic position seems related to health and mortality rates.   _____

Score (number right): _____

Look back at your score on the quiz in Exercise 1. Probably you got at least half of the questions right, perhaps more. This quiz was a test of the main ideas that were presented in this excerpt. You can see, then, that prereading does familiarize you with the chapter and enables you to identify and remember many of the main ideas it contains. Actually, each part of the chapter that you read while prereading provided you with specific information about the organization and content of the chapter. The following exercise emphasizes how each step in the prereading process gives you useful information about the material to be read.

 EXERCISE 2

DIRECTIONS   Listed below are various parts of an actual textbook chapter or article to which you would refer in prereading. For each item, read the parts and then answer the question that follows.

1. *Sample article*

Title:	"Psychologists Have Proof of ESP"
Source:	*Today's Women* magazine
Question:	Answer with yes or no. Would you expect this article to

   a. be technical?
   b. be highly factual with careful references?
   c. contain accounts of individuals with ESP?
   d. contain opinions?
   e. contain references for further study?

2. *Sample text*

Section heading:	Culture and Technology
Subheadings:	Historical Roots and Trends
	Recent Technological Changes
	Predicted Long-Range Effects
Question:	What clues do you have about how the author arranged ideas in this section of the text?

_____

_____

_____

3. *Sample text*

Title:	*Diversity in Families*
Chapter title:	"The Social Construction of Intimacy"
Chapter introduction:	

Intimacy, like other social relations, is shaped by our surroundings. Therefore, we cannot understand it in isolation from the rest of social life. This chapter is about intimate relationships and the ways in which they are embedded in social circumstances. Intimacy exists in relationships based on friendship, romantic love, and parenthood; it even exists among co-workers (Risman and Schwartz, 1989:x). Intimacy concerns both women and men, in homosexual as well as heterosexual relationships. Although intimacy need not include either sex or love, our focus is on relationships that encompass both.

In this chapter, we examine intimacy through a sociological lens. We begin by examining the changing historical and societal context giving rise to intimacy as it is defined today. We then look at patterns of courtship and mate selection by connecting them to historical developments. Turning to sexuality, we underscore the macro structural conditions that shape our most private behaviors. Here, we review the facts and trends pertaining to sex in contemporary U.S. society. We also consider some of the social connections between sexual practices and public health and policy issues. Finally, we turn our attention to the ways in which love and sex are patterned differently for various groups.

—Zinn and Eitzen, *Diversity in Families,* p. 205

Questions: a. List the topics the chapter will cover in the order in which you expect they will be covered.

_____

_____

_____

_____

_____

b. Which of the following will the chapter emphasize?
   (1) how intimacy has changed over the past several decades
   (2) that intimacy is affected by other aspects of social life
   (3) the importance of intimacy in long-term relationships
   (4) why courtship and mate selection depend on traditional values

4. *Sample text*

Title:	*Our Changing Economy*
Subtitle:	*An Introduction to Economics*
Chapter title:	"Why Are There Economic Systems?"
Graphic aids:	The chapter includes the following graphic aids:

a. a graph showing the relationship between the production of various types of goods and price
b. a "Beetle Bailey" cartoon that illustrates that choice is associated with cost
c. a picture of objects that have been used as money in various cultures throughout the world

Question: Consider what each graphic tells you about the chapter content.

a. _____

b. _____

c. _____

5. *Sample text*

Title:	*The World Today*
Subtitle:	*Its Patterns and Cultures*
Chapter title:	"Asia"
Section headings:	This chapter is divided into four major sections:

a. The Heritage of the Past in the Orient
b. How the People of the Orient Make a Living
c. New Directions for India, Pakistan, and Southeast Asia
d. The People's Republic of China, Democracy, and the Uncommitted Orient

Question: By noting the section titles within this chapter, what do you expect about the organization and content of the chapter?

_____

_____

_____

Type of Material	Special Features to Consider
Textbooks	Title and subtitle Preface Table of contents Appendix Glossary
Textbook chapters	Summary Vocabulary list Review and discussion questions
Articles and essays	TItle Introductory paragraphs Concluding paragraphs (see Chapter 7)
Research reports	Abstract
Articles without headings	First sentences of paragraphs
Tests and exams	Instructions and directions Number of items Types of questions Point distribution
Reference sources	Table of contents Index
Newspapers	Headline First few sentences Section headings
Internet Web site	Title Features listed on home page Links (see Chapter 9) Sponsor

Figure 5.2
How to Adjust Prereading to the Material

Prereading Specific Types of Material

Not all reading materials are organized in the same way, and not all reading materials have the same features or parts. Consequently, you must adjust the way you preread to the type of material you are working with. Figure 5.2 offers suggestions on how to adapt the prereading method to suit what you are reading.

Why Prereading Works

Research studies suggest that prereading increases comprehension and improves recall. Several studies show that prereading is a useful technique for reading textbook chapters. In a classic study done by McClusky, college students were divided into two groups.* One group was taught how to use headings and summaries for prereading; the other group received no instruction. Both groups were given a selection to read and comprehension questions to answer. Results of the study indicated that the group who used headings and summaries read 24 percent faster than, and just as accurately as, the students who did not preread. Prereading is effective for several reasons:

1. It helps you get interested in and involved with what you will read. It activates your thinking. Because you know what to expect, reading the material completely is easier.

*H.Y. McClusky, "An Experiment on the Influence of Preliminary Skimming on Reading," *Journal of Educational Psychology,* 25 (1934): 521–529.

2. It provides you with a mental outline of the material you are going to read. You begin to anticipate the sequence of ideas; you see the relationships among topics; you recognize what approach and direction the author has taken in writing about the subject.

3. It lets you apply several principles of learning. You identify what is important, thus establishing an intent to remember.

4. It functions as a type of rehearsal that enhances recall because it provides repetition of the most important points.

Prereading is used best with expository, factual material that is fairly well organized. Knowing this, you can see that prereading is not a good strategy to use when reading materials such as novels, poems, narrative articles, essays, or short stories. However, you will find it fairly easy to adapt the prereading technique to other kinds of writing.

DIRECTIONS   Select a chapter from one of your textbooks. To be practical, choose a chapter that you will be assigned to read in the near future. After prereading it, answer the following questions.

1. What is the major topic of the chapter?

_____

2. How does the author subdivide, or break down, this topic?

_____

3. What approach does the author take toward the subject? (Does he or she cite research, give examples, describe problems, list causes?)

_____

4. Construct a brief outline of the chapter.

_____

Making Predictions

Do you predict what a film will be about and whether seeing it will be worthwhile on the basis of a coming attractions preview? Do you anticipate what a party will be like before attending? This type of prediction or anticipation is typical and occurs automatically. Do you predict what a chapter will discuss before you read it?

Research studies of good and poor readers demonstrate that efficient readers frequently predict and anticipate, both before reading and while they read, both content and organization of the material. For example, from the title of a textbook chapter, you can predict the subject and, often, how the author will approach it. A business management textbook chapter titled "Schools of Management Thought: Art or Science?" indicates the subject—schools of management—but also suggests that the author will classify the various schools as artistic (creative) or scientific. Similarly, author, source, headings, graphics, photographs, chapter previews, and summaries, all of which you may check during prereading, provide additional information for anticipating content.

Making predictions is a way to expand and broaden your thinking beyond the Knowledge and Comprehension levels. Predicting forces you to apply your knowledge to new situations (Application), to examine how ideas fit together

(Analysis), and to put ideas together in unique ways (Synthesis). For a review of the Levels of Thinking, see Figure 2.3 on p. 46.

Efficient readers frequently make predictions about organization as well as content. That is, they anticipate the order or manner in which ideas or information will be presented. For instance, from a chapter section titled "The History of World Population Growth," you can predict that the chapter will be organized chronologically, moving ahead in time as the chapter progresses. A chapter titled "Behavioral *vs.* Situational Approaches to Leadership" suggests that the chapter will compare and contrast the two approaches to leadership.

As efficient readers read, they also confirm, reject, or revise their initial predictions. For example, a student who read the heading "Types of Managers" anticipated that the section would describe different management styles. Then he began reading:

Types of Managers

Now that you have an idea of what the management process is, consider the roles of managers themselves. It is possible to classify managers by the nature of the position they hold. This section will review some of the major categories of managers. The next section will identify how these differences affect a manager's job.

The student immediately revised his prediction, realizing that managers would be classified not by style but by the position they hold. Making predictions and anticipating content and organization are worthwhile because they focus your attention on the material. Further, the process of confirming, rejecting, or revising predictions is an active one—it forces you to concentrate and helps you to understand. Once you know what to expect in a piece of reading, you will find it easier to read.

EXERCISE 4

DIRECTIONS   For the textbook chapter described below, predict which of the following topics might appear in the chapter, and place a check mark next to each.

Textbook title: *Psychology: An Introduction*
Chapter: "Human Development Before Birth"
Headings: The Mechanics of Heredity
Prenatal Development: Influences before Birth

Topics:

_____   1.   Mental abilities of newborns

_____   2.   How sex is determined

_____   3.   How infants learn speech

_____   4.   Intellectual deficits

_____   5.   Fetal alcohol syndrome

_____   6.   Types of genes

_____   7.   Observing the development of emotions

_____   8.   Chromosome abnormalities

_____   9.   Siblings as behavioral role models

_____   10.   Upper body development

EXERCISE 5

DIRECTIONS Below are listed a textbook title, chapter title, and chapter headings. Place a check mark in front of the statements you predict will appear in the chapter. If possible, also indicate the section in which each statement is most likely to appear. (Indicate by marking 1, 2, 3, 4, or 5 to correspond to the headings in order.)

Textbook title: *America's Problems: Social Issues and Public Policy*
Chapter Title: "The Family"
Headings: Some Trends in Family Disruption
The Consequences of Family Disruption
Inequality in the Family: Division of Labor in the Home
Work, Family, and Social Supports
The Family as a Crucible of Violence

Statements:

_____ 1. Divorce creates social and personal stress for both children and parents.

_____ 2. Sex-role stereotypes dictate how much males contribute to housekeeping chores.

_____ 3. Street crime takes an enormous toll on citizens and only rarely results in prosecution by the courts.

_____ 4. Child and spouse abuse is aggravated by poverty and gender inequality.

_____ 5. The continued concentration of minorities in low-paying jobs is a reflection of inequality.

_____ 6. Lack of day care for single-parent families creates insurmountable problems.

_____ 7. Changing health care policies have reduced public responsibilities for family health care maintenance.

EXERCISE 6

DIRECTIONS Preread the textbook excerpt titled "Communication Between Women and Men," in Part Seven, p. 385. Then make a list of topics you predict it will cover. Next, read the selection. Then review your list of predictions and place a check mark next to those that were correct.

EXERCISE 7

DIRECTIONS Select a chapter from one of your textbooks. Preread the chapter, and then write a list of predictions about the chapter's content or organization.

DISCOVERING WHAT YOU ALREADY KNOW

Discovering what you already know about a topic will make learning easier because you will be connecting new information to old information already in place. You will find, too, that reading material becomes more interesting once you have connected its topic with your own experience. Comprehension will be easier, too, because you will have already thought about some of the ideas presented in the material.

Suppose you are studying a business textbook and are about to begin reading a chapter on advertising that discusses the objectives of advertising, the construction and design of ads, and the production of ads. Before you begin reading the chapter, you should spend a minute or two recalling what you already know about these topics. Try one or more of the following techniques.

1. *Ask questions and try to answer them.* You might ask questions such as "What are the goals of advertising?" In answering this question, you will realize you already know several objectives: to sell a product, to introduce a new product, to announce sales or discounts, and so on.

2. *Relate the topic to your own experience.* For a topic on the construction and design of ads, think about ads you have heard or read recently. What similarities exist? How do the ads begin? How do they end? This process will probably lead you to realize that you already know something about how ads are designed.

3. *Free-associate.* On a scrap sheet of paper, jot down everything that comes to mind about advertising. List facts and questions, or describe ads you have recently heard or seen. This process will also activate your recall of information.

At first, you may think you know very little—or even nothing—about a particular topic. However, by using one of the foregoing techniques, you will be surprised to find that there are very few topics about which you know nothing at all. For example, suppose you were about to read a biology chapter on genetics. At first you might think you know nothing about it. Complete Exercise 8 to discover what you do know about genetics.

EXERCISE 8

DIRECTIONS   For a chapter on genetics, write a list of questions, experiences, or associations that would help focus your mind on the topic. (Hint: Think of inherited family traits and characteristics; ask questions about eye and hair color.) When you have finished, compare your work with the student sample shown in Figure 5.3.

EXERCISE 9

DIRECTIONS   Discover what you already know about one of the following topics by using at least two of the techniques described in this section for each topic.

Topics

1. Creativity
2. Aggressive behavior
3. Body language

What eye color is dominant?
Is tendency to be overweight inherited?
What do genes do?
How many do we have?
What is genetic engineering?
Are aspects of personality inherited?
Can environment influence genetics?
Why do some women have facial hair?
Can genes be defective? If so, what happens?
What do chromosomes do?
Is hair loss hereditary?
Can a person have two eyes each of a different color?

Figure 5.3
A Student Sample

When you have finished, answer the following questions.

1. Did you discover you knew more about the topics than you first thought?
2. Which technique worked better? Why?
3. Might the technique you choose depend on your subject matter?

EXERCISE 10

DIRECTIONS In Exercise 6 you preread the textbook excerpt titled "Communication Between Women and Men." Discover what you already know about differences in the ways men and women talk and communicate using one of the techniques described in this section.

EXERCISE 11

DIRECTIONS Select a chapter from one of your textbooks. Preread it, and use one of the techniques described in this section to discover what you already know about the subject of the chapter.

DEFINING YOUR PURPOSES FOR READING

Have you ever read a complete page or more and then not remembered a thing? Have you wandered aimlessly through paragraph after paragraph, section after section, unable to remember key ideas you have just read, even when you were really trying to concentrate? If these problems sound familiar, you probably began reading without a specific purpose in mind. That is, you were not looking for anything in particular as you read. Guide questions can focus your attention and help you pick out what is important.

Developing Guide Questions

Most textbook chapters use boldface headings to organize chapter content. The simplest way to establish a purpose for reading is to convert each heading into one or more questions that will guide your reading. As you read, you then look for the answers. For a section with the heading "The Hidden Welfare System," you could ask the questions "What is the hidden welfare system?" and "How does it work?" As you read that section, you would actively search for answers. For a section of a business textbook titled "Taxonomy of Organizational Research Strategies," you could pose such questions as "What is a taxonomy?" and "What research strategies are discussed and how are they used?"

The excerpt that follows is taken from a social problems textbook chapter on problems of education. Before reading it, use the heading to formulate several guide questions and list them here. Then read the passage to find the answers, and fill them in after your questions.

Question 1: _____

_____

Answer: _____

_____

Question 2: _____

Answer: _____

_____

The Voucher System: Advantages and Disadvantages

The last two decades have been a time of ferment in our educational system, and there are literally dozens of proposals for restructuring our schools. One of the most popular among conservatives is the voucher system. Under most versions of this plan, automatic support for existing public schools would be withdrawn and parents would be given a voucher that could be "spent" at any school, public or private. Advocates of the voucher system claim it would stimulate competition among the schools and force schools and teachers to provide top-quality education or go out of business. Critics of these proposals, who include many of the nation's leading educators, say that such changes would create educational chaos as tens of thousands of independent schools spring up, with enormous differences in quality, curriculum, and objectives. California's superintendent of public instruction described the voucher proposals as "dangerous claptrap" that would produce the same disastrous results as the deregulation of the savings and loan industry, and Wisconsin's superintendent likened this approach to "nuking" the public school system.

—Coleman and Cressey, *Social Problems,* p. 113

You probably developed questions such as "What is the voucher system?" and "What are its advantages and disadvantages?" Then, as you read the section, you found out that the voucher system is a plan in which parents receive vouchers that can be spent at a school of their choice. You also discovered that the voucher system would stimulate competition and quality but might also create educational chaos. Did the guide questions help you focus your attention and make the passage easier to read?

You may find it helpful to jot down your guide questions in the margins of your texts, next to the appropriate headings. These questions are then available for later study. Reviewing and answering your questions is an excellent method of review.

Formulating the Right Questions

Guide questions that begin with *What, Why,* and *How* are especially effective. *Who, When,* and *Where* questions are less useful, because they can often be answered through superficial reading or may lead to simple, factual, or one-word answers. *What, Why,* and *How* questions require detailed answers that demand more thought, so they force you to read in greater depth.

For example, "The Fall of the Roman Empire," the title of a section in a history text, could be turned into a question such as "When did the Roman Empire fall?" For this question, the answer is merely a date. This question, then, would not guide your reading effectively. On the other hand, questions such as "How did the Roman Empire fall?" and "What brought about the fall of the Roman Empire?" and "What factors contributed to the fall of the Roman Empire?" would require you to recall important events and identify causes.

Here are a few examples of effective guide questions:

Heading	**Effective Guide Questions**
Management of Stress in Organizations	What types of stress occur? How is stress controlled?
Theories of Leadership	What are the theories of leadership? How are they applied or used?

Styles of Leader Behavior   What are the styles of leader
                                   behavior? How do they differ?
                                   How effective are they?

 **EXERCISE 12**

DIRECTIONS Assume that each of the following is a boldface heading within a textbook chapter and that related textual material follows. In the space provided, write questions that would guide your reading.

1. **Operating System Aids to Efficient Merging of Computer Files**

   _____

   _____

2. **Natural Immunity and Blood Types**

   _____

   _____

3. **Production of Electromagnetic Waves**

   _____

   _____

4. **Physical Changes in Adolescence**

   _____

   _____

5. **Sociological Factors Related to Delinquency**

   _____

   _____

Written Materials without Headings

In articles and essays without headings, the title often provides the overall purpose, and the first sentence of each paragraph can often be used to form a guide question about each paragraph. In the following paragraph, the first sentence could be turned into a question that would guide your reading.

> Despite its recent increase in popularity, hypnotism has serious limitations that restrict its widespread use. First of all, not everyone is susceptible to hypnotism. Second, a person who does not cooperate with the hypnotist is unlikely to fall into a hypnotic trance. Finally, there are limits to the commands a subject will obey when hypnotized. In many cases, subjects will not do anything that violates their moral code.

From the first sentence you could form the question "What are the limitations of hypnotism?" In reading the remainder of the paragraph, you would easily find its three limitations.

EXERCISE 13

DIRECTIONS Assume that each of the following sentences is the first sentence of a paragraph within an article that does not contain boldface headings. Beside each sentence, write a guide question.

1. Historically, there have been three branches of philosophical analysis.

   _____

   _____

2. Scientists who are studying earthquakes attribute them to intense pressures and stresses that build up inside the earth.

   _____

   _____

3. The way in which managers and employees view and treat conflict has changed measurably over the last 50 years.

   _____

   _____

4. Perhaps it will be easier to understand the nature and function of empathetic listening if we contrast it to deliberative listening.

   _____

   _____

5. In addition to the price of a good or service, there are dozens, perhaps hundreds, of other factors and circumstances that affect a person's decision to buy or not buy.

   _____

   _____

Are Guide Questions Effective?

A number of research studies have been conducted to test whether establishing purposes by forming guide questions improves understanding and recall of information. These studies confirm the effectiveness of guide questions and indicate that students who read with a purpose have a higher percentage of recall of factual information than students who read without a specific purpose. In one study, college students who wrote guide questions scored 19 percentage points higher on a recall test than students who read without doing so.

EXERCISE 14

DIRECTIONS   Turn to the Reading "Causes of Habitat Loss and Species Endangerment" in Part Seven on page 398. Form questions that would be useful in guiding your reading. (See Exercise 18, p. 102.)

EXERCISE 15

DIRECTIONS   Choose a three-to-four-page selection from one of your textbooks. Select pages that have already been assigned or that you anticipate will be assigned. For each heading, form and record guide questions that establish a purpose for reading. Then read the selection and answer your questions.

CHECKING YOUR COMPREHENSION

For many daily activities, you maintain an awareness, or check, on how well you are performing them. In sports such as racquetball, tennis, or bowling, you

*L. T. Frase and B. J. Schwartz, "Effects of Question Production and Answering on Prose Recall." *Journal of Educational Psychology*, 67 (1975): 628–635.

know if you are playing a poor game; you actually keep score and deliberately try to correct errors and improve your performance. When preparing a favorite food, you often taste it as you work to be sure it will turn out as you want. When washing your car, you check to be sure that you have not missed any spots.

A similar type of monitoring or checking should occur as you read. You should assess your performance. You need to keep score of how well you understand. Comprehension, however, is difficult to keep track of, because it is not always either good or poor. You may understand certain ideas you read and be confused by others. At times, comprehension may be incomplete—you may miss certain key ideas and not know you missed them.

Recognizing Comprehension Signals

Think for a moment about what occurs when you read material you can understand easily, and then compare this to what happens when you read complicated material that is difficult to understand. When you read certain material, does it seem that everything clicks—that is, do ideas seem to fit together and make sense? Is that click noticeably absent at other times?

Read each of the following paragraphs. As you read, be alert to your level of understanding of each.

Paragraph 1

In some ways, Americans are joiners. We form churches, fan clubs, hobby organizations, health groups—the lists seem endless. You can find a group to join for almost any purpose. We join together to share common experiences, to solidify common values, and to express feelings. Often group members share demographic characteristics. For example, doctors, lawyers, and dentists join professional societies based on occupational similarities. Consumer advocacy groups and support groups are united by purpose. Members of labor unions hold jobs and economic welfare in common. Homeowners' groups share geographic features. Political parties and religious groups attract people who share common values. Tee ball clubs, high school reunions, and associations of retired persons unite people who are similar in age. Groups share similar interests and goals that can be identified readily. Identifying these common interests is an important element of assessing your audience.

—Gronbeck et al., *Principles of Speech Communication,* p. 53

Paragraph 2

A pogonophoran lives within an upright tube of chitin and protein that it secretes around itself, with from one to many thousand tentacle-like branchiae protruding from the upper end of the tube. The branchiae are the "beard" of beard worms. Without their tubes many beard worms would look like threads that are badly frayed at one end. The branchiae are often called tentacles, but they absorb gases and are not used to capture solid food. In their typical cylindrical arrangement the branchiae resemble an intestine, complete with microvilli that increase the surface area.

—Harris, *Concepts in Zoology,* p. 573

Did you feel comfortable and confident as you read paragraph 1? Did ideas seem to lead from one to another and make sense? How did you feel while reading paragraph 2? Most likely you sensed its difficulty and felt confused. Unfamiliar words were used and you could not follow the flow of ideas, so the whole passage didn't make sense.

As you read paragraph 2, did you know that you were not understanding it? Did you feel confused or uncertain? Figure 5.4 lists and compares common signals that may help you assess your comprehension. Not all signals appear at the same time, and not all signals work for everyone. As you study the list, identify those positive signals you sensed as you read paragraph 1 on groups. Then identify the negative signals that you sensed when reading paragraph 2 about pogonophorans.

EXERCISE 16

DIRECTIONS   For "Causes of Habitat Loss and Species Endangerment," which you read in Exercise 14, answer the following questions.

1. How would you rate your overall comprehension? What positive signals did you sense? Did you feel any negative signals? Did you encounter unfamiliar vocabulary?
2. Test the accuracy of your rating in question 1 by answering the following questions based on the material you read.
   a. What is the primary cause of habitat loss, degradation, and fragmentation?
   b. What are the two aspects of habitat fragmentation?
   c. List at least three specific activities that destroy habitat.
   d. In what areas are certain human activities more harmful than in others? List at least two areas.
3. Check your answers in the Answer Key. In what sections was your comprehension strongest?
4. Did you feel at any time that you had lost, or were about to lose, comprehension? If so, go back to that section now. What made that section difficult to read?
5. Do you think prereading and writing guide questions strengthened your comprehension? If so, how?

Positive Signals	Negative Signals
Everything seems to fit and make sense; ideas flow logically from one to another.	Some pieces do not seem to belong; the material seems disjointed.
You understand what is important.	Nothing or everything seems important.
You are able to see where the author is leading.	You feel as if you are struggling to stay with the author and are unable to predict what will follow.
You are able to make connections among ideas.	You are unable to detect relationships; the organization is not apparent.
You read at a regular, comfortable pace.	You often slow down or reread.
You understand why the material was assigned.	You do not know why the material was assigned and cannot explain why it is important.
You can express the main ideas in your own words.	You must reread often and find it hard to paraphrase the author's ideas.
You recognize most words or can figure them out from the context.	Many words are unfamiliar.
You feel comfortable and have some knowledge about the topic.	The topic is unfamiliar, yet the author assumes you understand it.

Figure 5.4
Comprehension Signals

EXERCISE 17

DIRECTIONS   Select a three-to-four-page section of a chapter in one of your textbooks. Read the section, and then answer questions 1 and 4 in Exercise 16.

Evaluating Your Comprehension

At times, signals of poor comprehension do not come through clearly or strongly enough. In fact, some students think they have understood what they read until they are questioned in class or take an exam. Only then do they discover that their comprehension was incomplete. Other students find that they understand material on a surface, factual level but that they do not recognize more complicated relationships and implied meanings or do not see implications and applications. Use the following methods to determine whether you really understand what you read.

1. *Set checkpoints.* Race car drivers make pit stops during races for quick mechanical checks and repairs; athletes are subject to frequent physical tests and examinations. These activities provide an opportunity to assess performance and to correct any problems or malfunctions. Similarly, when you are reading, it is necessary to stop and evaluate.

As you preread a textbook assignment, identify reasonable or logical checkpoints: points at which to stop, check, and (if necessary) correct your performance before continuing. Pencil a check mark in the margin to designate these points. These checkpoints should be logical breaking points where one topic ends and another begins or where a topic is broken down into several subtopics. As you reach each of these checkpoints, stop and assess your work using the techniques described below.

2. *Use your guide questions.* Earlier in this chapter, you learned how to form guide questions by using boldface headings. These same questions can be used to monitor your comprehension while reading. When you finish a boldface-headed section, stop and take a moment to recall your guide question and answer it mentally or on paper. Your ability to answer your questions will indicate your level of comprehension.

3. *Ask connection questions.* To be certain that your understanding is complete and that you are not recalling only superficial factual information, ask connection questions. Connection questions are those that require you to think about content. They force you to draw together ideas and to discover relationships between the material at hand and other material in the same chapter, in other chapters, or in class lectures. Here are a few examples:

- What does this topic have to do with topics discussed earlier in the chapter?
- How is this reading assignment related to the topics of this week's class lectures?
- What does this chapter have to do with the chapter assigned last week?
- What principle do these problems illustrate?

Connection questions enable you to determine whether your learning is meaningful—whether you are simply taking in information or are using the information and fitting it into the scheme of the course. The best times to ask connection questions are before beginning and after you have finished a chapter or each major section.

4. *Use internal dialogue.* Internal dialogue—mentally talking to yourself—is another excellent means of monitoring your reading and learning. It involves rephrasing to yourself the message the author is communicating or the ideas you are studying. If you are unable to express ideas in your own words, your understanding is probably incomplete. Here are a few examples of the use of internal dialogue:

- While reading a section in a math textbook, you mentally outline the steps to follow in solving a sample problem.
- You are reading an essay that argues convincingly that the threat of nuclear war is real. As you finish reading each stage of the argument, you rephrase it in your own words.
- As you finish each boldface section in a psychology chapter, you summarize the key points.

EXERCISE 18

DIRECTIONS   Read "The Causes of Habitat Loss and Species Endangerment" in Part Seven on page 398. Answer the guide questions you wrote in Exercise 14, page 98.

EXERCISE 19

DIRECTIONS   Choose a section from one of your own textbooks. Read it, and then check your understanding by using both guide questions and connection questions. List your questions on a separate sheet of paper.

EXERCISE 20

DIRECTIONS   Select another section from one of your textbooks, and experiment with the technique of internal dialogue to assess your comprehension. In the space provided here, describe the technique you used and say whether or not it worked.

_____

_____

_____

_____

STRENGTHENING YOUR COMPREHENSION

You have learned how to recognize clues that signal strong or weak understanding of reading material and how to assess your comprehension. This section will offer some suggestions to follow when you realize you need to strengthen your comprehension.

1. *Analyze the time and place in which you are reading.* If you've been reading or studying for several hours, mental fatigue may be the source of the problem. If you are reading in a place with distractions or interruptions, you may not be able to understand what you're reading. (See the Success Workshop on page 12 for suggestions on how to monitor and improve your concentration.)

2. *Rephrase each paragraph in your own words.* You might need to approach complicated material sentence by sentence, expressing each in your own words.

3. *Read aloud sentences or sections that are particularly difficult.* Reading out loud sometimes makes complicated material easier to understand.

4. *Reread difficult or complicated sections.* At times, in fact, several readings are appropriate and necessary.

5. *Slow down your reading rate.* On occasion, simply reading more slowly and carefully will provide you with the needed boost in comprehension.

6. *Write guide questions next to headings.* Refer to your questions frequently and jot down or underline answers.

7. *Write a brief outline of major points.* This will help you see the overall organization and progression of ideas. (See Chapter 14 for specific outlining techniques.)

8. *Highlight key ideas.* After you've read a section, go back and think about and highlight what is important. Highlighting forces you to sort out what is important, and this sorting process builds comprehension and recall. (Refer to Chapter 13 for suggestions on how to highlight effectively.)

9. *Write notes in the margins.* Explain or rephrase difficult or complicated ideas or sections.

10. *Determine whether you lack background knowledge.* Comprehension is difficult—at times, it is impossible—if you lack essential information that the writer assumes you have. Suppose you are reading a section of a political science text in which the author describes implications of the balance of power in the Third World. If you do not understand the concept of balance of power, your comprehension will break down. When you lack background information, take immediate steps to correct the problem:

- Consult other sections of your text, using the glossary and index.
- Obtain a more basic text that reviews fundamental principles and concepts.
- Consult reference materials (encyclopedias, subject dictionaries, or biographical dictionaries).
- Ask your instructor to recommend additional sources, guidebooks, or review texts.

EXERCISE 21

DIRECTIONS   The following three paragraphs have been chosen because they are difficult. Assess your comprehension as you read each, paying attention to both positive and negative signals (Figure 5.4). After you have read each paragraph, list the signals you received, and indicate what you could do to strengthen your comprehension.

Paragraph 1

The extension of civil rights was not initiated by government act; civil rights were won through a long and bitter struggle of people determined to seize the citizenship that was their birthright. Deprived of political and business opportunities for a century, bright young black men and women turned to the black church to express their hopes, energies, and aspirations. This was particularly true in the segregated South. But during the 1950s the accumulation of change began to wear the edges of racial separation thin. When a young scholar, Martin Luther King, Jr., returned from Boston University to take up the ministry at Dexter Avenue Baptist Church in 1954 in Montgomery, Alabama, he had no hint that a nationwide civil rights movement would soon swirl around him or that his name would be linked with the great march on Washington of 1963 that would help open the floodgates of integration. What made King one of the most famous Americans of his day was the energy of a suppressed American culture, which he articulated into a momentous political and moral awakening. Its successes were his; its failures revealed his limitations and exposed the deepest barriers to equality in American life.

—Wilson et al., *The Pursuit of Liberty*, p. 422

Positive signals: _____

Negative signals: _____

Strengthen comprehension by: _____

Paragraph 2

In intermediary pricing, cost-plus pricing is the dominant mode among intermediaries in the marketing channel, wholesalers and retailers, where it is called *markup pricing.* These marketers deal with large assortments of products and do not have the resources to develop demand schedules for each item. . . . Channel members' prices are not totally unrelated to demand; they do assign different percentage markups to different items based upon sales experience and estimates of consumer price sensitivity. Wholesalers and retailers will quickly lower prices if an item is not selling. Also, the intermediary's price is based upon a markup on manufacturer's selling price, or discount from manufacturer's suggested retail price. The manufacturer may have researched demand and conducted a competitive analysis before setting the price and discount schedules.

—Kinnear, Bernhardt, and Krentler, *Principles of Marketing*, p. 637

Positive signals: _____

Negative signals: _____

Strengthen comprehension by: _____

Paragraph 3

As noted previously, one of the main motivations for zoologists to study development is that it provides insights regarding taxonomic relationships among groups of animals. In the early 19th century the Estonian biologist Karl Ernst von Baer made a number of observations that suggest such a relationship, although he explicitly rejected any evolutionary implications. What is known as von Baer's law states that embryonic development in vertebrates goes from general forms common to all vertebrates to increasingly specialized forms characteristic of classes, orders, and lower taxonomic levels. Thus the early embryos of all vertebrates, whether fish, frog, hog, or human, all look alike. Later it is possible to tell the human embryo from the fish but not from the hog, and still later one can see a difference between these two mammals.

—Harris, *Concepts in Zoology*, p. 130

Positive signals: _____

Negative signals: _____

Strengthen comprehension by: _____

EXERCISE 22

DIRECTIONS Select three brief sections from your most difficult textbook. Choose three of the suggestions for strengthening your comprehension and list them here. Try out each suggestion on one textbook section. Evaluate and describe the effectiveness of each.

	Suggestion	**Evaluation**
1.	_____	_____
2.	_____	_____
3.	_____	_____

LEARNING *Collaboratively*

DIRECTIONS Choose another student with whom to work. Each student should select, from one of his or her textbooks, a chapter that he or she has already read. The students should exchange textbooks, and each should preread the selected chapter. The textbook owner should quiz the textbook prereader about what he or she learned from the chapter by prereading. Then the prereader should make predictions about chapter content and organization. Finally, the owner should confirm or deny each prediction.

Applying YOUR LEARNING

Malcolm's reading assignment this week for his sociology class consists of a newspaper article, a journal article that does not contain a summary, an essay, and a short story. The class is studying the changing structure of the family during the twentieth century.

1. Describe how Malcolm should preread the newspaper article. What should he be looking for?
2. Describe how Malcolm should preread the journal article.
3. What should Malcolm pay attention to in prereading the essay?
4. The short story was written in 1941 by an American writer. A short story is an unusual assignment in a sociology class. Realizing this, how should Malcolm preread it? What predictions can he make about the story? What should he be looking for as he reads it?
5. Which assignment is most likely to present comprehension problems?
6. How should Malcolm evaluate his comprehension for each?

SELF-TEST SUMMARY

1. What is prereading?

Prereading is a technique that allows the reader to become familiar with the material to be read before beginning to read it completely. The technique involves checking specific parts of an article or textbook chapter that provide the reader with a mental outline of the content of the material. Prereading makes the actual reading of the material easier and helps the reader understand and remember what she or he reads.

2. How do you preread?

In prereading, the reader should note items such as the title and subtitle, the author and source, the publication or copyright date, the introduction or first paragraph; each major heading and the first sentence under it, typographical aids (italics, maps, pictures, charts, graphs), the summary or last paragraph, and any end-of-chapter or end-of-article materials.

3. Why is it helpful to make predictions about materials you are preparing to read?

Making predictions is a process of connecting what you already know about the subject with the clues you pick up during prereading. Efficient readers not only make predictions but also continually revise and modify them as they read.

4. Why is discovering what you already know valuable to do before reading?

Discovering what you already know about a topic before you read will increase your comprehension. Three methods of discovery are questioning, relating to previous experience, and free association.

5. How can I define a purpose for reading?

Before reading, establish a purpose by developing guide questions built from boldface headings and from first sentences of articles or essays without headings. Ask *what, why,* and *how* questions.

6. How can I keep track of comprehension while reading?

Keep track of both positive and negative signals by using these four techniques: establishing checkpoints, using guide questions, asking connection questions, and using internal dialogue.

Take a Road Trip to
New Orleans!

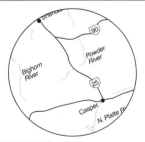

If your instructor has asked you to use the Reading Road Trip CD-ROM, be sure to visit the Active Reading module for multimedia tutorials, exercises, and tests.

CHAPTER 6

Understanding Paragraphs

Why Study Paragraphs?

▲ **You will learn to identify the important information in paragraphs in your reading assignments.**

▲ **You will see how the ideas in each paragraph fit together.**

▲ **You will improve your own writing with more effective paragraphs.**

Learning Experiment

Step 1

Read through list 1 below, spending a maximum of 15 seconds.

List 1	List 2	List 3	List 4
KQZ	BLT	WIN	WAS
NLR	FBI	SIT	THE
XOJ	SOS	LIE	CAR
BTK	CBS	SAW	RUN
YSW	NFL	NOT	OFF

Step 2

Now, cover list 1 with your hand or a piece of scrap paper and write down, in the space provided for list 1, as many items as you can remember.

List 1	List 2	List 3	List 4
_____	_____	_____	_____
_____	_____	_____	_____
_____	_____	_____	_____
_____	_____	_____	_____
_____	_____	_____	_____

Step 3

Follow steps 1 and 2 for each of the other three lists.

Step 4

Check to see how many items you had correct on each of the four lists.

The Results

Did you recall more items on list 2 than on list 1? Why? Did you remember more items on list 4 than on list 3? As you must now realize, after list 1, each list is more meaningful than the one before it. This lists progress from nonsense syllables to meaningful letter groups to words and, finally, to words that, when strung together, produce further meanings.

Learning Principle (What This Means to You)

You are able to remember information that is meaningful more easily than information that has no meaning. Once you understand how paragraphs are organized, they will become more meaningful and easier to remember. In this chapter you will learn the three essential parts of a paragraph and how they work together to create meaning.

THREE ESSENTIAL ELEMENTS OF A PARAGRAPH

The *paragraph* can be defined as a group of related sentences about a single topic. This chapter focuses on knowledge and comprehension of paragraph structure. It will help you understand and remember what you read. It will also help you write paragraphs more effectively. Once you know how a paragraph is structured, you will be able to apply your knowledge to paragraph writing.

The *topic,* the one thing the paragraph is about, is the unifying factor, and every sentence and idea contained in the paragraph is related to the topic. The *main idea,* what the author wants to communicate about the topic, is the central or most important thought in the paragraph. Every other sentence and idea in the paragraph is related to the main idea. The sentence that expresses this idea is called the *topic sentence. Details* are the proof, support, explanation, reasons, or examples that explain the paragraph's main idea.

Each of the following examples contains a group of sentences, but only one is a paragraph. Only that one has the three essential elements. Identify the paragraph.

> Cats frequently become aggressive when provoked. Some plants require more light than others as a result of coloration of their foliage. Some buildings, because of poor construction, waste a tremendous amount of energy.

> Some plants require more light than others as a result of coloration of their foliage. Some plants will live a long time without watering. Plants are being used as decorator items in stores and office buildings.

> Some plants require more light than others as a result of coloration of their foliage. Plants with shades of white, yellow, or pink in their leaves need more light than plants with completely green foliage. For example, a Swedish ivy plant with completely green leaves requires less light per day than a variegated Swedish ivy that contains shades of white, yellow, and green in its leaves.

In the first example, the sentences were unrelated; each sentence was about a different thing, and there was no connection among them.

In the second example, each sentence was about plants—the common topic; however, the sentences together did not prove, explain, or support any particular idea about plants.

In the third example, each sentence was about plants, and all the sentences were about one main idea: that some plants need more light than others because of the coloration of their leaves. Thus the third example is a paragraph; it has a topic—plants; a main idea—that plants require varying degrees of light due to coloration; and supporting details—the example of the Swedish ivy. The first sentence functions as a topic sentence.

In order to understand a paragraph, a reader must be able to identify the topic, main idea, and details easily. In the following paragraph, each of these parts is identified.

> Topic | As societies become industrialized, the distribution of workers   Topic: distribution
> sentence | among various economic activities tends to change in a predictable   of workers
>   way. In the early stages, the population is engaged in agriculture
>   and the collection of raw materials for food and shelter. But as tech-   Details
>   nology develops, agricultural workers are drawn into manufacturing
>   and construction.

This chapter will focus on identifying these essential elements of the paragraph and help you to read paragraphs more easily. Although the emphasis is on reading paragraphs, you will find this information useful in your own writing as well. Just as a reader must identify these elements, so must a writer structure his or her paragraphs by using these elements.

HOW TO IDENTIFY THE TOPIC

The topic of a paragraph is the subject of the whole paragraph. It is the one thing that the whole paragraph is about. Usually, the topic of a paragraph can be expressed in two or three words. To find the topic of a paragraph, ask yourself this question: What is the one thing the author is discussing throughout the paragraph? Read the following example.

> Magazines are a channel of communication halfway between newspapers and books. Unlike newspapers or books, however, many of the most influential magazines are difficult or impossible to purchase at newsstands. With their color printing and slick paper (in most cases), magazines have become a showplace for exciting graphics. Until the 1940s most consumer (general) magazines offered a diverse menu of both fiction and nonfiction articles and miscellany such as poetry and short humor selections. With television providing a heavy quotient of entertainment for the American home, many magazines discovered a strong demand for nonfiction articles, their almost exclusive content today.
>
> —Agee, Ault, and Emery, *Introduction to Mass Communication,* p. 153

In the example, the author is discussing one topic—magazines—throughout the paragraph. Notice how many times the word *magazines* is repeated in the paragraph. Frequently, the repeated use of a word can serve as a clue to the topic of a paragraph.

EXERCISE 1

DIRECTIONS Read each of the following paragraphs and then select the topic of the paragraph from the choices given.

1. Another reason that health care costs have risen so dramatically is high technology. A CT (computerized tomography) scanner costs around $1 million. An MRI (magnetic resonance imaging) scanner can cost over $2 million. A PET (positron emission tomography) scanner costs around $4 million. All of these machines became available in the 1990s and are desired throughout the country. Typical fees for procedures using them range from $300 to $500 for a CT scan to as high as $2,000 for a PET scan. The development of new technologies that help physicians and hospitals prolong human life is an ongoing process in an ever advancing industry. New procedures at even higher prices can be expected in the future.

    —Miller, *Economics Today,* p. 729

    a. the development of medical technology
    b. technology and health care costs
    c. CT and PET scans
    d. tomography and imaging

2. Children of Native American parents are traditionally socialized through an extensive network of relatives. Along with grandparents, uncles and aunts participate with parents in child care, supervision of children, and assurance of love, and cousins are thus considered as close as siblings. Members of this extended family also teach children their tribal values and beliefs or traditions and rituals. Reflecting a group-orientated culture, the values of cooperation and sharing are emphasized, while competitive behavior is discouraged. Children and adolescents are further encouraged to participate in tribal ceremonies and develop an appreciation for their cultural heritage.

    —Thio, *Sociology,* p. 155

    a. the structure of Native American families
    b. competitive behavior versus cooperation
    c. socialization of Native American children
    d. the importance of cultural heritage

3.   Slavery has taken a number of different forms. War captives and their descendants formed a class of slaves in some societies; in others, slaves were a commodity that could be bought and sold. The rights granted to a slave varied, too. In ancient Greece, a slave could marry a free person, but in the stratified society of the southern United States before the Civil War, slaves were not allowed even to marry each other, because they were not permitted to engage in legal contracts. Still, slaves in the South often lived together as husband and wife throughout their adult lives, forming nuclear families that remained tightly knit until they were separated at the auction block.

—Hicks and Gwynne, *Cultural Anthropology,* p. 270

a. rights of slaves
b. slavery in Greece
c. forms of slavery
d. slavery in the southern United States

4.   The simple word "to" has caused a great deal of confusion in many areas of science. For example, consider the phrase, "Birds migrate southward to escape winter." The statement seems harmless enough, but if interpreted literally, it implies that the birds have a goal in mind, or that they are moving under the directions of some conscious force that compels them to escape winter. Philosophers have termed such assumptions *teleology.* (*Teleos* is Greek for *end* or *goal.*) It is commonly used in reference to ideas that go beyond what is actually verifiable and generally implies some inner drive to complete a goal or some directing force operating above the laws of nature.

—Wallace, *Biology: The World of Life,* pp. 31–32

a. forces operating above the laws of nature
b. confusion in language
c. literally interpreted statements
d. teleological assumptions

5.   Earth's magnetic field is known to have reversed polarity many times in our planet's history. The *geographic* North and South Poles have of course remained in place, but the *magnetic* north and south poles have changed polarity continually. Marine geophysicists interpreted the magnetic seafloor patterns as indicating that the rock either solidified during a time when Earth's magnetic field was like it is today (a "positive" value) or solidified at another time, when the field was reversed (a "negative" value). In a way, the formation of these magnetic patterns in rocks is similar to a tape recording: the changes in Earth's magnetic field are the signal, which is being recorded on two very slowly moving "tapes" that spread in opposite directions from the ridge.

—Ross, *Introduction to Oceanography,* p. 48

a. polarity of the earth's magnetic field
b. patterns of rocks on the seafloor
c. geographic poles of the earth
d. work carried out by marine geophysicists

6.   All surfaces have textures that can be experienced by touching or through visual suggestion. Textures are categorized as either actual or simulated. *Actual* textures are those we can feel by touching, such as polished marble, wood, sand or swirls of thick paint. Simulated (or implied) textures are those created to look like something other than paint on a flat surface. A painter can simulate textures that

look like real fur or wood but to the touch would feel like smooth paint. Artists can also invent actual or simulated textures. We can appreciate most textures even when we are not permitted to touch them, because we know, from experience, how they would feel.

—Preble, Preble, and Frank, *Artforms,* p. 71

a. surface textures
b. feeling textures
c. painting textures
d. simulated textures

7. Many people believe that the only way to attain efficiency is through competition. One of the roles of government is to serve as the protector of a competitive economic system. Congress and the various state governments have passed *antitrust legislation.* Such legislation makes illegal certain (but not all) economic activities that might, in legal terms, restrain trade—that is, prevent free competition among actual and potential rival firms in the marketplace. The avowed aim of antitrust legislation is to reduce the power of *monopolies*—firms that have great control over the price of goods they sell. A large number of antitrust laws have been passed that prohibit specific anticompetitive business behavior. Both the Antitrust Division of the Department of Justice and the Federal Trade Commission attempt to enforce these antitrust laws. Various state judicial agencies also expend efforts at maintaining competition.

—Miller, *Economics Today,* p. 98

a. monopolies
b. promoting competition
c. economic efficiency
d. federal legislation

8. Businesses do not operate in a vacuum, but rather exist within a business environment that includes economic, legal, cultural, and competitive factors. Economic factors affect businesses by influencing what and how many goods and services consumers buy. Laws and regulations have an impact on many activities in a business. Cultural and social factors influence the characteristics of the goods and services sold by businesses. Competition affects what products and services a business offers, and the price it charges.

—Nickerson, *Business and Information Systems,* p. 30

a. economic factors in business
b. business activities
c. business environment
d. competition in business

9. Successful social movements almost always spark a reaction from groups that oppose their gains. These reaction groups are sometimes more powerful than the protest movement itself. The Civil Rights movement, for instance, sparked an antifederal government backlash among white southerners during the 1970s and 1980s that contributed to the success of such politicians as George Wallace and the rise of Republican party fortunes in that region. The Women's movement sparked a powerful backlash among fundamentalist religious groups. The successes of the Environmental movement during the 1970s energized a powerful, well-funded, and well-organized counteroffensive by America's leading corporations and business organizations.

—Greenberg and Page, *The Struggle for Democracy,* p. 291

a. successful social movements
b. the Civil Rights movement
c. the Republican party
d. reaction groups

10.   We know that changes in sea level have occurred in the past. In some instances, however, these were not related to changes in the volume of water, as was caused by melting or forming of glaciers. Rather, sea level shifted in response to changes in the shape of the ocean basin itself. Reducing the dimensions of the ocean basin (especially depth) by increasing the rates of subduction or seafloor spreading could cause a rise in sea level worldwide. An increase in the size of the ocean basin could cause a drop in sea level.

—Ross, *Introduction to Oceanography,* p. 62

a. glacier melting and formation
b. the shape of the ocean basin
c. rates of subduction
d. changes in sea level

EXERCISE 2

DIRECTIONS   For each of the following paragraphs, read the paragraph and write the topic in the space provided. Be sure to limit the topic to a few words.

1.   Energy conservation in the short run and long run will require creative solutions in all areas of business. A few innovative solutions have already surfaced which indicate that business understands the importance of saving energy. The makers of Maxwell House coffee developed a method to save natural gas. The first step in making instant coffee is to brew the coffee just as people do at home, except in 1000-gallon containers. The heat to brew the coffee had come from burning natural gas, and the process left Maxwell House with tons of coffee grounds. The company then had to use trucks (that burned gasoline) to cart the coffee grounds away. Maxwell House realized it could save most of the cost of the natural gas (and the gasoline cost) by burning the grounds to get the heat to brew subsequent batches of coffee. Natural gas is now used only to start the coffee grounds burning.

—Kinnear, Bernhardt, and Krentler, *Principles of Marketing,* pp. 79–81

Topic: _____

2.   The characteristic of speed is universally associated with computers. Power is a derivative of speed as well as of other factors such as memory size. What makes a computer fast? Or, more to the point, what makes one computer faster than another? Several factors are involved, including microprocessor speed, bus line size, and the availability of cache. A user who is concerned about speed will want to address all of these. More sophisticated approaches to speed include flash memory, RISC computers, and parallel processing.

—Capron, *Computers,* p. 82

Topic: _____

3.   The process of becoming hypnotized begins when the people who will be hypnotized find a comfortable body position and become thoroughly relaxed. Without letting their minds wander to other matters, they focus their attention on a specific object or sound, such as a metronome or the hypnotist's voice. Then, based on both what the hypnotherapist expects to occur and actually sees occurring, she or he tells the clients how they will feel as the hypnotic process continues. For instance, the hypnotist may say, "You are feeling completely

relaxed" or "Your eyelids are becoming heavy." When people being hypnotized recognize that their feelings match the hypnotist's comments, they are likely to believe that some change is taking place. That belief seems to increase their openness to other statements made by the hypnotist.

—Uba and Huang, *Psychology,* p. 148

Topic: _____

4.   Learning words is an important part of language acquisition. Yet the infinite productivity and flexibility of human language rest on much more than just words: they derive from people's ability to combine words in an incredibly large number of ways, according to rules understood by all users of that language, in order to express novel ideas and fine gradations of meaning. These rules are called syntax, or grammar. Children begin the task of acquiring syntax by expressing single relations such as possession ("Mommy's hat"). They progress to acquire more and more complex grammatical constructions (one child who was nearly 3 said, "I'm sorry I can't do that because it fell over when I pushed it").

—Newcome, *Child Development,* p. 223

Topic: _____

5.   Let's now deal with the fact that the human eye contains two distinctly different photoreceptor cells. Both rods and cones exist in our retinas, but they are not there in equal numbers. In one eye, there are approximately 120 million rods, but only 6 million cones; rods outnumber cones approximately 20 to 1. Not only are rods and cones found in unequal numbers, but they are not evenly distributed throughout the retina. Cones are concentrated in the center of the retina, at the fovea. Rods are concentrated in a band or ring surrounding the fovea, out toward the periphery of the retina. These observations have led psychologists to wonder if the rods and cones of our eyes have different functions.

—Gerow, *Essentials of Psychology,* p. 138

Topic: _____

6.   Although there were unions in the United States before the American Revolution, they have become major power blocks only in the last 60 years or so. Directly or indirectly, managerial decisions in almost all organizations are now influenced by the effect of unions. Managers in unionized organizations must operate through the union in dealing with their employees instead of acting alone. Decisions affecting employees are made collectively at the bargaining tables and through arbitration, instead of individually by the supervisor when and where the need arises. Wages, hours, and other terms and conditions of employment are largely decided outside of management's sphere of discretion.

—Mosley, Pietri, and Magginson, *Management: Leadership in Action,* p. 317

Topic: _____

7.   When a group is too large for an effective discussion or when its members are not well informed on the topic, a *panel* of individuals may be selected to discuss the topic for the benefit of others, who then become an audience. Members of a panel may be particularly well informed on the subject or may represent divergent views. For example, your group may be interested in UFOs (unidentified flying objects) and hold a discussion for your classmates. Or your group might tackle the problems of tenants and landlords. Whatever your topic, the audience should learn the basic issues from your discussion.

—Gronbeck et al., *Principles of Speech Communication,* p. 302

Topic: _____

8.   It seems obvious that power inequality affects the quality of people's lives. The rich and powerful live better than the poor and powerless. Similarly, power inequality affects the quality of *deviant* activities likely to be engaged in by people. Thus the powerful are more likely to perpetrate profitable crimes, such as corporate crime, while the powerless are more likely to commit unprofitable crimes, such as homicide and assault. In other words, power—or lack of it—largely determines the *type* of crime people are likely to commit.

—Thio, *Sociology,* p. 181

Topic: _____

9.   Automated radio has made large gains, as station managers try to reduce expenses by eliminating some of their on-the-air personnel. These stations broadcast packaged taped programs obtained from syndicates, hour after hour, or material delivered by satellite from a central program source. The closely timed tapes contain music and commercials, along with the necessary voice introductions and bridges. They have spaces into which a staff engineer can slip local recorded commercials. By eliminating disc jockeys in this manner, a station keeps its costs down but loses the personal touch and becomes a broadcasting automaton. For example, one leading syndicator, Satellite Music Network, provides more than 625 stations with their choice of seven different 24-hour music formats that include news and live disc jockeys playing records.

—Agee, Ault, and Emery, *Introduction to Mass Communications,* p. 225

Topic: _____

10.   Bone is one of the hardest materials in the body and, although relatively light in weight, it has a remarkable ability to resist tension and other forces acting on it. Nature has given us an extremely strong and exceptionally simple (almost crude), supporting system without giving up mobility. The calcium salts deposited in the matrix give bone its hardness, whereas the organic parts (especially the collagen fibers) provide for bone's flexibility and great tensile strength.

—Marieb, *Essentials of Human Anatomy and Physiology,* p. 119

Topic: _____

HOW TO FIND THE MAIN IDEA

The main idea of a paragraph tells you what the author wants you to know about the topic. The main idea is usually directly stated by the writer in one or more sentences within the paragraph. The sentence that states this main idea is called the *topic sentence.* The topic sentence tells what the rest of the paragraph is about. In some paragraphs, the main idea is not directly stated in any one sentence. Instead, it is left to the reader to infer, or reason out.

To find the main idea of a paragraph, first decide what the topic of the paragraph is. Then ask yourself these questions: What is the main idea—what is the author trying to say about the topic? Which sentence states the main idea? Read the following paragraph.

The Federal Trade Commission has become increasingly interested in false and misleading packaging. Complaints have been filed against many food packagers because they make boxes unnecessarily large to give a false impression of quantity. Cosmetics manufacturers have been accused of using false bottoms in packaging to make a small amount of their product appear to be much more.

In the preceding paragraph, the topic is false packaging. The main idea is that the Federal Trade Commission is becoming increasingly concerned about false or misleading packaging. The author states the main idea in the first sentence, so it is the topic sentence.

WHERE TO FIND THE TOPIC SENTENCE

Although the topic sentence of a paragraph can be located anywhere in the paragraph, there are several positions where it is most likely to be found. Each type of paragraph has been diagrammed to help you visualize how it is structured.

First Sentence

The most common position of the topic sentence is first in the paragraph. In this type of paragraph, the author states the main idea at the beginning of the paragraph and then elaborates on it.

> The good listener, in order to achieve the purpose of acquiring information, is careful to follow specific steps to achieve accurate understanding. First, whenever possible the good listener prepares in advance for the speech or lecture he or she is going to attend. He or she studies the topic to be discussed and finds out about the speaker and his or her beliefs. Second, on arriving at the place where the speech is to be given, he or she chooses a seat where seeing, hearing, and remaining alert are easy. Finally, when the speech is over, an effective listener reviews what was said and reacts to and evaluates the ideas expressed.

Usually, in this type of paragraph, the author is employing a deductive thought pattern in which a statement is made at the beginning and then supported throughout the paragraph.

Last Sentence

The second most common position of the topic sentence is last in the paragraph. In this type of paragraph, the author leads or builds up to the main idea and then states it in a sentence at the very end.

> Whenever possible, the good listener prepares in advance for the speech or lecture he or she plans to attend. He or she studies the topic to be discussed and finds out about the speaker and his or her beliefs. On arriving at the place where the speech is to be given, he or she chooses a seat where seeing, hearing, and remaining alert are easy. And when the speech is over, he or she reviews what was said and reacts to and evaluates the ideas expressed. Thus, an effective listener, in order to achieve the purpose of acquiring information, takes specific steps to achieve accurate understanding.

The thought pattern frequently used in this type of paragraph is inductive. That is, the author provides supporting evidence for the main idea first and then states it.

Middle of the Paragraph

Another common position of the topic sentence is in the middle of the paragraph. In this case, the author builds up to the main idea, states it in the middle of the paragraph, and then goes on with further elaboration and detail.

> Whenever possible, the good listener prepares in advance for the speech or lecture he or she plans to attend. He or she studies the topic to be discussed and finds out about the speaker and his or her beliefs. <u>An effective listener, then, takes specific steps to achieve accurate understanding of the lecture.</u> Furthermore, on arriving at the place where the speech is to be given, he or she chooses a seat where it is easy to see, hear, and remain alert. Finally, when the speech is over, the effective listener reviews what was said and reacts to and evaluates the ideas expressed.

First and Last Sentences

Sometimes an author uses two sentences to state the main idea or states the main idea twice in one paragraph. Usually, in this type of paragraph, the writer states the main idea at the beginning of the paragraph, then explains or supports the idea, and finally restates the main idea at the very end.

> <u>The good listener, in order to achieve the purpose of acquiring information, is careful to follow specific steps to achieve accurate understanding.</u> First, whenever possible the good listener prepares in advance for the speech or lecture he or she is going to attend. He or she studies the topic to be discussed and finds out about the speaker and his or her beliefs. Second, on arriving at the place where the speech is to be given, he or she chooses a seat where seeing, hearing, and remaining alert are easy. Finally, when the speech is over, he or she reviews what was said and reacts to and evaluates the ideas expressed. <u>Effective listening is an active process in which a listener deliberately takes certain actions to ensure that accurate communication has occurred.</u>

Exercise 3

DIRECTIONS   Read each of the following paragraphs and underline the topic sentence.

1.   First, language consists of a large number of *symbols*. The symbols that make up a language are commonly referred to as *words*. They are the labels that we have assigned to the mental representation of our experiences. When we use the word *chair* as a symbol, we don't use it to label any one specific instance of a chair. We use it to represent our concept of what a chair is. Note that, as symbols, words do not have to stand for real things in the real world. With language, we can communicate about owls and pussycats in teacups; four-dimensional, time-warped hyperspace; and a cartoon beagle that flies his doghouse into battle against the Red Baron. Words are used to stand for our cognitions, our concepts, and we have a great number of them.

—Gerow, *Essentials of Psychology*, p. 289

2.   One important reality with which marketers must contend is that people have *selective perception.* That is, we actually perceive only a very small proportion of all the stimuli with which we are constantly bombarded. For example, most consumers are exposed to countless advertisements every day on billboards, in magazines and newspapers, and on television or the radio, but they actually are conscious of very few of them. Thus, an important goal for marketers is to make sure that the advertisements for their products are perceived by their target markets.

—Kinnear, Bernhardt, and Krentler, *Principles of Marketing*, p. 191

3. Many people assume that the law is based on the consent of citizens, that it treats citizens equally, and that it serves the best interest of society. If we simply read the U.S. Constitution and statutes, this assumption may indeed be justified. But focusing on the *law on the books,* as William Chambliss (1969) pointed out, may be misleading. The law on the books does indeed say that the authorities ought to be fair and just. But are they? To understand crime, Chambliss argued, we need to look at the *law on action,* at how legal authorities actually discharge their duty. After studying the law in action, Chambliss concluded that legal authorities are actually unfair and unjust, favoring the rich and powerful over the poor and weak.

—Thio, *Sociology,* p. 180

4. The functions of desktop publishing software are similar to those of word processing programs, except that some capabilities are more sophisticated. A user can enter text using the desktop publishing program in the same way that he or she can enter text with a word processing program. In addition, the user can retrieve text from a file created by another program. For example, the user may enter, edit, and save text using a word processing program and then retrieve the saved text using the desktop publishing program.

—Nickerson, *Business and Information Systems,* p. 249

5. Verbal and nonverbal communications exist in a context, and that context to a large extent determines the meaning of any verbal or nonverbal behavior. The same words or behaviors may have totally different meanings when they occur in different contexts. For example, the greeting, "How are you?" means "Hello" to someone you pass regularly on the street but means "Is your health improving?" when said to a friend in the hospital. A wink to an attractive person on a bus means something completely different from a wink that signifies a put-on or a lie. Similarly, the meaning of a given signal depends on the behaviors it accompanies or is close to in time. Pounding a fist on the table during a speech in support of a politician means something quite different from that same gesture in response to news of a friend's death. Divorced from the context, it is impossible to tell what meaning was intended just from examining the signals. Of course, even if you know the context in detail, you still may not be able to decipher the meaning of the verbal or nonverbal message.

—DeVito, *Human Communication,* p. 110

6. The rate of cooling of an object depends on how much hotter the object is than the surroundings. The temperature change per minute of a hot apple pie will be more if the hot pie is put in a cold freezer than if put on the kitchen table. When the pie cools in the freezer, the temperature difference between it and its surroundings is greater. A warm home will leak heat to the cold outside at a greater rate when there is a large difference in the inside and outside temperatures. Keeping the inside of your home at a high temperature on a cold day is more costly than keeping it at a lower temperature. If you keep the temperature difference small, the rate of cooling will be correspondingly low.

—Hewitt, *Conceptual Physics,* p. 279

7. The pawnshop industry has been in decline in most parts of the world. In Great Britain in 1900 there were 3,000 pawnshops; in the 1990s there are fewer than 150. In the United States, however, the pawnshop business actually grew during the same time period, from under 2,000 to more than 7,000 today. Pawnshops in this country currently make about 40 million loans a year with an aggregate dollar amount over $1 billion. Most of these pawnshops are in the Southeast and Rocky Mountain areas. One of the reasons for the growth of pawnshops is

that many states have relaxed their restrictions (called *usury laws*) on the maximum interest rates that can be charged. Pawnshops in these states can now legally charge the high rates needed to stay in business. Further, the percentage of U.S. citizens classified as low-income has risen in recent decades. These individuals cannot get loans from mainstream financial institutions, such as banks and savings and loan associations, and so must turn to alternatives, one of which is the pawnshop.

—Miller, *Economics Today,* p. 213

8. Because faces are so visible and so sensitive, you pay more attention to people's faces than to any other nonverbal feature. The face is an efficient and high-speed means of conveying meaning. Gestures, posture, and larger body movements require some time to change in response to a changing stimulus, whereas facial expressions can change instantly, sometimes even at a rate imperceptible to the human eye. As an instantaneous response mechanism, it is *the* most effective way to provide feedback to an ongoing message. This is the process of using the face as a regulator.

—Weaver, *Understanding Interpersonal Communication,* p. 220

9. Color, a component of light, affects us directly by modifying our thoughts, moods, actions, and even our health. Psychologists, as well as designers of schools, offices, hospitals, and prisons, have acknowledged that colors can affect work habits and mental conditions. People surrounded by expanses of solid orange or red for long periods often experience nervousness and increase blood pressure. In contrast, some blues have a calming effect, causing blood pressure, pulse, and activity rates to drop to below normal levels.

—Preble, Preble, and Frank, *Artforms,* p. 64

10. During photosynthesis in green plants, as the energy of sunlight falls on the green pigment in the leaves, carbon dioxide and the hydrogens of water are used to make food, and water and oxygen are released. The release of oxygen by those first photosynthesizers was a critical step in the direction of life's development. In a sense, the production of oxygen falls into the "good news-bad news" category. It's good news for us, of course, since we need oxygen, but as oxygen began to become a prevalent gas in the atmosphere, it sounded the death knell for many of the early organisms. This is because oxygen is a disruptive gas, as demonstrated by the process of rusting metal. So, in the early days of life on the planet, many life forms were destroyed by the deadly and accumulating gas.

—Wallace, *Biology: The World of Life,* p. 167

RECOGNIZING DETAILS

The details in a paragraph are those facts and ideas that prove, explain, support, or give examples of the main idea of the paragraph. Once the topic and main idea have been identified, recognizing the supporting details is a relatively simple matter. The more difficult job is selecting the few key, or most important, details that clearly support the main idea.

All details in a paragraph are related to, and in some way expand, the paragraph's main idea, but not all these details are crucial to the author's central thought. Some details are just meant to describe; others are meant to provide added, but not essential, information; still others are intended merely to repeat or restate the main idea.

On the other hand, the key supporting details within a paragraph are those statements that carry the primary supporting evidence needed to back up the main idea. To find the key supporting details in a paragraph, ask yourself the question: What are the main facts the author uses to back up or prove what she or he said about the topic?

In the following paragraph, the topic sentence is underlined twice; the key supporting details are underlined once. Notice how the underlined details differ, in the type and importance of the information they provide, from the remaining details in the paragraph.

> <u>The larger-scale and more technologically sophisticated a society, the weaker its ties of marriage,</u> for several reasons. First, in large-scale societies, especially mobile ones like Western society, <u>individuals continually meet new people of the opposite sex.</u> Second, people are likely to <u>live longer</u> in technologically advanced societies, and longevity sometimes <u>leads to marital discontent.</u> Third, <u>many of the functions of marriage</u> in large-scale, technologically sophisticated societies <u>are fulfilled by other institutions.</u> A married person's economic support, for example, does not depend on cooperation with a spouse when both spouses earn paychecks outside their joint household and can continue to do so even if they part.
>
> —Hicks and Gwynne, *Cultural Anthropology,* p. 258

All the underlined details give the primary reasons why marriage ties are weaker in larger-scale, more technologically sophisticated societies. The details in the remainder of the paragraph offer examples or explain these reasons further.

 **EXERCISE 4**

DIRECTIONS   Each of the following statements could function as the topic sentence of a paragraph. After each statement are sentences containing details that may be related to the main idea statement. Read each sentence and make a check mark beside those with details that can be considered primary support for the main idea statement.

1. *Topic sentence:*

   Licorice is used in tobacco products because it has specific characteristics that cannot be found in any other single ingredient.

   Details:

   _____   a. McAdams & Co. is the largest importer and processor of licorice root.

   _____   b. Licorice blends with tobacco and provides added mildness.

   _____   c. Licorice provides a unique flavor and sweetens many types of tobacco.

   _____   d. The extract of licorice is present in relatively small amounts in most types of pipe tobacco.

   _____   e. Licorice helps tobacco retain the correct amount of moisture during storage.

2. *Topic sentence:*

Many dramatic physical changes occur during adolescence between the ages of 13 and 15.

Details:

_____ a. Voice changes in boys begin to occur at age 13 or 14.

_____ b. Facial proportions may change during adolescence.

_____ c. The forehead tends to become wider, and the mouth widens.

_____ d. Many teenagers do not know how to react to these changes.

_____ e. Primary sex characteristics begin to develop for both boys and girls.

3. *Topic sentence:*

The development of speech in infants follows a definite sequence or pattern of development.

Details:

_____ a. By the time an infant is six months old, he or she can make twelve different speech sounds.

_____ b. Before the age of three months, most infants are unable to produce any recognizable syllables.

_____ c. During the first year, the number of vowel sounds a child can produce is greater than the number of consonant sounds he or she can make.

_____ d. During the second year, the number of consonant sounds a child can produce increases.

_____ e. Parents often reward the first recognizable word a child produces by smiling or speaking to the child.

4. *Topic sentence:*

The two main motives for attending a play are the desire for recreation and the need for relaxation.

Details:

_____ a. By becoming involved with the actors and their problems, members of the audience temporarily suspend their personal cares and concerns.

_____ b. In America today, the success of a play is judged by its ability to attract a large audience.

_____ c. Almost everyone who attends a play expects to be entertained.

_____ d. Plays allow the audience to release tension, which facilitates relaxation.

_____ e. There is a smaller audience that looks to theater for intellectual stimulation.

5. *Topic sentence:*

In some parts of the world, famine is a constant human condition and exists for a variety of reasons.

Details:

_____ a. In parts of Africa, people are dying of hunger by the tens of thousands.

_____ b. Famine is partly caused by increased population.

_____ c. Advances in medicine have increased life expectancies, keeping more people active for longer periods of time.

_____ d. Agricultural technology has not made substantial advances in increasing the food supply.

_____ e. Because of the growth of cities, populations have become more dense, and agricultural support for these population centers is not available.

6. *Topic sentence:*

The amount of alcohol a person consumes has been found to depend on a number of socioeconomic factors such as age, sex, ethnic background, and occupation.

Details:

_____ a. Some religions prohibit consumption altogether, and most encourage moderation.

_____ b. The lowest proportion of drinkers is found among people with an educational level of below sixth grade.

_____ c. People in a lower socioeconomic level drink more than people in a higher socioeconomic level.

_____ d. In some cultures drinking is common at meals, but these same cultures disapprove of drunkenness.

_____ e. Farm owners have the highest proportion of nondrinkers, while professionals and businessmen have the highest proportion of drinkers.

7. *Topic sentence:*

An individual deals with anxiety in a variety of ways and produces a wide range of responses.

Details:

_____ a. Anxiety may manifest itself by such physical symptoms as increased heart activity and labored breathing.

_____ b. Fear, unlike anxiety, is a response to real or threatened danger.

_____ c. Psychologically, anxiety often produces a feeling of powerlessness, or lack of direct control over the immediate environment.

_____ d. Temporary blindness, deafness, and loss of the sensation of touch are examples of extreme physical responses to anxiety.

_____ e. Some people cannot cope with anxiety and are unable to control the neurotic behavior associated with anxiety.

8. *Topic sentence:*

An individual's status or importance within a group affects his or her behavior in that particular group.

Details:

_____ a. High-status individuals frequently arrive late at social functions.

_____ b. Once a person achieves high status, he or she attempts to maintain it.

_____ c. High-status individuals demand more privileges.

_____ d. Low-status individuals are less resistant to change within the group structure than persons of high status.

_____ e. There are always fewer high-status members than low-status members in any particular group.

9. *Topic sentence:*

An oligopoly is a market structure in which only a few companies sell a certain product.

Details:

_____ a. The automobile industry is a good example of an oligopoly, although it gives the appearance of being highly competitive.

_____ b. The breakfast cereal, soap, and cigarette industries, although basic to our economy, operate as oligopolies.

_____ c. Monopolies refer to market structures in which only one industry produces a particular product.

_____ d. Monopolies are able to exert more control and price fixing than oligopolies.

_____ e. In the oil industry, because there are only a few producers, each producer has a fairly large share of the sales.

10. *Topic sentence:*

Advertising can be used to expand consumer choice as well as to limit it.

Details:

_____ a. Food stores that typically advertise their "specials" each Wednesday in the local paper are encouraging consumer choice.

_____ b. Department store advertising often makes the consumer aware of new products and styles, as well as of current prices of products.

_____   c. Misleading or excessive advertising is usually rejected by the consuming public.

_____   d. Exaggerated claims made by some advertisers serve to limit the consumer's actual knowledge and free choice of products.

_____   e. Advertising that provides little or no factual information, but merely attempts to make the brand name well known, actually restricts consumers' free choice.

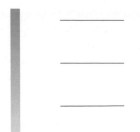

EXERCISE 5

DIRECTIONS   Read each paragraph and identify the topic and the main idea. Write each in the space provided. Then underline the key supporting details.

1.   The extent to which parents will sacrifice for their offspring is familiar to anyone who has watched either a robin tirelessly bringing worms to a nest full of gaping mouths or a human parent writing checks to pay for tuition. Humans are apt to interpret such selflessness as a manifestation of love, but many ethological studies suggest that in birds, at least, the behavior is a motor program. In many species of birds, any gaping mouth will evoke feeding by parents, whether the mouth belongs to their own young or not. European cuckoos and other brood parasites exploit this motor program to their own advantage. A further sign that parental behavior in birds is automatic can be seen when the chicks of gulls stray outside the nest. The parents apparently do not recognize a chick outside the nest, because they stand idly by while they starve to death or are eaten by predators.

—Miller, *Economics Today,* p. 84

Topic: _____

Main idea: _____

2.   There are a number of reasons why there has been an increase in the demand for nurses, not the least of which is the aging of the U.S. population. Older people use hospitals more and have chronic ailments that require more nursing. Moreover, as hospitals reduce the length of stay of patients, people who are discharged earlier than in previous years need more home care, usually provided by nurses. At the same time as demand has been rising, the supply of nurses has decreased somewhat. The age distribution of women between 18 and 24 has decreased in the past decade. Because this is the group from which nurses traditionally come, there have been fewer potential nurses. In addition, women have more alternatives in the labor market than they did years ago.

—Miller, *Economics Today,* p. 84

Topic: _____

Main idea: _____

3.   Perhaps we can best describe a theory by showing how one can be developed. Suppose someone comes up with an idea—one that explains certain observed phenomena in nature. At first, it is regarded as just that, an idea. But after it has been carefully described and its premises precisely defined, it may then become a *hypothesis*—an idea that can be tested. In a sense, the hypothesis is the first part of an "if . . . then" statement. The "then" predicts the result of the hypothesis, so one can know by testing if the hypothesis is sound. A hypothesis can also stand as a provisional statement for which more data are needed. If rigorous, carefully controlled testing supports the hypothesis, more confidence will be placed in it, until it finally gains the status of a theory. The theory itself, however,

may remain unproven and unprovable. A hypothesis, then, is a possible explanation to be tested, whereas a *theory* is a more-or-less verified explanation that accounts for observed phenomena in nature.

—Wallace, *Biology: The World of Life,* p. 28

Topic: _____

Main idea: _____

4.   With young infants, especially those under a year old, it is not possible to assess all components of the emotions we know in adulthood. Lack of language in infancy makes it difficult to know if they are aware of bodily changes such as increased heart rate or if they have thoughts regarding such things as the possibility of being hurt. Thus, developmental psychologists have concentrated on studying the changes in the brain and body of the infant that follow encounters with situations that would lead to an emotion in an adult, such as stimuli that would elicit pain (e.g., an inoculation), or happiness (e.g., social interaction). They have also coded the facial expressions shown by infants in such situations.

—Newcombe, *Child Development,* p. 152

Topic: _____

Main idea: _____

5.   When accomplished writers use the word revision, they don't mean the sort of superficial changes implied in the old elementary school phrase "Copy it over in ink." Revision doesn't even mean writing your paper over again. Instead, it means reading your draft carefully in order to make principled, effective changes in the existing text. It means stepping outside the draft you've created; assessing its strengths and weaknesses as if you were a reader seeing it for the first time; and deciding what parts of the draft need to be expanded, clarified, elaborated, illustrated, reworded, restructured, modified—or just plain cut.

—Anson and Swegler, *The Longman Handbook for Writers and Readers,* p. 78

Topic: _____

Main idea: _____

6.   The final component of a computer is secondary storage, also called auxiliary storage, which stores data not currently being processed by the computer and programs not currently being performed. Its function differs from that of primary storage, which stores the data and instructions that are currently being processed by the computer. For example, if the computer is currently doing payroll processing, then the employee data and the payroll computation program would be stored in the computer's primary storage. Other data and programs that are not currently being used, such as would be needed for sales analysis, would be stored in secondary storage and brought into primary storage when needed. Primary storage is temporary storage, and anything stored in it is lost when the power to the computer is turned off. Secondary storage, however, is permanent storage; anything stored in secondary storage remains there until it is changed even if the power is turned off.

—Nickerson, *Business and Information Systems,* p. 66

Topic: _____

Main idea: _____

7. In any given presidential election, in fact, only a handful of candidates are serious possibilities. So far in American history, these have virtually always been middle-aged or elderly white men, with extensive formal education, fairly high income, and substantial experience as public figures—usually as government officials (especially governors or senators) or military heroes. Movie stars, media commentators, business executives, and others who would be president almost always have to perform lesser government service until they are seriously considered for the presidency. Ronald Reagan, for example, most of whose career was spent acting in motion pictures and on television, served as governor of California before being elected president. Women and racial minorities have been conspicuous by their absence. Civil rights activist and congresswoman Shirley Chisholm made a run for the Democratic party presidential nomination in 1972 but did not get very far. Representative Pat Schroeder of Colorado tested the waters in 1988 but decided to withdraw. General Colin Powell was among the favorites for the Republican presidential nomination in 1996, according the public opinion polls, but he decided against making a run.

    —Greenberg and Page, *The Struggle for Democracy*, p. 190

Topic: _____

Main idea: _____

8. One of the most common targets of populist sentiment has been concentrated economic power and those who exercise it. Andrew Jackson mobilized this sentiment in his fight against the Bank of the United States in the 1830s. The Populist movement of the 1890s directed its political and legislative efforts against the new corporations of the day, especially the banks and the railroads. Corporations were the target of popular hostility during the dark days of the Great Depression and also in the 1970s, when consumer groups made the lives of some corporate executives extremely uncomfortable. Contemporary public opinion polls find strong popular support for free enterprise existing side by side with negative feelings about corporations and corporate leaders.

    —Greenberg and Page, *The Struggle for Democracy*, pp. 107–108

Topic: _____

Main idea: _____

9. As in previous periods, both push and pull factors are involved in people's emigration decisions. As subsistence economies are dismantled in the periphery, impoverished peasants are forced out of their home areas. At the same time, the hope of better wages, improved life chances, and jobs in factories that have recently been relocated from the core to the periphery are the primary magnets that draw the rural poor to the squatter camps of the cities (Mingione and Pugliese, 1994). At present, Latin America is experiencing the highest levels of urban growth, "where 8 to 10 million people annually are either migrating to cities or being born there" (Eitzen and Baca Zinn, 1994: 66).

    —Thompson and Hickey, *Society in Focus: An Introduction to Sociology*, p. 227

Topic: _____

Main idea: _____

10. Mexico City, with a population of 14 to 20 million, leads the world's cities in population. Situated in a high altitude with mountains forming a rim around it, Mexico City is primed for air pollution. Add to this the millions of vehicles without air-pollution control devices, the use of leaded fuel, and the 35,000

industrial sites spewing forth pollutants. A recent ozone reading of 0.35 parts per million was four times the level considered safe in California. Mexico City is attempting to address this severe problem by starting to equip cars with emission controls, eliminating diesel buses, and so forth. However, with the population of the city growing at such a high rate, such attempts may be "too little, too late."

—Glynn, Hohm, and Stewart, *Global Social Problems*, p. 222

Topic: _____

Main idea: _____

TRANSITIONS

Transitions are linking words or phrases used to lead the reader from one idea to another. Figure 6.1 presents a list of commonly used transitions. If you get in the habit of recognizing transitions, you will see that they often guide you through a paragraph, helping you to read it more easily.

In the following paragraph, notice how the underlined transitions lead you from one important detail to the next.

You need to take a few steps to prepare to become a better note-taker. First, get organized. It's easiest to take useful notes if you have a system. A loose leaf notebook works best because you can add, rearrange, or remove notes for review. If you use spiral or other permanently bound notebooks, use a separate notebook for each

Type of Transition	Example	What They Tell the Reader
Time–sequence	first, later, next, finally	The author is arranging ideas in the order in which they happened.
Example	for example, for instance, to illustrate, such as	An example will follow.
Enumeration	first, second, third, last, another, next	The author is marking or identifying each major point (sometimes these may be used to suggest order of importance).
Continuation	also, in addition, and, further, another	The author is continuing with the same idea and is going to provide additional information.
Contrast	on the other hand, in contrast, however	The author is switching to a different, opposite, or contrasting idea than previously discussed.
Comparison	like, likewise, similarly	The writer will show how the previous idea is similar to what follows.
Cause–effect	because, thus, therefore, since, consequently	The writer will show a connection between two or more things, how one thing caused another, or how something happened as a result of something else.
Summation	thus, in short, to conclude	The writer will state or restate his or her main point.

Figure 6.1
Common Transitions

subject to avoid confusion and to allow for expansion. <u>Second,</u> set aside a few min-utes each day to review the syllabus for your course, to scan the assigned readings, and to review your notes from the previous class period. If you do this just before each lecture, you'll be ready to take notes and practice critical thinking. <u>Finally,</u> pre-pare your pages by drawing a line down the left margin approximately two inches from the edge of the paper. Leave this margin blank while you take notes so that later you can use it to practice critical thinking.

—Gronbeck et al., *Principles of Speech Communication*, pp. 32–33

Not all paragraphs contain such obvious transitions, and not all transitions serve as such clear markers of major details. Transitions may be used to alert you to what will come next in the paragraph. If you see the phrase *for instance* at the beginning of a sentence, then you know that an example will follow. When you see the phrase *on the other hand,* you can predict that a different, opposing idea will follow. Figure 6.1 lists some of the most common transitions used within paragraphs and indicates what they tell you. In the next chapter, you will see that these transitional words also signal the author's organization.

EXERCISE 6   ■ **DIRECTIONS**   Underline each transition used in the paragraphs in Exercise 5.

UNSTATED MAIN IDEAS

Occasionally, a writer does not directly state the main idea of a given paragraph in a topic sentence. Instead, he or she leaves it up to the reader to infer, or reason out, what the main idea of the paragraph is. This type of paragraph contains only details or specifics that are related to a given topic and substantiate an unstated main idea. To read this type of paragraph, start as you would for para-graphs with stated main ideas. Ask yourself the question for finding the topic: What is the one thing the author is discussing throughout the paragraph? Then try to think of a sentence about the topic that all the details included in the paragraph would support.

Read the paragraph in the following example. First, identify the topic. Then study the details and think of a general statement that all the details in the para-graph would support or prove.

> Suppose a group of plumbers in a community decide to set standard prices for repair services and agree to quote the same price for the same job. Is this ethical? Suppose a group of automobile dealers agree to abide strictly by the used car blue book prices on trade-ins. Is this ethical? Two meat supply houses serving a large university submit identical bids each month for the meat contract. Is this ethical?

This paragraph describes three specific instances in which there was agree-ment to fix prices. Clearly, the main idea of the author is whether price collusion is ethical, but that main idea is not directly stated in a sentence anywhere within the passage.

EXERCISE 7   ▌ **DIRECTIONS**   In the following paragraphs the main idea is not directly stated. Read each paragraph, identify the topic, and write it in the space provided. Then write a sentence that expresses the main idea of the passage.

1. In 1950, only two cities, London and New York, had populations over 8 million; today there are 20 of these huge cities, 14 of them in developing countries. At present, the total urban population of the developing countries is an estimated 1.3 billion people—more than the total populations of Europe, Japan, and North America combined. At a growth rate of 50 million new urbanites every year, due both to natural increases in resident populations and immigration from rural areas, over half the people in the developing world will live in cities by the year 2020.

    —Hicks and Gwynne, *Cultural Anthropology,* p. 144

    Topic: _____

    Main idea: _____

2. When a homemaker is killed in an auto accident, that person's family can often sue for the value of the services that were lost. Attorneys (who rely on economists) are often asked to make an attempt to estimate this value to present to the court. They add up the cost of purchasing babysitting, cooking, housecleaning, and tutoring services. The number turns out to be quite large, often in excess of $30,000 a year. Of course one of the problems in measuring the value of unremunerated housework in such a way is that we could often purchase the services of a full-time live-in housekeeper for less money than if we paid for the services of the various components of housekeeping. And what about quality? Some homemakers serve fabulous gourmet meals; others simply warm up canned and frozen foods. Should they be valued equally? Another problem lies in knowing when to stop counting. A person can hire a valet to help him or her get dressed in the morning. Should we therefore count the time spent in getting dressed as part of unpaid work? Both men and women perform services around the house virtually every day of the year. Should all of those unremunerated services be included in a "new" measure of GDP? If they were, measured GDP would be increased dramatically.

    —Miller, *Economics Today,* p. 185

    Topic: _____

    Main idea: _____

3. Most anthropologists make their living by teaching in universities, colleges, and community colleges, and by carrying out university-based research. But a substantial and increasing proportion of anthropologists find employment in nonacademic settings. Museums, for example—especially museums of natural history, archaeology, and art and folklore—have long relied on the expertise of anthropologists. In recent years, anthropologists have been welcome in a greater variety of public and private positions: in government agencies concerned with welfare, drug abuse, mental health, environmental impact, housing, education, foreign aid, and agricultural development; in the private sector as personnel and ethnic relations consultants and as management consultants for multinational firms; and as staff members of hospitals and foundations.

    —Harris, *Cultural Anthropology,* pp. 3–4

    Topic: _____

    Main idea: _____

4. By 1932 the value of industrial shares had fallen close to 60 percent on the New York and Berlin markets. Unemployment doubled in Germany, and 25 percent of the labor force was out of work in the United States. The middle class, which had

invested in the stock market, saw their investments and savings wiped out. In nation after nation, industry declined, prices fell, banks collapsed, and economies stagnated. In the western democracies the depression heightened the feelings of uneasiness that had existed since 1918. In other countries, the tendency to seek authoritarian solutions became even more pronounced. Throughout the world people feared a future marked by lowered standards of living, unemployment, and hunger.

—Wallbank et al., *Civilization Past and Present,* p. 831

Topic: _____

Main idea: _____

5.   During the 1960s, police went from walking "beats" to riding in squad cars. While squad cars provided a faster response to emergency calls, they also changed the nature of social interaction between police officers and the public. Much police work had been highly personal, as officers strolled the sidewalks talking to storekeepers and homeowners, but it became much more impersonal, with less contact between officers and citizens. Since the 1960s, technological advances have provided more elaborate means of communication and surveillance, better-equipped squad cars, and more sophisticated weaponry. Unfortunately criminals have benefited from increased technology as well. This increased technology and other developments have led many city leaders to question contemporary policing practices and some to accentuate the need to reemphasize police–community relations.

—Thompson and Hickey, *Society in Focus,* p. 162

Topic: _____

Main idea: _____

6.   Severe punishment may generate such anxiety in children that they do not learn the lesson the punishment was designed to teach. Moreover, as a reaction to punishment that they regard as unfair, children may avoid punitive parents, who therefore will have fewer opportunities to teach and guide the child. In addition, parents who use physical punishment provide aggressive models. A child who is regularly slapped, spanked, shaken, or shouted at may learn to use these forms of aggression in interactions with peers.

—Newcombe, *Child Development,* p. 354

Topic: _____

Main idea: _____

7.   In 1920 there was one divorce for every seven marriages in the United States. Fifty years later the rate had climbed to one divorce for every three marriages, and today there is almost one divorce for every two marriages. The divorce rate in the United States is now the highest of any major industrialized nation, while Canada is in a rather distant second place.

—Coleman and Cressey, *Social Problems,* p. 130

Topic: _____

Main idea: _____

8. In 1970 the federal government passed the Comprehensive Drug Abuse, Prevention and Control Act (also known as the Controlled Substance Act). That act did not contain a rigid penalty system but rather established only upper bounds for the fines and prison terms to be imposed for offenses. In 1984 the act was amended in order to impose fixed penalties, particularly for dealers. For anyone caught with more than 1 kilogram of heroin, 50 grams of cocaine base, or 1,000 kilograms of marijuana, the applicable penalty was raised to imprisonment from 10 years to life plus a fine of $4 million. A variety of other prison penalties and fines were outlined in that amendment. Another amendment passed in 1988 included the death penalty for "drug kingpins." Such increased penalties have led to more rather than less violence. To understand why, we must reexamine the concept of marginal cost.

—Miller, *Economics Today,* p. 513

Topic: _____

Main idea: _____

9. People's acceptance of a product is largely determined by its package. The very same coffee taken from a yellow can was described as weak, from a dark brown can too strong, from a red can rich, and from a blue can mild. Even our acceptance of a person may depend on the colors worn. Consider, for example, the comments of one color expert: "If you have to pick the wardrobe for your defense lawyer heading into court and choose anything but blue, you deserve to lose the case. . . ." Black is so powerful it could work against the lawyer with the jury. Brown lacks sufficient authority. Green would probably elicit a negative response.

—DeVito, *Messages,* p. 153

Topic: _____

Main idea: _____

10. Just consider that from 1985 to 1994, defense spending fell by more than one-fifth. By the year 2000 the defense budget will be considerably lower. The Pentagon's prime contractors—McDonnell Douglas, Northrop, Lockheed, General Dynamics, Rockwell, and Grumman—have taken the hardest hits; so too will General Motors (which owns Hughes Aircraft), General Electric (which builds submarines), and Boeing. Each of these large businesses is supported by small subcontractors, many of whom will also be hurt.

—Miller, *Economics Today,* p. 27

Topic: _____

Main idea: _____

DIRECTIONS Turn to the reading "Losing Your Good Name Online," in Part Seven, p. 408. Read each paragraph and identify the topic and main idea. Then place brackets around the topic and underline the sentence that expresses the main idea. If the main idea is unstated, write a brief statement of the main idea in the margin.

EXERCISE 9

DIRECTIONS Select a three-page section from a textbook that you have been assigned to read. After reading each paragraph, place brackets around the topic and then underline the sentence that states the main idea. If any paragraph has an unstated main idea, write a sentence in the margin that summarizes the main idea. Continue reading and marking until you have completed the three pages.

LEARNING *Collaboratively*

DIRECTIONS Working in pairs, exchange the textbook sections you chose in Exercise 9. Review and critique each other's marking.

Applying YOUR LEARNING

Jason is having trouble distinguishing topic sentences from details in his sociology textbook. Imagine that you are Jason's study partner and that he has asked you for help. You have decided that the best way to help him is to explain by using some sample paragraphs.

1. Using "From Bear Teeth to Pearls: Why We Adorn Ourselves" in Part Seven, p. 379, select several paragraphs you could use as samples.
2. Outline the advice you will give Jason about distinguishing topic sentences from details.

SELF-TEST SUMMARY

1. What is a paragraph?	A paragraph is a group of related sentences about a single topic. It provides explanation, support, or proof for a main idea (expressed or unexpressed) about a particular topic.
2. What are the essential elements of a paragraph?	A paragraph has three essential elements. a. Topic: the one thing the entire paragraph is about b. Main idea: a direct statement or an implied idea about a topic c. Details: the proof, reasons, or examples that explain or support the paragraph's main idea
3. Where is the topic sentence most likely to be found?	A topic sentence expressing the main idea of the paragraph may be located anywhere within the paragraph, but the most common positions for this sentence are first, last, in the middle, and both first and last.
4. How can you identify main ideas that are not stated in a topic sentence?	Occasionally an author will write a paragraph in which the main idea is not stated in any single sentence. Instead, it is left up to the reader to infer, or reason out, the main idea. To find the main idea when it is unstated, ask yourself the following question: What is the one thing (topic) this paragraph is about, and what is the author saying about this thing (main idea)?

Take a Road Trip to
Maine and St. Louis!

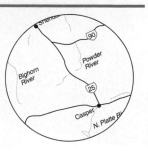

If your instructor has asked you to use the Reading Road Trip CD-ROM, be sure to visit the Main Idea and Supporting Details modules for multimedia tutorials, exercises, and tests. You may also want to visit the Great Lakes to practice your inference skills.

CHAPTER 7

Following Thought Patterns

Why Learn about Thought Patterns?

▲ **Patterns provide a framework for comprehending what you read.**

▲ **They enable you to anticipate a writer's flow of thought.**

▲ **Patterns help you remember what you read.**

Learning Experiment

Step 1

Study the following five diagrams for a minute. Then cover the diagrams with your hand and draw as many of the diagrams as you can recall.

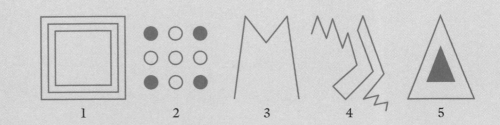

1   2   3   4   5

Step 2

Compare your drawings to the original diagrams.

The Results

Did you get the first, second, fourth, or fifth drawing correct? Why didn't you get the third one correct? Diagram 4 had no organization or pattern; the other four diagrams had an organization that you could identify.

Learning Principle (What This Means to You)

You are able to remember information better if it is organized or if you can detect a pattern. The above experiment demonstrated that you can recall a *diagram* more easily if you can detect a pattern. The same principle applies to ideas. If you can recognize how a writer has organized his or her ideas, you will be able to remember them more easily.

In college you will read a variety of materials; however, most of what you read will be textbooks, which are unique, highly organized information sources. If you become familiar with their organization and structure and learn to follow the writers' thought patterns, you will find that you can read them more easily. This chapter focuses on important features of textbook chapters and essays: (1) their overall structure or progression of ideas, (2) the types of details used to explain each idea, and (3) organizational patterns (how the ideas fit together).

THE ORGANIZATION OF TEXTBOOK CHAPTERS

Reading a chapter can be compared to watching a football game. You watch the overall progression of the game from start to finish, but you also watch individual plays and notice how each is executed. Furthermore, you observe how several plays work together as part of a game strategy or pattern. Similarly, when reading a chapter, you are concerned with the progression of ideas. But you are also concerned with each separate idea and how it is developed and explained. This chapter focuses on important features of textbook chapters and essays.

A textbook is divided into parts, each successively smaller and more limited in scope than the one before it. As a general rule, the whole text is divided into chapters; each chapter may be divided into sections; each section is subdivided by headings into subsections; and each subsection is divided into paragraphs. Each of these parts has a similar structure. Just as each paragraph has a main idea and supporting information, each subsection, section, or chapter has its own key idea and supporting information.

Locate the Controlling Idea and Supporting Information

The controlling idea in a textbook section is the broad, general idea the writer is discussing throughout the section. It is the central, most important thought that is explained, discussed, or supported throughout the section. It is similar to the main idea of a paragraph but is a more general, more comprehensive idea that takes numerous paragraphs to explain.

The controlling idea, then, is developed or explained throughout the section. In this chapter, the section you are reading is called "The Organization of Textbook Chapters." Subheadings are often used to divide a section into smaller units. Each subsection, or group of paragraphs, explains one idea or major concept, the central thought. This subsection is titled "Locate the Controlling Idea and Supporting Information." Each paragraph within a subsection provides one main idea that supports or explains the central thought. As you read each paragraph, you should understand its function and its connection to the other paragraphs in the section. The end of each section is an ideal checkpoint for monitoring your comprehension. Although the number of subheadings and paragraphs will vary, the structure of textbook sections is usually consistent (see Figure 7.1).

Read the section in Figure 7.2, "Learning," from a chapter in a biology book titled *Biology: The Network of Life.* (Note: Ellipses [. . .] indicate places where text has been omitted from the original.)

Note that paragraph 1 of the section introduces the subject: learning. The paragraph then defines learned behavior and states that only recently has it been studied in animals. The last sentence of the first paragraph states the controlling idea of the section: There are five types of learning. The subheadings divide the remaining text, and each identifies one category of learning. Each group of paragraphs under a subheading explains one type of learning (its central thought). In the first subsection on imprinting, the third sentence in paragraph 1 states the central thought of that section.

This example shows that the subheadings divided the section into five parts, or subsections. The section began with a general discussion of the subject and was divided into five smaller topics. This progression of ideas from large to small, general to particular, is typical of most textbooks. When you are familiar with and can follow this progression, your textbooks will seem more logical and systematic and will be easier to read.

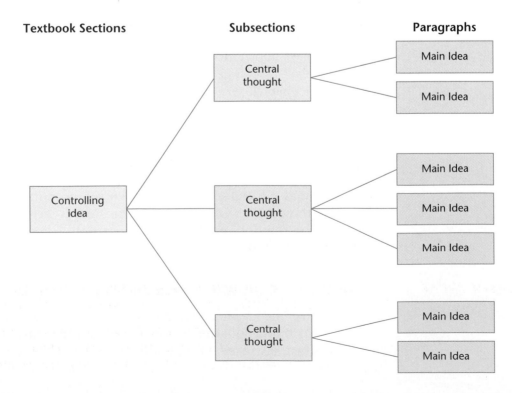

Figure 7.1
Organization of a Textbook Section

LEARNING

Introduction of subject

Learned behavior occurs when animals change their responses as a result of experience. Psychologists did a considerable amount of the early work on learning. They have primarily been concerned with human learning, and even when their research has been on animals, it has been with an eye toward using animals to understand human behavior. More recently, biologists have focused directly on animal learning. Although studies on learning have been carried out on a relatively small number of species, a vast amount of information has been generated. Scientists now recognize five major categories of learning: imprinting, habituation, associative learning, latent learning, and insight.

Controlling idea of section

Imprinting

Central thought of subsection

Imprinting is a highly specialized form of learning. In many species, it takes place during the early stages of an animal's life, when attachment to parents, the family, or a social group is critical for survival. Imprinting is a process whereby a young animal forms an association or identification with another animal, object, or class of items. The best-known type of imprinting, called filial imprinting, concerns the behavior of young in following a "mother object." During a critical sensitive period, a young animal is susceptible to imprinting.

Topic sentence

Young animals are not completely indiscriminate in what they follow. For example, a mallard duckling will follow a moving object for the first two months after hatching. It will show a preference, however, for yellow-green objects (the color of its parents) over objects of different colors. Young animals may also be sensitive to sound as well as to sights. Wood ducks respond to a species-specific call in exiting from their nests.

Topic sentence

Imprinting is an important form of learning, because it has both short-term effects on the immediate parent–offspring relationship and long-term effects that become evident in adult animals. For example, lack of imprinting has been shown to result in abnormal adult social behavior in some species. Also, the breeding preferences of many birds are a consequence of early imprinting experiences. As adults, they prefer to mate with birds of their imprinted parents' color or markings. This form of imprinting, which has considerable evolutionary significance as a reproductive isolating mechanism, is called sexual imprinting. The phenomenon can be tested by experiments that allow a bird to be raised by foster parents of a different species. When these young birds mature, they show a sexual preference for mates with the color of their foster parents. Sexual imprinting can have some unusual outcomes, as when hand-reared birds become sexually imprinted on people.

Habituation

Habituation is a simple form of learning . . .

Associative Learning

Habituation is learning that results in the loss of a response that is not relevant or useful to the animal. Associative learning, in contrast, is . . .

Latent Learning . . .

Insight . . .

Figure 7.2
Excerpt from *Biology: The Network of Life*

EXERCISE 1

DIRECTIONS Turn to "Causes of Habitat Loss and Species Endangerment" in Part Seven on page 398 of this text and complete the following instructions.

1. Where is the controlling idea of this article expressed? Underline it.
2. The dark-print headings divide the chapter into two parts, and the first heading is further divided by subheadings. How many main points are included under it?

EXERCISE 2

DIRECTIONS Read the excerpt "Communication Between Women and Men" in Part Seven on page 385 taken from a sociology textbook chapter. Complete the following instructions.

1. What subject does the article discuss?
2. What is the controlling idea?
3. Underline the central idea of each of the two subsections.
4. Underline the topic sentence of each paragraph.

EXERCISE 3

DIRECTIONS Choose a three- to four-page section from one of your textbooks that you have already read, and answer the following questions.

1. What is the overall topic or subject discussed in this section?

   _____

2. What is the controlling idea?

   _____

3. Is the section divided by subheadings? If so, underline the central thought in each subsection.

THE STRUCTURE OF ARTICLES AND ESSAYS

An article or essay usually begins with an *introduction* that presents the thesis statement (or controlling idea). Then one or more paragraphs are devoted to each supporting idea. The main part of the essay, often called the *body,* presents ideas and information that support the thesis statement. A *conclusion* makes a final statement about the subject and draws the article or essay to a close.

You can visualize the organization of an article or essay as follows.

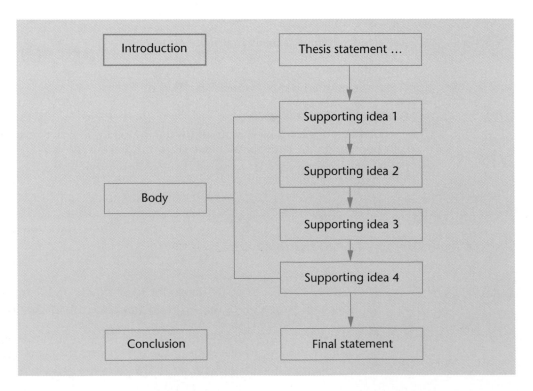

DIRECTIONS   Assume you have been assigned the essay below, "Holes in the Sky," by your biology instructor. Read it to answer the following questions.

Introduction:

1. How do the authors try to interest you in the subject?

_____

2. What is the subject of the essay?

_____

3. What is the authors' thesis?

_____

Body:

4. What main supporting ideas do the authors offer to support their thesis?

_____

_____

Conclusion:

5. What is the authors' final statement on CFCs?

_____

_____

Holes in the Sky

Now let's explore the relationship between underarm deodorants and the death of the oceans. Believe it or not, one may exist. The propellant in underarm sprays is, in many cases, a class of molecules called chlorofluorocarbons (CFCs). These are essentially carbon molecules to which are attached chlorine and/or fluorine atoms. Chlorofluorocarbons are used in a variety of manufactured products, such as air-conditioning, refrigeration, insulating foams, plastics, and industrial solvents.

The problem is [that] these molecules are very stable. So after you spray under your arms, or after the refrigerant escapes, these long-lived little molecules are released into the air. Because they're light, they eventually, perhaps a few years later, end up in the upper atmosphere.

Paradoxically, these molecules would be safer for life if they stayed closer to earth mingling with living things. It turns out, though, that they threaten life precisely because they drift upward, away from it. The reason is [that] at an altitude of 15 miles, the CFCs break down the ozone layer. Ozone is O_3, formed, in nature, by the sun breaking down atmospheric O_2 molecules, allowing them to rejoin as ozone. The chlorine in the CFCs attacks the ozone, breaking it back down into its components. There isn't much ozone up there to begin with. At sea level, all of it together would form a layer over the earth about as deep as a pencil lead is thick.

The ozone, though, is critical to life on earth. Primarily, it functions by blocking destructive ultraviolet light from the sun. Those rays are destructive on three primary bases. First, they increase the risk of skin cancer, particularly among light-skinned people. Second, they depress the immune systems of humans, setting the stage for a host of illnesses. Third, they destroy the algae that form the first step in the ocean's food chains. Ultraviolet light may be more destructive, in fact, than we now imagine. Andrew Blaustein and his group at Oregon State University have correlated frog egg failure in ponds with the amount of UV light they receive, signaling what may be an impending crisis for other life forms.

> Although ozone depletion was first discovered over the Antarctic, "holes" have now been found at midlatitude, in northern temperate regions. In fact, the ozone depletion in this area is now reaching 3–5% per decade. It has been calculated that a loss of 1% translates into 12,000 to 30,000 new skin cancers in the United States alone.
>
> The manufacturers of CFCs have been reluctant to take action to reduce the levels of these chemicals over the earth. Some have tried to paint a brighter face on it.
>
> [One company that] makes CFCs took out ads in newspapers saying that the danger to the ozone layer has just recently improved. The company has now agreed to phase out the manufacture of CFCs, but the phasing out will not be complete until the year 2000. Since the United States makes only 30% of the world's CFCs, the effort will have to be global, demanding more cooperation than one often finds among industrial nations.
>
> —Ferl, Wallace, and Sanders, *Biology,* p. 870

TYPES OF SUPPORTING INFORMATION

Authors use various types of supporting information to explain the controlling idea of a textbook section. Recognizing these types of supporting information is the key to understanding *how* the author develops and connects his or her ideas.

Examples

Usually a writer gives an example in order to make an idea practical and understandable. An example shows how a principle, concept, problem, or process works or can be applied in a real situation. In the following paragraph, notice how the writer explains the concept of motivation to make a purchase by giving a specific example.

> Motivation is defined as activity toward a goal. It is the basis of all consumer behavior. A basic question marketers must answer is, "What will motivate people to buy my product or service?" When a consumer is motivated, he exists in a state called drive. Drive is generated by tension, which is caused by an unfulfilled need. Consumers strive to reduce the tension by satisfying the need. The need is thus a critical component in the motivation process. When a need is aroused, it becomes a motive or drive stimulating behavior. For example, hunger is a basic need that, when aroused, becomes a motive for satisfying the need, perhaps by stopping at a McDonald's restaurant. Of course, the consumer could satisfy hunger in many other ways. The specific decision to stop at McDonald's is influenced, in turn, by many additional factors.
>
> —Kinnear, Bernhardt, and Krentler, *Principles of Marketing,* p. 143

As you read examples, be sure to look for the connection between the example and the concept it illustrates. Remember that examples are important only for the ideas they illustrate.

Reasons

Certain types of main ideas are most easily explained by giving reasons. Especially in argumentative and persuasive writing, you will find that a writer supports an opinion, belief, or action by discussing why it is appropriate. In the following paragraph, the writer gives reasons *why* some people oppose government programs that would provide vouchers or certificates that can be used to help individuals pay for private or parochial school tuition.

> Supporters of the voucher system argue that it would equalize education opportunity while providing for greater freedom of choice than currently exists. Opponents claim that by drawing students away from public schools, the proposed voucher system would drain badly needed revenues from public schools, whose funding is tied to enrollments. Furthermore, critics claim, the amount of the vouchers will prove insufficient to enable lower-income families to send their children to costly private schools. The result would be to further segregate schools along the lines of class, race, and ethnicity, with predominantly white middle class families using their vouchers to help defray the cost of private school education, while all others are forced to send their children to financially strapped public schools.
>
> —Appelbaum and Chambliss, *Sociology,* p. 424

You can see that the writer offers two basic reasons against the voucher system: it would place a financial burden on public schools and lead to further school segregation.

Description

An author uses description to help you visualize the appearance, organization, or composition of an object, a place, or a process. Descriptions are usually detailed and are intended to help you create a mental picture of what is being described. Read the following description of how movement is depicted in a particular thirteenth-century sculpture.

> To give lifelike feeling, artists often search for ways to create a sense of movement. Sometimes movement itself is the subject or a central quality of the subject. One of the world's most appealing depictions of movement is that of the Dancing Krishna, portraying a moment in India's ancient legend of the god Krishna when Krishna, as a playful child, has just stolen his mother's butter supply and now dances with glee. Bronze provides the necessary strength to hold the dynamic pose as the energy-radiating figure stands on one foot, counterbalancing arms, legs, and torso.
>
> —Preble, Preble, and Frank, *Artforms,* p. 60

You should be able to visualize the pose depicted in this bronze sculpture and even, perhaps, Krishna's facial expression. Each detail contributes to the description a bit of information that, when added to other bits, reveals its appearance.

Facts and Statistics

Another way to support an idea is to include facts or statistics that provide information about the main or controlling idea. Read the following passage, and notice how facts and statistics are used to support the idea that an increasing percentage of federal tax receipts comes from payroll taxes.

> An increasing percentage of federal tax receipts is accounted for each year by taxes (other than income taxes) levied on payrolls. These taxes are for Social Security, retirement, survivors' disability, and old-age medical benefits (Medicare). As of mid–1993 the Social Security tax was imposed on earnings up to $57,600 at a rate of 6.2 percent on employers and 6.2 percent on employees. That is, the employer matches

your "contribution" to Social Security. (The employer's contribution is really paid, at least in part, in the form of a reduced wage rate paid to employees.) A Medicare tax was imposed on earnings up to $135,000 at a combined rate of 2.9 percent. These taxes and the base on which they are levied will rise in the next decade.

—Miller, *Economics Today,* p. 112

When reading factual support or explanations, remember these questions: *What? When? Where? How?* and *Why?* They will lead you to the important facts and statistics contained in the passage.

Citation of Research Evidence

In many fields of study, authors support their ideas by citing research that has been done on the topic. Authors report the results of surveys, experiments, and research studies in order to substantiate theories or principles or to lend support to a particular viewpoint. The following excerpt from a family life textbook reports the results of research conducted to determine what problems working parents face.

> More recent studies show that despite the hype about family-friendly policies, working parents are having the same old problems. A survey conducted by the Women's Bureau of the U.S. Department of Labor in 1994 asked a quarter of a million women what it means to be a working woman in the United States today. The report, called *Working Women Count,* paints a complex portrait of U.S. working women in the 1990s. Most women reported pride and satisfaction at being breadwinners for their families. Seventy-nine percent of respondents said they either "love" or "like" their jobs overall. Yet the report also reveals a consensus among working women about what is wrong with their jobs and what needs to be fixed, namely, workplace support of family needs. This consensus crosses all occupations and incomes, all generations and races, and all regions of the country. The study reported that "the difficulty of balancing work and family obligations is the number one issue women wanted to bring to the president's attention" (U.S. Department of Labor, Women's Bureau, 1994).

—Zinn and Eitzen, *Diversity in Families,* pp. 199, 201

When reading research reports, keep the following questions in mind. They will help you see the relationship between the research results and the author's controlling idea.

1. Why was the research done?
2. What did it show?
3. Why did the author include it?

EXERCISE 5

DIRECTIONS Read the following passages and identify the type of supporting information or detail that is used in each.

1.   Three ceramic jars made in different villages in the late nineteenth and early twentieth centuries illustrate similarities and variations within the regional pottery style of the Pueblo peoples of New Mexico. The jars are similar in size and shape, but are different in surface decoration, with each bearing a design that is typical of the pottery produced by the artists of its Pueblo.

    The jar from Acoma Pueblo is decorated in large swaths—the brick-red elements seem to wander over the entire surface, draping over the shoulders of the jar like a garland. This undulating form divides the pot into irregularly shaped large areas.

On the Zuni jar the design is divided by vertical lines into sections in which other lines define circular triangular areas.

In San Ildefonso Pueblo, Maria Marinez and her husband developed another distinctive style, seen in our third example. The San Ildefonso jar has contrasting curvilinear and rectilinear shapes. This jar also features the subtle contrast of matte black and shiny black areas.

—Preble, Preble, and Frank, *Artforms,* pp. 98–99

Type of detail: _____

2. The more developed countries use a disproportionate amount of the world's food, but their behavior cannot be called simple looting because they also grow most of the world's food. Furthermore, they tend to grow more food with each passing year. Interestingly, the poorer and less industrialized developing countries, too, have been growing more food. In fact, from 1950 to 1990, the less developed countries steadily increased their food production, but they actually became hungrier because their populations increased at more than twice the rate of the more affluent nations. In fact, the more developed countries increased per capita food production nearly three times faster than the rest of the world. (The American population increased by a third while we doubled our food production.) The less developed countries, however, did not suffer as greatly as one might think because they had resources that they were able to trade for food. Of course, this meant that instead of the less developed countries receiving the technology they need so desperately, they were forced to trade for food, just to try to feed their booming populations.

It has been calculated that the difference between more developed countries and less developed countries in per capita consumption of calories and proteins from plant products is only about 13 percent. From plants alone, the poor receive an average of 2016 calories per person per day, near the minimum average requirement. However, the difference in consumption of the more expensive animal proteins was quite striking; the richer countries consumed about five times as much as the poorer ones.

—Wallace, *Biology, The World of Life,* p. 785

Type of detail: _____

3. Polls help political candidates detect public preferences. Supporters of polling insist that it is a tool for democracy. With it, they say, policymakers can keep in touch with changing opinions on the issues. No longer do politicians have to wait until the next election to see if the public approves or disapproves of the government's course. If the poll results suddenly turn, government officials can make corresponding midcourse corrections. Indeed, it was George Gallup's fondest hope that polling could contribute to the democratic process by providing a way for public desires to be felt at times other than elections.

Critics of polling, by contrast, think it makes politicians more concerned with the following than leading. Polls might have told the constitutional convention delegates that the Constitution was unpopular, or told Jefferson that people did not want the Louisiana Purchase. Certainly they would have told William Seward not to buy Alaska, known widely at the time as "Seward's Folly." Polls may thus discourage bold leadership.

—Edwards, Wattenberg, and Lineberry, *Government in America,* p. 156

Type of detail: _____

4.   In simple, preindustrial societies, most interactions occur in primary groups of kin, friends, and neighbors. By contrast, in present-day industrial societies, secondary-group interactions are very important. A secondary group *consists of two or more people who interact formally and impersonally to accomplish a specific objective.* Sociologists call these activities *instrumental behavior,* because people's interaction with others is not an end in itself, but a means of achieving specific goals. In most secondary relationships, interactions are limited and often brief, rules are important, and people relate to one another in terms of specific roles. For example, professors and students may get to know each other pretty well during a semester, but only in their reciprocal roles. It is rare for either to know where the other lives, the names of her or his spouse and children, or how the other spends her or his leisure time. Secondary groups may be small or large, but all large groups in which regular face-to-face interaction is impossible are secondary groups.

If you examine your daily routine, you will discover that, whereas a few hours each day may be devoted to family and friends, much of the day's activities are embedded in secondary groups. When you visit a restaurant, attend class, shop at the mall, go to church, participate in a club meeting, or have a brief chat with the mail carrier, you are engaging in secondary-group activities. The distinction between primary and secondary groups, however, is not always clear-cut, and in everyday life, groups may include elements of each *ideal type.* For example, when co-workers begin to see each other after work and engage in multifaceted relationships, office relationships may come to include both primary and secondary traits, and primary groups may emerge. When this occurs, co-workers often bend the rules and may sometimes even subvert the group's formal objectives in order to accommodate each other's individual talents, interests, and needs.

—Thompson and Hickey, *Society in Focus,* pp. 135–136

Type of detail: _____

5.   There has been a definite shift away from goods-producing and toward service-producing jobs during the past two decades. In fact, nearly 92 percent of the 33 million new jobs created during the last 15 years were in services. Retail and wholesale trade, together with finance, insurance, and real estate, creates around 2 million new jobs each year.

It is expected that fully 81 percent of all U.S. civilian employees will be performing services by the year 2005. And while the total number of jobs is expected to grow by 21 percent, the number of service-producing jobs should escalate by around 27 percent, while goods-producing jobs will grow by only 1 percent.

Over the last century, there has also been a marked shift from blue-collar to white-collar jobs, especially from operative types of jobs to technical and professional positions. Around 52 percent of all jobs are now white-collar positions, and this proportion is expected to increase to around 53 percent by the year 2005.

—Mosley, Pietri, and Megginson, *Management,* p. 289

Type of detail: _____

6.   Behavioral and social-learning theorists agree that traditional learning principles cannot account for all aspects of gender socialization, but they have identified many of the subtle reinforcers that do affect behavior. For example, sociobiologists (and many parents) believe that males are naturally more aggressive than females, and that this difference appears too early to be a result of systematic patterns of reinforcement. But even at 1 year of age, boys and girls *whose behavior is the same* are treated differently by adults. Beverly Fagot and her colleagues (1985) observed the reactions of teachers to "assertive acts" and "communicative acts" of 12- to 16-month-old children. Although there were no

differences between the boys and girls in the frequency of these acts, the teachers responded far more often to assertive boys and to verbal girls. When the researchers observed the same children a year later, a gender difference was now apparent, with boys behaving more assertively and girls talking more to teachers.

Similarly, the aggressiveness of boys gets more attention and other rewards from teachers and peers than does aggressiveness in girls, again even when the children start out being equally aggressive. In one observational study of preschool children, peers or teachers paid attention to the aggression of boys 81 percent of the time, compared to only 24 percent of the time for the girls' aggression. When girls and boys behaved dependently, however, such as by calling for help from the teacher, the girls got attention far more often (Fagot, 1984).

—Wade and Tavris, *Psychology*, p. 494

Type of detail: _____

7.   The first stage of the purchase decision process is problem recognition. It occurs when a person perceives a difference between some ideal state and his or her actual state at a given moment. Consider, for example, a student who is in the market to rent an apartment. For her, the problem-recognition stage may have started when she decided that her dorm was too noisy or perhaps after an argument with her roommate. For a product like shampoo, problem recognition may occur when a consumer sees his favorite brand on sale, or it may be triggered when he notices that the bottle in his shower is almost empty.

Problem recognition may occur gradually. Several weeks may have passed before our student realized how much the noise in the dorm was bothering her. Sometimes, it occurs very quickly. When standing in the check-out line at the grocery store you see your favorite movie star on the cover of *People* and impulsively buy the magazine, you have experienced nearly instantaneous problem recognition. In fact, you have gone through virtually the entire purchase decision process in a matter of moments.

—Kinnear, Bernhardt, and Krentler, *Principles of Marketing*, p. 180

Type of detail: _____

8.   According to its proponents, a national primary would bring directness and simplicity to the process for the voters as well as the candidates. The length of the campaign would be shortened and no longer would votes in one state have more political impact than votes in another. The concentration of media coverage on this one event, say its advocates, would increase not only political interest in the nomination decision, but also public understanding of the issues involved.

—Edwards, Wattenberg, and Lineberry, *Government in America*, p. 230

Type of detail: _____

9.   When the government sets out to measure the size of the labor force or the number of unemployed, its statisticians obviously cannot interview every single worker or potential worker. Survey data must be used. Although the survey technique is extensive—consisting of almost 60,000 households in almost 2,000 counties and cities in all 50 states and the District of Columbia—it is imperfect. One of the main reasons, argue some economists, is because of the *underground economy.* The underground economy consists of individuals who work for cash payments without paying any taxes. It also consists of individuals who engage in illegal activities such as prostitution, gambling, and drug trafficking.

Some who are officially unemployed and are receiving unemployment benefits do nonetheless work "off the books." Although they are counted as unemployed by the BLS, they really are employed. The same analysis holds for anyone who works and does not report income earned. The question, of course, is, How big is the underground economy? If it is small, the official unemployment statistics may still be adequate to give a sense of the state of the national economy. Various researchers have come up with different estimates of the size of the underground economy. Professor Peter Guttman believes that it is at least 10 percent of the size of the national economy. Other researchers have come up with estimates ranging from 5 to 15 percent. In dollars and cents that may mean that the underground economy represents between $300 billion and $900 billion a year. How many members of the true labor force work in this economy and their effect on the true unemployment rate is anyone's guess.

—Miller, *Economics Today*, p. 117

Type of detail: _____

10.   An enlarger can produce a print of any size—larger, smaller, or the same size as a negative, so it is sometimes more accurately called a projection printer. Most often, however, it is used to enlarge an image. An enlarger operates like a slide projector mounted vertically on a column. Light from an enclosed lamp shines through a negative and is then focused by a lens to expose an image of the negative on printing paper placed at the foot of the enlarger column. Image size is set by changing the distance from the enlarger head (the housing containing lamp, negative, and lens) to the paper; the greater the distance, the larger the image. The image is focused by moving the lens closer to or farther from the negative. The exposure time is controlled by a timer. To regulate the intensity of the light, the lens has a diaphragm aperture with f-stops like those on a camera lens.

—London and Upton, *Photography*, p. 134

Type of detail: _____

RECOGNIZING ORGANIZATIONAL PATTERNS

You have seen that textbook sections are structured around a controlling idea and supporting information and details. The next step in reading these materials effectively is to become familiar with how information is organized.

Recognition of organizational patterns is a useful learning device. It is based on the principle of meaningfulness, which states that things that are meaningful are easier to learn and remember than those that are not. When you fit details into a pattern, you connect them so that each one helps you recall the rest. By identifying how the key details in a paragraph or passage form a pattern, you are making them more meaningful to you and, as a result, making them easier to remember.

Patterns are forms of schemata, or sets of familiar information. Once you recognize that a paragraph or passage follows a particular pattern, its organization becomes familiar and predictable.

Six organizational patterns are commonly used in textbook writing: definition, time sequence, comparison–contrast, cause–effect, problem–solution, and enumeration. A chart that summarizes these patterns is shown in Figure 7.3 on page 159.

To help you visualize each pattern, a diagram will be presented for each. Later, in Chapter 14, you will see that these diagrams, also called maps, are useful means of organizing and retaining information.

These patterns may also appear together in various combinations, producing a mixed pattern. For each of these patterns, particular words and phrases are used to connect details and lead from one idea to another. These words are called *directional words* because they indicate the direction or pattern of thought. A chart (Figure 7.4) giving examples of types of directional words appears on page 160.

Definition

One of the most obvious patterns is definition, which you will find in textbooks of most academic subjects. Each academic discipline has its own language or specialized terminology (see Chapter 11). One of the primary tasks of authors of introductory course textbooks, then, is to introduce their readers to this new language. Therefore, you will find many textbook sections in which new terms are defined.

Suppose you were asked to define the word *comedian* for someone unfamiliar with the term. First, you would probably say that a comedian is a person who entertains. Then you might distinguish a comedian from other types of entertainers by saying that a comedian is an entertainer who tells jokes and makes others laugh. Finally, you might mention as examples the names of several well-known comedians who have appeared on television. Although you may have presented it informally, your definition would have followed the standard, classic pattern. The first part of your definition tells what general class or group the term belongs to (entertainers). The second part tells what distinguishes the term from other items in the same class or category. The third part includes further explanation, characteristics, examples, or applications.

This pattern can be visualized as follows.

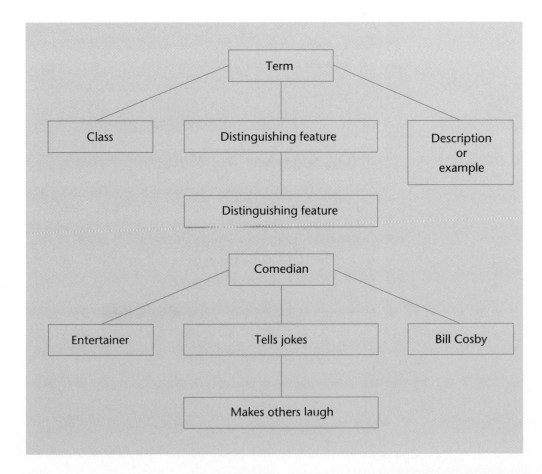

Read the following definition of *society* taken from a sociology textbook.

Society has traditionally been defined as the interacting people who share a common culture—that is, any group of people who speak a common language, share common beliefs and customs, belong to the same institutions and organizations, use the same tools and technology, and consume the same goods. Although the term "society" is sometimes also used to refer to people with a common culture who share the same territory, we prefer not to emphasize this geographical dimension: in modern society it is increasingly possible to share a common culture with people who are geographically dispersed.

—Appelbaum and Chambliss, *Sociology,* p. 55

This definition has three parts: (1) The general class is stated first, (2) the distinguishing characteristics are then described, and (3) further explanation and examples are given. The first sentence states the general class—group of people, interacting people. The same sentence also gives distinguishing characteristics. The remainder of the passage gives further explanation of the term *society.* When reading definitions, be sure to look for each of these parts. Passages that define often use directional words and phrases such as:

refers to	can be defined as
means	consists of
is	

EXERCISE 6

DIRECTIONS   Define each of the following terms by identifying the class it belongs to and describing its distinguishing characteristics.

1. Adolescence
2. Automatic teller machine (ATM)
3. Cable television
4. Computer
5. Advertising

Time Sequence

One of the clearest ways to describe events, processes, procedures, and development of theories is to present them in the order in which they occurred. The event that happened first appears first in the passage; whatever occurred last is described last in the passage.

The time sequence pattern can be visualized as follows.

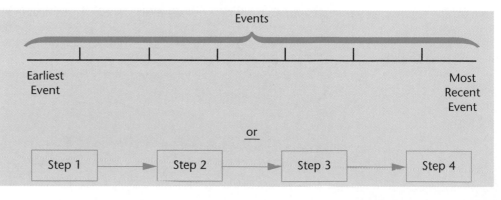

The first drawing is often called a *time line;* the second a *process diagram.*

Notice in the following example how the writer proceeds through time, describing the process of communication among members of an organization.

A Business Communication Model

People, not organizations, communicate. An organization's communication system therefore reflects a variety of individuals with different backgrounds, education levels, beliefs, cultures, moods, and needs. When individuals in an organization communicate, what exactly takes place? Let us examine a basic communication model so that we will be better able to understand why communication fails so frequently and what actions managers can take to improve their communication effectiveness. This model illustrates the six most important elements involved in communication between and among organization members:

The *source,* or originator of the message, takes the first step in the communication process. Some event stimulates the need for transmitting ideas, information, or feelings to someone else.

The second step—*encoding*—involves choosing some verbal or nonverbal communication that is capable of transferring meaning, such as spoken or written words, gestures, or actions. One must think not only of what is going to be communicated but also of *how* it will be presented to have the desired effect on the receiver. Thus, the message must be adapted to the level of understanding, interest, *and* needs of the receiver to achieve the desired consequences.

The third step—*transmitting,* or sending the communication from the source to the receiver—reflects the communicator's choice of medium or *distribution channel.* Oral communication may be transmitted through many channels—in person, by telephone, by audio- or videotape. It may take place privately or in a group setting. Written communication may be transmitted by means such as memos, letters, reports, notes, bulletin boards, company manuals, and newsletters. Written communication has the advantage of providing a record for future reference, but the major disadvantage is that it does not allow spontaneous, face-to-face feedback.

The fourth step is *receiving* the message. People receive messages through their five senses—sight, hearing, taste, touch, and smell. Full transmission has not occurred unless a party actually *receives* a message. Many important attempts at communication have failed because the message never got to its intended receiver.

The fifth step of the communication process is *decoding,* which involves providing meaning to the message by the receiver or his or her representative. This meaning is a product of such variables as the receiver's heritage, culture, education, environment, prejudices, and biases, as well as distractions in the surroundings. There is always the possibility that the source's message, when decoded by the receiver, will yield a meaning far different from the one the sender intended. The receiver thus shares a large responsibility for communication effectiveness, for *communication is a two-way street.* Managers and subordinates may occupy both source and receiver roles throughout an interaction.

Step 6 of the process is *feedback*—the responses the receiver gives by further communicating with the sender. Communication is thus a continuous and perpetual process. A person communicates, the receiver responds by further communicating with the original sender or another person, and so forth.

—Mosley, Pietri, and Megginson, *Management,* pp. 333–336

This excerpt could be visualized as follows.

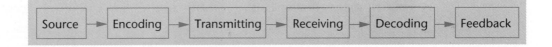

Material presented in terms of a time sequence is relatively easy to read because you know what order the writer will follow. When reading sequential, organized material, pay attention to the order of and connection between events. When studying this material, remember that the order is often as important as the events themselves. To test your memory and to prepare information for study, list ideas in this correct order, or draw a process diagram or time line.

The time sequence pattern uses directional words to connect the events described or to lead you from one step to another. The most frequently used words are:

first	before	following
second	after	last
later	then	during
next	finally	when
as soon as	meanwhile	until

EXERCISE 7

DIRECTIONS For each of the following topic sentences, make a list of directional words you expect to be used in the paragraph.

1. Advertising has appeared in magazines since the late 1700s.
2. Large numbers of European immigrants first began to arrive in the United States in the 1920s.
3. The first step in grasping a novel's theme is reading it closely for literal content, including plot and character development.
4. After he left Spain, strong winds blew Columbus and his ships into the middle of the Atlantic.
5. The life cycle of a product consists of the stages a product goes through from when it is created to when it is no longer produced.

Comparison–Contrast

Many fields of study involve the comparison of one set of ideas, theories, concepts, or events with another. These comparisons usually examine similarities and differences. In anthropology, one kinship category might be compared with another; in literature, one poet might be compared with another; in biology, one theory of evolution might be compared with another. You will find that the comparison–contrast pattern appears regularly in the textbooks used in these fields. The comparison–contrast pattern can be visualized in several ways. For material that considers both similarities and differences, the following map is effective.

Topics A and B

Similarities   *Differences*

_____   _____

_____   _____

_____   _____

For example:

Professor Miller and Professor Wright

Similarities   *Differences*

both require class attendance   Miller assigns term paper

both give essay exams   Wright demands class participation

both have sense of humor   age

For material that focuses primarily on differences, you might use the following.

	Topic A	**Topic B**
Feature 1	_____	_____
Feature 2	_____	_____
Feature 3	_____	_____

For example:

Feature	*Professor Smith*	*Professor Jones*
teaching style	lecture	discussion
class atmosphere	formal	casual
type of exam	multiple choice	essay

A comparison–contrast pattern can be organized in one of three ways. A writer comparing two famous artists, X and Y, could use any of the following procedures.

1. Discuss the characteristics of artist X and those of artist Y, and then summarize their similarities and differences.
2. Consider their similarities first, and then discuss their differences.
3. Consider both X and Y together for each of several characteristics. For instance, discuss the use of color by X and Y, then discuss the use of space by X and Y, and then consider the use of proportion by X and Y.

Read the following paragraph, and try to determine which of the preceding patterns is used.

In their original work both Darwin and that other great innovator who followed him, Gregor Mendel, used deductive reasoning to great effect. Both these giants of biology had been trained in theology. As a result, they were well acquainted with an intellectual tradition based on deduction. And since induction is difficult to apply in a field where so little can be directly observed, perhaps theology provided some of the essential intellectual tools both men needed to develop a viewpoint so different from prevailing theological thinking.

Darwin and Mendel are linked in another fundamental way. Darwin could not explain how successful traits are passed on to successive generations, exposing his theory of natural selection to growing criticism. When Mendel was rediscovered, geneticists were paying a lot of attention to mutations. They still felt that natural selection of variants had a minor part in evolution. The major factor, they believed, was sudden change introduced by mutation. Not until the 1930s did biologists realize, at last, that Darwin's theory of natural selection and Mendel's laws of genetics were fully compatible. Together the two form the basis of population genetics, a major science of today.

—Laetsch, *Plants: Basic Concepts in Botany,* p. 393

Darwin and Mendel

Similarities

both trained in theology

both developed different viewpoint

both giants of biology

held compatible theories

The passage compares the characteristics of the work of Darwin and the work of Mendel. The first paragraph presents their use of deductive reasoning. The second paragraph describes the compatibility of their theories.

In comparison–contrast passages, the way ideas are organized provides clues to what is important. In a passage that is organized by characteristics, the emphasis is placed on the characteristics. A passage that groups similarities and then differences emphasizes the similarities and differences themselves rather than the characteristics.

Directional words indicate whether the passage focuses on similarities, differences, or both.

Similarities	Differences
also	unlike
similarly	one the other hand
like	instead
likewise	despite
too	nevertheless
as well as	however
both	in spite of

EXERCISE 8

DIRECTIONS For each of the following topic sentences, predict the content of the paragraph. Will it focus on similarities, differences, or both? Also, if you predict that the passage will discuss both similarities and differences, predict the organization of the paragraph that will follow. (Identify the type of organization by its number in the list on page 151 for the comparison–contrast pattern.)

1. Two types of leaders can usually be identified in organizations: informal and formal.

   Content: _____   *Organization:* _____

2. The human brain is divided into two halves, each of which is responsible for separate functions.

   Content: _____   *Organization:* _____

3. Humans and primates, such as gorillas and New World monkeys, share many characteristics but are clearly set apart by others.

   Content: _____   *Organization:* _____

4. Interpersonal communication is far more complex than intrapersonal communication.

   Content: _____   *Organization:* _____

5. Sociology and psychology both focus on human behavior.

   Content: _____   *Organization:* _____

Cause–Effect

Understanding any subject requires learning *how* and *why* things happen. In psychology it is not enough to know that people are often aggressive; you also need to know why and how people show aggression. In physics it is not enough to know the laws of motion; you also must understand why they work and how they apply to everyday experiences.

The cause–effect pattern arranges ideas according to why and how they occur. This pattern is based on the relationship between or among events. Some passages discuss one cause and one effect—the omission of a command, for example, causing a computer program to fail.

This relationship can be visualized as follows.

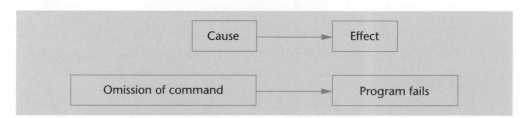

Most passages, however, describe multiple causes or effects. Some may describe the numerous effects of a single cause, such as unemployment producing an increase in crime, family disagreements, and a lowering of self-esteem.

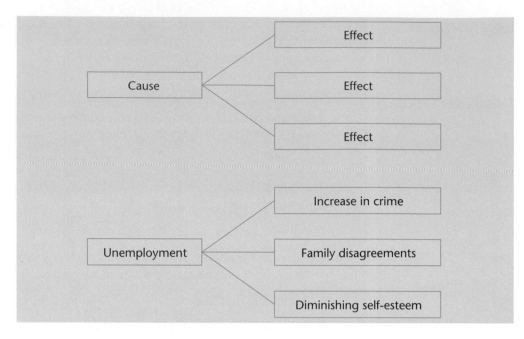

Others may describe the numerous causes of a single effect, such as increased unemployment and poverty along with decreased police protection causing a high crime rate.

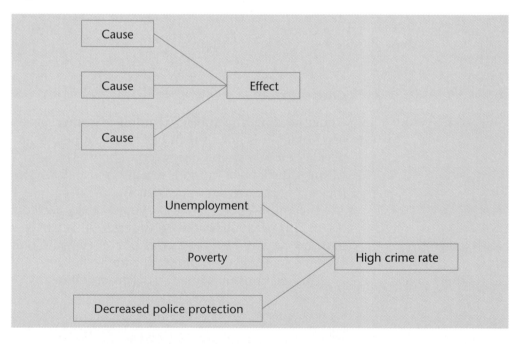

Still others may present multiple causes and effects, such as unemployment and poverty producing an increase in crime and in family disputes.

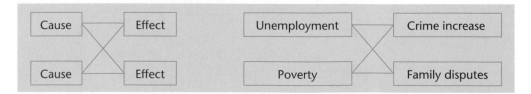

Read the following passage, which is taken from a business marketing text, and determine which of the following patterns is used.

- single cause–single effect
- multiple causes–single effect
- single cause–multiple effects
- multiple causes–multiple effects

Then draw a diagram in the margin, describing this relationship.

Eventually, product class sales begin to decline, sometimes even rapidly. The causes of the decline may be market saturation, new technology, or changes in social values. Since most homes have smoke detectors, sales in that product class have slowed considerably. Compact disc players have significantly slowed sales of cassette tape players. Health conscious consumers have caused a significant decrease in beef consumption in the United States. The decline in volume often results in higher costs. At this stage marketers must eliminate products that are no longer profitable or find ways of cutting operational and marketing costs. Some of these include eliminating marginal dealers and distributors, cutting advertising and sales promotion, and minimizing production costs. These cuts could result in renewed profitability. In effect, the product is "milked"; that is, it is allowed to coast with decreased marketing support as long as it remains profitable.

Of course it is possible that reducing marketing support will hasten the product's demise, and thus decline has been viewed as a self-fulfilling prophecy. Brands that have developed strong consumer loyalty decline slower than products that have not been differentiated from their competitors. It is even possible for individual competitors to do well for quite some time while the product class is in decline. They may be able to garner a larger market share, albeit of a smaller market, as other competitors drop out. Technics and Pioneer continue to produce stereo turntables although distribution is limited.

—Kinnear, Bernhardt, and Krentler, *Principles of Marketing,* p. 290

The passage offers numerous reasons why product sales decline. Numerous causes, then, produce a single effect.

When you read and study ideas organized in a cause–effect pattern, focus on the connection between or among events. To make relationships clearer, determine which of the four cause–effect patterns is used. Directional words can help you determine the cause–effect relationship.

Causes	Effects
because	consequently
because of	as a result
since	one result is
one cause is	therefore
one reason is	thus

EXERCISE 9

DIRECTIONS   From the following list of section headings from an American government textbook, predict which sections will be developed using the cause–effect pattern. Place a check mark in front of those you select.

_____   1.   How Public Policies Affect Income

_____   2.   Explaining the Decline of Isolationism in America

_____   3.   Tasks of Political Parties

_____   4.   The Affirmative Action Issue

_____   5.   Political Parties: How Party Loyalty Shifts

_____   6.   Why Bureaucracies Exist

_____   7.   The Organization of National Political Parties

_____   8.   How Lobbyists Shape Policy

_____   9.   Types of Special-Interest Groups

_____   10.   The Nature of the Judicial System

Enumeration

The primary function of textbooks is to present information. If there is a relationship or connection between or among ideas, this connection is usually emphasized and used to organize information. Many types of information, however, have no inherent order or connection. Lists of facts, characteristics, parts, or categories can appear in any order; thus writers use a pattern called *enumeration.* In this pattern, the information is often loosely connected with a topic sentence or controlling idea: "There are several categories of . . ." or "There are three types of . . ." and so forth. This listing pattern, sometimes called *classification,* divides a topic into subgroups or groups items according to a common characteristic.

Read the following paragraph, observing how the pattern proceeds from one type of flaw to another.

> The U.S. deposit-insuring agencies have serious design flaws. First, the price of deposit insurance to individual depository institutions was until recently relatively low; the depository institutions are subsidized by the depository insurers. Second, the insurance premium is the same percentage of total deposits for all depository institutions, regardless of the riskiness of the institution's portfolio. Also until recently, all deposit-insuring agencies charged a depository institution about .25 percent of the institution's total (not just insured) deposits. For example, federally insured commercial banks pay a flat fee for the FDIC guarantee of the first $100,000 of each deposit account in the bank. The flaw in this pricing structure is that an individual depository institution's premium is set without regard to its probability of failure, the riskiness of its portfolio, or the estimated cost to the insurer should the institution fail.
>
> —Miller, *Economics Today,* p. 335

One key to reading and studying this pattern is to be aware of how many items are enumerated so you can check your recall of them. It is also helpful to note whether the information is listed in order of importance, frequency, size, or any other characteristic. This will help you organize the information for easier recall.

Directional words are very useful in locating items in a list. As a writer moves from one item in a list to another, he or she may use directional words to mark or identify each point.

one	first
another	second
also	finally
too	for example
for instance	in addition

DIRECTIONS   For each of the following topic sentences, supply three pieces of information that might be contained in the paragraph.

1. There are magazines designed for almost every possible special interest and every conceivable type of person.
2. Humans have more than just five senses; within the broad category of touch, there are many different kinds of sensation that can be felt.
3. The category of mammals contains many widely different kinds of animals.
4. Scientists find life hard to define, except by describing its characteristics.
5. Because the purpose of a résumé is to sell the qualities of the person writing it, it should include several important kinds of information.

Problem–Solution

Many academic disciplines are concerned with defining problems, conducting research, and examining possible solutions. Consequently, problem–solution is a common pattern used in textbooks. For example, an ecology text may describe various solutions to environmental pollution. A mathematics text formally presents solutions to various problems.

The problem–solution pattern is closely tied to the cause–effect pattern because the solutions of problems are related to their causes. The overall pattern often hinges on "if . . . then" relationships. For example,

Solution

If chemical waste dumping is outlawed, *then* there will be less

pollution in the local rivers.

Problem

More than one step or action may be necessary to produce a solution, and at times several conditions that contribute to the problem may exist simultaneously. Other times, an author may analyze a problem and identify causes but not offer a direct solution. For example, a social problems text may analyze conditions that create abuse of the welfare system but not propose a comprehensive solution.

Read the following excerpt, identify the problem, and sketch how it might be most effectively mapped. In this excerpt, the problem discussed is women's persistent poverty.

Many women find themselves placed in an inescapable poverty syndrome. Numerous factors contribute to this persistence of poverty. First, many women without higher education or skilled training are relegated to low-paying jobs, usually within the service or agricultural fields. Factors within our economy and social system prevent these women from advancing beyond their entry level, low-paying jobs. These jobs do not provide fringe benefits such as overtime pay, vacations, leaves, or unemployment or medical insurance. Lacking these benefits, many women are unable to seek further education or retraining. Sexual division of labor within the home requires many women to spend long hours in childcare and household upkeep, again preventing them from seeking advancement through education.

It could be diagrammed as follows.

Causes	Problem
1. job segregation	women's persistent poverty
2. women's economy	
3. sexual division of labor in family	

The following map is effective in visualizing and recalling ideas presented in problem–solution patterns. Do not always expect to be able to fill in both causes and solutions.

Causes	Problem	Solution(s)
_____	_____	_____
_____	_____	_____
_____	_____	_____

Directional words for the problem–solution pattern include some of the words that suggest a cause–effect pattern as well as the following.

the problem is . . .	causes
Why does . . .	What happens when
if . . . then . . .	suppose

EXERCISE 11

DIRECTIONS   For each of the following topic sentences, identify the problem and predict whether the paragraph will focus on causes, solutions, or both.

1. There is growing controversy today about the need to cut trees in national forests for commercial lumber production; numerous alternative proposals are currently under discussion.
2. The overcrowding in federal and state prisons had led some social scientists to consider other methods of crime deterrence.
3. Steps can be taken to restore or identify damaged fossils that archeologists discover.
4. When writing the Constitution, its framers recognized that the fundamental rights of the people had to be protected by the government.
5. Perhaps the most difficult part of a job interview is being asked an unexpected question for which you do not have a ready answer.

Mixed Patterns

In many texts, sections and passages combine one or more patterns. In defining a concept or idea, a writer might explain a term by comparing it with something similar or familiar. In describing an event or process, a writer might include reasons for or causes of an event or might explain why the steps in a process must be followed in the prescribed order.

Read the following paragraph and determine which two patterns are used.

> The error of ascribing to animals the thoughts, emotions, and motivations of humans is now rejected by most behavioral scientists as anthropomorphic (from the Greek words meaning "man" and "form"). The banishing of anthropomorphism was due largely to the behaviorist school of psychology, which argued that one could only observe animal behavior, not try to infer the mental states underlying it. Later behaviorists, like B. F. Skinner, went even further, arguing that mental states, such as free will, did not occur even in humans. The behaviorist approach to animal behavior has produced more experimentally testable theories than the anthropomorphic approach, but most of these theories have been based on studies of the albino laboratory rat under extremely artificial conditions. Behaviorists have therefore been accused of replacing the anthropomorphic view of animals with a "ratomorphic" view of humans. For zoologists, the behavior of rats under laboratory conditions is not only a poor model for the behavior of humans, it is also a poor model for the natural behavior of rats.
>
> —Harris, *Concepts in Zoology,* p. 402

Two approaches to the study of animal behavior—*anthropomorphic* and *behaviorist*—are defined, but for purposes of explanation, the terms are also compared. Therefore, the paragraph combines a definition pattern with a comparison–contrast pattern.

When reading mixed patterns, do not be overly concerned with identifying or labeling each pattern. Instead, look for the predominant pattern that carries the overall organization.

Figures 7.3 (below) and 7.4 (next page) present a review of the organizational patterns and of directional words commonly used with each pattern. Although this chapter has focused on the use of these patterns in textbook writing, you will find such patterns in other academic situations as well. For example, your professor may organize her or his lecture by using one or more of these patterns and may use directional words to enable you to follow the line of thought. On exams, especially essay exams, you will find questions that require you to organize information in terms of one or more of the organizational patterns. (Refer to Chapter 17 for more information on essay exam questions.)

Pattern	Characteristics
Definition	Explains the meaning of a term or phrase; consists of class, distinguishing characteristics, and explanation
Time sequence	Describes events, processes, procedures
Comparison–contrast	Discusses similarities and/or differences among ideas, theories, concepts, objects, or persons
Cause–effect	Describes how one or more things cause or are related to another
Problem–solution	Focuses on "if . . . then" relationships; identifies problems, discusses causes and solutions
Enumeration	Organizes lists of information: characteristics, features, parts, or categories

Figure 7.3
Summary of Organizational Patterns

Thought Pattern		Directional Words
Definition		refers to, means, can be defined as, consists of
Time sequence		first, second, later, before, next, as soon as, after, then, finally, meanwhile, following, last, during, when, until
Comparison–contrast	*Similarities:*	also, similarly, like, likewise, too, as well as, both
	Differences:	unlike, on the other hand, instead, despite, nevertheless, however, in spite of
Cause–effect	*Causes:*	because, because of, since, one cause is, one reason is
	Effects:	consequently, as a result, one result is, therefore, thus
Problem–solution		why does . . . , if . . . then, causes, suppose, what happens when . . .
Enumeration		one, another, also, too, for instance, first, second, finally, for example, in addition

Figure 7.4
**Summary of
Directional Words**

Organizational patterns and directional words are also useful in organizing your own ideas and presenting them effectively in written form. As you write papers and complete written assignments, these patterns will provide a basis for relating and connecting your ideas and presenting them in a clear and understandable form. The directional words are useful as transitions, leading your reader from one idea to another.

EXERCISE 12

DIRECTIONS Assume that each of the following sentences or groups of sentences is the beginning of a textbook section. On the basis of the information contained in each, predict what organizational pattern is used throughout the passage. Look for directional words to help you identify the pattern.

1. In large businesses, clerical jobs are usually very specialized in order for the work to be accomplished to be done in the most efficient manner. As a result, clerical work is very often routine and highly repetitive. _____

2. There are clear limitations to population growth and the use of natural resources. First, the food supply could be exhausted as a result of water, mineral, and soil depletion. _____

3. Unlike the statues of humans, the statues of animals found at Stone Age sites are quite lifelike. _____

4. When a patient enters a mental hospital, he is carefully tested and observed for 24 hours. Then a preliminary decision is made concerning medication and treatment. _____

5. One shortcoming of the clinical approach in treating mental illness is that definitions of normal behavior are subjective. Another shortcoming of the approach is that it assumes that when a patient has recovered, he will be able to return to his previous environment. _____

6. Most of the world's news is transmitted by Western news agencies. Third World nations regard this dominance as oppressive and feel that action must be taken to develop their communication networks.   _____

EXERCISE 13

DIRECTIONS   Read each of the following passages and identify the main organizational pattern used in each.

1.   TAMPERING WITH GENES, OR GENETIC ENGINEERING?   Genetic engineering, as the name implies, involves manipulating genes to achieve some particular goal. Some people object to the entire idea of tailoring molecules with such profound implications for life. Where could it lead? Would we have the wisdom not to unleash something terrible on the earth?

Perhaps the greatest threat of recombinant techniques, some would say, lies in [their] very promise. The possibilities of such genetic manipulation seem limitless. For example, we can mix the genes of anything—say, an ostrich and a German shepherd. This may bring to mind only images of tall dogs, but what would happen if we inserted cancer-causing genes into the familiar *E. coli* that is so well adapted to living in our intestines? What if the gene that makes botulism toxin, one of the deadliest poisons known, were inserted into the DNA of friendly *E. coli* and then released into some human population? One might ask, "But who would do such a terrible thing?" Perhaps the same folks who brought us napalm and nerve gas.

Another, less cynical concern is that well-intended scientists could mishandle some deadly variant and allow it to escape from the laboratory. Some variants have been weakened to prevent such an occurrence; but we should remember that even though smallpox was "eradicated" from the earth, there were two minor epidemics in Europe caused by cultured experimental viruses that had escaped from a lab. One person died of a disease that technically didn't exist.

—Ferl, Wallace, and Sanders, *Biology: The Realm of Life,* pp. 252–253

Organizational pattern: _____

2.   GROWING DIVERSITY   Ours is an ethnically, religiously, and racially diverse society. The white European Protestants, black slaves, and Native Americans who made up the bulk of the U.S. population when the first census was taken in 1790 were joined by Catholic immigrants from Ireland and Germany in the 1840s and 1850s. In the 1870s, Chinese migrated to America, drawn by jobs in railroad construction. Around the turn of the twentieth century, most immigration was from eastern, central, and southern Europe, with its many ethnic, linguistic, and religious groups. Today, most immigration is from Asia and Latin America.

The rate of migration to the United States has accelerated in recent years. If illegal entrants are included in the total, over 10 million people immigrated to the United States during the 1980s, the highest total in any decade in American history, and the numbers are even higher in the 1990s. As a result, the percentage of foreign-born people in the United States doubled between 1970 and 1996; the 24.5 million total means that 10 percent of people in the United States today are foreign-born (compared to 13.5 percent in 1910). In California, over one-fourth of the population today was born abroad.

—Greenberg and Page, *The Struggle for Democracy,* p. 71

Organizational pattern: _____

3.   PERMANENT SETTLERS   Numerous factors account for the growing number of immigrants, worldwide. First, as noted, the planet has been experiencing tremendous population growth, mostly in the less developed regions which do not
have sufficient numbers of jobs for the working-age population. One option for
unemployed or underemployed citizens in the LDCs (Less Developed Countries)
is to migrate to an MDC (More Developed Country) in the hope of finding
work. For example, World Bank labor force figures suggest that 10 percent of
Mexico's domestic labor force resides in the United States. A second reason for
increased migration from LDCs to MDCs is the loss of jobs in LDCs caused by
modern electronic machines that displace human beings. Increased mechaniza-
tion characterizes the labor forces of LDCs just as it does the MDCs. A third
reason for the increase in worldwide migration is environmental degradation.
Environmental problems such as deforestation, desertification, and polluted
water supplies often result in people moving to other countries to escape these
problems.

—Glynn, Hohm, and Stewart, *Global Social Problems,* p. 154

Organizational pattern: _____

4.   THE MARXIAN ANALYSIS   Karl Marx was born in Trier, Germany, to middle-class
Jewish parents who had converted to Protestantism. He attended the University
of Berlin as a doctoral candidate in philosophy, instead of studying law as his
father desired. At the university he joined a circle that followed some aspects of
Hegel's thought. After finishing his degree, he could not find a university position and so returned to the Rhineland where he began writing for a local newspaper. The injustices he saw around him and his reading of the French socialists
Henri de Saint-Simon and Pierre Joseph Proudhon led him to concentrate on
the economic factors in history. He went to Paris to continue his studies, met
Engels, and was expelled by the authorities in 1845. From there he went first to
Belgium and finally to England where, after 1848, he spent most of the rest of
his life.

An uncompromising hostility to capitalism drove Marx's work. He stated in
the *Manifesto* that communists "openly declare that their ends can be attained
only by the forcible overthrow of all existing social conditions." Virtually every
day he made his way to the British Museum where he waged intellectual war on
capitalism by doing research for his major works, especially *Das Kapital.*

—Wallbank et al., *Civilization Past and Present,* vol. 2, p. 671

Organizational pattern: _____

5.   PROTEINS   *Proteins* are much more complex in structure than carbohydrates or
lipids and are involved in numerous physiological activities. Proteins are largely
responsible for the structure of body cells. Some proteins in the form of enzymes
function as catalysts to speed up certain chemical reactions. Enzymes are very
important in regulating chemical reactions in cells to help maintain homeostasis.
Other proteins assume an important role in muscular contraction. Antibodies are
proteins that defend the body against invading microbes. Some types of hor-
mones are proteins.

Chemically, proteins always contain carbon, hydrogen, oxygen, and
nitrogen, and sometimes sulfur. *Amino acids* are the building blocks of proteins.
There are at least 20 different amino acids. In protein formation, amino acids
combine to form more complex molecules; the bonds formed between amino
acids are called *peptide bonds.*

—Tortora, *Introduction to the Human Body,* p. 30

Organizational pattern: _____

6.   COUNCILS AND COMMITTEES   Councils and committees are advisory groups found in many different kinds of societies. We have briefly mentioned *councils* among the Shavante, Tetum, and Qashgai. They meet in public and are usually made up of informally appointed elders. *Committees* differ from councils in that they meet privately. Moreover, whereas councils are typical of simpler political organizations, committees are more characteristic of states. But the two kinds of groups can and often do coexist within the same political organization. When this occurs, councils are superior to committees, whose tasks and powers are delegated to them by councils.

     Councils tend to be consensus-seeking bodies, while committees are more likely to achieve agreement by voting (although either kind of body may reach decisions in either way). Consensus seeking is typical of small social groups whose members have frequent personal interaction. Once a council or committee increases to more than about 50 members, decision by consensus is no longer possible. Voting is typical of larger groups whose members do not see much of one another in daily life and who owe their main allegiance not to other group members but to people (perhaps many millions) outside the council or committee. Members may in fact represent these outside people, as is the case with the U.S. Congress.

Hicks and Gwynne, Cultural Anthropology, p. 304

Organizational pattern: _____

7.   BELIEFS   Beliefs consist of a system of propositions and assertions about the nature of reality. They provide people and societies with a fundamental orientation to the world and answer questions about human origins, proper relations among people, and the destiny of humans and the universe. Simple societies answer these questions with myth and folklore; complex societies answer them with religion and science. Beliefs also include simple observations about the physical and social worlds, or "truths" about nature and people.

     Beliefs are social constructions. Although they are typically accepted as truths by the members of a society, beliefs are based not only on objective reality but on social agreement. Moreover yesterday's beliefs and the common sense of the present are the falsehoods and "myths" of tomorrow. For example, the word "lunatic" is derived from the popular nineteenth-century belief that a full moon causes madness, a belief that has folk origins in Europe and even deeper associations in simple cultures. Today, such thinking is derisively labeled "superstition."

—Thompson and Hickey, Society in Focus, p. 65

Organizational pattern: _____

8.   INTERPERSONAL VERSUS MASS COMMUNICATION   Personal or interpersonal channels of communication can occur in social settings when friends or acquaintances share information. Such word-of-mouth communication is a very powerful source of information for consumers. Word-of-mouth communication is usually not under the control of the marketer. Commercial sources of interpersonal communication usually come in the form of personal selling efforts.

     Nonpersonal channels of communication, as defined earlier, do not involve direct communication between sender and receiver. Instead, information is shared through mass communication. Advertising, sales promotion, and publicity use nonpersonal techniques. Both interpersonal and mass communication are important in marketing.

     A mass communication, such as an advertisement in a magazine, can more accurately deliver the same message to a larger audience than can an interpersonal communication such as a salesperson's presentation to a customer. The latter changes with each attempt to communicate. The cost of reaching an individual through the mass media is substantially lower as well. However, mass communication is one-way, it is less likely to gain the potential audience's selective attention, and it suffers from slow and, many times, inaccurate feedback.

Interpersonal communication has the benefits of being fast, and allowing two-way feedback. A buyer can respond instantly to a salesperson's presentation, and the salesperson can ask for clarification of the response. The greater flexibility in feedback allows the communicator to counter objections from the buyer and thus attain a greater change in attitude and behavior than is possible with mass communication. Interpersonal communication is much more efficient than mass communication. Unfortunately, when used for a large audience, interpersonal communication is slow and very expensive. Hence marketers must compare the efficiency of using a particular type of communication with the cost involved. This comparison is referred to as the *communication-promotion paradox*.

—Kinnear, Bernhardt, and Krentler, *Principles of Marketing*, pp. 475–476

Organizational pattern: _____

9.   OBSERVATIONAL LEARNING   Much social learning occurs in situations where learning would not be predicted by traditional conditioning theory, because a learner has made no active response and has received no tangible reinforcer. The individual, after simply watching another person exhibiting behavior that was reinforced or punished, later behaves in much the same way, or refrains from doing so. This is known as observational learning. Cognition often enters into observational learning in the form of expectations. In essence, after observing a model, you may think, "If I do exactly what she does, I will get the same reinforcer to avoid the same punisher." A younger child may be better behaved than his older sister because he has learned from the sister's mistakes.

This capacity to learn from watching as well as from doing is extremely useful. It enables you to acquire large, integrated patterns of behavior without going through the tedious trial-and-error process of gradually eliminating wrong responses and acquiring the right ones. You can profit immediately from the mistakes and successes of others. Researchers have demonstrated that observational learning is not special to humans. Even octopuses are capable of changing their behavior after merely observing the performances of another member of the species.

—Zimbardo and Gerrig, *Psychology and Life*, p. 337

Organizational pattern: _____

10.   INNATE HUMAN CHARACTERISTICS   Because of our common evolutionary history, many abilities, traits, and characteristics are universal in human beings and are either present at birth or develop as the child matures, given certain experiences. For example, babies are born with a number of reflexes, such as sucking and grasping (see Chapter 13). In addition, an attraction to novelty seems to be part of our evolutionary heritage, and that of many other species, as well. If a rat has had its dinner, it will prefer exploring an unfamiliar wing of a maze rather than the familiar wing where food is. Human babies, too, reveal a surprising interest in looking at and listening to unfamiliar things—which, of course, includes most of the world. A baby will even stop nursing if someone new enters his or her range of vision. A third innate characteristic in birds and mammals is a motive to explore and manipulate objects. Primates especially like to "monkey around" with things, taking them apart and scrutinizing the pieces, apparently for the sheer pleasure of it (Harlow, Harlow, & Meyer, 1950).

Many species, including our own, seem to have an innate motive to play, to fool around, and to imitate others (Huizinga, 1950). Think of kittens and lion cubs, puppies and pandas, and all young primates, who will play with and pounce on each other all day until hunger or naptime calls. Some researchers argue that play and exploration are biologically adaptive because they help members of a species find food and other necessities of life and learn to cope with their environment. Indeed, the young of many species enjoy practice play, behavior that will later be used for serious purposes when they are adults (Vandenberg, 1985). A kitten, for example, will stalk and attack a ball of yarn. In human beings, play is part of a child's socialization, teaching children how to get along with others and giving them a chance to practice their motor and linguistic skills (Harlow & Harlow, 1966; Pelligrini & Galda, 1993).

—Wade and Tavris, *Psychology,* p. 86

Organizational pattern: _____

EXERCISE 14   ■ **DIRECTIONS**   Read "The Talk of the Sandbox" in Part Seven on p. 387. Identify the organizational pattern that is used throughout the reading.

LEARNING *Collaboratively*

DIRECTIONS   Locate and mark, in one of your textbooks or in Part Seven of this text, several paragraphs that are clear examples of thought patterns discussed in Chapter 7. Write the topic sentence of each paragraph on a separate index card. Once your instructor has formed small groups, choose a group "reader" who will collect all the cards and read each sentence aloud. Groups should discuss each and predict the pattern of the paragraph from which the sentence was taken. The "finder" of the topic sentence should then confirm or reject the choice and quote sections of the paragraph if necessary.

Applying YOUR LEARNING

Suzanne is writing a research paper on "male and female language" for her sociology class. She has collected a great deal of information through research and interviews, but she is having difficulty organizing it. Some of the subtopics on which she has collected information are listed below.

Subject of Paper:
Male and Female Language

Subtopics:
• Research studies on use of language in adolescent sex-separate peer groups
• Men's language patterns
• Women's language patterns
• Stages of language development in infants and children
• Physical differences in areas of men's and women's brains that control language functioning
• Types of games children play and how they involve language

1. What possible *overall* organizational pattern could her paper follow?
2. What organizational pattern(s) might she follow in developing the section of her paper that deals with each of the topics above?
3. What types of details do you anticipate that Suzanne will include to develop each subtopic?

SELF-TEST SUMMARY

1. Why is it important to become familiar with the organization of your textbooks?

Textbooks are unique, highly organized sources of information. Becoming familiar with their organization and structure and learning to follow the writer's thought patterns are important textbook reading skills. A textbook is divided into parts: chapters, sections, subsections, and paragraphs. Although each is successively smaller in size and more limited in scope, each follows a similar organization and is built around a single idea with details that support and explain it.

2. What types of supporting information are used in textbooks and how are they organized?

Textbook writers explain ideas by providing various types of supporting information: examples, description, facts and statistics, and citation of research evidence. These supporting details are often organized into one or more organizational patterns: definition, time sequence, comparison–contrast, cause–effect, problem–solution, and enumeration.

3. How can you tell which organizational pattern is being used in a section or paragraph?

By paying close attention to the specific words and phrases a writer uses to connect ideas and lead from one idea to another, you can usually identify the pattern being used. These *directional words* that show the direction or pattern of thought are different for each of the common organizational patterns.

4. Why is it helpful to recognize the pattern or organization of a paragraph or passage you are reading?

When you recognize that what you are reading follows a specific pattern, you will be better able to follow the ideas being presented and to predict what will be presented next. You will find that you have connected the important details so that recalling one idea will help you recall the others, and as a result, it will be easier to learn and remember them.

Take a Road Trip to
Ellis Island and the Statue of Liberty!

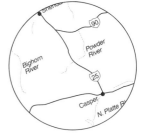

If your instructor has asked you to use the Reading Road Trip CD-ROM, be sure to visit the Patterns of Organization module for multimedia tutorials, exercises, and tests.

CHAPTER 8

Reading Graphics and Technical Writing

Why Read Graphics?

▲ Graphics—pictures of information—help you study complex ideas quickly and efficiently.

▲ Graphics condense and organize information that may be complicated and difficult to remember.

▲ Graphics display trends and patterns in a clear form so you can better see differences or changes.

Learning Experiment

Step 1

Read the following paragraph and answer the question that follows.

> In 1996 the population of the United States was 73.2% white, 10.6% Hispanic, 12.1% African American, 3.4% Asian, and 0.7% Native American. By the year 2006 it is projected that the population will be divided as follows: 69.5% white, 12.8% Hispanic, 12.4% African American, 4.5% Asian, and 0.8% Native American. By 2015, the population is projected to be 66.1% white, 15.1% Hispanic, 12.7% African American, 5.3% Asian, and 0.8% Native American.

Question: What group is projected to steadily decline in population?

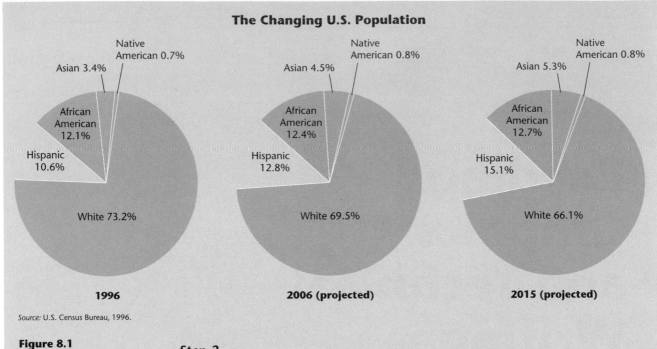

The Changing U.S. Population

1996

Native American 0.7%
Asian 3.4%
African American 12.1%
Hispanic 10.6%
White 73.2%

2006 (projected)

Native American 0.8%
Asian 4.5%
African American 12.4%
Hispanic 12.8%
White 69.5%

2015 (projected)

Native American 0.8%
Asian 5.3%
African American 12.7%
Hispanic 15.1%
White 66.1%

Source: U.S. Census Bureau, 1996.

Figure 8.1
Circle Graphs[1]

Step 2

Study the circle graphs in Figure 8.1 and answer the question that follows.

Question: What group is projected to steadily increase in population?

The Results

For which question was it easier to locate the answer? Which took less time to answer? Why? The second question was easier because the graphs presented a visual representation. You could "see" the changes in population, as the pieces of the pie grew larger.

Learning Principle (What This Means to You)

Visualization enables you to grasp ideas, see relationships, and recall information easily. At times, textbook authors will present information visually; other times you may have to create your own visual images. In this chapter you will learn to use visual aids as a learning tool.

READING GRAPHICS

Highly detailed specific information is often an integral part of course content. For instance, a sociology course may involve crime-rate statistics, a chemistry course is concerned with the characteristics of atomic particles, and an art history course focuses on historical periods.

These kinds of highly specialized information are presented in two unique ways: (1) graphics and (2) technical writing. The term *graphics* refers to all forms of visual representation of information, including maps, charts, tables, and diagrams. Textbooks in many academic disciplines use graphics to organize and present information. *Technical writing* is the compact, precise, and detailed presentation of factual information intended for practical use or application. Applications may include, for example, solving a problem in chemistry, writing a computer program, or operating a fax machine. College courses in the sciences, applied technologies, business, and specialized careers all demand technical reading skills. The purpose of this chapter is to present strategies for reading graphics and for approaching technical writing.

Some students are tempted to skip over graphs, tables, and diagrams. Stopping to study graphics requires time and seems to interrupt the flow of reading. Others think, incorrectly, that because the accompanying text explains the graphic, the graphic is unimportant. Actually, graphics are usually *more* important than the paragraphs that surround them. They are included to call your attention to, emphasize, and further explain the subject at hand.

Reading graphics enables you to analyze and synthesize information. It is never enough (and it is often unnecessary) to know each individual piece of information presented in a graph or chart. Instead, you must draw together the information to determine what it *means*.

Here is a general strategy for reading graphics. More specific suggestions for each type of graphic will follow.

1. *Read the title or caption.* The title will identify the subject and may suggest what relationship is being described.
2. *Determine how the graphic is organized.* Read the column headings or labels on the horizontal and vertical axes.
3. *Identify the variables.* Decide what is being compared to what or what relationship is being described.
4. *Anticipate the purpose.* On the basis of what you have seen, predict what the graphic is intended to show. Is its purpose to show change over time, describe a process, compare costs, or present statistics?
5. *Determine scale, values, or units of measurement.*
6. *Study the data to identify trends or patterns.* Note changes, unusual statistics, and any unexplained variations.
7. *Draw connections with the chapter content.* Take a moment to discover why the graphic was included and what concepts or key points it illustrates or explains.
8. *Make a brief summary note.* In the margin, jot a brief note about the trend or pattern the graphic emphasizes. Writing will crystallize the idea in your mind, and your note will be useful when you review.

Applying Levels of Thinking

Graphics and Levels of Thinking

Reading graphics involves several levels of thinking. Your first task is to comprehend the information presented in the graphic. Then you move to analysis, synthesis, and evaluation by focusing on what the graph means or how it can be interpreted. Here is a list of questions to guide your thinking about graphics.

Level of Thinking	Question
Knowledge and Comprehension	What factual information does the graphic present?
Application	How can this information be applied to ideas presented in the chapter or to my own experience?
Analysis	What changes or variations occur in the data?
Synthesis	What trends or patterns are evident?
Evaluation	Of what use or value are these trends or patterns?

Human Population Trends, 1900-2100

	POPULATION (MILLIONS)					
	1900	1950	1985	2000	2025	2100
Developing regions (total)	1,070	1,681	3,657	4,837	6,799	8,748
Africa	133	224	555	872	1,617	2,591
Asia[a]	867	1,292	2,679	3,419	4,403	4,919
Latin America	70	165	405	546	779	1,238
Developed regions (total)	560	835	1,181	1,284	1,407	1,437
Europe, USSR, Japan, Oceania[b]	478	669	917	987	1,062	1,055
Canada, United States	2	166	264	297	345	382
World total	1,630	2,516	4,837	6,122	8,206	10,185

[a]Excludes Japan.
[b]Includes Australia and New Zealand.

Figure 8.2
A Sample Table[2]

TYPES OF GRAPHICS

There are many types of graphics; each accomplishes specific purposes for the writer, and each describes a particular relationship.

Tables

A table is an organized display of factual information, usually numbers or statistics. Its purpose is to present large amounts of information in a condensed and systematically arranged form. It's easy to make comparisons between or among data. Take a few minutes to study the table in Figure 8.2. Then use the tips listed below.

1. *Determine how the data are classified or divided.* The table shown in Figure 8.2 classifies population growth by year and subdivides it by region (developing or developed).
2. *Make comparisons and look for trends or patterns.* This step involves looking at the rows and columns, noting how each compares with the others. Look for similarities, differences, and sudden changes or variations. Underline or highlight unusual or outstanding data. Try to note increases or decreases that seem unusually high or low. Also note trends in the data. For example, in Figure 8.2, you might note that the population of Latin America between 1950 and 1985 more than tripled, while the population of Asia only doubled, and the population of the developed regions didn't even do that. Or you might note that Asia has the highest population by far at every point or that population growth is projected to slow down in the twenty-first century in developed regions.

PARTY IDENTIFICATION IN THE UNITED STATES 1952–1996[3]

YEAR	DEMOCRATS	INDEPENDENTS	REPUBLICANS
1952	48.6	23.3	28.1
1956	45.3	24.4	30.3
1960	46.4	23.4	30.2
1964	52.2	23.0	24.8
1968	46.0	29.5	24.5
1972	41.0	35.2	23.8
1976	40.2	36.8	23.0
1980	41.7	35.3	23.0
1984	37.7	34.8	27.6
1988	35.7	36.3	28.0
1992	35.8	38.7	25.5
1994	34.6	34.8	30.5
1996	36.4	35.0	28.6

[3]In percentage of people; the small percentage who identify with a minor party or who cannot answer the question are excluded.
SOURCE: 1952–1994 National Election Studies conducted by the University of Michigan; 1996 from *New York Times*/CBS News polls.

Figure 8.3
A Table[3]

3. *Draw conclusions.* Decide what the data mean and what they suggest about the subject at hand. Examine the paragraphs that correspond to the table for clues, or sometimes direct statements, about the purpose of the graph. You can conclude from Figure 8.2 that the world population in general has grown tremendously since 1900 and that a vast majority of the growth has occurred in developing countries.

EXERCISE 1

DIRECTIONS   Study the table in Figure 8.3 and answer the questions that follow.

1. From 1952 to 1996, which political party had the largest increase in people identifying with it?
2. Which one showed an overall decrease in party identification?
3. With which political party did the most people identify in 1964?
4. With which party has party identification remained the same from 1952 to 1996?
5. In what year did more people identify with the Independent party than with the other two?

Graphs

There are two primary types of graphs: bar graphs and linear graphs. Each plots a set of points on a set of axes.

Bar Graphs

A bar graph makes comparisons between quantities or amounts. It is particularly useful in showing changes that occur with passing time. Bar graphs usually are designed to emphasize differences. The graph shown in Figure 8.4 displays the percentage of the world's population living in urban areas. It makes it easy to see at a glance how the percentage of city dwellers will increase until the year 2025.

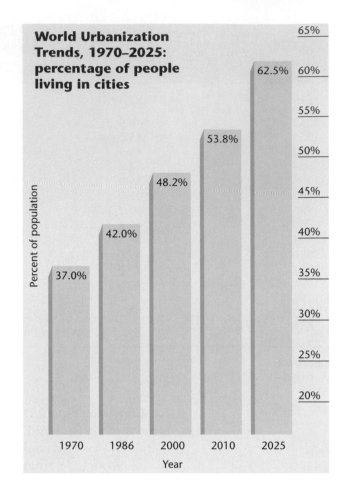

Figure 8.4
A Sample Bar Graph[4]

Multiple Bar Graphs

A multiple bar graph displays at least two or three comparisons simultaneously. Figure 8.5 compares male and female preferences for private-brand food products by age group.

Stacked Bar Graphs

In a stacked bar graph, instead of bars being arranged side by side, they are placed one on top of another. This variation is often used to emphasize whole/part relationships—that is, to show what part of an entire group or class a particular item accounts for. Stacked bar graphs also make numerous comparisons possible. The graph in Figure 8.6 enables you to compare responses to a question about care of elderly parents by religion and race and shows a national response as well.

Linear Graphs

In a linear graph, or line graph, points are plotted along a vertical and a horizontal axis and then connected to form a line. A linear graph allows more data points than a bar graph. Consequently, it is used to present more detailed and/or larger quantities of information. A linear graph may represent the relationship between two variables; if so, it consists of a single line. More often, however, linear graphs are used to compare relationships among several sets of variables, and multiple lines are included. The graph shown in Figure 8.7 on page 174 shows fishing efficiency for the freshwater catch, the ocean catch, and the total catch each year from 1940 through 1990.

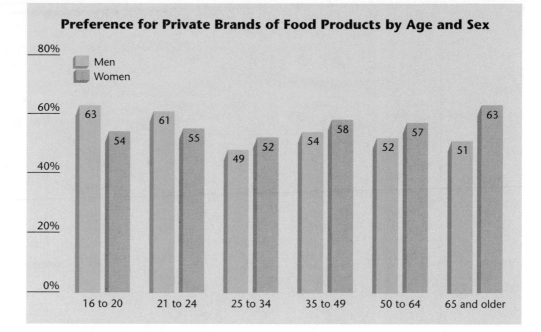

**Figure 8.5
A Sample Multiple
Bar Graph**[5]

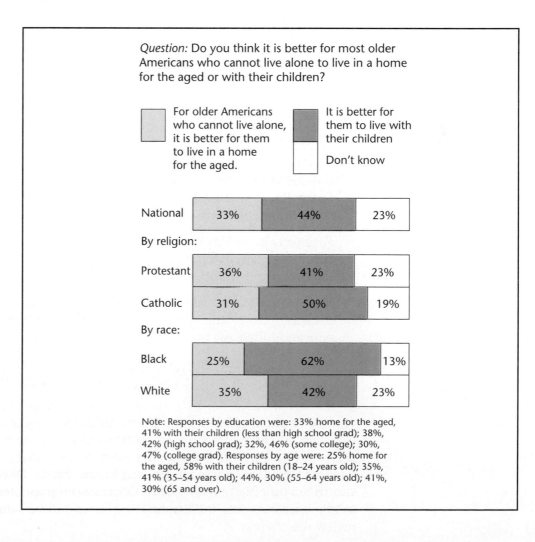

**Figure 8.6
A Sample Stacked
Bar Graph**[6]

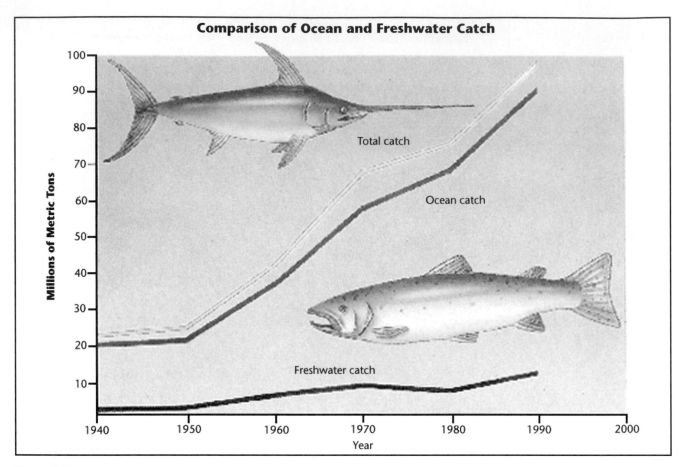

Figure 8.7
A Sample Linear Graph⁷

Linear graphs are generally used to display continuous data—data that are connected in time or events that occur in sequence. The data in Figure 8.7 are continuous as they move from 1940 to 1990.

Single linear graphs can display one of three general relationships: positive, negative, or independent. Each of these is shown in Figure 8.8.

Positive relationship. When the variables increase or decrease at the same time, the relationship is positive and is shown by a line that climbs up from left to right. In graph A, as years in school increase, so does income.

Inverse (or negative) relationship. When one variable increases as the other decreases, the relationship is inverse or negative. In graph B, as the years of education increase, the number of children decreases.

Independent relationship. When the variables have no effect on each other, the relationship is independent. In graph C, years in school have no effect on number of house pets.

The linear graph in Figure 8.7 shows an overall positive relationship between year and all three categories of catch recorded (total, ocean, and freshwater). Between 1970 and 1980, we can see a slightly negative, or perhaps independent, relationship between decade and freshwater catch. Once you know the trend and the nature of the relationship that a linear graph describes, jot them down in the margin next to the graph. These notes will be valuable timesavers as you review the chapter.

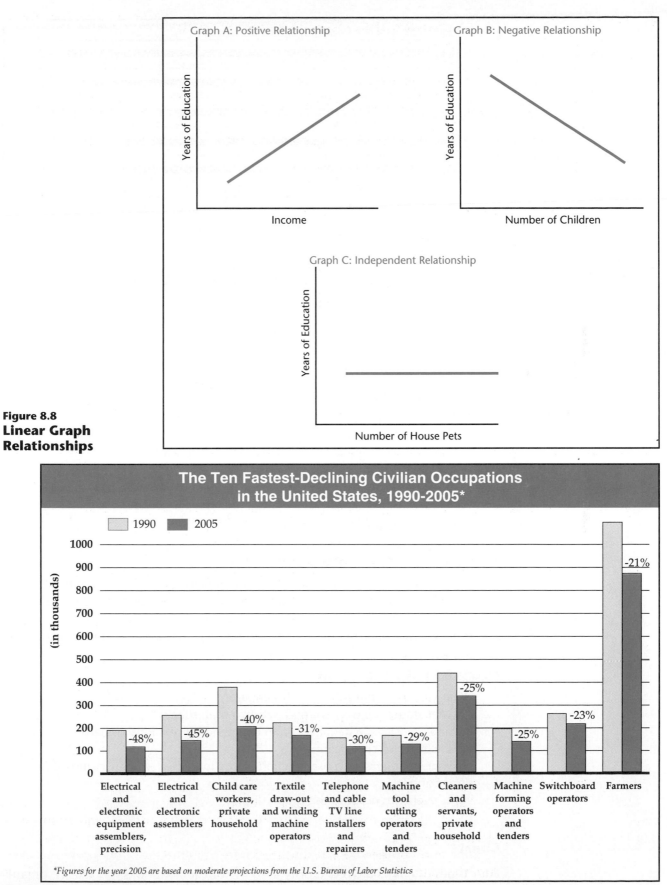

Figure 8.8
Linear Graph
Relationships

Figure 8.9
A Sample Multiple Bar Graph[8]

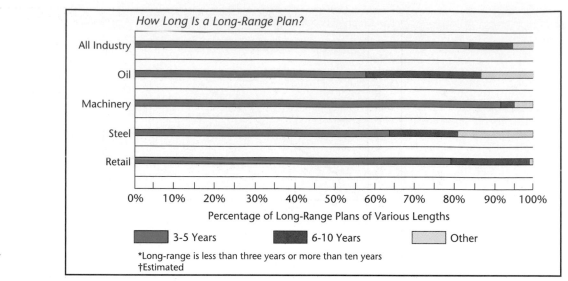

Figure 8.10
A Stacked Bar
Graph[9]

> **EXERCISE 2**

DIRECTIONS   Study the graphs shown in Figures 8.9 through 8.11 and answer the corresponding questions.

Figure 8.9: A Multiple Bar Graph

1. What is the purpose of the graph in Figure 8.9 on the previous page?
2. What occupation will decline the most by 2005? Which will rank second?
3. Among these occupations, which will decline the least?
4. Which declining occupation will employ the most workers in 2005?
5. How many machine forming operators and tenders were employed in 1990?
6. What conclusions can you draw about the types of occupations that are represented among the ten fastest declining?

Figure 8.10: A Stacked Bar Graph

1. What industry has the largest percentage of plans in the 3–5-year range?
2. For all industries considered together, what percentage of plans tends to be 3–5-year plans?
3. What industry has the smallest percentage of plans in the 6–10-year range?

Figure 8.11: A Linear Graph

1. What variables does Figure 8.11 compare?
2. At what stages are women more satisfied than men?
3. Is there a positive, a negative, or an independent relationship between marital satisfaction and child rearing?
4. At what stage(s) is men's satisfaction increasing while women's satisfaction is decreasing?
5. What overall trend does this graph display?

Charts

Four types of charts are commonly used in college textbooks: pie charts, organizational charts, flowcharts, and pictograms. Each is intended to display a relationship, either quantitative or cause–effect.

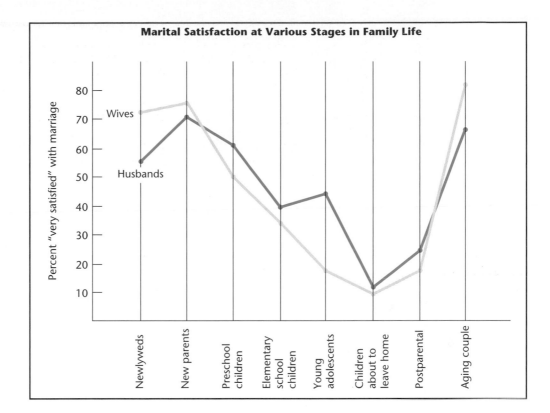

Figure 8.11
A Linear Graph[10]

Pie Charts

Pie charts, sometimes called circle graphs, are used to show whole/part relationships or to show how given parts of a unit have been divided or classified. They let the reader compare the parts to each other as well as compare each part to the whole. Figure 8.12, taken from a criminal justice textbook, shows the percentages of law enforcement officers killed in the line of duty by various causes. It provides a clear visual as well as a statistical comparison of these seven different categories.

Organizational Charts

An organizational chart divides an organization, such as a corporation, a hospital, or a university, into its administrative parts, staff positions, or lines of authority. Figure 8.13 on the next page shows the organization of the marketing

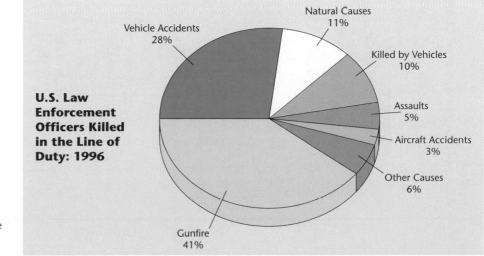

Figure 8.12
A Sample Pie Chart[11]

Source: Officer Down Memorial Page on the World Wide Web, http://www.odmp.org.

Figure 8.13
A Sample Organizational Chart[12]

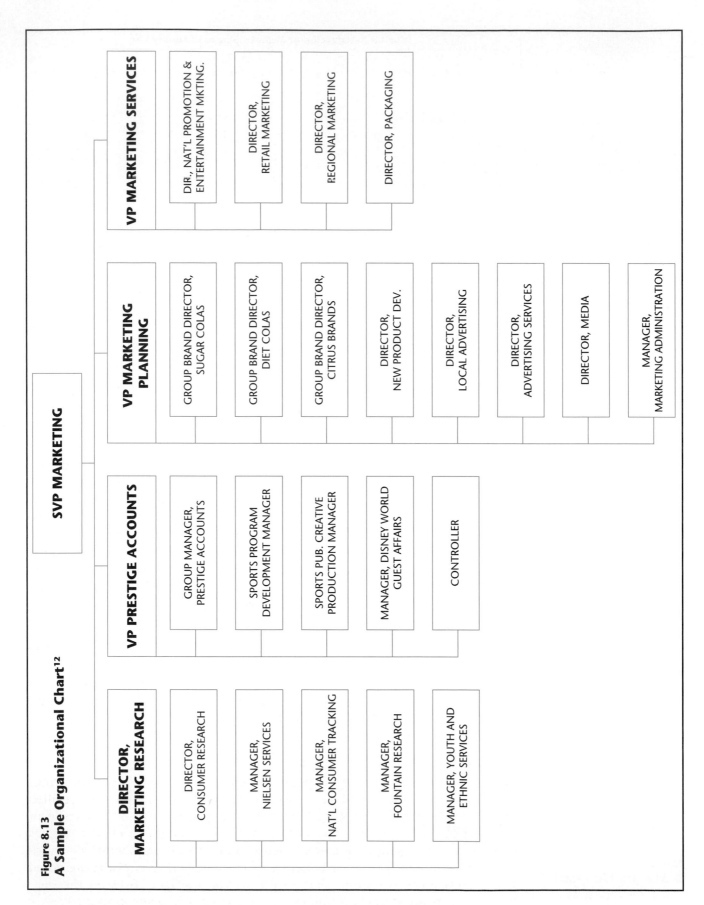

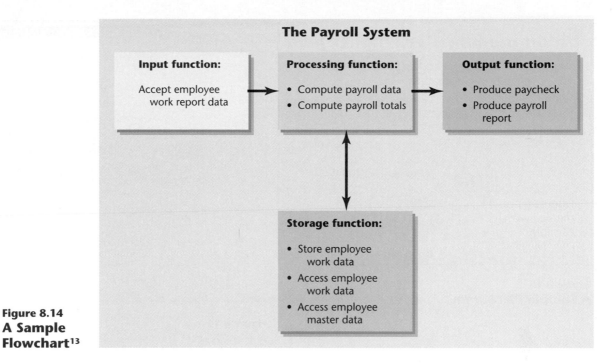

**Figure 8.14
A Sample
Flowchart**[13]

division of Coca-Cola. It indicates that there are four major subdivisions and depicts divisions of responsibility for each.

Flowcharts

A flowchart is a specialized type of chart that shows how a process or procedure works. Lines or arrows are used to indicate the direction (route or routes) through the procedure. Various shapes (boxes, circles, rectangles) enclose what is done at each stage or step. You could draw, for example, a flowchart to describe how to apply for and obtain a student loan or how to locate a malfunction in your car's electrical system. The flowchart shown in Figure 8.14, taken from a business information systems textbook, describes how a payroll system functions. The chart reveals a four-step process and describes the parts of each step. To read flowcharts effectively, use the following suggestions.

1. Decide what process the flowchart shows.
2. Next, follow the chart, using the arrows and reading each step. Start at the top or far left of the chart.
3. When you've finished, describe the process in your own words. Try to draw the chart from memory without referring to the text. Compare your drawing with the chart, and take note of anything you forgot or misplaced.

Pictograms

A combination of a chart and a graph, a pictogram uses symbols or drawings (such as books, cars, or buildings), instead of bars or lines, to represent specified amounts. This type of chart tends to be visually appealing, makes statistics seem realistic, and may carry an emotional impact. For example, a chart that uses stick-figure drawings of pregnant women to indicate the number of abortions performed each year per state may have a greater impact than statistics presented in numerical form. A sample pictogram is shown in Figure 8.15 on the next page. This pictogram uses two wooden beams as symbols to represent the weekly

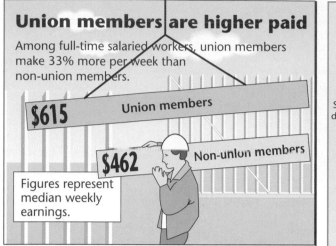

Figure 8.15
A Sample Pictogram[14]

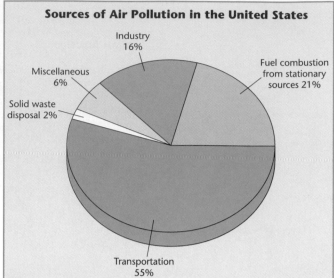

Figure 8.16
A Pie Chart[15]

earnings of union and non-union workers. The difference in the lengths of these beams provides a visual comparison of the average weekly salaries of these two groups of workers.

EXERCISE 3

DIRECTIONS   Study the charts shown in Figures 8.16 and 8.17 and answer the corresponding questions.

Figure 8.16: A Pie Chart

1. What is the largest source of air pollution in the U.S.?
2. What is the smallest source of air pollution?
3. Is this chart more effective than a bar graph displaying the same data? Why or why not?

Figure 8.17: A Flowchart

1. What process does this flowchart describe?
2. List the steps in the order in which they occur.
3. What steps are included in primary treatment?
4. What happens to water after secondary treatment is completed?

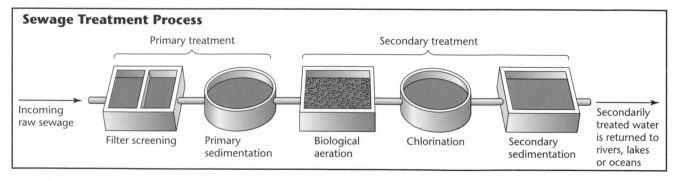

Figure 8.17
A Flowchart[16]

Diagrams

Diagrams often are included in technical and scientific as well as business and social science texts to explain processes. Diagrams are intended to help you see relationships between parts and understand what follows what. Figure 8.18, taken from a biology textbook, depicts a plant stem and shows how a plant's history is revealed by stem growth.

Reading diagrams differs from reading other types of graphics in that diagrams often correspond to fairly large segments of text, and you have to switch back and forth frequently between the text and the diagram to determine what part of the process each paragraph refers to.

Because diagrams of processes and their corresponding text are often difficult, complicated, or highly technical, plan on reading these sections more than once. Use the first reading to grasp the overall process. In later readings, focus on the details of the process, examining each step and understanding the progression to the next.

One of the best ways to study a diagram is to redraw it without referring to the original, including as much detail as possible. Or test your understanding and recall of the process explained in a diagram by explaining it, step by step in writing, using your own words.

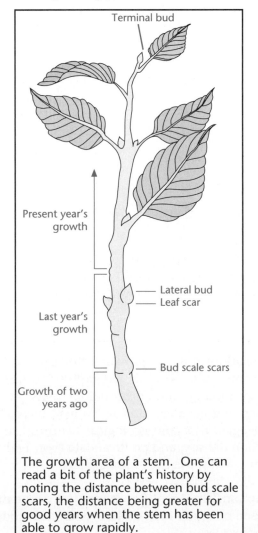

Terminal bud

Present year's growth

Last year's growth

Lateral bud

Leaf scar

Bud scale scars

Growth of two years ago

The growth area of a stem. One can read a bit of the plant's history by noting the distance between bud scale scars, the distance being greater for good years when the stem has been able to grow rapidly.

Figure 8.18
A Sample Diagram[17]

HOW THE CONSTITUTION CAN BE AMENDED

The Constitution sets up two alternative routes for proposing amendments and two for ratifying them. One of the four possible combinations has been used in every case but one, but there are persistent calls for a constitutional convention to propose some new amendment or another. Amendments to permit prayer in schools, to make abortion unconstitutional, and to require a balanced national budget are recent examples.

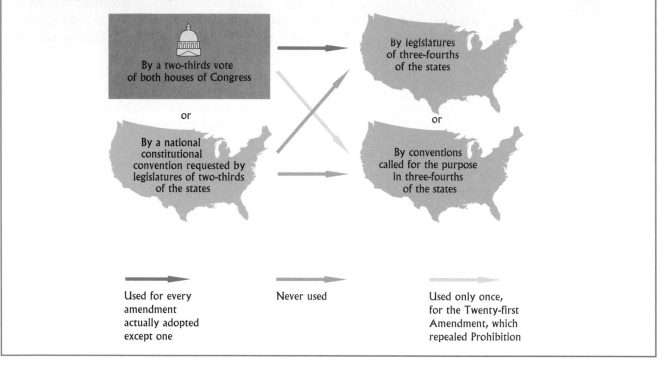

By a two-thirds vote of both houses of Congress

or

By a national constitutional convention requested by legislatures of two-thirds of the states

By legislatures of three-fourths of the states

or

By conventions called for the purpose in three-fourths of the states

Used for every amendment actually adopted except one

Never used

Used only once, for the Twenty-first Amendment, which repealed Prohibition

Figure 8.19
A Diagram[18]

EXERCISE 4

DIRECTIONS   Study the diagram shown in Figure 8.19 and answer the questions that follow.

1. What is the purpose of the diagram?
2. What amendment process is most commonly used?
3. Name two processes that have never been used.

Maps

Maps describe relationships and provide information about location and direction. They are commonly found in geography and history texts, and they also appear in ecology, biology, and anthropology texts. Although most of us think of maps as describing distances and locations, maps also are used to describe placement of geographical and ecological features such as areas of pollution, areas of population density, and political data (voting districts).

When reading maps, use the following steps.

1. Read the caption. This identifies the subject of the map.
2. Use the legend or key to identify the symbols or codes used.
3. Note distance scales.

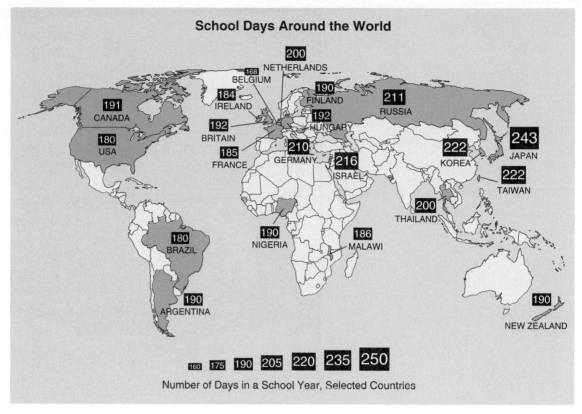

Figure 8.20
A Sample Map[19]

4. Study the map, looking for trends or key points. Often the text that accompanies the map states the key points that the map illustrates.
5. Try to create a mental picture of the map.
6. As a learning and study aid, write, in your own words, a statement of what the map shows.

Now look at the map shown in Figure 8.20. Its key depicts boxes with various numbers of days in a school year; the more days per year, the larger the box. Using this code, you can quickly locate those countries with the most and fewest school days by looking for the largest and smallest boxes. For example, Japanese students attend school the most days (243), whereas Belgian students attend the fewest (168). You can also observe that in general, nations in the Far East have the most school days, whereas students in North and South America attend far fewer days.

Cartoons

Cartoons are included in textbooks to make a point quickly or simply to lighten the text by adding a touch of humor about the topic at hand. Cartoons usually appear without a title or legend and there is usually no reference within the text to the cartoon.

Cartoons can make abstract ideas and concepts concrete and real. Pay close attention to cartoons, especially if you are a visually oriented learner. They may help you recall ideas easily by serving as a recall clue that triggers your memory of related material.

Figure 8.21
A Sample Cartoon[20]

College of Positive Self-Image 7.
University of Low Self-Esteem 0.

The cartoon shown in Figure 8.21 appears in a sociology textbook chapter titled "Personality." It appears on a page that defines self-concept and discusses positive and negative self-concepts.

Photographs

Although sometimes considered an art form instead of a graphic, photographs, like other graphics, can be used in place of words to present information. Photographs also are used to spark your interest and, often, to draw out an emotional response or feeling. The caption on a photograph often provides a clue to its intended meaning. As you study a photograph, ask "What is my first overall impression?" and "What details did I notice first?" These questions will lead you to discover the purpose of the photograph.

EXERCISE 5

DIRECTIONS   Study the photographs shown in Figure 8.22 and answer the questions that follow.

1. What are the photographs intended to emphasize?
2. What does this set of photographs show that a paragraph could not?
3. List several cultural differences that these photographs reveal.

Figure 8.22
Photographs[21]

DIRECTIONS   Indicate what type(s) of graphic(s) would be most useful in presenting each of the following sets of information.

1. Damage done to ancient carved figures by sulfur dioxide in the air
2. A comparison of the types of products the United States imports with those it exports
3. Changes in worker productivity each year from 1970 through 1990 in Japan, France, Germany, and the United States
4. The probabilities of being murdered for various racial and ethnic groups in the United States
5. Foreign revenue, total revenue, foreign operating profit, foreign assets, and total assets for the ten largest American multinational corporations
6. Living arrangements (one parent, two parents, neither parent) for white, black, and Spanish-origin children under 18 years of age in 1960, 1970, 1980, and 1990
7. The basic components of a robot's manipulator arm
8. A description of how the AIDS virus affects the immune system
9. Sites of the earliest Neanderthal discoveries in Western Europe
10. Number of receipts of, and profits for, three types of businesses: sole proprietorships, partnerships, and corporations

READING TECHNICAL WRITING

Technical writing is commonly thought of as something science or engineering students read. Actually, technical writing is by no means restricted to traditional technical or scientific fields. Technical writing is what most of us are called on to read in our daily lives as well as in many academic courses. Here are a few examples of situations, both everyday and academic, that require reading technical writing.

Everyday Situations

1. Reading directions to set up your programmable telephone
2. Assembling a bicycle from printed instructions
3. Consulting a repair manual to troubleshoot problems in your car's engine

Academic Situations

1. Reading end-of-the-year financial reports to assess a corporation's financial health for a business class project
2. Consulting the *Journal of Abnormal Psychology* to complete a psychology term paper on characteristics of the manic-depressive personality
3. Referring to a technical manual to find out how to save a file in a new word-processing program

Technical writing, then, is an important part of everyday activities and of many academic disciplines. Technical reading skills are essential in both the everyday and the academic world. This portion of the chapter will discuss and describe technical writing and offer suggestions for reading it effectively.

How Technical Writing Is Different

You already know that technical writing is different, but do you know how it differs from other types of writing? Take a moment now and think about what you already know about technical writing.

Now expand your knowledge by comparing several sample pieces of writing, one of which is a technical one. All of the following excerpts concern the same topic: birds. After you have read all three, complete Exercise 7.

Sample 1

"You would know the heron if you saw it," the stranger continued eagerly. "A queer tall white bird with soft feathers and long thin legs. And it would have a nest perhaps in the top of a high tree, made of sticks, something like a hawk's nest."

Sylvia's heart gave a wild beat; she knew that strange white bird, and had once stolen softly near where it stood in some bright green swamp grass, away over at the other side of the woods. There was an open place where the sunshine always seemed strangely yellow and hot, where tall, nodding rushes grew, and her grandmother had warned her that she might sink in the soft black mud underneath and never be heard of more. Not far beyond were the salt marshes just this side the sea itself, which Sylvia wondered and dreamed much about, but never had seen, whose great voice could sometimes be heard above the noise of the woods on stormy nights.[22]

Sample 2

At once a voice arose among
    The bleak twigs overhead
In a full-hearted evensong
    Of joy unlimited;
An aged thrush, frail, gaunt, and small
    In blast-beruffled plume,
Had chosen thus to fling his soul
    Upon the growing gloom.[23]

Sample 3

THRUSH. In the large thrush family of birds are some of the finest singers—the robin, the bluebird, and the nightingale, as well as those commonly known as thrushes. Although most of them are feathered in browns and buffs, some thrushes—such as the robin and the bluebird—have bright colors.

Whatever the color of the parent birds, all young thrushes have spotted breasts until their first autumn molt. Some species nest and live in trees, others on the ground; some feed on insects, others on fruits. In England the mavis, or song thrush, the missel thrush, and the nightingale are the best-known species. In the United States the wood thrush, the hermit thrush, and the veery are among the best known of the family. These are slender brown birds.

The wood thrush often nests in wooded city lots. The hermit prefers secluded northern forests. The veery's home is in low, wet woodlands with dense underbrush. They lay three or four greenish-blue eggs. The willow thrush is a western subspecies of the veery. (See also *Birds; Bluebird; Nightingale; Robin.*)

The scientific name of the thrush family is Turdidae; of the wood thrush, *Hylocichla mustelina;* of the hermit thrush, *H. guttata;* of the veery and willow thrush, *H. fuscescens.* [24]

Sample 1, an excerpt from an essay titled "A White Heron," presents an everyday description of the heron—a sense of oddness and awkwardness is revealed through the description.

Sample 2 is an excerpt from a poem titled "The Darkling Thrush," by Thomas Hardy. Here the bird and its song are presented in contrast to a gloomy depressing scene.

Sample 3, an excerpt from an encyclopedia entry on thrushes, presents factual information about the bird's appearance and habitat.

EXERCISE 7

DIRECTIONS   By comparing and contrasting the three samples just given, list additional features of technical writing that you have discovered. Then compare your list with the information that appears in Figure 8.23.

Tips for Reading Technical Material

Use the following suggestions when reading technical material.

Adjust Your Reading Rate

Because technical writing is factual and contains numerous illustrations, diagrams, and sample problems, you should read more slowly. Plan on spending twice as long reading a technical textbook as you spend reading nontechnical texts.

Plan on Rereading

Do not expect to understand everything the first time you read the assignment. It is helpful to read an assignment once rather quickly to get an overview of it. Then reread it to learn the details.

Preread Carefully

Because technical material often deals with unfamiliar subject matter about which you have little or no background knowledge, prereading is a particularly important skill.

Characteristic	Description
Purpose	To supply the reader with needed information. To perform a task, understand a situation, solve a problem, make a decision.
Fact density	Facts are abundant and usually are presented as compactly as possible.
Exact word choice	Meaning must be clear and without possibility of confusion or misinterpretation.
Technical/specialized vocabulary	Because meaning must be exact, technical or specialized vocabulary is often introduced. These words have specific meanings within the field or discipline and often serve as shortcuts to the lengthy descriptions or details that would be necessary if nonspecialized language were used.
Abbreviations and notation systems	An extensive system of abbreviation and notations (signs and symbols) is used. These are also shortcuts to writing out complete words or meanings and are often used in diagrams, formulas, and drawings.
Graphics	Most technical writing contains numerous drawings, charts, tables, diagrams, or graphs. They are included to clarify, help you to visualize, and emphasize key information.
Examples and sample problems	Technical textbooks often contain numerous examples and sample problems. These are included to illustrate how information is used and instructions are applied.
Specific formats	Technical writing often follows specific formats. A lab report has a specific organization. A psychologist's case report has specific categories. Research reports in the sciences typically include a statement of problem, a description of experimental design, and so forth.

Figure 8.23
Characteristics of Technical Writing

Alternate between Reading Text and Studying Graphics

Drawings and illustrations are referred to frequently in surrounding text. Consequently, it is often necessary to alternate between text and graphics. Page arrangement is often confusing, and a diagram and the paragraph that explains it may not be on the same page. Other times, a diagram may appear before it is referred to in the text. Use the following strategy.

1. Notice the types of illustrations and drawings as you preread the material.
2. As soon as a graphic is mentioned in the text, locate and study it. Titles, captions, and labels are important.
3. If a graphic appears before its text reference, notice its title, and keep reading until it is introduced.
4. Plan to stop reading frequently to refer to graphics. For instance, when reading about the function of specific parts of a piece of equipment, each time a specific part is mentioned, refer to the diagram and locate the part. Then read the description of its function.

Use Visualization

Visualization is a process of creating mental pictures or images. As you read, try to visualize the process or procedure being described. Make your image as specific and detailed as possible. Visualization will make reading these descriptions easier, as well as improve your ability to recall details. Here are a few examples of how students use visualizations:

- A nursing student reading about methods of arranging intravenous tubing for administering two solutions simultaneously visualized the arrangement of clamps, tubing, and bottles
- A communications student studying types of nonverbal communication visualized himself using each form

Now read the following description of paramecia and try to visualize as you read.

> If you should find yourself with a microscope and unable to resist examining the water of a scummy pond, you would likely find great numbers of tiny protozoans. Some of these would be covered with tiny, hairlike cilia. Protists that bear cilia at some stage in the life cycle comprise the phylum ciliophora. The most familiar of these are the Paramecia. Paramecia (singular, Paramecium) are recognizable by their slipper shape, which is maintained by their outer thickened membrane, the pellicle. The pellicle, while holding its form, is flexible enough to enable the paramecium to bend around objects as it furiously swims through the water propelled by the wavelike actions of the cilia covering its body. Behind its rounded anterior (or front) end lies a deep oral groove into which food is swept by other cilia. The food is then forced through a mouthlike pore (cytostome) at the end of the groove and into a bulbous opening, which will break away and move into the cytoplasm as a food vacuole.[25]

Tips for Studying Technical Material

Use the following suggestions to learn technical material.

Study Daily

Because technical material is unfamiliar, frequent contact with the material is necessary if you are to remember it.

Reserve Large Blocks of Time

Large blocks of time are often necessary to complete projects, lab write-ups, or problem sets. Also, technical material requires a particular mind-set, which, once you've established it, is worth continuing.

Learn Technical Vocabulary

Understanding the technical vocabulary in your discipline is essential. For technical and applied fields, it is especially important to learn to pronounce technical terms and use them in your speech and writing. To establish yourself as a professional in the field and to communicate effectively with other professionals, it is vital to speak and use the language. Use the suggestions in Chapter 11 for learning specialized terminology.

Study by Drawing Diagrams and Pictures

Although your textbook may include numerous drawings and illustrations, there is not sufficient space to have drawings for every process. An effective learning strategy is to draw diagrams and pictures whenever possible. These should be fast sketches; be concerned with describing parts or processes, and do not worry about artwork or scale drawings. For example, a student studying air conditioning and refrigeration repair drew a quick sketch of a unit he was to repair in his lab before he began to disassemble it, and he referred to sketches he had drawn in his notebook as he diagnosed the problem.

Focus on Concepts and Principles

Because technical subjects are so detailed, many students get lost in details and lose sight of the concepts and principles to which the details relate. Keep in the front of your notebook, for easy reference, a sheet on which you record information you need to refer to frequently. Include constants, conversion formulas, metric equivalents, and commonly used abbreviations.

Integrate Lab, Lecture, and Classroom Activities

Many technical courses have a required lab. Because the lab is scheduled separately from the lecture and has its own unique format, you may fail to see the lab as an integral part of the course. The lab is intended to help you understand and apply principles and techniques used in your course and gives you an opportunity to ask questions. Use the following tips for handling lab work.

- Be prepared before going to lab. Read the manual or assignment once to understand its overall purpose and a second time to understand the specific procedures. Make notes or highlight key information.
- Ask questions before you make a mistake. Because procedures can be time-consuming to repeat, ask questions first.
- Be sure you understand the purpose of each step before you perform it.
- Analyze your results and do the follow-up report as soon as possible. The best time to study your results is while the experiment and procedures are still fresh in you mind. If you finish the lab work early, stay and discuss results and interpretations with other students or your lab instructor.
- Follow the required format closely when writing your report.

Use the Glossary and Index

Because of the large number of technical terms, formulas, and notations you will encounter, it is often necessary to refer to definitions and explanations. Place a paper clip at the beginning of the glossary and a second at the index so you can find them easily.

Highlight Selectively

Everything looks (and often is) important in texts, and it is easy to fall into the habit of overhighlighting. Avoid this pitfall by reading a whole paragraph or section before highlighting. Then go back and mark only key terms and concepts. Do not try to highlight all useful facts. Refer to Chapter 13 for suggestions on how to highlight effectively.

Use Outlining

Many students find outlining to be an effective study and review technique. Some texts include chapter outlines, but even though your text may have one, make your own. It is the process of making the outline that is important. Outlining forces you to decide what pieces of information are important and how they are related and then to express the ideas in your own words. Refer to Chapter 14 for specific suggestions on taking outline notes.

Learn Processes and Procedures

Procedures, directions, installations, repairs, instructions, and diagnostic checking procedures all follow the process pattern. To read materials written in this pattern, you must not only learn the steps but also learn them in the correct order. To study process material, use the following tips.

1. Prepare study sheets that summarize each process. For example, a psychology student learning the steps in motor development of infants wrote the summary shown in Figure 8.24.
2. Test your recall by writing out the steps from memory. Recheck periodically by mentally reviewing each step.

Month(s)	Activity
1–2	raise head—45 degrees
3	roll—front to back
4	sit with support
6	sit alone
7–12	crawl and creep
7	pull to stand
9	sidestepping
11	stand alone
12	walk

**Figure 8.24
A Sample Summary Sheet**

3. For difficult or long procedures, write each step on a separate index card. Shuffle the pack and practice putting the cards in the correct order.
4. Be certain you understand the logic behind the process. Figure out why each step is done when it is.

EXERCISE 8

DIRECTIONS Turn to the article titled "Communication Between Women and Men" in Part Seven on page 385. Write a brief outline for the section titled "Speaking Different Genderlects."

LEARNING *Collaboratively*

DIRECTIONS   Bring a copy of your local newspaper, a magazine, or *USA Today* to class. After your instructor forms groups, each group should select and tear out four or five graphics. For each graphic, your group should identify the type of graphic, analyze its purpose, and identify the trend or pattern it reveals. In your group, discuss what other types of graphics could be used to accomplish the author's purpose. Working together, your group should choose one graphic to submit to the instructor with a brief summary of your analysis.

Applying **YOUR LEARNING**

Elaine is a liberal arts major who is taking a biology class to fulfill her science requirement. Her reading assignment for this week includes a chapter on plant reproduction and development. It includes numerous complicated diagrams of reproductive life cycles of conifers (a type of evergreen tree) and flowering plants. Elaine is unsure how to approach reading and understanding the material. She is also frustrated because some of the diagrams appear before the part of the chapter that explains them. The chapter also describes, but does not illustrate, the reproductive stages of ferns, mosses, and algae.

1. Give some suggestions to help Elaine read and study the chapter.
2. How should she read and study the diagrams in the chapter?
3. How can Elaine learn and understand the life cycles not illustrated in the chapter?
4. What general suggestions would you offer to help Elaine succeed in a science course that contains a great deal of technical material?

SELF-TEST SUMMARY

1. What steps can be taken to read graphic material more effectively?	Graphics condense information and enable the reader to see patterns, identify trends, observe variations, and interpret information. To get the most from all types of graphics, you should begin by reading the title or caption and determining how the graphic is organized, what its purpose is, what variables are being presented, and what scale, values, or units of measurements are being used. You should then study the data to identify trends and patterns and to draw connections with the content of the chapter. Finally, making marginal notes will aid your further reading and review.
2. How is technical writing different from other types of writing?	Technical writing is unique and distinct from other types of writing. It is action-oriented, supplying information that the reader needs to perform a task, solve a problem, or make a decision. Technical writing presents many facts in a small space, so it is precise in word choice, uses a technical, specialized vocabulary, includes special abbreviations and notations, and contains graphics, examples, and sample problems for clarity. Finally, different types of technical writing follow their own specific formats that are different from most other types of writing.
3. How should technical material be read?	When reading technical material, you should plan to read at about half the speed you use with nontechnical writing. You should preread carefully and read the material at least twice. It is important to study any graphics carefully as you are reading the text, and it is helpful to visualize and create a mental picture of what is being described.
4. How can technical material be studied more effectively?	To study technical material more effectively, it is important to study daily in large blocks of time in order to stay focused. You should make an extra effort to learn technical vocabulary by referring frequently to your text's glossary and index. Focusing on concepts and principles, on integrating information from labs, lectures, and classroom activities, and on drawing diagrams and pictures will keep you from getting lost in details. When reading and reviewing, highlight selectively or outline, and prepare study sheets on the important information, procedures, or processes.

Take a Road Trip to
Wall Street!

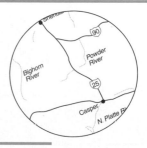

If your instructor has asked you to use the Reading Road Trip CD-ROM, be sure to visit the Graphics and Visual Aids module for multimedia tutorials, exercises, and tests.

CHAPTER 9

Reading Electronic Sources

Why Learn to Read Electronic Sources?

▲ **A computer screen is different from a printed page and needs to be approached differently.**

▲ **An increasing number of college instructors expect their students to use electronic sources.**

▲ **Computers are an important means of communication and source of information in the workplace.**

▲ **Some useful sources of information are available only online.**

Learning Experiment

Step 1

Study the following formula for converting temperature from Celsius (C) to Fahrenheit (F). Then without looking back write it in the space provided on the next page.

$$F = 1.8C + 32$$

Formula: _____

Step 2

Study the following cartoon. What does it say about human and animal communication?

"ALTHOUGH HUMANS MAKE SOUNDS WITH THEIR MOUTHS AND OCCASIONALLY LOOK AT EACH OTHER, THERE IS NO SOLID EVIDENCE THAT THEY ACTUALLY COMMUNICATE WITH EACH OTHER."

©2000 by Sidney Harris.

Step 3

Briefly describe how you studied each of the above tasks. Did you complete them in the same way?

The Results

You probably studied the formula differently than the cartoon. You may have repeated the formula or rewrote it until you remembered it. However, with the cartoon you had to look for a meaning implied by its caption and the drawing.

Learning Principle (What This Means to You)

You study different types of material differently, depending on the nature of the material and on what you are expected to do once you have studied it. In this chapter you will learn to read and study electronic sources differently than you do print sources.

Increasingly, college students are finding the Internet to be a valuable and useful resource. The Internet is a worldwide network of computers through which you can access a wide variety of information and services. Through the Internet, you can access the World Wide Web, a system of Internet servers that allow exchange of information of specially formatted documents. It connects a vast array of resources (documents, graphics, and audio and visual files) and allows users to move between and among them easily and rapidly.

Although in most courses your textbook is still your primary source of information, more and more instructors are expecting their students to use the Internet to supplement their textbook or obtain additional, more current information by visiting Web sites on the Internet. (Textbooks, no matter how up-to-date they may be, often do not contain information from the past year.)

Other instructors encourage or require their students to use CD-ROMs that accompany their textbooks or use the CD-ROMs available in computer labs. Still other instructors expect their students to consult Internet sources in researching a topic for a research paper. Many students, too, are finding valuable information on personal or special interests on the Internet.

For example, Maria Valquez, a student majoring in liberal arts, over the course of a week conducted the following activities using electronic sources.

- Ordered a music CD from Amazon.com, an online book and music store
- Visited an online writing center (http://www.purdue.edu), for help with an English paper
- Searched for Web sites on the topic of tattooing for a sociology research paper
- Used a CD-ROM tutorial to help her solve problems for her math class
- Sent and received e-mail from friends
- Checked the weather in her hometown, in anticipation of a weekend trip
- Visited a Latino student Web site for ideas for organizing a Latino student group on her campus

Electronic sources are becoming increasingly important in many students' academic and personal lives. Therefore, it is important to know how Web sites are structured, how to locate useful sources, how to evaluate the sources you locate, how they differ from print sources, and how to navigate through them in an efficient way.

Although this chapter focuses on using electronic sources, you should realize that the Internet is not always the best source of information. Sometimes it is easier and quicker to find a piece of information in a book or other traditional sources.

THE FEATURES OF A WEB SITE

A Web site is a location on the World Wide Web where you can obtain information on a particular subject. It is a collection of related pages linked together. Each page is called a *Web page* and stands for a set of information. (It can be any length and is not restricted to a single screen or printed page.) The first page you see when you access a Web site is called its *home page*.

Major corporations such as Hertz, Burger King, and General Motors have Web sites, as do many universities, government agencies, nonprofit organizations, and local businesses. Web sites are created for a variety of purposes: to sell products, present information, promote a particular viewpoint, share creative work, and so forth.

Web sites have recently been established by textbook publishers and authors to provide information and activities that supplement the textbook. A Web site for a biology text, for example, may contain reviews of recent research and discoveries not included in the text. A Web site for an English composition textbook may contain additional current readings or up-to-date information on documenting electronic sources or exercises that relate to specific portions of the textbook.

◀ **EXERCISE 1**

DIRECTIONS Visit two of the following Web sites by typing in the Internet addresses listed below. Then answer the questions that follow.

http://www.ucc.vt.edu/stdysk

http://www.usps.gov

http://www.amazon.com

http://www.bbg.org

(If any of the above sites no longer exist, substitute another site.)

1. What is the purpose of each site?
2. In what ways are they similar and in what ways do they differ?

Parts of a Web Site

A Web site begins with a home page which is the first screen (and possibly more) of the site; it serves as the introduction to the site. You can also think of it as a master directory. A sample home page for Career Magazine is shown in Figure 9.1 on page 198. You can move to other pages on the site by using either navigational buttons or links. *Navigational buttons* are graphic icons such as symbols, arrows, pictures, or buttons. They usually appear at the top, bottom, or on one side of each page. Clicking on these buttons allows you to move to different pages within the site. On the sample home page in Figure 9.1, the icon "Win $10,000" is a button, as is the list of items at the left side of the screen. *Links* are highlighted words or phrases within a document that take you to other pages within the site (relative links) or to other Web sites (remote links).

Notice that the Career Magazine home page has numerous links throughout. Because it is easy to get lost when navigating through a site, many sites include buttons on all secondary pages that take the reader back to the home page.

Well-designed Web sites tend to cluster chunks of related information together. The more important information often appears in the top left or right of the screen, since readers of English use a left-to-right eye movement pattern.

Web Site Addresses

Each Web site has its own address, known as its URL (Uniform Resource Locator). Here's how to read a URL for the *San Francisco Chronicle*:

Transfer Format   Host Computer   Directory Path   File Name

http://www.sfgate.com/chronicle/index.shtml

CAREERMagazine

JOB OPENINGS

EMPLOYERS

ARTICLES

RESUME BANK

MESSAGE BOARD

ON CAMPUS

DIVERSITY

Be Your Own Boss

Job Fairs

Recruiter Directory

Consultant Directory

Products & Services

Relocation Resources

Career Links

Advertising Information

Corporate Access

Alliances

Get excited
Click Here!

Browse
Faster

WORKING
WOUNDED

feature of the week

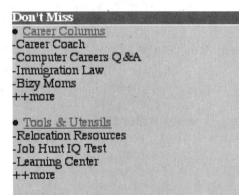

Maternity leave is over and it's time to return to work. Click here for tips on how to blend work with motherhood.

today's hot topics

job search:	15 tips for writing winning resumes.
on the job:	How families influence our career paths.
for employers:	Tips for exploring alternatives to downsizing.
management:	Are you responsible for handling sexual harassment claims?
entrepreneurs:	How to bring fun, focus and fulfillment to every workday.
communication:	Why is "why?" so important?

Don't Miss
- Career Columns
-Career Coach
-Computer Careers Q&A
-Immigration Law
-Bizy Moms
++more

- Tools & Utensils
-Relocation Resources
-Job Hunt IQ Test
-Learning Center
++more

- Today's News

quote of the day
"If you apply reason and logic to this career of mine, you're not going to get very far. You simply won't. The journey has been incredible from its beginning. So much of life, it seems to me, is determined by pure randomness."
- Sidney Poitier

*Need a little laugh to brighten your day? Click here.

Figure 9.1
A Sample Home Page

The *transfer format* identifies the type of server the document is located on and indicates the type of transfer format that is to be used. The second names the host computer. The *directory path* is the "address" part of the Web site. The last is the document name.

Many sites can be contacted using only the transfer format and the host computer address. Then, once you have contacted the site, you can move to different locations and files within the Web site. For example, suppose you are looking for information on an author, and all you know is that she teaches at Tufts University. You could search for the URL of Tufts University and then get to the University home page. Once there you could look under "Faculty" and you might find information about the author.

Anyone can place a Web site on the Internet. Consequently, you must be cautious and verify that the sources are reliable. A Web page may contain a heading, called a header, that serves as a title for the information on that page. It often appears in bigger, bolder type than the rest of the text on the page. These headers can sometimes serve as valuable, concise descriptions of the contents of the page. If they are descriptive, use them to decide whether the page contains the information you need and if it is worth reading.

HOW TO LOCATE ELECTRONIC SOURCES ON THE WEB

Begin by gaining access to the Internet. In addition to a computer you will need a modem and a browser, such as Microsoft Explorer or Netscape Navigator. You will also need an Internet service provider (ISP) to connect your computer to the Internet. Your college's computer center, your telephone or cable company, or a commercial service provider such as America Online can connect you. You will need a name you use online, called a *username,* and a password. If you need help getting started, check with the staff in your college's computer lab.

Identifying Keywords

To search for information on a topic, you need to come up with a group of specific words that describe your topic; these are known as *keywords*. It is often necessary to narrow your topic in order to identify specific keywords. For example, if you searched the topic "home-schooling," you would find thousands of sources. However, if you narrowed your topic to "home-schooling of primary grade children in California," you would identify far fewer sources.

There are three basic groups of search tools you can use to locate information: subject directories, search engines, and meta-search engines.

Using Subject Directories

Subject directories classify Web resources by categories and subcategories. Some offer reviews or evaluations of sites. Use a subject directory when you want to browse the Web using general topics or when you are conducting a broad search.

A subject directory is helpful if you are looking for sites about parenting issues or want to find a list of organizations for animal welfare. Here are several useful directories:

INFOMINE	http://infomine.ucr.edu
Lycos	http://www.lycos.com
Yahoo	http://www.yahoo.com

Using a Search Engine

A search engine is a computer program that helps you locate information on a topic. Search engines search for keywords and provide connections to documents that contain the keywords you instruct it to search for. Depending on your topic, some search engines are more useful than others. In addition, each search engine may require a different way of entering the keywords. For example, some may require you to place quotations marks around a phrase ("capital punishment"); other times you may need to use plus signs between keywords ("home schooling" + "primary grades" + "California"). The quotation marks around "home schooling" will create a search for those words as a phrase, rather than as single terms. Be sure to use the "help" feature when you use a new search engine to discover the best way to enter keywords.

Other useful search engines include:

Alta Vista:	http://altavista.com
Excite:	http://www.excite.com
HotBot:	http://www.hotbot.com
NetSearch:	http://home.netscape.com/home/internet-search.html
Metacrawler:	http://www.metacrawler.com

Most search engines have help sections that include instructions about how to use them.

Using Meta-Search Engines

You can search a number of search engines at the same time and combine all the results in a single listing using a meta-search engine. Use these types of engines when you are searching for a very specific or obscure topic or one for which you are having trouble finding information. Here are two common ones:

DogPile	http://dogpile.com
PROFUsion	http://profusion.com

EXERCISE 2

DIRECTIONS Use one of the search tools listed above to locate three sources on one of the following topics. Then use a different search engine or subject directory to search the same topic again. Compare your results. Which search tool was easier to use? Which yielded more sources?

1. The Baseball Hall of Fame
2. Telecommuting
3. Your favorite musical group
4. Parenting issues

HOW TO EVALUATE INTERNET SOURCES

Although the Internet contains a great deal of valuable information and resources, it also contains rumor, gossip, hoaxes, and misinformation. In other words, not all Internet sources are trustworthy. You must evaluate a source before accepting it. Here are some guidelines to follow when evaluating Internet sources.

1. *Check the publisher or sponsor of the site.* If a site is sponsored or provided by a well-known organization, a reputable newspaper such as the *New York Times* for example, the information is apt to be reliable. One way to discover the sponsoring organization is to check the URL. The last part of a URL, called the domain, reveals something about the nature of a Web site's sponsor. Here is a list of common domains and their abbreviation as used in a URL:

Commercial	.com	(Internet providers, AOL, for example; companies, or anyone trying to sell something)
Education	.edu	(public schools, colleges, universities, students' home pages, term papers)*
Government	.gov	(state, federal agencies)
Network	.net	
Nonprofit organization	.org	(nonprofit groups)
Military	.mil	
Other countries	.ca	(Canada)
	.uk	(United Kingdom)

2. *Check the author.* For Web sites, look for professional credentials or affiliations. Often the author's professional affiliation will be included at the end of an article he or she has written. Usually, you can trust a reputable sponsor to feature only credible authors. To find out about an author through an Internet search, use a search engine. Type the author's full name in the search box. Place the full name in quotation marks, or choose phrase searching if it is available.

   For newsgroups or discussion groups (see p. 210), check to see if the author has given his or her name and a signature (a short biographical description included at the end of messages).
3. *Check the date of the posting.* Be sure you are obtaining current information. A credible Web site usually includes the date on which it was last updated.
4. *Discover the purpose of the posting.* Many Web sites are written with an agenda, such as to sell a product, promote a cause, advocate a position, and so forth. Look for bias in the reporting of information.

---

*The .edu abbreviation used to be a good indicator of a higher education academic site, but that is no longer the case. Be sure to check the source.

5. *Check links (addresses of other sources suggested by the Web site).* If these links are no longer working, the Web site you are visiting may be outdated or not reputable.

6. *Cross-check your information.* If you have doubts about the accuracy of information you have found, try to find the same information in another source.

Exercise 3

DIRECTIONS   Evaluate each of the sites you located for Exercise 2. Assign a rating of 1–5 (1 = low reliability; 5 = high reliability). Be prepared to discuss your ratings.

Exercise 4

DIRECTIONS   Visit a Web site and become familiar with its organization and content. Evaluate it using the suggested criteria. Then write a brief paragraph explaining why the Web site is or is not a reliable source.

WHY ELECTRONIC TEXT REQUIRES NEW READING STRATEGIES

Reading electronic text (also called hypertext) is very different from reading traditional printed text such as textbooks or magazines or newspaper articles. The term electronic text, as used in this chapter, refers to information presented on a Web site. It does not refer to articles and essays that can be downloaded from Searchbank or from an e-journal, for example. Because Web sites are unique, they require a different mind-set and different reading strategies. If electronic text is new or unfamiliar to you, you need to change the way you read and the way you think when approaching Web sites. If you attempt to read Web sites the same way you read traditional text, you may lose focus or perspective, miss important information, or become generally disoriented. Text used on Web sites, often called hypertext, is different in the following ways from traditional print text.

- **Reading Web sites involves paying attention to sound, graphics, and movement, as well as words.** Your senses, then, may pull you in several different directions simultaneously. Recorded or artificial sounds may compete with animated sequences, flashing graphics, and colorful drawings or photos for your attention. Some Web sites are available in two formats—graphical and text-only. This is most common for academic sites. If you are distracted by the sound and graphics, check to see if a text-only version of the site is available.

- **Text on Web sites comes in brief, independent screenfuls, sometimes called nodes.** These screenfuls tend to be brief, condensed pieces of information. Unlike traditional text, they are not set within a context, and background information is often not supplied. They do not depend on other pages for meaning either. In traditional print text, paragraphs and pages are dependent—you often must have read and understood a previous one in order to comprehend the one that follows it. Electronic pages are often intended to stand alone.

- **Text on Web sites may not follow the traditional main idea, supporting details organization of traditional paragraphs.** Instead, the screen may appear as a group of topic sentences without detail.

- **Web sites are multidirectional and unique; traditional text progresses in a single direction.** When reading traditional text a reader usually follows a single direction, working through the text from beginning to end as written by the author. Web site text is multidirectional; each electronic reader creates his or her own unique text, by following or ignoring different paths. Two readers of the same Web site may read entirely different material, or the same material in a different order. For example, one user of the Career Magazine Web site in Figure 9.1 might begin by reading the feature of the week; another user might start by taking the survey; a third might begin by clicking on the Job Fairs link.

- **Web site text requires readers to make decisions.** Because screens have menus and links, electronic readers must always make choices. They can focus on one aspect of the topic and ignore all others, for example, by following a path of links. Readers of print text, however, have far fewer choices to make.

- **Web sites allow readers the flexibility to choose the order in which to receive the information.** Partly due to learning style, people prefer to acquire information in different sequences. Some may prefer to begin with details and then, from the details, come to understand underlying rules or principles. Others may prefer to begin in the opposite way. Electronic sources allow readers to approach the text in any manner compatible with their learning style. A pragmatic learner may prefer to move through a site systematically, either clicking or ignoring links as they appear on the screen from top to bottom, for example.

- **Web sites use new symbol systems.** Electronic texts introduce new and sometimes unfamiliar symbols. A flashing or blinking light may suggest a new feature on the site or an underlined word or a word in a different color may suggest a link. Sound effects, too, may have meanings. For example, on a children's Web site a child can have a book read aloud. The auditory signal may indicate when to turn the page. Icons and drawings may be used in place of words. A drawing of a book, for example, may indicate that print sources are available.

 **EXERCISE 5**

DIRECTIONS   Visit one of the Web sites suggested for one of the World Wide Web activities in Part Seven of this book (p. 383, p. 392, p. 405, p. 411, p. 418) or locate a different Web site on one of the topics. Write a list of characteristics that distinguish it from the print articles in Part Seven on the same topic.

Changing Your Reading Strategies for Reading Electronic Text

Reading electronic text is relatively new to the current generation of college students. (This will no doubt change with the upcoming generations who, as children, will learn to read both print and electronic text.) Most current college students and teachers first learned to read using print text. We have read print text for many more years than electronic text; consequently, our brains have developed numerous strategies or "work orders" for reading traditional texts. Our work orders, however, are less fully developed for electronic text. Electronic texts have a wider variety of formats and more variables to cope with than traditional texts. A textbook page is usually made up of headings, paragraphs, and an occasional photo or graphic. Web sites have vibrant color, animation, sound, and music as well as words.

Reading is not only different, but it also tends to be slower on the computer screen than on print sources. One expert estimates reading a screen is 25 percent slower than reading paper. In a book your eyes can see the layout of two full pages. From the two pages you can see headings, division of ideas, and subtopics. By glancing at a print page, you get an initial assessment of what it contains. You can tell, for example, if a page is heavily statistical (your eye will see numbers, dates, symbols) or is anecdotal (your eye will see capitalized proper names, quotation marks, and numerous indented paragraphs for dialogue, for example). Because you have a sense of what the page contains and how it is organized, you can read somewhat faster. Because a screen holds fewer words, you get far less feedback before you begin to read.

DEVELOPING NEW WAYS OF THINKING AND READING

Reading electronic sources demands a different type of thinking than print sources. A print source is linear—it goes in a straight line from idea to idea. Electronic sources, due to the presence of links, tend to be multidirectional; you can follow numerous paths.

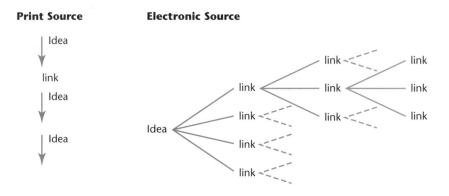

Reading electronic text also requires new strategies. The first steps to reading electronic text easily and effectively are to understand how it is different (see previous section) and realize that you must change and adapt how you read. Some specific suggestions follow.

Focus on Your Purpose

Focus clearly on your purposes for visiting the site. What information do you need? Because you must create your own path through the site, unless you fix in mind what you are looking for, you may wander aimlessly, wasting valuable time, or even become lost, following numerous links that lead you farther and farther away from the site at which you began.

Get Used to the Site's Design and Layout

Each Web site has unique features and arranges information differently.

1. *When you reach a new site, spend a few minutes getting used to it and discovering how it is organized.* Scroll through it quickly to determine how it is organized and what information is available. Ask yourself the following questions.
   - What information is available?
   - How is it arranged on the screen?

2. *Expect the first screen to grab your attention and make a main point.* (Web site authors know that many people [up to 90 percent] who read a Web page do not scroll down to see the next page.)

3. *Get used to the colors, flashing images, and sounds before you attempt to obtain information from the site.* Your eye may have a tendency to focus on color or movement, rather than on print. Because Web sites are highly visual, they require visual as well as verbal thinking. The author intends you to respond to photos, graphics, and animation.

4. Consider both the focus and limitations of your learning style. Are you a spatial learner? If so, you may have a tendency to focus too heavily on the graphic elements of the screen. If, on the other hand, you are a verbal learner, you may ignore important visual elements or signals. If you focus *only* on the words and ignore color and graphics on a particular screen, you will probably miss information or may not move through the site in the most efficient way. Review your learning style (p. 39) and consider both your strengths and limitations as they apply to electronic text.

DIRECTIONS   In groups of two or three students, consider one aspect of learning style. For each, discuss the tendencies, limitations, and implications this particular learning style may have for reading electronic text. How would a pragmatic learner approach a Web site? How might it differ from how a creative learner might approach it?

Exercise 7

DIRECTIONS   Locate two Web sites that you think are interesting and appealing. Then answer the following questions.

1. How does each use color?
2. How does each use graphics?
3. Is sound or motion used? If so, how?

Pay Attention to How Information Is Organized

Because you can navigate through a Web site in many different ways, it is important to have the right expectations and to make several decisions before you begin.

Some Web sites are much better organized than others. Some have clear headings and labels that make it easy to discover how to proceed; others do not and will require more thought before beginning. For example, when you are reading an article with ten to fifteen underlined words (links), there is no prescribed order to follow and these links are not categorized in any way. Figure 9.2 on the next page shows an excerpt from a Web site titled "Gender and Society" sponsored by Trinity University. Notice that is has numerous links built into paragraphs. Use the following suggestions to grasp a site's organization.

1. *Use the site map, if provided, to discover what information is available and how it is organized.* A sample site map for Virginia Tech is shown in Figure 9.3 on page 207. Notice that the links are categorized according to who might use the information (students, faculty, visitors, etc.).

2. *Consider the order in which you want to take in information.* Choose an order in which to explore links; avoid randomly clicking on link buttons. Doing so is somewhat like randomly choosing pages to read out of a reference book.

GENDER AND SOCIETY

The desire of a man for a woman is not directed at her because she is a human being, but because she is a woman. That she is a human being is of no concern to him.

--Immanuel Kant

In addition to age, gender is one of the universal dimensions on which status differences are based. Unlike sex, which is a biological concept, gender is a social construct specifying the socially and culturally pre-scribed roles that men and women are to follow. According to Gerda Lerner in *The Creation of Patriarchy,* gender is the "costume, a mask, a straitjacket in which men and women dance their unequal dance" (p. 238). As Alan Wolfe observed in "The Gender Question" (*The New Republic,* June 6:27–34), "of all the ways that one group has systemati-cally mistreated another, none is more deeply rooted than the way men have subordinated women. All other discriminations pale by contrast." Lerner argues that the subordination of women preceded all other sub-ordinations and that to rid ourselves of all of those other "isms"— racism, classism, ageism, etc.—it is sexism that must first be eradicated.

Women have always had lower status than men, but the extent of the gap between the sexes varies across cultures and time (some arguing that it is inversely related to social evolution). In 1980, the United Nations summed up the burden of this inequality: Women, who com-prise half the world's population, do two thirds of the world's work, earn one tenth of the world's income and own one hundredth of the world's property. In Leviticus, God told Moses that a man is worth 50 sheikels and a woman worth 30—approximately the contemporary salary differentials of the sexes in the United States. What might be the socio-cultural implications if men were to also be the child bearers? Follow the first human male pregnancy at www.malepreg-nancy.com.

And the significance of the stamps above? A recent U.S. Postal Service publication, "Women on Stamps," holds some interesting methodological possibilities. Putting a deceased individual's likeness on a stamp is one way by which political immortality is conferred. Of the hundreds of Americans so immortalized only a handful are women: 16, to be precise, through 1960; 19 through 1970; and 29 through 1980 (any connection between this 50% increase with the ERA movement of the seventies?). An enterprising student may wish to investigate and compare how this female proportion of immor-talized citizens varies across countries and time.

Matters of gender are scattered throughout these pages, including gender differences in household duties, in in voting during the 1996 Presidential election, and in suicide rates cross-nationally. Take advantage of this site's search engine by first entering "gender" and next "sex" as the search words.

Figure 9.2
Sample Web Site with Links

Quick VT Search [   ] **Locator & Directories Page**

SITEMAP

Students	Faculty/Staff	Alumni/Friends	Prospective Students	Visitors	Info Center
Academics	Administrative Services	Alumni Association	Admissions	About Virginia Tech	About Virginia Tech
Money Matters	Intranet	VT Magazine	Graduate Admissions	Campus Guide	Sites of Interest
Rules/Regs	Academics	VT NetLetter	Veterinary Medicine	Accommodations	News
Services	Employment	Development	Academics	Resources	University Facts
Extracurricular	Forms	Career Services	Money Matters	Academics	Electronic Publications
Housing/Dining	Governance	Sports	Housing/Dining	University Administration	Research and Outreach
New Students	University News	VT Snapshots	Campus Guide	Career Services	Library
Sports	Electronic publications	VT Picture Postcards	Sports	VT Snapshots	Resources
Computing	University Administration			VT Picture Postcards	
Libraries	Provost News			Local Weather	
	Libraries			Employment	
	Computing			Alternative Access Methods	

Figure 9.3
A Sample Site Map

Do you need definitions first? Do you want historical background first? Your decision will be partly influenced by your learning style.

3. *Consider writing brief notes to yourself as you explore a complicated Web site.* Alternatively, you could print the home page and jot notes on it.

4. *Expect shorter, less detailed sentences and paragraphs.* Much online communication tends to be briefer and more concise than in traditional sources. As a result, you may have to mentally fill in transitions and make inferences about relationships among ideas. For example, you may have to infer similarities and differences or recognize cause and effect connections.

EXERCISE 8   ▌ **DIRECTIONS**   Visit two Web sites on the same topic. Write a few sentences comparing and contrasting their organization and design.

Use Links to Find the Information You Need

Links are unique to electronic text. Following are some suggestions for how best to use them.

1. *Plan on exploring links to find complete and detailed information.* Links, both remote links (those that take you to another site) and related links within a site are intended to provide more detailed information on topics introduced on the home page.
2. *As you follow links, be sure to bookmark your original site and other useful sites you come across so you can find them again.* Bookmarking is a feature on your Internet browser that allows you to record Web site addresses and access them later by simply clicking on the site name. Different search engines use different terms for this function. Netscape uses the term, *Bookmarks,* Microsoft Explorer calls it *Favorites.* In addition, Netscape has a "GO" feature that allows a user to retrace the steps of the current search.
3. *If you use a site or a link that provides many pages of continuous paragraphs, print the material and read it offline.*
4. *If you find you are lacking background on a topic, use links to help fill in the gap or search for a different Web site on the same topic that is less technical.*
5. *If you get lost, most Internet browsers have a history feature. It allows you to back-track or retrace the links your followed in a search.* On Netscape, for example, click on "Back," it will take you back one link at a time; "History" keeps track of all searches over a given period and allows you to go directly to a chosen site, rather than backtracking step by step.

EXERCISE 9

DIRECTIONS   For one of the Web sites you visited earlier in the chapter or a new site of your choice, follow at least three links and then answer the following questions.

1. What type of information did each contain?
2. Was each source reliable? How do you know?
3. Which was the easiest to read and follow? Why?

ELECTRONIC LEARNING AIDS

In addition to the Web sites on the Internet, you may use many other electronic sources and services as well: CD-ROMs, computer tutorial software, e-mail, list-servs, and newsgroups. Each of the following are described below along with suggestions for how to use them.

CD-ROMs that Accompany Textbooks

A CD-ROM may be included with a textbook when you purchase it or it may be available in your college's academic computer labs. For example, the *Reading Road Trip* multimedia reading and study skills CD-ROM is available with this textbook. (Not all textbooks have CD-ROM accompaniments.) CD-ROMs contain a wealth of information, activities, and learning resources. Here is an example of what a CD-ROM that accompanies a psychology text contains:

- Review of key topics
- A "click here" function for more information on terms, concepts, etc.
- Demonstrations and experiments

- Matching games and other learning activities
- Review quizzes
- Glossary of key terms
- Student notepad (for recording your own ideas)
- Reference sources

The best part of CD-ROMs is that they are interactive and engaging. The sound, dialogue, and visuals hold your interest and are well suited to the auditory, spatial, or pragmatic learner. They also allow you to choose what and how you want to learn. If you need to review a topic such as learning theory, you click on an icon and are guided through a learning sequence. You can access more information if you need it. When you have finished, you can choose or not choose to take a review quiz to assess what you have learned. Additionally, many of the activities are interactive—you get involved with the material by responding to rather than merely reading it.

Here are a few guidelines for using CD-ROMs that accompany textbooks:

1. *Try whatever is available.* Even if you have never used a computer before, if software is available, try it out. College computer labs are usually staffed with friendly, helpful people (sometimes other students) who can show you how to get started.
2. *Use them with, but not in place of, your text.* CD-ROMs are supplements. Although they are fun to use, you must still read your textbook.
3. *Use the CD-ROM as a chapter preview.* View the CD-ROM on a particular topic to get an overview of it before reading the corresponding text material.
4. *Use the CD-ROM for review and practice.* After you have read the text, use the CD-ROM to help you learn the material.
5. *Use the quiz or self-test modules when studying for an exam.* Use the quizzes to discover which topics you need to study further. Keep a record of your progress. Many programs will do this for you and allow you to print a progress report. This record will enable you to see your strengths and weaknesses, plan further study, and review troublesome topics.
6. *If the CD-ROM has a notepad (a place where you can write your own notes), use it.* You will learn more efficiently if you express what you have learned in your own words.
7. *Space out your practice.* Because many software programs are fun and engaging, some students work on them for hours at a time. To get maximum benefit from the time you are spending, limit your work to an hour or so. Beyond that, many activities become routine; your mind switches to "automatic pilot," and learning ceases to occur.
8. *Consolidate your learning.* When you finish a module or program segment, do not just exit and shut off the machine. Stop and reflect on what you have learned. If you worked on an algebra module about the multiplication of polynomials, stop and recall the techniques you learned. Write notes or summarize the process in a separate section of your course notebook reserved for this purpose.

E-mail

E-mail (electronic mail) enables you to send messages to another person or place using your computer. A variety of computer programs are available that allow you to send and receive messages electronically, as well as to print them for future reference. There are many academic uses for e-mail. Students in a class may collaborate on a project or critique each others' papers using e-mail. Other times, instructors and students communicate through e-mail. In completing a research paper, it is possible to contact professors or other students doing research on the topic you are studying. It is also possible to transmit word processing files by attaching them to an e-mail message.

Most e-mail follows a consistent format and, consequently, is easy to read. Messages begin with a memo format in which the topic of the message, date the message was sent, sender, and receiver are identified as "Subject" or "Re," "Date," "From," and "To." The message follows this introductory identifying information. Transmittal information that tracks the electronic path through which the message was sent may accompany the message. This information, if it appears, can be ignored unless you wish to verify the source of the sender.

The style of e-mail messages tends to be more casual and conversational than the traditional print forms of communication (letters and memos) but more formal than phone or in-person conversations. Because e-mail is intended to be a rapid, expedient means of communication, some formalities of written communication are relaxed. Expect to find a briefer introduction, more concise sentences, and few or no concluding remarks. Consequently, e-mail requires close attention; unlike print forms of communication, there is little repetition and fewer cues as to what is important.

Reading lengthy e-mail messages may be easier if you print them first. Figure 9.4 shows a sample e-mail message. Notice that the message is a concise yet effective form of communication.

Newsgroups

Newsgroups are collections of people interested in a particular topic or issue who correspond to discuss it. Participants post messages on a given topic; other participants read and respond. Read postings with a critical mind-set. Most postings are written by average people expressing their opinions; their ideas may be informative, but they may also contain incorrect information, bias, and unsubstantiated opinion. At times, you also may find postings that are mindless ranting and raving. Here are some tips for reading newsgroup postings:

- Separate fact from opinion (see Chapter 10, p. 221). Take into account the bias, motivation, and prejudices of the author.
- Verify any information you get from a newsgroup with a second source.
- Use newsgroups to explore the range of opinion on a topic or issue.

Usually newsgroups are open forums; anyone can lurk or "listen in" to the discussion. Newsgroups can yield additional sources of information, as well as a variety of interesting perspectives on a topic. A specialized form of newsgroup is known as a listserv. Participation is limited to those who have subscribed. Academic discussion groups are considered listservs. Directories are available to help you locate useful newsgroups and listservs. These include:

Directory of professional and scholarly e-conferences
http://www.n2h2.com/KOVACS/

E-mail discussion lists
http://alabanza.com/kabacoff/Inter-Links/listserv.html

Usenet news groups
http://www.liszt.com/news/

```
Subj:        Research on learning styles
Date:        98-02-23  11:49:34  EST
From:        Maryrod@daemon.edu (Mary Rodriguez)
Reply to:    Maryrod@daemon.edu
To:          KateAppP@daemon.edu
-----------------------------------------------------

Dear Kate,
In response to your request for recent research
on the learning styles of university versus
community college students, I do know of one
article that may be useful as a starting point:

Henson, Mark, and Schemeck, R.R. "Learning
Styles of Community College Versus University
Students," Perceptual Motor Skills, 76 (1), 118.

Good luck on your research project.

Mary
```

Figure 9.4
A Sample E-mail Message

EXERCISE 10   **DIRECTIONS**   Visit a newsgroup and either lurk or participate in the discussion. Then answer the following questions.

1. What was the topic of discussion?
2. Were the postings largely fact or opinion?
3. Did you detect bias or prejudice?
4. How useful is the newsgroup as a source of information?

LEARNING *Collaboratively*

DIRECTIONS   Working with another student, select a topic of mutual interest. Discuss it, narrow it down, and write two or three specific research questions. Working independently, use the Internet to locate answers to your research questions. When you have finished, compare your answers and the sources from which you obtained them.

Applying YOUR LEARNING

Robert has been assigned to write a paper on a contemporary issue. He chooses the topic of gun control. He uses a search engine, finds the Web site of the National Rifle Association, and bases his paper on the information he finds there.

1. Discuss what is wrong with Robert's research strategy.
2. Offer suggestions for what he could do to improve his paper.

SELF-TEST SUMMARY

1. What are the key parts of a Web site?	A Web site includes a home page and links to other sites within the site and/or outside the Web site.
2. How do you locate sources on the World Wide Web?	To locate sources, identify keywords and use a search engine.
3. How can I evaluate a Web site?	Check the publisher or sponsor, author, date of posting, and links. Also, discover the purpose of the site. Cross-check any suspicious information.
4. In what ways are Web sites different from print text?	Web sites involve graphics, sound, color, and animation. Language tends to be brief; screens are independent. Due to the use of links, Web sites are multidirectional. They require decision making and permit flexibility.
5. How should I read an electronic text?	Identify the purpose of the source or site. Familiarize yourself with the site's design and layout. Pay attention to how information is organized, and use links to find the information you need.
6. What other electronic learning aids are available?	CD-ROMs accompany many textbooks and are valuable learning aids. E-mail is useful to communicate with classmates and professors. Newsgroups provide a variety of perspectives on a topic.

Take a Road Trip!

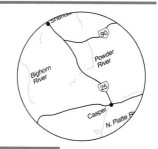

If your instructor has asked you to use the Reading Road Trip CD-ROM, be sure to use the CD throughout the course for multimedia tutorials, exercises, and tests.

10

Critical Thinking and Reading

thinking outside of your usually of Heink

A analizing

Why Learn to Read and Think Critically?

▲ **You will understand your reading assignments more fully if you become a critical thinker. Textbook reading requires critical thinking.**

▲ **You will become more successful at taking tests if you read and think critically. Taking tests requires critical thinking.**

▲ **You will write more effective papers if you apply critical thinking skills.**

Learning Experiment

Step 1

Read the following paragraph on school voucher systems and highlight important ideas.

> In the late 1960s, a new idea began to receive considerable publicity. It was vintage USA: If there were more competition among schools, perhaps schools would be better. After all, people were entitled to more freedom in choosing where their children would be educated. This idea inspired proposals for voucher plans. Public schools have a virtual monopoly on public funds for education, and children attend schools depending, for the most part, on where they live. A voucher plan can change this situation. In a sense, parents, not schools, receive public money. They receive it in the form of a *voucher,* which they use to pay for their children's attendance at the schools of their choice. The schools receive money from the government in return for the vouchers. The greater the number of parents who choose a particular school, the more money it receives. The idea is to force the public schools to compete with each other, and with private and parochial schools, for "customers." Presumably, good schools would attract plenty of students, and poor schools would be forced either to improve or close.

—Thio, *Sociology,* pp. 376–377

Step 2

Read the following paragraph on home schooling and then answer the questions that follow, either alone, as part of a classroom discussion group, or with a friend or classmate.

> There has been phenomenal growth in the number of children who receive their formal education at home. In the late 1970s there were only about 12,500 such children, but today the number has soared to more than 500,000 and is still increasing rapidly. Before 1994, most of the home schooling parents were fundamentalist Christians who believed that religion was either abused or ignored in the public school. But today two thirds of the families reject public education for secular reasons: poor teaching, crowded classrooms, or lack of safety. Many of the older children, though, enroll in public schools part time, for a math class or a chemistry lab, or for after-school activities such as football or volleyball. Most home-schooling parents have some college education, with median incomes between $35,000 and $50,000. Over 90 percent are white.
>
> —Thio, *Sociology*, p. 377

1. What are the advantages and disadvantages of home schooling for the child?
2. What credentials should parents be required to demonstrate in order to teach their own children?
3. Do you think a home-schooled child would learn as much or more than a traditionally schooled child? Why?

Step 3

On which topic—voucher systems or home schooling—do you feel you would be better prepared to write a paper, make a speech, or lead a discussion group?

The Results

You most likely feel better prepared to work with the topic of home schooling. Why? Probably because the discussion questions that you answered after reading provoked your thinking and opened up your mind to new ideas. By discussing the topic of home schooling, you used the principle of elaboration.

Learning Principle (What This Means to You)

Elaborating, or thinking about and reacting to what you read, helps you to remember more of what you read and prepares you to write about and discuss the ideas. This chapter will show you how to improve your critical reading skills by reacting to and analyzing what you read. You will learn to make inferences, ask critical questions, and analyze arguments effectively. You will learn to handle exam questions, class discussions, and written assignments that demand critical reading and thinking more effectively.

MAKING INFERENCES

The photograph shown above was taken from a sociology textbook. What do you think is happening? Where is it happening? How do the participants feel toward one another?

To answer these questions, you used what you saw in the photo to make reasonable guesses. The process you went through is called making an inference. An *inference* is a reasoned guess about what you don't know based on what you do know. We all make inferences throughout our daily lives. If a friend is late, you may predict that she was delayed in traffic, especially if you know she often is so delayed. If you see a seated man frequently checking his watch, you can infer that he is waiting for someone who is late.

As you read, you also need to make inferences frequently. Authors do not always directly state exactly what they mean. Instead, they may only hint at or suggest an idea. You have to reason out or infer the meaning an author intends (but did not say) on the basis of what he or she did say. For instance, suppose a writer describes a character as follows.

> As Agatha studied Agnes, she noticed that her eyes appeared misty, her lips trembled slightly, and a twisted handkerchief lay in her lap.

From the information the author provides, you may infer that Agnes is upset and on the verge of tears. Yet the writer does not say any of this. Instead, the author implies her meaning through the description she provides.

How to Make Inferences

There are no specific steps to follow in making inferences. Each inference depends on the situation and the facts provided as well as on your knowledge and experience with the situation. Following are a few general guidelines for making inferences.

1. *Be sure you understand the literal meaning first.* You need knowledge and comprehension of the stated ideas and facts before you can move to higher levels of thinking, of which making inferences is a part. For each paragraph, then, you should identify the topic, main idea, supporting details, and organizational pattern.

2. *Ask yourself a question.* Ask yourself questions such as:
   • What is the author trying to suggest through the stated information?
   • What do all the facts and ideas point toward or seem to add up to?
   • For what purpose did the author include these facts and details?

   To answer these questions, you must add together the individual pieces of information to arrive at an inference. Making an inference is somewhat like putting together a complicated picture puzzle, in which you try to make each piece fit with all the rest of the pieces to form something recognizable.

3. *Use clues provided by the writer.* A writer often provides numerous hints that point you toward accurate inferences. For instance, a writer's choice of words often suggests his or her attitude toward a subject. Try to notice descriptive words, emotionally charged words, and words with strong positive or negative connotations. Here is an example of how the choice of words can lead you to an inference:

   Grandmother had been an <u>unusually attractive</u> young woman, and she carried herself with the <u>graceful confidence</u> of a natural charmer to her last day.

   The underlined phrases *unusually attractive, graceful confidence,* and *natural charmer* suggest that the writer feels positive about her grandmother. However, in the following example, notice how the underlined words and phrases create a negative image of the person.

   The <u>withdrawn</u> child <u>eyed</u> her teacher with a hostile disdain. When directly spoken to, the child responded in a <u>cold</u> but carefully respectful way.

   In this sentence, the underlined words suggest that the child is unfriendly and that he or she dislikes the teacher.

4. *Consider the author's purpose.* An awareness of the author's purpose is often helpful in making inferences. If an author's purpose is to convince you to purchase a particular product, as in an advertisement, you already have a clear idea of the types of inferences the writer hopes you will make as you begin reading. For instance, here is a magazine ad for a stereo system:

   If you're in the market for true surround sound, a prematched system is a good way to get it. The components in our system are built for each other by our audio engineers. You can be assured of high performance and sound quality.

   It is clear that the writer's purpose is to encourage you to buy a prematched stereo system.

5. *Verify your inference.* Once you have made an inference, be sure to check that it is accurate. Look back at the stated facts to be sure you have sufficient evidence to support the inference. Also, be sure you have not overlooked other equally plausible or more plausible inferences that could be drawn from the same set of facts.

EXERCISE 1

DIRECTIONS   Read the following passages and then answer the questions. The answers are not directly stated in the passage; you will have to make inferences in order to answer the questions.

Passage A

The Lion's Share

The lion, the jackal, the wolf, and the hyena had a meeting and agreed that they would hunt together in one party and share equally among them whatever game they caught.

They went out and killed an antelope. The four animals then discussed which one of them would divide the meat. The lion said, "Whoever divides the meat must know how to count."

Immediately the wolf volunteered, saying, "Indeed, I know how to count."

He began to divide the meat. He cut off four pieces of equal size and placed one before each of the hunters.

The lion was angered. He said, "Is this the way to count?" And he struck the wolf across the eyes, so that his eyes swelled up and he could not see.

The jackal said, "The wolf does not know how to count. I will divide the meat."

He cut three portions that were small and a fourth portion that was very large. The three small portions he placed before the hyena, the wolf, and himself. The large portion he put in front of the lion, who took his meat and went away.

"Why was it necessary to give the lion such a large piece?" the hyena said. "Our agreement was to divide and share equally. Where did you ever learn how to divide?"

"I learned from the wolf," the jackal answered.

"Wolf? How can anyone learn from the wolf? He is stupid," the hyena said.

"The jackal was right," the wolf said. "He knows how to count. Before, when my eyes were open, I did not see it. Now, though my eyes are wounded, I see it clearly."

—Dresser, *The Rainmaker's Dog,* pp. 110–111

1. What did the jackal learn from the wolf?
2. Although "The Lion's Share" is a folktale, it does make a point. Summarize the message this story offers.

Passage B

What's Best for the Child

In many states, there are no regulations governing the number of infants a staff member may care for. In those where there are, many states allow five or six. In Wisconsin, where I live, the maximum is four infants per worker. [According to the National Association for the Education of Young Children, 29 states require this four-to-one ratio, while only three—Kansas, Maryland, and Massachusetts—require a three-to-one ratio. Most of the remaining states have five-to-one or six-to-one ratios.]

Consider the amount of physical care and attention a baby needs—say 20 minutes for feeding every three hours or so, and 10 minutes for diapering every two hours or so, and time for the care giver to wash her hands thoroughly and sanitize the area after changing each baby. In an eight-and-a-half-hour day, then, a care giver working under the typical four-to-one ratio will have 16 diapers to change and 12 feedings to give. Four diaper changes and three feedings apiece is not an inordinate amount of care over a long day from the babies' point of view.

But think about the care giver's day: Four hours to feed the babies, two hours and 40 minutes to change them. If you allow an extra two and a half minutes at each changing to put them down, clean up the area, and thoroughly wash your hands, you can get by with 40 minutes for sanitizing. (And if you think about thoroughly washing your hands 16 times a day, you may begin to understand why epidemics of diarrhea and related diseases regularly sweep through infant-care centers.)

That makes seven hours and 20 minutes of the day spent just on physical care—if you're lucky and the infants stay conveniently on schedule.

Since feeding and diaper changing are necessarily one-on-one activities, each infant is bound to be largely unattended during the five-plus hours that the other three babies are being attended to. So, if there's to be any stimulation at all for the child, the care giver had better chat and play up a storm while she's feeding and changing.

Obviously, such a schedule is not realistic. In group infant care based on even this four-to-one ratio, babies will not be changed every two hours and they will probably not be held while they're fed.

They also will not get the kind of attention and talk that is the foundation of language development. If a child is deprived of language stimulation for eight to ten hours a day, how much compensation—how much "quality time"—can concerned parents provide in the baby's few other waking hours at home?

—Conniff, *The Progressive*

1. What is the author's attitude about infant care in a typical day care program?
2. What is the author implying when in the third paragraph she says ". . . if you think about thoroughly washing your hands 16 times a day, you may begin to understand why epidemics of diarrhea and related diseases regularly sweep through infant-care centers"?
3. In paragraph 7, what is the author's purpose in using the word *compensation* in referring to the parents' time with their babies at home?
4. Do you think the author would favor laws that mandate infant–worker ratios? Why?

Passage C

Stiff Laws Nab Deadbeats

The sight of deadbeat dad king Jeffrey Nichols nabbed, cuffed and jailed in New York for ducking $580,000 in child support ought to shake up other scofflaws.

A few years ago, Nichols almost surely would have escaped his responsibilities. His wealth enabled him to run to Toronto, Boca Raton, Fla., and Charlotte, Vt., and he got away with it for five years. He defied three states' court orders to pay up.

He was finally caught because in the past few years local, state and federal governments have finally gotten serious about child support.

A law Congress passed in 1992 required the FBI to chase child-support cheats when they cross state lines. Nichols became a target, culminating in his arrest.

As the scale of such enforcement has grown, it has prompted occasional criticism—particularly about use of Internal Revenue Service records to track down deadbeats. But there's no doubt it's needed.

There are 7 million deadbeat parents, 90% of them dads. If all paid what they are supposed to, their children would have $34 billion more—money that sometimes has to come from the taxpayers instead.

—McMiller, *USA Today*

1. In paragraph 1, the author states that the sight of Nichols jailed "ought to shake up other scofflaws." What is the author implying?
2. Why do you think Nichols became a target of the FBI?
3. Why would the use of Internal Revenue Service records to track down deadbeats receive criticism?
4. Why do you think 90 percent of deadbeat parents are dads?
5. In what way(s) is money taken from the taxpayers when deadbeat parents do not meet their payments?

ASKING QUESTIONS: THE KEY TO CRITICAL THINKING

One morning a sociology instructor opened her class with the question "What was your reaction to the reading assignment on public education reform?" No one responded. Everyone seemed surprised by the question. Although most students had *read* the assignment, no one felt prepared *to react* to it or say what they really thought of it. The students were prepared to respond at the knowledge and comprehension levels of thinking but had not stretched their thinking to the higher levels of analysis, synthesis, and evaluation (see p. 46).

The instructor expressed her disappointment; then she began asking students questions that encouraged them to react. For example, she asked, "Did the author succeed in proving his point? Why or why not? What kinds of evidence did he provide? What inferences can be made about educational reforms? What additional information do you need?" Each day the instructor began the class by asking students to ask questions about their reading. Eventually, everyone in the class was participating in lively discussions about the reading assignment. The students had learned to analyze, interpret, and evaluate their assignments. They were reading and thinking critically. The key to developing a critical mind-set, then, is to ask questions that focus your attention on higher levels of thinking—analysis, synthesis, and evaluation.

1. What is the source of the material?
2. What are the author's qualifications?
3. Is the material fact or opinion?
4. What is the author's purpose?
5. Is the author biased?
6. What is the tone?

What Is the Source of the Material?

Textbook information can usually be accepted as reliable and well researched. Not all other sources, however, are as worthy of your trust. Not all authors and publishers apply equally high standards of research and verification of information. Not all sources are equal in their levels of detail and technical accuracy, which depend in part on their intended audience. Consequently, checking the source can help you evaluate the accuracy and completeness of the information it contains. Suppose you were doing a research paper on the economic advantages of waste recycling. You found that each of the following sources contained information on recycling. Which do you predict would contain the type of information that would be most useful in writing a term paper?

- An article in *Reader's Digest* titled "Stiffer Laws for Waste Recycling"
- A newspaper editorial titled "Why I Recycle"
- A brochure published by the Waste Management Corporation explaining the benefits of recycling to its potential customers
- An article in *Business Week* titled "Factors Influencing an Economic Boom: Recycling and Waste Management"

The *Reader's Digest* article is limited to discussing laws that regulate recycling and will not focus on its advantages. The newspaper editorial is likely to contain personal opinion rather than factual information. The brochure may be biased (see p. 225), because it was written to convince potential customers that they need the company's services. The best source will be the article in *Business Week.* It is concerned with economic effects of recycling and is likely to contain fairly detailed factual information.

Knowledge and awareness of your sources, then, can help you locate information and evaluate material you are given to read. Suppose you are asked to read an article from *Time* magazine on the relationship between diet and heart disease. You would not expect it to have the same level of detail or analysis as an article in the *Journal of the American Medical Association.*

If you are unfamiliar with a source, you can still evaluate it in several ways. One way is to look for footnotes, endnotes, or a list of references. These features suggest that the author consulted other sources and/or authorities to write his or her article. Another approach is to verify the information by checking additional sources. A third is to check with college librarians; they are familiar with a variety of sources and may be able to tell you whether a particular source is considered reliable.

◤ EXERCISE 2

DIRECTIONS   Predict how useful and appropriate each of the following sources will be for the situation described. Rate each as "Very Appropriate," "Possibly Useful," or "Not Appropriate."

1. *Source:* A *Time* magazine article on American eating habits
   Situation: You are collecting information for a research paper on food cravings for your health and nutrition class.

2. *Source:* A book titled *Junk and Collectibles: The History of Flea Markets*
   Situation: You are preparing a speech on flea markets for your public speaking class.

3. *Source:* The *Human Ecologist,* a periodical dealing with environmental health issues
   Situation: You are writing a letter to the editors of your local newspaper opposing the construction of a chemical waste treatment plant in your neighborhood; you need evidence about possible dangers.

4. *Source:* A classified ad for a Toyota
   Situation: You are shopping for a used car.

5. *Source:* A newsletter published by the Sierra Club, a group devoted to environmental protection
   Situation: You are writing a paper evaluating whether the lumber industry acts responsibly toward the environment.

What Are the Author's Qualifications?

To evaluate printed material, the competency of the author also must be considered. If the author lacks expertise in or experience with the subject, the material he or she produces may not meet an acceptable level of scholarship and accuracy.

Depending on the type of material you are using, you have several means of checking the qualifications of an author. In textbooks, the author's credentials may be described in one of two places. The author's college or university affiliation, and possibly his or her title, may appear on the title page beneath the author's name. Second, in the preface of the book, the author may indicate or summarize his or her qualifications for writing the text. In nonfiction books and general market paperbacks, a synopsis of the author's credentials and experiences may be included on the book jacket or the back cover. However, in other types of material, little effort is made to identify the author or his or her qualifications. In newspapers, magazines, and reference books, the reader is given little or no information about the writer. You are forced to rely on the judgment of the editors or publishers to assess an author's authority.

If you are familiar with an author's work, then you can anticipate the type of material you will be reading and predict the writer's approach and attitude toward the subject. If, for example, you found an article on world banking written by former President Carter, you could predict it will have a political point of view. If you were about to read an article on John Lennon written by Ringo Starr, one of the other Beatles, you could predict the article might possibly include details of their working relationship from Ringo's point of view.

Is the Material Fact or Opinion?

When working with any source, try to determine whether the material is factual or an expression of opinion. Facts are statements that can be verified—that is, proved to be true or false. Opinions are statements that express feelings, attitudes, or beliefs and are neither true nor false. Here are a few examples of each:

Facts

1. More than one million teenagers become pregnant every year.
2. The costs of medical care increase every year.

Opinions

1. Government regulation of our private lives should be halted immediately.
2. By the year 2025, most Americans will not be able to afford routine health care.

Facts that are taken from a reputable source or verified can be accepted and regarded as reliable information. Opinions, on the other hand, are not reliable sources of information and should be questioned and carefully evaluated. Look for evidence that supports the opinion and indicates that it is reasonable. For example, opinion 2 above is written to sound like a fact, but look closely. What basis does the author have for making that statement?

Some authors are careful to signal the reader when they are presenting an opinion. Watch for words and phrases such as:

apparently	this suggests	in my view	one explanation is
presumably	possibly	it is likely that	according to
in my opinion	it is believed	seemingly	

Other authors do just the opposite; they try to make opinions sound like facts, as in opinion 2 above.

In the following excerpt from a social problems textbook, notice how the author carefully distinguishes factual statements from opinion by using qualifying words and phrases (underlined).

Economic Change, Ideology, and Private Life

<u>It seems clear</u> that there has been a major change in attitudes and feelings about family relationships since the eighteenth century. <u>It is less clear</u> how and why the change came about. One question debated by researchers is: In what social class did the new family pattern originate—in the aristocracy, as Trumbach (1978) believes, or in the upper gentry, as Stone (1977) argued, or in the working class, as Shorter (1975) contended? Or was the rise of the new domesticity a cultural phenomenon that affected people in all social categories at roughly the same time? Carole Shammas (1980) <u>has found evidence</u> of such a widespread cultural change by looking at the kinds of things people had in their homes at various times in the past, as recorded in probate inventories. She found that in the middle of the eighteenth century all social classes experienced a change in living habits; even working-class households now contained expensive tools of domesticity, such as crockery, teapots, eating utensils, and so on. Thus, <u>according to Shammas,</u> the home was becoming an important center for social interaction, and family meals had come to occupy an important place in people's lives.

—Skolnick, *The Intimate Environment: Exploring Marriage and the Family,* p. 95

Other authors, however, mix fact and opinion without making clear distinctions. This is particularly true in the case of informed opinion, which is the opinion of an expert or authority. Ralph Nader represents expert opinion on consumer rights, for example. Textbook authors, too, often offer informed opinion, as in the following statement from an American government text.

> The United States is a place where the pursuit of private, particular, and narrow interests is honored. In our culture, following the teachings of Adam Smith, the pursuit of self-interest is not only permitted but actually celebrated as the basis of the good and prosperous society.

—Greenberg and Page, *The Struggle for American Democracy,* p. 186

The author of this statement has reviewed the available evidence and is providing his expert opinion on what the evidence indicates about American political culture. The reader, then, is free to disagree and offer evidence to support an opposing view.

EXERCISE 3

DIRECTIONS   Read each of the following statements and identify whether it sounds like fact, opinion, or informed opinion.

_____ 1. United Parcel Service (UPS) is the nation's largest deliverer of packages.

_____ 2. United Parcel Service will become even more successful because it uses sophisticated management techniques.

_____ 3. UPS employees are closely supervised; new drivers are accompanied on their rounds, and time logs are kept.

_____ 4. The best way to keep up with world news is to read the newspaper.

_____ 5. A community, as defined by sociologists, is a collection of people who share some purpose, activity, or characteristic.

_____ 6. The mayor of our city is an extraordinarily honest person.

_____ 7. To a dieter, food is a four-letter word.

_____ 8. According to a leading business analyst, most television advertising is targeted toward high-spending consumer groups.

_____ 9. Americans spend $13.7 billion per year on alternative medicine and home remedies.

_____ 10. A survey of Minnesota residents demonstrated that lotteries are played most frequently by those who can least afford to play.

EXERCISE 4

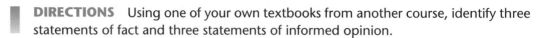

DIRECTIONS   Read or reread "The Talk of the Sandbox: How Johnny and Suzy's Chatter Prepares Them for Life at the Office" in Part Seven on page 387. Tannen is a nationally known expert on the communication styles of men and women. Underline five statements of informed opinion contained in the excerpt.

EXERCISE 5

DIRECTIONS   Using one of your own textbooks from another course, identify three statements of fact and three statements of informed opinion.

What Is the Author's Purpose?

Author's purpose refers to the reason(s) a writer has for writing. Here are a few examples: Textbook authors write to inform and present information. Advertising copy writers write to sell products or services. Comic strip writers write to amuse, entertain, or provide social commentary. Essay writers write to inform, describe, or persuade.

Recognizing an author's purpose can help you decide what critical questions to ask. It can also provide a means of evaluating the material. Ask yourself: How effectively did the author accomplish what he or she set out to accomplish?

For many types of material, the author's purpose is obvious. You know, for example, that the directions on a toy carton are written to tell you how to assemble it and that an advertisement is written to sell a product or service. Other times, the author's purpose is less obvious. To find the author's purpose, use the following suggestions.

1. *Consider the source and intended purpose.* A writer may want to reach a general-interest audience (anyone who is interested in the subject) or appeal to specific segments of the population. Most newspapers and periodicals such as *Time* and *Newsweek* appeal to a general-interest audience. The *Journal of American Medicine, Skiing Today,* and the *World of Antiques* appeal to specific audiences with specialized interests. Also, a writer may intend his or her writing for an audience with particular political, moral, or religious attitudes. Articles in the *Atlantic Monthly* often appeal to the conservative political viewpoint, whereas the *Catholic Digest* appeals to a particular religious group. The source can suggest certain biases, priorities, or political views. If the source does not clearly identify the intended audience, then the level of language, the choice of words, and the complexity of the ideas, examples, or arguments used will often suggest the audience the writer has in mind. Once you have identified a potential audience, you can begin to consider what it is the writer wants to communicate to that audience.

2. *Consider the point of view.* Point of view is the perspective from which an article or essay is written. A review of a rock concert, for example, may be described from the point of view of someone in the music industry or from that of someone who is a classical music fan. A controversial issue may be discussed from a more objective point of view, examining both sides of the issue, or from a more subjective point of view, in which the author favors one side of the issue. Point of view might be described as the way an author looks at or approaches his or her subject. Accordingly, point of view can often suggest the author's purpose in writing.

3. *Decide whether the writer tries to prove anything about the subject.* Try to determine whether the article is written to persuade you to accept a certain point of view or to perform a certain action. For instance, a writer may write to convince you that inflation will cause a national disaster, or that inflicting

the death penalty is morally wrong, or that the best jobs are available in health-related fields.

DIRECTIONS   For each of the following passages, identify the author's purpose.

Passage 1

Legal Issues and the Internet

Can existing laws solve problems on the Internet that involve libel, privacy, censorship, and copyright? Is it possible, or desirable, to regulate the content of millions of communication acts that take place daily on this international highway? If so, to whom should the laws primarily apply—to the operators of the online services or to their users? And how can the rights of the creators of those materials be protected?

These are some of the questions still largely unanswered in the complex, almost anarchic, cyberspace world of the 1990s.

—Agee et al., *Introduction to Mass Communication,* p. 466.

Purpose: _____

_____

Passage 2

Hunger in Rural America

Rural America is where the highest percentages of hungry people are to be found, says George Sanders, director of the Alabama Coalition Against Hunger. The irony is not lost on him: People in rural communities—where the United States raises most of the food it uses to feed not only its own citizens but much of the world as well—go hungry themselves. That's because the infrastructure of rural communities is designed to get food out, not to distribute it within, says Sanders.

Many rural people, though they are eligible, do not get food stamps or other government food support. One reason is that social service agencies don't have offices in small communities, so visiting the right government office to maintain the paperwork can mean a 100-mile odyssey.

Also, people in rural towns are sometimes unwilling to apply for food stamps because it's hard to protect their privacy. Those who do may travel to other communities to avoid using food stamps at the grocery where they've shopped all their lives.

And while urban food pantries can expect monthly shipments of food surpluses from the federal government, rural pantries get shipments only quarterly, making planning difficult. That is, it would be difficult, Sanders says, if rural communities *had* pantries. Most don't. Sparsely populated counties are hard pressed to maintain a volunteer staff at a food pantry, says Sanders.

He and other advocates say that hunger cannot be eliminated unless policy-makers reappraise the nation's current food-assistance system, which simply doesn't work anymore.

—Clarke, *Salt*

Purpose: _____

_____

Passage 3

Momentum and Energy

Nearly two decades before Newton's *Principia* was published, the Royal Society of London called for experimental studies of the behavior of colliding objects. Responses were received from several of Newton's contemporaries, including Sir Christopher Wren and Christian Huygens (1629–1695). Their observations led to the discovery of laws governing the exchange of momentum and energy between two colliding objects. These ideas were known to Newton and influenced his work. Their most important result was the law of conservation of linear momentum. According to this law, the total momentum after a collision is the same as the total momentum before the collision. This law made a key contribution to the growing understanding of mechanics.

Momentum as stated in Newton's second law is often called linear momentum to distinguish it from the angular momentum associated with rotational motion, which we will discuss in Chapter 9. The independent laws concerning the conservation of energy and of linear momentum are among the most basic laws in contemporary physics. Although we will derive these laws from Newton's laws of motion, in some respects they are even more fundamental and far-reaching than Newton's laws. For example, even in situations where Newton's laws do not apply, such as speeds approaching the speed of light or dimensions on atomic scales, these conservation laws are still valid. The use of conservation laws is one of the most fundamental ways of describing nature.

For simplicity, we focus on one conservation law at a time. Here we want to emphasize the conservation of momentum. However, in some cases we will first apply conservation of momentum and then use conservation of mechanical energy. In the next chapter we will examine collisions in which the laws of conservation of momentum and of conservation of kinetic energy are applied simultaneously.

—Jones and Childers, *Contemporary College Physics,* p. 188

Purpose: _____

_____

Is the Author Biased?

Bias refers to an author's partiality, inclination toward a particular viewpoint, or prejudice. A writer is biased, for example, if she or he takes one side of a controversial issue and does not recognize opposing viewpoints. Perhaps the best example of bias occurs in advertising. A magazine advertisement for a new snack cracker, for instance, describes only positive selling features: taste, low cholesterol, convenience, and crunch. The ad does not recognize the cracker's negative features: high in calories, high in fat, and so on. In some material, the writer is direct and forthright in expressing his or her bias; other times the bias is less obvious and is left for the reader to discover through careful analysis.

Read the following description of rock and rap music.

People used to tap their feet and smile when they listened to American popular music. Now many of us sit open-mouthed and stare: at "speed metal" rockers with roadkill hair who, despite a certain virtuosity on guitar, treat music as a form of warfare; at "grunge" bands in thrift-shop flannels who throw tantrums and smash their instruments; at "gangsta" rappers in baggy gear who posture as rapists, drug dealers, prostitutes, murderers, and terrorists. Tune in to MTV, and you will occasionally come across something wonderful. But more likely the sonic abuse and verbal–visual ugliness will appall and repel you.

"Turn that racket down," we yell, realizing that we sound just like our parents. So we chalk the problem up to age, telling ourselves that people prefer the music of their youth, and that's all there is to it. But this explanation conjures up a most unlikely prospect: today's teenagers 60 years from now attending Saturday-night dances in their retirement communities, their eyes misting over to the sounds of Megadeth, Sonic Youth, and Niggaz With Attitude. Such a future seems unlikely for the obvious but underappreciated reason that much of today's popular music evokes only the more intense, unsettling emotions of youth: anxiety, lust, anger, aggression. In the narrow gauge of its effects, such music could not be more different from the best of American popular music, which balances those emotions with tenderness, grace, and wit. Indeed, the great vigor of our music has always been its ability to blend opposites.

—Bayles, *Wilson Quarterly*

In this passage, the author's bias against rock and rap music is clear. The author's choice of words—*sonic abuse, verbal–visual ugliness,* and *roadkill hair*—reveals a negative attitude. Note, too, that the author's selection of detail is biased; no positive aspects of rock or rap are mentioned.

To identify bias, apply the following steps.

1. *Pay attention to emotional language.* Does the author use numerous positive or negative terms to describe the subject?
2. *Notice descriptive language.* What impression is created? How does the author make you feel?
3. *Look for opposing viewpoints.* Does the author present or ignore disadvantages, limitations, and alternative solutions?

DIRECTIONS   Read the following passage. Underline words and phrases that reveal the author's bias.

Jerry's Got to be Kidding

Why Disabled People Aren't Laughing

People with disabilities are outraged by the backward practices of telethons, the worst of which is the Jerry Lewis Muscular Dystrophy Association (MDA) Telethon. Some of us demonstrated against last fall's Labor Day telethon. As a writer–activist and a severely disabled person who must use a power wheelchair to get around, I helped lead a vigil outside the telethon in Los Angeles, as did others in Chicago, Denver, and other cities.

Do I watch the telethon? Yes, on tape, in manageable doses to avoid a stroke. Jerry Lewis' comedy career began with crude imitations of disabled people. He continues with smarmy, self-glorifying performances of songs like "The Wind Beneath My Wings" while mugging, beaglelike, at the camera or one of his disabled "kids." He encapsulates everything that disabled people wish to escape.

I have polio, not muscular dystrophy. Nevertheless, the stigma created by the telethon smears *all* physically disabled people. And those without muscular dystrophy do not even receive any of the MDA's stingy services.

—*In These Times*

What Is the Tone?

In speech, a speaker's tone of voice often reveals his or her attitude toward the subject and contributes to the overall message. Tone is also evident in a piece of writing, and it too contributes to meaning. Recognizing an author's tone is often important because tone can reveal feelings, attitudes, or viewpoints not directly stated by the author. An author's tone is achieved primarily through word choice and stylistic features such as sentence pattern and length.

Tone, then, often reveals feelings. Many human emotions can be communicated through tone—disapproval, hate, admiration, disgust, gratitude, and forcefulness are examples. Now read the following passage, paying particular attention to the feeling it creates.

What You Don't Know About Indians

Native American Issues Are Not History

Most Americans, even those deeply concerned about issues of justice, tend to speak of Indian issues as tragedies of the distant past. So ingrained is this position that when the occasional non-Indian does come forward on behalf of *today's* Indian cause—Marlon Brando, William Kunstler, Robert Redford, Jane Fonda, David Brower—they are all dismissed as "romantics." People are a bit embarrassed for them, as if they'd stepped over some boundary of propriety.

The Indian issue is *not* part of the distant past. Many of the worst anti-Indian campaigns were undertaken scarcely 80 to 100 years ago. Your great-grandparents were already alive at the time. The Model-T Ford was on the road.

And the assaults continue today. While the Custer period of direct military action against Indians may be over in the United States, more subtle though equally devastating "legalistic" manipulations continue to separate Indians from their land and their sovereignty.

—Mander, *Utne Reader*

Here the author's tone is concerned and serious. He is concerned about Native American issues and current legal manipulations.

An author's bias is often revealed in his or her tone. To identify an author's tone, ask yourself: How does the author feel about his or her subject and how are these feelings revealed?

 **EXERCISE 8**

DIRECTIONS   Describe the tone of each of the following passages.

1. The caller's voice does not hold together well. I can tell he is quite old and not well. He is calling from Maryland.

"I want four boxes of the Nut Goodies," he rasps at me after giving me his credit card information in a faltering hurry.

"There are 24 bars in each box," I say in case he doesn't know the magnitude of his order. Nut Goodies are made here in St. Paul and consist of a patty of maple cream covered with milk chocolate and peanuts. Sort of a Norwegian praline.

"OK, then make it five boxes but hurry this up before my nurse gets back."

He wants the order billed to a home address but sent to a nursing home.

"I've got Parkinson's," he says. "I'm 84."

"OK, sir. I think I've got it all. They're on the way." I put a rush on it.

"Right. Bye," he says, and in the pause when he is concentrating God knows how much energy on getting the receiver back in its cradle, I hear a long, dry chuckle.

One hundred and twenty Nut Goodies.

Way to go, buddy.

—Swardson, *City Pages*

Tone: _____

_____

2. Gleanings

So these three economists are on one of those Washington week-in-review shows. You know, the kind where reliable gray men with bad haircuts wear sincere gray suits and everybody talks to each other with pained grimaces like they're reunited school chums harboring a deadly secret ("She's *all* of our problem now, Finchley"). At prediction time, the grayest of the men says the economy is about to shoot toward unprecedented growth, the slate-colored one warns of triple-dip recession-sugar cone extra and the steely guy says "no change." Three different pointy heads, one economy, three totally different predictions. These are the experts? What the hell kind of job is that?

—*Utne Reader*, "Gleanings"

Tone: _____

_____

3. **What You Need**

You need a large wooden frame and enough space to accommodate it. Put comfortable chairs around it, allowing for eight women of varying ages, weight, coloring, and cultural orientation. It is preferable that this large wood frame be located in a room in a house in Atwater or Los Banos or a small town outside Bakersfield called Grasse. It should be a place that gets a thick, moist blanket of tule fog in the winter and be hot as blazes in the summer. Fix plenty of lemonade. Cookies are a nice complement.

When you choose your colors, make them sympathetic to one another. Consider the color wheel of grammar school—primary colors, phenomena of light and dark; avoid antagonism of hues—it detracts from the pleasure of the work. Think of music as you orchestrate the shades and patterns; pretend that you are a conductor in a lush symphony hall, imagine the audience saying *Ooh* and *Ahh* as they applaud your work.

—Otto, *How to Make an American Quilt*

Tone: _____

_____

ANALYZING ARGUMENTS

Writers often use argument to establish and evaluate positions on controversial issues. An argument is a logical presentation of ideas that makes a claim about an issue and supports that claim with evidence. In a philosophy course, for example, you might read arguments on the issues of individual rights, the rights of the majority, or the existence of God. The claim is the point the writer tries to prove about the issue. Arguments deal with issues on which there are two or more positions or opinions. For instance, on the issue of gun control there are several claims.

- All handguns should be legal.
- No handguns should be legal.
- Some handguns should be legal for certain individuals.

Consider the issue of abortion. Three possible claims are:

- No abortions should be allowed.
- All abortions should be legal.
- Some abortions should be allowed under special circumstances.

An argument takes one position on an issue and provides reasons and evidence that the claim is sound or believable.

EXERCISE 9

DIRECTIONS   For each of the following issues, identify at least two positions and write a sentence expressing each.

1. Immigration laws restricting entry into the United States

   _____

   _____

2. Drug testing in the workplace

   _____

   _____

3. Smoking in public places

   _____

   _____

Evaluating the Reasons and Evidence

Once you have understood a writer's argument by identifying what is asserted and how, the next step is to evaluate the soundness, correctness, and worth of the reasons and evidence that supports the assertion. As a critical reader, your task is to assess whether the evidence is sufficient to support the claim. Let's look at a few types of evidence that are often used.

Facts

Be sure the facts are taken from a reliable source and are verifiable.

Personal Experience

Writers often substantiate their ideas through experience and observation. Although a writer's personal account of a situation may provide an interesting perspective on an issue, personal experience should not be accepted as proof. The observer may be biased or may have exaggerated or incorrectly perceived a situation.

Examples

Examples can illustrate or explain a principle, concept, or idea. To explain what aggressive behavior is, your psychology instructor may offer several examples: fighting, punching, and kicking. Examples should not be used by themselves to prove the concept or idea they illustrate, as is done in the following passage.

> The American judicial system treats those who are called for jury duty unfairly. It is clear from my sister's experience that the system has little regard for the needs of those called as jurors. My sister was required to report for jury duty the week she was on vacation. She spent the entire week in a crowded, stuffy room waiting to be called to sit on a jury and never was called.

The sister's experience does sound unfair, but it, by itself, does not prove anything about the entire judicial system.

Statistics

Many people are impressed by statistics—the reporting of figures, percentages, averages, and so forth—and assume that they are irrefutable proof. Actually, statistics can be misused, misinterpreted, or used selectively to give other than the most objective, accurate picture of a situation. Suppose you read that magazine X has increased its readership by 50 percent while magazine Y had only a 10 percent increase. From this statistic, some readers might assume that magazine X has a wider readership than magazine Y. However, obtaining complete information may well reveal that this is not true. The missing, but crucial, statistic is the total readership of each magazine prior to the increase. If magazine X had a readership of 20,000 and increased it by 50 percent, its readership would total 30,000. However, if magazine Y's readership was already 50,000, a 10 percent increase (bringing the new total to 55,000) would still give it the larger readership, despite the fact that it made the smaller increase. Always approach statistical evidence with a critical, questioning attitude.

Statistics are often presented in graphical form. Writers use graphs to make points dramatically. At times they may exaggerate certain data by manipulating how the graph is drawn or by their choice of what scale to use.

Comparisons and Analogies

Comparisons and analogies (extended comparisons) serve as illustrations and are often used in argument. Their reliability depends on how closely the comparison corresponds, or how similar it is, to the situation to which it is being compared. For example, Martin Luther King, Jr., in his famous letter from the Birmingham jail, compared nonviolent protesters to a robbed man. To evaluate this comparison, you would need to consider how the two are similar and how they are different. In general, no two things are exactly the same.

Appeal to Authority

A writer may quote a well-known person or expert on the issue. Unless the well-known person is knowledgeable or experienced with the issue, his or her opinion is not relevant. Whenever an expert is cited, be certain that the expert offers support for her or his opinion.

Cause–Effect Relationships

A writer may argue that when two events occurred in close sequence, one caused the other. In other words, a writer may assume a cause–effect relationship when none exists. For example, suppose unemployment decreased the year a new town mayor was elected. The mayor may claim she brought about the decrease in unemployment. However, the decrease may have been caused by factors the mayor was not involved with, such as a large corporation opening a branch within the town and creating new jobs.

Relevancy and Sufficiency of Evidence

Once you have identified the evidence used to support an argument, the next step is to decide whether the writer has provided enough of the right kind of evidence to lead you to accept his or her claim. This is always a matter of judgment; there are no easy rules to follow. You must determine (1) whether the evidence provided directly supports the statement and (2) whether sufficient evidence has been provided.

Suppose an article in your campus newspaper argues for eliminating mathematics as a required course at your college. As evidence, the student offers the following.

Mathematics does not prepare us for the job market. In today's world, calculators and computer programs have eliminated the need for the study of mathematics.

This argument neither directly supports the statement nor provides sufficient evidence. First, calculators and computer programs do not substitute for an understanding of mathematical principles. Second, the writer does nothing to substantiate his claim that mathematics is irrelevant to the job market. For the argument to be regarded seriously, the writer would need to provide facts, statistics, expert opinion, or other forms of documentation.

Reading an Argument

When reading arguments, use the following steps.

Reading Arguments

1. Identify the issue. What controversial question or problem does the argument address?

2. Identify the claim-position, idea, or action the writer is trying to convince you to accept. Often, a concise statement of this key point appears early in the argument or in the introduction of a formal essay. The author often restates this key point.

3. Read the entire article or essay completely, more than once if necessary. Underline key evidence that supports the author's claim.

4. Evaluate the types of evidence the author provides. Does he or she offer statistics, facts, or examples? Is the evidence relevant and sufficient?

5. Watch for conclusions. Words and phrases such as *since, thus, therefore, accordingly, it can be concluded, it is clear that, it follows that,* and *hence* are signals that a conclusion is about to be given.

6. Reread the argument and examine its content and structure. What is stated? What is implied or suggested?

7. Write a brief outline of the argument, listing its key points.

Now read the following brief article, applying the steps we have just listed.

David Bianculli: In Defense of TV

I'm both amazed and infuriated by the number of people who, at social gatherings or in casual conversation, remark rather proudly that they (a) never watch television or (b) don't even have a TV set. To me, that's no less a boastful admission of ignorance than to announce, with an arrogant air of superiority, that one is either illiterate or an intentional abstainer from books and magazines.

Yes, 90 percent of television is junk, pure and simple. But so are 90 percent of the books being printed, and the movies being made, and no one seems to be upset about the ratio of quantity to quality in those media. But TV gets dumped on from all directions, blamed for every social ill, and generally given no respect.

Yet dismissing TV because of *Gilligan's Island* and *Studs* is no more fair than dismissing print because of Judith Krantz and *Penthouse*. TV is the enemy of literacy, and of intelligent viewing, only if parents, teachers, and young viewers use television indiscriminately and stupidly. Wonderful banquets can be made from what TV has to offer, if only people would look past the junk food.

One quick example where TV and reading have walked hand-in-hand in my own household: After one of the annual showings of *The Wizard of Oz,* my daughter, then less than 3, used her videotaped copy of the movie to watch certain sections (the ones with the Wicked Witch, who scared her) over and over again, partly for enjoyment and partly to overcome her fears.

I was not at all upset about her desire for repetition, because I'd seen the same behavior at night when reading her bedtime stories and fairy tales. Familiarity, in some cases, breeds not contempt, but contentment.

Years later, I showed that same daughter the telemovie *The Dreamer of Oz,* a fanciful yet tasteful and well-researched dramatization of the life and work of author L. Frank Baum, and how he came to write the "Oz" books. I also showed her *Return to Oz,* a film incorporating later stories and characters from the "Oz" series—at which time my daughter became hooked and started burning her way through the original books.

On other occasions, I've used videodiscs and tapes of *West Side Story* and TV's *Peter Pan* to prepare my kids for a trip to see *Jerome Robbins' Broadway.* I've seen their enjoyment of the *Anne of Green Gables* TV miniseries lead directly to the purchase and perusal of the original novels.

At whatever age, TV offers special and very literate fare to those willing to search for it. Preschoolers have *Sesame Street* and Shelly Duvall's *Bedtime Stories* and *Faerie Tale Theatre* series. Preteens have *Reading Rainbow,* and all of them have *Buy Me That!* HBO's amazing *Consumer Reports* documentary series that teaches TV literacy itself—showing young viewers how to watch TV, and especially what to watch for (and watch out for) during the ads.

Finally, I think TV should be taught in the schools on the university level, where first-year students can learn critical skills by analyzing the "texts" of programs with which they already are fluent. Those skills can then be used on less familiar subjects, like Shakespeare, rather than having students grapple with both subjects and methods simultaneously.

And much earlier, at the grade school level, TV can be used in the classroom in two ways: to motivate kids to read and learn, and to teach kids how to "read" TV as skeptical yet appreciative young viewers.

Before that happens, of course, the teachers themselves will have to learn the lesson that TV is not bad for you. Only bad TV is.

—Bianculli, *Reading Today*

The issue discussed is the value of television. Bianculli takes the position that some television programs can be worthwhile and that all programs should not be considered worthless because some programs are bad. The author supports this position by offering examples. Specifically, he names worthwhile programs and explains their value. He also argues that some programs are valuable because they can be used in elementary classroom instruction. The action called for is a college course on critical television-watching skills.

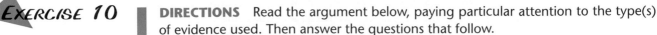

EXERCISE 10

DIRECTIONS   Read the argument below, paying particular attention to the type(s) of evidence used. Then answer the questions that follow.

Let's Tell the Story of All America's Cultures

America's bittersweet legacy of struggling and failing and getting another step closer to democratic ideals of liberty and equality and justice for all wasn't for the likes of me, an immigrant child from Korea. The history books said so.

Well, the history books were wrong.

Educators around the country are finally realizing what I realized as a teenager in the library, looking up the history I wasn't getting in school. America is a multicultural nation, composed of many people with varying histories and varying traditions who have little in common except their humanity, a belief in democracy and a desire for freedom.

America changed them, but they changed America too.

A committee of scholars and teachers gathered by the New York Department of Education recognizes this in their recent report, "One Nation, Many Peoples: A Declaration of Cultural Interdependence."

They recommend that public schools provide a "multicultural education, anchored to the shared principles of a liberal democracy."

What that means, according to the report, is recognizing that America was shaped and continues to be shaped by people of diverse backgrounds. It calls for students to be taught that history is an ongoing process of discovery and interpretation of the past, and that there is more than one way of viewing the world.

Thus, the westward migration of white Americans is not just a heroic settling of an untamed wild, but also the conquest of indigenous peoples. Immigrants were not just white, but Asian as well. Blacks were not merely passive slaves freed by northern whites, but active fighters for their own liberation.

In particular, according to the report, the curriculum should help children "to assess critically the reasons for the inconsistencies between the ideals of the U.S. and social realities. It should provide information and intellectual tools that can permit them to contribute to bringing reality closer to the ideals."

In other words, show children the good with the bad, and give them the skills to help improve their country. What could be more patriotic?

Several dissenting members of the New York committee publicly worry that America will splinter into ethnic fragments if this multicultural curriculum is adopted. They argue that the committee's report puts the focus on ethnicity at the expense of national unity.

But downplaying ethnicity will not bolster national unity. The history of America is the story of how and why people from all over the world came to the United States, and how in struggling to make a better life for themselves, they changed each other, they changed the country, and they all came to call themselves Americans.

E pluribus unum. Out of many, one.

This is why I, with my Korean background, and my childhood tormentors, with their lost-in-the-mist-of-time European backgrounds, are all Americans. It is the unique beauty of this country. It is high time we let all our children gaze upon it.

—Yuhfill, *Philadelphia Inquirer*

1. What is the issue?
2. What is the claim?
3. What types of evidence are used?
4. Is the evidence convincing?
5. Is there sufficient evidence?
6. What other types of evidence could have been used to strengthen the argument?

LEARNING *Collaboratively*

DIRECTIONS   Bring to class a brief (two- to three-paragraph) newspaper article, editorial, film review, etc. Working in groups of three or four students, each student should read his or her piece aloud or distribute copies. The group should discuss and evaluate (1) the source of the material, (2) the author's qualifications, (3) whether more facts or opinions are represented, (4) the author's purpose, (5) any bias, and (6) the tone of the passage. Your group should choose one article and submit your findings to the class or instructor.

Applying YOUR LEARNING

Ian is taking a business course in which he is studying forms of business owner-ship: sole proprietorships, partnerships, corporations, cooperatives, syndicates, and joint ventures. He read and highlighted his textbook and attended all class lectures. To prepare for an essay exam, Ian made a study sheet summarizing the characteristics of each form of ownership. When Ian read the following exam question, he knew he was in trouble.

Exam Question

Suppose you are the sole proprietor of a successful car wash. The owner of a competing car wash suggests that you form a partnership. Another competitor suggests that you enter into a joint venture to explore expansion opportunities. And a major car wash chain offers you a management position and stock in the corporation if you sell out. Write an essay explaining what factors you would consider in making a decision.

1. What levels of thinking did Ian use in preparing for the exam?
2. Why was Ian in trouble? That is, what types of thinking does the question demand?
3. How should Ian have prepared for the exam?

SELF-TEST SUMMARY

1. How can you learn to make better inferences?	Begin with a firm grasp of the literal meaning of what you read. Become aware of the author's purpose, and watch for clues along the way. Adding up all the facts should also help you make accurate inferences.
2. How can you become a critical reader?	The key to becoming a critical reader is to ask questions. Asking and answering the following questions can help you develop your critical reading skills. What is the source of the material? What are the author's qualifications? Is the material fact or opinion? What is the author's purpose? Is the author biased? What is the tone?
3. What is the key to analyzing arguments?	An argument is a common method of expressing ideas that deal with an issue and take a position on that issue. When reading an argument, be sure to evaluate the relevance and sufficiency of the evidence that is offered in support of the claim.
4. What are the common types of evidence used in arguments?	To support their positions in arguments, writers use many types of evidence. In addition to facts, the most common types of evidence are personal experience, examples, statistics, comparisons and analogies, appeal to authority, and cause–effect relationships.

Take a Road Trip to the
American Southwest!

If your instructor has asked you to use the Reading Road Trip CD-ROM, be sure to visit the Critical Thinking module for multimedia tutorials, exercises, and tests.

11 CHAPTER

Expanding
Your
Vocabulary

Why Expand Your Vocabulary?

▲ **Your vocabulary is a reflection of you, and a strong vocabulary creates a positive image.**

▲ **Broadening your vocabulary will improve the clarity of your thinking.**

▲ **Your reading and writing skills will improve as your vocabulary improves.**

▲ **A strong vocabulary will contribute to both academic and career success.**

Learning Experiment

Step 1

Study the following list of words and meanings (list A) for one to two minutes.

List A

contrive—to plan with cleverness; to devise

comprise—to consist of

revulsion—feeling of violent disgust or hatred

retaliate—to pay back, to get even with

repertoire—a collection of skills, aptitudes; a collection of items to be performed

inhibit—to hold back, restrain

Step 2

Study list B for one to two minutes. Then, for each word, write a sentence using the word.

List B

ambivalent—uncertain or undecided about a course or action

infallible—incapable of making a mistake

mundane—commonplace, ordinary

relentless—unyielding, unwilling to give in

déjà vu—the impression of having seen or experienced something before

Step 3

Wait two days and then take the following quiz. Cover the two lists above before you begin the quiz.

Match each word in column A with its meaning in column B. Write the letter from column B in the blank provided.

	Column A	Column B
_____	1. revulsion	a. to pay back
_____	2. comprise	b. undecided
_____	3. repertoire	c. feeling of hatred
_____	4. contrive	d. feeling of experiencing something again
_____	5. retaliate	e. collection of items or skills
_____	6. ambivalent	f. to consist of
_____	7. relentless	g. ordinary
_____	8. infallible	h. incapable of error
_____	9. déjà vu	i. to create a clever plan
_____	10. mundane	j. unwilling to give in

Step 4

Check your answers using the key on p. 445.

The Results

Questions 1–5 were based on list A; Questions 6–10 were based on list B. You probably got more questions right for list B than for list A. Why? For list B, you used each word in a sentence. By using each word in a sentence you were practicing it. Practice is a part of a technique known as rehearsal, which means going back over material you are attempting to learn.

Learning Principle (What This Means to You)

Rehearsal improves both your ability to learn and your ability to recall information. To expand your vocabulary, be sure to practice using words you identify as important to learn, whether they are part of your general vocabulary or the specialized terminology of your courses. This chapter will help you to identify the words you need to add to your vocabulary and to use the resources that can expand your vocabulary.

GENERAL APPROACHES TO VOCABULARY EXPANSION

Expanding your vocabulary requires motivation, a positive attitude, and skills, and the first of these is the most important. To improve your vocabulary, you must be willing to work at it, spending both time and effort to notice and learn new words and meanings. Unless you intend to remember new words you hear or read, you will probably forget them. Your attitude toward reading will also influence the extent to which your vocabulary develops. If you enjoy reading and you read a broad range of subjects, you will frequently encounter new words. On the other hand, if you read only when required to do so, your exposure to words will be limited. Finally, your skills in using reference sources, in handling specialized terminology, and in organizing a system for learning new words will influence your vocabulary development.

The remainder of this chapter will focus on the skills you need to build your vocabulary. Before you continue, however, read the following suggestions for expanding your vocabulary.

Read Widely

One of the best ways to improve your vocabulary is by reading widely and diversely, sampling many different subjects and styles of writing. Through reading, you encounter new words and new uses for familiar words. You also see words used in contexts that you have not previously considered.

College is one of the best places to begin reading widely. As you take elective and required courses, you are exposed to new ideas as well as to the words that express them clearly and succinctly. While you are a student, use the range of required and elective reading to expand your vocabulary.

Use Words You Already Know

Most people think they have just one level of vocabulary and that this can be characterized as large or small, strong or weak. Actually, everyone has at least four levels of vocabulary, and each varies in strength.

1. Words you use in everyday speech or writing
   Examples: *sharp, teeth, parent, visit, steak, illness*

2. Words you know but seldom or never use in your own speech or writing
   Examples: *lethal, legitimate, lawful, landscape, laid-back*

3. Words you've heard or seen before but cannot fully define
Examples: *logistics, lament, lackadaisical, latent, latitude*

4. Words you've never heard or seen before
Examples: *lanugo, lagniappe, laconic, lactone, lacustrine*

In the spaces provided, list five words that fall under each of these four categories. It will be easy to think of words for category 1. Words for categories 2 through 4 may be taken from the following list.

activate	delicate	impartial
alien	delve	impertinent
attentive	demean	liberate
congruent	focus	logic
connive	fraught	manual
continuous	garbanzo	meditate
contort	gastronome	osmosis
credible	havoc	resistance
deletion	heroic	voluntary

Category 1	Category 2	Category 3	Category 4
_____	_____	_____	_____
_____	_____	_____	_____
_____	_____	_____	_____
_____	_____	_____	_____
_____	_____	_____	_____

To build your vocabulary, try to shift as many words as possible from a less familiar to a more familiar category. This task is not easy. You start by noticing words. Then you question, check, and remember their meanings. Finally, and most important, you use these new words often in your speech and writing.

Look for Five-Dollar Words to Replace One-Dollar Words

Some words in your vocabulary are general and vague. Although they convey meaning, they are not precise, exact, or expressive. Try to replace these one-dollar words with five-dollar words that convey your meaning more directly. The word *good* is an example of a much-overused word that has a general, unclear meaning in the following sentence.

The movie was so good, it was worth the high admission price.

Try substituting the following words in the preceding sentence: *exciting, moving, thrilling, scary, inspiring*. Each of these gives more information than the word *good*. These are the types of words you should strive to use in your speech and writing.

Build Your Word Awareness

Get in the habit of noticing new or unusual words when reading and listening. Learn to pay attention to words and notice those that seem useful. One of the first steps in expanding your vocabulary is to develop a word awareness. At the college level, many new words that you learn do not represent new concepts or ideas. Instead, they are more accurate or more descriptive replacements for simpler words and expressions that you already know and use. Once you begin to notice words, you will find that many of them automatically become part of your vocabulary.

Your instructors are a good resource for new words. Both in formal classroom lectures and in more casual discussions and conversations, many instructors use words that students understand but seldom use. You will hear new words and technical terms that are particular to a specific discipline.

Other good sources are textbooks, collateral reading assignments, and reference materials. If you are like most students, you understand many more words than you use in your own speech and writing. As you read, you will encounter many words you are vaguely familiar with but cannot define. When you begin to notice these words, you will find that many of them become part of your vocabulary.

Consider Working with a Vocabulary Improvement Program

If you feel motivated to make improvements in a concentrated program of study, consider setting aside a block of time each week to work with a vocabulary improvement program. A variety of paperbacks on the market are designed to help you improve your vocabulary. The average bookstore should have several to choose from. Computer programs, some in game formats, have also been designed to strengthen general vocabulary. Check with your college's learning lab or library to see what is available.

USING REFERENCE SOURCES

Once you have developed a sense of word awareness and have begun to identify useful words to add to your vocabulary, the next step is to become familiar with the references you can use to expand your vocabulary.

Dictionaries: Which One to Buy

Students often ask, "Which dictionary should I buy?" There are several types of dictionaries, each with its own purpose and use. A pocket or paperback dictionary is an inexpensive, shortened version of a standard desk dictionary. It is small enough to carry with you to your classes and is relatively inexpensive.

A desk dictionary is a larger, more inclusive dictionary. Although a pocket dictionary is convenient, it is also limited. A pocket edition lists about 55,000 words, whereas a standard desk edition lists up to 150,000 words. The desk edition also provides much more information about each word. Desk dictionaries are usually hardbound and cost over $20.

Several standard dictionaries are available in both desk and paperback editions. These include the *Random House Dictionary of the English Language,*

Webster's Collegiate Dictionary, and the *American Heritage Dictionary of the English Language.*

Another type is the unabridged dictionary, which can be found in the reference section of any library. The unabridged edition provides the most information on each word in the English language.

Whether you purchase a desk or a pocket dictionary will depend on your needs as well as on what you can afford. It would be ideal to have both. A pocket dictionary is sufficient for checking spelling and for looking up common meanings of unfamiliar words. To expand your vocabulary by learning additional meanings of words or to do any serious word study, you need a desk dictionary.

Use of the Dictionary

Most students are familiar with the common uses of a dictionary: (1) to look up the meaning of words one doesn't know and (2) to check the spelling of words. A dictionary can be useful in many other ways because it contains much more than just word meanings. For most entries you will find a pronunciation key, word origin, part(s) of speech, variant spellings, and synonyms. At the beginning or end of many desk dictionaries, you will find information on language history and manuscript form, lists of symbols, and tables of weights and measures.

A dictionary is the basic tool for expanding your vocabulary. Get in the habit of consulting your dictionary whenever you see or hear a somewhat familiar word that you don't use and can't define precisely. Locate the word, read each meaning, and find the one that fits the way the word was used when you read or heard it. Use the vocabulary card system suggested later in this chapter to record and learn these words.

EXERCISE 1

DIRECTIONS   Use a desk dictionary to answer the following questions.

1. What does the abbreviation *obs.* means?

   _____

2. What does the symbol *c.* stand for?

   _____

3. How many meanings are listed for the word *fall*?

   _____

4. How is the word *phylloxera* pronounced? (Record its phonetic spelling.)

   _____

5. What is the plural spelling of *addendum*?

   _____

6. Can the word *protest* be used other than as a verb? If so, how?

   _____

7. The word *prime* can mean first or original. List some of its other meanings.

   _____

8. What does the French expression *savoir faire* mean?

   _____

9. List three synonyms for the word *fault.*

   _____

10. List several words that are formed using the word *dream.*

   _____

Thesauruses

A thesaurus, or dictionary of synonyms, is a valuable reference for locating a precise, accurate, or descriptive word to fit a particular situation. Suppose you are searching for a more precise term for the expression *looked over,* as used in the following sentence.

> My instructor looked over my essay exam.

The thesaurus lists the synonyms given in Figure 11.1. Right away you can identify a number of words that are more specific than the phrase *looked over.* The next step, then, is to choose from the list the word that most closely suggests the meaning you want to convey. The easiest way to do this is to test out, or substitute, various choices in your sentence to see which one is most appropriate; check the dictionary if you are not sure of a word's exact meaning.

Many students misuse the thesaurus by choosing words that do not fit the context. *Be sure to use words only when you are familiar with all their shades of meaning.* Remember, a misused word is often a more serious error than a wordy or imprecise expression.

VERBS **12. see, behold, observe, view, witness, perceive, discern, spy,** espy, descry, **sight,** have in sight, make out, spot [coll.], twig [coll.], discover, notice, distinguish, recognize, ken [dial.], **catch sight of,** get a load of [slang, U.S.], take in, look on *or* upon, cast the eyes on or upon, **set** *or* **lay eyes on, clap eyes on** [coll.]; pipe, lamp, nail, peg [all slang]; **glimpse,** get *or* catch a glimpse of; see at a glance, see with half an eye; see with one's own eyes.

13. look, peer, direct the eyes, turn *or* bend the eyes, lift up the eyes; **peek, peep,** pry, take a peep *or* peek; play at peekaboo *or* bopeep; get an eyeful [coll., U.S.].

14. look at, take a look at, take a gander at [slang, U.S.], have a looksee [slang, U.S.], look on *or* upon, gaze at *or* upon; **watch, observe,** pipe [slang], **view, regard;** keep in sight *or* view, hold in view; look after, follow; spy upon.

15. scrutinize, survey, eye, ogle, contemplate, look over, give the eye [slang], give the once-over *or* double-O [slang, U.S.]; examine, **inspect 484.31;** size up [coll.], take one's measure [slang].

16. gaze, gloat, fix~, fasten *or* rivet the eyes upon, keep the eyes upon; eye, ogle; **stare,** look [coll.], goggle, **gape, gawk** [coll.], gaup *or* gawp [dial.], gaze open-mouthed; crane, crane the neck; rubber, **rubberneck,** gander [all slang, U.S.]; look straight in the eye, look full in the face, hold one's eye *or* gaze, stare down; strain the eyes.

17. glare, glower, look daggers.

18. glance, glimpse, glint, cast a glance, glance at *or* upon, take a glance at, take a slant *or* squint at [slang].

19. look askance *or* **askant,** give a side-long look, cut one's eye [slang], glime [dial.]; squint, look asquint; cock the eye; **look down one's nose** [coll.].

20. leer, leer the eye, look leeringly, give a leering look.

21. look away, avert the eyes; look another way, break one's eyes away, stop looking, turn away from, turn the back upon; drop one's eyes *or* gaze, cast one's eyes down; avoid one's gaze, cut eyes [coll.].

Figure 11.1
A Sample Thesaurus Entry

The most widely used thesaurus was originally compiled by the English scholar Peter Roget and is known today as *Roget's Thesaurus;* it is readily available in an inexpensive paperback edition.

EXERCISE 2

DIRECTIONS   Replace the underlined word or phrase in each sentence with a more descriptive word or phrase. Use a thesaurus to locate your replacement.

1. When Sara learned that her sister had committed a crime, she was <u>sad.</u>
2. Compared to earlier chapters, the last two chapters in my chemistry text are <u>hard.</u>
3. The instructor spent the entire class <u>talking about</u> the causes of inflation and deflation.
4. The main character in the film was a <u>thin,</u> talkative British soldier.
5. We went to see a <u>great</u> film that won the Academy Award for the best picture.

Subject Area Dictionaries

Many academic disciplines have specialized dictionaries that list important terminology used in that field. They have specialized meanings and suggest how and when to use a word. For the field of music there is the *New Grove Dictionary of Music and Musicians,* which lists and defines the specialized vocabulary of music. Other subject area dictionaries include *Taber's Cyclopedic Medical Dictionary, A Dictionary of Anthropology,* and *A Dictionary of Economics.*

Be sure to find out whether there is a subject area dictionary for your courses and area of specialization. Most of these dictionaries are available only in hardbound copies, and they are likely to be expensive. Many students, however, find them to be worth the initial investment. You will find that most libraries have copies of specialized dictionaries in their reference section.

EXERCISE 3

DIRECTIONS   List below each course you are taking this term. Using your campus library or the Internet, find out whether a subject area dictionary is available for each discipline. If so, list their titles below.

Course   **Subject Area Dictionary**

_____   _____

_____   _____

_____   _____

_____   _____

LEARNING SPECIALIZED TERMINOLOGY

Each subject area can be said to have a language of its own—its own set of specialized words that makes it possible to describe and discuss accurately topics, principles and concepts, problems, and events related to the subject area.

One of the first tasks that both college instructors and textbook authors face is the necessity of introducing and teaching the specialized language of an academic field. This task is especially important in introductory, first-semester courses in which a student studies or encounters the subject area for the first time. In an introduction to psychology course, for instance, you often start by learning the meaning of *psychology* itself—what the study is devoted to, what it encompasses, how it approaches situations, events, and problems. From that point you move on to learn related terms: *behavior, observations, hypothesis, experiment, variables, subjects,* and so forth.

Often the first few class lectures in a course are introductory. They are devoted to acquainting students with the nature and scope of the subject area and to introducing the specialized language.

The first few chapters in a textbook are introductory, too. They are written to familiarize students with the subject of study and acquaint them with its specialized language. In one economics textbook, 34 new terms were introduced in the first two chapters (40 pages). In the first two chapters (28 pages) of a chemistry book, 56 specialized words were introduced. A sample of the words introduced in each of these texts is given below. From these lists you can see that some of the terms are common, everyday words that take on a specialized meaning; others are technical terms used only in that subject area.

New Terms: Economics Text	New Terms: Chemistry Text
capital	matter
ownership	element
opportunity cost	halogen
distribution	isotope
productive contribution	allotropic form
durable goods	nonmetal
economic system	group (family)
barter	burning
commodity money	toxicity

Recognition of specialized terminology is only the first step in learning the language of a course. More important is the development of a systematic way of identifying, marking, recording, and learning the specialized terms. Because new terminology is introduced in both class lectures and course textbooks, it is necessary to develop a procedure for handling the specialized terms in each.

EXERCISE 4

DIRECTIONS Turn to the reading "The Last of Their Kind," in Part Seven, p. 395. Identify as many new terms as you can, and record them in the space provided below.

Total number of specialized words: _____

Examples of specialized vocabulary: _____

_____

_____

_____

_____

EXERCISE 5

Academic Application

DIRECTIONS   Select any two textbooks you are currently using. In each, turn to the first chapter and check to see how many specialized terms are introduced. List the total number of such terms. Then list several examples.

Textbook 1: _____   Textbook 2: _____
                    (title)   (title)

Total number of specialized words: _____   Total number of specialized words: _____

Examples of Specialized Words   **Examples of Specialized Words**

1. _____   1. _____

2. _____   2. _____

3. _____   3. _____

4. _____   4. _____

5. _____   5. _____

6. _____   6. _____

7. _____   7. _____

Specialized Terminology in Class Lectures

As a part of your note-taking system, develop a consistent way of separating new terms and definitions from other facts and ideas. You might circle or draw a box around each new term; or, as you edit your notes (make revisions, changes, or additions to your notes after taking them), underline each new term in red; or mark "def." in the margin each time a definition is included. The mark or symbol you use is a matter of preference; the important thing is to find some way to identify definitions for further study. In addition, as part of your editing process, check each definition to be sure that it is complete and readable. Also, if you were not able to record any explanation or examples of new terms, add them as you edit. If the definitions you recorded are unclear, check with a friend or with your instructor. The last step in handling new terminology presented in class lectures is to organize the terms into a system for efficient study. One such system will be suggested later in this chapter.

Specialized Terminology in Textbooks

Textbook authors use various means to emphasize new terminology as they introduce it. In some texts, new vocabulary is printed in italics, boldface type, or colored print. Other texts indicate new terms in the margin of each page. The most common means of emphasis, however, is a new-terms list or vocabulary list at the beginning or end of each chapter.

While you are reading and highlighting important facts and ideas, you should also mark new terminology. Be sure to mark definitions and to separate them from other chapter content. (The mark or symbol you use is your choice.)

Occasionally in textbooks, you may meet a new term that is not defined or for which the definition is unclear. In this case, check the glossary at the back of the book for the meaning of the word. Make a note of the meaning in the margin of the page.

The glossary, a comprehensive list of terms introduced throughout the text, is an aid that can help you learn new terminology. At the end of the course, when you have covered all or most of the chapters, the glossary can be used to review terminology. Use the glossary to test yourself; read an entry, cover up the meaning and try to remember it; then check to see whether you were correct. As you progress through a course, however, the glossary is not an adequate study aid. A more organized, systematic approach to learning unfamiliar new terms is needed.

SYSTEMS OF LEARNING VOCABULARY

Here are two effective ways to organize and learn specialized or technical vocabulary for each of your courses.

The Vocabulary Card System

Once you have identified and marked new terminology, both in your lecture notes and in your textbook, the next step is to organize the words for study and review. One of the most efficient and practical ways to accomplish this is the vocabulary card system. Use a 3-inch-by-5-inch index card for each new term. Record the word on the front and the meaning on the back. If the word is particularly difficult, you might also include a guide to its pronunciation. Underneath the correct spelling of the word, indicate in syllables how the word sounds. For the word *eutrophication* (a term used in chemistry to mean "overnourishment"), you could indicate its pronunciation as "you-tro-fi-kay'-shun." On the back of the card, along with the meaning, you might want to include an example to help you remember the term more easily. A sample vocabulary card, front and back, is shown in Figure 11.2.

Use these cards for study, for review, and for testing yourself. Go through your pack of cards once, looking at the front and trying to recall the meaning on

Figure 11.2
A Sample Vocabulary Card

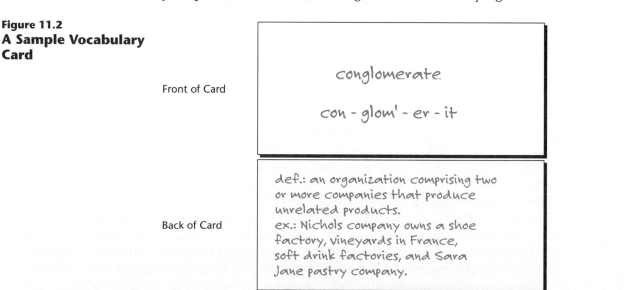

Front of Card

conglomerate

con - glom' - er - it

Back of Card

def.: an organization comprising two or more companies that produce unrelated products.
ex.: Nichols company owns a shoe factory, vineyards in France, soft drink factories, and Sara Jane pastry company.

the back. Then reverse the procedure; look at the meanings and see whether you can recall the terms. As you go through the pack in this way, sort the cards into two piles: words you know and words you don't know. The next time you review the cards, use only cards in the "don't know" pile for review. This sorting procedure will help you avoid wasting time reviewing words you have already learned. Continue to review the cards until you are satisfied that you have learned each new term. To prevent forgetting, review the entire pack of cards periodically.

The Computerized Vocabulary File

Using a word processing program, create a computer file for each of your courses. Daily or weekly, review both textbook chapters and lecture notes and enter specialized and technical terms that you need to learn. Use a two-column or table format, entering the word in one column, its meaning in the other. You might subdivide or code your file by textbook chapter so that you can review easily when exams or quizzes on particular chapters are announced.

Your files can be used in several different ways. If you alphabetize the words, you have created a glossary that will serve as a handy reference. Keep a print copy handy as you read new chapters and review lecture notes. When studying the words in your file, try scrambling the words to avoid learning them in a fixed order.

EXERCISE 6

DIRECTIONS Select two or three sets of notes on a particular topic from any course you are taking. Prepare a set of vocabulary cards for the new terms introduced. Review and study the cards.

EXERCISE 7

DIRECTIONS Select one chapter from any of the textbooks you are currently using. Prepare a vocabulary card for each new term introduced in the chapter. Review and study the cards.

LEARNING *Collaboratively*

DIRECTIONS After listing 20 unfamiliar words and their meanings on the chalkboard, the instructor will divide the class into two groups. Group 1 should record each word on an index card, writing the word on the front and the meaning on the back. Group 2 should copy the words in a list on a piece of notebook paper, writing the meaning to the right of each word. Both groups will be given five minutes to study the words (which have been erased from the chalkboard). Group 1 should study but not rewrite the list. During the next class, both groups should take a test on the words. Tally and compare scores of each group, and discuss what this experiment demonstrates about vocabulary learning.

Applying YOUR LEARNING

Erika is taking a human anatomy course and is having difficulty understanding and learning all the new vocabulary items. Her instructor uses many specialized words in lectures. Often Erika is unable to spell the words correctly, and sometimes she cannot write down the entire definition.

1. Is there a dictionary you would recommend that Erika use?
2. How can Erika separate out these new terms in her lecture notes?
3. How can Erika use the glossary in her textbook to help her study for exams?
4. How can she use the vocabulary card system to study?

SELF-TEST SUMMARY

1. What can you do to expand your overall vocabulary?

Expanding your vocabulary is a relatively simple process and does not require large investments of time or money. It will be most helpful to develop a sense of word awareness—to pay attention to and notice words. Wide reading can expose you to new words and new uses of familiar words. In your speech and writing, you should try to use more exact and expressive words to convey your meaning more clearly and directly. Finally, you might try a vocabulary building program, either book- or computer-based. You can obtain help and information at your college learning laboratory.

2. Which reference sources are helpful in vocabulary building?

References that are useful in expanding your vocabulary include the dictionary, the thesaurus, and subject-area dictionaries. Owning both a pocket and a desk dictionary is helpful for quick reference and serious word study. A good thesaurus is an indispensable reference for selecting the best word for a particular situation. Subject area dictionaries are very helpful in locating meanings and uses of specialized terms for the different academic disciplines.

3. How can you identify which specialized terms to learn?

Specialized terminology—those words used within an academic discipline—are especially important to learn. While taking notes and reading textbooks, pay special attention to these words. When taking lecture notes, it is helpful to distinguish new terms and definitions by circling them, highlighting them in a coded color, or labeling them in the margins of your notes. Your textbooks will often make special terms stand out by using italics, bold print, or color. You should also mark any other terms that are new to you. Further, you can consult each chapter's vocabulary list for terms to learn and can use your text's glossary as a study aid.

4. How can you use the vocabulary card system to help you learn new vocabulary?

Once general and specialized vocabulary have been identified, the vocabulary card system provides an easy and efficient way to learn each. In involves using 3-inch-by-5 inch cards for study, review, and self-testing. Each card should contain a word and its pronunciation on one side and its meaning and an example on the other. Study these cards by looking at one side and then at the other and then reversing the process. Sort them into piles: "words learned" and "words to be learned." Concentrate on the words you haven't learned until you master them all. Keep them fresh in your memory by reviewing them often and testing yourself frequently.

Take a Road Trip to the
Library of Congress!

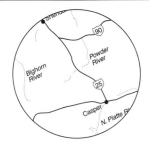

If your instructor has asked you to use the Reading Road Trip CD-ROM, be sure to visit the Vocabulary Development module for multimedia tutorials, exercises, and tests.

Using Context and Word Parts

Why Learn to Use Context and Word Parts?

▲ **These methods will help you learn more words faster than by simply memorizing individual meanings.**

▲ **They will save you time; you will not have to look up as many unfamiliar words in the dictionary.**

Learning Experiment

Step 1

Here are five words and their meanings:

List A

turmoil—complete confusion, uproar

subjective—involving judgment or feelings; not objective

eccentric—odd, strange

devious—shifty; not straightforward

corroborate—to strengthen or support with other evidence

Study the list until you have memorized it.

Step 2

When *hyper* is placed in front of a word it means *more than normal.*

Using the information above, learn the meaning of each of the following words.

List B

hyperactivity—overly active

hypersensitivity—overly sensitive

hypertension—abnormally high blood pressure

hyperextension—extension of a bodily joint beyond its normal range

hyperventilate—to breathe overly fast

The Results

Which list was easier and faster to learn? Probably the second list. Why? In list A, you had to learn five unrelated words; in list B, the words all began with the prefix (word beginning) *hyper.*

Learning Principle (What This Means to You)

You can learn things more easily if they are meaningful and related to one another (as the words in list B were). In this chapter you will learn two methods for finding and connecting the meanings of unfamiliar words.

A STRATEGY FOR LEARNING UNFAMILIAR WORDS

What should you do when you are reading a passage and you come to a word you don't know? If your instructor asked this question, you might reply, "I'd look the word up in the dictionary." And as you said this, you would know that in fact you don't often take the time to check the dictionary and were only giving an answer you thought your instructor wanted to hear and would agree with.

Actually, looking up a word in a dictionary is not the first thing to do when you meet a word you don't know. In fact, a dictionary is your last resort—somewhere to turn when all else fails. Instead, first try pronouncing the word aloud. Hearing the word may help you recall its meaning. If pronouncing the word does not help, try to figure out the meaning of the word from the words around it in a sentence, paragraph, or passage that you are reading. Very often, among these surrounding words are various clues that enable you to reason out the meaning of the unknown word. The words around an unknown word that contain clues to its meaning are referred to as the *context.* The clues themselves are called *context clues.* You can use four basic types of context clues in determining word meanings in textbook material: *definition, example/illustration, contrast,* and *logic of the passage.*

If a word's context does not provide clues to its meaning, you might try breaking the word into parts. Analyzing a word's parts, which may include its *prefix, root,* and *suffix,* also provides clues to its meaning. Finally, if word parts do not help, look the word up in a dictionary. Regardless of whatever method you use to find a word's meaning, be sure to record its meaning in the margin of the page. Later, transfer its meaning to a vocabulary log or computer file.

USING CONTEXT CLUES

Definition Context Clues

The most obvious type of context clue is an author's direct statement of the meaning of a new term. A textbook author does this when he or she is aware that a word is new to the reader and therefore takes the time to give an accurate definition of the term. Fox example, in the first chapter of a chemistry book, the term *chemical reaction* is defined.

> A <u>chemical reaction</u> is an interaction involving different atoms, in which chemical bonds are formed, or broken, or both.[1]

Some writers signal you directly that they are presenting a definition with expressions such as "Mass is . . ." or "Anthropology can be defined as ..." Other writers, however, are less direct and obvious when they include a definition. Parentheses may be used to give a definition, partial definition, or synonym of a word, as in the following sentence.

> <u>Deciduous trees</u> (trees bearing leaves that are shed annually) respond differently to heat and cold than <u>coniferous trees</u> (trees bearing cones).

Or, an author may use commas or dashes to set off a brief definition or synonym within the sentence.

> To begin with, he (Mendel) needed <u>true-breeding plants,</u> plants that showed little variation from generation to generation.[2]

> The <u>mean</u>—the mathematical average of a set of numbers—will determine whether grades will be based on a curve.

Finally, an author may simply insert a synonym directly within the sentence.

> Another central issue, that of the right of a state to withdraw or <u>secede</u> from the Union, was simply avoided.[3]

EXERCISE 1

DIRECTIONS   In each sentence, locate the part of the sentence that gives a definition or synonym of the underlined word. Underline this portion of the sentence.

1. A <u>democracy</u> is a form of government in which the people effectively participate.[4]
2. The amount of heat that it takes to melt one gram of any substance at its melting point is called the <u>heat of fusion.</u>[5]
3. <u>Linoleic acid</u> is an essential fatty acid necessary for growth and skin integrity in infants.[6]
4. When a gas is cooled, it <u>condenses</u> (changes to a liquid) at its condensation point.[7]
5. But neither a monkey nor an ape has thumbs long enough or flexible enough to be completely <u>opposable,</u> able to reach comfortably to the tips of all the other fingers, as is required for our delicate yet strong precision grip.[8]

Example/Illustration Context Clues

Authors frequently explain their ideas and concepts by giving specific, concrete examples or illustrations. Many times, when an example is given that illustrates or explains a new term, you can figure out the meaning of the term from the example. Suppose, for instance, that you frequently confuse the terms *fiction* and *nonfiction* and you are given the following assignment by your instructor: *Select any nonfiction book and write a critical review; you can choose from a wide range of books, such as autobiographies, sports books, how-to manuals, commentaries on historical periods, and current consumer-awareness paperbacks.* From the examples given, you can easily see that *nonfiction* refers to books that are factual, or true.

Writers sometimes give you an advance warning or signal that they are going to present an example or illustration. Phrases that signal an example or illustration to follow include *for example, for instance, to illustrate, such as, included are,* and so on. Read the following examples.

> Some everyday, common <u>solutions</u> include gasoline, antifreeze, soda water, seawater, vodka, and ammonia.

> Specifically, management of a New York bank developed a strategic plan to increase its customers by making them see banks as offering a large variety of services rather than just a few <u>specialized services</u> (cashing checks, putting money into savings accounts, and making loans).[9]

EXERCISE 2

DIRECTIONS   Read each sentence and write a definition or synonym for each underlined word. Use the illustration/example context clue to help you determine word meanings.

1. Maria enjoys all <u>equestrian</u> sports, including jumping, riding, and racing horses.

   _____

2. Murder, rape, and armed robbery are <u>reprehensible</u> crimes.

   _____

3. Psychological disturbances are sometimes traceable to a particular <u>trauma</u> in childhood. For example, the death of a parent may produce long-range psychological effects.

   _____

4. To <u>substantiate</u> his theory, Watson offered experimental evidence, case study reports, testimony of patients, and a log of observational notes.

   _____

5. Many <u>phobias</u> can seriously influence human behavior; the two most common are claustrophobia (fear of confined spaces) and acrophobia (fear of heights).

   _____

6. <u>Homogeneous</u> groups, such as classes made up entirely of boys, social organizations of people with high IQs, country clubs, and wealthy families, have particular roles and functions.

   _____

Contrast Context Clues

It is sometimes possible to figure out the meaning of an unknown word from a word or phrase in the context that has an opposite meaning. To use a simple example, in the sentence "Sam was thin, but George was obese," a contrast of opposites is set up between George and Sam. The word *but* signals that an opposite or contrasting idea is to follow. By knowing the meaning of *thin* and knowing that George is the opposite of thin, you figure out that *obese* means "not thin," or *fat.*

Most often when an opposite or contrasting meaning is given, a signal word or phrase in the sentence indicates a change in the direction of the thought. Most commonly used are these signal words or phrases: *on the other hand, however, although, whereas, but, nevertheless, on the contrary.* Note the following example.

> The Federalists, from their <u>pessimistic</u> viewpoint, believed the Constitution could protect them by its procedures, whereas the more positive Anti-Federalists thought of the Constitution as the natural rights due to all people.

In the preceding example, if you did not know the meaning of the word *pessimistic,* you could figure it out because a word appears later in the sentence that gives you a clue. The sentence is about the beliefs of two groups, the Federalists and the Anti-Federalists. The prefix *anti-* tells you that they hold opposite or differing views, and *whereas* also signals a contrast. If the Federalists are described as pessimistic and their views are opposite those of the Anti-Federalists, who are described as more positive, you realize that *pessimistic* means the opposite of positive, or negative.

Here is another example:

> Most members of Western society marry only one person at a time, but in other cultures <u>polygamy</u> is common and acceptable.

In this sentence, by the contrast established between Western society and other cultures, you can infer that *polygamy* refers to the practice of marriage to more than one person at a time.

EXERCISE 3

DIRECTIONS   Read each sentence and write a definition or synonym for each underlined word. Use the contrast context clue to help you determine the meaning of the word.

1. The philosopher was <u>vehement</u> in his objections to the new grading system; the more practical historian, on the other hand, expressed his views calmly and quietly.

   _____

2. The mayor was <u>dogmatic</u> about government policy, but the assistant mayor was more lenient and flexible in his interpretations.

   _____

3. Instead of evaluating each possible solution when it was first proposed, the committee decided it would <u>defer</u> judgment until all possible solutions had been proposed.

   _____

4. The two philosophical theories were <u>incompatible:</u> One acknowledged the existence of free will; the other denied it.

_____

5. Cultures vary in the types of behavior that are considered socially acceptable. In one culture, a man may be <u>ostracized</u> for having more than one wife, whereas in other cultures, a man with many wives is an admired and respected part of the group.

_____

Context Clues in the Logic of a Passage

One of the most common ways in which context provides clues about the meaning of an unknown word is through logic or general reasoning about the content of a sentence or about the relationship of ideas within a sentence. Suppose that before you read the following sentence you did not know the meaning of the word *empirical.*

> Some of the questions now before us are <u>empirical</u> issues that require evidence directly bearing on the question.[10]

From the way *empirical* is used in the sentence, you know that an empirical issue is one that requires direct evidence, and from that information you can infer, or reason, that *empirical* has something to do with proof or supporting facts.

Now suppose that you did not know the meaning of the term *cul-de-sac* before reading the following sentence.

> A group of animals hunting together can sometimes maneuver the hunted animal into a <u>cul-de-sac:</u> out onto a peak of high land, into a swamp or river, or into a gully from which it cannot escape.[11]

From the mention of the places into which a hunted animal can be maneuvered—a gully, a peak, or a swamp—you realize that the hunters have cornered the animal and that *cul-de-sac* means a blind alley or a situation from which there is no escape.

EXERCISE 4

DIRECTIONS Read each of the following sentences and write a synonym or definition for each underlined word or term. Look for context clues in the logic of the passage to help you figure out the meaning of each.

1. Religious or ethical convictions make the idea of capital punishment, in which a life is willingly, even legally, extinguished, a <u>repugnant</u> one.

_____

2. The former Berlin Wall, originally built with enough force and strength to separate East and West Germany, was <u>impervious</u> to attack.

_____

3. When the judge pronounced the sentence, the convicted criminal shouted <u>execrations</u> at the jury.

_____

4. The police officer was <u>exonerated</u> by a police review panel of any possible misconduct or involvement in a case of police bribery.

_____

5. The editor would not allow the paper to go to press until certain passages were <u>expunged</u> from an article naming individuals involved in a political scandal.

_____

EXERCISE 5

DIRECTIONS   Each of the following sentences contains an underlined word or phrase whose meaning can be determined from the context. Underline the part of the sentence that contains the clue to the meaning of the underlined words. Then, in the blank below, identify what type of context clue you used.

1. <u>Separation of powers</u> is the principle that the powers of government should be separated and put in the care of different parts of the government.[12]

_____

2. Samples of moon rock have been analyzed by <u>uranium dating</u> and found to be about 4.6 billion years old, or about the same age as the earth.[13]

_____

3. Like horses, human beings have a variety of <u>gaits;</u> they amble, stride, jog, and sprint.[14]

_____

4. In the past, <u>malapportionment</u> (large differences in the populations of congressional districts) was common in many areas of the country.[15]

_____

5. Tremendous <u>variability</u> characterizes the treatment of the mentally retarded during the medieval era, ranging from treatment as innocents to being tolerated as fools to persecution as witches.[16]

_____

EXERCISE 6

DIRECTIONS   Read each of the following paragraphs. For each underlined word, use context to determine its meaning. Write a synonym or brief definition in the space provided.

1.   The homeless are among the extremely poor. They are by definition people who sleep in streets, parks, shelters, and places not intended as <u>dwellings,</u> such as bus stations, lobbies, or abandoned buildings. Homelessness is not new. There have always been homeless people in the United States. But the homeless today differ in some ways from their <u>counterparts</u> of the 1950s and 1960s. More than 30 years ago, most of the homeless were old men, only a handful were women, and <u>virtually</u> no families were homeless. Today, as has been mentioned, the homeless are younger, and include more women and families with young children. Today's homeless also are more <u>visible</u> to the general public because they are much more likely to sleep on the streets or in other public places in great numbers. They also suffer greater <u>deprivation.</u> Although in the past homeless men on Skid Row were undoubtedly poor, their average income from casual and

intermittent work was three to four times more than what the current homeless receive. In addition, many of the older homeless men in the past had small but <u>stable</u> pensions, which today's homeless do not have (Rossi, 1989).

—Thio, *Sociology,* p. 235

a. dwellings _____

b. counterparts _____

c. virtually _____

d. visible _____

e. deprivation _____

f. stable _____

2.   **Territoriality**

Many animals that live in groups share a home range. In winter, for example, many birds flock together in a home range. After the spring migration to their new habitats, however, most male birds undergo a Jekyll-to-Hyde <u>transformation</u> and establish a territory that they vigorously defend against other males of their species. As noted before, sticklebacks, as well as numerous other animals, also establish territories. The essential difference between a home range and a territory is that the territory is, by definition, defended against <u>encroachment</u> by others of the same species. Male birds <u>advertise</u> possession of their territories by songs and visual displays. An <u>intruding</u> male's song or plumage is the releaser for territorial aggression by the resident. Resident males will often attack a tape recorder playing another male's song or a <u>tuft</u> of feathers the same color as the male's breeding plumage. The only way for a male bird to lurk about within the territory of another is to keep quiet and out of sight. Such "lurkers" are less likely to breed, however, because the songs and display are also required to attract females.

In some species a territory may be occupied by two or more males and their mates. Wolves are the classic illustration of a species that defends a group territory. The average wolf pack is an extended family of from five to eight individuals with a territory of a few hundred square kilometers. An <u>alpha male</u> and an <u>alpha female</u> lead the pack. They define the pack's territory by releasing a pheromone during a characteristic raised-leg urination about every 450 meters as they patrol its perimeter. To wolves from neighboring territories these <u>olfactory</u> boundary markers are, in one sense at least, nothing to sniff at. Packs of wolves have been seen abandoning a deer chase rather than cross into another pack's territory.

—Harris, *Concepts in Zoology,* p. 417

a. transformation _____

b. encroachment _____

c. advertise _____

d. intruding _____

e. tuft _____

f. alpha male _____

g. alpha female _____

h. olfactory _____

3.   Many animals communicate by chemical signals, which have the unique advantage of <u>persisting</u> for some time after the messenger has left the area. They also have the advantage that they will be detected only by those with receptors that respond to the chemical, so they are less likely to attract predators. Some chemical messages have a hormone-like ability to <u>induce</u> specific behavioral responses in recipients in the same species. Such chemical messages are called <u>pheromones.</u> The best-known pheromones are insect sex attractants, many of which have been isolated and chemically analyzed. The first such pheromone to be studied was bombykol, which is produced in minute amounts by glands near the anus of the female silk moth *Bombyx mori.* The glands from half a million females had to be processed to yield 12 mg of pheromone. (One lab worker was reportedly overheard complaining, "The end is always in sight, but the work is never done.") A single molecule of bombykol is enough to <u>evoke</u> an action potential from the antenna of a male silk moth, and several hundred molecules are enough to make the male fly upwind, toward the female.

—Harris, *Concepts in Zoology,* pp. 408–409

a. persisting _____

b. induce _____

c. pheromones _____

d. evoke _____

4.   Certain personal <u>characteristics</u> may explain who among the extremely poor are more likely to become homeless. These characteristics have been found to include chronic mental problems, alcoholism, drug addiction, serious criminal behavior, and physical health problems. Most of the extremely poor do not become homeless because they live with their relatives or friends. But those who suffer from any of the personal <u>disabilities</u> just mentioned are more likely to wear out their welcome as <u>dependents</u> of their parents or as <u>recipients</u> of aid and money from their friends. After all, their relatives and friends are themselves likely to be extremely poor and already living in crowded housing. We should be careful, though, not to <u>exaggerate</u> the <u>impact</u> of personal disabilities on homelessness. To some degree, personal disabilities may be the <u>consequences</u> rather than the cause of homelessness.

—Thio, *Sociology,* p. 235

a. characteristics _____

b. disabilities _____

c. dependents _____

d. recipients _____

e. exaggerate _____

f. impact _____

g. consequences _____

ANALYZING WORD PARTS

Mark and Elaine were taking a course in biology. While walking to class one day, Mark complained to Elaine, "I'll never be able to learn all this vocabulary!" They agreed that they needed some system, because learning each new word separately would be nearly impossible. Have you felt the same way in some of your courses?

The purpose of this section is to present a system of vocabulary learning. This system works for specific courses in which a great deal of new terminology is presented, as well as for building your overall, general vocabulary. The approach is based on analyzing word parts. Many words in the English language are made up of word parts called *prefixes, roots,* and *suffixes.* Think of these as beginnings, middles, and endings of words. These word parts have specific meanings, and when added together, they can help you figure out the meaning of the word as a whole. Let's begin with a few words from biology.

poikilotherm   homeotherm   endotherm   ectotherm

You could learn the definition of each term separately, but learning would be easier and more meaningful if you could see the relationship among the terms.

Each of the four words has as its root *-therm,* which means "heat." The meaning of the prefix, or beginning, of each word is given below.

poikilo- = changeable

homeo- = same or constant

endo- = within

ecto- = outside

Knowing these meanings can help you determine the meaning of each word.

poikilotherm = organism with variable body temperature
(i.e., cold-blooded)

homeotherm = organism with stable body temperature
(i.e., warm-blooded)

endotherm = organism that regulates its temperature internally

ectotherm = organism that regulates its temperature by taking in heat from the environment or giving off heat to the environment

When you first start using this method, you may not feel that you're making progress; in this case, you had to learn four prefixes and one root to figure out four words. However, what may not yet be obvious is that these prefixes will help unlock the meanings of numerous other words, not only in the field of biology but also in related fields and in general vocabulary usage. Here are a few examples of words that include each of the word parts we have analyzed:

therm-	poikilo-	homeo- (homo-)	ecto-	endo-
thermal	poikilocyte	homeostasis	ectoparasite	endocytosis
thermodynamics	poikilocytosis	homogeneous	ectoderm	endoderm

The remainder of this section will focus on commonly used prefixes, roots, and suffixes that are used in a variety of academic disciplines. In various combinations, these will unlock the meanings of thousands of words. For example, more than 10,000 words begin with the prefix *non-.*

**Figure 12.1
A Sample List
of Prefixes**

Psychology

neuro– nerves, nervous system   path– feeling, suffering
phob– fear   homo– same
auto– self   hetero– different

Once you have mastered the prefixes, roots, and suffixes given in this chapter, you should begin to identify word parts that are commonly used in each of your courses. For example, Figure 12.1 shows a partial list made by one student for a psychology course. Keep these lists in your course notebooks or use index cards, as described later in this chapter.

Before learning specific prefixes, roots, and suffixes, it is useful to be aware of the following points.

1. In most cases, a word is built on at least one root.
2. Words can have more than one prefix, root, or suffix.
   - Words can be made up of two or more roots (*geo* / *logy*).
   - Some words have two prefixes (*in* / *sub* / ordination).
   - Some words have two suffixes (beauti / *ful* / *ly*).
3. Words do not always have both a prefix and a suffix.
   - Some words have neither a prefix nor a suffix (read).
   - Others have a suffix but no prefix (read / *ing*).
   - Others have a prefix but no suffix (*pre* / read).
4. Roots may change in spelling as they are combined with suffixes. Some common variations are noted on page 262.
5. Sometimes you may identify a group of letters as a prefix or root but find that it does not carry the meaning of the prefix or root. For example, in the word *internal*, the letters *inter* should not be confused with the prefix *inter-*, meaning "between." Similarly, the letters *mis* in the word *missile* are part of the root and are not the prefix *mis-*, which means "wrong" or "bad."

Prefixes

Prefixes, appearing at the beginning of many English words, alter or modify the meaning of the root to which they are connected. In Figure 12.2 on the next page, common prefixes are grouped according to meaning.

◄ *EXERCISE 7*

DIRECTIONS   Use the prefixes listed in Figure 12.2 to help determine the meaning of each of the underlined words in the following sentences. Write a brief definition or synonym for each. If you are unfamiliar with the root, you may need to check a dictionary.

1. The instances of <u>abnormal</u> behavior reported in the mass media are likely to be extreme.

   _____

2. The two theories of language development are not fundamentally <u>incompatible,</u> as originally thought.

   _____

3. When threatened, the ego resorts to <u>irrational</u> protective measures, which are called defense mechanisms.

_____

4. Freud viewed the <u>interplay</u> among the id, ego, and superego as of critical importance in determining behavioral patterns.

_____

5. The long-term effects of continuous drug use are <u>irreversible.</u>

_____

Prefix	Meaning	Sample Word
Prefixes indicating direction, location, or placement		
circum-	around	circumference
com-, col-, con-	with, together	compile
de-	away, from	depart
ex-/extra-	from, out of, former	ex-wife
hyper-	over, excessive	hyperactive
inter-	between	interpersonal
intro-/intra-	within, into, in	introduction
mid-	middle	midterm
post-	after	posttest
pre-	before	premarital
re-	back, again	review
retro-	backward	retrospect
sub-	under, below	submarine
super-	above, extra	supercharge
tele-	far	telescope
trans-	across, over	transcontinental
Prefixes referring to amount or number		
bi-	two	bimonthly
equi-	equal	equidistant
micro-	small	microscope
mono-	one	monocle
multi-	many	multipurpose
poly-	many	polygon
semi-	half	semicircle
tri-	three	triangle
uni-	one	unicycle
Prefixes meaning "not" (negative)		
a-, an-, ab-	not	asymmetrical
anti-	against	antiwar
contra-	against, opposite	contradict
dis-	apart, away, not	disagree
mis-	wrong, bad	misunderstand
non-	not	nonfiction
pseudo-	false	pseudoscientific
un-	not	unpopular

Figure 12.2
Common Prefixes

EXERCISE 8

DIRECTIONS   Write a synonym or brief definition for each of the following underlined words. Check a dictionary if the root is unfamiliar.

1. a <u>substandard</u> performance _____

2. to <u>transcend</u> everyday differences _____

3. <u>telecommunications</u> equipment _____

4. a <u>hypercritical</u> person _____

5. a <u>retroactive</u> policy _____

6. <u>superconductive</u> metal _____

7. <u>extracurricular</u> activities _____

8. <u>postoperative</u> nursing care _____

9. a blood <u>transfusion</u> _____

10. <u>antisocial</u> behavior _____

11. to <u>misappropriate</u> funds _____

12. a <u>microscopic</u> organism _____

13. a <u>monotonous</u> speech _____

14. a <u>pseudointellectual</u> essay _____

15. a <u>polysyllabic</u> word _____

Roots

Roots carry the basic or core meaning of a word. Hundreds of root words are used to build words in the English language. Thirty of the most common and most useful are listed in Figure 12.3 on the next page. Knowing the meanings of these roots will assist you in unlocking the meanings of many words. For example, if you know that the root *dic-* or *dict-* means "tell" or "say," then you have a clue to the meanings of such words as *predict* (to tell what will happen in the future), *contradiction* (a statement that is contrary or opposite), and *diction* (wording or manner of speaking).

EXERCISE 9

DIRECTIONS   Write a synonym or brief definition for each of the underlined words. Consult Figures 12.2 and 12.3 as necessary.

1. a <u>monotheistic</u> religion _____

2. a <u>subterranean</u> tunnel _____

3. a <u>chronicle</u> of events _____

4. a <u>conversion</u> chart _____

5. <u>exportation</u> policies _____

6. leading an <u>introspective</u> life _____

7. to <u>speculate</u> on the results _____

8. <u>sensuous</u> music _____

9. a <u>versatile</u> performance _____

10. an <u>incredible</u> explanation _____

11. infant <u>mortality</u> rates _____

12. the <u>tensile</u> strength of a cable _____

13. a <u>vociferous</u> crowd _____

14. a logical <u>deduction</u> _____

15. a <u>corporate</u> earnings report _____

Root	Meaning	Sample Word
aster, astro	star	astronaut
aud, audit	hear	audible
bio	life	biology
cap	take, seize	captive
chron(o)	time	chronology
corp	body	corpse
cred	believe	incredible
dict, dic	tell, say	predict
duc, duct	lead	introduce
fact, fac	make, do	factory
geo	earth	geophysics
graph	write	telegraph
log, logo, logy	study, thought	psychology
mit, miss	send	dismiss
mort, mor	die, death	immortal
path	feeling, disease	sympathy
phone	sound, voice	telephone
photo	light	photosensitive
port	carry	transport
scop	seeing	microscope
scribe, script	write	inscription
sen, sent	feel	insensitive
spec, spic, spect	look, see	retrospect
tend, tent, tens	stretch, strain	tension
terr, terre	land, earth	territory
theo	god	theology
ven, vent	come	convention
vert, vers	turn	invert
vis, vid	see	invisible
voc	call	vocation

Figure 12.3
Common Roots

Suffixes

Suffixes are word endings that often change the part of speech of a word. For example, adding the suffix *-y* to a word changes it from a noun to an adjective and shifts the meaning—for example, *cloud, cloudy.* Often several different words can be formed from a single root word with the addition of different suffixes. Here is an example:

Root: *Class*

classify

classification

classic

Common suffixes are grouped according to meaning in Figure 12.4.

Suffix	Sample Word
Suffixes that refer to a state, condition, or quality	
-able	touchable
-ance	assistance
-ation	confrontation
-ence	reference
-ic	aerobic
-ible	tangible
-ion	discussion
-ity	superiority
-ive	permissive
-ment	amazement
-ness	kindness
-ous	jealous
-ty	loyalty
-y	creamy
Suffixes that mean "one who"	
-ee	employee
-eer	engineer
-er	teacher
-ist	activist
-or	editor
Suffixes that mean "pertaining to" or "referring to"	
-al	autumnal
-ship	friendship
-hood	brotherhood
-ward	homeward

Figure 12.4
Common Suffixes

EXERCISE 10

DIRECTIONS   Write a synonym or brief definition of each of the underlined words. Consult a dictionary if necessary.

1. acts of <u>terrorism</u> _____

2. a <u>graphic</u> description _____

3. a <u>materialistic</u> philosophy _____

4. <u>immunity</u> to disease _____

5. <u>impassable</u> road conditions _____

6. a speech <u>impediment</u> _____

7. <u>intangible</u> property _____

8. <u>instinctive</u> behavior _____

9. <u>interrogation</u> techniques _____

10. the communist <u>sector</u> _____

11. obvious <u>frustration</u> _____

12. <u>global</u> conflicts _____

13. in <u>deference</u> to _____

14. <u>piteous</u> physical ailments _____

15. Supreme Court <u>nominee</u> _____

EXERCISE 11

DIRECTIONS   The following terms were taken from the "The Decorated Body" in Part Seven, pp. 381–383. Locate the term in the reading and write a brief definition of each. Use both context clues and word parts and a dictionary, if necessary.

1. unbearable (para. 1) _____

2. transformed (para. 2) _____

3. millennia (para. 3) _____

4. aesthetically (para. 4) _____

5. unornamented (para. 5) _____

6. communal (para. 5) _____

7. pretexts (para. 8) _____

8. inscription (para. 9) _____

9. brutish (para. 10) _____

10. homogeneous (para. 12) _____

EXERCISE 12

DIRECTIONS From a chapter in one of your textbooks make a list of words with multiple word parts. Using Figures 12.2, 12.3, and 12.4, define as many as you can. Check the accuracy of your definitions using your book's glossary or a dictionary.

LEARNING *Collaboratively*

DIRECTIONS The instructor will choose a reading selection from Part Seven and divide the class into groups. In your groups, locate and underline at least five difficult words in the selection that can be defined by analyzing word parts and/or using context clues. Work together with group members to determine the meaning of each word, checking a dictionary to verify and expand meanings.

Applying YOUR LEARNING

Imagine that Jon is taking one of your courses with you. He is having difficulty figuring out and remembering new terms presented in the text and in lectures.

1. Photocopy several pages from your notes and from your text where new terms are introduced.
2. Explain to Jon what context clues the professor and the author are using.
3. Share with Jon your system for building up a content-specific vocabulary.

SELF-TEST SUMMARY

1. What is a context clue?	The context—the words around an unknown word—frequently contains clues that help you figure out the meaning of the unknown word.
2. What are the four basic types of context clues? Define each.	There are four basic types of context clues. a. *Definition:* A brief definition or synonym of an unknown word may be included in the sentence in which the word is used. b. *Example/illustration:* Writers may explain their words and ideas by giving specific, concrete examples. c. *Contrast:* The meaning of an unknown word can sometimes be determined from a word or phrase in the context that has the opposite meaning. d. *Logic of the passage:* The meaning of an unknown word can sometimes be determined through reasoning or by applying logic to the content of the sentence or paragraph.
3. How can learning word parts improve your vocabulary?	Learning word parts enables you to figure out the meaning of an unknown word by analyzing the meanings of its parts—prefixes, roots, and suffixes.

Take a Road Trip to the
Library of Congress!

If your instructor has asked you to use the Reading Road Trip CD-ROM, be sure to visit the Vocabulary Development module for multimedia tutorials, exercises, and tests.

Textbook Highlighting and Marking

CHAPTER 13

Why Learn to Highlight and Mark Your Textbooks?

▲ Highlighting and marking force you to sort ideas, deciding which are important and which are not.

▲ Highlighting and marking keep you physically active while you read and help focus your attention on the material.

▲ Highlighting and marking help you remember what you read.

▲ Highlighting and marking force you to weigh and evaluate what you read.

▲ Highlighting and marking help you see the organization of facts and ideas and connections between them.

Learning Experiment

Step 1

Study the following diagram of the human brain. Estimate how long it would take you to learn all the parts of the brain shown in the diagram.

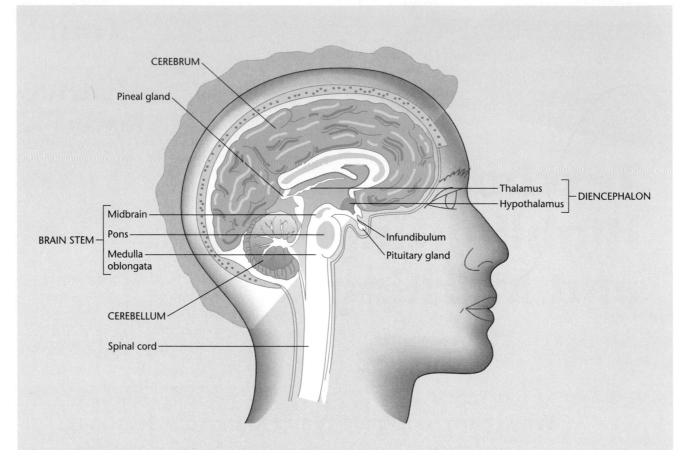

Principal Parts of the Human Brain

Step 2

Now, using the same diagram, estimate how long would it take you to learn only the four principal parts of the brain.

The Results

No doubt your estimate was much lower for step 2. Why? You had less information to learn.

Learning Principle (What This Means to You)

You can make studying textbooks easier if you are selective about what to learn. In most courses, you are not expected to learn and recall every detail and example in your textbook. Instead, you are responsible for learning the more important ideas. In this chapter you will learn how to identify what is important in a textbook chapter and develop a system of highlighting and marking.

THE PROBLEM OF TEXTBOOK REVIEW

As you have already discovered, most college courses involve lengthy and time-consuming reading assignments. Just completing the reading assignments is a big job. Have you begun to wonder how you will ever go back over all those textbook chapters when it's time for an exam?

Let's suppose that it takes you at least 4 hours to read carefully a 40-page chapter for one of your courses. Assume that your text has ten chapters of approximately 40 pages each. It would take a total of 40 hours, then, to read completely through the text once. Suppose that your instructor is giving a final exam that will cover the entire text. If the only thing you did to prepare for the final was to reread the whole text, then it would take close to another 40 hours to study for the exam; and one additional reading is no guarantee that you will pass the exam.

Now consider this: If you had highlighted and marked important ideas and facts as you were first reading the chapters, when you were ready to review, you would have to read and study only what you marked. If you had marked or highlighted 15 to 20 percent of the chapter material, you would have cut your rereading time by 80 to 85 percent, or 32 hours! Of course, to prepare effectively for the exam, you would have to review in other ways besides rereading, but you would have time left to do this.

HOW TO HIGHLIGHT TEXTBOOKS

To learn how to highlight textbooks effectively, start with the following guidelines.

1. *Read first; then highlight.* As you are reading to develop skill in highlighting, it is better to read a paragraph or section first and then go back and highlight what is important to remember and review. Later, when you've had more practice highlighting, you may be able to highlight while you read.
2. *Read the boldface headings.* Headings are labels, or overall topics, for what is contained in that section. Use the headings to form questions that you expect to be answered in the section.
3. *After you have read the section, go back and highlight the parts that answer your questions.* These will be parts of sentences that express the main ideas, or most important thoughts, in the section. In reading and highlighting the following section, you could form questions like those suggested and then highlight as shown.

Questions to Ask
What are primary groups?
What are secondary groups?

Primary and Secondary Groups
It is not at all surprising that some students used their families as a reference group. After all, families are the best examples of the groups Charles Cooley (1909) called *primary* chiefly because they "are fundamental in forming the social nature and ideals of the individual." In a primary group the individuals interact informally, relate to each other as whole persons, and enjoy their relationship for its own sake. This is one of the two main types of social groups. In the other type, a secondary group, the

individuals interact formally, relate to each other as players of particular roles, and expect to profit from each other.

—Thio, *Sociology,* p. 100

4. *As you identify and highlight main ideas, look for important facts that explain or support the main idea, and highlight them too.*
5. *When highlighting main ideas and details, do not highlight complete sentences.* Highlight only enough so that you can see what is important and so that your highlighting makes sense when you reread. Note how only key words and phrases are highlighted in the following passage.

Causes of Homelessness

The causes of homelessness can be categorized into two types: larger social forces and personal characteristics. One social force is the shortage of inexpensive housing for poor families and poor unattached persons. This shortage began in the 1970s and accelerated in the 1980s. Another social force is the decreasing demand for unskilled labor in the 1980s, which resulted in extremely high unemployment among young men in general and blacks in particular. A third social force is the erosion of public welfare benefits over the last two decades. These three social forces do not directly cause homelessness. They merely enlarge the ranks of the extremely poor, thereby increasing the chances of these people becoming homeless.

—Thio, *Sociology,* p. 232

ASPECTS OF EFFECTIVE HIGHLIGHTING

For your highlighting to be effective and useful to you as you study and review, it must follow four specific guidelines.

1. The right amount of information must be highlighted.
2. The highlighting must be regular and consistent.
3. It must be accurate.
4. It must clearly reflect the content of the passage.

Suggestions for implementing these guidelines and examples of each are given in the following paragraphs.

Highlight the Right Amount

Students frequently make the mistake of highlighting either too much or too little. If you highlight too much, the passages you have marked will take you too long to reread when you are studying later. If you highlight too little, you won't be able to get any meaning from your highlighting as you review it.

Too Much Highlighting

Iran, which had served as an area of competition between the British and the Russians since the nineteenth century, became a bone of contention between the United States and the Soviet Union after World War II. As the result of an agreement between the British and the Russians in 1941, Shah Mohammad Reza Pahlavi (1919–1980) gained the Iranian throne. After the war he asked foreign troops to withdraw from his country, but following the slow return of the Soviet army to its borders, aggressive activities of the Iranian Communist party (Tudeh), and an assassination attempt on the Shah's life, Iran firmly tied itself to the West.

—Wallbank et al., *Civilization Past and Present,* pp. 1012–1013

Too Little Highlighting

Iran, which had served as an area of competition between the British and the Russians since the nineteenth century, became a bone of contention between the United States and the Soviet Union after World War II. As the result of an agreement between the British and the Russians in 1941, Shah Mohammad Reza Pahlavi (1919–1980) gained the Iranian throne. After the war he asked foreign troops to withdraw from his country, but following the slow return of the Soviet army to its borders, aggressive activities of the Iranian Communist party (Tudeh), and an assassination attempt on the Shah's life, Iran firmly tied itself to the West.

Effective Highlighting

Iran, which had served as an area of competition between the British and the Russians since the nineteenth century, became a bone of contention between the United States and the Soviet Union after World War II. As the result of an agreement between the British and the Russians in 1941, Shah Mohammad Reza Pahlavi (1919–1980) gained the Iranian throne. After the war he asked foreign troops to withdraw from his country, but following the slow return of the Soviet army to its borders, aggressive activities of the Iranian Communist party (Tudeh), and an assassination attempt on the Shah's life, Iran firmly tied itself to the West.

Almost all of the first passage is highlighted. To highlight nearly all of the passage is as ineffective as not highlighting at all, because it does not distinguish important from unimportant information. In the second passage, only the main point of the paragraph is highlighted, but very sketchily—not enough detail is included. The highlighting in the third passage is effective; it identifies the main idea of the paragraph and includes enough details to make the main idea clear and understandable.

As a rule of thumb, try to highlight no more than one-quarter to one-third of each page. This figure will vary, of course, depending on the type of material you are reading. Here is another example of effective highlighting. Note that approximately one-third of each paragraph is highlighted.

Living with Pain

Temporary pain is an unpleasant but necessary part of life, a warning of disease or injury. Chronic pain, which is ongoing or recurring, is another matter, a serious problem in itself. Back injuries, arthritis, migraine headaches, serious illnesses such as cancer—all can cause unrelieved misery to pain sufferers and their families. Chronic pain can also impair the immune system, and such impairment can put patients at risk of further complications from their illnesses.

At one time, the only way to combat pain was with drugs or surgery, which were not always effective. Today, we know that the experience of pain is affected by attitudes, and that treatment must take into account psychology as well as biology. Even social roles can influence a person's response to pain. For example, although women tend to report greater pain than men do, a real-world study of people who were in pain for more than six months found that men suffered more severe psychological distress than women, possibly because the male role made it hard for them to admit their pain.

—Wade and Tarvis, *Invitation to Psychology,* p. 182

Develop a Regular and Consistent System of Highlighting

As you develop your textbook highlighting skills, you should focus on this second guideline: Develop a system for deciding what type of information you will highlight and how you will mark it. First, decide what type of information you want to mark. Before marking anything, decide whether you will mark only main ideas or mark main ideas and details. You should also decide whether you will highlight or mark definitions of new terminology and, if so, how you will distinguish them from other information marked in the paragraph. Second, it is important to use consistently whatever system and type of highlighting you decide on so that you will know what your highlighting means when you review it. If you sometimes mark details and main ideas and other times highlight only main ideas, at review time you will find that you are unsure of what passages are marked in what way, and you will be forced to reread a great deal of material.

You may decide to develop a system for separating main ideas from details, major points from supporting information. When you review highlighting done this way, you will immediately know what is the most important point of the paragraph or section, and you will not get bogged down in the details—unless you need to. One such system uses one color of marker for main points and a different color for details. Another approach is to use asterisks and brackets to call attention to the main points.

Each of the following paragraphs has been highlighted using one of the suggested systems. You will notice that the paragraphs vary in the type of information marked in each.

Version 1: Use of Color

Barriers to Listening

There are several reasons why people are poor listeners. One reason is that the complex human mind can comprehend many more words per minute than speakers can produce. Listeners can process more than 400 spoken words per minute, yet the average speaker only produces between 125 and 175 words per minute. This time lag between slower speaking rates and faster rates of thinking is known as the **speech–thought differential.** Stated in a different way, the listener needs only 15 seconds of every minute to comprehend the spoken message. The resulting time lag creates special problems. In this excess time, listeners' thoughts may begin to stray. Can you recall a time when you began listening to a speaker, but soon found yourself thinking about lunch, or an upcoming test, or a date? This tendency for our thoughts to stray poses many problems for the speaker trying to convey an understandable message, especially if the subject matter is complex.

—Gronbeck et al., *Principles of Speech Communication,* p. 25

Version 2: Use of Brackets and Asterisks

Barriers to Listening

* There are several reasons why people are poor listeners. One reason is that the complex human mind can comprehend many more words per minute than speakers can produce. Listeners can process more than 400 spoken words per minute, yet the average speaker only produces between 125 and 175 words per minute. This time lag between slower speaking rates and faster rates of thinking is known as the * **speech–thought differential.** Stated in a different way, the listener needs only 15 seconds of every minute to comprehend the spoken message. The resulting time lag creates special problems. In this excess time, listeners' thoughts may begin to stray. Can you recall a time when you began listening to a speaker, but soon found yourself thinking about lunch, or an upcoming test, or a date? This tendency for our thoughts to stray poses many problems for the speaker trying to convey an understandable message, especially if the subject matter is complex.

EXERCISE 1

DIRECTIONS   Read the following passage. Then evaluate the effectiveness of the highlighting, making suggestions for improvement.

Scarcity of Human Fossils

Unfortunately humans are a maddeningly poor source of fossils. In 1956, the paleontologist G. H. R. von Koenigswald calculated that if all the then-known fragments of human beings older than the Neanderthal people were gathered together they could be comfortably displayed on a medium-sized table. Although many more fossils of early hominids have been found since then, discoveries are still rare.

Why are human fossils so scarce? Why can one go to good fossil sites almost anywhere in the world and find millions of shell remains or thousands of bones of extinct reptiles and mammals, while peoples earlier than Neanderthal are known from only a handful of sites at which investigators, working through tons of deposits, pile up other finds by the bushel basket before recovering a single human tooth?

There are many reasons. First, the commonness of marine fossils is a direct reflection of the abundance of these creatures when they were alive. It also reflects the tremendous span of time during which they abounded. Many of them swarmed through the waters of the earth for hundreds of millions of years. Whey they died, they sank and were covered by sediments. Their way of life—their life in the water—preserved them, as did their extremely durable shells, the only parts of them that now remain. Humans, by contrast, have never been as numerous as oysters and clams. They existed in small numbers, reproduced slowly and in small numbers, and lived a relatively long time. They were more intelligent than, for example, dinosaurs and were perhaps less apt to get mired in bogs, marshes, or quicksands. Most important, their way of life was different. They were not sea creatures or exclusively riverside browsers but lively, wide-ranging food-gatherers and hunters. They often lived and died in the open, where their bones were gnawed by scavengers, were trampled on, and were bleached and decomposed by the sun and rain. In hot climates, particularly in tropical forests and woodlands, the soil is likely to be markedly acid. Bones dissolve in such soils, and early humans who lived and died in such an environment had a very poor chance of leaving remains that would last until today. Finally, human ancestors have been on earth only a few million years. There simply has not been as much time for them to leave their bones as there has been for some of the more ancient species of animals.

—Campbell and Loy, *Humankind Emerging,* pp. 22–23

 **EXERCISE 2**

DIRECTIONS   Read each passage and then highlight the main ideas and important details in each. You may want to try various systems of highlighting as you work through this exercise.

1. **The Relationship Between Publicity and Public Relations**
   Publicity and public relations are closely related. While the public-relations role in organizations involves many communications approaches including institutional advertising and personal selling by senior corporate executives, publicity is often the cornerstone of a company's public-relations efforts. A firm's successful public-relations efforts, for example, might be largely the result of publicity it has managed to attract. When Chevron Oil sponsors research aimed at improving the environment, news reports that carry the story (publicity) are instrumental in furthering the image of the company (public relations).

   Publicity is generally a short-term strategy whereas a firm's public relations are ongoing. It is also important to note that a firm controls its public-relations efforts. The company designs its public-relations program to provide positive information about itself and its products. Because publicity is not generated internally, the organization cannot control it.

   Both publicity and public relations are important components of an organization's integrated marketing communications. When carefully planned, with an understanding of the target audience's interests, publicity and public relations can effectively promote a company with little expense.

   —Kinnear, Bernhardt, and Krentler, *Principles of Marketing,* p. 537

2. Beliefs

Beliefs consist of a system of propositions and assertions about the nature of reality. They provide people and societies with a fundamental orientation to the world and answer questions about human origins, proper relations among people, and the destiny of humans and the universe. Simple societies answer these questions with myth and folklore; complex societies answer them with religion and science. Beliefs also include simple observations about the physical and social worlds, or "truths" about nature and people.

Beliefs are social constructions. Although they are typically accepted as truths by the members of a society, beliefs are based not only on objective reality but on social agreement. Moreover yesterday's beliefs and the common sense of the present are the falsehoods and "myths" of tomorrow. For example, the word "lunatic" is derived from the popular nineteenth-century belief that a full moon causes madness, a belief that has folk origins in Europe and even deeper associations in simple cultures. Today, such thinking is derisively labeled "superstition."

The belief systems of simple societies are generally well integrated and stable and contain few contradictions. In contrast, complex societies—in particular, industrial societies—include multiple and competing belief systems that usually contain many contradictions. For example, Fundamentalist Christianity and science each contain a logically consistent body of beliefs and underlying premises, but the two present very different views of reality. Because of competing ideologies, or beliefs that support, rationalize, or legitimize various social arrangements, people in industrial societies are often more critical of their beliefs than are people in simple societies. Their beliefs are also apt to change at a much faster rate.

—Thompson and Hickey, *Society in Focus,* p. 65

3. Policies to Reduce Unemployment

The Employment Act of 1946 gave the U.S. government responsibility for establishing policies to achieve the maximum practical level of employment in the nation. Before deciding on a policy for full employment, it is necessary to identify the causes of unemployment. Then policymakers can design programs to remedy each type. Economists classify unemployment into three categories, depending on the cause: frictional, cyclical, and structural.

Frictional Unemployment. Some portion of total unemployment includes workers who are unemployed because of "frictions" in the movement of workers from job to job or among workers entering the labor force for the first time.

Frictional unemployment is common in a growing economy and reflects the healthy expansion or decline of different sectors of the economy. Markets and production techniques are constantly changing to reflect changes in consumer demand. Workers must move out of declining industries and into expanding industries. If there were no frictional unemployment, expanding industries would have to bid up the wages of employed workers, aggravating tendencies toward inflation.

In recent years, frictional unemployment has come to constitute a larger portion of total employment. This is primarily because of the growing numbers of married women and teenagers in the job market, with typically higher rates of entry and reentry into the labor force than adult male workers.

Frictional unemployment is, by definition, temporary. Its effects may be relieved by better job information and aids to worker mobility. For example, workers can be provided job counseling, or they can be paid grants to finance a move to a new location where jobs are more plentiful.

Cyclical Unemployment. A more serious problem than frictional unemployment is cyclical unemployment—unemployment associated with cycles of economic activity. The Great Depression provides the most obvious example of cyclical unemployment. During the Great Depression, the unemployment rate reached as high as 25 percent of the labor force.

Typically, economic activity grows in spurts. Periods of growth and prosperity are followed by slower growth or decline. Once homes are equipped with all the latest consumer gadgets, demand for consumer goods diminishes. Retailers cut back on inventories and cancel orders to wholesalers. The whole economic system seems to pause before the next round of innovations creates new gadgets, and the cycle begins again.

Cyclic swings in employment are most severe in industries producing durable goods. Purchase of a VCR, microwave oven, or personal computer can be postponed if consumers are worried about their jobs. Cyclical swings are less severe in industries producing nondurable goods and services. Purchases of food, clothing, and health services, for instance, cannot generally be postponed.

In past business cycles, blue-collar production workers were more likely to suffer unemployment than white-collar professional or supervisory workers. Professional and supervisory workers have specialized functions and, often, employment contracts that formerly made dismissal difficult. These workers suffered severely in the recession of 1990–91, however.

Expansionary fiscal and monetary policy make prolonged cyclical unemployment less a threat to our economic system today than in former years.

Structural Unemployment. The kind of unemployment that is most damaging to our prosperity and social health is the growing problem of structural unemployment. *Structural unemployment* is caused by an imbalance between the structure of the labor force, on the one hand, and the requirements of modern industry, on the other. Unless available labor skills correspond to the needs of business firms, there will be unemployment. In fact, there may be severe unemployment at the same time there are job vacancies. Structural unemployment is worsened by the entry of untrained workers (such as teenagers) into the labor force.

The greatest needs in business today are for skilled workers and for workers in the growing service sector. For example, there are extreme shortages of workers in machine trades, some types of engineering, nursing, and transportation.

Policies to remedy structural unemployment include federal and state programs to train workers in new skills, better job information and counseling, and private on-the-job training.

—McCarty, *Dollars and Sense: An Introduction to Economics*, pp. 272–273

Highlight Accurately

A third guideline for marking textbooks is to be sure that the information you highlight accurately conveys the content of the paragraph or passage. In a rush, students often overlook the second half of the main idea expressed in a paragraph, miss a crucial qualifying statement, or mistake an example or (worse yet) a contrasting idea for the main idea. Read the following paragraph and evaluate the accuracy of the highlighting.

It has long been established that the American legal court system is an open and fair system. Those suspected to be guilty of a criminal offense are given a jury trial in which a group of impartially selected citizens are asked to determine, based upon evidence presented, the guilt or innocence of the person on trial. In actuality, however, this system of jury trial is fair to everyone except the jurors involved. Citizens are expected and, in many instances, required to sit on a jury. They have little or no choice as to the time, place, or any other circumstances surrounding their participation. Additionally, they are expected to leave their job and accept jury duty pay for each day spent in court in place of their regular on-the-job salary. The jury must remain on duty until the case is decided.

In the preceding paragraph, the highlighting indicates that the main idea of the paragraph is that the legal system that operates in American courts is open and fair. The paragraph starts out by saying that the legal system has long been established as fair, but then it goes on to say (in the third sentence) that the system is actually unfair to one particular group—the jury. In this case, the student who did the highlighting missed the real main statement of the paragraph by mistaking the introductory contrasting statement for the main idea.

Make Your Highlighting Understandable for Review

As you highlight, keep the fourth guideline in mind: Be certain that your highlighting clearly reflects the content of the passage so that you will be able to reread and review it easily. Try to highlight enough information in each passage so that the passage reads smoothly when you review it.

Read these two examples of highlighting of the same passage. Which highlighting is easier to reread?

Version 1

Capital may be thought of as manufactured resources. Capital includes the tools and equipment that strengthen, extend, or replace human hands in the production of goods and services. Hammers, sewing machines, turbines, bookkeeping machines, and component parts of finished goods—all are capital goods. Even the specialized skills of trained workers can be thought of as a kind of human capital. Capital resources permit "roundabout" production: producing goods indirectly by a kind of tool rather than directly by physical labor.

To construct a capital resource requires that we postpone production of consumer goods and services today so that we can produce a tool that will enable us to produce more goods and services in the future. To postpone production of wanted goods and services is sometimes a painful decision, particularly when people are poor and in desperate need of goods and services today.

—McCarty, *Dollars and Sense*, pp. 213–214

Version 2

Capital may be thought of as manufactured resources. Capital includes the tools and equipment that strengthen, extend, or replace human hands in the production of goods and services. Hammers, sewing machines, turbines, bookkeeping machines, and component parts of finished goods—all are capital goods. Even the specialized skills of trained workers can be thought of as a kind of human capital. Capital resources permit "roundabout" production: producing goods indirectly with a kind of tool rather than directly by physical labor.

To construct a capital resource requires that we postpone production of other goods and services today so that we can produce a tool that will enable us to produce more goods and services in the future. To postpone production of wanted goods and services is sometimes a painful decision, particularly when people are poor and in desperate need of goods and services today.

A good way to check to see if your highlighting is understandable for review is to reread only your highlighting. If parts are unclear right after you read it, you can be sure it will be more confusing when you reread it a week or a month later. Be sure to fix ineffectual highlighting in one paragraph before you continue to the next paragraph.

TESTING YOUR HIGHLIGHTING

As you are learning highlighting techniques, it is important to check to be certain that your highlighting is effective and will be useful for review purposes. To test the effectiveness of your highlighting, take any passage that you have highlighted in Exercise 2 and reread only the highlighting. Then ask yourself the following questions.

1. Have I highlighted the right amount or do I have too much or too little information highlighted?
2. Have I used a regular and consistent system for highlighting?
3. Does my highlighting accurately reflect the meaning of the passage?
4. As I reread my highlighting, is it easy to follow the train of thought or does the passage seem like a list of unconnected words?

DIRECTIONS Read the section titled "Effects of Habitat Destruction and Degradation on Species" in the Part Seven reading "Causes of Habitat Loss and Species Endangerment," on p. 404. Highlight the main ideas and important details. When you have finished, test your highlighting by asking the four preceding questions. Make any changes that will make your highlighting more consistent, accurate, or understandable.

DIRECTIONS Choose a three- to four-page passage from one of your textbooks. Read the selection and highlight the main ideas, the important details, and any key terms that are introduced. When you have finished, test your highlighting by asking the four questions listed above, and make any changes that will improve your highlighting.

MARKING A TEXTBOOK

As you were highlighting paragraphs and passages in the earlier part of this chapter, you may have realized that highlighting alone is not sufficient, in many cases, to separate main ideas from details and both of these from new terminology. You may have seen that highlighting does not easily show the relative importance of ideas or indicate the relationship between facts and ideas. Therefore, it is often necessary to mark, as well as highlight, selections that you are reading. Suggestions for marking are shown in Figure 13.1 on the next page.

Two versions of the same paragraph, excerpted from *Messages* by DeVito, follow. The first version contains only highlighting, whereas both highlighting and marking are used in the second. Which version more easily conveys the meaning of the passage?

Version 1

Cultural Time

Two types of cultural time are especially important in nonverbal communication. In American culture, *formal time* is divided into seconds, minutes, hours, days, weeks, months, and years. Other cultures may use phases of the moon or the seasons to delineate time periods. In some colleges courses are divided into 50- or 75-minute periods that meet two or three times a week for 14-week periods called semesters. Eight semesters of 15 or so 50-minute periods per week equal a college education.

Other colleges use quarters or trimesters. As these examples illustrate, formal time units are arbitrary. The culture establishes them for convenience.

Informal time refers to the use of general time terms—for example, "forever," "immediately," "soon," "right away," "as soon as possible." This area of time creates the most communication problems because the terms have different meanings for different people.

Attitudes toward time vary from one culture to another. In one study, for example, the accuracy of clocks was measured in six cultures—Japanese, Indonesian, Italian, English, Taiwanese, and North American (U.S.). The Japanese had the most accurate and Indonesians had the least accurate clocks. A measure of the speed at which people in these six cultures walked found that the Japanese walked the fastest, the Indonesians the slowest.

—DeVito, *Messages*, pp. 161–162

Type of Marking		Example
Circling unknown words	def	. . .redressing the apparent ⃝asymmetry⃝ of their relationship . . .
Marking definitions	def	To say that the balance of power favors one party over another is to introduce a disequilibrium.
Marking examples	ex	. . .concessions may include negative sanctions, trade agreements . . .
Numbering lists of ideas, causes, reasons, or events		. . .components of power include ①self-image, ②population, ③natural resources, and ④geography
Placing asterisks next to important passages	*	Power comes from three primary sources . . .
Putting question marks next to confusing passages	?→	. . .war prevention occurs through institutionalization of mediation . . .
Making notes to yourself	check def in soc text	. . .power is the ability of an actor on the international stage to . . .
Marking possible test items	T	There are several key features in the relationship . . .
Drawing arrows to show relationships		. . .natural resources . . . control of industrial manufacturing capacity
Writing comments, noting disagreements and similarities	Can terrorism be prevented through similar balance?	. . .war prevention through balance of power is . . .
Marking summary statements	sum	. . .the greater the degree of conflict, the more intricate will be . . .

Figure 13.1
Textbook Marking

Version 2

Cultural Time

def

examples

Two types of cultural time are especially important in nonverbal communication. In American culture, formal time is divided into seconds, minutes, hours, days, weeks, months, and years. Other cultures may use phases of the moon or the seasons to delineate time periods. In some colleges courses are divided into 50- or 75-minute periods that meet two or three times a week for 14-week periods called semesters. Eight semesters of 15 or so 50-minute periods per week equal a college education. Other colleges use quarters or trimesters. As these examples illustrate, formal time units are arbitrary. The culture establishes them for convenience.

def

Informal time refers to the use of general time terms—for example, "forever," "immediately," "soon," "right away," "as soon as possible." This area of time creates the most communication problems because the terms have different meanings for different people.

cultural differences

research study

Attitudes toward time vary from one culture to another. In one study, for example, the accuracy of clocks was measured in six cultures—Japanese, Indonesian, Italian, English, Taiwanese, and North American (U.S.). The Japanese had the most accurate and Indonesians had the least accurate clocks. A measure of the speed at which people in these six cultures walked found that the Japanese walked the fastest, the Indonesians the slowest.

As you can see, in version 2 the two types of cultural time are easy to identify. Boxing the two types makes them immediately noticeable and distinguishes them from the remainder of the passage.

Critical Comments

When you highlight, you are operating at the knowledge and comprehension levels of thinking (see Chapter 2, p. 46). Marking is an opportunity to record your thinking at other levels.

Applying Levels of Thinking

Marking and Levels of Thinking

Here are some examples of the kinds of marginal notes you might make.

Level of Thinking	Marginal Notes
Application	Jot notes about how to use the information.
Analysis	Draw arrows to link related material.
Synthesis	Record ideas about how topics fit together; make notes connecting material to lectures; condense ideas into your own words.
Evaluation	Comment on the worth, value, relevance, and timeliness of ideas.

Writing Summary Notes

Writing summary words or phrases in the margin is one of the most valuable types of textbook marking. It involves pulling ideas together and summarizing them in your own words. This process forces you to think and evaluate as you read and makes remembering easier. Writing summary phrases is also a good test of your understanding. If you cannot state the main idea of a section in your own words, you probably do not understand it clearly. This realization can serve as an early warning signal that you may not be able to handle a test question on that section.

The following sample passage has been included to illustrate effective marking of summary phrases. First, read through the passage. Then look at the marginal summary clues.

Cross-Cultural Conclusions

At this juncture, after analyzing organized crime in various societies, we may reach several conclusions about the subject.

hierarchical

First, organized crime is basically the same across societies in being a *hierarchical* organization that engages in crime activities. Organized crime differs from one society to another only in intraorganizational unity and criminal activities. Members' loyalty to the crime organization seems stronger in Japan and Hong Kong than in the United States and Italy today. The Hong Kong Triads engage in drug trafficking much more extensively than their counterparts in other countries. The Triads, along with their peers in Japan, Italy, and Russia, seem to have penetrated legitimate business and politics more deeply than the crime organizations in the United States.

not uniquely American

Second, there is no validity to the suggestion of Bell's well-known theory that organized crime is a uniquely American way for ambitious poor people in the United States to realize the American dream. There is nothing unique about American organized crime as a ladder of success for the ambitious poor. Organized crime serves the same function in other countries.

stronger outside U.S.

Third, organized crime is more pervasive, influential, or powerful in Italy, Japan and Hong Kong than in the United States. The reason may be partly cultural in that organized crime in foreign countries is more socially acceptable and integrated into the legitimate world of business and politics. The reason may also be partly economic: the less mature the capitalism of a country is, the less controllable and hence more prevalent its organized crime is. This point shows most clearly in the contrast between the United States and Russia.

difficult to get rid of

Fourth, it is extremely difficult, if not impossible, to get rid of organized crime, as shown by the failure of anti-syndicate measures in various countries. This is particularly true in Japan and Hong Kong because of the underworld's deeper penetration into the conventional upperworld. By comparison, however, the American authorities are more successful in prosecuting mobsters, especially in recent years. Does this mean that we can ever hope to eradicate organized crime in the United States? Let us take closer look at this issue.

—Thio, *Deviant Behavior*, pp. 311–312

Summary notes are most effectively used in passages that contain long and complicated ideas. In these cases, it is simpler to write a summary phrase in the margin than to highlight a long or complicated statement of the main idea and supporting details.

To write a summary clue, try to think of a word or phrase that accurately states, in brief form, a particular idea presented in the passage. Summary words should trigger your memory of the content of the passage.

EXERCISE 5

DIRECTIONS   Read the following textbook selection. Then mark as well as highlight important information contained in the passage.

Basis of Social Organization

Although monkeys and apes differ from each other in important ways, they share many characteristics. Of these, certainly the most interesting is that they are all social species (except perhaps the orangutan) and their societies are highly organized. We first need to ask ourselves several questions. What are the advantages of social life? Why are so many mammal and bird species social and why have the Hominoidea developed this characteristic to such lengths? Four kinds of advantage are usually proposed by zoologists:

1. Several pairs of eyes are better than one in the detection of predators and in their avoidance. Defense by a group is also far more effective. Three or four male baboons constitute an impressive display and can frighten any predator, even a lion. A lone baboon is a dead baboon.

2. Competing for large food patches is more successful when done by groups rather than by individuals. We shall see that some monkeys' social groups subdivide when food is sparse and widely scattered.

3. Reproductive advantages accrue from social groups because regular access to the opposite sex is ensured.

4. Social groups permit extensive socialization with peers and elders and the opportunity to learn from them. Among animals such as the higher primates, this is a factor of the greatest importance.

These factors are probably the most important in bringing about the selection of social life in animals such as primates. Although considerable variation may occur within a species, especially under different environmental conditions, only a few Old World primate species (including the gibbons and siamang, a large gibbon) normally live in groups consisting only of an adult male, a female, and their young. The orang is unique in being more-or-less solitary. The remaining Old World monkeys and apes all live in social groups that number as high as 500 individuals but most commonly number between 10 and 50.

But how are these societies organized? Far from being a structureless collection of rushing, squalling animals, primate societies are remarkably complex and stable. Order is maintained in primate societies through a complex interrelationship of several factors. One factor is the animals' prolonged period of dependence: infant apes and monkeys, like human infants, are far from self-sufficient, and maintain a close relationship with their mothers longer than most other animals.

—Campbell and Loy, *Humankind Emerging*, pp. 127–128

EXERCISE 6

DIRECTIONS   Turn to the reading on p. 404 in Part Seven that you highlighted to complete Exercise 3. Review the section and add marking and summary words that would make the section easier to study and review.

EXERCISE 7

DIRECTIONS   Choose a three- or four-page excerpt from one of your textbooks. Highlight and mark main ideas, important details, and key terms. Include summary words, if possible.

LEARNING *Collaboratively*

DIRECTIONS   Your instructor will choose a reading from Part Seven and divide the class into two groups for an out-of-class assignment. One group should highlight the reading but make no other markings. The second group should both highlight and mark the reading. During the next class session, students may quiz each other to determine which group is better prepared for (1) an essay exam, (2) a multiple-choice exam, and (3) class discussion.

Applying YOUR LEARNING

Jin Lon always highlights her psychology textbook but often wonders whether her highlighting is effective. She usually highlights complete sentences because she is afraid she will miss something important. Sometimes she uses just one marker, and other times she uses two different colored markers. She usually highlights about half of each paragraph. As she reads, she notices things that she thinks could be on an exam, makes a mental note, and continues reading. She doesn't make any notes in the margins because she is unsure what to write.

1. How could Jin Lon determine whether her highlighting is effective?
2. Evaluate Jin Lon's highlighting technique.
3. Should she continue to use two highlighting systems?
4. How could she make better note of possible exam questions?
5. What advice could you give her on marking her textbooks?

SELF-TEST SUMMARY

1. Why should you highlight and mark chapters when you read them?

Reading textbook chapters is a long and time-consuming process. As you read, you encounter a great deal of information that you know you will need to study and review for your next exam or quiz. To be able to locate this information quickly when you study, it is necessary to highlight and mark important information as you read. Without a system of highlighting and marking, you need to reread an entire chapter in order to review it effectively.

2. What guidelines should you follow for effective highlighting?

Highlight the right amount. Develop a regular and consistent system of highlighting. Highlight accurately. And make your highlighting understandable for later review. It is also wise to have a system for marking as well as highlighting.

3. Why should you supplement your textbook highlighting with marking?

Marking involves the use of marginal notes, summary words, and symbols that can make a passage easier to review. Marking can help you to organize the information you have highlighted by showing the relative importance of, or the relationships between, facts and ideas.

4. Why do highlighting and marking work as a way to prepare for study?

Highlighting and marking are an effective way to prepare yourself for study because they take advantage of a number of learning principles. This method forces you to focus your concentration by keeping you physically active, makes you think about and evaluate the information, helps you grasp the organization of the material, and provides you with a way to check your understanding.

Take a Road Trip to
Seattle!

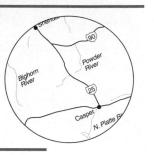

If your instructor has asked you to use the Reading Road Trip CD-ROM, be sure to visit the Annotating Textbooks and Taking Lecture Notes module for multimedia tutorials, exercises, and tests.

Methods of Organizing Information

Why Organize Information from Your Textbooks?

▲ **You will learn the material as you organize it.**

▲ **You will develop useful study aids.**

▲ **You will increase the amount of material you can remember.**

Learning Experiment

Step 1

Read the following description of the steps involved in a conversation.

> Conversation takes place in at least five steps: opening, feedforward, business, feedback, and closing. It is convenient to divide any act—and conversation is no exception—into chunks or stages and view each stage as requiring a choice of what to say and how to say it. In this model the conversation process is divided into five stages, each of which requires that you make a choice as to what you'll do. The first step is to open the conversation, usually with some kind of greeting: "Hi. How are You?" "Hello, this is Joe." It is a message that establishes a connection between two people and opens the channels for more meaningful interaction. At the second step, you usually provide some kind of feedforward, which gives the other person a general idea of the conversation's focus: "I've got to tell you about Jack," "Did you hear what happened in class yesterday?" or "We need to talk about our vacation plans." At the third step, you talk "business," the substance or focus of the conversation. The term "business" is used to emphasize that most conversations are goal directed; you converse to fulfill one or several of the general purposes of interpersonal communication: to learn, relate, influence, play or help. The fourth step is the reverse of the second. Here you reflect back on

the conversation to signal that as far as you're concerned the business is completed: "So you want to send Jack a get-well card," "Wasn't that the craziest class you ever heard of?" or "I'll call for reservations, and you'll shop for what we need."

—DeVito, *The Interpersonal Communication Book,* p. 266

Step 2

Now, draw a diagram or write an outline that explains the process of conversation.

The Results

Did drawing the diagram or writing an outline help you learn or understand the steps in conversation? Why? In order to diagram or outline, you had to grasp the process and make it fit within a framework. Through these activities you were consolidating, or putting together, the information. You organized it and made connections among the ideas presented.

Learning Principle (What This Means to You)

Consolidation is a process in which information settles, gels, or takes shape. The key to learning large amounts of information is to organize and consolidate it. Basically, this involves looking for patterns, differences, similarities, or shared characteristics and then grouping, rearranging, and reducing the information into manageable pieces. In this chapter you will learn three methods of consolidating information from either textbooks or lectures: outlining, summarizing, and mapping.

ORGANIZING BY OUTLINING

Outlining is an effective way of organizing the relationships among ideas. It involves both analysis and synthesis of ideas. From past experiences, many students think of an outline as an exact, detailed, organized listing of all information in a passage; they consider outlining as routine copying of information from page to page and, therefore, avoid doing it.

Actually, an outline should *not* be a recopying of ideas. Think of it, instead, as a means of pulling together important information and recording it to show how ideas interconnect. It is a form of note taking that provides a visual picture of the structure of ideas within a textbook chapter.

Outlining has many advantages, one being that you learn while you do it. Outlining forces you to think about the material you read and to sort out the important ideas from those that are less important. Because it requires you to express ideas in your own words and to group them, outlining reveals whether you have understood what you read. Finally, thinking about, sorting, and expressing ideas in your own words is a form of repetition, or rehearsal, that helps you to remember the material.

How to Develop an Outline

To be effective, an outline must show (1) the relative importance of ideas and (2) the relationship between ideas. The easiest way to achieve this is to use the following format.

I. Major topic

   A. First major idea

      1. First important detail

      2. Second important detail

   B. Second major idea

      1. First important detail

         a. Minor detail or example

      2. Second important detail

II. Second major topic

   A. First major idea

Note that the more important ideas are closer to the left margin, whereas less important details are indented toward the middle of the page. A quick glance at an outline indicates what is most important and how ideas support or explain one another.

Here are a few suggestions for developing an effective outline.

1. Don't get caught up in the numbering and lettering system. Instead, concentrate on showing the relative importance of ideas. How you number or letter an idea is not as important as showing what other ideas it supports or explains. Don't be concerned if some items don't fit exactly into outline format.
2. Be brief; use words and phrases, never complete sentences. Abbreviate words and phrases where possible.
3. Use your own words rather than lifting most of the material from the text. You can use the author's key words and specialized terminology.
4. Be sure that all information underneath a heading supports or explains it.
5. All headings that are aligned vertically should be of equal importance.

Now study the sample outline in Figure 14.1, which is based on the first five paragraphs of "Communication Between Women and Men" in Part Seven on page 385.

How Much Information to Include

Before you begin to outline, decide how much information to include. An outline can be very brief and cover only major topics, or, at the other extreme, it can be very detailed, providing an extensive review of information.

How much detail you include in an outline should be determined by your purpose in making it. For example, if you are outlining a collateral reading assignment for which your instructor asked that you be familiar with the

I. Communication between Women and Men
   A. Differences
      1. Men—use language of status and independence
      2. Women—use language of connection & intimacy
   B. Genderlects
      1. def—different linguistic styles between men and women
      2. failure to understand genderlects creates problems
         a) ex—Linda & Josh
            1. Linda—wanted to be involved
            2. Josh—wanted to be independent
      3. purposes of communication
         a. men—to give information
         b. women—to express feelings
         c. men & women—cross purposes = miscommunication
      4. Public communication
         a. men—topics: business, food, sports
         b. women— topics: people, business, health
         c. mixed groups—topics: follow style of men only groups

Figure 14.1
A Sample Outline

author's viewpoint and general approach to a problem, then little detail is needed. On the other hand, if you are outlining a section of an anatomy and physiology text for an upcoming objective exam, a much more detailed outline is needed. To determine the right amount of detail, ask yourself: What do I need to know? What type of test situation, if any, am I preparing for?

Outlining Using a Computer

Word processing programs are particularly helpful for writing outlines. The tab key makes indenting easy and systematic, and you can devise a system by which you use different typefaces to designate the relative importance of ideas. For example, you might use capital letters and boldface for major topics, lowercase boldface for the most important supporting ideas, and regular type for details and examples. An example is shown in Figure 14.2 on the next page. Alternatively, you might use symbols to distinguish various types of information—an asterisk for important ideas, brackets for key definitions, and so forth.

Word processing programs enable you to move text readily. Consequently, you can rearrange information easily, grouping ideas on a specific topic together. You will find this capability particularly useful when preparing study sheets for essay exams (see p. 327) and when writing papers (see pp. 429–437).

> **I. ARGUMENTATION**
>
> **A. Definition—process of putting forth a claim or proposition supported by reasons**
> 1. others examine the argument and offer counterarguments
> 2. rule governed—unlike other forms of public speaking
> 3. is a form of "mutual truth-testing"
>
> **B. Four Social Conversions That Arguments Follow**
> I. *Bilaterality*—requires 2 people or 2 messages
>   a. message of open for examination by the other person
>   b. arguer understands that others may offer opposing messages
>   (1) ex. seller of new car
>   (2) candidates for political office
> II. *Self-risk*—opening ideas to others involves risk
>   a. ideas may fail

Figure 14.2
A Sample Computer Outline

When to Use Outlining

Outlining is useful in a variety of situations.

1. When you are using reference books or reading books you do not own, outlining is an effective way of taking notes.
2. When you are reading material that seems difficult or confusing, outlining forces you to sort ideas, see connections, and express them in your own words.
3. When you are asked to write an evaluation or critical interpretation of an article or essay, it is helpful to outline briefly the factual content. The outline will reflect the development and progression of thought and will help you analyze the writer's ideas.
4. In courses where order or process is important, an outline is particularly useful. In a data processing course, for example, in which various sets of programming commands must be performed in a specified sequence, making an outline is a good way to organize the information.
5. In the natural sciences, in which classifications are important, outlines help you record and sort information. In botany, for example, one important focus is the classification and description of various plant groups. Making an outline will enable you to list subgroups within each category and to keep track of similar characteristics.

EXERCISE 1

DIRECTIONS Turn to the article titled "No Secrets: Computers and Privacy" in Part Seven on p. 406. Write a brief outline of the section titled "The Privacy Problem."

EXERCISE 2

DIRECTIONS Write a brief outline of Chapter 15 of this text, "Study and Review Strategies." Assume you are preparing for an essay exam on the chapter.

EXERCISE 3   **DIRECTIONS**   Write a brief outline of this chapter. Assume you are preparing for a multiple-choice exam on the chapter.

EXERCISE 4   **DIRECTIONS**   Choose a section from one of your textbooks and write a brief outline that reflects the organization and content of that section.

Academic Application

SUMMARIZING

A *summary* is a brief statement or list of ideas that identifies the major concepts in a textbook section. Its main purpose is to record the most important ideas in an abbreviated and condensed form. It is a synthesis of ideas. A summary is briefer and less detailed than an outline. It goes one step beyond an outline by pulling together the writer's thoughts and making general statements about them. In writing a summary or making summary notes, you may indicate how the writer makes his or her point or note the types of supporting information the writer provides.

Writing a summary forces you to go beyond separate facts and ideas and consider what they mean as a whole. Summarizing encourages you to consider such questions as "What is the writer's main point?" and "How does the writer prove or explain his or her ideas?" It is also a valuable study technique that will clarify the material.

How to Summarize

Although most students think of a summary as a correctly written paragraph, a summary written for your own study and review purposes may be in either paragraph or note format. If you choose a note format, however, be sure that you record ideas and not just facts. Here are a few suggestions for writing useful summaries:

1. Start by identifying the author's main point, and then write a statement that expresses it.
2. Next, identify the most important information the writer offers to support or explain his or her main point. Include these main supporting ideas in your summary.
3. Include any definitions of key terms or important new principles, theories, or procedures that are introduced.
4. The amount of detail you include, if any, will depend on your purpose for writing the summary and on the type and amount of recall you need.
5. Although examples are usually not included in a summary, include several representative examples if you feel the material is complex and cannot be understood easily without them.
6. Depending on the type of material you are summarizing, it may be appropriate to indicate the author's attitude and approach toward the subject and to suggest his or her purpose for writing.
7. Try to keep your summary objective and factual. Think of it as a brief report that should reflect the writer's ideas, not your evaluation of them.
8. Let your purpose guide and determine the amount and type of information you include in your summary.

9. Consider using a word processor to write summaries. You'll find it easy to make revisions and changes. You can move and rearrange ideas or group summaries on related topics together.

Now read the summary in Figure 14.3, which is based on the section of "Communication Between Women and Men" that begins on page 385. After you have studied the sample summary, compare it with the outline of the same material shown in Figure 14.1.

When to Use Summaries

Summaries are particularly useful in learning situations in which factual, detailed recall is not needed.

Preparing for Essay Exams

Summarizing ideas to be learned for possible exam topics is an excellent way to study for an essay exam. Because essay exam questions often require you to summarize information you have learned on a particular topic, writing summaries is a good way to practice taking the exam.

Reading Literature

When reading literature, you are most often required to interpret and react to the ideas presented. To do so, you must be sure you are familiar with the basic plot (in fiction) or literal presentation of ideas (in nonfiction). Writing a plot summary (describing who did what, when, and where) for fiction and a content summary for nonfiction will help you be certain you have mastered the literal content.

Collateral Reading Assignments

In many undergraduate courses, instructors give additional reading assignments in sources other than your own text. These assignments may be given to supplement information in the text, to present a different or opposing viewpoint, to illustrate a concept, or to show practical applications. Usually, in-depth recall of particular facts and information is not expected. Your instructor probably wants

Figure 14.3
A Sample Summary

> One difference in the communication between men and women is their use of language. Men use language to demonstrate status and independence, while women use it to establish connections and intimacy. Genderlects refers to the differences in the way men and women use language. Men often communicate to give information, while women communicate to express feelings; miscommunication often results. In public, men and women communicate differently as well, each discussing different topics. In mixed groups, topics are usually those preferred by males.

you to understand the main points and their relation to topics covered in the text or in class; therefore, a brief summary is a useful study aid for collateral readings.

Laboratory Experiments/Demonstrations

A summary is a useful means of recording the results of a laboratory experiment or class demonstration in a natural science course. Although laboratory reports usually specify a format that includes careful reporting of procedures and listing of observations, a summary is often included. Reviewing summaries is an efficient way of recalling the purposes, procedures, and outcomes of lab and classroom experiments conducted throughout the semester.

EXERCISE 5

> **DIRECTIONS** Write a brief summary of the textbook excerpt subtitled "Observational Learning" on page 164 of this text.

EXERCISE 6

> **DIRECTIONS** Write a summary of "Body Adornment," which begins on page 376 in Part Seven.

EXERCISE 7

> **DIRECTIONS** Refer to the section from one of your textbooks that you used to complete Exercise 4 on page 291. Write a summary of the information presented in this section.

MAPPING: A VISUAL MEANS OF ORGANIZING IDEAS

Mapping is a visual method of organizing information. It involves drawing diagrams to show how ideas or concepts in an article or chapter are related. Mapping provides a picture, or visual representation, of how ideas are developed and connected. Maps group and consolidate information and make it easier to learn. How much you use mapping will depend on your learning style. Some students, especially those with a visual learning style, prefer mapping to outlining. Other students find mapping to be freer and less tightly structured than outlining. The degree to which you use mapping will also depend on the types of courses you are taking. Some types of information are more easily learned by using mapping than are others.

Maps can take numerous forms. You can draw them in any way that shows the relationships among ideas. They can be hand drawn or drawn using a word processor's capability to box and block type. Figure 14.4 (page 294) shows the types of information to include in a map, depending on the desired level of detail. Figure 14.5 on page 295 shows two sample maps. Each was drawn to show the organization of the section "Checking Your Comprehension" in Chapter 5 of this book. Refer to pages 98–102; then study each map.

How to Draw Maps

Think of a map as a picture or diagram that shows how ideas are connected. Use the following steps in drawing a map.

1. Identify the overall topic or subject, and write it in the center or at the top of the page.

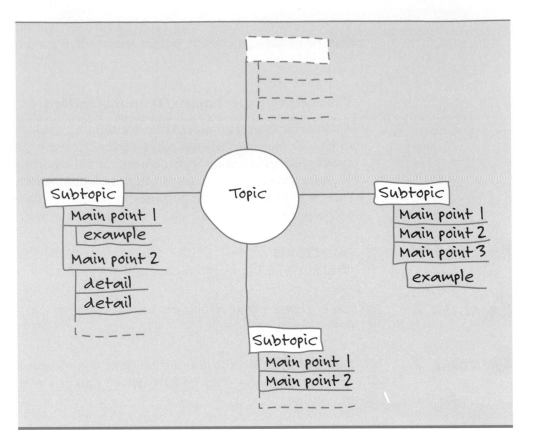

Figure 14.4
A Model Map

2. Identify the major supporting information that is related to the topic. Write each fact or idea on a line connected to the central topic.
3. As you discover a detail that further explains an idea already mapped, draw a new line branching from the idea it explains.

How you arrange your map will depend on the subject matter and how it is organized. Like an outline, it can be either quite detailed or very brief, depending on your purpose.

EXERCISE 8   **DIRECTIONS**   Draw a map showing the organization of any section of Chapter 1 in this text.

EXERCISE 9   **DIRECTIONS**   Turn to the reading "Losing Your Good Name Online" on p. 408 in Part Seven. Draw a map showing how the article is organized.

EXERCISE 10   **DIRECTIONS**   Select a section from one of your textbooks. Draw a concept map that reflects its organization.

Academic Application

Specialized Types of Maps

Concept maps may take numerous forms. This section presents five types of maps useful for organizing specific types of information: time lines, process diagrams, part/function diagrams, organizational charts, and comparison–contrast charts.

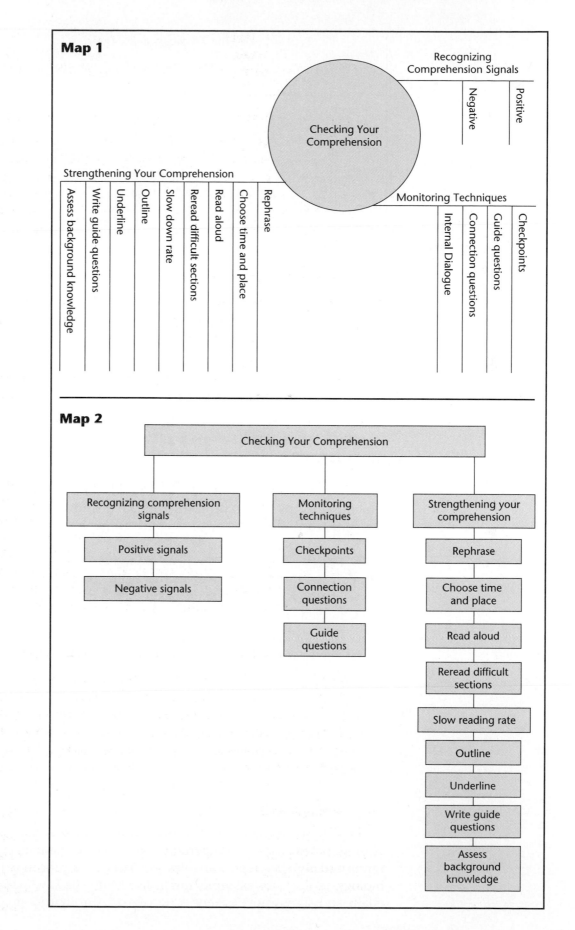

Figure 14.5
Sample Maps

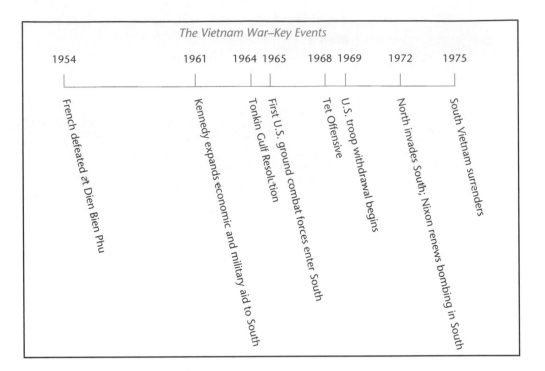

Figure 14.6
A Time Line

Time Lines

In a course in which chronology of events is the central focus, a time line is a useful way to organize information. To visualize a sequence of events, draw a single horizontal line and mark it off in yearly intervals, just as a ruler is marked off in inches, and then write events next to the appropriate year. The time line in Figure 14.6, for example, was developed for an American history course in which the Vietnam War was being studied. It shows the sequence of events and helps you to visualize the order in which things happened.

EXERCISE 11

DIRECTIONS   The following passage reviews the ancient history of maps. Read the selection and then draw a time line that helps you visualize these historical events. (Remember that B.C. refers to time before Christ, and such numbers increase as time moves back in history.)

In Babylonia, in approximately 2300 B.C., the oldest known map was drawn on a clay tablet. The map showed a man's property located in a valley surrounded by tall mountains. Later, around 1300 B.C., the Egyptians drew maps that detailed the location of Ethiopian gold mines and that showed a route from the Nile Valley. The ancient Greeks were early mapmakers as well, although no maps remain for us to examine. It is estimated that in 300 B.C. they drew maps showing the earth to be round. The Romans drew the first road maps, a few of which have been preserved for study today. Claudius Ptolemy, an Egyptian scholar who lived around 150 A.D., drew one of the most famous ancient maps. He drew maps of the world as it was known at that time, including 26 regional maps of Europe, Africa, and Asia.

Process Diagrams

In the natural sciences, as well as other courses such as economics and data processing, processes are an important part of course content. A diagram that presents visually the steps, variables, or parts of a process will aid learning. A biology student, for example, might use Figure 14.7, which describes the food chain and shows how energy is transferred through food consumption. Note

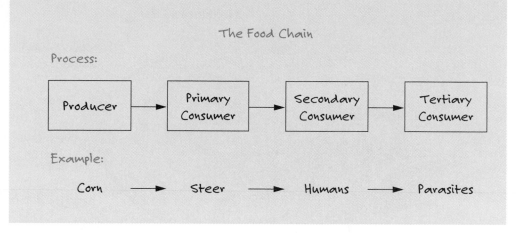

Figure 14.7
A Process Diagram

that this student included an example, as well as the steps in the process, to make the diagram clearer.

EXERCISE 12

DIRECTIONS The following paragraph describes the process through which malaria is spread by mosquitoes. Read the paragraph, and then draw a process diagram that shows how this process occurs.

> Malaria, a serious tropical disease, is caused by parasites, or one-celled animals, called protozoa. These parasites live in the red blood cells of humans as well as in female anopheles mosquitoes. These mosquitoes serve as hosts to the parasites and carry and spread malaria. When an anopheles mosquito bites a person who already has malaria, it ingests the red blood cells that contain the malaria parasites. In the host mosquito's body, these parasites multiply rapidly and move to its salivary glands and mouth. When the host mosquito bites another person, the malaria parasites are injected into the victim and enter his or her bloodstream. The parasites again multiply and burst the victim's blood cells, causing anemia.

Part/Function Diagrams

In courses that deal with the use and description of physical objects, labeled drawings are an important learning tool. In a human anatomy and physiology course, for example, the easiest way to study the parts and functions of the inner, middle, and outer ear is to use a drawing of the ear. Study the material and make a sketch of the ear; then test your recall of ear parts and their function. Refer to Figure 14.8 on the next page for a sample part/function diagram.

EXERCISE 13

DIRECTIONS The following paragraph describes the Earth's structure. Read the paragraph, and then draw a diagram that will help you visualize how the Earth's interior is structured.

> At the center is a hot, highly compressed *inner core,* presumably solid and composed mainly of iron and nickel. Surrounding the inner core is an *outer core,* a molten shell primarily of liquid iron and nickel with lighter liquid material on the top. The outer envelope beyond the core is the *mantle,* of which the upper portion is mostly solid rock in the form of olivine, an iron–magnesium silicate, and the lower portion chiefly iron and magnesium oxides. A thin coat of metal silicates and oxides (granite), called the *crust,* forms the outermost skin.
>
> —Berman and Evans, *Exploring the Cosmos,* p. 145

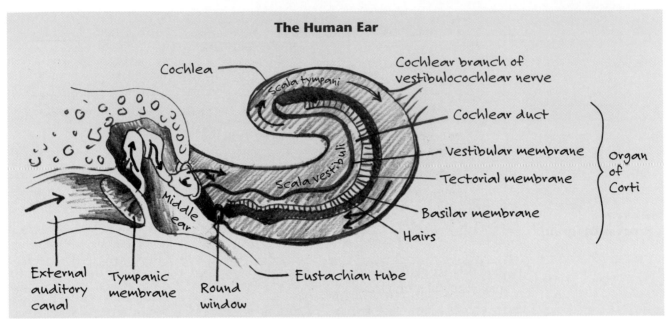

Figure 14.8
A Sample Part/
Function Diagram

Organizational Charts

When you are reviewing material that is composed of relationships and structures, organizational charts are useful study aids. Suppose that in a business management course, you are studying the organization of a small temporary clerical employment agency. If you drew and studied the organizational chart shown in Figure 14.9, the structure would become apparent and easy to remember.

DIRECTIONS   The following paragraph describes one business organizational structure that is studied in management courses. Read the paragraph, and then draw a diagram that will help you visualize this type of organization.

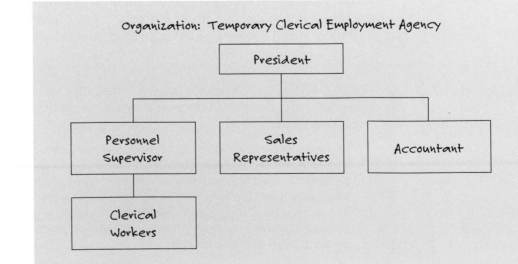

Figure 14.9
An Organizational
Chart

It is common for some large businesses to be organized by *place,* with a department for each major geographic area in which the business is active. Businesses that market products for which customer preference differs from one part of the country to another often use this management structure. Departmentalization allows each region to focus on its own special needs and problems. Often the president of such a company appoints several regional vice-presidents, one for each part of the country. Then each regional office is divided into sales districts, each supervised by a district director.

Comparison–Contrast Charts

A final type of visual aid that is useful for organizing factual information is the comparison–contrast chart. Based on the categorization principle of learning, this method of visual organization divides and groups information according to similarities or common characteristics. Suppose that in a marketing and advertising course, you are studying three types of market survey techniques: mail, telephone, and personal interview surveys. You are concerned with factors such as cost, level of response, time, and accuracy. In your text, this information is discussed in paragraph form. To learn and review this information in an efficient manner, you could draw a chart such as the one shown in Figure 14.10.

EXERCISE 15

DIRECTIONS   The following passage describes the major physical differences between humans and apes. Read the selection, and then arrange the information into a chart that would make the information easy to learn.

Numerous physical characteristics distinguish humans from apes. While apes' bodies are covered with hair, the human body has relatively little hair. While apes often use both their hands and feet to walk, humans walk erect. Apes' arms are longer than their legs, while just the reverse is true for humans. Apes have large teeth, necessary for devouring coarse, uncooked food, and long canine teeth for self-defense and fighting. By comparison, human teeth are small and short. The ape's brain is not as well developed as that of the human being. Humans are capable of speech, thinking,

Market Survey Techniques			
Type	Cost	Response	Accuracy
Mail	usually the cheapest	higher than phone or personal interview	problems with misunderstanding directions
Phone	depends on phone service	same as personal interview	problems with unlisted phones and homes w/out phones
Personal interview	most expensive	same as phone	problems with honesty when asking personal or embarrassing questions

Figure 14.10
A Comparison–Contrast Chart

and higher-level reasoning skills. These skills enable humans to establish culture, thereby placing the quality and level of human life far above that of apes.

Humans are also set apart from apes by features of the head and face. The human facial profile is vertical, while the ape's profile is *prognathous,* with jaw jutting outward. Humans have a chin; apes have a strong lower jaw, but no chin. Human nostrils are smaller and less flaring than those of the ape. Apes also have thinner, more flexible lips than human beings.

Man's upright walk also distinguishes him from apes. The human spine has a double curve to support his weight, while an ape's spine has a single curve. The human foot is arched both vertically and horizontally but, unlike the ape's, is unable to grasp objects. The human torso is shorter than that of apes. It is important to note that many of these physical traits, while quite distinct, differ in degree rather than in kind.

EXERCISE 16   **DIRECTIONS**   Draw a process diagram that shows how dams adversely affect the environment in which they are built. Refer to the reading "Causes of Habitat Loss and Species Endangerment," in Part Seven, p. 398. Use the section titled "Water Development" on p. 402.

EXERCISE 17   **DIRECTIONS**   Draw a comparison–contrast chart showing the differences in communication between men and women. Use the reading "Communication Between Women and Men" in Part Seven, p. 385, as your source.

LEARNING *Collaboratively*

DIRECTIONS   Your instructor will choose a reading from Part Seven and divide the class into three groups. Members of one group should outline the material, another group should draw maps, and the third should write summaries. When the groups have completed their tasks, the class members should review each other's work. Several students should read their summaries, draw their maps, and write their outlines on the chalkboard. Discuss which of the three methods seemed most effective for the material and how well prepared each group feels for (1) an essay exam, (2) a multiple-choice exam, and (3) a class discussion.

Applying YOUR LEARNING

Ken's courses this semester include the History of the British Empire, Business Management, Biology, and Introduction to Anthropology. The history course requirements include several collateral reading assignments from books placed on reserve in the library and an essay final exam. The anthropology text contains several chapters and lectures explaining how humans evolved and the relationships of other species to humans; a short-answer and essay final exam will be given. The biology course involves textbook reading, lectures, labs, and multiple-choice exams. The business management course focuses, in part, on the organization and structure of corporations; two multiple-choice and true-false exams will be given.

1. In which course(s) do you think Ken will need to use outlining? Why?
2. In which course(s) do you think Ken will need to use summarizing? Why?
3. Recommend a mapping strategy Ken might use for each course. Explain why each recommended approach is appropriate.

SELF-TEST SUMMARY

1. What is an outline and what are its advantages?

Outlining is a way to organize information to indicate the relative importance of ideas and the relationships among them. When done correctly, it helps you to sort ideas, test your understanding, and recall the material.

2. What is a summary and what are its advantages?

Summarizing is the process of recording a passage's most important ideas in a condensed, abbreviated form. A summary not only helps you to organize the facts and ideas presented in the text but also enables you to go beyond the facts and react to them critically.

3. What are concept maps and what are their advantages?

Mapping creates a visual representation of the information and shows relationships. Five types of concept maps are time lines, process diagrams, part/function diagrams, organizational charts, and comparison–contrast charts. Mapping is versatile in that it enables you to adjust to both the type of information you are recording and its unique organization. Grouping and consolidating information in different ways makes it easier to learn and remember.

Take a Road Trip to
Florida (Spring Break)!

If your instructor has asked you to use the Reading Road Trip CD-ROM, be sure to visit the Outlining, Summarizing, Mapping, and Paraphrasing module for multimedia tutorials, exercises, and tests.

Study and Review Strategies

Why Learn Review Strategies?

▲ **Forgetting occurs rapidly unless you review what you have learned.**

▲ **If you review what you have learned regularly, you won't have to cram before exams.**

Learning Experiment

Step 1

Make a list of five to ten tasks (sports, hobbies, household duties, etc.) you can perform well. For each, indicate how you know you are proficient at the task.

Step 2

Make a list of two to five things you might want to learn to do at some point in your lifetime (write a novel, ride horseback, race cars, etc.). For each, indicate how you will measure your success.

The Results

For each task, either those at which you are proficient or those you would like to learn, you were able to suggest some measure or yardstick by which you can evaluate your proficiency or success.

Learning Principle (What This Means to You)

To know whether you have accomplished something, you need some measurement standard. To know whether you have learned something, you also need to test or measure your learning. **For academic learning, self-testing, often through writing, is an effective way to measure what you have learned.** In this chapter you will discover several learning strategies that involve review and self-testing. Even though you have read a textbook chapter and highlighted or outlined it, you cannot be certain that you have learned the material or will be able to apply it on exams. Study and review must follow reading and organizing.

LEARNING THROUGH WRITING

Writing is a form of recoding or processing information by rearranging, rephrasing, or regrouping it so that it becomes more meaningful and easier to recall. Outlining, summarizing, and mapping, each described in the previous chapter, are forms of writing and recoding and do contribute to learning. This section will discuss three other ways to use writing to learn: paraphrasing, self-testing, and keeping a learning journal.

Paraphrasing

A paraphrase is a restatement of a passage's ideas in your own words. The author's meaning is retained, but your wording, *not* the author's, is used. We use paraphrasing frequently in everyday speech. For example, when you relay a message from one person to another, you convey the meaning but do not use the person's exact wording. A paraphrase can be used to make a passage's meaning clearer and often more concise. A paraphrase, then, moves you from a knowledge level in which you can recall information to a comprehension level in which you understand the ideas presented. Paraphrasing is also an effective learning and review strategy in several situations.

First, paraphrasing is useful for portions of a text for which exact, detailed comprehension is required. For example, you might paraphrase the steps in solving a math problem, the process by which a blood transfusion is administered, or the levels of jurisdiction of the Supreme Court. Figure 15.1 on the next page shows a paraphrase written by a biology student studying the functioning of the human heart.

Paraphrasing is also a useful way to be certain you understand difficult or complicated material. If you can express the author's ideas in your own words, you can be certain you understand it, and if you find yourself at a loss for words—except for those of the author—you will know your understanding is incomplete. Figure 15.2 on page 305 shows two students' paraphrases of an excerpt from a difficult passage. Paraphrase 1 shows that the student had difficulty—the student wrote in generalities and was unable to connect ideas. In contrast, paraphrase 2 carries the meaning of the passage and demonstrates the student's high level of understanding.

Paraphrasing is a useful strategy when working with material that is stylistically complex, poorly written, or overly formal, awkward, or biased. Many technical manuals, for example, are poorly written and require the reader to

Passage	Paraphrase
What does the separation of the two halves of the heart have to do with efficiency? The two halves are essentially two hearts, one serving the lungs, the other serving the body. When CO_2-laden blood enters the right atrium from the large veins (the *superior vena cava* from above and the inferior vena cava from below), it is pumped from the atrium to the right ventricle. Contraction of the right ventricle sends the blood through the *pulmonary arteries* to the lungs. Here the blood picks up oxygen and releases carbon dioxide before returning to the left atrium via the *pulmonary veins*. The left atrium pumps the blood into the left ventricle, which then contracts to send the blood into the large aorta, which immediately branches before looping down-ward, carrying the blood on the first leg of its long journey through the body, bearing its gift of oxygen. —Wallace, p. 434	Blood-filled CO_2 enters the right atrium of the heart from the superior vena cava and the inferior vena cava. It is pumped to the right ventricle, where a contraction moves it through the pulmonary arteries into the lungs, where it exchanges CO_2 for O_2 and then returns through the pulmonary veins to the left atrium. From the left atrium it is pumped to the left ventricle, then to the large aorta, and from there it carries O_2 to the rest of the body.

Figure 15.1
A Sample Paraphrase

struggle to obtain meaning. An essay written in the 1700s may use language pat-terns different from those you are accustomed to. In such situations, it is helpful to cut through the language barrier and express the content as simply as possible in your own words. Figure 15.3 shows how a student simplified a complicated discussion about the disappearance of oral poetry from Germany.

Use the following suggestions to paraphrase effectively.

1. Read slowly and carefully.
2. Read the material through entirely before writing anything.
3. As you read, pay attention to exact meanings and relationships among ideas.
4. Paraphrase sentence by sentence.
5. Read each sentence and express the key idea in your own words. Reread the original sentence; next, look away and write your own sentence. Then reread the original and add anything you missed.
6. Don't try to paraphrase word by word. Instead, work with ideas.
7. For words or phrases that you are unsure of or are not comfortable using, check a dictionary to locate a more familiar meaning.
8. You may combine several original sentences into a more concise paraphrase.
9. Follow the author's arrangement (order) of ideas unless you have a specific reason for changing them.
10. When finished, reread your paraphrase and compare it with the original for completeness and accuracy.

EXERCISE 1

DIRECTIONS Write a paraphrase for each of the following excerpts. (Exercise 1 excerpts continue on page 306.)

1. The tides are important for several reasons. Tidal mixing of nearshore waters removes pollutants and recirculates nutrients. Tidal currents also move floating animals and plants to and from their usual breeding areas in estuaries to deeper waters. People who fish frequently follow tidal cycles to improve their catch, because strong tidal

Passage: Neurons

Individual neurons do not form a continuous chain, with each neuron directly touching another, end to end. If they did, the number of connections would be inadequate for the vast amount of information the nervous system must handle. Instead, individual neurons are separated by a minuscule space called the synaptic cleft, where the axon terminal nearly touches a dendrite or the cell body of another. The entire site—the axon terminal, the cleft, and the membrane of the receiving dendrite or cell body—is called a synapse. Because a neuron's axon may have hundreds or even thousands of terminals, a single neuron may have synaptic connections with a great many others. As a result, the number of communication links in the nervous system runs into the trillions or perhaps even the quadrillions.

Although we seem to be born with nearly all the neurons we will ever have, many synapses have not yet formed at birth. Research with animals shows that axons and dendrites continue to grow as a result of both physical maturation and experience with the world, and tiny projections on dendrites called spines increase both in size and in number. Throughout life, new learning results in the establishment of new synaptic connections in the brain, with stimulating environments producing the greatest changes (Greenough & Anderson, 1991; Greenough & Black, 1992). Conversely, some unused synaptic connections are lost as cells or their branches die and are not replaced (Camel, Withers, & Greenough, 1986). The brain's circuits are not fixed and immutable; they are continually developing and being pruned in response to information and to challenges and changes in the environment.

—Wade and Tavris, pp. 124–125

Paraphrase 1: Demonstrates Lack of Understanding

Neurons don't connect with each other because it would be too much information for the nervous system. They have trillions or even quadrillions of links and hundreds or thousands of terminals. They also have clefts, membranes, and synapses—the receiving dendrite or cell body. We seem to be born with all of them that we will ever have. Spines or dendrites become more and bigger, and some of their branches aren't replaced. The brain's circuits cannot be fixed, but are pruned.

Paraphrase 2: Demonstrates Understanding

Neurons are separated from each other by tiny spaces or clefts between the axon of one and the dendrite of another. These three parts make up a synapse. Because of synapses, neurons can make more connections with each other than if they had to touch. This allows for trillions of links in the nervous system. The number of synapses we have is constantly changing. Unused connections vanish, and learning causes our axons and dendrites to grow and make new synaptic connections.

Figure 15.2
A Comparison of Paraphrases

Passage

The heroic oral poetry of the ancient Germanic peoples, which survived in Iceland and was there committed to writing, disappeared gradually from among the continental Germans in the course of the Middle Ages, and for a long time no adequate substitute took its place. Heathen gods and heathen manners were honored in those poems, and the Church could not approve of either, much less foster their preservation in writing. Thus the numerous German dialects came to be represented during their "old" period, roughly from 500 A.D. to 1000 A.D. almost exclusively by utilitarian and devotional works, and no secular literature worthy of the name was created.

—Parzival

Paraphrase

Germanic heroic oral poetry, although written down in Iceland, disappeared from Germany in the Middle Ages because it celebrated heathen religion, which would not be tolerated by the Church. German dialects were thus not written until they became old (500 A.D. to 1000 A.D.) and then only in religious and practical contexts.

Figure 15.3
Paraphrasing to Simplify

currents concentrate bait and smaller fish, thus attracting larger fish. When sailing ships were more common, departures or arrivals in a harbor had to be closely linked to the tidal cycle.

—Ross, *Introduction to Oceanography,* p. 239

2. The *stomach* is a muscular sac that churns the food as it secretes mucus, hydrochloric acid, and enzymes that begin the digestion of proteins. The food is meanwhile sealed in the stomach by two sphincters, or rings of muscles, one at either end of the stomach. After the mixing is completed, the lower sphincter opens and the stomach begins to contract repeatedly, squeezing the food into the small intestine. A fatty meal, by the way, slows this process and makes us feel "full" longer. This is also why we're hungry again so soon after a low-fat Chinese dinner.

The *small intestine* is a long convoluted tube in which digestion is completed and through which most nutrient products enter the bloodstream. Its inner surface is covered with tiny, fingerlike projections called *villi,* which increase the surface area of the intestinal lining. Furthermore, the surface area of each villus is increased by about 3000 tiny projections called *microvilli.* Within each villus is a minute lymph vessel surrounded by a network of blood capillaries. While the digested products of certain fats move directly into the lymph vessel, the products of protein and starch digestion move into the blood capillaries.

—Wallace, *Biology: The World of Life,* p. 443

3. *Section 7.* (1). All bills for raising revenue shall originate in the House of Representatives; but the Senate may propose or concur with amendments as on other bills.

(2). Every bill which shall have passed the House of Representatives and the Senate, shall, before it become a law, be presented to the President of the United States; if he approve he shall sign it, but if not he shall return it, with his objections to that House in which it shall have originated, who shall enter the objections at large on their journal, and proceed to reconsider it. If after such reconsideration two thirds of that House shall agree to pass the bill, it shall be sent, together with the objections, to the other House, by which it shall likewise be reconsidered, and if approved by two thirds of that House, it shall become a law. But in all such cases the votes of both Houses shall be determined by yeas and nays, and the names of the persons voting for and against the bill shall be entered on the journal of each House respectively. If any bill shall not be returned by the President within ten days (Sundays excepted) after it shall have been presented to him, the same shall be a law, in like manner as if he had signed it, unless the Congress by their adjournment prevent its return, in which case it shall not be a law.

—U.S. Constitution

EXERCISE 2

DIRECTIONS   Write a paraphrase of the first paragraph of "The Rapid Loss of Species" in Part Seven, on p. 394.

EXERCISE 3

DIRECTIONS   Write a paraphrase of a two- to three-paragraph excerpt from one of your textbooks. Choose a passage that is difficult or stylistically complex.

Self-Testing

Have you ever taken an exam for which you studied hard and felt prepared, only to find out you earned just an average grade? Although you spent time reviewing, you did not review in the right ways; you probably focused on recalling factual information. Many college professors demand much more of their students than factual recall of textbook and lecture content. They expect their students to react, evaluate, and apply ideas. They require their students to be able to compare and synthesize sources and integrate ideas.

Consequently, a study approach that includes only factual recall is inadequate. Strategies such as rereading, underlining, writing an outline, and drawing maps are useful and important because they enable you to learn literal content. However, you must use additional and different strategies to focus on higher levels of thinking: application, analysis, synthesis, and evaluation.

Writing can facilitate and clarify your thinking. Writing is a way of seeing your ideas. Once you've seen some, others will follow. Writing will help you generate ideas, discover relationships, and grasp applications.

Self-testing is a study strategy that uses writing to discover and relate ideas. It involves writing possible exam questions and drafting answers to them. This activity combines the use of factual recall with interpretation and evaluation. Self-testing is an active strategy that gets you involved with the material and forces you to think about, organize, and express (in your own words) ideas. Self-testing is also a sensible and effective way to prepare for an exam. How would you prepare for a typing or keyboarding exam? By keyboarding. How would you prepare to run a marathon? By running. Similarly, you should prepare for an exam by testing yourself.

Applying Levels of Thinking

Self-Testing and Levels of Thinking

When you use the strategy of self-testing, be sure to ask questions at all six levels of thinking.

Level of Thinking	Types of Questions to Ask
Knowledge	What is . . . ? When did . . . ? Who was . . . ?
Comprehension	Explain how . . . Define . . . Describe the process by which . . .
Application	Given an example of how . . . Think of a situation in which . . . How can I use . . . ?
Analysis	Why does . . . ? What trends are evident?
Synthesis	How is _____ related to _____? What are the similarities or differences between _____ and _____ ?
Evaluation	What is the value, importance, or significance of _____ ? How effectively does . . . ?

Constructing potential test questions is fun and challenging and can be done with a classmate or in groups. It is usually best to write answers yourself, however, to get maximum benefit from the technique. After writing, compare and discuss your answers with classmates. If you prefer to work alone, be sure to verify your answers by referring to your text and/or lecture notes.

Type of Material	Questions
Report of research studies and experiments	What was the purpose of the study? What are the important facts and conclusions? What are its implications? How can these results be used?
Case studies	What is it intended to illustrate? What problems or limitations does it demonstrate? To what other situations might this case apply?
Models	How was the model derived? What are its applications? What are its limitations? Do other models of the same process exist?
Current events	What is the significance of the event? What impact will this have in the future? Is there historical precedent?
Supplementary readings	Why did your instructor assign the reading? How is it related to course content? What key points or concepts does the reading contain? Does the reading present a particular viewpoint?
Sample problems	What processes or concepts does the problem illustrate? What is its unique feature? How is it similar to and how different from other problems?
Historical data (historical reviews)	Why were the data presented? What trends or patterns are evident? How is this information related to key concepts in the chapter or article?
Arguments	Is the argument convincing? How is the conclusion supported? What persuasive devices does the author use? Do logical flaws exist? Is the author's appeal emotional?
Poetry	What kinds of feelings does the poem evoke? What message or statement is the poet making? How does the poet use language to create feelings?
Essays	What is the author's purpose? What thought patterns are evident? How does the author support his or her key point (thesis)?
Short stories	What does the title mean? Beyond the plot, what does the story really mean? (What is the theme?) What kinds of comments does it make about life? How do the plot, setting, and tone contribute to the overall meaning?

Figure 15.4
Questions to Provoke Thought

What kinds of questions you ask depends on the type of material you are learning as well as on the type or level of analysis your instructor expects. Sample questions for various types of material that you may be required to study are listed in Figure 15.4.

To construct and answer possible test questions, use the following hints.

1. Do not waste time writing multiple-choice or true-false questions. They are time-consuming to write, and you know the answer before you start.
2. Matching tests are useful, but they are limited to information that requires only factual recall.

3. Open-ended questions that require sentence answers are best, because they tend to require more levels of thought.

4. Consult Figure 15.4 for ideas on how to word your questions.

5. You are interested in long-term retention of information, so it is best to write the questions one day and answer them a day or two later.

6. As you answer your questions, respond in complete sentences. Writing complete sentences usually involves more careful and deliberate thought and therefore leads to more effective learning.

7. Take time to review and critique your answers. This process will also contribute to learning.

8. Rewrite any answers that you found to be poorly done or incomplete. This repetition will facilitate learning.

9. Save your answers, and review them once again the evening before the exam.

Many students who use self-testing as a review strategy are pleasantly surprised when they take their first exam: They discover that some (or many!) of their questions actually appear on the exam. This discovery boosts their confidence during the exam and saves them time as well. As you will see later in this chapter, self-testing is an important part of the SQ3R system—a systematic approach to learning and study.

EXERCISE 4

DIRECTIONS Write a list of questions that might be asked on an exam covering one of the chapters in this book that you have already read. Answer them and then verify the correctness of your answers by consulting the chapter.

EXERCISE 5

DIRECTIONS Write a list of questions for an upcoming exam in one of your courses. Answer each. Save your questions, and after you have taken the exam, mark those that appeared on the exam. (Do not expect the actual questions to use the same wording or format as those you constructed.)

Academic Application

Keeping a Learning Journal

As you have seen throughout this book, there is a wide range of study and review alternatives. Do not expect to know right away what strategies will work for you or what modifications to make. Instead, you will need to experiment with different variations until you are satisfied with the results. Some students find it effective to keep a learning journal—an informal written record of the techniques they have tried, how well these techniques worked, and what problems they encountered. Writing the journal helps you to sort and evaluate techniques. The journal also serves as a record and is useful to reread as you revise or consider new approaches. Keep a separate journal—perhaps a spiral or steno notebook or section for each of your most challenging courses. A sample learning journal entry is shown in Figure 15.5 on the next page. It was written as the student applied several of the techniques in this chapter to her biology textbook.

Your journal may include a wide range of observations, comments, and reactions. Consider including the following.

General reactions to course content

Unique features of assignments

What you like and what you don't like about the course

Problems encountered with a particular assignment

Figure 15.5
Sample Learning Journal

Paraphrasing It is difficult not to use the same words. I was unable to find a paraphrase for scientific words. I learned the material very well, though, because I spent so much time thinking about it.

Self-testing This was very helpful and helped me to focus on important parts of the chapter. I'm going to keep the questions I wrote and use them while studying for the final exam.

SQ3R This was really effective, and I improved on it by highlighting the answer I found to the question I asked. This helped to focus my reading. Asking and answering the question out loud also helped since I am an auditory learner. I also drew maps and diagrams and I read them over out loud.

Techniques that worked (and *why*)

Techniques that didn't work (and *why*)

New ideas for approaching the material

Changes you made in using various techniques

Analysis and reactions to exams after you take them and again when they are returned

Be sure to date your entries and indicate the particular chapters or assignments to which they apply. Some students also find it helpful to record the amount of time spent on each assignment.

Once you've made several entries for a particular course, reread your entries and look for patterns. Try to discover what you are doing right, what needs changing, and what changes you'll make. Then write an entry summarizing your findings.

EXERCISE 6

DIRECTIONS For each course you are taking this semester, create a learning journal. Experiment with self-testing as a means of reviewing a particular chapter in each. Then write a journal entry describing how you used self-testing, how you modified the technique to suit the course, and how effective you felt it to be.

A CLASSIC SYSTEM: SQ3R

In 1941, a psychologist named Francis P. Robinson developed a study-reading system called SQ3R that integrates study and review with reading. The SQ3R system, which is based on principles of learning theory, was carefully researched and tested. Continuing experimentation has confirmed its effectiveness. Since that time, SQ3R has been taught to thousands of college students and has become widely recognized as the classic study-reading system.

As a step toward developing your own personalized system, look at SQ3R as a model. Once you see how and why SQ3R works, you can modify or adapt it to suit your own academic needs.

Steps in the SQ3R System

The SQ3R system involves five basic steps that integrate reading and study techniques. As you read the following steps, some of them will seem similar to the skills you have already learned.

S—Survey

Try to become familiar with the organization and general content of the material you are to read.

1. Read the title.
2. Read the lead-in or introduction. (If it is extremely long, read just the first paragraph.)
3. Read each boldface heading and the first sentence that follows it.
4. Read titles of maps, charts, or graphs; read the last paragraph or summary.
5. Read the end-of-chapter questions.
6. After you have surveyed the material, you should know generally what it is about and how it is organized.

The Survey step is the technique of prereading that you learned in Chapter 5.

Q—Question

Try to form questions that you can answer as you read. The easiest way to do this is to turn each boldface heading into a question. (The section of Chapter 5 titled "Defining Your Purposes for Reading" discusses this step in depth.)

R—Read

Read the material section by section. As you read each section, look for the answer to the question you formed from the heading of that section.

R—Recite

After you finish each section, stop. Check to see whether you can answer your question for the section. If you can't, look back to find the answer. Then check your recall again. Be sure to complete this step after you read each section.

R—Review

When you have finished the whole reading assignment, go back to each heading; recall your question and try to answer it. If you can't recall the answer, be sure to look back and find the answer. Then test yourself again.

The SQ3R method ties together much of what you have already learned about active reading. The first two steps activate your background knowledge and establish questions to guide your reading. The last two steps provide a means of monitoring your comprehension and recall.

Why SQ3R Works

Results of research studies overwhelmingly suggest that students who are taught to use a study-reading system understand and remember what they read much better than students who have not been taught to use such a system.

In a classic study designed to test the effectiveness of the SQ3R system,* the reading rates and comprehension levels of a group of college students were

*F. P. Robinson, *Effective Study* (New York: Harper & Row, 1941), p. 30.

measured before and after they learned and used the SQ3R system. After students learned the SQ3R method, the average reading rate increased by 22 percent; the comprehension level increased by 10 percent.

If you consider for a moment how people learn, it becomes clear why study-reading systems are effective. One major way to learn is through repetition. Consider the way you learned the multiplication tables. Through repeated practice and drills, you learned $2 \times 2 = 4$, $5 \times 6 = 30$, $8 \times 9 = 72$, and so forth. The key was repetition. Study-reading systems provide some of the repetition necessary to ensure learning. Compared with the usual once-through approach to reading textbook assignments, which offer one chance to learn, SQ3R provides numerous repetitions and increases the amount learned.

SQ3R has many psychological advantages over ordinary reading. First, surveying (prereading) gives you a mental organization or structure—you know what to expect. Second, you always feel that you are looking for something specific rather than wandering aimlessly through a printed page. Third, when you find the information you're looking for, it is rewarding; you feel you have accomplished something. And if you can remember the information in the immediate- and long-term recall checks, it is even more rewarding.

EXERCISE 7

DIRECTIONS   Read the article titled "Causes of Habitat Loss and Species Endangerment," beginning on page 398, using the SQ3R method. The following SQ3R worksheet will help you get started. Fill in the required information as you go through each step.

SQ3R Worksheet

S—Survey: Read the title of the chapter, the introduction, each boldface heading, and the summary, and look at any pictures or graphs that appear.

1. What is the chapter about?

   _____

2. What major topics are included?

   _____

Q—Question 1: Turn the first heading into a question.

_____

_____

R—Read: Read the material that follows the first heading, looking for the answer to your question.

R—Recite: Reread the heading and recall the question you asked. Briefly answer this question in your own words without looking at the section. Check to see whether you are correct.

_____

_____

Q—Question 2: Turn the second heading into a question.

_____

_____

R—Read: Read the material that follows the second heading, looking for the answer to your question.

R—Recite: Briefly answer the question.

_____

_____

Q—Question 3: Turn the third heading into a question.

_____

_____

R—Read: Read the material that follows the third heading, looking for the answer to your question.

R—Recite: Briefly answer the question.

_____

_____

Continue using the question, read, and recite steps until you have finished each part of the chapter. Then complete the review step.

R—Review: Look over the total chapter by rereading the headings. Try to answer the question you made from each heading.

Answer to Question 1:

_____

_____

Answer to Question 2:

_____

_____

Answer to Question 3:

_____

_____

Check to see that your answers are correct.

UPDATING AND REVISING THE SQ3R SYSTEM

Now that you are familiar with the basic SQ3R system, it is time to modify it to suit your specific needs. As mentioned previously, the SQ3R method was developed in the 1940s, more than 50 years ago. Over these many years, considerable research has been done and much has been discovered about the learning process. Consequently, it is now possible to expand on the original SQ3R method by adding more recent techniques and strategies. Figure 15.6 lists the steps in the SQ3R method and indicates how you can expand each step to make it work better for you. Most of the techniques listed have been described in previous chapters, as indicated in the table.

SQ3R Steps	Additional Strategies
Survey	Preread (Chapter 4)
	Activate your background and experience (Chapter 4)
	Predict (Chapter 4)
Question	Ask guide questions (Chapter 6)
Read	Check your understanding (Chapter 6)
	Highlight and mark (Chapter 11)
	Anticipate thought patterns (Chapter 8)
Recite	Outline (Chapter 12)
	Summarize (Chapter 12)
	Map (Chapter 12)
Review	Paraphrase (Chapter 13)
	Self-test (Chapter 13)
	Review highlighting, outlines, and maps (Chapter 11, 12)

Figure 15.6
Expanding SQ3R

As shown in Figure 15.6, the Survey step is really a get-ready-to-read step, along with the Question step. The Read step becomes much more than simply the see-words step. It involves interacting with the text, thinking, anticipating, and reacting. The Recite step can involve much more than answering the questions posed in the Question step. As you identify important information, grasp relationships, and understand key concepts, you might change your highlighting, add to your marking, write notes or questions, self-test, summarize, outline, or draw maps. The final step, Review, can be expanded to include paraphrasing, self-testing, and the review of highlighting, annotation, outlines, and maps.

One popular modification of the SQ3R system is the addition of a fourth R— "Rite"—creating an SQ4R system. SQ4R recognizes the importance of writing, note taking, outlining, and summarizing in the learning process.

Add an "Evaluate" Step

Because critical thinking is an important part of learning, many students add an Evaluate step to the SQ3R system. The Review step assures you that you have mastered the material at the knowledge and comprehension levels of thinking. An Evaluate step encourages you to sit back and *think* about what you have read. To get started, ask yourself questions such as:

Why is this information important?

How can I use it?

How does it fit with the class lectures?

How is this chapter related to previously assigned ones?

Does the author provide enough evidence to support his or her ideas?

Is the author biased?

What are the author's tone and purpose?

Consider Your Learning Style

In Chapter 2, you completed a learning style questionnaire to discover characteristics of your learning style. These characteristics are important to consider in deciding how to modify SQ3R to work best for you. For instance, if you are a visual learner, you might sketch a map showing the organization of the chapter as part of the Survey step. Then, as part of the Recite step, include additional mapping. An auditory learner, during the Survey step, might predict and tape-record what he or she expects the chapter to cover and replay the tape before and after reading. The questions could also be taped during the Question step and then played back and answered as part of the Recite step.

DIRECTIONS   Review the results of the Learning Style Questionnaire on page 33. Then write a list of the changes you might make in the SQ3R method for one of your courses.

ADAPTING YOUR SYSTEM FOR DIFFERENT ACADEMIC DISCIPLINES

Various academic disciplines require different kinds of learning. In an English composition and literature class, for example, you learn skills of critical interpretation, whereas in a chemistry course you learn facts, principles, and processes. A history course focuses on events, their causes, their significance, and long-term trends.

Because different courses require different types of learning, they also require different types of reading and study; therefore, you should develop a specialized study-reading approach for each subject. The following subjects are some of the academic disciplines most commonly studied by beginning college students, for which changes in a study-reading system are most important. For each, possible modifications in a study-reading system are suggested.

Mathematics

Sample problems are an important part of most math courses; therefore, you would add a Study the Problems step, in which you would try to see how the problems illustrate the theory or process explained in the chapter. This step might also include working through or reviewing additional practice problems.

Literature

When reading novels, essays, short stories, or poetry in a composition and literature class, you are usually asked to interpret, react, and write about what you read. For reading literature, then, you might drop the Recite step, use the Review step for the literal content (who did what, when, and where?), and add two new steps: Interpret and React. In the Interpret step, you would analyze the characters, their actions, and the writer's style and point of view to determine the writer's theme or message. In the React step, you might ask questions such as "What meaning does this have for me? How effectively did the writer communicate his or her message? Do I agree with this writer's view of life?" You should make notes about your reactions, which can be a source of ideas if a paper is assigned.

Sciences

Prereading is particularly important when you are reading and studying biology, chemistry, physics, or another science, because most of the material is new. You might quickly read each end-of-chapter problem to discover what principles and formulas are emphasized in that chapter. The sciences emphasize facts, principles, formulas, and processes; therefore, build in a Write or Record step in which you highlight, outline, or write study sheets.

Social Sciences

Introductory courses in the social sciences (psychology, sociology, anthropology, economics, political science, and the like) often focus on a particular discipline's basic problems or topics. These courses introduce specialized vocabulary and the basic principles and theories on which the discipline operates.

For social science courses, then, build a Vocabulary Review step into your study-reading system. A Write or Highlight step is also needed to provide an efficient method for review and study.

Other Academic Disciplines

This brief chapter does not permit discussion of modifications for every academic discipline. Probably you are taking one or more courses that we have not mentioned. To adapt your study-reading system to these courses, ask yourself the following questions.

1. What type of learning is required? What is the main focus of the course? (Often the preface or the first chapter of your text will answer these questions. The instructor's course outline or objectives may be helpful.)
2. What must I do to learn this type of material?

Learn to "read" the instructor of each course. Find out what each expects, what topics and types of information each feels are important, and how your grades are determined. Talk with other students in the course or with students who have already taken the course to get ideas for useful ways of studying.

EXERCISE 9

DIRECTIONS   Four textbook excerpts appear in Part Seven (pages 376, 385, 394, and 406). Each represents a different academic discipline. How would you modify the SQ3R system to study-read each textbook excerpt?

1. Anthropology

_____

_____

_____

_____

2. Communication

_____

_____

_____

_____

3. Biology

_____

_____

_____

_____

4. Business

_____

_____

_____

_____

EXERCISE 10

Academic Application

DIRECTIONS   List each of the courses you are taking. Then briefly indicate what changes in your study-reading system you intend to make for each course.

_____

_____

_____

_____

_____

_____

LEARNING *Collaboratively*

DIRECTIONS   Your instructor will divide the class into three groups and select one of the readings in Part Seven. As an out-of-class assignment, the members of one group should *only* read the assignment (they should not use SQ3R or preread or review). A second group should preread (see Chapter 5) but should not review. A third group should use the SQ3R system. During the next class meeting, your instructor will quiz you and will report which group earned the highest scores. The class should evaluate their scores and draw conclusions about the relative effectiveness of the study methods used.

Applying YOUR LEARNING

Sharon is a visual, conceptual, and pragmatic learner. She is taking an astronomy course and is finding the textbook complicated. She is having difficulty understanding and completing reading assignments. Exams in astronomy are a combination of multiple-choice and essay. She is also taking Introduction to Women's Studies. Many of the readings are newspaper articles about current events and essays about the history of women's roles. The exam will be an essay exam.

1. What reading techniques and learning strategies using writing would you recommend to Sharon to help her with her astronomy text?
2. How can Sharon prepare for her essay exam? What specific suggestions can you make on the basis of the types of readings assigned for the course?
3. How might Sharon adapt SQ3R for her astronomy course?
4. How might Sharon adapt SQ3R for Introduction to Women's Studies?

SELF-TEST SUMMARY

1. Why is paraphrasing a useful study strategy?	Paraphrasing, the restatement of a passage's ideas in your own words, is a particularly useful strategy for recording the meaning and checking your comprehension of detailed, complex, precise, or poorly or unusually written passages. When you use your own words rather than the author's, the meaning of the passage is expressed in a clearer and more concise way than the original, making it easier to study and review.
2. What are the advantages of self-testing?	Self-testing emphasizes interpretation and application of the information being learned. Writing possible exam questions and drafting answers to them causes you to think about and organize ideas and to express them in your own words. It also gives you a way to practice for an upcoming exam.
3. How can a learning journal help you find the study techniques that work for you?	By keeping a written record of your reactions, comments, and assessments of learning strategies for individual courses, you can discover which strategies work best for you and how to modify them to be even more useful. Rereading your journal entries periodically and summarizing your impressions can help you see what is working, what needs changing, and how to change it.
4. What is the SQ3R study system?	The SQ3R method is a classic five-step method of study and review. The steps are Survey, Question, Read, Recite, and Review.
5. Why is it effective?	The SQ3R study method has several advantages over ordinary reading. By building a mental framework on which to fit information, searching actively for important facts, going through the repetitions involved in the three R's, and feeling rewarded when you find the answers to your questions, you can improve your comprehension and recall of study material.
6. How can you adapt your reading-study system for different academic disciplines?	The SQ3R method should be adapted to suit the unique characteristics of various academic disciplines. The system can also be expanded to include additional and/or newer techniques and strategies. Considering the focus of the course, the type of learning required, and what you must do to learn the material will guide you in adapting and expanding your reading-study system.

Take a Road Trip to
Florida (Spring Break)!

If your instructor has asked you to use the Reading Road Trip CD-ROM, be sure to visit the Outlining, Summarizing, Mapping, and Paraphrasing module for multimedia tutorials, exercises, and tests.

CHAPTER **16**

Preparing
for Exams

Why Learn to Prepare for Exams?

▲ **Preparing well for exams helps you tie together the facts and concepts you have learned.**

▲ **Better preparation for exams will help you achieve better grades.**

▲ **If you prepare well for your exams, you will minimize stress.**

Learning Experiment

You are taking a statistics class and must learn to calculate the median of a set of numbers.

Step 1

Read the following paragraph defining the term *median*.

> Because it can be affected by extremely high or low numbers, the mean is often a poor indicator of central tendency for a list of numbers. In cases like this, another measure of central tendency, called the **median**, can be used. The *median* divides a group of numbers in half; half the numbers lie above the median, and half lie below the median.
>
> Find the median by listing the numbers *in order* from *smallest* to *largest*. If the list contains an *odd* number of items, the median is the *middle number*.
>
> If a list contains an *even* number of items, there is no single middle number. In this case, the median is defined as the mean (average) of the *middle two* numbers.

Step 2

Applying the definition above, circle the median in each of the following groups of numbers.

> 17, 24, 6, 9, 10, 2, 44

> 7, 13, 9, 4

Which step was more useful in helping you learn the formula?

The Results

Most students find step 2 more useful. Why? In step 1 all you do is read. In step 2 you apply the explanation to several sets of numbers. Step 2 forces you to use and apply the information contained in step 1. By practicing computing the median, you come to understand it.

Learning Principle (What This Means to You)

One of the best ways to prepare for a test is to simulate the test conditions. To prepare for an exam, then, practice answering the types of questions you think will be on the test. Do not just read or reread as step 1 required you to do. This chapter will offer many ideas on preparing for exams and will show you ways to study by simulating test conditions for both objective and essay tests. You will also learn how to organize your review, identify what to study, analyze and synthesize information, and learn and remember what is important.

ORGANIZING YOUR STUDY AND REVIEW

Studying is the most important thing you can do to increase your chance of passing an exam. When exam papers are returned, you may hear comments like "I spent at least ten hours studying. I went over everything, and I still failed the exam!" Students frequently complain that they spend large amounts of time studying and do not get the grades they think they deserve. Usually the problem is that although they did study, they did not study the best way. The first thing to do, well in advance of the exam, is to get organized. The timing of your review sessions is crucial to achieving good test results. Organize your review sessions, using the suggestions discussed in the following sections.

Organize Your Time

1. Schedule several review sessions at least a week in advance of an exam. Set aside specific times for daily review, and incorporate them into your weekly schedule. If you are having difficulty with a particular subject, set up extra study times.

2. Spend time organizing your review. Make a list of all chapters, notes, and handouts that need to be reviewed. Divide the material, planning what you will review during each session.

3. Reserve time the night before the exam for a final, complete review. Do not study new material during this session. Instead, review the most difficult material, checking your recall of important facts or information for possible essay questions.

Find Out about the Exam

When studying for an exam or test, find out whether it will be objective, essay, or a combination of both. If your instructor does not specify the type of exam when he or she announces the date, ask during or after class. Most instructors are willing to tell students what type of exam will be given—sometimes they simply forget to mention it when announcing the exam. If an instructor chooses not to tell you, do not be concerned; at least you have shown that you are interested and are thinking ahead.

Be sure you know what material the exam will cover. Usually your instructor will either announce the exam topics or give the time span that the exam will cover. Also, find out what your instructor expects of you and how he or she will evaluate your exam. Some instructors expect you to recall text and lecture material; others expect you to agree with their views on a particular subject; still others encourage you to recall, discuss, analyze, or disagree with the ideas and information they have presented. You can usually tell what to expect by the way quizzes have been graded or classes have been conducted.

Attend the Class before the Exam

Be sure to attend the class prior to the exam. Cutting class to spend the time studying, although tempting, is a mistake. During this class, the instructor may give a brief review of the material to be covered or offer last-minute review suggestions. Have you ever heard an instructor say, "Be sure to look over . . ." prior to an exam? Also, listen carefully to how the instructor answers students' questions; these answers will provide clues about what the exam will emphasize.

Consider Studying with Others

Depending on your learning style, it may be helpful to study with another person or with a small group of students from your class. Be sure to weigh the following advantages and disadvantages of group study. Then decide whether group study suits your learning style.

Group study can be advantageous for the following reasons.

1. Group study forces you to become actively involved with the course content. Talking about, reacting to, and discussing the material aids learning. If you have trouble concentrating or staying with it when studying alone, group study may be useful.

2. One of the best ways to learn something is to explain it to someone else. By using your own words and thinking of the best way to explain an idea, you are analyzing it and testing your own understanding. The repetition

involved in explaining something you already understand also strengthens your learning.

Group study can, however, have disadvantages.

1. Unless everyone is serious, group study sessions can turn into social events in which very little study occurs.
2. Studying with the wrong people can produce negative attitudes that will work against you. For example, the "None of us understands this and we can't all fail" attitude is common.
3. By studying with someone who has not read the material carefully or attended classes regularly, you will waste time reviewing basic definitions and facts that you already know, instead of focusing on more difficult topics.

EXERCISE 1

DIRECTIONS   Plan a review schedule for an upcoming exam. Include material you will study and when you will study it.

IDENTIFYING WHAT TO STUDY

In preparing for an exam, review every source of information—textbook chapters and lecture notes—as well as sources sometimes overlooked, such as old exams and quizzes, the instructor's handouts, course outlines, and outside assignments. Talking with other students about the exam can also be helpful.

Textbook Chapters

You must review all chapters that were assigned during the period covered by the exam or that are related to the topics covered in the exam. Review of textbook chapters should be fairly easy if you have kept up with weekly assignments, used your own variation of a study-reading system, and marked and underlined each assignment.

Lecture Notes

In addition to textbook chapters, review all relevant notes. This, too, is easy if you have used the note-taking and editing system presented in Chapter 4.

Previous Exams and Quizzes

Be sure to keep all old tests and quizzes, which are valuable sources of review for longer, more comprehensive exams. Most instructors do not repeat the same test questions, but old quizzes list important facts, terms, and ideas. The comprehensive exam will probably test your recall of the same information through different types of questions.

Look for Patterns of Error

Pay particular attention to items that you got wrong; try to see a pattern of error.

1. Are you missing certain types of questions? If so, spend extra time on these questions.

Level of Question	Exam 1 Wrong Answers	Exam 2 Wrong Answers			
Knowledge	0	1			
Comprehension	2	0			
Application	7	5			
Analysis	1	2			
Synthesis	0	0			
Evaluation	1	0			

Figure 16.1
Sample Grid for Analysis of Errors

2. Are there certain topics on which you lost most of your points? If so, review these topics.
3. Are you missing questions at a particular level of thinking? Use a grid like the one shown in Figure 16.1 to analyze what type of questions you are getting wrong. If you discover, for example, that you are getting knowledge and comprehension questions wrong, include more factual review in your study plans. On the other hand, if you are missing numerous synthesis questions, you need to focus more on drawing connections between and among your study topics.

Identify the Levels of Thinking Your Instructor Emphasizes

The grid shown in Figure 16.2 can also be used to identify the level of thinking your instructor requires on exams. For example, some instructors may emphasize application; others may focus on analysis and synthesis of information. You can see that the exam analyzed in Figure 16.2 emphasized comprehension and applications questions. To discover your instructor's emphasis, go through a previous exam, question by question, identifying and marking its type in the grid. Once you have discovered your instructor's emphasis, adjust your study methods accordingly. Include more factual review if knowledge and comprehension are emphasized. Be sure to consider practical situations and uses if application questions are frequently asked.

Instructor's Handouts

Instructors frequently distribute duplicated sheets of information, such as summary outlines, lists of terms, sample problems, maps and charts, or explanations of difficult concepts. Any material that an instructor prepares for distribution is

Level of Thinking	Exam 1 Question Numbers	Exam 2 Question Numbers
Knowledge	5, 8, 25	
Comprehension	1, 3, 18, 19, 21, 22, 24	
Application	2, 5, 6, 7, 10, 11, 12, 20, 14, 16	
Analysis	4	
Synthesis	9, 15, 23	
Evaluation	13, 17	

Figure 16.2
Sample Grid for Determining Your Instructor's Emphasis

bound to be important. As you review these sheets throughout the course, date them and label the lecture topic to which they correspond. Keep them together in a folder or in the front of your notebook so that you can refer to them easily.

Outside Assignments

Out-of-class assignments might include problems to solve, library research, written reactions or evaluations, or lectures or movies to attend. If an instructor gives an assignment outside of class, the topic is important. Because of the limited number of assignments that can be given in a course, instructors choose only those that are most valuable. You should therefore keep your notes on assignments together for easy review.

Talk with Other Students

Talking with classmates can help you identify the right material to learn. By talking with others, you may discover a topic that you have overlooked or recognize a new focus or direction.

EXERCISE 2

Academic Application

DIRECTIONS   Construct a grid like the one shown in Figure 16.2. Use it to analyze the level(s) of thinking your instructor emphasized on one of your previous exams.

ANALYZING AND SYNTHESIZING INFORMATION

Once you have identified what material to learn, the next step is to draw together, analyze, and synthesize the information. Synthesis is an important critical-thinking skill because it forces you to see connections among ideas. In your close study of chapters and lecture notes, it is easy to get lost in details and lose sight of major themes or processes. When concentrating on details, you can miss significant points and fail to see relationships. Exams often measure your awareness of concepts and trends as well as your recall of facts, dates, and definitions. The following suggestions will help you learn to synthesize information.

Get a Perspective on the Course

To avoid focusing too narrowly on details and to obtain perspective on the course material, step back and view the course from a distance. Imagine that all your notes, textbook chapters, outlines, and study sheets are arranged on a table and that you are looking down on them from a peephole in the ceiling. Then ask yourself: What does all that mean? When put together, what does it all show? Why is it important?

Look for Relationships

Study and review consist of more than just learning facts. Try to see how facts are related. In learning the periodic table of chemical elements, for example, you should do more than just learn names and symbols. You should understand how elements are grouped, what properties the members of a group share, and how the groups are arranged.

Look for Patterns and the Progression of Thought

Try to see why the material was covered in the order in which it was presented. How is one class lecture related to the next? To what larger topic or theme are several lectures connected? For class lectures, check the course outline or syllabus that was distributed at the beginning of the course. Because it lists major topics and suggests the order in which they will be covered, your syllabus will be useful in discovering patterns.

Similarly, for textbook chapters, try to focus on the progression of ideas. Study the table of contents to see the connection between chapters you have read. Often chapters are grouped into sections based on similar content.

Watch for the progression or development of thought. Ask yourself: What is the information presented in this chapter leading up to? What does it have to do with the chapter that follows? Suppose that in psychology you had covered a chapter on personality traits and next were assigned a chapter on abnormal and deviant behavior. You would want to know what the two chapters have to do with each other. In this case, the first chapter on personality establishes the standards or norms by which abnormal and deviant behavior are determined.

Interpret and Evaluate

Do not let facts and details camouflage important questions. Remember to ask yourself: What does this mean? How is this information useful? How can this be applied to various situations? Once you have identified the literal content, stop, react, and evaluate its use, value, and application.

Prepare Study Sheets

The study sheet system is a way of organizing and summarizing complex information by preparing a mini-outline. It is most useful for reviewing material that is interrelated, or connected, and needs to be learned as a whole rather than as separate facts. Types of information that should be reviewed on study sheets include:

1. Theories and principles
2. Complex events with multiple causes and effects
3. Controversial issues—pros and cons
4. Summaries of philosophical issues
5. Trends in ideas or data
6. Groups of related facts

Look at the sample study sheet in Figure 16.3 on the next page, which was made by a student preparing for a psychology exam that would cover a chapter on stress. You will note that the study sheet organizes information on two approaches to coping with stress and presents them in a form that permits easy comparison.

To prepare a study sheet, first select the information to be learned. Then outline the information, using as few words as possible. Group together important points, facts, and ideas related to each topic.

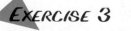

DIRECTIONS   Prepare a study sheet for the selection "No Secrets: Computers and Privacy," which begins on page 406 in Part Seven. Use the following headings in your study sheet: The Issue, Benefits, Risks.

	Problem-Focused Approach	Emotion-Focused Approach
Purpose	solving the problem causing stress	changing or managing the emotions the problems caused
Example	learning about a disability and how to live with it	expressing grief and anger to get it out of your system
How it is accomplished	1. defining the problem 2. learn about problem and how to fix it 3. take steps to fix the problem	1. reappraisal 2. comparisons 3. avoidance 4. humor

Figure 16.3
A Sample Study Sheet

EXERCISE 4

Academic Application

DIRECTIONS Prepare a study sheet for a topic you are studying in one of your courses. Include all the information you need to learn in order to prepare for an exam.

LEARNING AND MEMORIZING

The methods and procedures you use to learn and to remember depend on the type of exam for which you are preparing. You would study and learn information differently for a multiple-choice test than for an essay exam.

Exams can be divided into two basic types: objective and essay. Objective tests include short-answer tests in which you choose one or more answers from several that are given or supply a word or phrase to complete a statement. Multiple-choice, true/false, matching, and fill-in-the-blank questions are objective tests. In each of these, the questions are constructed so that the answers you choose are either right or wrong; scoring is completely objective, or free from judgment.

Essay tests require you to answer questions in your own words. You have to recall information, organize it, and present it in an acceptable written form. This is different from recognizing the correct answer among several choices or recalling a word or phrase. Because essay exams differ from objective tests, you must use different methods in preparing and reviewing for them.

Review for Objective Tests

Objective tests usually require you to recognize the right answer. On a multiple-choice test, for example, you have to pick the correct answer from the choices given. In matching tests, you have to recognize which two items go together.

One goal in reviewing for objective tests, then, is to become so familiar with the course material that you can recognize and select the right answers.

Use Highlighting and Marking

Your highlighting of reading assignments can be used in several ways for review. First, reread your highlighting in each chapter. Second, read the chapter's bold-face headings and form a question for each, as you did in the Question step in the SQ3R system. Try to answer your question; then check your highlighting to see whether you were correct. Finally, review special marks you may have included. If, for example, you marked new or important definitions with a particular symbol, then you should go through the chapter once and note these terms, checking your recall of their meanings.

Use the Recall Clues in Your Lecture Notes

Go back through each set of lecture notes and check your recall by using the marginal recall clue system. Test yourself by asking questions and trying to remember answers. Mark in red ink things you have trouble remembering. Then use ink of a different color the second time you go through your notes, marking information you still can't recall.

Use Study Aids

Use all study sheets, outlines, summaries, and organizational charts and diagrams that you have prepared to review and learn course content. To learn the information on a study sheet or outline, first read through it several times. Then take the first topic, write it on a sheet of paper, and see whether you can fill in the information under the topic on your study sheet or outline. If you can't recall all the information, test yourself until you have learned it. Continue in this way with each topic.

Use the Index Card System

The index card system is an effective way of reviewing for objective tests. Using 3-inch-by-5 inch index cards (or just small sheets of paper), write part of the information on the front, the remainder on the back. To review the dates of important events, write the date on the front, the event on the back; to review vocabulary, put each term on the front of one card and its definition on the back. See the sample index cards shown in Figure 16.4 on the next page, which were made by a student preparing for an objective exam in biology.

To study these cards, look at the front of each and try to remember what is written on the back. Then turn the card over to see whether you are correct. As you go through your pack of cards, sort them into two stacks—those you know and those you don't remember. Then go back through the stack of those you don't know, study each, and retest yourself, again sorting the cards into two stacks. Continue this procedure until you are satisfied that you have learned all the information. Go through your cards in this manner two or three times a day for three or four days before the exam. On the day of your exam, do a final, once-through review so that the information is fresh in your mind.

The index card system has several advantages. First, it is time-efficient; by sorting the cards, you spend time learning what you do not know and do not waste time reviewing what you have already learned. Second, by having each item of information on a separate card rather than in a list on a single sheet of

Figure 16.4
Sample Study Cards

poikilotherm

An organism whose body temperature varies with the environment.

homeotherm

An organism that maintains a stable body temperature regardless of the environment.

primary sources of heat gain

1. Radiant energy
2. Cellular metabolism

paper, you avoid the danger of learning the items in a certain order. If you study a list of items, you run the risk of being able to remember them only in the order in which they are written on the list. When a single item appears out of order on an exam, you may not remember it. By sorting and occasionally shuffling your index cards, you avoid learning information in a fixed order. A third advantage of the index card system is that these cards are easy to carry in a pocket or purse. It is therefore easier for you to space your review of the material. If you carry them with you, you can study in spare moments—even when you don't have textbooks or notebooks with you. Moments usually wasted waiting in supermarket lines, doctors' offices, gas stations, or traffic jams can be used for study.

The index card system is more appropriate for learning brief facts than for reviewing concepts, ideas, and principles or for understanding sequences of events, theories, and cause–effect relationships. For this reason, it works best when you are studying for objective tests that include short-answer questions such as fill-in-the-blanks.

Test Yourself

Check to be sure you have learned all the necessary facts and ideas. By testing yourself before the instructor tests you, you are preparing in a realistic way for the exam. If you were entering a marathon race, you would prepare for the race by running—not by playing golf. The same is true of test taking; you should prepare for a test by testing yourself—not by simply rereading chapters or pages of notes. You can test yourself in any of the following ways.

- Use recall clues for your lecture notes (see Chapter 4, p. 78).
- Draw and label maps (see Chapter 14, p. 293).
- Write partially completed outlines. Fill in the blanks from memory.
- Use vocabulary cards (see Chapter 11, p. 247).
- Work with a classmate, testing each other by making up sample questions and answering them.

EXERCISE 5

DIRECTIONS   Prepare a set of index cards (at least 20) for a chapter or section of a chapter you are studying in one of your courses. Then learn the information on the cards, using the sorting technique described previously.

Review for Essay Exams

Essay exams demand extensive recall. Starting with a blank sheet of paper, you are required to retrieve from your memory all the information that answers the question. Then you must organize that information and express your ideas about it in acceptable written form.

To review for an essay exam, first identify topics that may be included in the exam. Then predict actual questions and write outline or rough-draft answers.

Select Probable Topics

In choosing topics to study, you attempt to predict what questions will be included on the exam. There are several sources from which you can choose topics. First, you can use boldface textbook headings to identify important topics or subtopics. End-of-chapter discussion questions and recall clues written in the margins of your lecture notes may also suggest topics. Remember to check the course outline distributed by your instructor at the beginning of the course. This outline frequently contains a list of major topics covered in the course.

Study the Topics Selected

Once you have made your choices, identify which aspects of the topics might be tested. Perhaps the best source of information is your instructor, who probably has been consciously or unconsciously giving clues all semester about what the most important topics are. Train yourself to watch and listen for these clues. Specifically, look for your instructor's approach, focus, and emphasis with respect to the subject matter. Does your history instructor emphasize causes and dates of events? Or is he or she more concerned with the historical importance and lasting effects of events? Is your ecology instructor concerned with specific changes that a pollutant produces or its more general environmental effects?

Write Possible Questions

Next, write actual questions that you think your instructor might ask. Study the sample essay questions in Figure 17.1 on page 346 to get an idea of how they are written. Be sure to predict questions at all levels of thinking.

Applying Levels of Thinking

Preparing for Essay Exams and Levels of Thinking

Level of Thinking	What to Ask
Knowledge and Comprehension	These levels require recall of facts; remembering dates, names, definitions, and formulas falls into these categories. The five "W" questions—Who? What? Where? When? and Why?—are useful to ask.
Application	This level of thinking requires you to use or apply information. The following two questions best test this level: In what practical situations would this information be useful? What does this have to do with what I already know about the subject?
Analysis	Analysis involves seeing relationships. Ask questions that test your ability to take ideas apart, find cause–effect relationships, and discover how things work.
Synthesis	This level involves pulling ideas together. Ask questions that force you to look at similarities and differences.
Evaluation	This level involves making judgments and assessing value or worth. Ask questions that challenge sources, accuracy, long-term value, importance, and so forth.

Write Outline or Rough-Draft Answers

Once you have identified possible exam questions, the next step is to practice answering them. Do not take the time to write out full, complete sentences. Instead, collect and organize the information you would include in your answer, and record it in brief note or outline form, listing the information you would include.

If you are using a computer to organize lecture notes and notes taken from textbook chapters, it is easy to prepare a study sheet. You can copy sections from both sources to create a study sheet on each topic.

Use Key-Word Outlines

As a convenient way to remember what your draft answer includes, make a key-word outline of your answer. For each item in your draft, identify a key word that will trigger your memory of that idea. Then list and learn these key words. Together, these words form a mini-outline of topics and ideas to include in an essay on this topic. A key-word outline is shown in Figure 16.5.

Predicting and answering possible examination questions is effective for several reasons. Predicting forces you to analyze the material, not just review it. Drafting answers forces you to express ideas in written from. Through writing, you will recognize relationships, organize your thoughts, and discover the best way to present them.

Figure 16.5
A Sample Key-Word Outline

> Problem vs. Emotion
> purpose
> example
> how accomplished

EXERCISE 6

Academic Application

DIRECTIONS   Assume you are preparing for an essay exam in one of your courses. Predict several questions that might be asked for one textbook chapter and write them in the space provided.

_____

_____

_____

_____

_____

EXERCISE 7

Academic Application

DIRECTIONS   Choose one of the essay exam questions that you wrote in Exercise 6. Prepare a study sheet that summarizes the information on the topic. Then reduce that information on your study sheet to a key-word outline.

LEARNING *Collaboratively*

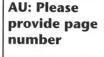

DIRECTIONS   Each student should write five essay questions based on the three readings included in Thematic Group D, "Computers and Privacy," in Part Seven, pp. 406–410. Working in groups of three or four students, compare and evaluate your questions, revise several strong ones, and categorize each question using the levels of thinking included in Chapter 1 (p. 46). Finally, choose one question to submit to the class. After each group has presented its question, the class will identify the level(s) of thinking that each question demands and discuss which is the hardest and which the easiest.

> **AU: Please provide page number**

Applying **YOUR LEARNING**

Art is taking a psychology course in which grades are based on four multiple-choice exams. Each exam contains fifty items worth 2 points and is machine-scored. When exams are returned, students receive their answer sheets but do not receive the questions themselves. On the first exam, Art earned 68 points, which is a high D grade. For the second exam, he spent more time studying but only earned 72, a C−. When Art visited his instructor in her office and asked for advice on how to improve his grade, the instructor handed Art copies of the first two exams and said, "Spend a half hour or so with each of these; I'm sure you'll discover what's going wrong."

1. What things should Art look for in the exams?
2. What kinds of notes should he make, if any, about the exams?
3. How should Art use each of the following in preparing for his next multiple-choice exam?
   - index cards
   - lecture notes
   - summaries of textbook chapters

SELF-TEST SUMMARY

1. How can you get organized to study and review for exams?

Organizing for study and review requires planning and scheduling your time so that all the material is reviewed carefully and thoroughly. You should begin at least a week before the exam to plan what material you will study each day and at what specific times you will study, and you should plan time for a complete review the evening before the exam. Attending the last class before the exam can provide you with useful hints, and group study can be helpful for certain individuals and circumstances.

2. How can you identify what to study?

In order to identify what to study, it is important to review all of your sources of information. To determine what material is to be learned, you should review all textbook chapters assigned; lecture notes, exams, and quizzes you have taken; classroom handouts, and notes on outside assignments. From these sources and discussion with other students, you will arrive at the topics most likely to be covered in the exam.

3. How can you organize these facts and ideas and synthesize them into a meaningful body of information to be studied?

To synthesize the information presented in a course, it is helpful to "step back" and look at the larger picture of the meaning of the course. Look at relationships between ideas, note patterns in the course syllabus and your textbook's table of contents, and see past the details to the important questions regarding the use, value, and application of this information. Preparing study sheets or mini-outlines can help in this process.

4. How can you best learn and memorize the information for objective and essay exams?

Learning and memorizing, the final steps in preparing for exams, require learning the material in a manner that is most appropriate for the type of exam to be taken. For objective exams, you should review all highlighting and marking, the recall clues in your lecture notes, and any study aids you have prepared throughout the course. By using the index card system and testing yourself, you can be sure you have learned all the important facts and ideas. For essay exams, you should begin by predicting probable exam questions. Next, you should study the topics selected by preparing a study sheet from which you can review and write a clear, concise essay. Finally, prepare a key-word outline or mini-outline that will guide your writing of answers to the questions you predicted earlier.

Take a Road Trip to
Hollywood!

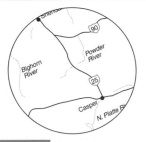

If your instructor has asked you to use the Reading Road Trip CD-ROM, be sure to visit the Test Taking and Preparation module for multimedia tutorials, exercises, and tests.

CHAPTER 17

Taking Exams

Why Learn How to Take Exams?

▲ **You will take plenty of exams in your college career.**

▲ **Exams may be an important part of admission to graduate school, the job application process, and licensing and certification for various careers.**

▲ **Knowing how to approach an exam can earn you extra points.**

Learning Experiment

Step 1

Here is a multiple-choice test item from a psychology exam:

> Modern psychological researchers maintain that the mind as well as behavior can be scientifically examined primarily by
>
> a. observing behavior and making inferences about mental functioning
> b. observing mental activity and making inferences about behavior
> c. making inferences about behavior
> d. direct observation of behavior
>
> If you know the correct answer, circle it now.

Step 2

If you did not know the correct answer, use your reasoning skills to determine the best answer and circle it.

Hints:

1. Which choices do *not* refer to both the mind and behavior?
   (Answer: choices c and d)
2. Which choice contains an activity that cannot be easily done?
   (Answer: b—mental activity cannot be observed without specialized medical equipment.)

The Results

Using the hints above, you probably were able to eliminate choices b, c, and d.

Learning Principle (What This Means to You)

Although you did not know the correct answer, you were able to figure it out. **When taking exams trust your reasoning skills to help you figure out correct answers.** In this chapter you will learn how to sharpen your reasoning skills for all types of exams. The manner in which you approach an exam, how you read and answer objective questions, and how carefully you read, organize, and write your answers to an essay exam can influence your grade. This chapter discusses each of these aspects of becoming test-wise and also considers a problem that interferes with many students' ability to do well on exams: test anxiety.

GENERAL SUGGESTIONS FOR TAKING EXAMS

The following suggestions will help you approach classroom exams in an organized, systematic way.

Bring Necessary Materials

When going to any exam, be sure to take along any materials you might be asked or allowed to use. Be sure you have an extra pen, and take a pencil in case you must make a drawing or diagram. Take paper—you may need it for computing figures or writing essay answers. Take along anything you have been allowed to use throughout the semester, such as a pocket calculator, conversion chart, or dictionary. If you are not sure whether you may use them, ask the instructor.

Get There on Time

It is important to arrive at the exam room on time, or a few minutes early, to get a seat and get organized before the instructor arrives. If you are late, you may miss instructions and feel rushed as you begin the exam.

If you arrive too early (15 minutes ahead), you risk anxiety induced by panic-stricken students questioning each other, trading last-minute memory tricks, and worrying about how difficult the exam will be.

Sit in the Front of the Room

If you have a choice, the most practical place to sit in an exam room is at the front. There you often receive the test first and get a head start. There, also, you are sure to hear directions and corrections and can easily read any changes written on the chalkboard. Finally, it is easier to concentrate at the front of the room. At the back, you are exposed to distractions, such as a student dropping papers or cheating, or the person in front who is already two pages ahead of you.

Preread the Exam

Before you start to answer any of the questions, quickly page through the exam, noting the directions, the length, the types of questions, and the general topics covered. Prereading provides an overview of the whole exam. Prereading also helps eliminate the panic you may feel if you go right to the first few questions and find that you are unsure of the answers.

Plan Your Time

After prereading the exam, you will know the numbers and types of questions included. You should then estimate how much time you will spend on each part of the exam. The number of points each section is worth (the point distribution) should be your guide. If, for example, one part of an exam has 20 multiple-choice questions worth 1 point each and another part has two essays worth 40 points each, you should spend much more time answering the essay questions than working through the multiple-choice items. If the point distribution is not indicated on the test booklet, you may want to ask the instructor what it is.

As you plan your time, be sure to allow a minute or two to preread the exam. Also allow three to four minutes at the end of the exam to review what you have done, answering questions you skipped, and making any necessary corrections or changes.

To keep track of time, wear a watch. Many classrooms do not have wall clocks, or you may be sitting in a position where the clock is difficult to see.

If you were taking an exam with the following distribution of questions and points, how would you divide your time? Assume the total exam time is 50 minutes.

Type of Question	Number of Questions	Total Points
Multiple-choice	25 questions	25 points
True/false	20 questions	20 points
Essay	2 questions	55 points

You should probably divide your time like this:

Prereading	1–2 minutes
Multiple-choice	15 minutes
True/false	10 minutes
Essay	20 minutes
Review	3–4 minutes

Because the essays are worth twice as many points as either of the other two parts of the exam, it is necessary to spend twice as much time on the essay portion.

Read the Questions Carefully

Most instructors word their questions so that what is expected is clear. A common mistake students make is to read more into the question than is asked for. To avoid this error, read the question several times, paying attention to how it is worded. If you are uncertain what is asked for, try to relate the question to the course content. Don't anticipate hidden meanings or trick questions.

◣ EXERCISE 1

DIRECTIONS   For each of the exams described below, estimate how you would divide your time.

1. Time limit: 75 minutes

Type of Question	Number of Questions	Total Points
Multiple-choice	20 questions	40 points
Matching	10 questions	10 points
Essay	2 questions	50 points

How would you divide your time?

Prereading   _____ minutes

Multiple-choice   _____ minutes

Matching   _____ minutes

Essay   _____ minutes

Review   _____ minutes

2. Time limit: 50 minutes

Type of Question	Number of Questions	Total Points
True/false	15 questions	30 points
Fill-in-the-blank	15 questions	30 points
Short answer	10 questions	40 points

How would you divide your time?

Prereading   _____ minutes

True/false   _____ minutes

Fill-in-the-blank   _____ minutes

Short answer   _____ minutes

Review   _____ minutes

HINTS FOR TAKING OBJECTIVE EXAMS

When taking objective exams—usually multiple choice, true/false, or matching—remember the following hints, which may net you a few more points.

Read the Directions

Before answering any questions, read the directions. Often an instructor may want the correct answer marked in a particular way (underlined rather than circled). The directions may contain crucial information that you must know in order to answer the questions correctly. If you were to ignore directions such as the following and assume the test questions were of the usual type, you could lose a considerable number of points.

True/False Directions

Read each statement. If the statement is true, mark a T in the blank to the left of the item. If the statement is false, add and/or subtract words in such a way as to make the statement correct.

Multiple-Choice Directions

Circle all the choices that correctly complete the statement.

Without reading the true/false directions, you would not know that you should correct incorrect statements. Without reading the multiple-choice directions, you would not know that you are to choose more than one answer.

Leave Nothing Blank

Before turning in your exam, be sure you have answered every question. If you have no idea about the correct answer to a question, guess—you might be right. On a true/false test, your chances of being correct are 50 percent; on a four-choice multiple-choice question, your odds are 25 percent.

Students frequently turn in tests with some items unanswered because they leave difficult questions blank, planning to return to them later. Then, in the rush to finish everything, they forget to go back to them. The best way to avoid this problem is to enter what look like the best answers and mark the question numbers with an X or a check mark; then, if you have time at the end of the exam, you can give them more thought. If you run out of time, at least you will have attempted to answer them.

Look for Clues

If you encounter a difficult question, choose what seems to be the best answer, mark the question so that you can return to it, and keep the item in mind as you go through the rest of the exam. Sometimes you will see some piece of information later in the exam that reminds you of a fact or idea. At other times you may notice information that, if true, contradicts an answer you had already chosen.

Don't Change Answers without Good Reason

When reviewing your exam answers, don't make a change unless you have a specific reason for doing so. If a later test item made you remember information for a previous item, by all means make a change. If, however, you are just having second thoughts about an answer, leave it alone. Your first guess is usually the best one.

Hints for Taking True/False Tests

When taking true/false tests, watch for words that qualify or change the meaning of a statement; often, just one word makes it true or false. Consider the following oversimplified example.

All dogs are white.

Some dogs are white.

The first statement is obviously false, whereas the second is true. In each statement, only one word determined whether the statement was true or false. Of course, the words and statements are much more complicated on college true/false exams, but you will find that one word often determines whether a statement is true or false. Read the following examples.

> *All* paragraphs must have a stated main idea.

> Spelling, punctuation, and handwriting *always* affect the grade given to an essay answer.

> When taking notes on a lecture, try to write down *everything* the speaker says.

In each of these examples, the italicized words modify—or limit—the truth of the statement. When reading a true/false statement, look carefully for any limiting words, such as *all, some, none, never, always, usually, frequently,* and *most of the time.* Overlooking these words may cost you several points on an exam.

Read Two-Part Statements Carefully

Occasionally you may find a statement with two or more parts. In answering these items, remember that both or all parts of the statement must be true in order for it to be correctly marked true. If part of the statement is true and another part is false, then mark the statement false. Here is an example:

> The World Health Organization (WHO) has been successful in its campaign to eliminate smallpox and malaria.

Although it is true that WHO has been successful in eliminating smallpox, malaria is still a world health problem and has not been eliminated. Because only part of this statement is true, it should be marked false.

Look for Negative and Double-Negative Statements

Test items that use negative words or word parts can be confusing. Words such as *no, none, never, not,* and *cannot* and beginnings of words such as *in-, dis-, un-, it-,* and *ir-* are easy to miss and always alter the meaning of the statement. For items that contain negative statements, make it a habit to underline or circle them as you read.

Statements that contain two negatives, such as the following, are even more confusing.

> It is not unreasonable to expect Vietnam veterans to continue to be angry about their exposure to Agent Orange.

In reading these statements, remember that two negatives balance or cancel out each other. "Not unreasonable," then, can be interpreted to mean "reasonable."

Make Your Best Guess

When all else fails and you are unable to reason out the answer to an item, use these three last-resort rules of thumb:

1. Absolute statements tend to be false. Because there are very few things that are always true and for which there are no exceptions, your best guess is to mark statements that contain words such as *always, all, never,* or *none* as false.

2. Mark any item that contains unfamiliar terminology or facts as false. If you've studied the material thoroughly, trust that you would recognize as true anything that was a part of the course content.

3. When all else fails, it is better to guess true than false. It is more difficult for instructors to write false statements than true statements. As a result, many exams have more true items than false.

EXERCISE 2

DIRECTIONS   The following true/false test is based on content presented in the reading "The Rapid Loss of Species" in Part Seven on p. 394. Read each item. Then find and underline the single word that, if changed or deleted, could change the truth or falsity of the statement. In the space provided at the left, indicate whether the statement is true or false by marking T for true and F for false.

_____   1.   Key deer is a species found only in the Florida Keys.

_____   2.   Key deer were nearly exterminated in the late 1900s.

_____   3.   Motorists are the primary threat to the key deer's survival.

_____   4.   Scientists estimate that within the next century less than half of the Earth's current species will become extinct.

_____   5.   Tropical forests alone may house 80 percent of the world's plants and animals.

_____   6.   Many living species are yet to be discovered and named.

_____   7.   Habitat loss threatens the greatest number of species.

_____   8.   Whale hunting is still allowed in many underdeveloped countries.

_____   9.   There has been a population increase in species of songbirds in Central and South America.

_____   10.   Deforestation is not a threat to migratory birds.

Hints for Taking Matching Tests

Matching tests require you to select items in one list that can be paired with items in a second list. Use the following tips to answer matching tests.

1. Before answering any items, glance through both lists to get an overview of the subjects and topics the test covers. Next, try to discover a pattern. Are you asked to match dates with events, terms with meanings, people with accomplishments?

2. Answer the items you are sure of first, lightly crossing off items as they are used.

3. Don't choose the first answer you see that seems correct; items later in the list may be better choices.

4. If the first column consists of short words or phrases and the second is made up of lengthy definitions or descriptions, save time by "reverse matching"; that is, look for the word or phrase in column 1 that fits each item in column 2.

Hints for Taking Short-Answer Tests

Short-answer tests require you to write a brief answer, usually in list or sentence form. Here is an example:

> List three events that increased U.S. involvement in the Vietnam War.

In answering short-answer questions, be sure to:

1. Use point distribution as a clue to how many pieces of information to include. For a 9-point item asking you to describe the characteristics of a totalitarian government, give at least three ideas.
2. Plan what you will say before starting to write.
3. Use the amount of space provided, especially if it varies for different items, as a clue to how much you should write.

Hints for Taking Fill-in-the-Blank Tests

Items that ask you to fill in a missing word or phrase within a sentence require recall of information rather than recognition of the correct answer. It is important, therefore, to look for clues that will trigger your recall.

1. Look for key words in the sentence, and use them to decide what subject matter and topic the item covers.
2. Decide what type of information is required. Is it a date, name, place, new term?
3. Use the grammatical structure of the sentence to determine the type of word called for. Is it a noun, verb, or qualifier?

Hints for Taking Multiple-Choice Tests

Multiple-choice exams are among the most frequently used types of exams and are often the most difficult. The following suggestions should improve your success in taking multiple-choice tests.

Read all choices first, considering each.

Do not stop with the second or third choice, even if you are sure that you have found the correct answer. Remember, on most multiple-choice tests, your job is to pick the *best* answer, and the last choice may be better than the preceding answers.

Some multiple-choice tests include combinations of previously listed choices.

See the following test item.

> Among the causes of slow reading is (are)
>   a. lack of comprehension
>   b. reading word by word rather than in phrases
>   c. poorly developed vocabulary
>   d. making too few fixations per line
>   e. a and b
>   f. a, b, and c
>   g. a, b, c, and d

The addition of choices that are combinations of previous choices tends to be confusing. Treat each choice, when combined with the stem, as a true or false statement. As you consider each choice, mark it true or false. If you find more than one true statement, select the choice that contains the letters of all the true statements you identified.

Use logic and common sense.

Even if you are unfamiliar with the subject matter, it is sometimes possible to reason out the correct answer. The following item is taken from a history exam on Japanese–American relations after World War II.

Prejudice and discrimination are
a. harmful to our society because they waste our economic, political, and social resources
b. helpful because they ensure against attack from within
c. harmful because they create negative images of the United States in foreign countries
d. helpful because they keep the majority pure and united against minorities

Through logic and common sense, it is possible to eliminate choices b and d. Prejudice and discrimination are seldom, if ever, regarded as positive, desirable, or helpful, because they are inconsistent with democratic ideals. Having narrowed your answer to two choices, a or c, you can see that choice a offers a stronger, more substantial reason why prejudice and discrimination are harmful. What other countries think of the United States is not as serious as the waste of economic, political, and social resources.

Study any items that are very similar.

When two choices seem very close and you cannot decide between them, stop and examine each. First, try to express each in your own words. Then analyze how they differ. Often this process will lead you to recognize the correct answer.

Look for qualifying words.

As in true/false tests, the presence of qualifying words is important. Because many statements, ideas, principles, and rules have exceptions, you should be careful in selecting items that contain such words as *best, always, all, no, entirely,* and *completely,* all of which suggest that something is always true, without exception. Also be careful of statements that contain such words as *none, never,* and *worst,* which suggest things that without exception are never true. Items containing words that provide for some level of exception or qualification are more likely to be correct; a few examples are *often, usually, less, seldom, few, more,* and *most.*

In the following example, note the use of italicized qualifying words.

In most societies
a. values are *highly* consistent
b. people *often* believe and act on values that are contradictory
c. *all* legitimate organizations support the values of the majority
d. values of equality *never* exist alongside prejudice and discrimination

In this question, items c and d contain the words *all* and *never,* suggesting that those statements are true without exception. Thus if you did not know the answer to this question based on content, you could eliminate items c and d on the basis of the level of qualifiers.

Some multiple-choice questions require application of knowledge or information.

You may be asked to analyze a hypothetical situation or to use what you have learned to solve a problem. Here is an example taken from a psychology test:

> Carrie is uncomfortable in her new home in New Orleans. When she gets dressed up and leaves her home and goes to the supermarket to buy the week's groceries, she gets nervous and upset and thinks that something is going to happen to her. She feels the same way when walking her four-year-old son Jason in the park or playground.
>   Carrie is suffering from
>   a. shyness
>   b. a phobia
>   c. a personality disorder
>   d. hypertension

In answering questions of this type, start by crossing out unnecessary information that can distract you. In the preceding example, distracting information includes the woman's name, her son's name, where she lives, why she goes to the store, and so forth.

Answer the items using your own words.

If a question concerns steps in a process or the order in which events occur or any other information that is likely to confuse you, ignore the choices and use the margin or scrap paper to jot down the information as you can recall it. Then select the choice that matches what you wrote.

Avoid selecting answers that are unfamiliar or that you do not understand.

A choice that looks complicated or uses difficult words is not necessarily correct. If you have studied carefully, a choice that is unfamiliar to you is probably incorrect.

Pick the choice that seems most complete.

As a last resort, when you do not know the answer and are unable to eliminate any of the choices as wrong, guess by picking the one that seems complete and contains the most information. This is a good choice because instructors are always careful to make the best answer completely correct and recognizable. Such a choice often becomes long or detailed.

Make educated guesses.

In most instances, you can eliminate one or more of the choices as obviously wrong. Even if you can eliminate only one choice, you have reduced your odds of being correct on a four-choice item from 1 in 4 to 1 in 3. If you can eliminate two choices, you have reduced your odds to 1 in 2, or 50 percent. Don't hesitate to play the odds and make a guess—you may gain points.

HINTS FOR TAKING STANDARDIZED TESTS

At various times in college, you may be required to take a standardized test, which is a commercially prepared, timed test used nationally or statewide to measure skills and abilities. Your score compares your performance to that of large numbers of other students throughout the country or state. The SAT and ACT are examples of standardized tests; many graduate schools require a standardized test as part of their admission process. Following are a few suggestions for taking this type of test.

1. Most standardized tests are timed, so the pace you work at is a critical factor. You need to work at a fairly rapid rate, but not so fast as to make careless errors.
2. Don't plan on finishing the test. Many of the tests are designed so that no one finishes.
3. Don't expect to get everything right. Unlike classroom tests or exams, you are not expected to get most of the answers correct.
4. Find out if there is a penalty for guessing. If there is none, then use the last 20 or 30 seconds to randomly fill in an answer for each item that you have not had time to do. The odds are that you will get one item correct for every four items that you guess.
5. Get organized before the timing begins. Line up your answer sheet and test booklet so you can move between them rapidly without losing your place.

HINTS FOR TAKING ESSAY EXAMS

Essay questions are usually graded on two factors: what you say and how you say it. It is not enough, then, simply to include the correct information. The information must be presented in a logical, organized way that demonstrates your understanding of the subject you are writing about. There can be as much as one whole letter grade difference between a well-written and a poorly written essay, although both contain the same basic information. This section offers suggestions for getting as many points as possible on essay exams.

Read the Question

For essay exams, reading the question carefully is the key to writing a correct, complete, and organized answer.

Read the Directions First

The directions may tell you how many essays to answer and how to structure your answer, or they may specify a minimum or maximum length for your answer.

Study the Question for Clues

The question usually includes three valuable pieces of information. First, the question tells you the *topic* you are to write about. Second, it contains a *limiting word* that restricts and directs your answer. Finally, the question contains a *key word* or phrase that tells you how to organize and present answers. Read the essay question in this example:

(key word)   (limiting word)   (topic)   (limiting word)   (topic)

Compare the causes of the Vietnam War with the causes of the Korean War.

In this example you have two topics—the Vietnam War and the Korean War. The question also contains a limiting word that restricts your discussion to these

Key Words	Example	Information to Include
Comprehension		
Discuss	Discuss Laetrile as a treatment for cancer.	Consider important characteristics and main points.
Enumerate	Enumerate the reasons for U.S. withdrawal from Vietnam.	List or discuss one by one.
Define	Define thermal pollution and include several examples.	Give an accurate meaning of the term with enough detail to show that you really understand it.
Application		
Illustrate	State Boyle's law and illustrate its use.	Explain, using examples that demonstrate or clarify a point or idea.
Analysis		
Compare	Compare the causes of air pollution with those of water pollution.	Show how items are similar as well as different; include details or examples.
Contrast	Contrast the health care systems in the United States with those in England.	Show how the items are different; include details or examples.
Explain	Explain why black Americans are primarily city dwellers.	Give facts, details, or reasons that make the idea or concept clear and understandable.
Describe	Describe the experimentation that tests whether plants are sensitive to music.	Tell how something looks or happened, including how, who, where, and why.
Justify	Justify former President Carter's attempt to rescue the hostages in Iran.	Give reasons that support an action, event, or policy.
Synthesis		
Trace	Trace the history of legalized prostitution in Nevada.	Describe the development or progress of a particular trend, event, or process in chronological order.
Summarize	Summarize the arguments for and those against offering sex education courses in public schools.	Cover the major points in brief form; use a sentence-and-paragraph form.
Evaluation		
Evaluate	Evaluate the strategies our society has used to treat mental illness.	React to the topic in a logical way. Discuss the merits, strengths, weaknesses, advantages, or limitations of the topic.
Criticize	Criticize the current environmental controls to combat air pollution.	Make judgments about quality or worth; include both positive and negative aspects.
Prove	Prove that ice is a better cooling agent than water when both are at the same temperature.	Demonstrate or establish that a concept or theory is correct, logical, or valid.

Figure 17.1
Key Words Used in Essay Questions

topics and tells you what to include in your answer. In this sample question, the limiting word is *causes*. It tells you to limit your answer to a discussion of events that started, or caused, each war. Do not include information about events of the war or its effects. The key word in the sample question is *compare*. It means you should consider the similarities, and possibly the differences, between the causes of the two wars. When directed to compare, you already have some clues as to how your answer should be written. One possibility is to discuss the causes of one war and then the causes of the other and finally to make an overall statement about their similarities. Another choice is to discuss one type of cause for each of the wars, and then go on to discuss another type of cause for each. For instance, you could discuss the economic causes of each and then the political causes of each.

There are several common key words and phrases used in essay questions. They are listed in Figure 17.1. Some questions require only knowledge and comprehension, but most require the higher-level thinking skills of application, analysis, synthesis, and evaluation.

Watch for Questions with Several Parts

A common mistake that students often make is to fail to answer all parts of an essay question, perhaps because they get involved with answering the first part and forget about the remaining parts. Questions with several parts come in two forms. The most obvious form is as follows.

> For the U.S. invasion of Grenada, discuss the
> a. causes
> b. immediate effects
> c. long-range political implications

A less obvious form that does not stand out as a several-part question is the following.

> Discuss *how* the Equal Rights Amendment was developed and *why* its passage has aroused controversy.

When you find a question of this type, underline or circle the limiting words to serve as a reminder.

Make Notes as You Read

As you read a question the first time, you may begin to formulate an answer. When this occurs, jot down a few key words that will bring these thoughts back when you are ready to organize your answer.

EXERCISE 3

DIRECTIONS   Read each of the following essay questions. For each question, underline the topic, circle the limiting word, and place a box around the key word.

1. Discuss the long-term effects of the trend toward a smaller, more self-contained family structure.
2. Trace the development of monopolies in the late nineteenth and early twentieth centuries in America.

3. Explain one effect of the Industrial Revolution on each of three of the following:
   a. transportation
   b. capitalism
   c. socialism
   d. population growth
   e. scientific research
4. Discuss the reason why, although tropical plants have very large leaves and most desert plants have very small leaves, cactus grows equally well in both habitats.
5. Describe the events leading up to the War of 1812.
6. Compare and contrast the purpose and procedures in textbook marking and lecture note taking.
7. Briefly describe a complete approach to reading and studying a textbook chapter that will enable you to handle a test on that material successfully.
8. List four factors that influence memory or recall ability and explain how each can be used to make study more efficient.
9. Summarize the techniques a speaker or lecturer may use to emphasize the important concepts and ideas in a lecture.
10. Explain the value and purpose of the prereading technique and list the steps involved in prereading a textbook chapter.

DIRECTIONS   Write ten possible essay questions for a course you are taking. *Be sure to write at least one question at each level of thinking.*

Organize Your Answer

As mentioned earlier, a well-written, organized essay often gets a higher grade than a carelessly constructed one. Read each of these examples and notice how they differ. Each essay was written in response to this instruction on a psychology final exam: Describe the stages involved in the memory process.

Example 1

Memory is important to everybody's life. Memory has special ways to help you get a better recollection of things and ideas. Psychologists believe that memory has three stages: encoding, storage, and retrieval.

In the encoding stage, you are putting facts and ideas into a code, usually words, and filing them away in your memory. Encoding involves preparing information for storage in memory.

The second stage of memory is storage. It is the stage that most people call memory. It involves keeping information so that it is accessible for use later in time. How well information is stored can be affected by old information already stored and newer information that is added later.

The third step in memory is retrieval, which means the ability to get back information that is in storage. There are two types of retrieval—recognition and recall. In recognition, you have to be able to identify the correct information from several choices. In recall, you have to pull information directly from your memory without using the recognition type of retrieval.

Example 2

Memory is very complicated in how it works. It involves remembering things that are stored in your mind and being able to pull them out when you want to remember them. When you pull information out of your memory it is called retrieval. How well you can remember something is affected by how you keep the information in your mind and how you put it in. When keeping, or storing, information you have to realize that this information will be affected by old information already in your memory. Putting information in your memory is called encoding, and it means that you store facts and ideas in word form in your memory. Information stored in your memory can also be influenced by information that you add to your memory later.

There are two ways you can retrieve information. You can either recognize it or recall it. When you recognize information you are able to spot the correct information among other information. When you recall information you have to pull information out of your head. Recall is what you have to do when you write an essay exam.

While these two essays contain practically the same information, the first will probably receive a higher grade. In this essay, it is easy to see that the writer knows that the memory process has three stages and knows how to explain each. The writer opens the essay by stating that there are three stages and then devotes one paragraph to each of the three stages.

In the second essay, it is not easy to identify the stages of memory. The paragraphs are not organized according to stages in the memory process. The writer does not write about one stage at a time in a logical order. Retrieval is mentioned first; then storage and retrieval are discussed further. At the end, the writer returns to the topic of retrieval and gives further information.

Here are a few suggestions to help you organize your answer:

1. Think before you start to write. Decide what information is called for and what you will include.
2. Make a brief word or phrase outline of the ideas you want to include in your answer.
3. Study your word outline and rearrange its order. You may want to put major topics and important ideas first and less important points toward the end, or you may decide to organize your answer chronologically, discussing events early in time near the beginning and mentioning more recent events near the end. The topic you are discussing will largely determine the order of presentation.
4. If the point value of the essay is given, use that information as a clue to how many separate points or ideas may be expected. For an essay worth 25 points, for example, discussion of five major ideas may be expected.

Use Correct Paragraph Form

Be sure to write your answers in complete, correct sentences and to include only one major point in each paragraph. Each paragraph should have a main idea, usually expressed in one sentence. The remainder of the paragraph should explain, prove, or support the main idea you state. Also, use correct spelling and punctuation.

Begin Your Answer with a Thesis Statement

Your first sentence should state what the entire essay is about and suggest how you intend to approach it. If a question asks you to discuss the practical applications of Newton's three laws of motion, you might begin by writing, "Newton's laws of motion have many practical applications." Then you should proceed to name the three laws and their practical applications, devoting one paragraph to each law. If you have time, your final paragraph may summarize or review the major points you covered in the essay.

Make Your Main Points Easy to Find

Because many essay exam readers have a large number of papers to read in a short period of time, they tend to skim (look for key ideas) rather than read everything; therefore, state each main point at the beginning of a new paragraph. For lengthy answers or multipart questions, you might use headings or the same numbering used in the question. Use space (two lines) to divide your answers into different parts.

Include Sufficient Explanation

Instructors often criticize essay answers because they fail to explain or to support ideas fully. If you include only one major idea per paragraph, you avoid this danger and force yourself to explain major points. Also, if you answer an essay question with the intent of convincing your instructor that you have learned the material, then you are likely to include enough explanation. Another rule of thumb is also useful: Too much information is better than too little.

Avoid Opinions and Judgments

Unless the question specifically asks you to do so, do not include your personal reaction to the topic. When you are asked to state your reactions and opinions, include reasons to support them.

Make Your Answer Readable

An instructor cannot help having personal reactions to your answer. Try to make those reactions positive by handing in a paper that is as easy to read as possible. It is annoying to an instructor to try to read poor handwriting and carelessly written answers.

1. Use ink—it is easier to read than pencil and does not smear.
2. Use clean, unwrinkled 8½-by-11-inch paper. Reading a handful of small sheets is difficult and confusing.
3. Number your pages and put your name on each sheet.
4. Do not scratch out sentences you want to omit. Draw a single line through each and write *omit* in the margin.
5. If the paper is thin or the ink runs, write on only one side.
6. Leave plenty of space between questions. Leave a 1- to 2-inch margin at each side. The instructor will need space to write comments.

Proofread Your Answer

After you have written an essay, read it twice. Before reading your essay the first time, read the question again. Then check to see that you have included all necessary facts and information and that you have adequately explained each fact. Add anything you feel improves your answer. Then read the essay a second time, checking and correcting all the mechanical aspects of your writing. Check for hard-to-read words and errors in spelling and punctuation. Again, make all necessary corrections.

If You Run Out of Time

Despite careful planning of exam time, you may run out of time before you finish writing one of the essays. If this happens, try to jot down the major ideas that you would discuss fully if you had time. Often, your instructor will give you partial credit for this type of response, especially if you mention that you ran out of time.

If You Don't Know the Answer

Despite careful preparation, you may forget an answer. If this should happen, do not leave a blank page; write something. Attempt to answer the question—you may hit upon some partially correct information. The main reason for writing something is to give the instructor a chance to give you a few points for trying. If you leave a blank page, your instructor has no choice but to give you zero points. Usually when you lose full credit on one essay, you automatically eliminate your chance to get a high passing grade.

EXERCISE 5

DIRECTIONS   Organize and write a response to one of the following essay questions.

1. Six organizational patterns are commonly used in textbook writing: comparison–contrast, definition, time sequence, cause–effect, problem–solution, and enumeration. Discuss the usefulness of these patterns in predicting and answering essay exam questions.
2. Describe three strategies that have improved your reading skills. Explain why each is effective.
3. Describe your approach to time management. Include specific techniques and organizational strategies that you have found effective.

CONTROLLING TEST ANXIETY

Do you get nervous and anxious just before an exam begins? If so, your response is normal; most students feel some level of anxiety before an exam. In fact, research indicates that some anxiety is beneficial and improves your performance by sharpening your attention and keeping you alert.

Research also shows that very high levels of anxiety can interfere with test performance. Some students become highly nervous and emotional and lose their concentration. Their minds seem to go blank, and they are unable to recall material they have learned. They also report physical symptoms: Their hearts pound, it is difficult to swallow, or they break out in a cold sweat.

Test anxiety is a complicated psychological response to a threatening situation, and it may be related to other problems and past experiences. The following suggestions are intended to help you ease test anxiety. If these suggestions do not help, the next step is to discuss the problem with a counselor.

Be Sure Test Anxiety Is Not an Excuse

Many students say they have test anxiety when actually they have not studied and reviewed carefully or thoroughly. The first question, then, that you must answer honestly is this: Are you in fact *unprepared* for the exam, and do you therefore have every reason to be anxious?

Get Used to Test Situations

Psychologists who have studied anxiety use processes called "systematic desensitization" and "simulation" to reduce test anxiety. Basically, these are ways of becoming less sensitive to or disturbed by tests by putting yourself in testlike conditions. These techniques are complicated processes often used by trained therapists, but here are a few ways you can use these processes to reduce test anxiety.

1. Become familiar with the building and room in which the test is given. Visit the room when it is empty and take a seat. Visualize yourself taking a test there.
2. Develop practice or review tests. Treat them as real tests, and do them in situations as similar as possible to real test conditions.
3. Practice working with time limits. Set an alarm clock and work only until it rings.
4. Take as many tests as possible, even though you dislike them. Always take advantage of practice tests and make-up exams. Buy a review book for the course you are taking or a workbook that accompanies your text. Treat each section as an exam, and have someone else correct your work.

Control Negative Thinking

Major factors that contribute to test anxiety are self-doubt and negative thinking. Just before and during an exam, test-anxious students often think, "I won't do well." "I'm going to fail." "What will my friends think of me when I get a failing grade?" This type of thinking predisposes you to failure; you are telling yourself that you expect to fail. By thinking in this way, you undermine your own chances for success.

One solution to this problem is to send yourself positive rather than negative messages, such as, "I have studied hard and I deserve to pass." "I know that I know the material." "I know I can do it!" And remember, being well prepared is one of the best ways to reduce test anxiety.

Compose Yourself before the Test Begins

Don't take an exam on an empty stomach; you will feel queasy. Have something light or bland to eat. Some students find that a brisk walk outside before going to an exam helps to reduce tension.

Before you begin the test, take 30 seconds or so to calm yourself, to slow down, and to focus your attention. Take several deep breaths, close your eyes, and visualize yourself calmly working through the test. Remind yourself that you have prepared carefully and have every reason to do well.

Answer Easy Questions First

To give yourself an initial boost of confidence, begin with a section of the test that seems easy. This will help you to work calmly, and you will prove to yourself that you can handle the test.

LEARNING *Collaboratively*

DIRECTIONS   Each member of the class should write an answer to the following essay question, which is based on the reading "The Talk of the Sandbox: How Johnny and Suzy's Playground Chatter Prepares Them for Life at the Office" in Part Seven, p. 387.

> Explain how the roles boys and girls assume when they play is similar to the roles they will assume in the workplace.

You may not refer to the reading as you write your answer. Working in pairs, compare your answers, noting strengths and weaknesses of the essays. Then rewrite and combine your answers to produce a stronger or more nearly complete response.

Applying **YOUR LEARNING**

Maria is taking an American history course. The instructor announced that the next exam will cover only three chapters on the Constitution—its origins, history, and current applications and interpretations. Further, students are allowed to bring their textbook and both lecture and study notes to class and use them during the exam. As most students breathed a sigh of relief, the instructor cautioned, "It's not as easy as you think!" Still, many students in the class are not preparing for this exam at all. Maria knows she should prepare, but she is uncertain about what to do.

1. What type of questions (multiple-choice, true/false, short answer, or essay) do you think Maria's exam will contain?
2. Why would the instructor allow students to bring materials to the exam? What types of learning is she emphasizing? What is she not emphasizing?
3. How should Maria prepare for this exam?

SELF-TEST SUMMARY

1. How can you improve the way you take most exams?	You can improve your exam grades by approaching tests in a systematic, organized manner. This involves taking the necessary materials, arriving on time, deliberately choosing a seat in a nondistracting section of the room, prereading the exam, planning the time you will devote to various sections of the exam, and reading the questions carefully.
2. What can you do to improve the way you take most objective exams?	In taking any type of objective exam, read the directions carefully, leave nothing blank, and look for clues that will help you recall the information. When taking true/false tests, you should also read two-part statements carefully and be aware of negative words or word

parts. When you have no idea of the answer, make your best guess by marking extreme statements and those that contain unfamiliar terms as false and all others as true.

For multiple-choice tests, you should make educated guesses by reading the choices carefully, narrowing them down by using reasoning power, paying attention to qualifying words, and considering the choices in light of what you know about the topic. When all else fails, eliminate unfamiliar or confusing items and choose an answer that seems complete.

When taking short-answer tests, use the point distributions and amount of space provided to determine how much to write and plan what to write beforehand.

For fill-in-the-blank tests, decide what kind of information is being asked for by the key words in and grammatical structure of the sentence.

3. What can you do to improve the way you take essay exams?

When taking an essay exam, it is important to read the question carefully, reading the directions, noting all parts, and looking for clues in the question to determine exactly what type of response your instructor wants. Essay answers should be carefully organized and written in an easy-to-read form. This can be achieved by including a topic sentence in each paragraph, using numbering and headings, including enough information to prove your point, and stating opinions and judgments only when the question asks for them. Take pains to make your answer readable, and carefully proofread for accuracy, grammar, and mechanics. If you run out of time or your memory fails, you can earn some credit by jotting an outline or writing something on the page.

4. How can you control test anxiety?

Too much test anxiety can seriously affect your performance on exams. You can relieve it by being prepared for the exam; becoming familiar with the testing location, conditions, and time limits; controlling negative thoughts; taking time to compose yourself near the time of the exam; and beginning with the easy questions for an initial boost.

Take a Road Trip to
Hollywood!

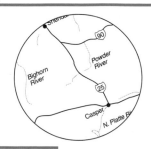

If your instructor has asked you to use the Reading Road Trip CD-ROM, be sure to visit the Test Taking and Preparation module for multimedia tutorials, exercises, and tests.

CHAPTER **18**

Improving Your Reading Rate and Flexibility

Why Learn to Improve Your Reading Rate?

▲ **Reading takes time; if you can learn to read faster, you'll save time.**

▲ **Not everything on a page is equally important. If you can learn to read selectively, you will save time.**

Learning Experiment

Step 1

The following paragraph discusses one method by which new products are developed. Read the paragraph only until you get to the words "STOP HERE."

> Me-toos are products that are new to a firm but not new to the marketplace. Companies create "me-toos" because they believe there is room in the market for another competitor, and the projected returns outweigh the risks. For example, STOP HERE when McDonald's decided to enter the fast-food breakfast business, its product was new to the company even though a fast-food breakfast was not new to the market. Procter & Gamble has entered the "me-too" game with both disposable training pants and ultra-thin diapers—two offerings that enable the firm to play catch-up with diaper developments by Kimberly-Clark.

Step 2

Based on what you read, predict what the remainder of the paragraph will contain and write it below.

_____

_____

_____

_____

Step 3

Now, go back and check: Did you predict accurately?

The Results

You have probably discovered that you can predict the content of paragraphs from their topic sentences. The above experiment demonstrates that some parts of a paragraph are more important than others.

Learning Principle (What This Means to You)

Successful students read and learn selectively. You should not read every paragraph in the same way. Instead, you should vary your technique and approach depending on the nature of the assignment and what you are expected to learn from it. This chapter will show you how to adjust your reading rate and reading technique to suit the material you are reading and your purpose for reading it. You will also learn how to skim and scan, alternatives to reading a text in its entirety.

BUILDING YOUR READING RATE

Reading rate, the speed at which you read, is measured in words per minute (wpm). What should be your reading rate? Is it better to be a fast reader or a slow reader? Does a good reader read every word? You should be able to read at 100, 200, 300, and 400 wpm; you should be both a fast _and_ a slow reader; good readers are often "word skippers." These answers may seem strange or even contradictory, but they are nevertheless true. You should strive to improve your reading rate in order to become a more efficient reader, but you should also be able to change your rate and method of reading to fit different situations and different types of reading material.

To read faster, you must improve your capacity to process information rapidly. Instead of thinking about your eyes and how they move, concentrate on getting information quickly from the printed page. Reading at a faster rate involves understanding ideas and how they interrelate.

By working through this book, you have learned skills and techniques that have improved your comprehension. Many techniques that improve comprehension also improve rate. Reading faster is often a combination of pushing yourself to higher reading speeds on different types of materials and learning and applying several new techniques. The following suggestions will help you to read faster.

Avoid Roadblocks to Reading Efficiency

Certain poor reading habits often carry over from when you first learned to read. These are (1) moving your head as you read, (2) moving your lips as you read, and (3) using your finger or pen to keep your place on the line. Each of these habits can slow you down and contribute to poor comprehension.

Moving Your Head

Moving your head rather than just your eyes across the line of print prevents you from reading at even a normal reading rate and also creates strain and muscle fatigue. Ask someone to check to see whether you move your head while reading; this person should check when you are not consciously thinking about the problem. One of the easiest ways to break this habit is to sit with your elbow up on your desk with your hand cupping your chin. If you start to move your head, you will feel you hand and forearm move, and this will remind you to correct the habit.

Moving Your Lips

Moving your lips limits your reading rate. The average adult rate of speech (pronouncing words out loud) is 125 words per minute, whereas the average adult rate for silent reading is 250 to 300 words per minute. Thus moving your lips can really slow your silent reading down—by as much as half. However, there is one situation in which lip movement may be appropriate. When you are reading something that is extremely difficult or complicated, you may find that moving your lips or even whispering aloud as you read helps you to understand the material.

To eliminate this habit, sit in a position in which part of your hand or your fingers touch your lips. If you move your lips while reading, you will feel the movement on your hand or fingers.

Keeping Your Place on the Line

Another bad habit is keeping your place on a line of print by moving your finger or a pen or pencil across the line as you read. This practice causes very slow, word-by-word reading. The solution is simple—tightly grasp the book with both hands. This will prevent you from following across the line with your finger or another object. Be careful you don't cheat and slide your thumb down the margin as a guide to where you are on the page. If you have tried unsuccessfully to control this habit, an eye exam is advisable. Inability to keep one's place on the line is one symptom of a need for corrective lenses.

Preread to Familiarize Yourself with the Material

In Chapter 5, you learned that prereading is a means of improving your comprehension by becoming familiar with the organization and content of material before you begin to read it. In addition to improving your comprehension, prereading increases your reading speed. Because prereading enables you to anticipate the flow of ideas, you will find yourself able to read the material more rapidly.

Try to Eliminate Regressions

As your eyes move across a line, they normally proceed from left to right. Occasionally, instead of moving to the next word, your eyes move backward, or regress, to a word in the same line or in a line already read. Regressions (backward movements) scramble word order, thus creating confusion that slows your pace. Although even very good readers make regressions, your rate and comprehension will improve if you can reduce the number of regressions. The following suggestions will help you eliminate or reduce regressions.

1. Be conscious of the tendency to regress, and force yourself to continue reading. Do not allow yourself to regress until you have finished a sentence. Then, if the meaning is still unclear, reread the entire sentence.
2. If you frequently regress to a word or phrase on a previous line, you might try sliding a 5-inch-by-8-inch index card down the page as you read. Use the card to cover the lines you have finished reading. This technique will help you break the habit of regression because when you look back, the line will be covered.

Read in Meaning Clusters

Most college students read word by word, looking at each word and then moving to the next one. A more efficient way to read is to combine words that naturally go together. Try not to think of a sentence as a string of single words. Instead, think of it as several word clusters, or phrases. Look at the following sentence.

> The math instructor told her class about the quiz.

"The" does not convey any meaning by itself. While "math" does have meaning, it is intended to describe the next word, "instructor." Rather than reading the first three words separately, try to think of them together as a meaningful phrase—"the math instructor." The remainder of the sentence could then be read as two additional phrases: "told her class" and "about the quiz."

The following brief paragraph has been divided into meaningful word groups separated by slashes. Read the paragraph; as you read, try to see and think of each cluster as a unit of thought rather than as two or three separate words.

> In order / to protect themselves / against loss / drivers purchase / liability insurance. / There are / two types of / liability insurance. / Bodily injury liability / provides payment / if you / are injured / in an accident. / Property damage liability / covers you / when your car / damages the property / of others.

Note that words that make sense together are grouped together. Words are grouped with the words they explain or modify.

To see whether you can group words into meaningful clusters, divide the following paragraph with slashes. The first two lines have been done for you.

> The United States / has changed / in the past one hundred years / from an agricultural economy / to an industrial economy / and has become / the world's first / ser-

vice economy. What does the term *service* mean? There is no widely accepted definition in marketing. In fact, there is no clear distinction between those firms that are part of a marketing channel for products and those firms that market services. Restaurants are often classified as food distributors because they compete with supermarkets, but restaurants also provide services to customers.

—Kinnear, Bernhardt, and Krentler, *Principles of Marketing,* p. 654

Once you begin reading in word clusters, you will find that meaning falls into place more easily, thus enabling you to read somewhat faster.

Learn to Pace Yourself

An established method of improving your reading rate is *pacing,* which requires maintaining a preestablished rate. Pacing means pushing yourself to read faster than your normal speed while maintaining your level of comprehension. There are numerous ways to pace yourself in order to increase your speed; the following are among the most common methods.

1. *Use an index card.* Slide a 3-inch-by-5-inch card down the page as you read, moving it so that it covers up lines as you read them. This technique will force you along and keep you moving rapidly. Move the card down the page at a fixed pace, and try to keep up while reading. How fast you move the card will depend on the size of the print and the length of the line, so it will vary for each new piece of material you read. At first you will need to experiment to find an appropriate pace. Try to move at a pace that is slightly uncomfortable and that you are not sure you can maintain.
2. *Use your hand or index finger, or a pen or pencil.* Use your hand or index finger, or a pen or pencil, in the same manner as the index card. Using your hand does not completely obstruct your view of the page and allows you to pick up clues from the layout of the page (to see that a paragraph is ending, that a graphic example is to follow, and so on).
3. *Use a timer or clock.* Start by measuring what portion of a page you can read in a minute. Then set a goal for yourself: Determine how many pages you will attempt to read in a given period of time. Set your goal slightly above what you measured as your current rate. For example, suppose that in a particular book you can read half a page in a minute. You might set as your goal to read five pages in 9 minutes (forcing yourself to read a little more than a half-page per minute). The next day, try to read five pages in 8 or 8½ minutes. Use an alarm clock or timer to let you know when you have used up your time.

EXERCISE 1

DIRECTIONS   Select a magazine or newspaper article that you are interested in or a section of a paperback you are reading. Using one of the pacing techniques described in this section, try to increase your current reading speed by approximately 50 wpm. Record your results in the space provided.

Article title: _____

Estimated number of words: _____

Finishing time: _____

Starting time: _____

Reading time: _____

Words per minute: _____

Estimated level of comprehension: _____

Use Rereading to Build Speed

Although rereading is not an effective way to learn, it is an effective method of building your reading speed. Rereading at a slightly faster pace prepares you for reading new material faster. Rereading gets you moving at a faster rate and serves as a practice or trial run for reading new material faster.

To reread for speed increase, use the following steps.

1. Select an article or passage, and read it as you normally would for careful or leisure reading.
2. Time yourself and compute your speed in words per minute after you finish reading.
3. Take a break (five minutes or so). Then reread the same selection. Push yourself to read faster than you read the first time.
4. Time yourself and compute your speed again. You should be able to reread the selection at a faster rate than you read it initially.
5. Read a new selection, pushing yourself to read almost as fast as you *re*read the first selection.

EXERCISE 2

Academic Application

DIRECTIONS   Choose two magazine or newspaper articles that you are interested in reading. Follow the preceding steps for rereading to build speed. Record your results below.

Article 1

Title: _____

Estimated number of words: _____

First reading _____

Time: _____

Words per minute: _____

Second reading _____

Time: _____

Words per minute: _____

Article 2

Title: _____

Estimated number of words: _____

First reading _____

Time: _____

Words per minute: _____

DEVELOPING YOUR READING FLEXIBILITY

The way writers write, the words they use, how they put words together, and how clearly they can express ideas all contribute to how easy it is to read a passage and to how fast it can be read. The type of material you are reading also has a major influence on how fast you can read with good comprehension. Finally, your purpose for reading is an important factor related to both rate and comprehension. If you are reading a magazine article for enjoyment, your purpose is different from when you are reading a textbook chapter to prepare for an exam. If you are paging through the newspaper, your purpose differs from your purpose when you are reading a poem for your English literature class.

As you can see from Figure 18.1, no one should have just one reading rate. Instead, your reading rate should vary according to *what* you are reading and *why* you are reading it. Adjusting your rate in response to the material and to your purpose for reading is called *reading flexibility.*

Learning to adjust your rate according to style, content, and purpose will require a conscious effort at first. If you are now in the habit of reading everything at the same pace, as most college students are, then you will need to force yourself to make an assessment of the particular reading material before deciding how fast you can read it. When you use the technique of prereading, you are only a small step away from adjusting your rate. By prereading, you familiarize yourself with the overall content and organization of the material. You may also include, as part of your prereading, a step in which you pay particular attention to the overall difficulty of the material. While prereading, you will sample enough of the actual writing to be able to assess the level of complexity of both the language and the content.

Deciding how much to speed up or slow down for a particular article is a matter of judgment. Through experience, you will become able to judge how much you can afford to alter your speed. It is not important to know precisely how much to increase your speed. Rather, the important thing is to develop *flexibility.* Here is a step-by-step procedure you can follow that will help you build the habit of varying your reading rate.

Method of Reading	Range of Speed	Purpose in Reading	Types of Material
Analytical	Under 100 wpm	Detailed comprehension: analysis, evaluation, critique	Poetry, argumentative writing
Study reading	150–250 wpm	High comprehension and high recall	Textbooks, library research
Casual reading	250–400 wpm	Moderate comprehension of main ideas, entertainment, enjoyment, general	Novels, newspapers, magazines
Accelerated reading	Above 600 wpm	Overview of material; rapid location of a specific fact	Reference material, magazines, novels, nonfiction

Figure 18.1
Types of Reading

1. Choose a time and place for reading that will help rather than hinder your concentration. Choose a time when you are alert and your state of mind is conducive to study.
2. Preread the material. As you preread, assess the difficulty of both the writing style and the content. Are there a lot of difficult words? Are the sentences long and complicated? How factual is the material? How much background information do you have on the subject?
3. Define your overall purpose for reading. Your purpose will determine the level of comprehension and the degree of retention that you require. Are you reading for enjoyment, looking up facts, or reading a text chapter to prepare for an exam?
4. Decide what rate would be appropriate for reading this particular material.
5. After you've finished the first page of the reading material, stop and evaluate. Are you understanding and remembering what you are reading? Can you summarize the ideas in your own words?

You Don't Have to Read Everything

Before you begin to read flexibly, you must accept the notion that there is nothing sacred about the printed word. Many students erroneously believe that anything that appears in print must be true, valuable, and worth reading. Actually, the importance and value of printed information are affected by whether you need to learn it or whether you can use it in a practical way. Depending on the kind of material and on your purpose for reading it, many times you may need to read only some parts and skip over others. You might read selectively in the following situations.

1. *A high level of comprehension is not needed.* If you are not trying to remember a major portion of the facts and details, then you might concentrate on reading only main ideas. This method of reading only main ideas is called *skimming.* Specific techniques for skimming are presented later in the chapter.
2. *You are searching for specific information.* If you are looking up the date of a historical event in your history text, you skip over everything in the chapter except the exact passage that contains the information. This technique of skipping everything except the specific information for which you are looking is called *scanning.* Practice in scanning techniques is included later in the chapter.
3. *You are familiar with what you are reading.* In a college chemistry course, for example, you might find that the first few chapters of your text are very basic if you have already studied high school chemistry. You can therefore afford to skip basic definitions and explanations and examples of principles that you already know. Do not, however, decide to skip an entire chapter or even large sections within it; there just may be some new information included. You may find that more exact and detailed definitions are given or that a new approach is taken toward a particular topic.
4. *The material does not match your purpose in reading.* Suppose that, in making an assignment in your physics text, your instructor told you to concentrate only on theories, laws, and principles presented in the chapter. As you begin reading the chapter, you find that the first topic discussed is Newton's law of

motion, but the chapter also contains a biographical sketch of Newton giving detailed information about his life. Because your purpose in reading the chapter is to focus on theories, laws, and principles, it is appropriate to skip over much of the biographical information.

5. *The writer's style allows you to skip information (portions).* Some writers include many examples of a particular concept or principle. If, after reading two or three examples, you are sure that you understand the idea being explained, just quickly glance at the remaining examples. Unless they present a new aspect or different point of view, skip over them. Other writers provide detailed background information before getting into a discussion of the intended topic. If a chapter starts out by summarizing information that was covered in a chapter you just read last week, it is not necessary to read this information again carefully unless you feel you need to review.

EXERCISE 3

DIRECTIONS   Each of the following items suggests a reading situation and describes the material to be read. After reading each item, decide whether the reader should (a) read the material completely, (b) read parts and skip other parts, or (c) skip most of the material.

1. Your history instructor has assigned each student to read a historical novel for the purpose of getting a realistic picture of what life was like and how people lived during a certain period. As you are reading, you come to a detailed two-page description of the types of gowns Southern women wore to a particular party. How should you read these two pages?   _____

2. You are doing research for a sociology term paper on the world population explosion. You are looking for information and statistics on recent population trends. You have located several books from the 1940s on the topic of population growth in the United States. How should you read these books?   _____

3. Your nursing instructor has just returned a test on a chapter describing the nursing process. She indicates that the class's overall performance on this test was poor and suggests that the chapter be reviewed. You received a grade of 79 on the test. How should you reread this chapter?   _____

4. Your biology professor has assigned a number of brief outside readings along with the chapters in your regular textbook. He has put them on reserve in the college library for the use of all his classes. This is the only place where they can be used. He did not say whether you would be tested on these readings. How should you read them?   _____

5. You have just attended English class, where your instructor discussed Milton's *Paradise Lost.* During his discussion, he made numerous references to Dante's *Inferno.* You have never read this second work but think it's important to know something about it. How should you read it?

Skimming Techniques

As you know, the term *skimming* refers to the process of reading only main ideas within a passage and simply glancing at the remainder of the material. Skimming is used to get an overall picture of the material, to become generally familiar with the topics and ideas presented, or to get the gist of a particular work. Usually skimming is an end in itself; that is, skimming is all you intend to do with the article. You do not intend to read it more intensively later. You are willing to settle for an overview of the article, giving up a major portion of the details.

At this point, you may be thinking that skimming seems similar to the technique of prereading. If so, you are correct. Prereading is actually a form of skimming. To be more precise, there are three forms of skimming: *preread skimming, skim-reading,* and *review skimming.* Preread skimming assumes that you plan to read the entire article or chapter and that you are prereading as a means of getting ready to read. Skim-reading refers to situations in which skimming is the only coverage you plan to give the material. Review skimming assumes that you have already read the material and are going back over it as a means of study and review.

We discussed prereading in Chapter 5. Methods of review after reading are part of the reading-study systems, such as SQ3R, discussed in Chapter 15. This chapter will focus on skim-reading techniques.

Demonstration of Skimming

The sample article in Figure 18.2 has been included to demonstrate what skimming is like. The parts of the passage that should be read while skimming are shaded. Taken from a psychology textbook chapter on thought and language, the article is a boxed feature at the end of the chapter. It is intended to create interest and to give a perspective on or interpretation of the topics discussed in the chapter itself.

How to Skim-Read

Your purpose in skimming is to get an overall impression of the content of a reading selection. The technique of skimming involves selecting and reading those parts of the selection that contain the most important ideas and merely glancing at the rest of the material. Below is a step-by-step procedure to follow in skimming for main ideas.

1. Read the title. If the piece is an article, check the author, publication date, and source.

Has Television Killed Off Reading—And If So, So What?

You find yourself with a free evening and decide to spend a quiet, cozy evening at home. A novel someone gave you for your birthday beckons the bookshelf. The TV listings tempt you with a new sitcom. Which do you pick, the book or the tube?

A growing number of academics, writers, and social commentators think you'll make the wrong choice. We bet you can guess what it is.

Reading, the critics say, appears to be going out of fashion. More books are being published than ever before, but many are sold as gifts and are not necessarily read or even skimmed. In an article called "The Death of Reading," writer Mitchell Stephens (1991) notes that more and more people are reading no books at all, and fewer and fewer people say they read yesterday's newspaper. Poet and writer Katha Pollitt (1991) contends that college teachers get as worked up as they do about which literary works to teach—the traditional Western "classics" or works from many cultures by both sexes—in part because they assume students won't read anything else. "While we have been arguing so fiercely about which books make the best medicine," Pollitt says, "the patient has been slipping deeper and deeper into a coma." The curriculum debate, says Pollitt, misses the point that if students don't read on their own, they won't like reading and will forget the books on the required reading list the minute they finish them, no matter what the books are.

One reason people are reading less these days is that they are doing something else instead: watching TV, typically for 20 to 30 hours a week. The problem, say many critics, is not just television's content, which is often mindless, but the medium itself, which creates mindlessness. We watch TV primarily to amuse ourselves, but in fact, far from cheering us up, television has a negative impact on both mood and alertness. In a series of studies involving 1,200 subjects, Robert Kubey and Mihalyi Csikszentmihalyi (1990) found that although television relaxes people while they are watching, afterward they are likely to feel more tense, bored, irritable, and lonely than they did before, and less able to concentrate. In contrast, reading tends to leave people more relaxed, in a better mood, and with improved concentration.

Television may also discourage the development of imagination and creativity. Patricia Greenfield and Jessica Beagles-Roos (1988) found that children *remember* more of a story when they see it on TV than when they hear it on radio (because visual images help memory), but their thinking becomes more *imaginative* when they hear the story on radio (because they have to imagine what the characters look like and what they are doing). The researchers fear that children who are raised on television "may have more information but be less imaginative, less verbally precise, and less mentally active" than earlier generations raised with only radio.

The medium that supplies our information about the world may also influence our ability to think critically. In his book *Amusing Ourselves to Death,* Neil Postman (1985) notes that because television lumps serious issues with silly ones, sells politicians the same way it sells cereal, and relies on a format of quick cuts and hot music, it discourages sustained, serious thought. Mitchell Stephens (1991) makes a similar point: "All television demands," he writes, "is our gaze." We can make dinner, play with the cat, or even daydream while watching it.

Television, say these critics, teaches us to judge not only products but also politicians by their ability to divert us. If an argument is too complex, if it takes more of our time than a "sound bite," we can just switch the channel. In contrast, reading gives us the opportunity to examine connections among statements and spot contradictions. It requires that we sit still and follow extended arguments. If frees us from the here and now and encourages us to think in terms of abstract principles and not just personal experience.

Defenders of television feel the criticisms are unfair. There are many possible causes of reading's decline: the press of modern life, the popularity of outdoor sports and physical fitness, the time demands of juggling work and family responsibilities. Television not only entertains but also supplies information and intellectual enrichment (especially through public television programming). It gives families something to do together. It provides a diverse population with a common culture. *Mindful*

Figure 18.2
An Example of Skimming

television viewing, in which you analyze and discuss what you're seeing, can be mentally enriching (Langer & Piper, 1988). And who knows, perhaps television will eventually be put to better use, in ways that haven't yet been thought of; after all, it took a century and a half after the printing press was invented for someone to think of producing novels and newspapers (Stephens, 1991).

What do you think of these arguments? Are there books you can't wait to read, or has reading become a chore (and if so, why)? Would you read more books if you watched less television? Do you know as much about world events after watching the nightly news as you do after reading a newspaper? Is disapproval of television just a reactionary, backward-looking response to successful new technology? If not, what can be done to see that people control the TV knob instead of allowing themselves to be controlled by it? Think about it.

—Wade and Tavris, *Psychology*, pp. 284–285

Figure 18.2 (continued)

2. Read the introduction. If it is very long, read only the first paragraph completely. Read the first sentence of every other paragraph. Usually the first sentence is a statement of the main idea of that paragraph.
3. Read any headings and subheadings. When taken together, the headings form an outline of the main topics that are covered in the material.
4. Notice any pictures, charts, or graphs; these are usually included to emphasize important ideas, concepts, or trends.
5. If you do not get enough information from the headings or if you are working with material that does not have headings, read the first sentence of each paragraph.
6. Glance at the remainder of the paragraph.
   • Notice any italicized or boldfaced words or phrases. These are key terms used throughout the selection.
   • Look for any lists of ideas within the text of the material. The author may use numerals, such as 1, 2, and 3, to organize the list or may include signal words such as *first, second, one major cause, another cause,* and the like.
   • Look for unusual or striking features of the paragraph. You may notice a series of dates, many capitalized words, or several large-figure numbers.
7. Read the summary or last paragraph.

EXERCISE 4

DIRECTIONS   Skim each of the following selections. Then summarize each article in the space provided.

Selection 1: "Are There Perfect Answers About Greenness?"

_____

_____

_____

Selection 2: "Aromatherapy: The Nose Knows?"

_____

_____

_____

Selection 3: "Tobacco and Global Markets: An Ethical Issue?"

_____

_____

_____

1. **Are There Perfect Answers about Greenness?**

A growing list of U.S. firms have decided—for public relations, staff morale, and other reasons—to be socially responsible about the environment. This is called going "green." For example, Lever Brothers, a manufacturer of household products, has led the pack in recycling plastic bottles. DuPont has campaigned for chemical companies to take voluntary environmental initiatives. Monsanto, a chemical giant, took the lead in reducing air pollution long before passage of the Clean Air Act of 1990. Downy Fabric Softener can now be purchased in a "refill" pack.

Also, small firms in many businesses—bakers, painters, dry cleaners, any printing companies—have taken steps to comply with the law. Kinko's, a copying and business service firm, recycles paper and toner. Hannaford Brothers supermarkets, located in New England, offers shoppers canvas bags rather than plastic or paper bags. There is a lot of interest in and action toward being a responsible business and in achieving a "green," livable environment. However, there is also some debate about what is best.

In November 1990 McDonald's Corporation said it would phase out its use of polystyrene foam containers in favor of paper. McDonald's decision was based on evidence suggesting that the chemicals used in producing polystyrene were harmful to the environment. Now studies and researchers have suggested that the foam containers may be better for the environment than paper ones because the loss of trees used to produce paper is environmentally destructive. To settle similar debates, researchers have used a life-cycle analysis procedure to tote up every environmental risk associated with making, using, and disposing of products. In an unpublished study It sponsored, McDonald's claims that paper has lower environmental costs in most, if not all, respects. Therefore McDonald's will stick with paper.

The environmentally correct decision regarding greenness is equally unclear in the diaper industry. In a study sponsored by Procter & Gamble, the manufacturer of Luvs and Pampers disposable diapers, it was found that cloth diapers consume more than three times as much energy, cradle to grave, as disposables do. But a study sponsored by the National Association of Diaper Services found the opposite.

The diaper duel illustrates the toughest issue in life-cycle analysis; how to compare different kinds of environmental harm. Cloth diapers use about 60 percent more water and [create a] greater volume of water pollution than disposables do. But disposables generate more than seven times as much trash, hence filling landfills, and they take more energy to produce. Biodegradable disposables, the hoped-for compromise, only biodegrade in the sunlight, not when buried in a landfill.

Can all products be separated into good and bad categories? The public would like simple answers: foam or paper? disposables or cloth? It doesn't appear, however, that life-cycle analysis or any present analytical methodology is going to provide simple answers. Costs, green benefits, research to support and oppose, common sense, and leadership are all factors that society, the government, and individuals will have to weigh in making decisions about ecological issues.

—Kinnear, Bernhardt, and Krentler, *Principles of Marketing*, p. 61

2. **Aromatherapy: The Nose Knows?**

Humans rely much less on their sense of smell than do other mammals, for whom smells may be the chief way of perceiving the environment, more so than hearing or vision. But we do distinguish (and react in various ways to) a wide range of smells. The aroma of apples cooking with cinnamon calls up homey visions; a sour smell warns us that the milk has spoiled, an acrid one that something is burning. All sensations are important to cooks, lovers, physicians, and a host of others. Yet most people today live in a scent-impoverished world, thanks largely to indoor plumbing, soap, hot running water, and washable fabrics.

Back to Nature?

It's not surprising that the idea of "aromatherapy"—using inhaled or applied scents to influence behavior and mood or even to treat disease—has recently surfaced or, more correctly, resurfaced. The contemporary version of it, according to J. R. King, a psychologist at the University of Warwick, England, is part of the "back to nature" movement and the backlash against scientific medicine. Modern aromatherapy originated in France, rose to prominence throughout Europe (especially the United Kingdom), and is now growing in popularity in the U.S. and Canada. It's based on people's prior psychological associations with specific smells.

Aromatherapy involves the use of "essential oils"—that is, essences of different plant fragrances. Those believed to have stimulating or relaxing effects include nutmeg, lily-of-the-valley, neroli oil (from orange blossoms), valerian oil, and many, many others. These natural oils are not quite as natural as their vendors claim. To produce an oil such as lavender or gardenia, the plant must be highly processed—pounded, steamed, and heated. These oils can then be diffused in the air—you can paint your light bulbs with them, for example, or sprinkle your linens. They can also be applied to the skin as ointment or during massage.

Some aromatherapy claims are truly extravagant: that essential oils can fight bacteria as effectively as antibiotics, can boost immunity, alleviate arthritis pain, and (applied topically) cure herpes simplex and shingles. Most promoters of aromatherapy don't go this far. A recent catalogue offering essential oils ($12 for a tiny 10-milliliter bottle), plastic aromatherapy diffusers ($34), and a "decoder card" for essential oils ($10) makes no medical claims but alludes simply to "healthier states of mind," "tranquillity," and "coaxing the mind and body into harmonious balance."

The Adaptive Nose

It wouldn't be hard to demonstrate that lavender oil won't cure herpes, but not much scientific work has been done on the psychological effects of aromatherapy, which tends to be backed up by personal testimonial. There's no argument, of course, that the sense of smell has emotional connections, or that it can influence mood. Smells can also affect mental and physical performance. Some malls and stores waft scents toward shoppers, hoping to soften customer resistance—a kind of Muzak for the nostrils. Like Muzak itself, it might strike some people as an infringement of personal privacy.

One problem in studying the effect of aromatherapy is that a person's belief is very important—if you think bergamot oil smells wonderful, you'll probably feel soothed by it—and it's hard to disguise this scent so as to have a "blinded" experiment. Another problem in designing a study is that we tend to get used to odors rapidly. The odor that overwhelms us one moment may hardly be apparent to us five minutes later. Also, reactions to scents are highly personal. What smells sweet and clean to one nose may be sharp and unpleasant to another. Essential oils are not universally pleasant or benign. Some are toxic if swallowed, or can cause skin irritation or induce headache and nausea in some people. In *Aromatherapy: An A–Z*, Patricia Davis lists 35 essential oils (including tansy, wintergreen, wormwood, savory, sassafras, and bitter almond) that should never be used in therapy. Fennel, hyssop, sage, and wormwood, she says, can trigger attacks in epileptics.

Pro-Aroma vs. No Aroma

And there's always the question of allergies. Cosmetics with fragrances cause skin eruptions in some people. Indeed, the trend in cosmetics these days is "fragrance-free," since such products are less likely to cause problems. Actually, as aromatherapy has grown in popularity, another movement is menacing it. People who believe they have "multiple chemical sensitivities" have campaigned to ban perfumes from public areas. Some California cities already have ordinances restricting the use of fragrances. Who indeed does not gag at certain aromas, maybe even gardenia oil? This dispute may well be beyond a rational solution.

Dollars and Scents

The chief benefit of aromatherapy so far has been not so much for the public as for marketers—perfuming mall air, adding supposedly alluring scents to thousands of products from furniture waxes to new cars, and the marketing of essential oils and various gadgets to diffuse them. This is usually harmless, unless you're allergic. But smells don't cure diseases, nor is aromatherapy an adjunct to medicine or an essential component of a healthy life.

—*Berkeley Wellness Letter,* May 1995

3. **Tobacco and Global Markets: An Ethical Issue?**

Are the ethics of U.S. based tobacco companies, as well as the ethics of the U.S. government when it comes to the tobacco industry, going up in smoke? Consider the facts.

Tobacco companies in the United States have significantly increased their marketing efforts in global markets. These efforts appear to be in response to marketing research indicating that the cigarette business in the United States is getting weaker each year. Markets in Latin America, Europe, Africa, and Asia have been targeted. The Asian market, for example, where $90 billion worth of cigarettes are sold each year, has received considerable attention from U.S. producers Philip Morris and R. J. Reynolds. The companies have received support in their efforts from the U.S. government, which has pressured South Korea, Japan, and Taiwan to open their markets to the U.S. companies. The result of all these efforts? Smoking related deaths have overtaken communicable diseases as Asia's top killer.

Another global market that tobacco firms have targeted for growth is Eastern Europe and the former Soviet Bloc. Seven hundred billion cigarettes are sold annually in this market, making it 40 percent larger than the U.S. market. Philip Morris and R. J. Reynolds, along with B.A.T. Industries of Britain and Reemstma of Germany, have entered this part of the world with a variety of operational methods. Philip Morris (PM), for example, invested $200 million in 1993 to acquire direct ownership of the Kazakhstan government-owned cigarette factory. The world's largest tobacco company, PM has also acquired factories in Russia, Krasanodar, Lithuania, Hungary, and the Czech Republic. Competitor R. J. Reynolds has acquired direct ownership in Russia, Poland, and Hungary, and set up two joint ventures in the Ukraine.

Promotion in these countries typically emphasizes the allure of western culture. For example, L & M cigarettes are touted as The Way America Tastes. Despite the efforts of world health organizations to stop them, tobacco companies continue to advertise on television in such countries as the Czech Republic and Hungary.

Tobacco companies, of course, are looking to make a profit. Thus, market development in global markets is an understandable, if easily criticized, strategy as western markets look less and less attractive. The actions of the U.S. government regarding this controversial industry may be more difficult to understand. Its signals appear mixed at best.

On one hand, the United States federal government, as well as state governments and local municipalities, have passed a myriad of legislation aimed at supporting the message Americans have received for years, namely, Smoking is hazardous to health. Smoking is now banned in most workplaces and in most public buildings in the country. It is also banned on all domestic airline flights with durations of fewer than six hours, which is enough time to get from coast to coast. In most states, cigarettes cannot legally be sold to individuals under 18 years of age, and by law every pack of cigarettes sold has to carry a warning from the U.S. Surgeon General. Furthermore, tobacco companies cannot advertise on television. However, while the government states that it supports anti-smoking campaigns, it provides millions of dollars in subsidies to U.S. tobacco growers and pressures foreign countries to open their markets to U.S. tobacco companies.

—Kinnear, Bernhardt, and Krentler, *Principles of Marketing,* p. 138

Scanning Techniques

Scanning is a method of selective reading that is used when you are searching for a particular fact or the answer to a question. Scanning can best be described as a looking rather than a reading process. As you look for the information you need, you ignore everything else. When you finish scanning a page, the only thing you should know is whether it contained the information you were looking for. You should *not* be able to recall topics, main ideas, or details presented on the page. You already use the technique of scanning daily: you regularly scan telephone books, television listings, and indexes. The purpose of this section is to help you develop a rapid, efficient approach for scanning.

Use the following step-by-step procedure to become more skilled in rapidly locating specific information.

1. State in your mind the specific information you are looking for. Phrase it in question form if possible.
2. Try to anticipate how the answer will appear and what clues you might use to help you locate the answer. If you are scanning to find the distance between two cities, you might expect either digits or numbers written out as words. Also, a unit of measurement, probably miles or kilometers, will appear after the number.
3. Determine the organization of material: It is your most important clue to where to begin looking for information. Especially when you are looking up information contained in charts and tables, the organization of the information is crucial to rapid scanning.
4. Use headings and any other aids that will help you identify which sections might contain the information you are looking for.
5. Selectively read and skip through likely sections of the passage, keeping in mind the specific question you formed and your expectations of how the answer might appear. Move your eyes down the page in a systematic way. There are various eye movement patterns, such as the "arrow pattern" (straight down the middle of the page) and the "Z pattern" (zig-zagging down the page). It is best to use a pattern that seems comfortable and easy for you.
6. When you reach the fact you are looking for, the word or phrase will stand out, and you will notice it immediately.
7. When you have found the needed information, carefully read the sentences in which it appears in order to confirm that you have located the correct information.

EXERCISE 5

DIRECTIONS Scan each paragraph or passage to locate and underline the answer to the question stated at the beginning of each.

1. *Question:* Why was an Irish militia supposedly formed?

Passage

Revolution in America also brought drastic changes to Ireland. Before 1775, that unhappy island, under English rule, had endured centuries of religious persecution, economic exploitation, and political domination. During the war, however, Henry Gratton (1746–1820) and Henry Flood (1732–91), two leaders of the Irish Protestant gentry, exploited English weakness to obtain concessions. An Irish militia was formed, supposedly to protect the coasts against American or French attacks. With thousands of armed Irishmen behind them, the two leaders resorted successfully to American methods. In February 1782, a convention in Dublin, representing 80,000 militiamen, demanded legislative independence, which the English Parliament subsequently granted. An Irish legislature could now make its own laws, subject to veto only by the English king. Ireland thus acquired a status denied the American colonies in 1774.

—Wallbank et al., *Civilization Past and Present*, Vol. 2, p. 533

2. Question: How does the cost of in-home retailing compare with suburban rates?

Passage

In-home retailing involves the presenting of goods to customers in a face-to-face meeting at the customer's home or by contacting the customer by telephone. This solicitation can be done without advance selection of consumers or follow-ups based upon prior contact at stores, or by phone or mail. The well-known Tupperware party fits in this category. Here a person has a social gathering where everyone knows a sales presentation will be made. Besides Tupperware, the largest companies operating in this type of retailing are Avon (cosmetics), Electrolux (vacuum cleaners), Amway (household products), World Book (encyclopedia and books), Shaklee (food supplements), Home Interiors and Gifts (decorative items), L. H. Stuart (jewelry and crafts), Stanley Home Products (household products), and Kirby (vacuum cleaners). Despite the great cost savings of having no store and no inventory, labor costs make this form of retailing expensive. Expenses are estimated to average about 50 percent of sales, compared to about 26 percent for all retailing.

—Kinnear, Bernhardt, and Krentler, *Principles of Marketing*, p. 388

3. *Question:* Who are secondary relatives?

Passage

Generally, relations with kin outside the parent-child unit play a significant role in American family life. But the strength of those ties and the functions they serve are extremely diverse. They vary according to the kind of relationship—parent, grandparent, cousin, uncle—as well as with social class, ethnic group, occupation, and region of the country. Indeed, in rural areas of the United States today, many families are still focused on extended kin—not just grandparents, but "secondary relatives" like aunts, uncles, cousins, and others. Table 5.1 illustrates the contrasts between this extended kin version of family values, and the kind of familism centered around nuclear or primary family relationships—husbands and wives, parents and children.

—Skolnick, *The Intimate Environment: Exploring Marriage and the Family*, p. 107

4. *Question:* What is a spiff?

Passage

Manufacturers often sponsor *contests* with prizes like free merchandise, trips, and plaques to dealers who reach certain specified sales levels. Additionally, they may get free *merchandise allowances* or even *money bonuses* for reaching sales performance goals. Once in a while, there is a sweepstakes, where "lucky" dealers can win substantial prizes. For example, Fisher-Price Toys had great success with a sweepstakes that gave cooperating dealers a chance to win a trip to Puerto Rico. These types of programs may also be directed at in-store sales personnel for their individual sales performances. A direct payment by a manufacturer to a channel member salesperson is called a *spiff*. This is very common at the consumer level for consumer durables and cosmetics, and at the wholesale level for beer and records. Another version of a spiff is when retailers pay their salespeople to push certain items. Clearly, this practice makes it possible for consumers to be deceived by a salesperson attempting to earn *push money.* As a result, these types of payments are controversial.

—Kinnear, Bernhardt, and Krentler, *Principles of Marketing,* p. 495

5. *Question:* What were the objectives of the New Deal?

Passage

In the 1932 elections, Franklin D. Roosevelt, only the third Democrat to be elected to the presidency since 1860, overwhelmed Hoover by assembling a coalition of labor, intellectuals, minorities, and farmers. The country had reached a crisis point by the time he was to be inaugurated in 1933, and quick action had to be taken in the face of bank closings. Under his leadership, the New Deal, a sweeping, pragmatic, often hit-or-miss program, was developed to cope with the emergency. The New Deal's three objectives were relief, recovery, and reform. Millions of dollars flowed from the federal treasury to feed the hungry, create jobs for the unemployed through public works, and provide for the sick and elderly through such reforms as the Social Security Act. In addition, Roosevelt's administration substantially reformed the banking and stock systems, greatly increased the rights of labor unions, invested in massive public power and conservation projects, and supported families who either needed homes or were in danger of losing the homes they inhabited.

—Wallbank et al., *Civilization Past and Present,* Vol. 2, p. 781

LEARNING *Collaboratively*

Your instructor will assign one of the readings in Part Seven or distribute an article of his or her choice. Choose a partner to work with. One student should read the article completely; the other should skim it. Then quiz each other and draw conclusions about the relative efficiency of skimming compared to that of reading. Also, list situations in which skimming would and would not be an appropriate strategy.

Applying YOUR LEARNING

Carla has been assigned a term paper for her business marketing class. In the paper, Carla is supposed to select a popular product, such as Pepsi or Reebok sneakers, survey its marketing history, analyze and critique its current marketing strategies, and make recommendations for widening the product's market. Carla began with encyclopedias and then checked the online card catalog, searched the shelves for related books, checked the *Reader's Guide to Periodical Literature,* and consulted the *Business Index* to locate journal articles.

1. Identify the reading strategies Carla might use for each source.
   • Encyclopedia: _____
   • Card catalog: _____
   • Shelved books: _____
   • *Reader's Guide to Periodical Literature:* _____
   • *Business Index:* _____
2. Evaluate Carla's approach to research for this assignment.

SELF-TEST SUMMARY

1. What techniques can be used to improve overall reading rate?	Reading rate can be improved by eliminating roadblocks, prereading, eliminating regression, reading in meaning clusters, pacing, and rereading for speed increase.
2. What factors influence reading flexibility?	The type of material being read, the way the writer's ideas are expressed, and your purpose for reading all influence the rate and method of reading you use.
3. Is it always necessary to read every word on a page?	Many types of material do not require a thorough, beginning-to-end, careful reading. There are also many situations in which reading everything is not necessary; reading some parts is more appropriate.
4. When should I read selectively?	It is effective to read selectively in situations in which you need only main ideas, you are looking for specific facts or the answer to a question, you are highly familiar with the content of the material, or the material contains information that is not related to your purpose. Finally, with certain types of material and styles of writing, you can skip information.
5. What is skimming?	Skimming is a process of reading only main ideas and simply glancing at the remainder of the material. There are three basic types of skimming: preread skimming, skim-reading, and review skimming. The type of skimming used depends on the reader's purpose.
6. What is scanning?	Scanning is a method of selective reading that is used when one is searching for a particular fact or the answer to a question.

Take a Road Trip to the
Indianapolis Speedway!

If your instructor has asked you to use the Reading Road Trip CD-ROM, be sure to visit the Reading Rate module for multimedia tutorials, exercises, and tests.

PART
SEVEN

Thematic
Readings

THEME A

SOCIOLOGY/CULTURAL ANTHROPOLOGY
BODY ADORNMENT 376

THEME B

COMMUNICATION
MEN'S AND WOMEN'S COMMUNICATION 385

THEME C

BIOLOGY
ENDANGERED AND EXTINCT SPECIES 394

THEME D

BUSINESS/COMPUTER TECHNOLOGY
COMPUTERS AND PRIVACY 406

THEME E

HUMANITIES/LITERATURE
MULTICULTURAL IDENTITY 412

SOCIOLOGY/CULTURAL ANTHROPOLOGY
BODY ADORNMENT

A–1 TEXTBOOK EXCERPT: BODY ADORNMENT

David Hicks and Margaret A. Gwynne

1   We use the term *body adornment* to refer to the voluntary and reversible (as opposed to permanent) changes people make to the outward appearance of their bodies. These changes include wearing clothing and jewelry, using cosmetics (which in many societies are applied to the body as well as to the face), and styling and coloring the hair.

Clothing

2   Human beings almost completely lack the external physical protection from the natural environment that other animals possess, such as tough hides, hard shells, layers of feathers, or thick coats of fur. Even people living in tropical climates, where no insulation against cold weather is needed, must protect their bodies from the sun, rain, stinging insects, thorny vegetation, or rough surfaces. No doubt for this reason, the vast majority of people wear clothes. The native people of Australia, called the Aborigines, were an exception; most were reportedly naked when first contacted by Westerners. But (as far as we know) for practical reasons, few societies in the past, and none today, completely lack a tradition of clothing the body.

3   Garments protect their wearers, but have another, equally important, function as well: to convey messages, both about individual clothes wearers and about the culture or subculture of which they are a part (Barnes and Eicher 1992; Kaiser 1990). One of these is the message of sexual identity. Few societies depend totally on anatomical differences to distinguish males from females. In most, different styles of clothing confirm the differences between the two sexes. Contemporary Western society is unusual in that certain items of casual wear, such as jeans, T-shirts, and jogging shoes are considered appropriate for both males and females. In India, women wear saris, men wear dhotis—never the reverse.

4   Wearing clothes seems not to depend on any innate human sense of modesty, for there is no universal agreement about which parts of the body should be kept hidden from view. In many (but by no means all) societies, the sexual organs, especially those of adults, are kept covered, but in other societies they are intentionally exposed. Sometimes clothing both covers and accentuates simultaneously; Western women's bras and Pacific men's penis sheaths both conceal and emphasize parts of the body. Depending on the society, other parts of the body—the hair, the lower part of the face, the ankles, the female midsection (to name just a few)—are either well hidden or intentionally exposed to public view.

5   Another message clothes convey is self-identity. If you were shown close-up photographs of the faces—and only the faces—of two young males, you might be able to determine their approximate ages, ethnic origins, states of health, and moods, but you would have trouble determining which was the face of a punk rocker and which a preppy. Whole-body photographs of the same two males, however—one in a metal-studded leather jacket, combat boots, and spiked hairdo; the other in an oxford-cloth shirt, madras slacks, deck

In some cultures, women traditionally wear garments that hide both their faces and bodies. Faces may be shielded by light fabric through which women can see enough to get about, heavier fabric in which eye holes have been cut, or full masks of leather or even metal. In the Hadramaut region of South Yemen (see map on page 378), a woman wears her culture's traditional garb.

shoes, and short, slicked-down hair—would give you a great deal of information about the different interests and values of these two individuals, provided the cultural context was one with which you were familiar.

6 The interests and values expressed by the appearances of these two individuals are not merely personal. Clothing reflects cultural as well as personal beliefs and ideals, and it is the cultural rather than the personal aspects of clothing that most interest anthropologists. What can we learn about the worldview of a given society from the way its members dress? In what values do the society's members collectively believe? What can clothes tell us about who is socially, politically, or economically dominant in the society and who is not? About the relationships between the sexes in the society and the attitudes of members of one sex toward members of the other? About the people's sense of national or ethnic identity, their conservative or liberal inclinations, even their religious beliefs?

7 Head coverings are a good example of the range of ideas that can be transmitted by a single item of clothing. The custom of covering the head, and sometimes the face as well, with a piece of cloth is widespread among females in Middle Eastern societies. Women wear headcloths ranging in size from small kerchiefs to large, enveloping semicircles of cloth that cover the entire body, including the head and sometimes much of the face. These veils are the external expression of deeply rooted Middle Eastern customs and collective ideas (Fernea and Fernea 1987), some of which find their origins in the Muslim religion.

8 The Middle Eastern custom of veiling originated in the time of the prophet Muhammad (A.D. 570–632), founder of Islam, as an outward symbol of religious identity. Muhammad's wives, so the story goes, were once mistaken for slaves—a grievous insult. To avoid future confusion, female followers of Muhammad began to wear veils (Fernea and Fernea 1987:106). But if its first cultural message was one of religious identity, veiling soon began to send a message about social status as well. Because it obstructed both movement and vision, the veil made performing certain tasks very difficult. A poor woman obliged to labor in the fields could not wear one. Thus, wearing this garment soon began to suggest a privileged life-style and high social status. This notion remains widely held today.

9 Veiling delivers other cultural messages too. Many Middle Easterners believe that females have strong sexual appetites and that their sexual behavior reflects directly on the honor of their families. For some, a family's honor rests in part on controlling women's sexuality (Lindholm and Lindholm 1985:234). To protect women from sexual temptation, and males from the uncontrollable lust of dangerous women who might ruin their good names, the physical seclusion of women, a custom known as purdah, has been practiced since the time of Muhammad. Houses may be surrounded by high walls, and women may spend their entire lives virtually imprisoned behind them. Wrapping a woman in a garment that conceals her body from public view is another reflection of the same idea. Today, a Middle Eastern woman wearing a veil on a

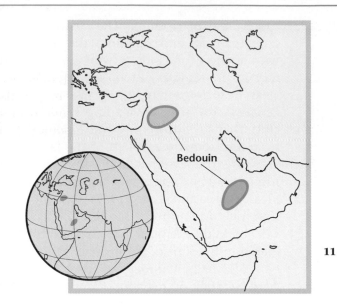

public street is signaling "hands off!" A man who approaches a veiled woman invites serious trouble, for he is shaming both the woman and her family. This does not mean that a woman wearing a veil is necessarily repressed, inhibited, or even ultraconservative. A modern Muslim woman's veil may conceal a T-shirt, jeans, and sneakers.

10   Another cultural notion associated with veiling is modesty. Among the Bedouin, Arabic-speaking nomads of the Middle East, modesty is an essential component of personal honor and respectability (Abu-Lughod 1986, 1987). The honorable person keep his or her distance from members of the opposite sex

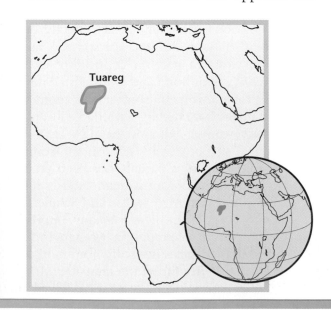

(except for close relatives); casts the eyes shyly downward; moves with formality; and refrains from eating, smoking, talking, or laughing in certain social situations. Young, unmarried women show that they are modest and respectable by wearing kerchiefs on their heads. Married women wear black headcloths that can be drawn protectively across the face when they are in the presence of certain men, such as in-laws. To display one's modesty in this way is a matter of pride for the Bedouin, who consider this behavior "a sign of respect for the social and moral system" (1987:29).

11   These examples show that in the Middle East, the cultural meanings attached to wearing a veil (or not wearing one) are many. Depending on where and in what style it is being worn, the veil can symbolize a woman's faith, the idea of protection (both from danger and from temptation), the notion of women as temptresses who must not be allowed to distract men, status and wealth, and personal modesty. And although we have been discussing the veil as an article of female apparel, among the Tuareg, camel pastoralists of North Africa, men wear veils because lips are considered obscene.

12   Westerners, too, convey messages with their clothing. In church, a woman's hat or kerchief is a mark of her religious faith; at a party, her expensive beaded dress suggests her wealth and thus her social status. Her white bridal gown symbolizes her purity, and her bridal veil her modesty. When she wears a bikini she does so not to express faith, wealth, social status, purity, or modesty but rather to show off her attractive body. Her message is one of good health, self-discipline, self-esteem, and interest in attracting the attention of the opposite sex.

Source: Cultural Anthropology, pp. 373–376.

A–2: FROM BEAR TEETH TO PEARLS: WHY WE ADORN OURSELVES

Catherine Clifford

1 Suppose you were given a choice: You could have makeup and accessories or you could have clothes, but not both. If you took the clothes, you might be smart, but you'd make a lousy cavewoman. Because while we regard food, clothing and shelter as basic necessities, earlier Homo Sapiens apparently sported baubles, bangles and proto-cosmetics long before they bothered with body coverings.

2 What's the big deal about a bunch of junk jewelry and body paint that made it more important than keeping warm? It's that the seemingly frivolous art of decorating yourself—be it with bear teeth or bugle beads—has roots that go deep into human identity. And there's a paradox at the heart of why we daub and decorate our bodies: Self-ornamentation is a visual resume of our societal roles, written in our culture's language, yet it can also be one of the most potent mediums to express individuality.

3 The point of puttin' on the Ritz for primitives was simple: In a nonliterate society, what you wore or how you were painted, scarred or tattooed told volumes about who you were. "Adornment was really a mode of communication, and the message always had to do with group life," explains Ruth P. Rubinstein, professor of sociology at the Fashion Institute of Technology (FIT) in New York City. "In some societies, for example, adornment was used the way we use wedding rings: to identify marital status and establish membership in a particular segment of society." It might say where you were from (to this day, some Moroccan women wear tattoos on their face and hands that identify their village) or what your role was.

4 "Adornment was always something both men and women used," adds Valerie Steele, author of *Paris Fashion: A Cultural History* (Oxford University Press, 1988) and an adjunct professor at FIT. "If anything, men favored ornamentation more because it sym-bolized their position as chief or priest or warrior." This at-a-glance inventory might also convey sexual information—although it must have been hard to guess wrong about gender if no one wore clothes.

Cultural Creations

5 One crucial component is, of course, getting everyone to agree about who wears what. "There are no universal symbols—they are necessarily culturally created—but some things, by their form, are chosen to express certain attributes, like a shape that naturally suggests a phallic symbol," says Steele. "Or the color red—every culture does something different with it, but since it's the color of blood, it's frequently connected with life force, sexuality, passion or anger." Similarly, gold (the element, that is) seems to be worn for unusually consistent reasons. "Jewelry arose out of a desire to integrate supernatural powers," says Rubinstein. "It was thought that through gold you could adopt the power of the sun, and through stones, the powers of the underlying universe."

6 But when you get right down to it, the rules that this says that about you had to originate somewhere. "Whoever was in authority might create rules based on their associations," says Rubinstein. For instance, the New Testament gave jewelry a second meaning by proscribing it as seductive centuries ago. But an individual might also adopt certain ornaments that he felt would make him more powerful, and others copied him.

7 The mix of motivations—to stress similarity yet also stand out—is largely responsible for fashion pressures on women. "The importance—and speed—of fashion changes in Western culture over the past few centuries seem related to a new value being placed on individual expression," says Claudia Brush Kidwell, curator of costumes for the Smithsonian's American History Museum and coeditor of *Men and Women: Dressing the Part*

(Smithsonian Institution Press, 1989). "When individual accomplishment and setting one-self apart become critical, trying new things with clothes and adornment is a logical exten-sion." At the same time, as the growth of capi-talism caused men to view their role and therefore their appearance as strictly business, that left women, by default, with the job of enhancing everyone's social scenery. "As men's fashions became more restricted, women not only continued the tradition of playing with materials and trimmings and cre-ating their 'look,' but also it became more important," explains Kidwell. "The duty to be beautiful is a 19th-century concept that is still promoted and commercialized." So two of the strongest directives women get are: Be an indi-vidual. And/but be beautiful. Using accou-trements from snazzy shoes to sequined hair bows is one way to satisfy both.

Personal Talismans

8   What makes one woman choose shoes while another goes with bows? The experts' answer: Who knows? "We can look at society and what certain choices mean in a cultural context," says Rubinstein. "For instance, bows imply a restriction of sexuality, something that can be opened but is held back. Polka dots came from the Roman tradition of a circle representing continuity. But we can't explain why you wear something, because that's too personal. Our sense of what is pretty or appealing dates back to early childhood, to what we saw our mothers, grandmothers or fathers wearing. We may favor very different styles than they did, but the real markers of personality—a prefer-ence for a specific color blue or a particular kind of jewelry—come from very individual associations."

9   Some trappings are so rich with resonance that they become modern-day equivalents of primitive talismans. A given item could be family-linked or it could be something you wore when you were at a weight you liked or on the night you met your boyfriend. Whatever, its magic is so private that it's an amulet no one else would recognize and that

you might not be entirely aware of yourself. But much as we still don ceremonial robes like bridesmaid's dresses or gray funeral suits, many of us continue to practice a semi-serious mysticism with our sartorial frills.

10   Even the most direct statements in self-dec-oration can be obscure, since the culturewide sources of possible associations are endless. Bits and pieces of various ethnic heritages may show up on our ears or around our necks. Borrowing from other cultures could be a way of displaying qualities that are supposedly characteristic—Latin flamboyance, Eastern mystery—or simply showing worldliness.

11   Gold indicates wealth, whether you're an inner-city teenager or a society matron, but obviously within very different contexts. Status-y trappings may be an attempt to imi-tate the upper classes or a flat-out Trump-like brag about being rich enough to buy extrava-gant trinkets. (Incidentally, why is it that, when it comes to displays of wealth, more is more up to a point, beyond which it is too much? Because, according to Steele, in the 17th century middle-class people started acquiring more money than many aristocrats, who then scrambled to find new ways of showing superiority that money couldn't buy—in fact, negated. "It takes a certain sensi-bility to really believe that less is more," says Steele.) As each force in fashion—safari, status, ethnic, athletic, animal print, high-tech—rip-ples out from its source, it retains less and less of its original message and starts slapping against other waves.

12   On top of all that, points out Steele, there's irony: the current tendency to play any theme not straight but with a wink—wearing an armful of fake "status" watches—so that your kind of people (those who get the joke) recog-nize you as a kindred sprit. That we still use ornamental objects to signal our identities is unarguable, but not only is the message often less exact, it also tends to vary. "The woman who wears elegant gold earrings one day may wear big pink plastic hoops the next," says Steele. "She hasn't changed, nor has her cul-ture, but there are so many choices now, all of which are acceptable, that there's more

freedom to emphasize different aspects of yourself."

13   And that's where you get, finally, to the real fun. Medium and message aside, fooling around with your exterior decoration is being frivolous in the best sense. "Indulging in extra makeup or crazy jewelry says 'Look at me!' in a way—a healthy way—that we might not be comfortable saying straight out," says New York City psychologist Arlene Kagle. "Taking pleasure in resembling a hot rocker one night out of the year doesn't mean you secretly want to put Madonna out of business. It's just that there's a little slice of you that, with the right decoration, you can let out to play. It's similar to one reason people have affairs—they want to experience something new."

14   There's also a pleasure even more primitive than playing with identity: exploring the senses. "Little children are sensual beings," says Kidwell. "They like the feel of soft stuff, they like to drape things around their necks, they like feathers, they like to dab themselves with paint. It doesn't matter whether they're male or female. What matters is the fun of stimulating the senses, the fun of creation."

15   It's worth remembering. The reasons for painting and primping and decorating ourselves like Christmas trees are serious and significant . . . to a point. But there's a wild-card element that makes it all unpredictable and, sometimes, pure pleasure—a visual and emotional perk that's one part science, one part art.

Source: Health, August 1989.

A–3: THE DECORATED BODY

France Borel

1   Human nakedness, according to social custom, is unacceptable, unbearable, and dangerous. From the moment of birth, society takes charge, managing, dressing, forming, and deforming the child—sometimes even with a certain degree of violence. Aside from the most elementary caretaking concerns—the very diversity of which shows how subjective the motivation is—an unfathomably deep and universal tendency pushes families, clans, and tribes to rapidly modify a person's physical appearance.

2   One's genuine physical makeup, one's given anatomy, is always felt to be unacceptable. Flesh, in its raw state, seems both intolerable and threatening. In its naked state, body and skin have no possible existence. The organism is acceptable only when it is transformed, covered with signs. The body only speaks if it is dressed in artifice.

3   For millennia, in the four quarters of the globe, mothers have molded the shape of their newborn babies' skulls to give them silhouettes conforming to prevalent criteria of beauty. In the nineteenth century, western children were tightly swaddled to keep their limbs straight. In the so-called primitive world, children were scarred or tattooed at a very early age in rituals which were repeated at all the most important steps of their lives. At a very young age, children were fitted with belts, necklaces, or bracelets; their lips, ears, or noses were pierced or stretched.

4   Some cultures have designed sophisticated appliances to alter physical structure and appearance. American Indian cradleboards crushed the skull to flatten it; the Mangbetus of Africa wrapped a knotted rope made of bark around the child's head to elongate it into a sugarloaf shape, which was considered to be aesthetically pleasing. The feet of very young Chinese girls were bound and spliced, intentionally and irreversibly deforming them, because this was seen to guarantee the girls' eventual amorous and matrimonial success.[1]

5   Claude Lévi-Strauss said about the Caduveo of Brazil: "In order to be a man, one had to be painted; whoever remained in a natural state was no different from the beasts."[2] In Polynesia, unless a girl was tattooed, she would not find a husband. An unornamented hand could not cook, nor dip into the communal food bowl. Pink lips were despicable and ugly. Anyone who refused the test of the tattoo was seen to be marginal and suspect.

6   Among the Tivs of Nigeria, women called attention to their legs by means of elaborate scarification* and the use of pearl leg bands; the best decorated calves were known for miles around. Tribal incisions behind the ears of Chad men rendered the skin "as smooth and stretched as that of a drum." The women would laugh at any man lacking these incisions, and they would never accept him as a husband. Men would subject themselves willingly to this custom, hoping for scars deep enough to leave marks on their skulls after death.

7   At the beginning of the eighteenth century, Father Laurent de Lucques noted that any young girl of the Congo who was not able to bear the pain of scarification and who cried so loudly that the operation had to be stopped was considered "good for nothing."[3] That is why, before marriage, men would check to see if the pattern traced on the belly of their intended bride was beautiful and well-detailed.

8   The fact that such motivations and pretexts depend on aesthetic, erotic, hygienic, or even medical considerations has no influence on the result, which is always in the direction of transforming the appearance of the body. Such a transformation is wished for, whether or not it is effective.

9   The body is a supple, malleable, and transformable prime material, a kind of modeling clay, easily molded by social will and wish. Human skin is an ideal subject for inscription, a surface for all sorts of marks which make it possible to differentiate the human from the

*Scarification: the making of superficial incisions in the skin by cutting or scratching

animal. The physical body offers itself willingly for tattooing or scarring so that, visibly and recognizably, it becomes a social entity.

10   The absolutely naked body is considered as brutish, reduced to the level of nature where no distinction is made between man and beast. The decorated body, on the other hand, dressed (if even only in a belt), tattooed, or mutilated, publicly exhibits humanity and membership in an established group. As Theophile Gautier said, "The ideal disturbs even the roughest nature, and the taste for ornamentation distinguishes the intelligent being from the beast more exactly than anything else. Indeed, dogs have never dreamed of putting on earrings."

11   So, it is by their categorical refusal of nakedness that human beings are distinguished from nature. The "mark makes unremarkable"—it creates an interval between what is biologically and brutally given in the animal realm and what is won in the cultural realm. The body is tamed continuously; social custom demands, at any price—including pain, constraint or discomfort—that wildness be abandoned.

12   Each civilization chooses—through a network of elective relationships which are difficult to determine—which areas of the body deserve transformation. These areas are as difficult to define and as shifting as those of eroticism or modesty. An individual alone eludes bodily modifications; they are the expression of a homogeneous collectivity which, at a chosen moment, comes to a tacit agreement to attack one or another part of the anatomy.

13   Whatever the choices, options, or differences may be, that which remains constant is the transformation of appearance. In spite of our contemporary western belief that the body is perfect as it is, we are constantly changing it: clothing it in musculature, suntan, or makeup; dying its head hair or pulling out its bodily hair. The seemingly most innocent gestures for taking care of the body very often hide a persistent and disguised tendency to make it adhere to the strictest of norms, reclothing it in a veil of civilization. The total

nudity offered at birth does not exist in any region of the world. Man puts his stamp on man. The body is not a product of nature, but of culture.

Notes

1. Of course, there are also many different sexual mutilations, including excisions and circumcisions, which we will not go into at this time as they constitute a whole study in themselves.

2. C. Lévi-Strauss, *Tristes Tropiques* (Paris: Plon, 1955), p. 214.

3. J. Cuvelier, *Relations sur le Congo du Père Laurent de Lucques* (Brussels: Institut royal colonial belge, 1953), p. 144.

Source: Parabola, fall 1994.

Making Connections

1. Define the term *body adornment.* Does the term have the same meaning for each author? Give examples to support your answer.
2. Each author offers reasons why people adorn their bodies. First, write a list of reasons. Then decide whether the authors are in agreement on the purposes of body adornment.
3. What types of body adornment do humans use? Make a list of the types discussed in each reading. Are there types of adornment not discussed by any of the authors?
4. Compare the tone used in each of the readings. Which is more serious? Which is more academic?
5. What further information would you need in order to write a paper or make a speech on body adornment?

World Wide Web Activity

Keyword Searches

Experiment to see how much information you can find on the topic of body adornment by completing the following activities.

1. Reread one of the articles on body adornment and list five possible keywords or phrases that you might use to find related information on the World Wide Web. For example, from the first article, the phrases "body adornment," "head coverings and customs," or "Middle Eastern veils" might be used.

2. Select a search engine such as Lycos, Yahoo!, AltaVista, or another. Use only one search engine as you try the following steps.

   a. Examine the Help page to learn the method for doing a keyword search on the search engine you selected. Follow the directions for how to type in keyword phrases.

b. In the Search box, type in one of your possible keyword phrases. When the list of resources appears on your search page, scroll down through the list, skimming the titles of articles and names of Web sites to see what kinds of sites you have found. Make notes on what kinds of sites and how many of them the keyword phrase led you to. Follow the same steps for each keyword phrase.

3. Share your keyword phrases and search results with your classmates. Which keyword phrases uncovered which kinds of sources? Were any of the keyword phrases particularly useful?

COMMUNICATION
MEN'S AND WOMEN'S COMMUNICATION

B–1 TEXTBOOK EXCERPT: COMMUNICATION BETWEEN WOMEN AND MEN

Alex Thio

1   In the world of women, connection and intimacy are the primary goals of life, and individuals cultivate friendship, minimize differences, seek consensus, and avoid the appearance of superiority. On the other hand, status and independence are the primary goals of life in men's world, so individuals seek status by telling others what to do, attain freedom from others' control, avoid taking orders, and resist asking for help. Thus, when the two sexes communicate with each other, women tend to use the language of connection and intimacy, and men the language of status and independence. Both may use the same English language, but in effect they speak and hear different dialects called **genderlects**, linguistic styles that reflect the different worlds of women and men (Tannen, 1994a; 1990).

Speaking Different Genderlects

2   Failure to understand each other's genderlects can spell trouble for intergender communication. Consider a married couple, Linda and Josh. One day Josh's old high school buddy from another city called to announce that he would be in town the following month. Josh invited him to stay for the weekend. When he told Linda that they were going to have a houseguest, she was upset. Often away on business, she had planned to spend that weekend with Josh alone. But what upset her the most was that Josh had extended the invitation without first discussing it with her. Linda would never make plans without first checking with Josh. "Why can't you do the same with me?" Linda asked, But Josh responded, "I can't say to my friend, 'I have to ask my wife for permission!'" To Josh, who lives in the men's world of status, checking with his wife means seeking permission, giving up his independence, or having to act like a kid asking his mom if it's okay to play with a friend. In Linda's female world of connection, checking with her husband has nothing to do with permission. In fact, Linda likes to tell others, "I have to check with Josh," because it makes her feel good to reaffirm that she is involved with someone, that her life is bound up with someone else's (Tannen, 1990). In short, Linda and Josh speak and hear different genderlects, one having to do with connection and intimacy, the other with status and independence.

3   There are other ways the different genderlects can throw a monkey wrench into the communication between women and men. Accustomed to speaking for the purpose of giving *information* only, men tend to misunderstand women by taking literally what women say. On the other hand, women, more habituated to talking for the purpose of expressing *feelings,* tend to misunderstand men by reading emotional meanings into what men say.

4   Thus women and men tend to communicate at cross-purposes. If a woman says to her husband, "We never go out," he may upset her by responding, "That's not true. We went out last week." The husband fails to grasp the feeling the wife is trying to convey. In saying "we never go out," she in effect says something like "I feel like going out and doing

something together. We always have such a fun time, and I enjoy being with you. It has been a few days since we went out." If on another occasion the woman asks her husband, "What's the matter?"? and gets the answer, "I'm okay," she may respond by saying, "I know something's wrong. What is it? Why aren't you willing to share your problem with me? Let me help you." The wife fails to understand that, by saying "I'm okay," her husband means "I am okay; I can deal with my problem. I don't need any help, thank you" (Gray, 1992). In his male world, dealing with one's own problem is a hallmark of independence, which he tries to assert, and getting help from others is a sign of weakness, which he tries to avoid.

5   Genderlects are not confined to communication between intimates. They also influence communication in public. Sitting alone in a dining room where bank officers had lunch, sociolinguist Alice Deakins listened to what they were talking about at adjacent tables. When no woman was present, the men talked mostly about business and rarely about people. The next most popular topics were food, sports, and recreation. When women talked alone, their most frequent topic was people, especially friends, children, and partners in personal relationships. Business was next, and then health, including weight control. Together, women and men tended to avoid the topic that each group liked best and settle on topics of interest to both, *but they followed the style of the men-only conversations.* They talked about food the way men did, focusing on the food and restaurant rather than diet and health. They talked about recreation the way men did, concentrating on sports figures and athletic events rather than on exercising. And they talked about housing the way men did, dealing mostly with location, property values, and commuting time, rather than whether the house is suitable for the family, how safe the neighborhood is for the children, and what kinds of people live next door. In other words, in public communication between the sexes, the male genderlect tends to dominate, mostly centering on things and activities, thus ignoring the female genderlect, which primarily concerns people and relationships (Tannen, 1994a; 1990).

Playing the Gendered Game of Proxemics

6   In gender-mixed groups, men's proxemics differs from women's. Men usually sprawl with legs spread apart and hands stretched away from the body, taking up considerable space around them. Women are more likely to draw themselves in, using only little space with "ladylike" postures such as closing or crossing the legs and placing the hands near the body.

7   A more direct way for men to dominate women in proxemics involves invading their personal space. As has been suggested, men often let their hands rest on women's shoulders but women rarely do the same to men. A similar proxemic domination prevails in interactions of mutual affection. When an intimate couple walk down the street, the man may place his arm around the woman's shoulders, but the woman is far less likely to put her arm around the man's shoulders. Doesn't this merely reflect the fact that the man is usually taller so that it would be uncomfortable for the sexes to reverse positions? No. The same ritual of man playing the powerful protector and woman the helpless protected is often observed when both are of about the same height or even when the man is slightly shorter. If the man is too short to stretch his arm around the woman's shoulders, they still will not reverse positions but will instead settle for holding hands. If a tall woman does put her arm around a shorter man's shoulders, chances are that she is a mother and he is her child (Tannen, 1994a; 1990). In the world of gender inequality, a man is likely to cringe if his girlfriend or wife treats him like a child by putting her arms around his shoulders.

8   Even in the most intimate moments between a man and a woman, male domination reigns. When both lie down in bed, he typically lies on his back, flat and straight, but she lies on her side, her body nestled against his. She further places her head on his shoulder,

The proxemics of body language differs between women and men. In gender-mixed groups, men are likely to sprawl in open positions, whereas women are likely to draw themselves in, sitting in "ladylike" positions.

and he his arm around her. It is a picture of an unequal relationship, with the man appearing strong and protective and the woman weak and protected (Tannen, 1994a; 1990).

Questions for Discussion and Review

1. What are genderlects, and how do they affect the communication between women and men?
2. How do men and women play the gendered game of proxemics?

Source: Sociology, pp.121–131.

B–2: THE TALK OF THE SANDBOX: HOW JOHNNY AND SUZY'S PLAYGROUND CHATTER PREPARES THEM FOR LIFE AT THE OFFICE

Deborah Tannen

1 Bob Hoover of the Pittsburgh Post-Gazette was interviewing me when he remarked that after years of coaching boys' softball teams, he was now coaching girls and they were very different. I immediately whipped out my yellow pad and began interviewing him—and discovered that his observations about how girls and boys play softball parallel mine about how women and men talk at work.

2 Hoover told me that boys' teams always had one or two stars whom the other boys treated with deference. So when he started coaching a girls' team he began by looking for the leader. He couldn't find one. "The girls who are better athletes don't lord it over the others," he said. "You get the feeling that everyone's the same." When a girl got the ball, she didn't try to throw it all the way home as a strong-armed boy would; instead, she'd throw it to another team member, so they all became better catchers and throwers. He went on, "If a girl makes an error, she's not in the doghouse for a long time, as a boy would be."

3 "But wait," I interrupted. "I've heard that when girls make a mistake at sports, they often say 'I'm sorry,' whereas boys don't."

4 That's true, he said, but then the girl forgets it—and so do her teammates. "For boys, sports is a performance art. They're concerned with how they look." When they make an error, they sulk because they've let their teammates down. Girls want to win, but if they lose, they're still all in it together—so the mistake isn't as dreadful for the individual or the team.

5 What Hoover described in these youngsters were the seeds of behavior I have observed among women and men at work.

6 The girls who are the best athletes don't "lord it over" the others—just the ethic I found among women in positions of authority. Women managers frequently told me they were good managers because they did not act in an authoritarian manner. They said they did not flaunt their power, or behave as though they were better than their subordinates. Similarly, linguist Elisabeth Kuhn found

that women professors in her study informed students of course requirements as if they had magically appeared on the syllabus ("There are two papers. The first paper, ah, let's see, is due . . . It's back here [referring to the syllabus] at the beginning"), whereas the men professors made it clear that they had set requirements ("I have two midterms and a final").

7   A woman manager might say to her secretary, "Could you do me a favor and type this letter right away?" knowing that her secretary is going to type the letter. But her male boss, on hearing this, might conclude she doesn't feel she deserves the authority she has, just as a boys' coach might think the star athlete doesn't realize how good he is if he doesn't expect his teammates to treat him with deference.

8   I was especially delighted by Hoover's observation that, although girls are more likely to say, "I'm sorry," they are actually far less sorry when they make a mistake than boys who don't say it, but are "in the doghouse" for a long time. This dramatizes the ritual nature of many women's apologies. How often is a woman who is "always apologizing" seen as weak and lacking in confidence? In fact, for many women, saying "I'm sorry" often doesn't mean "I apologize." It means "I'm sorry that happened."

9   Like many of the rituals common among women, it's a way of speaking that takes into account the other person's point of view. It can even be an automatic conversational smoother. For example, you left your pad in someone's office; you knock on the door and say, "Excuse me, I left my pad on your desk," and the person whose office it is might reply, "Oh, I'm sorry. Here it is." She knows it is not her fault that you left your pad on her desk; she's just letting you know it's okay.

10   Finally, I was intrigued by Hoover's remark that boys regard sports as "a performance art" and worry about "how they look." There, perhaps, is the rub, the key to why so many women feel they don't get credit for what they do. From childhood, many boys learn something that is very adaptive to the workplace: Raises and promotions are based on "perfor-

mance" evaluations and these depend, in large measure, on how you appear in other people's eyes. In other words, you have to worry not only about getting your job done but also about getting credit for what you do.

11   Getting credit often depends on the way you talk. For example, a woman told me she was given a poor evaluation because her supervisor felt she knew less than her male peers. Her boss, it turned out, reached this conclusion because the woman asked more questions: She was seeking information without regard to how her queries would make her look.

12   The same principle applies to apologizing. Whereas some women seem to be taking undeserved blame by saying "I'm sorry," some men seem to evade deserved blame. I observed this when a man disconnected a conference call by accidentally elbowing the speakerphone. When his secretary re-connected the call, I expected him to say, "I'm sorry; I knocked the phone by mistake." Instead he said, "Hey, what happened?! One minute you were there, the next minute you were gone!" Annoying as this might be, there are certainly instances in which people improve their fortunes by covering up mistakes.

13   If Hoover's observations about girls' and boys' athletic styles are fascinating, it is even more revealing to see actual transcripts of children at play and how they mirror the adult workplace. Amy Sheldon, a linguist at the University of Minnesota who studies children talking at play in a day care center, compared the conflicts of pre-school girls and boys. She found that boys who fought with one another tended to pursue their own goal. Girls tended to balance their own interests with those of the other girls through complex verbal negotiations.

14   Look how different the negotiations were:

15   Two boys fought over a toy telephone: Tony had it; Charlie wanted it. Tony was sitting on a foam chair with the base of the phone in his lap and the receiver lying beside him. Charlie picked up the receiver, and Tony protested, "No, that's my phone!" He grabbed the telephone cord and tried to pull the

receiver away from Charlie, saying, "No, that—uh, it's on MY couch. It's on MY couch, Charlie. It's on MY couch. It's on MY couch." It seems he had only one point to make, so he made it repeatedly as he used physical force to get the phone back.

16   Charlie ignored Tony and held onto the receiver. Tony then got off the couch, set the phone base on the floor and tried to keep possession of it by overturning the chair on top of it. Charlie managed to push the chair off, get the telephone and win the fight.

17   This might seem like a typical kids' fight until you compare it with a fight Sheldon videotaped among girls. Here the contested objects were toy medical instruments: Elaine had them; Arlene wanted them. But she didn't just grab for them; she argued her case. Elaine, in turn, balanced her own desire to keep them with Arlene's desire to get them. Elaine lost ground gradually, by compromising.

18   Arlene began not by grabbing but by asking and giving a reason: "Can I have that, that thing? I'm going to take my baby's temperature." Elaine was agreeable, but cautious: "You can use it—you can use my temperature. Just make sure you can't use anything else unless you can ask." Arlene did just that; she asked for the toy syringe: "May I?" Elaine at first resisted, but gave a reason: "No, I'm gonna need to use the shot in a couple of minutes." Arlene reached for the syringe anyway, explaining in a "beseeching" tone, "But I—I need this though."

19   Elaine capitulated, but again tried to set limits: "Okay, just use it once." She even gave Arlene permission to give "just a couple of shots."

20   Arlene then pressed her advantage, and became possessive of her property: "Now don't touch the baby until I get back, because it is MY BABY! I'll check her ears, okay?" (Even when being demanding, she asked for agreement: "okay?")

21   Elaine tried to regain some rights through compromise: "Well, let's pretend it's another day, that we have to look in her ears together." Elaine also tried another approach that would give Arlene something she wanted: "I'll have

to shot her after, after, after you listen—after you look in her ears," suggested Elaine. Arlene, however, was adamant: "Now don't shot her at all!"

22   What happened next will sound familiar to anyone who has ever been a little girl or overheard one. Elaine could no longer abide Arlene's selfish behavior and applied the ultimate sanction: "Well, then, you can't come to my birthday!" Arlene uttered the predictable retort: "I don't want to come to your birthday!"

23   The boys and girls followed different rituals for fighting. Each boy went after what he wanted; they slugged it out; one won. But the girls enacted a complex negotiation, trying to get what they wanted while taking into account what the other wanted.

24   Here is an example of how women and men at work used comparable strategies.

25   Maureen and Harold, two managers at a medium-size company, were assigned to hire a human-resources coordinator for their division. Each favored a different candidate, and both felt strongly about their preferences. They traded arguments for some time, neither convincing the other. Then Harold said that hiring the candidate Maureen wanted would make him so uncomfortable that he would have to consider resigning. Maureen respected Harold. What's more, she liked him and considered him a friend. So she said what seemed to her the only thing she could say under the circumstances: "Well, I certainly don't want you to feel uncomfortable here. You're one of the pillars of the place." Harold's choice was hired.

26   What was crucial was not Maureen's and Harold's individual styles in isolation but how they played in concert with each other's style. Harold's threat to quit ensured his triumph—when used with someone for whom it was a trump card. If he had been arguing with someone who regarded this threat as simply another move in the negotiation rather than a non-negotiable expression of deep feelings, the result might have been different. For example, had she said, "That's ridiculous; of course you're not going to quit!" or matched it

("Well, I'd be tempted to quit if we hired your guy"), the decision might well have gone the other way.

27   Like the girls at play, Maureen was balancing her perspective with those of her colleague and expected him to do the same. Harold was simply going for what he wanted and trusted Maureen to do likewise.

28   This is not to say that all women and all men, or all boys and girls, behave any one way. Many factors influence our styles, including regional and ethnic backgrounds, family experience and individual personality. But gender is a key factor, and understanding its influence can help clarify what happens when we talk.

29   Understanding the ritual nature of communication gives you the flexibility to consider different approaches if you're not happy with the reaction you're getting. Someone who tends to avoid expressing disagreement might learn to play "devil's advocate" without taking it as a personal attack. Someone who tends to avoid admitting fault might find it is effective to say "I'm sorry"—that the loss of face is outweighed by a gain in credibility.

30   There is no one way of talking that will always work best. But understanding how conversational rituals work allows individuals to have more control over their own lives.

Source: The Washington Post, December 11, 1994.

B–3: COMMUNICATION BETWEEN SEXES: A WAR OF THE WORDS?

Barbara Ash

1   Dave Davis draws a blank when asked if he notices any differences in the way women and men communicate on the job. "I don't find any," says Davis, a researcher for Florida TaxWatch. "I think that's a stereotype that died, or should have died, years ago. In my experience working with state government, the women I see in meetings communicate just as well as males, are just as persuasive and as appreciated as males. I don't think it's an issue anymore."

2   Jayne Hoffman doesn't know Davis, but his response doesn't surprise her. "I'd imagine a man would say that," says Hoffman with a laugh. "Men have been running things, setting the pace and communication style from the beginning. When women started encroaching on their territory, men didn't have to change their style. We had to adjust ours to fit in," says the budget director at the Department of Highway Safety and Motor Vehicles. "Of course, it's not an issue for men."

3   But conversational style should be an issue for everyone, particularly women, because even the simplest exchanges at work can be, in a sense, a test, says Deborah Tannen, author of the best-seller *You Just Don't Understand: Men and Women in Conversation.* "What we say as we do our work can become the evidence on which we are judged, and the judgments may surface in the form of raises (or denials of raises), promotions (or lack of them), and favorable (or unfavorable) work assignments," Tannen says.

4   The hardest part about communication style is that everyone assumes they're communicating the same way, says Micki Kacmar, a Florida State University business professor and organizational communications consultant. "But people interpret the same message differently, and that causes problems. Unless the person you're communicating with understands your style, you won't be successful." That's why it's hard to grin and bear it when:

- You say something at a meeting and it's ignored, but then a man says the same thing and it's embraced as a wonderful idea.
- You speak up at the conference table and you're constantly interrupted by the men on your team, whose voices are louder, deeper, and more authoritative.
- You've worked overtime on a project, but don't get the credit.
- You give what you think are clear instructions, but the job doesn't get done.

5   People in positions of authority are judged by how they use that authority. That can pose a special challenge for women managers because the ways women are expected to talk are at odds with our traditional images of authority, Tannen says. In fact, the way women communicate, issue orders, and make decisions are often misinterpreted as a lack of confidence or even competence. "Women tend to be more polite and congenial. They want everything to be pleasant, and that doesn't always work because not everyone is playing by the same rules," says Darlene Long, a data-processing manager with the Agency for Health Care Reform.

6   A main difference between men and women's styles, Tannen says and many Tallahassee working women agree, is that men are more goal-oriented, while women are more people-oriented. "I'm more likely to take into consideration an employee's family situation and if the deadline is an important one before I make them work overtime to get a job done," says Hoffman, who supervises both men and women. "If a man takes personal issues into consideration, it doesn't show. He's going to want to get the job done no matter what," Hoffman said.

7   Denise Rains, a public-affairs officer for the U.S. Forest Services, recalls that in a previous job she and other women on her leadership team would get a man to present suggestions. "We felt there was a better chance that people would listen to him," Rains admitted. "More than once, a woman would say something and the people at the meeting would say, 'OK,' ignore it, and go on. Then a man would say the exact same thing in a different way, and

everyone would act like it's a new, great idea." Examples like this leave women feeling invisible.

8   "Women have told me they often come away from meetings feeling empty, feeling they haven't gotten across what they want to get across," says Tallahassee marriage and family therapist Kristen Overman, who counsels men and women on communication. Women tend to personalize experiences, thinking this is happening only to them, Overman said. "When they understand this is a general dynamic, they can use our good minds to develop methods of communicating our ideas in a way that will be heard," Overman says.

9   Like Tannen, Overman and Kacmar don't consider men's communication style superior to women's, just different. In fact, adopting men's style for the most part doesn't work for women. Men tend to be more direct, more goal-oriented. They also tend to speak louder, longer, interrupt more, and speak more authoritatively at meetings. Men are more likely to start sentences with, "It's obvious that . . . ," "The facts show . . . ," "This will work if we . . ." Women, on the other hand, are more likely to speak less at meetings, apologize for taking up time, try to draw everyone into the decision-making process, ask opinions, and thank co-workers for listening to them. "We shouldn't be forced into a style or thought process that we're not comfortable with," Rains says.

10   Some women say you're damned if you act businesslike, and damned if you don't. Realtor Joan Raley says that if she approaches peers in a professional manner and is direct, like men tend to be, or if she displays annoyance or anger, she's viewed as "grumpy, grouchy, or bitchy." "People react to men's anger or irritability differently," she says. "They accept that as a part of their role as an assertive executive." "I'm just trying to get work done in a businesslike manner, which is how a top-flight male executive would approach his business. It's okay for a male to do that, but not a woman. Both men and women expect women to communicate and behave a certain way—to

be quieter, not as direct, not as assertive. They expect us to be nurturing."

11   Overman and Kacmar agree that women and men don't have to change their communication styles. Instead, they need to be mindful of other conversational styles, and develop flexibility. "You must have a large repertoire of tactics to communicate effectively," she says. "You can keep your style as long as you know you're making your point." One tactic Long, the data-processing manager, has adopted is to continue talking when someone interrupts her. "When you're talking and men cut you off, I've learned to do what they do," she says. "I'll continue talking until they realize what they're doing. I've had to be more assertive because if you're not, you'll end up being ignored."

12   Overman says she sees a lot of women who are frustrated and depressed because they feel their talents are devalued, and they're not listened to at work or at home. "At work a woman's communication may be misinterpreted by a male subordinate because she's been raised to give directives in a polite, respectful manner," Overman says. "For instance, the female boss may say, 'You might want to consider making these changes in this report.' Her intention is to communicate that she wants something done." But the man may interpret that as a suggestion, rather than a directive, and may not follow it. The woman interprets his inaction as insubordination, and with good reason, Overman says. But he's unaware he was given a directive, and is perplexed at her anger. Men need to be spoken to directly, with specific requests.

13   "The frustration at work carries over to home," Overman says. "Home should be a place where the people who love you listen to you, but many women express frustration that their partners don't listen well either. "What frustrates men and women is when they misinterpret each other. They need to become familiar with each other's styles."

Source: Knight-Ridder Tribune News Service, February 13, 1996.

Making Connections

1. All three authors agree that men and women communicate differently. Specifically, what differences does each author identify?
2. Think of an example from your own experience that illustrates one of the differences discussed by one or more of the authors.
3. Which reading did you find most enjoyable and interesting? Why?
4. Which article seems most detailed and most carefully researched? Support your answer by referring to the readings.
5. Two of the readings appeared in newspapers. How do these two readings differ from the third, which was taken from a college textbook?

World Wide Web Activity

A Researcher's Home Page

In the first reading about communication between women and men, two research studies by Tannen are cited in the first paragraph: Tannen, 1994a, 1990.

The second reading, "The Talk of the Sandbox," is by Deborah Tannen. The third reading refers to a best-selling book that Tannen wrote called *You Just Don't Understand: Men and Women in Conversation.* From this group of readings, you can reason that Deborah Tannen is a well-known researcher in the area of men's and women's communication.

Suppose you are writing a paper on this topic, and you'd like to know more about Tannen's research. Do a World Wide Web search using "Deborah Tannen" as your keyword phrase to find the official Web site of Deborah Tannen. When you find it, answer the following questions.

1. How many books has Tannen written? How many of them seem to be on the topic of men's and women's communication? Where did you find this information?

2. Where does the link to her book *Talking from 9 to 5* take you? Where does the link to her Ph.D. degree take you? Are these related or remote links? How do you know?

3. In the list of "General Audience Publications" Tannen has written, which articles seem to be most relevant to the topic of women's communication at work? How do you know?

BIOLOGY
ENDANGERED AND EXTINCT SPECIES

C–1 TEXTBOOK EXCERPT: THE RAPID LOSS OF SPECIES

Campbell et al.

1   The key deer, a miniature subspecies of the whitetail deer, is about the size of a German shepherd dog (Figure A). It is found only in the Florida Keys and is a population with a unique gene pool. Key deer were cut off from whitetail populations on the mainland when the sea level rose after the last ice age. Confined to a few islands, key deer have never been numerous and were nearly exterminated by poachers in the early 1900s. Conservation efforts brought the population back from fewer than 50 animals to about 400 in the early 1970s. Key deer are now declining again as the human population in the Florida Keys mushrooms. Housing developments are reducing the habitat, while motorists on new highways have become the main threat to the deer's survival. Now down to some 240 individuals, the deer are dying on the roads faster than they can reproduce.

2   In many ways, the plight of the key deer illustrates the effect of modern human culture worldwide. We are now presiding over an alarming **biodiversity crisis**, a rapid decrease in Earth's great variety of life. Animal and plant species are now being lost at a rate that is unprecedented in the history of life. Some biologists estimate that within the next century, fully half of Earth's current species may pass into extinction. This would reduce biodiversity to the level of 60 million years ago, after mass extinctions, which occurred over a much longer period of time, reduced species numbers by about 75%.

3   Thus far, about 1.5 million living species have been discovered and named, and it is

A. Key deer

B. Black-market ivory confiscated by wildlife officials in Tanzania.

likely that there are at least another 2.5 million yet to be found. Tropical forests alone may house 80% of the world's plants and animals. The current rate of deforestation is so great that many tropical species may become extinct before scientists discover them. Deforestation also threatens migratory species. Scientists have documented serious population reductions in over half of the more than 200 species of songbirds that winter in Central and South America and migrate to the U.S. and Canada to breed. Destruction of forests in the tropics *and* in the United States and Canada is thought to be a major factor in the decline.

4   Habitat loss threatens the greatest number of species, but other factors are also important. Overhunting has eliminated many species and continues to threaten others. Whales, for example, have been hunted to near extinction, and a few countries continue to kill these huge mammals despite a nearly worldwide ban on whaling. Many animals and plants have also succumbed to competition from foreign species that humans have introduced. In East Africa, hundreds of species of tropical fishes in Lake Victoria are currently threatened by the nile perch, a large species (up to 200 lb) that was introduced as a sport and food fish.

5   Often, as for the key deer, a combination of killing and habitat destruction has driven a species over the edge. In the past century, for instance, the Hawaiian Islands have lost half their bird species, mainly to overhunting, deforestation, and diseases carried by foreign bird species introduced into the islands. In Africa, elephants and rhinoceroses are being pushed toward extinction by habitat loss and by poachers catering to a black market for ivory and horns (Figure B).

6   Why should we worry about species losses? First of all, large-scale extinctions of other species may be a warning to us that we are altering the biosphere so fast that we ourselves are threatened. Secondly, we depend on many other species for food, clothing, shelter, oxygen, soil fertility—the list goes on and on. Finally, we might ask ourselves what right we have to destroy other species. Shouldn't we use our intelligence constructively and accept the responsibility of conserving as much of the biosphere and its diversity as possible?

Source: Biology Concepts and Connections, p. 763.

C–2: THE LAST OF THEIR KIND

Jim Motavalli and Jennifer Bogo

As the War on Wildlife Continues, We're Losing Species at an Incredible Rate

1 The big, slow-moving Galapagos tortoise is one of the most endangered animals on Earth, confined to dwindling populations on just five islands. On one of these islands so memorably visited by Charles Darwin, a solitary male tortoise survives. Galapagos tortoises, which can grow to over 500 pounds, live to 100 and take 20 years to reach sexual maturity, are protected today, but there is a long history of calamitous contact with the human race. Nineteenth-century whalers used to toss a clutch of live tortoises on their backs in the ships' holds, using them as a valuable source of fresh meat and oil. These days, the tortoise's main enemies are domestic animals, introduced species like goats, dogs and pigs.

2   The Galapagos tortoise's survival in the wild is in doubt, but that doesn't mean the wealthy are denied the pleasure of keeping one as a pet. The live reptile trade has grown enormously in recent years, and more than nine million turtles and snakes were exported from the U.S. in 1996. The Captive Bred Wildlife Foundation in Arizona (its slogan is "When Turtles Are Outlawed, Only Outlaws Will Have turtles") would be happy to sell you a young Galapagos tortoise for $3,500, and it's perfectly legal provided you have a federal permit. What's more, for just $20, you can get

a TROVAN microchip transponder implanted in its body so you're sure the valuable tortoise in question is your own. Jeff Gee, who runs the reptile farm, says that a species' value is "intrinsic, based on rarity or availability of the animal. I guarantee you could take a canary, put it on the Endangered Species list, and tomorrow it would be worth $250."

3   Endangered species remain global big business, despite worldwide treaties like the Convention on International Trade in Endangered Species of Wild Fauna and Flora (CITES) and the Species Survival Commission of the World Conservation Union (IUCN), as well as national protections like the Endangered Species Act, now undergoing a contentious renewal process. Protection on paper is no guarantee that a species will recover. Not only do all the laws and treaties contain loopholes, but enforcement on the ground is difficult at best. Endangered animals are slaughtered for trophies and traditional medicines, made homeless by development, caught up in wars and eaten as "bush meat."

4   Though species have a definite right to exist for their own reasons, it's also true that they're disappearing before we fully understand their ecological significance to the planet as a whole. That's a tragedy when applied to rare medicinal plants, but it's relevant for animals as well. An entirely new bird species was discovered in Tanzania in 1991. Unfortunately, the specimens were in a bird exporter's shop, and two were already dead and the other two dying. An increasingly endangered West African chimpanzee subspecies, Pan troglodytes troglodytes, was recently revealed to harmlessly harbor an AIDS-like virus that could solve the mystery of the disease's origins in humans—and lead to a cure.

5   The numbers are as stark as ever, pointing to what biologist E. O. Wilson calls a "sixth extinction" of species comparable to the mass die-off of dinosaurs. The Nature Conservancy (TNC) calculates that one-third of U.S. plants and animals are at risk of extinction. Since European discovery of North America, 110 irreplaceable flora and fauna have disappeared forever, and another 416 are "missing" and presumed lost. Almost 7,000 U.S. species are threatened. According to the U.S. Public Interest Research Group, 50,000 plants and animals become extinct worldwide every year. Within 50 years one-quarter of the world's species could be gone.

6   Larry Master, TNC's chief zoologist, says the group must perform a kind of triage, devoting resources only in specific instances where it thinks intervention will provide a survival edge. TNC's protected land, some nine million acres in the U.S. and Canada, is the only extant habitat for some severely depleted species. But for every modest success story, like the piping plover and the Peregrine falcon, there are many losses.

Compassion Fatigue

7 Just as "compassion fatigue" has been identified as an unfortunate syndrome, so too have warnings about imminent extinction sometimes fallen on deaf ears. "Save the Whales" is derided as a slogan from the 1960s, and as a crusade whose goals have already been achieved. Whales are more popular than ever before—as symbols of the majesty of nature, or as entertainment—but whale-watching expeditions don't in themselves save species. One reason endangered whales aren't bouncing back from the brink is that illegal and irresponsible hunting still occurs. According to the journal Nature, Harvard biologists recently found, through DNA testing, that whale meat for sale in Japanese markets came from a rare hybrid bluefin whale caught off the coast of Iceland, supposedly for "scientific" purposes.

8   Americans can perhaps be forgiven for thinking that endangered species are yesterday's problem, since threatened "charismatic megafauna" (from bald eagles to cheetahs) are pervasive on television and in magazines, where their computer-manipulated images are used to sell products and create brand identities. A commercial featuring herds of rhinos and tigers thundering through Manhattan may convince viewers

that the real animal is not going to disappear. Writing in *Double Take,* Bill McKibben observed that we've already archived so much wildlife imagery that we need never disturb the real animals again.

9   The film "Fierce Creatures" satirized the growing corporate involvement in the world's zoos, which use endangered species as calling cards. The San Diego Zoo is hardly immune from this, having set up the giant Panda Research Station in partnership with Pacific Bell. The visiting public can get up to date on the latest news from Bai Yun and Shi Shi, who are on a 12-year loan from China, by calling the Giant Panda Hotline.

10   The zoo calls its arrangement with Chinese authorities a "research loan," but that belies the pandas' role as a major zoo attraction. San Diego's Georgeanne Irvine admits that the pandas are "one of our most popular animals," but she insists that the zoo is also gaining valuable insights into panda communications and breeding activity. In addition to scientific studies of panda scent markers, DNA and stress physiology, the zoo sends $1 million annually to aid China in habitat preservation efforts. Delegations from the zoo travel frequently to the Wolong Giant Panda Preserve in China to study pandas in the wild. But if casual zoo visitors can buy an encounter with such rare animals along with their modest admission price, not to mention a plush talking version in the gift shop, are they going to worry about the species' long-term survival?

11   The role of zoos in endangered species protection gets more complex when one considers that, for some species, they have become the best hope for survival. In too many cases, zoos and research institutions hold the most viable breeding populations as natural habitats are devastated. That's certainly the case with the once-plentiful black-footed ferret. But can a species be truly said to have "survived" if it no longer has any wild identity?

12   And reintroducing captive-bred animals to the wild is a frustrating and often-heartbreaking business. Efforts to repopulate the thick-billed parrot into Arizona, for instance, have recently failed because birds raised in zoos or by breeders lack the vital herding instincts that keep them safe from predators. A plan to bring the lynx back to what had become unfamiliar territory in New York State also ended disastrously.

13   But scarcity in the wild is actually a plus to wildlife traders. As Jeff Gee notes, a brutal law of supply and demand is in effect when it comes to endangered species—the fewer there are, the more they're worth. Simon Habel, director of TRAFFIC North America, an arm of the World Wildlife Fund that tracks the endangered animal trade, says the business fluctuates according to "the flavor of the month." Collectors have what Habel calls "a postage stamp mentality" meaning they'll pay almost anything to get a rare specimen, sometimes alive or dead. The CITES Appendix I-listed (the most endangered) Australian palm cockatoo, which is difficult to breed in captivity, sells for up to $20,000 a pair.

14   Some countries are tightening penalties. Chinese panda smugglers get life sentences. In the U.S., traders can now be prosecuted for even claiming that their products contain the bones of tigers or other endangered species—even if the claims prove to be untrue. "All over the world, there's an effort to clamp down," says Habel, who adds that TRAFFIC is helping to educate practitioners of traditional medicine in humane alternatives. "We're finding that people who buy these products don't realize there is a direct connection with tigers poached in the wild," he adds.

15   Despite some positive enforcement steps, the illegal wildlife trade is still very profitable and, in most countries, the penalties for getting caught are not very severe. In 1996, Hector Ugalde pleaded guilty to federal conspiracy charges in the smuggling of Brazil's critically endangered Hyacinth macaw, which can fetch $8,000 on the open market. His sentence: three years of probation and a $10,000 fine.

16   TRAFFIC produces highly-detailed—and very depressing—reports showing how wasteful the wild-caught trade can be. When a

Senegalese bird dealer makes the two-day trip along rutted roads from Kedougou to Dakar, for instance, he is expected to lose a third of his 15,000 passengers. And the damage isn't limited to the birds themselves. In Argentina, and in many other countries, the most popular way to catch valuable parrots is to cut down their nesting trees, which in Argentina alone accounted for the loss of 100,000 quebracho trees in the 1980s.

17   Although habitat destruction is probably the major factor pushing endangered species into extinction, civil unrest plays a part, too. Our unstable world has little respect for Habitat Conservation Plans. Aside from their incredible human toll, the ethnic massacres in Rwanda threatened the last bastion of the 400 surviving mountain gorillas. Sometimes the killing is officially sanctioned: The Tanzanian Army has been implicated in the killing of Ugandan elephants for "bush meat." Other times, the damage is collateral: Jungle fighting in the Asian country of Myanmar last January scattered a herd of 97 wild elephants, sending them fleeing into neighboring Thailand. Conflict in the Congo late in 1998 may have decimated the last few Northern white rhinos in the wild.

18   It's hard to escape the conclusion that many of our critically endangered species are on an unstoppable downward spiral. But there are occasional bright spots. President Clinton recently proposed a $100 million plan to save the rapidly dwindling population of Pacific salmon. And, in 1998, The Nature Conservancy announced that seven U.S. species thought to have disappeared entirely (the list included three snails and two freshwater mussels) had been rediscovered, still clinging to life. TNC scientists failed to locate 72 other threatened species, so the applause should be somewhat muted.

19   After the heedless depredations of the 19th century, it is perhaps good news that we're at least trying to save our endangered species. Unfortunately, we're losing the battle on many fronts. To save our wild future, we'll have to try harder.

Source: E, May, 1999

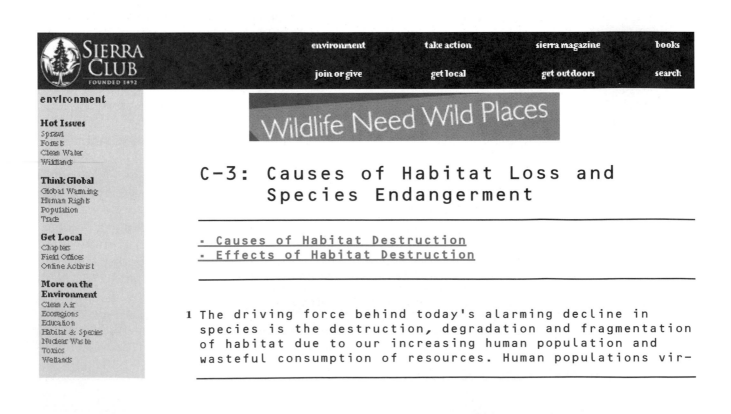

C-3: Causes of Habitat Loss and Species Endangerment

- Causes of Habitat Destruction
- Effects of Habitat Destruction

1 The driving force behind today's alarming decline in species is the destruction, degradation and fragmentation of habitat due to our increasing human population and wasteful consumption of resources. Human populations vir-

tually all around the globe are on the rise. All of these people require living space, clean water and food. Because Americans consume so much more energy, food and raw materials than our counterparts in other developed countries, our impact on our environment is proportionally much greater. As a result, wildlife and wild places in the U.S. are being pushed to the brink of extinction.

2 While the U.S. does not currently face as significant an increase in population as other countries, the movement of our population to new areas and the ensuing development has resulted in the destruction of species and their habitat. Thus, not surprisingly, there is a high correlation between human population and economic development trends in the U.S. and species decline and ecosystem destruction.

3 In the Southeast, Southwest, Pacific Northwest and Rocky Mountain states, population growth is higher than in the Northeast and Midwest. In particular, Nevada, Arizona, Arkansas, Florida, California and Washington have the greatest percentage of population growth. These are the same areas that have the greatest rate of species extinction and decline.

4 While population growth is the ultimate threat to species and the ecosystems they rely upon, there are other threats facing species in the interim. These threats revolve around the way we use the earth's resources and consequences of that use. Human exploitation of our resources is the primary cause of habitat loss, degradation and fragmentation.

5 While habitat loss and degradation are obvious threats to species survival, habitat fragmentation is a less obvious but more insidious threat. Habitat fragmentation has two parts: (1) a decrease in the habitat type and (2) the apportionment of the remaining habitat into smaller, more isolated pieces. The problems that arise from habitat fragmentation include smaller populations due to small amounts of habitat, isolation of populations in the fragmented parts, and potential increase in predators, competitors and parasites. As a result, habitat fragmentation is one of the greatest threats to species and the ecosystems they rely upon for survival.

Causes of Habitat Destruction, Degradation and Fragmentation

6 Human activities that cause habitat destruction and fragmentation include intensive corporate farming, urbanization, logging, grazing, mining, road building, damming and channelizing of streams, pollution, the introduction of non-native species, fire suppression and recreation. All of these activities have contributed to the decline of our forests, rangelands and aquatic habitats. The following is a review of how each of these activities adversely impact species and their habitat:

Corporate Farming

7 Approximately 45 percent of the U.S. land area is used for agricultural purposes, with 472 million acres in cropland and 587 million acres in range or pasture. Agricultural development, particularly the conversion of the small family farm into the massive single crop agribusiness, is the leading cause of habitat destruction in this country, substantially impacting our forests, rangelands and wetlands. In fact, nearly 90 percent of recent wetland losses are attributable to agriculture.

8 The damage caused by corporate farming comes from the conversion of small family farms into large industry farms, the shift to planting only one crop, wetland drainage and the elimination of the practice of allowing fields to lie fallow between plantings. These practices have resulted in the reduction of habitat diversity (e.g., a decline in the amount of undisturbed grass-dominated cover), acceleration of soil erosion, increase in water pollution from agricultural runoff and creation of a greater dependence on fertilizers and pesticides.

Urban Development

9 While agribusiness development tops the list of activities responsible for habitat destruction for endangered plants and animals, a review of recovery plans for endangered and threatened plants identified urban development as the greatest threat to the plants' continued survival. Urban sprawl replaces species' habitat with development projects, fragmenting and depleting the remaining habitat.

10 In the early 1990s, urban sprawl in California had reduced the indigenous coastal sage scrub ecosystem, home to the threatened California gnatcatcher, by more than 90 percent. The remaining 10 percent of sage scrub is severely fragmented. For example, in 1931, an aerial photograph of Orange, Riverside and San Diego counties would have revealed 180 distinct patches of coastal sage scrub; by 1990, there were four times as many patches, with each patch averaging less than one-tenth of its 1931 size. The region's chaparral, grassland and riparian habitats were likewise fragmented.

Logging

11 In less developed areas, logging, grazing and mining are the major threats to endangered ecosystems and species. Logging activities have devastating impacts on wildlife and habitat. Approximately 3,000 species of animals and 10,000 species of plants are found in national forests, including 260 threatened and endangered species. Poorly planned clearcuts and logging roads destroy habitat by removing large stands of trees and surrounding habitat. Logging and the construction of timber roads also cause erosion and even landslides. The resulting erosion can clog streams with silt, degrading water quality for downstream users, including municipalities, and harming fish

populations. Logging and the construction of timber roads are one of the biggest threats facing the grizzly bear today.

Grazing

12 Livestock grazing is one of the most insidious and pervasive threats to biodiversity on rangelands. It is also the most widespread of the federally subsidized, private commercial practices operating on public lands, occurring on 270 million acres of rangeland managed by the federal government. Livestock grazing exacts a terrible toll on wildlife and its habitat, changing the species composition of native ecological communities and significantly impacting riparian areas. Grazing strips the banks of rivers and streams, which in turn leads to erosion and degradation of aquatic ecosystems. In addition to directly destroying habitat, grazing has a number of indirect impacts from the management of livestock. For example, many ranchers try to kill predators or species that may compete with livestock for food. These efforts have been so successful that many predators, such as the mountain lion, wolf and bear, have been extirpated from a majority of their range.

Mining

13 Mining significantly impacts ecosystems by destroying habitat and polluting and degrading streams and waterways. Mining also leads to road building and surface mining, which destroy the surface ecosystem. In addition, mining requires a large amount of underground material to be brought to the surface. These materials, when exposed to rain, create runoff that is highly acidic or has high concentrations of metal ore, both of which are highly toxic to aquatic species. For example, a northern Idaho gold mine has been leaking toxic cyanide into a tributary of the South Fork Salmon River, poisoning the breeding grounds of the threatened chinook salmon.

Road Building

14 Road building associated with agriculture, logging, mining and urban development seriously impacts ecosystems in a number of ways. Dirt roads, which are usually built in forest or mining operations, cause erosion and landslides, and degrade water quality in streams and rivers. Paved roads, on the other hand, do not permit any infiltration of water, forcing water to be drained elsewhere, often polluted with lead, oil, and gasoline. In addition, when roads cut through an ecosystem, further habitat degradation and fragmentation results. Finally, the introduction of roads in the wilderness increases the chance of species being hit by cars or killed by legal or illegal hunting or trapping. The sum total of the damage caused by roads is an ecosystem that is less hospitable to species. For example, wolf researchers have found that wolf populations decline if the concentration of roads in an area exceeds one mile of road for each square mile of area.

Water Development

15 Water development adversely impacts species in a number of ways. The natural flow of rivers and streams is disrupted by the construction and maintenance of dams, impoundments and other barriers on streams and rivers, flood control projects, stream channelization for navigation, and dredging of waterways. This results in an increase in water temperatures and salinity, the removal of important nutrients and silt, and the alteration of upstream and downstream habitat, including wetlands and marshes. Water diversion projects for the transport of water for agriculture, commercial or residential development also divert water to other areas, reducing the total volume of water downstream. This reduction in water creates problems with water flow, temperature and salinity. It also alters river and stream habitat, wetlands and estuaries.

16 Water projects have resulted in serious declines in aquatic species. In the Pacific Northwest, the damming and diverting of many rivers, including the Columbia, have devastated salmon populations. In the Southwest, the damming and diversion of the Colorado River has brought its native fish populations to the brink of extinction. In California, the diversion of water for agriculture has created a build-up of selenium, a naturally occurring trace element in western soils which is toxic even in small amounts. When soils are irrigated, the selenium is flushed into the Kesterson National Wildlife Refuge, causing a massive die-off of waterfowl.

Introduction of Non-Native Species

17 After habitat destruction, the invasion of non-native species is the greatest threat to rare and native species and ecosystems. Non-native species alter habitat by changing the vegetation, competing with native species, and preying on native species. Hawaii, California and Florida have the most severe problem with exotic species. In Hawaii, introduced species are now considered to be the single greatest cause of extinction of the state's native fauna and flora. For example, the introduction of cattle to Hawaii has destroyed many plant communities, causing species such as the hau hele 'ula (or Hawaiian tree cotton) to be placed on the threatened and endangered species list.

18 Another example is the introduction of the opossum shrimp in Flathead Lake in Montana and in other lakes and reservoirs in the West to provide an extra food source for economically important salmon. Unfortunately, the shrimp was such a successful predator of small crustaceans, which were the primary food source of salmon, that the salmon fishery collapsed, adversely affecting bald eagles and grizzly bears, which eat salmon.

Pollution

19 Pollution damages ecosystems through the introduction of sulfur compounds, ozone, pesticides and heavy metals. Airborne pollutants such as ozone and acid precipitation often impact natural communities miles away from the source. For example, acid rain and acid fog destroy northern forests, lakes and streams. Many species have been seriously impacted by chemicals humans have thoughtlessly introduced to the environment. For example, more than a billion pounds of toxic chemicals were discharged directly into America's waters between 1990 and 1994, according to the Environmental Protection Agency's Toxics Release Inventory data, analyzed in the U.S. PIRG/ Environmental Working Group report "Dishonorable Discharge." Thirty million pounds of these chemicals were carcinogens, reproductive toxins or persistent toxic metals.

20 These chemicals (including mercury, lead, PCBs and DDT) kill species by poisoning them and interfering with their immune, nervous and reproductive systems. Indeed, many well known endangered species--like the bald eagle, peregrine falcon and brown pelican--were imperiled largely because of reproduction failures linked to the use of the pesticide DDT. Species such as the piping plover and bald eagle continue to be threatened by the use of pesticides, which either directly kills the birds or interferes with their reproductive ability.

Fire Suppression

21 The suppression of fire has caused the decline of many of our most endangered ecosystems--grasslands, savannas, barrens, and open forests. While a commonly held belief is that fire only destroys, in many ecosystems, the contrary is true. Fire is actually an integral part of many ecosystems, maintaining the ecosystem's natural vegetation. In fact, there are many plant species that require fire to trigger the release of their seeds. Fire also clears out the underbrush in forests, and the prevention of all forest fires actually leads to fires that burn hotter and longer due to the accumulation of underbrush. Thus the suppression of all fires leads to habitat destruction and degradation. If handled judiciously to protect life and property, some fires should be allowed to burn to reproduce the ecosystem's natural state.

Recreation

22 Recreation also takes a toll on wildlife and habitats. Probably the most harmful form of outdoor recreation is the use of off-road vehicles. These vehicles provide access to remote wilderness areas, resulting in the harassment of wildlife and an increase in legal and illegal hunting and trapping. They also result in the killing of wildlife (e.g., crushing of desert tortoises or the eggs of sea turtles and piping plover), acceleration of soil compaction and erosion, pollution of water and air, and destruction of vegetation.

Effects of Habitat Destruction and Degradation on Species
===

23 According to recent studies, habitat destruction is the leading cause of species endangerment, threatening 80 percent or more of federally listed species. Indeed, habitat destruction and degradation is at least part of the reason why more than 95 percent of listed species are imperiled. Studies show that logging affects approximately 14–17 percent of listed species, grazing impacts 19–22 percent, water development affects 29–33 percent, recreation affects 23–26 percent, and mining impacts 14–21 percent.

24 Habitat destruction and degradation is a factor in the decline of every category of species. For example, an examination of recovery plans for 98 plant species currently listed as threatened or endangered revealed that habitat destruction by human activities was the primary cause of endangerment of 83 percent of the species. For migrant bird populations, the decline of close to 40 percent is directly linked to habitat destruction. For amphibians, declining populations are linked to habitat destruction, introduction of exotic species, water pollution and ozone depletion.

25 Habitat destruction was also a contributing factor in the extinction of at least 73 percent of freshwater fish in North America and the leading threat to fish species considered threatened, endangered or of special concern. In California, habitat degradation (especially from water diversions for agriculture) and the introduction of non-indigenous plants are primarily responsible for the decline in native fish. In the Northwest, dams, logging, roads and grazing all contribute to the decline of salmon.

26 While certain human activities impact certain species more than others, the same can be said about certain activities' impacts on particular regions. In peninsular Florida, the Eastern Gulf Coast, and Central and Southern California, the primary cause of species endangerment is urban development. In the Arizona Basin and Colorado/Green River Plateau, the primary reason for declining species is grazing. In the East, intensive land use activities are the reason species are decreasing. More specifically, in Southern Appalachia, agriculture is the leading cause of imperilment while, in Florida, urban development, forest clearing and fire suppression are all causes of species decline. Finally, in the West, species are becoming endangered due to the collection of rare plants, surface mining, oil and gas development, the introduction of exotic species and water diversion.

Source: http://www.sierraclub.org/habitatloss.asp

Making Connections

1. Each reading discusses causes for the loss and endangerment of species. On which causes to do the authors agree?
2. Why is biodiversity important? Summarize how each author might answer this question.
3. What are the consequences and dangers of species loss? Summarize what you have learned from the readings in this unit.
4. Which of the three readings was easiest to read? Why? Which was most difficult? Why? Which was most interesting and engaging? Why?
5. Based on what you learned in this unit, what actions do you think should be taken to protect endangered species?

World Wide Web Activity

A Government Web Site

The bald eagle, a national symbol of the United States, was for many years listed as an endangered species by the U.S. Fish & Wildlife Service (FWS). The FWS now wants to take the bald eagle off the endangered species list. Should they?

To get more information, go to the Endangered Species Home Page, which you can access by going to http://www.fws.gov/ and clicking on the Endangered Species link. Find the following information on the Web site to decide whether the bald eagle is still endangered or not. (Note: If the FWS Endangered Species page is unavailable or does not contain the information you need, use a search engine to locate other sites that will help you complete this activity.)

1. How many bald eagles were there when the birds were put on the Endangered Species list? How many bald eagles are there today?
2. What main threats did the bald eagle face back then? Are these threats still a problem?
3. If the bald eagle is taken off the list, are there any other laws to protect them?

Write several paragraphs on why or why not the bald eagle should be taken off the Endangered Species list. Be sure to give several reasons to support your argument.

BUSINESS/COMPUTER TECHNOLOGY
COMPUTERS AND PRIVACY

D–1 TEXTBOOK EXCERPT: NO SECRETS: COMPUTERS AND PRIVACY

Beckman

1 Advanced technology has created new opportunities for America as a nation, but it has also created the possibility for new abuses of the individual American citizen. Adequate safeguards must always stand watch so that man remains master and never the victim of the computer.

—Richard Nixon, 37th president of the U.S., Feb. 23, 1974

2 Instant airline reservations, all-night automated banking, overnight mail, instant library searches—databases provide us with conveniences that were unthinkable a generation ago. But convenience isn't free. In the case of databases the price we pay is our privacy.

The Privacy Problem

3 We live in an information age, and data is one of the currencies of our time. Businesses and government agencies spend billions of dollars every year to collect and exchange information about you and me. More than 15,000 specialized marketing databases contain 2 billion consumer names, along with a surprising amount of personal information. The typical American consumer is on 25 marketing lists. Many of these lists are organized by characteristics like age, income, religion, political affiliation, and even sexual preference—and they're bought and sold every day.

4   Marketing databases are only the tip of the iceberg. Credit and banking information, tax records, health data, insurance records, political contributions, voter registration, credit

The Internal Revenue Service workers shown here enter taxpayers' personal financial information into massive computer databases. When you shop by phone, respond to a survey, or fill out a warranty card, it's likely that a clerk somewhere will enter that data into a computer.

card purchases, warranty registrations, magazine and newsletter subscriptions, phone calls, passport registration, airline reservations, automobile registrations, arrests, Internet explorations—they're all recorded in computers, and we have little or no control over what happens to most of those records once they're collected.

5   For most of us this data is out of sight and out of mind. But lives are changed because of these databases. Here are three representative stories:

6 • When members of Congress investigated ties between President Jimmy Carter's

brother Billy and the government of Libya, they produced a report that detailed, among other things, the exact time and location of phone calls placed by Billy Carter in three different states. The phone records, which revealed a great deal about Billy Carter's activities, were obtained from AT&T's massive network of data-collecting computers. Similar information is available on every phone company customer.

7 • When a credit bureau mistakenly placed a bankruptcy filing in the file of a St. Louis couple, banks responded by shutting off loans for their struggling construction business, forcing them into *real* bankruptcy. They sued but lost because credit bureaus are protected by law from financial responsibility for "honest" mistakes!

8 • A Los Angeles thief stole a wallet and used its contents to establish an artificial identity. When the thief was arrested for a robbery involving murder, the crime was recorded under the wallet owner's name in police databases. The legitimate owner of the wallet was arrested five times in the following 14 months and spend several days in jail before a protracted court battle resulted in the deletion of the record.

9 Privacy violations aren't new, and they don't always involve computers. The German Nazis, the Chinese Communists, and even Richard Nixon's 1972 campaign committee practiced surveillance without computers. But the privacy problem takes on a whole new dimension in the age of high-speed computers and databases. The same characteristics that make databases more efficient than other information storage methods—storage capacity, retrieval speed, organizational flexibility, and ease of distribution of information—also make them a threat to our privacy.

Big Brother and Big Business

10 If all records told the same tale, then the lie passed into history and became truth.

—*George Orwell, in* 1984

11 In George Orwell's *1984,* information about every citizen was stored in a massive database controlled by the ever-vigilant Big Brother. As it turns out, this kind of central computer is no longer necessary for producing computerized dossiers of private citizens. With networked computers it's easy to compile profiles by combining information from different database files. As long as the files share a single unique field, like Social Security number, **record matching** is trivial and quick. And when database information is combined, the whole is often far greater than the sum of its parts.

12 Sometimes the results are beneficial. Record matching is used by government enforcement agencies to locate criminals ranging from tax evaders to mass murderers. Because credit bureaus collect data about us, we can use credit cards to borrow money wherever we go. But these benefits come with at least three problems:

13 • *Data errors common.* A study of 1,500 reports from the three big credit bureaus found errors in 43 percent of the files.

14 • *Data can become nearly immortal.* Because files are commonly sold and copied, it's impossible to delete or correct erroneous records with absolute certainty.

15 • *Data isn't secure.* A *Business Week* reporter demonstrated this in 1989 by using his computer to obtain then Vice President Dan Quayle's credit report. Had he been a skilled criminal, he might have been able to *change* that report.

16 Protection against invasion of privacy is not explicitly guaranteed by the U.S. Constitution. Legal scholars agree that the **right to privacy**—freedom from interference in the private sphere of a person's affairs—is implied by other constitutional guarantees, although debates rage about what this means. Federal and state laws provide forms of privacy protection, but most of those laws were written years ago. Most European countries have had strong privacy protection laws for years. The 1998 European Data Protection

Directive guarantees that all countries in the European Union will guarantee a basic set of privacy rights to citizens—rights that go far beyond those of American citizens. The directive allows citizens to have access to all personal data, to know where that data originated, to have inaccurate data rectified, to seek recourse in the event of unlawful processing, and to withhold permission to use their data for direct marketing. The American legislature has refused to pass similar laws because of intense lobbying by business interests. When it comes to privacy violation in America, technology is far ahead of the law.

17   Database technology clearly poses a threat to personal privacy, but other information technologies amplify that threat. The rapid growth of networking technology, described in the next two chapters, makes it possible for personal data to be transmitted almost anywhere instantly. The Internet is particularly fertile ground for collecting personal information about individuals. Workplace monitoring technology, described in a later chapter, allows managers to know more than ever before about the work habits and patterns of workers. Smart cards and other intelligent personal devices, described in the last three chapters of this book, allow us to trade convenience for personal privacy.

18   Democracy depends on the free flow of information, but it also depends on the protection of individual rights. Maintaining a balance is not easy, especially when new information technologies are being developed at such a rapid pace. With information at our fingertips it's tempting to think that more information is the answer. But in the timeless words of populist philosopher Will Rogers, "It's not the things we don't know that get us into trouble, it's the things we do know that ain't so."

Source: Computer Confluence, pp. 203–206.

D–2: LOSING YOUR GOOD NAME ONLINE

Jared Sandberg

1   After leasing two high-end sport utility vehicles in just two days last spring, Kenneth Morse was finally stopped by a third dealership on the third day. Noting Morris's suspicious SUV-buying spree through a credit check, the New Jersey Mercedes dealer said no deal. It was a good thing, because the real Kenneth Morse was more than 250 miles away, pushing papers at his desk in upstate New York. With just his name and Social Security number, someone had hijacked Morse's credit-worthiness and was joy riding it for all it was worth. The cops, who weren't much help, knew enough to suspect he had given out his Social Security number somewhere online. The suspect was ultimately caught, and Morse's name was cleared—as best as he can tell. He still doesn't know exactly how it all happened. And he still drives his old Camry, a rusty beater with 160,000 miles.

2   Morse was a victim of the worst kind of privacy violation—the theft of his identity. This alarming prospect is poised to be an increasingly common nightmare as the tendrils of the Internet take root ever deeper in our daily lives. All is takes is your name and your Social Security number, and your identity can be plucked from you easier than a coat from a closet. With Social Security numbers being used as account identifiers by financial-service firms, healthcare companies and motor-vehicle departments—all of which are going online—it is becoming easier for impostors to put on your happy face. Once it's stolen, count on bureaucratic torture: a seemingly endless telephone and letter-writing campaign trying to atone for your alter ego's sins. Peter Neumann of the R&D firm SRI International calls identity theft the "hidden downside of computing."

3   For crooks, however, it's payday. The Internet hasn't caused the problem—people

still rummage through dumpsters to reconstruct personal details from trash—but the Web has allowed criminals to lock onto marriage licenses, property records and motor-vehicle information with a mouse-click. "Before, you had to go to the county courthouse to find that information," says Beth Grossman, identity-theft program manager (yes, there is such a person) at the Federal Trade Commission. "Not anymore." Computers are powerful enough now to pry open widely used software safeguards, compounding the problem.

4   The advent of e-commerce is, however inadvertently, endangering privacy. Companies have long boasted about the efficiency, convenience and personalized service that distinguish commerce online. But that promise hinges on the merchants' intimate knowledge of their customers' tastes and behavior. For starters, they know who their customers are, where they live and their credit-card numbers. And the more someone buys, the more the seller finds out about him: likes bourbon and trash novels; sends someone not his wife flowers every Wednesday.

5   Any Web-site operator can reconstruct a visitor's every move on his site: what pages he viewed, what information he entered and the Internet service he uses. Privacy advocates warn that most online companies won't fight subpoenas seeking access to those logs. Security guru Richard Smith, founder of Phar Lap Software, likens Web sites to VCRs "constantly recording when you come in, who you talked to and maybe what you talked about."

6   Getting your identity stolen online isn't as unusual as you might think. Three weeks ago John Aravosis, a Washington, D.C., Internet consultant, logged onto AOL and found an e-mail warning that his account was involved in criminal activity in certain chat rooms. Realizing someone had been logging into his account, he wanted to make sure AOL knew it wasn't him in the event any records became public. He began a weeklong lobbying effort, calling AOL, privacy groups and a senator's office. Ultimately, he found out that the "criminal" activity was software piracy, and

he's still waiting for a letter from AOL that clears his name.

7   Aravosis says he never gave out his password, nor did he download a malicious program, but AOL staffers suspect he did. Using AOL's Instant Messenger service, online cons can send a user a missive posing as an AOL employee who needs the user's password for some reason or another. "We are experiencing difficulties with our records . . . I need you to verify your logon password to me to that I can validate you as a user." If you don't fall for that ploy, you could become the unwitting victim of a "Trojan horse" program—an innocuously named e-mail attachment that stores your password when you open it. The program then e-mails the information to the perp.

8   So you have to be digitally vigilant. Guard your Social Security number as if it were the master key to your life, which it is. And plead with your insurance company and financial institution not to use the number as your account ID (good luck).

9   Paranoid, maybe, but it could have saved William Bergau. In May 1998 the 35-year-old college recruiter and his wife had their wallets stolen from their car and returned the next day. But the thief kept checks and Bergau's Social Security card, which he used to obtain a fraudulent driver's license by telling the DMV he had lost the original. He successfully purchased goods and withdrew money. But the real problem hit Bergau when the pretender started getting arrested, under Bergau's name, for drunken driving, marijuana possession and grand-theft auto. A year after the theft, when Bergau was on vacation with his wife and kids in Arizona, thousands of miles from home, he was pulled over for speeding. "His" record—for driving under the influence—came up, and the cop wanted to lock him up. "The kids are in the van thinking Daddy's going to jail," he says. But Bergau explained the theft of his identity and, after more letters and calls, he finally got off the hook. He wasn't ensnared online, but the Internet makes his predicament more imaginable for the rest of us.

10   Now Bergau carries around a series of letters from agencies and the police explaining

his plight. But the notes give him little comfort: "I'm going to spend my whole life picking up the pieces of this guy's dirty work." For him—and anybody whose identity is lifted in cyberspace—it's hard to see if he'll ever truly get his name back.

Source: Newsweek, September 20, 1999.

D–3: FOOD FOR THOUGHT ABOUT INTERNET ADVERTISING

Jake Kirchner

1 Anyone who buys groceries from a reasonably modern market has experienced this bit of personalized advertising. You pay for your milk, eggs, Minute Maid orange juice, and the rest of your foodstuffs, and when you get home you find in the bag a coupon for Tropicana juice that says something like, "Did you know that Tropicana has 25 percent more vitamin C than Minute Maid? Use this coupon to get 50 cents off your next half-gallon of Tropicana Pure Premium."

2 Of course Tropicana knows that the coupon is going to a Minute Maid buyer, because that information was scanned into the store's checkout system, which spit out the coupon when it printed your register receipt and credit card slip. Tropicana can afford to offer you a nice rebate, because the company has saved a ton of money by being able to target you, a prime potential customer, without mailing millions of coupons to people who might never drink orange juice.

3 Pretty nifty use of technology. And pretty harmless. Or maybe not. Think of the possibilities if some database somewhere were to track everything you buy. It's unlikely any single database—other than your credit card company—will have significant amounts of information about your purchases. But it's not farfetched to imagine databases being linked across the Internet for a detailed profile of your buying preferences.

4 Even today there are companies that can deliver targeted ads to your e-mail address or, in real time, to your Web browser based on the sites you're visiting. Privacy and security on the Web are hot topics. Many parties are working to secure Web transactions, and there are multiple schemes for limiting the personal information we pass along. But not as much thought is being given to the legitimate but ancillary uses of the data that we volunteer or that we inadvertently provide by buying something online.

5 Advertisers are willing to pay big bucks for such buyer access. According to International Data Corp., the business transacted over the Web is expected to grow from $2.6 billion last year to over $220 billion during 2001.

6 You can't buy on the Web without revealing personal info. You don't just buy airline tickets; you specify the person you're buying them for. You don't just buy flowers; you specify the recipient and the occasion. When you buy books, videos, and CDs, you reveal a great deal about your preferences—far more than you realize, because that information can be combined with census-type data to build a very accurate profile.

7 It's one thing to have BarnesandNoble.com alert you to the next thriller in a series you've been following, but think how you'll feel when Department store.com e-mails you a message that says, "Hey, big spender, it's your anniversary. The little lady will appreciate the diamond pin that's 20 percent off this month. After the toaster oven you got her last year, don't you think she deserves it? And don't make us send her an e-mail about the pearl earrings you had us deliver to that young thing in your accounting department!"

You think Internet ads are annoying now? Wait till they start getting personal!

Source: PC Magazine, November 18, 1997.

Making Connections

1. Explain how computers have created an invasion of privacy. Give several examples.
2. Explain both the benefits and risks of online shopping.
3. What solutions, if any, did the authors suggest?
4. Which reading was most informative and detailed? Why?
5. What further information would you need in order to write a paper or give an oral presentation on the topic of computer privacy?

World Wide Web Activity

An Organizational Web Site

Who should be able to read your medical records? Should a future employer have access to them? Should an insurance company? Should your bank be able to access your records? Why or why not?

Go to the American Civil Liberties Union (ACLU) page on Privacy at http://www.aclu.org/privacy/ to get more ideas about this topic. Also visit their page on Workplace Rights by following the related links. The ACLU page also contains remote links to other organizational sites on this topic through the Other Resources link. (Note: If the ACLU Privacy page is unavailable or does not contain the information you need, use a search engine to locate other sites that will help you complete this activity.)

Here are two questions to get you started:

1. What is the ACLU's general stance on computers and privacy? Which amendment of the Bill of Rights does this organization base their position on? Do you agree with their position?
2. What are some examples of how employers and/or insurance companies use the medical information they find in ways the ACLU considers unethical? Are there any ethical uses you can think of?

Discuss your findings with a group of classmates.

HUMANITIES/LITERATURE
MULTICULTURAL IDENTITY

E–1 POEM: CHILD OF THE AMERICAS

Aurora Morales

> I am a child of the Americas,
> A light-skinned Mestiza of the Caribbean,
> A child of many diaspora, born into this continent
> At a crossroads.

5
> I am a Caribbean, island grown,
> Spanish is in my flesh, ripples from my tongue,
> Lodges in my hips: the language of garlic and mangoes,
> The singing in my poetry, the flying gestures of my hands.
> I am of Latinoamerica, rooted in the history of my continent
10
> I speak from that body.

> I am not African, Africa is in me,
> But I cannot return.
> I am not Taina, Taino is in me,
> But there is no way back.
15
> I am not European, Europe lives in me,
> But I have no home there.

> I am new. History made me.
> My first language was Spanglish.
> I was born at the crossroads,
20
> And I am whole.

Source: http://www.cs.tufts.edu/~wvargus/poems.html

Search results for: "On Being Blackanese"

E-2: On Being Blackanese

Mitzi Uehara-Carter

1 "Umm . . . Excuse me. Where are you from?"

2 "I'm from Houston, Texas."

3 "Oh . . . but your parents, where are they from?"

4 (Hmm. Should I continue to play stupid or just tell them.) "My dad is from Houston, and my mom is from Okinawa, Japan."

5 "And your dad is black then?"

6 "Yup."

7 "So do you speak Japanese?"

8 "Some."

9 "Wow. Say something."

10 This is not a rare conversation. I cannot count the number of times I've pulled this script to rehearse with random people who have accosted me in the past. "That's so exotic, so cool that you're mixed." It's not that these questions or comments bother me or that I am offended by their bluntness. I think it's more of the attitudes of bewilderment and the exoticism of my being and even the slight bossiness to do something "exotic" that annoy me. I think I am also annoyed because I am still exploring what it means to be both Japanese and Black and still have difficulty trying to express what that means to others.

11 In many ways and for many years I have grappled with the idea of being a product of two cultures brought together by an unwanted colonization of American military bases on my mother's homeland of Okinawa. Author of "In the Realm of a Dying Emperor," Norma Field expressed these sentiments more clearly than I ever could. "Many years into my growing up, I thought I had understood the awkward piquancy of biracial children with the formulation, they are nothing if not the embodiment of sex itself; now, I

modify it to, the biracial offspring of war are at once more offensive and intriguing because they bear the imprint of sex as domination." Of course this is not how I feel about myself all the time, but rather it is the invisible bug that itches under my skin every now and then. It itches when I read about Okinawan girls being raped by U.S. Servicemen, when I see mail order bride ads, when I notice the high divorce or separation rate among Asian women and GI's who were married a few years after WWII, when I see the half-way hidden looks of disgust at my mother by other Japanese women when I walk by her side as a daughter. Our bodies, our presence, our reality is a nuisance to some because we defy a definite and demarcated set of boundaries because they don't know how to include us or exclude us. We are blackanese, hapas, eurasians, multiracial.

12 My mother has been the center of jokes and derogatory comments since my older sister was born. She was the one who took my sister by the hand and led her through the streets of Bangkok and Okinawa as eyes stared and people gathered to talk about the sambo baby. She was the one who took all my siblings to the grocery stores, the malls, the park, school, Burger King, hospitals, church. In each of these public arenas we were stared at either in fascination because we were a new "sight" or stared at with a look of disgust or both. Nigga-chink, Black-Jap, Black-Japanese mutt. The neighborhood kids, friends, and adults labeled my siblings and me with these terms especially after they recognized that my mother was completely intent on making us learn about Okinawan culture. On New Year's Day, we had black eyed peas and mochi. We cleaned the house to start the year fresh and clean. "Don't laugh with your mouth too wide and show yo teeth too much," my mom would always tell us. "Be like a woman." I had not realized that I covered my mouth each time I laughed until someone pointed it out in my freshman year in college. When we disobeyed my mother's rule or screamed, we were being too "American." If I ever left the house with rollers in my hair, my mom would say I shouldn't do American things. "Agijibiyo . . . Where you learn this from? You are Okinawan too. Dame desuyo. Don't talk so much like Americans; listen first." There were several other cultural traits and values that I had inevitably inherited (and cherish) being raised by a Japanese mother.

13 Growing up in an all black neighborhood and attending predominately Black and Latino schools until college influenced my identity also. I was definitely not accepted in the Japanese circles as Japanese for several reasons, but that introduces another subject on acceptance into Japanese communities. Now this is not to say that the Black community I associated with embraced me as Blackanese, even though I think it is more accepting of multiracial people than probably any other group (because of the one-drop rule, etc.). There is still an exclusion for those who wish to encompass all parts of their her-

itage with equal weight, and there is also a subtle push to identify more with one's black heritage than the other part because "society won't see you as mixed or Japanese but BLACK." I can't count the number of times I have heard this argument. What I do know is that no society can tell me that I am more of one culture than another because of the way someone else defines me. I am Blackanese--a mixture of the two in ways that cannot be divided. My body and mentality is not split down the middle where half is black and the other half is Japanese. I have taken the aspects of both worlds to create my own worldview and identity. Like Anna Vale said in Itabari Njeri's article "Sushi and Grits," my mother raised me the best way she knew how, "to be a good Japanese daughter."

14 My father on the other hand never constantly sat down to "teach" us about being Black. We were surrounded by Blackness and lived it. He was always tired when he came home from work. He'd sit back in his sofa and blast his jazz. My mom would be in the kitchen with her little tape player listening to her Japanese and Okinawan tapes my aunt sent every other month from California. My siblings and I would stay at my grandmother's house once in a while (she cooked the best collard greens), and when my mom came to pick us up she'd teach her how to cook a southern meal for my father. Our meals were somewhat of an indicator of how much my mom held onto her traditions. My father would make his requests for chicken, steak or okra and my mom had learned to cook these things, but we always had Japanese rice on the side with nori and tofu and fishcake with these really noisome beans that are supposed to be good for you (according to my mom. I swear she knows what every Japanese magazine has to say about food and health.) It was my mother who told us that we would be discriminated against because of our color, and it was my Japanese mother to whom we ran when we were called niggers at the public swimming pool in Houston. To say to this woman, "Mom, we are just black" would be a disrespectful slap in the face. The woman who raised us and cried for years from her family's coldness and rejection because of her decision to marry interracially, cried when my father's sister wouldn't let her be a part of the family picture because she was a "Jap." This woman who happens to be my mother will never hear "Mom, I'm just Black" from my mouth because I'm not and no person-- society or government--will force me to do that and deny my reality and my being, no matter how offensive I am to their country or how much of a nuisance I am to their cause. I am Blackanese.

Source: http://www.webcom.com/~intvoice/mitzi.html

E–3: KIPLING AND I

Jesús Colón

1 Sometimes I pass Debevoise Place at the corner of Willoughby Street . . . I look at the old wooden house, gray and ancient, the house where I used to live some forty years ago . . .

2 My room was on the second floor at the corner. On hot summer nights I would sit at the window reading by the electric light from the street lamp which was almost at a level with the windowsill.

3 It was nice to come home late during the winter, look for some scrap of old newspaper, some bits of wood and a few chunks of coal, and start a sparkling fire in the chunky four-legged coal stove. I would be rewarded with an intimate warmth as little by little the pigmy stove became alive puffing out its sides, hot and red, like the crimson cheeks of a Santa Claus.

4 My few books were in a soap box nailed to the wall. But my most prized possession in those days was a poem I had bought in a five-and-ten-cent store on Fulton Street. (I wonder what has become of these poems, maxims and sayings of wise men that they used to sell at the five-and-ten-cent stores?) The poem was printed on gold paper and mounted in a gilded frame ready to be hung in a conspicuous place in the house. I bought one of those fancy silken picture cords finishing in a rosette to match the color of the frame.

5 I was seventeen. This poem to me than seemed to summarize, in one poetical nutshell, the wisdom of all the sages that ever lived. It was what I was looking for, something to guide myself by, a way of life, a compendium of the wise, the true and the beautiful. All I had to do was to live according to the counsel of the poem and follow its instructions and I would be a perfect man—the useful, the good, the true human being. I was very happy that day, forty years ago.

6 The poem had to have the most prominent place in the room. Where could I hang it? I decided that the best place for the poem was on the wall right by the entrance to the room. No one coming in and out would miss it. Perhaps someone would be interested enough to read it and drink the profound waters of its message . . .

7 Every morning as I prepared to leave, I stood in front of the poem and read it over and over again, sometimes half a dozen times. I let the sonorous music of the verse carry me away. I brought with me a handwritten copy as I stepped out every morning looking for work, repeating verses and stanzas from memory until the whole poem came to be part of me. Other days my lips kept repeating a single verse of the poem at intervals throughout the day.

8 In the subways I loved to compete with the shrill noises of the many wheels below by chanting the lines of the poem. People stared at me moving my lips as though I were in a trance. I looked back with pity. They were not so fortunate as I who had as a guide to direct my life a great poem to make me wise, useful and happy.

9 And I chanted:

If you can keep your head when all about you
Are losing theirs and blaming it on you . .

If you can wait and not be tired by waiting,
  Or being lied about, don't deal in lies,
Or being hated don't give way to hating . . .

If you can make one heap of all your winnings;
  And risk it on one turn of pitch-and-toss,
And lose, and start again at your beginnings . . .

10 "If—," by Kipling, was the poem. At seventeen, my evening prayer and my first morning thought. I repeated it every day with the resolution to live up to the very last line of that poem.

11 I would visit the government employment office on Jay Street. The conversations among the Puerto Ricans on the large wooden benches in the employment office were always on the same subject. How to find a decent place to live. How they would not rent to Negroes or Puerto Ricans. How Negroes and Puerto Ricans were given the pink slips first at work.

12   From the employment office I would call door to door at the piers, factories and storage houses in the streets under the Brooklyn and Manhattan bridges. "Sorry, nothing today." It seemed to me that that "today" was a continuation and combination of all the yesterdays, todays and tomorrows.

13   From the factories I would go to the restaurants, looking for a job as a porter or dishwasher. At least I would eat and be warm in a kitchen.

14   "Sorry" . . . "Sorry" . . .

15   Sometimes I was hired at ten dollars a week, ten hours a day including Sundays and holidays. One day off during the week. My work was that of three men: dishwasher, porter, busboy. And to clear the sidewalk of snow and slush "when you have nothing else to do." I was to be appropriately humble and grateful not only to the owner but to everybody else in the place.

16   If I rebelled at insults or at a pointed innuendo or just the inhuman amount of work, I was unceremoniously thrown out and told to come "next week for your pay." "Next week" meant weeks of calling for the paltry dollars owed me. The owners relished this "next week."

17   I clung to my poem as to a faith. Like a potent amulet, my precious poem was clenched in the fist of my right hand inside my secondhand overcoat. Again and again I declaimed aloud a few precious lines when discouragement and disillusionment threatened to overwhelm me.

If you can force your heart and nerve and sinew
  To serve your turn long after they are gone . . .

18   The weeks of unemployment and hard knocks turned into months. I continued to find two or three days of work here and there. And I continued to be thrown out when I rebelled at the ill treatment, overwork and insults. I kept pounding the streets looking for a place where they would treat me half decently, where my devotion to work and faith in Kipling's poem would be appreciated. I remember the worn-out shoes I bought in a secondhand store on Myrtle Avenue at the corner of Adams Street. The round holes in the soles that I tried to cover with pieces of carton were no match for the frigid knives of the unrelenting snow.

19   One night I returned late after a long day of looking for work. I was hungry. My room was dark and cold. I wanted to warm my numb body. I lit a match and began looking for some scraps of wood and a piece of paper to start a fire. I searched all over the floor. No wood, no paper. As I stood up, the glimmering flicker of the dying match was reflected in the glass surface of the framed poem. I unhooked the poem from the wall. I reflected for a minute, a minute that felt like an eternity. I took the frame apart, placing the square glass upon the small table. I tore the gold paper on which the poem was printed, threw its pieces inside the stove and, placing the small bits of wood from the frame on top of the paper, I lit it, adding soft and hard coal as the fire began to gain strength and brightness.

I watched how the lines of the poem withered into ashes inside the small stove.

Source: A Puerto Rican in New York

Making Connections

1. What problems, frustrations, and feelings do any of the authors share?
2. This unit contains a poem, as essay, and a short story. Which genre (method of expression) did you find most effective? That is, which most effectively explained to you the issue of multicultural identity?
3. How would you contrast Colón's experiences with those of Morales?
4. Compare Uehara-Carter's attitude on interracism with that of Morales.
5. If you could interview each of the authors, what questions would you ask each?

World Wide Web Activity

An Online Newsjournal

The essay "On Being Blackanese" was printed on the Interracial Voice newsjournal Web site, whose URL is http://www.webcom.com/~intvoice/. Go to the site and respond to the following questions in writing.

1. What is the purpose of this newsjournal? Who publishes it? Where did you find this information?
2. Describe the general content of each of the following parts of the site: Point 2 Point, Research, Media, Essays, Poems.
3. Who are the intended readers of Interracial Voice? What information did you gather from the site that supports your view?
4. How useful would this site be if you were researching a topic for your literature class on Latino-American poetry from the 1970s? How do you know?

SUCCESS
Workshops

Stay Healthy and Relaxed

Use Computers as a Learning Tool

Make Effective Oral Presentations

Work with Your Classmates

STAY HEALTHY AND RELAXED

Why?

Learning to handle the many demands of college life can be stressful, especially if you are trying to raise a family or work a job at the same time. If you stay healthy and learn to manage stress, you will find that your life becomes more enjoyable and fun.

Think about Your General Health

1. How much sleep do you usually get each night? _____

2. How much time do you spend exercising each week? _____

3. How often do you eat regular, healthy meals? _____

4. Do you smoke or drink alcohol? If so, how much? _____

Think about Your Stress Level

5. Do you spend most of your time either studying or worrying about not studying? _____

6. Have you ever noticed that you get sick when you can least afford it? _____

7. Do you have a tendency to skip meals, eat junk food, stay up late, or skip exercise when you are overworked? _____

8. Do you often feel impatient or irritable without knowing why? _____

9. Do you feel stressed-out? _____

Focus on the elements of this workshop that will help you the most in moving toward a healthier, more relaxed lifestyle.

Reflecting . . .
Do Your Habits Work for You?

Regardless of how busy you are, be sure to:

Get enough sleep. The amount of sleep a person needs is highly individual. Discover how much you need by noticing patterns. For several weeks, analyze how well your day went and consider how much sleep you had the night before. Then adjust your schedule to make sure you get the right amount of sleep for you each night.

Get regular exercise. Exercising three times a week for about 15 minutes each time is a good way to get

420

started on a regular fitness program. Whenever you find yourself getting tense, for example when your shoulders or neck start tensing, take a few minutes immediately to stretch or go for a brief walk.

Eat regular, healthy meals. Give yourself time to eat three meals a day. For snacks in between, eat fruit or vegetables. Avoid a diet heavy in fats, and try to eat balanced meals rather than junk food.

Reduce or eliminate smoking and drinking alcohol. Check with a counselor at the student health center for a program that will help you.

Learn to say "No" to unreasonable requests from friends and family. Explain your schedule to your family, and make sure they understand your academic goals. Then when you need to turn down unreasonable requests, they will understand why.

Take breaks. Constantly pushing yourself compounds stress. Slow down and do nothing for a brief period, even if just for five minutes. If you practice deep breathing on your breaks, you will relax even more. Breathe in through your nose; then breathe out completely through your mouth.

Planning . . .
How Can You Improve Your Habits?

Examine your weekly schedule of classes, study, work, and family activities. Look for short time periods that you could use for exercise, better meals, and breaks. Look for ways to increase the amount of sleep you're getting, if that's an issue. Make a plan for improving your health and relaxation by writing the necessary changes into your schedule.

Changing . . .
Does Your Thinking Help You?

When you feel as if you don't have enough time in your day to get everything done, don't think negatively—"I'll never be able to get this all done!" This leads to unnecessary stress. Instead think positively— "It's going to feel great to accomplish this!"

▲ Visualize success. Imagine yourself getting everything done in an orderly, systematic way.

▲ Focus on the benefits of completing each task. How will completing each task help you or others?

▲ Develop a plan or schedule that will allow you to get everything done (refer to Chapter 1 for tips on time management).

Discovering . . .
Using Your Senses for Success

Success follows from working productively. Keeping your senses trained on the world around you, rather than on your personal thoughts, can help you focus on the task at hand and increase your productivity. Use this brief exercise to refocus your senses when you take a break from your work.

Stand up and move around your study area for three to five minutes. Look closely at the colors, shapes, and images in the room. As you are looking, listen carefully for all the sounds that you can hear: traffic sounds, music playing, appliances humming, people talking. While looking and listening, notice what you can feel around you: touch different objects, notice the air temperature, feel the floor under your feet. Examine what you are seeing, hearing, and feeling as if the sights, sounds, and sensations are all new to you.

When you return to your work, you will find that you are more able to put aside unrelated thoughts and complete your task more efficiently. During long study periods, repeat this exercise every 50 minutes and notice how much more you can accomplish!

Reflecting . . .
Every Week or Two, Check Again

▲ Am I getting enough sleep?

▲ Am I getting regular exercise?

▲ Am I eating regular, healthy meals?

▲ Am I taking brief breaks when I start to feel stressed?

▲ Am I focusing my senses on success?

▲ Am I focusing on the benefits of completing each task?

▲ Is my schedule allowing me to get everything done?

USE COMPUTERS AS A LEARNING TOOL

We live in an electronic age. If you have not already done so, it is time to move your study methods into the electronic age as well. If you need assistance in learning how to use a computer, check to see if your campus offers any courses—learning computer skills is one of the best investments you can make for school and work. Here are a few suggestions for how to use computers as a learning tool.

Use Word Processing to Write Papers

If you have ever used a typewriter, you know how frustrating it can be to finish typing a page only to discover one or two small errors that should have been corrected. Using a word processing program on a computer can save you hours of retyping. Word processors also make it easy to revise your ideas and your paper's organization as many times as you need to get it right. Once you have the basics down, you can also produce a much more professional looking paper by learning to take advantage of different typefaces and graphics.

Use Word Processing to Organize Your Lecture Notes

Lecture notes are, of course, recorded by hand as you listen to the lecture. Typing your notes into the computer is a means of editing and review. Once your notes are entered, you can rearrange and reorganize them as suggested below.

Use Word Processing to Organize Notes from Textbook Reading

As you take notes from reading, your notes tend to follow the organization of the text. That is, the order of ideas in your notes parallels the order of ideas presented in the text. At times, it is useful to reorganize and rearrange your notes. For example, you may want to pull together information on a certain topic that is spread throughout one or more chapters. Or, you may want to combine your lecture notes and your text notes.

The word processing program's cut-and-paste functions enable you to rearrange and reorganize notes or outlines easily without retyping. You must type your notes initially, but you can edit and review them as you type.

A Few Questions to Ask . . .
If You've Never Used Word Processing

Once you have learned how to turn on the computer, open the word processing program, and insert a floppy disk into the disk drive, there are some basic skills you must learn in order to use a word processor. (The answers will be slightly different depending on which program you are using.)

1. How do I open a new file? How do I open a file I already created?

2. How do I name a file? How long can the file name be?

3. How do I set the margins so the page will print correctly once I'm finished?

4. How do I choose the type size (how big the letters will look on the screen and on the page)?

5. How do I select single-spacing or double-spacing?

6. How do I indent to start a new paragraph?

7. How do I move text from one place in the document to another?

8. How do I delete text?

9. How do I underline, boldface, or italicize part of the text?

10. How do I save and close the file when I'm finished?

You can often learn these basic functions in a single workshop on using a word processor.

WORK WiTH YOUR CLASSMATES

Why?

▲ You can learn from other students. By discovering how other students approach a task or solve a problem, you sharpen your own thinking.

▲ It may be required. Instructors may assign group projects or require you to participate in group activities.

▲ It can be fun. You'll meet new people and form new friendships.

▲ It is good practice. You will have to work cooperatively with coworkers on the job, so begin polishing your collaborative skills now.

Reflecting . . .
Your Experiences as a Group Member

Most students have had some experience in working with a group, whether at school or at work. Share one of your experiences with a few other classmates. Figure out what made the group successful or unsuccessful in completing its task. What could you have done to help the group work together more effectively? Reflect on this question again once you have read this workshop.

Thinking Ahead . . .
How to Make It Work

1. Select alert, energetic classmates if you are permitted to choose group members.

2. Be an active, responsible participant. Accept your share of the work and expect others to do the same. Approach the activity with a serious attitude, rather than joking or complaining about the assignment. This will establish a serious tone and cut down on wasted time.

3. Because organization and direction are essential for productivity, every group needs a leader. Unless some other competent group member immediately assumes leadership, take a leadership role. Leadership may require more work, but you will be in control. (Remember, too, that leadership roles are valuable experiences for your career.) As the group's leader, you will need to direct the group in analyzing the assignment, organizing a plan of action, distributing work assignments, planning, and (in long-term projects), establishing deadlines.

4. Suggest that specific tasks be assigned to each group member and that the group agrees upon task deadlines.

5. Take advantage of individual strengths and weaknesses. For instance, a person who seems indifferent or is easily distracted should not be assigned the task of recording the group's findings. The most organized, outgoing member might be assigned the task of making an oral report to the class.

Problem Solving . . .
What to Do If It Doesn't Work

If a Group Member . . .	You May Want to Say . . .
hasn't begun to do the work she's been assigned	"You've been given a difficult part of the project. How can we help you get started?"
complains about the workload	"We all seem to have different amounts of work to do. Is there some way we might lessen your workload?"
has missed meetings	"To ensure that we all meet regularly, would it be helpful if I called everyone the night before to confirm the day and time?"
is uncommunicative and doesn't share information	"Since we are all working from different angles, let's each make an outline of what we've done so far, so we can plan how to proceed from here."

In This Case You Could . . .

| seems to be making you or other members do all the work. | Make up a chart with each member's responsibilities before the meeting. Give each member a copy and ask,

"Is there any part of your assignment that you have questions or concerns about? Would anyone like to change his or her completion date?" Be sure to get an answer from each member. |

MAKE EFFECTIVE ORAL PRESENTATIONS

Everyone has had experience listening to speakers, whether in a classroom, at a religious service, at a rally, or on radio or television. We have all heard speakers who are dynamic and exciting and those who are dull and lifeless. Write a list of characteristics of effective and ineffective speakers.

Effective	**Ineffective**
_____	_____
_____	_____
_____	_____
_____	_____
_____	_____

How To Make Strong Presentations

Oral presentations may be done in groups or individually. Groups may be asked to report their finds, summarize their research, or describe a process or procedure. Individual presentations are often summaries of research papers, reviews or critiques, or interpretations of literary or artistic works. Use the following suggestions to make effective oral presentations.

1. *Understand the purpose of the assignment.* Analyze the assignment carefully before beginning to work. Is the presentation intended to be informative? Are you to summarize, evaluate, or criticize?

2. *Research your topic thoroughly and organize your ideas.* Remember that listeners can grasp only one idea at a time, and make sure you organize your ideas so that one point flows naturally to the next.

3. *Prepare outline notes.* Use index cards (either 3-by-5-inch or 5-by-8-inch) to record only key words and phrases.

4. *Consider the use of visual aids.* Depending on the type of assignment as well as on your topic, diagrams, photographs, or demonstrations may be appropriate and effective in maintaining audience interest.

5. *Anticipate questions your audience may ask.* Review and revise your notes to include answers.

6. *Practice delivery.* This will build your confidence and help you overcome nervousness. First, practice your presentation aloud several times by yourself. Time yourself to be sure you are within any limits. Then practice in front of friends and ask for criticism. Finally, tape-record or video-tape your presentation. Play it back, looking for ways to improve.

7. *Deliver your presentation as effectively as possible.* Engage your audience's interest by maintaining eye contact; look directly at other students as you speak. Make a deliberate effort to speak slowly; when you are nervous, your speech tends to speed up. Be enthusiastic and energetic.

What If . . . Questions and Answers

Questions

What if I get nervous?

Answers

▲ Be sure to practice delivering your speech several times before you actually make your presentation in front of the class. Practice speaking slowly and distinctly, taking deep breaths and pausing.

▲ Visualize yourself giving your presentation in a relaxed manner to a receptive audience.

▲ Get excited about your topic. Focus on the points you want to make, and you won't have time to be nervous. Excitement is contagious; the more interested you are in your topic, the more involved your audience will become.

Questions	Answers
What if, during my presentation, the instructor and/or the class starts to show signs of boredom?	▲ Change the tone or pitch of your voice.
	▲ Maintain your audience's interest by engaging them in the presentation. Pose a question, for example.
	▲ Make eye contact with restless individuals.
What if I "go blank"?	▲ Write notes on index cards. If you suddenly "go blank," all you need to do is look at your notes.
	▲ Ask whether there are any questions. Even if there aren't, this pause will give you time to think about what to say next.

Remember . . .
Preparation Is the Key

▲ Begin planning your presentation as soon as it is assigned.

▲ Allow plenty of time to use your library and Internet resources if necessary to learn about your topic.

▲ If your first practice presentation seems difficult to follow, reorganize your ideas.

▲ Make sure your note cards list only the most important points, and make sure your notes are large enough to be readable quickly.

▲ If you will use visual aids, practice with them every time you practice your presentation.

APPENDIX

Preparing and Writing Research Papers

TIPS FOR GETTING STARTED

In assigning a research paper, your instructor is asking you to learn about a topic and then to organize and summarize what you have learned. Completing a research paper involves much more than just writing. It involves selecting a topic, locating appropriate sources of information, reading, taking notes, and organizing the information. In fact, writing is actually the final step in the process of acquiring and organizing information for a research paper.

The first college research paper you do is always the most difficult, because you are learning how to do the paper while doing it. Once you have mastered the techniques for writing research papers, later ones will be much easier and less time-consuming. Here are a few tips to help you get started:

1. Find out how important the research paper is by finding out how heavily the paper counts in your final grade. This information will help you determine how much time and effort you should put into the paper.

2. Get an early start. Even if the paper is not due until the end of the term, start working on it as soon as possible. Starting early may enable you to produce a good paper rather than a barely acceptable one. Also, if you have not done a research before, you will need time to become familiar with the process.

   Starting early has several other advantages. You will find books and references readily available in the library, whereas if you wait until everyone is working on papers, popular sources will be in use or checked out by other students. Starting early also gives you time to acquire information you may need from other libraries through interlibrary loan services. Finally, an early start allows you time to think, to organize, and even to make mistakes and correct them.

3. Ask your instructor for advice. If you have trouble, ask for help. Through their experience with the subject matter, instructors are often able to suggest alternative approaches to the topic, recommend a particular reference, or suggest a different organization. When you go to see your instructor, take your notes, outlines, and rough drafts.

STEPS IN WRITING A RESEARCH PAPER

There are eight steps in writing a research paper. If you follow each step, however, you will discover that you are carefully led through a fairly routine process of focusing your paper, collecting information, and writing the paper. The steps are as follows.

1. Narrow and focus your topic.
2. Locate and review appropriate sources of information.
3. Write a tentative thesis statement.
4. Collect information.
5. Form an outline.
6. Write and revise.
7. Prepare the final copy.
8. Prepare the list of references.

Step 1: Narrow and Focus Your Topic

Choosing and narrowing your topic are critical to producing a good paper. If you begin with an unmanageable topic, then regardless of how hard you work, you will be unable to produce an acceptable paper. Also, your task is much easier if you choose a manageable topic—one for which information is readily accessible and understandable.

The most important consideration in selecting a topic is to choose one that is neither too broad nor too narrow. If you choose a topic that is too broad, then it will be impossible for you to cover all its aspects adequately. On the other hand, if it is too specific, then you may have difficulty finding enough to write about. Most students have a tendency to select a topic that is too general.

Suppose you are taking a course in ecology and the environment and you have been assigned a 15-page research paper. Your instructor will allow you to choose any topic related to the course of study. You have always been interested in environmental pollution and decide to do your research paper on this subject. Because there are many causes of pollution, many types of pollution, and many effects of pollution, both immediate and long-term, you realize that the general topic of environmental pollution is much too broad. To narrow or limit this topic, you might choose one type of pollution—such as water pollution—and then decide to research its causes or effects. Or you might decide to limit your topic to a study of the different types of chemicals that pollute the air. It is often necessary to narrow your topic two or three times. The process of narrowing this pollution topic might be diagrammed as shown in Figure A.1.

Once you have a subject area or a broad topic in mind, try to think of ways in which your topic could be subdivided. Often you will first have to acquire some general background about the subject. For ideas to start with, check the

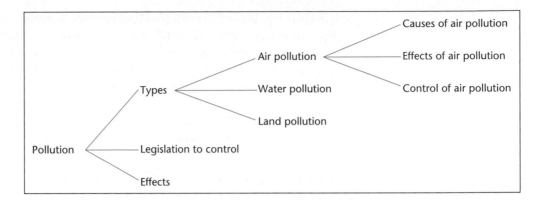

Figure A.1
Narrowing a Topic

card catalog in the library under your subject, and read the subject headings that immediately follow it to see how the subject is divided. Also, check an encyclopedia to see how the subject is divided, and then skim quickly through to learn a little about the topic. Depending on your subject, you may also wish to consult other texts in the subject area to get a brief overview of the field. Make a list of possible topics. As an alternative approach, make a list of questions that might be asked about the subject. Each of your questions suggests a possible division of your subject. You may find it necessary to limit these divisions further as you gather information.

Once you have narrowed your topic, you are ready to determine the focus of your paper. You should decide whether you want to prove something about your topic, inform others about it, or explain or analyze it. In some cases, your purpose may have already been defined by your instructor when he or she assigned the research paper. Most of the time, however, you will need to decide how to approach your topic. To determine your approach, ask yourself: What do I want to accomplish by writing this paper? Whatever approach you select will directly affect how you proceed from this point. The types of sources you consult, the amount of reading you do, and the thesis that you state and develop are all shaped by your purpose.

Step 2: Locate and Review Appropriate Sources of Information

Your campus library, its librarians, and its reference materials are the keys to locating appropriate sources of information on your topic. There are several rules of thumb to follow when locating sources of information.

1. Proceed from general to specific. Locate general sources of information first; then, once you have an overview of the topic, locate more detailed references on particular aspects of the topic.
2. Locate as many sources as possible. Your research paper is expected to cover your topic thoroughly. In collecting information, therefore, you must be sure that you do not overlook important aspects of the topic completely. Once you have read several sources, you can skim additional sources, checking to see what new information is provided.
3. Record all sources used. Many students waste valuable time by failing to keep a complete record of all the references they used. An important part of any research paper is the list of the references you used to write the paper (see step 8, page 436). A list of references is important because it gives credit to the sources you used and enables your reader to verify your information.

One easy way to record your references is to use a separate 3-inch-by-5-inch index card for each source. Record source information in the exact form in which it should appear in the list of references. Later you will see that the cards enable you to alphabetize your references easily.

4. Ask for assistance. If you have difficulty locating information or if you are not certain that you have looked at all possible sources, ask the reference librarian for assistance. Most librarians are ready and willing to guide serious students in their research.

Using the Computerized Card Catalog

The computerized card catalog is an easy-to-use listing of all the books the library owns. You type in the title, author, or subject you are interested in locating, and the information you need appears on screen, as shown in Figure A.2.

Using Reference Sources

In addition to its holdings of books and periodicals, libraries have a reference section that contains general references—sources that cannot be checked out. Among the most common reference materials are encyclopedias, dictionaries, periodical indexes, almanacs, biographical dictionaries, atlases, and statistical handbooks. Many of these are now available on CD-ROMs or can be accessed online. Also, many libraries contain a reserve section in which instructors reserve—or place on restricted use—important, useful sources to which many students need access. The reference librarian is available to assist you in using these sources.

Review Your Sources

Once you have located sources, skim them. Your purpose at this point is to learn enough about your topic to be able to refine the direction or focus of your paper. Again, a good starting point is the encyclopedia.

Because your purpose is to get an overview of the topic, do not try to read everything. You might read parts of the material and skip others. Do not try to take notes on your readings yet. Just jot down, on index cards, references that

Figure A.2
A Sample Card Catalog

Search Request: S=HOUDINI	U-CAT—University Library
BOOK-Record 10 of 12 Entries Found	Long View

Author: Brandon, Ruth.

Title: The life and many deaths of Harry Houdini/Ruth Brandon.

Edition: 1st ed.

Published: New York: Random House, 1993<i.e. c1994>

Description: x, 355 p.:ill.;24 cm.   *Number of pages, whether illustrated, size*

Subjects, Library of Congress (Use s=):   *Library of Congress headings*
   Houdini, Harry, 1874–1926.
   Magicians—United States—Biography.

Notes: Copyright date from bookjacket.
      Includes bibliographical references and index.   *Additional notes on contents*

ISBN: 0679424377   *Book number (useful for locating or purchasing)*

LOCATION:	CALL NUMBER:	STATUS:
MAIN LIB.	GV1545 .H8 B73 1994	Not checked out

would be useful for a later, more thorough reading. If you are working on a computer, bookmark useful Web sites so you can find them again easily. Also, jot down any ideas that might come to mind about how to approach, further limit, or organize your topic. Continue sampling general sources until you find that most of what you are reading is no longer new and that you have already read it in another source.

Step 3: Write a Tentative Thesis Statement

A thesis statement is a one-sentence summary of what your paper is about. It states the idea you will develop throughout the paper. You might think of a thesis statement as similar to the topic sentence of a paragraph or the central thought of a passage. These state, in a general way, what the paragraph or passage is about. Similarly, the thesis statement indicates to your reader what your paper will be about.

Here are a few examples of thesis statements that could be written for the topic of effects of air pollution:

> Air pollution is caused by many factors, including industrial waste and automobile exhaust.

> Air pollution has been the primary cause of numerous health-related problems for Americans.

> Because air pollution created from industrial waste has caused numerous health problems, private industries have been forced to change.

Note that each thesis statement specifies what the writer intends to show about air pollution and its effects.

Because you have done only preliminary reading and research so far, your thesis statement is tentative. You should expect to change, revise, or narrow this statement as you proceed through the remaining steps. Right now, your thesis statement should express the idea you think your paper will explain or discuss. In a sense, it further narrows your topic by limiting your paper to a specific focus or approach.

Step 4: Collect Information: Reading and Note Taking

Now that you have written a tentative thesis statement, the next step is to collect and record the information that supports your thesis.

Reading Reference Material

In reading reference material, you clearly define your purpose for reading; you are looking for facts and ideas that will help you prove, explain, or support your thesis statement. However, reading reference sources is very different from reading textbooks. In textbooks, you are reading for retention and recall of most of the information presented. When you are reading reference material, on the other hand, not all information is useful or important. Also, you are not trying to remember everything you read; instead, when you find a useful piece of information, you can write it down and use it later.

Prereading is a valuable skill when you are identifying sources that may contain information on your topic. Once you have located a book in the card catalog and then found it on the library shelves, take a few minutes to preview it to determine whether it contains useful information and is worth checking out. You can save yourself valuable time and avoid carrying home armloads of books by prereading to select only appropriate, usable sources.

Because high retention is not required in reading reference material, you can afford to skim, scan, or skip large portions of material (see Chapter 18 for skimming and scanning techniques). In fact, trying to read everything, regardless of whether you use it in your paper, would be an extremely inefficient use of time.

Taking Notes

The manner and form in which you take notes largely determines whether writing your paper will be a relatively simple or an extremely difficult, time-consuming task. The next two steps, developing an outline and writing the paper, require that the information you collect be in a form that can be rearranged or placed in a specific order.

One effective way to take notes is to use index cards; 5-inch-by-8-inch and 4-inch-by-6-inch sizes are best. Some students prefer to use separate full sheets of paper. Use a separate card or sheet of paper for each different subtopic or different aspect of your topic. Record in the upper right corner the author's last name and the pages you used. In the upper left corner, write the subtopic that the notes are concerned with. Be sure to write on only one side of the cards. A sample note card or sheet might look like the one shown in Figure A.3.

Another effective system is to use a computer to take and/or reorganize notes. Using the cut and paste commands, you can rearrange your notes to create a detailed outline of your paper.

Here are a few suggestions for taking good research notes:

1. Record the information in your own words instead of copying the author's words. By recording the author's wording, you run the risk of using that wording in your paper, perhaps without realizing that you have done so. Whenever you use an author's words instead of your own, you are required to give the author credit by indicating the author and the source from which the material was taken. The same rule applies when you use someone's idea, theory, or argument that is not common knowledge. Failure to give credit is known as *plagiarism* and means that you have borrowed someone else's

Figure A.3
A Sample Note Card

> Violence—how it's learned   Barlow p. 125-6
>   violence learned through imitation & modeling.
>   —experiments by Bandura show that children pick
> up behavior patterns of adults they know or respect.
>   ex. Child views film of woman beating/kicking a
>   doll/then child is given similar doll
>   Child performs similar violent behavior as woman
>   —patterns may be learned from watching adults
>   on T.V.
> patterns are retained through life & generalized to other
> situations
> reward & punishment play imp't role in this type of learning

words and ideas without acknowledging them. Plagiarism is a serious error, and many institutions penalize students who either knowingly or unknowingly plagiarize.

2. Try to summarize and condense information. You simply cannot record all the information you find, so try to state the facts and ideas as concisely and briefly as possible.

3. Record information only once. As you continue reading, eventually you will find the same information appearing and reappearing in various sources. Occasionally you may need to check back through your notes to see what you've already recorded. If you have already made a note once, do not spend time writing it again. You might, however, want to note the fact that there is common agreement in a number of sources about the information.

4. Record useful quotations. If you find a statement that strongly supports your thesis, you may want to quote it in your paper. Copy it down exactly, along with its source, and place it in quotation marks in your notes.

Instead of notes, you might use photocopies of research materials. You can highlight useful information and make marginal notations to record your reactions to the ideas presented.

Step 5: Form an Outline

Once you are satisfied that you have collected enough information, reread and organize your note cards. Try to group them together by subtopic. You many find some subtopics that overlap and others that can be grouped together under a more general subtopic. Remember to change the subtopic written in the upper left corner of the card for any cards that you reclassify.

Next, sort your cards in separate piles according to subtopic. Then, with each pack of cards or sheets laid out in front of you, try to arrange them in some logical order or sequence. You might arrange your subtopics chronologically, in order of importance, or by cause–effect. Often your purpose for writing, your thesis statement, or the content of the paper will dictate the order or arrangement. You can use the organizational patterns you learned to identify in reading paragraphs as a means of organizing your paper. Arrange your information in a manner that supports your thesis statement. Once you have done this, you have a tentative outline. To record this arrangement, list the subtopics in order. When you can see how the ideas are related to one another, reread your outline and revise it. Check each subtopic to be sure that it directly supports your thesis statement.

Step 6: Write and Revise

Using your outline as a guide and your note cards to provide the specific facts and information, start writing the first draft of your paper. Your paper should have a brief introduction of one or two paragraphs, a body, and a conclusion or summary. In the introduction, you should lead up to and state the thesis of the paper. Before stating it, you might lead up to it by supplying necessary background information or by providing a context.

The body, which makes up most of the paper, should explain and discuss the thesis statement. Each idea should be directly related to and support the thesis statement. Finally, in the conclusion or summary you should draw together the ideas you presented and bring the paper to a close. That is, in the last several paragraphs, try to review the major points you presented and connect them, yet again, to the thesis statement.

Once you have written a first draft, reread, evaluate, and revise it. If possible, wait a day or two before beginning your revision. As with any other type of paper, revision is a critical step and can make a difference in the grade you earn.

When revising your paper, ask yourself the following questions.

1. Does each paragraph directly support the thesis statement?
2. Are the ideas expressed clearly and concisely?
3. Are the major points connected to one another as well as to the thesis statement?
4. Is there sufficient explanation and support for the thesis statement?

After you have reread your paper and made changes, ask someone else to read it. Then ask the person to identify the thesis statement and to summarize the supporting information. If he or she is unable to do so or does so incorrectly, then you may not have communicated your message effectively.

Some students find it necessary to go through more than one revision, especially if their first drafts are weak or poorly organized. Also, you may sometimes find that you need more information, in which case you must go back to the research stage to check new sources. Do not be discouraged by these additional steps; remember that the first few times you write a research paper, you are learning *how* to do the assignment. Therefore, some extra time and effort may be required initially.

Step 7: Prepare the Final Copy

Once you are satisfied that you have made sufficient revision to produce a good research paper, you are ready to prepare the final copy for submission. Some instructors require printed copy; most prefer it to handwritten papers. If you have poor, illegible handwriting, your instructor may become annoyed while reading the paper and may unconsciously react to your paper negatively or critically. A printed copy, on the other hand, presents a neat appearance and suggests that you care enough about your work to present it in the best possible form.

An important part of preparing a final copy, whether it is handwritten or printed, is proofreading. Once your have prepared the final copy, be sure to take the time to read it through and correct spelling, punctuation, and grammar. If you are weak in one or more of these areas and cannot easily recognize your own errors, ask a friend to proofread your paper and point out or mark the errors.

Step 8: Prepare the List of References

The final steps in completing a research paper are to prepare a list of all the sources that you used to write the paper and to prepare any necessary endnotes. Endnotes list in consecutive order the sources from which you have taken quotations and those that contained unique or specialized information. Endnotes are called *footnotes* if they are placed at the bottom of each page rather than in a consecutive list at the end of the paper. You will need to consult a handbook to determine the specialized format required for endnotes.

As mentioned earlier, if you kept careful records as you collected your information, preparing your list of references is relatively easy. You simply list alphabetically all the sources you consulted. Also, you must use a consistent form for listing the information. Depending on your instructor, as well as on the subject area you are working in, different formats may be expected. Although each format requires basically the same information, arrangement of information as well as punctuation may vary. Some instructors specify a particular format; others accept any standard, consistent format. If your instructor prefers a particular format, use it.

It is well worth the initial cost to purchase a handbook or style guide that explains a particular format. In any case, be sure to consult the most recent edition. Two commonly used handbooks are the *MLA Handbook for Writers of Research Papers* and the *Publication Manual of the American Psychological Association.*

LIMITED ANSWER KEY

Note: Answers are not included in this key for exercises that require lengthy or subjective responses or the highlighting or marking of passages.

PART ONE
Succeeding In College

CHAPTER 1
Setting Goals and Managing Your Time

▲ EXERCISE 1

1. His choices include

   a. reducing work hours and seeking financial aid if needed;

   b. settling for less than a B average in some courses;

   c. asking a family member to accept additional household responsibilities;

   d. dropping one or more courses;

   e. dropping an activity or doing it in less time.

3. Mark's plan has two faults. First, he should not leave the most difficult assignment, which requires the greatest amount of concentration, until last. Second, he should not schedule his study of subjects according to likes or dislikes but should instead allot his time in accordance with the difficulty and types of assignments given.

5. Evaluate his study plan according to the suggestions given in the section "Building a Time Schedule." He should rearrange his schedule in accordance with these scheduling suggestions.

CHAPTER 2
Learning Style and Learning Strategies

▲ EXERCISE 4

1. Identify and jot down areas (topics, periods) of weakness; look for patterns, such as the types of questions missed; find out where the questions were taken from (text or lecture); use the exam as a review for the final exam.

3. Review the procedures before attending the lab; underline key steps in the lab manual.

▲ EXERCISE 5

1. Knowledge

3. Knowledge

5. Synthesis and evaluation

7. Application

9. Analysis

▲ EXERCISE 6

1. Knowledge:

   a. Speakers reveal and reflect their emotional states through nonverbal behavior.

   b. Speakers' nonverbal cues enrich or elaborate the message that comes through words.

   c. Nonverbal messages form a reciprocal interaction between speaker and listener.

3. Application: A man sitting hunched over with his hands over his face is revealing sadness or despair through his posture.

5. Synthesis: Answers may vary.

▲ EXERCISE 7

The questions that follow are suggested responses. Many others are possible.

Knowledge

What is body adornment?

Comprehension

Explain how clothes convey messages of self-identity.

Application

What are some examples of clothing that reflect religious beliefs of different groups in the United States?

Analysis

Why might two women attending the same social function dress differently?

Synthesis

Write a list of five clothing items and indicate what each item suggests in Western culture.

Evaluation

Was the information in this article helpful in understanding the cultural functions of clothing?

CHAPTER 3
Understanding How Learning and Memory Work

▲ EXERCISE 1

1. Approximately 25 percent

3. Although taking the notes would serve as a form of rehearsal, without further review you should expect your recall to be fairly poor.

▲ EXERCISE 2

1. Responses might include lighting, heating, color of walls, clock ticking, traffic in street, noise in corridor, and feeling of watch on wrist.

3. Items of information can be grouped into longer bits that can be recalled as one item.

5. It may take longer than 20 seconds to reach the phone, or the person may not have grouped the numbers together and cannot remember each separately.

▲ EXERCISE 3

1. Rote learning

3. Recoding

5. Recoding

▲ EXERCISE 4

1. The group that paraphrased used recoding. Highlighting is repetition of existing information. Alone it is an inefficient learning strategy for large quantities of information.

3. The film recodes and enables students to make elaborations.

▲ EXERCISE 5

1. Retrieval

3. Encoding and storage

5. Retrieval

▲ EXERCISE 6

1. a. She used only rote learning.

   b. She was not able to concentrate.

   c. She did not select what was important to learn.

3. The student did not selectively attend to the quiz announcement.

5. Selective attention

7. He is providing for elaborative rehearsal.

▲ EXERCISE 8

1. Group into political, economic, and social or short-, intermediate-, and long-term causes.

3. Group into importance to United States, to Western world, to world economy.

▲ EXERCISE 9

1. Ask questions about each step.

3. Group according to type or characteristic.

▲ EXERCISE 10

1. Immediate review, visualization, numerous sensory channels, connect with previous learning, retrieval clues, simulate retrieval

3. Elaboration (practical examples), categorize types (cybercrime, embezzlement), retrieval clues, connect with previous knowledge

CHAPTER 4
Taking Notes in Class

LEARNING EXPERIMENT

Paragraph 1: intimate, personal, social, public

Paragraph 2: attraction, taste, memory, identity

▲ EXERCISE 3

Recall clues: Freud's psychoanalytic theory, free association, repression, suppression, trauma, interpretation of dreams, three parts of personality

Questions: What is free association? What is repression? What is suppression? What is trauma? How can dreams be interpreted? What are the three parts of the personality? What does each do? What principle governs each part?

PART TWO
Reading Textbooks and Assignments

CHAPTER 5
Active Reading Strategies

▲ *Exercise 1*

1. T
2. T
3. F
4. F
5. T

▲ *Exercise 2*

1. a. No
   b. No
   c. Yes
   d. Yes
   e. No

3. a. Historical and societal background, patterns of courtship, trends and facts regarding sexuality, public health and policy issues, and group differences in love and sex.
   b. (2)

5. The chapter is organized chronologically; it moves from the historical events to the present to projections for the future. The chapter discusses the history and current economy of Asia and the directions and problems of the future.

▲ *Exercise 4*

Topics: 2, 5, 6, 8, 10

▲ *Exercise 5*

Statement 1: section 2
Statement 7: section 1 or 4

▲ *Exercise 6*

Possible topics include:

1. Differences in women's and men's communication.
2. What *genderlects* means
3. Problems that result from differences in genderlects
4. How genderlects affect public communication
5. Differences between men's and women's proxemics
6. Ways men invade women's personal space

▲ *Exercise 12*

1. What are the aids that help merge files? How do they work?

3. How are electromagnetic waves produced? What are they used for?

5. What sociological factors are related to delinquency? How are they related?

▲ *Exercise 13*

1. What are the three branches of philosophical analysis?

3. How has the treatment of conflict changed?

5. What factors influence a decision to buy? How are people influenced by circumstances when making a buying decision?

▲ *Exercise 16*

1. Answers will vary.

2. a. human exploitation of resources
   b. (1) decrease in habitat type
      (2) apportionment of the remaining
   c. logging, urban development, mining
   d. Central and Southern California—urban development; Southern Appalachia—agriculture

3.–5. Variable responses

▲ *Exercise 18*

Possible guide and connection questions include:

How does population movement in the United States relate to habitat destruction?

What is habitat fragmentation?

In what ways does corporate farming affect habitats?

CHAPTER 6
Understanding Paragraphs

▲ *Exercise 1*

1. b
3. c
5. a
7. b
9. a

▲ *Exercise 2*

1. Innovative solutions to energy conservation
3. The process of becoming hypnotized
5. Photoreceptor cells or rods and cones

7. Panel discussions

9. Automated radio programs

▲ EXERCISE 3

1. Second sentence

3. Sixth sentence

5. First sentence or second-to-last sentence

7. Second sentence

9. First sentence

▲ EXERCISE 4

1. b, c, e

3. a, b, c, d

5. a, b, c, d, e

7. a, c, d, e

9. a, b, e

▲ EXERCISE 5

1. *Topic:* Birds' care of their young
   Main Idea: Birds' selfless care of their young seems to be an automatic behavior.

3. *Topic:* Theory
   Main Idea: A theory is at first an idea, then a hypothesis, and finally a verified explanation.

5. *Topic:* The meaning of revision
   Main Idea: Revision means assessing the strengths and weaknesses of your writing and making effective changes in it.

7. *Topic:* Presidential election candidates
   Main Idea: In any presidential election only a handful of candidates are serious possibilities.

9. *Topic:* Emigration decisions
   Main Idea: Both push and pull factors are involved in people's emigration decisions.

▲ EXERCISE 6

1. But, a further (sign)

3. At first, but after however, then

5. Instead

7. For example

9. At the same time, at present

▲ EXERCISE 7

1. *Topic:* Urban population
   Main Idea: The world's population is becoming increasingly urban.

3. *Topic:* Careers in anthropology
   Main Idea: Anthropologists work in a variety of settings, both academic and nonacademic.

5. *Topic:* Police work
   Main Idea: Changes in police work since 1960 have had mixed results.

7. *Topic:* Divorce rates
   Main Idea: There has been a dramatic increase in divorce rates since 1920.

9. *Topic:* Effects of color
   Main Idea: Colors have a great influence on how we think of products and people.

CHAPTER 7
Following Thought Patterns

▲ EXERCISE 1
Paragraph 1, first sentence

▲ EXERCISE 2

1. Communication between men and women

3. First subsection: first sentence
   Second subsection: first sentence

▲ EXERCISE 4

1. By mentioning, in paragraph 1, the relationship between underarm deodorants and the death of the oceans

3. The use of CFCs is threatening life on earth.

5. Reducing CFC levels will require global cooperation, which seems unlikely.

▲ EXERCISE 5

1. Description

3. Reasons

5. Facts/statistics

7. Examples

9. Facts/statistics

▲ EXERCISE 6

1. Class: Period in human development
   Characteristic: Between puberty and maturity

3. Class: Communication medium
   Characteristic: For transmitting TV signals through cables

5. Class: Spoken or written language
   Characteristic: That attempts to sell

▲ Exercise 7

(Answers may vary.)

1. As soon as, next, later, before
3. Second, next, finally
5. First, second, finally

▲ Exercise 8

Content   Organization
1. Both
   1
3. Both
   2
5. Similarities

▲ Exercise 9

1, 2, 5, 6, 8

▲ Exercise 10

1. Sports, fashion, cooking
3. Whales, dogs, cows
5. Experience, education, career goal

▲ Exercise 11

1. Conservation of trees; both
3. Fossil damage; solutions
5. Unexpected questions; both

▲ Exercise 12

1. Cause–effect
3. Contrast
5. Enumeration

▲ Exercise 13

1. Enumeration
3. Cause–effect
5. Definition
7. Definition
9. Definition

▲ Exercise 14

Comparison-contrast

CHAPTER 8
Reading Graphics and Technical Writing

▲ Exercise 1
Figure 8.3:

1. The Independent Party
3. The Democratic Party. 1992

▲ Exercise 2
Figure 8.9:

1. To show how much decline in employment can be expected over a 15-year period in the ten least promising U.S. occupations.
3. Farming
5. 200,000

Figure 8.10:

1. Machinery
3. Machinery

Figure 8.11:

1. Marital satisfaction of wives and husbands at various stages of their life together
3. Negative
5. The postparental years are the best years for marital satisfaction for both wives and husbands. Child-rearing years tend to be less satisfying.

▲ Exercise 3
Figure 8.16:

1. Transportation
3. Yes. It is easier to see at a glance where each source of air pollution stands in the total causes of air pollution and in relation to other sources.

Figure 8.17:

1. Sewage treatment
3. Filter screening and primary sedimentation

▲ Exercise 4

1. To describe the process by which the constitution can be amended
3. a. Proposed by a national constitutional convention, requested by the legislatures of two-thirds of the states, and ratified by the legislatures of three-fourths of the states
   b. Proposed by a national constitutional convention requested by the legislatures of two-thirds of the states and ratified by conventions called for that purpose in three-fourths of the states.

▲ EXERCISE 5

1. Differences in the marriage ceremony in different cultures.

3. Cultural differences:
U.S.—gaiety, informal, one with community.
Southeast Asia—solemn, formal, sense of regal dignity, aloofness.

▲ EXERCISE 6

1. Photograph

3. Table, line graph

5. Table

7. Diagram

9. Map

▲ EXERCISE 8

Sample Outline

Speaking Different Genderlects

I. Leads to communication problems between intimates.

   A. Men

      1. Speak to give information only

      2. Tend to take what women say literally

   B. Women

      1. Speak to express feelings

      2. Tend to read emotional meaning into what men say

II. Genderlects influence public communication.

   A. Topics of conversation when alone

      1. Men—things and activities

      2. Women—people and relationships

   B. Male genderlect dominates when together

      1. Topics of interest to both

      2. Style of men-only conversations

CHAPTER 9

Reading Electronic Sources

Answers will vary.

CHAPTER 10

Critical Thinking and Reading

▲ EXERCISE 1

Passage A

1. That the lion should be given the largest share.

Passage B

1. She regards it as a form of deprivation that can be harmful to infants' development.

3. She means to suggest than an infant's time in day care must in some way be "made up for" in order to undo the damage done in day care.

Passage C

1. That what finally happened to Nichols will deter other deadbeat dads from refusing to make payments for child support.

3. Many people regard those records as private information not to be shared by the IRS with agencies or individuals.

5. The mother often requires public assistance to support the child. When welfare is involved, the cost of feeding, clothing, housing, and providing medical care comes from taxes. In addition, if a welfare mother isn't working, she isn't contributing taxes for her child's public education or for government services she shares with other citizens.

▲ EXERCISE 2

1. Possibly useful

3. Possibly useful

5. Possibly useful

▲ EXERCISE 3

1. Fact

3. Fact

5. Informed opinion

7. Opinion

9. Fact

▲ EXERCISE 4

1. "What Hoover described in these youngsters were the seeds of behavior I have observed among women and men at work."

3. "From childhood, many boys learn something that is very adaptive to the workplace: Raises and promotions are based on 'performance' evaluations and these depend, in large measure, on how you appear in other people's eyes."

5. "Whereas some women seem to be taking undeserved blame by saying 'I'm sorry,' some men seem to evade deserved blame."

7. "There is no one way of talking that will always work best. But understanding how conversational rituals work allows individuals to have more control over their own lives."

▲ EXERCISE 6

Passage 1: To motivate the reader to consider some legal problems associated with the Internet.

Passage 3: To inform the reader about laws of momentum and energy, and to explain how they will be discussed.

▲ EXERCISE 8

1. Humorous, sympathetic
3. Humorous, good-natured, with a fondness

▲ EXERCISE 9

1. Immigration laws are too lenient. Immigration laws are too strict.
3. Smoking in all public places should be banned. All public places should have designated smoking areas

▲ EXERCISE 10

1. Multicultural education
3. Personal opinion, New York Department of Education report
5. No; more details and facts about the curriculum are needed

PART THREE
Developing Your Vocabulary

CHAPTER 11
Expanding Your Vocabulary

Learning Experiment

1. c 2. f 3. e 4. i 5. a 6. b
7. j 8. h 9. d 10. g

▲ EXERCISE 1

1. Obscure or Obsolete
3. Answers will vary: Webster's New World Dictionary lists 70.
5. Addenda
7. Best, favorable, earliest part, highest quality
9. Failing, weakness, foible, vice

▲ EXERCISE 2

1. Distressed, despondent, disheartened, sorrowful, grief-stricken
3. Explaining, discussing, describing, arguing, debating, illustrating
5. Excellent, praiseworthy, pleasing, superior, laudable

▲ EXERCISE 4

Microchip transponder, pan troglodytes, flora, fauna, extant habitat

CHAPTER 12
Using Context and Word Parts

▲ EXERCISE 1

1. A form of government in which the people effectively participate
3. An essential fatty acid necessary for growth and skin integrity in infants
5. Able to reach comfortably to the tips of all the other fingers

▲ EXERCISE 2

1. Pertaining to horses
3. Negative emotional experience
5. Fears

▲ EXERCISE 3

1. Strong, forceful, excited
3. Delay, put off
5. Banished, excluded from a group

▲ EXERCISE 4

1. Disgusting, offensive
3. Curses, expressions of abhorrence
5. Struck out, removed

▲ EXERCISE 5

The underlined parts should be as follows (context clues are given in parentheses):

1. The principle that the powers of government should be separated and put in the care of different parts of government (definition)
3. Amble, stride, jog, and sprint (example/illustration)

5. Ranging from treatment as innocents to being tolerated as fools to persecution as witches (example/illustration)

▲ EXERCISE 6

1. a. Homes, houses
   b. Similar people, equivalents
   c. Nearly, practically
   d. Noticeable, obvious
   e. Hardship, need
   f. Dependable, secure, predictable
3. a. Lasting
   b. Cause, bring forth
   c. Chemical messages
   d. Bring about

▲ EXERCISE 7

1. Not normal, deviant
3. Not logical or reasonable
5. Unchangeable, not able to reverse

▲ EXERCISE 8

1. Below standard, unacceptable
3. Communication over distance by radio, telephone, television, etc.
5. Taking effect at a specified date in the past
7. Not part of the required course of study
9. To transfer or introduce blood into a vein
11. Dishonest or incorrect use
13. Tiresome, lacking variety
15. Having several syllables

▲ EXERCISE 9

1. Belief in only one god
3. Historical record, narrative
5. Process of carrying or removing goods from one country to another
7. Orderly process of reasoning about the unknown
9. Competent in many features, able to change or adapt
11. The proportion of deaths per 1,000 people
13. Loud, noisy
15. Belonging to a corporation

▲ EXERCISE 10

1. Use of force to intimidate or control
3. Preoccupation with material rather than intellectual or spiritual things
5. Not able to pass, blocked
7. Not touchable
9. Questioning, examining
11. Condition of being flustered (nervous, befuddled)
13. Out of regard or respect for
15. One who is nominated to an office

▲ EXERCISE 11

1. Intolerable
3. Spans of one thousand years
5. Not decorated
7. Professed purposes, excuses
9. Crude in feeling or manner

PART FOUR
Studying Textbooks

CHAPTER 13
Textbook Highlighting and Marking
Answers will vary.

CHAPTER 14
Methods of Organizing Information

▲ EXERCISE 5

Observational learning is a type of social learning that results from observing the successes and mistakes of others. It does not fit traditional learning theory because one learns from watching; rather than actually experiencing reward or punishment for certain behaviors. This type of learning allows one to develop complex behaviors immediately, without the time needed for trial-and-error learning.

CHAPTER 15
Study and Review Strategies

▲ EXERCISE 1

1. There are a number of reasons why tides are important. They mix the waters near shore,

taking out pollutants and moving nutrients around. The currents from tides move floating animals and plants back and forth between the shallow waters where they usually breed and deeper waters. Fishermen use these tidal changes to catch more fish by looking for big fish where the strong currents cause little fish and other bait to collect. In the days when ships used sails, sailors had to depend on the tides when leaving or entering harbors.

3. (1) All bills for raising revenue Begin in the House of Representatives. The Senate may offer amendments.

(2) Having passed the House of Representatives and the Senate, every bill must be presented to the President of the United States before it becomes a law; if the President does not sign it, he returns the bill with his reasons for not accepting it to the house it came from to be reconsidered. Then, after each house again looks at the bill considering the objections raised by the President, the bill must be accepted by two-thirds of both houses in order to become a law. Both the affirmative and negative votes of members of both houses shall be recorded. The bill is then returned to the President for his signature. In the event that a bill is not returned to the President within 10 days after he has reviewed it, it will become a law without his signature unless the bill is detained by an adjournment of Congress; then it will not become a law.

▲ EXERCISE 2

Sample paraphrase

The key deer of the Florida Keys is a small version of the whitetail deer, and it stands only as tall as a large dog. These deer have an unusual gene pool because a rise in sea level stranded them on a few islands, and they didn't breed with mainland whitetails. There were never very many of them, and poachers almost wiped them out in the early 1900s. Less than 50 survived, but, thanks to conservation, they reached about 400 by the 1970s. Today more people are moving to the Florida Keys, homes are taking over the deer's range, and many deer are being killed by cars. Because they are being killed faster than they can reproduce, their numbers are now down to 240.

▲ EXERCISE 9

Anthropology: Add a Highlighting step; make a list of the functions of clothing.

Communication: Add a Highlighting step; add a Summary step.

Biology: Spend more time than usual prereading; outline; prepare summary sheet.

Business: Add a Mapping step or outline step.

PART FIVE
Studying for Exams

CHAPTER 16
Preparing for Exams
Answers will vary.

CHAPTER 17
Taking Exams

▲ EXERCISE 1

1. 1, 20, 5, 45, 4
(Other, similar time plans may be correct.)

▲ EXERCISE 2

1. only
3. primary
5. alone
7. greatest
9. increase

▲ EXERCISE 3

1. Topic: Trend
Limiting words: long-term effects
Key word: discuss

3. Topic: Industrial Revolution
Limiting words: one effect
Key word: explain

5. Topic: War of 1812
Limiting word: events
Key word: describe

7. Topic: Textbook chapter
Limiting word: approach
Key word: describe

9. Topic: lecturer
Limiting word: techniques
Key word: summarize

PART SIX
Reading Flexibility

CHAPTER 18
Improving Your Reading Rate and Flexibility

▲ *EXERCISE 3*

1. c

3. a

5. b

▲ *EXERCISE 4*

1. As more U.S. firms are becoming environmentally conscious, there is growing debate about how best to achieve "greenness." What seem to be simple answers may not be the environmentally correct ones.

3. As the tobacco industry's advertising and marketing strategies are being limited in the United States, tobacco companies are significantly expanding their efforts around the world. Our government is playing a major role in this expansion, even though it promotes anti smoking campaigns at home.

▲ *EXERCISE 5*

1. To protect the coasts against attack

3. Aunts, uncles, cousins, and others

5. Relief, recovery, and reform

CREDITS

Photo Credits: Page 5TR, © Bettmann/Corbis; 5BR, © AP/Wide World Photos; 5BL, © Karen Garber/The Coming Leader/Sipa Press; 6BR, © Stewart Cohen/Stone; 6TR, © Joseph Schulyer/Stock, Boston; 6BL, © Joseph Schulyer/Stock, Boston; 6C, © Bruce Ayers/Stone; © 6TL, © J. Moore/The Image Works; 9TL, © Bob Daemmrich Photography; 9TR, © David Young-Wolff/PhotoEdit; 9BR, © R. Lord/The Image Works; 9BL, © Bob Daemmrich/The Image Works; 9MR, © Bob Daemmrich Photography; 13, © Judy Gelles/Stock, Boston; 32, © Bob Daemmrich/Stock, Boston; 16, © Barbara Stitzer/PhotoEdit; 185T, © Jean-Claude Lejeune/Stock, Boston; 185B, © Nadirsh Naoroji/The Image Works; 215, © Bob Daemmrich/Stone; 377, © Hubertus Kanus/Photo Researchers; 387, © Bob Daemmrich/The Image Works; 394T, © Animals Animals©Zig Leszczynski; 394B, © Tom Stoddart/KatzPix/Woodfin Camp & Associates; 406, © Bob Daemmrich/Stone; 420T, © Jean-Cleaude Lejeune/Stock, Boston; 420M, © Lawrence Migdale/Stock, Boston; 420B, © Lori Adamski Peek/Stone; 422, © David Hanover/Stone; 424, © Bob Mahoney/The Image Works/ 426 © Hugh Rogers/Monkmeyer.

Text Credits

Chapter 2

Bloom, Benjamin, *Taxonomy of Educational Objectives: Cognitive Domain.* New York: McKay, 1956.

Gronbeck, Bruce E., et al., from *Principles of Speech Communication,* 11th Brief Instructor's Edition, pp. 217–218. Copyright © 1992 by HarperCollins Publishers. Reprinted by permission of Addison-Wesley Educational Publishers, Inc.

Chapter 3

Katz, Jane, *Swimming for Total Fitness: A Progressive Aerobic Program,* p. 99. Garden City, NY: Dolphin Books/Doubleday & Company, Inc., 1981

Chapter 5

Coleman, James William and Donald R. Cressey, from *Social Problems,* 6th ed., p. 98. Copyright © 1996 by HarperCollins College Publishers. Reprinted by permission of Addison-Wesley Educational Publishers, Inc.

Gronbeck, Bruce E., et al., from *Principles of Speech Communication,* 12th ed., p. 53. Copyright © 1995 by HarperCollins College Publishers. Reprinted by permission of Addison-Wesley Educational Publishers, Inc.

Harris, C. Leon, from *Concepts in Zoology,* 2nd ed., pp. 130, 573. Copyright © 1996 by HarperCollins College Publishers. Reprinted by permission of Addison-Wesley Educational Publishers, Inc.

Kinnear, Thomas C., Kenneth L. Bernhardt, and Kathleen A. Krentler, from *Principles of Marketing,* 4th ed., p. 637. Copyright © 1995 by HarperCollins Publishers. Reprinted by permission of Addison-Wesley Educational Publishers, Inc.

Wade, Carole, and Carol Tavris, from *Psychology,* 5th ed., pp. 545–548. Copyright © 1998 by Addison-Wesley Educational Publishers, Inc. Reprinted by permission.

Wilson, R. Jackson, et al., from *The Pursuit of Liberty: A History of the American People,* 3rd ed., Vol. 2, p. 422. Copyright © 1996 by HarperCollins College Publishers. Reprinted by permission of Addison-Wesley Educational Publishers, Inc.

Zinn, Maxine and Stanley D. Eitzen, from *Diversity in Families,* 4th ed., p. 205. Copyright © 1996 by HarperCollins College Publishers. Reprinted by permission of Addison-Wesley Educational Publishers, Inc.

Chapter 6

Agee, Warren K., Phillip H. Ault, and Edwin Emery, from *Introduction to Mass Communications,* 12th ed., pp. 153, 225. Copyright © 1997 by Addison-Wesley Educational Publishers, Inc. Reprinted by permission.

Anson, Chris M., and Robert A. Schwegler, *The Longman Handbook for Writers and Readers,*

Ross, David A., from *Introduction to Oceanography,* pp. 48, 62. Copyright © by David A. Ross. Reprinted by permission of Addison-Wesley Educational Publishers, Inc.

Thio, Alex, from *Sociology,* 4th ed., pp. 181, 180. Copyright © 1996 by HarperCollins College Publishers. Reprinted by permission of Addison-Wesley Educational Publishers, Inc.

Thio, Alex, from *Sociology,* 5th ed., p. 155. Copyright © 1998 by Addison-Wesley Educational Publishers, Inc. Reprinted by permission.

Thompson, William E., and Joseph Hickey, from *Society in Focus: An Introduction to Sociology,* 2nd ed., pp. 227, 162. Copyright © 1996 William E. Thompson and Joseph V. Hickey. Reprinted by permission of Addison-Wesley Educational Publishers.

Uba, Laura, and Karen Huang, *Psychology,* p. 148. New York: Addison-Wesley Educational Publishers, Inc., 1999.

Wallace, Robert A., from *Biology: The World of Life,* 6th ed., pp. 31–32, 28. Copyright © 1992 by HarperCollins Publishers. Reprinted by permission of Addison-Wesley Educational Publishers, Inc.

Wallace, Robert A., from *Biology: The World of Life,* 7th ed., p. 167. Copyright © 1997 by Addison-Wesley Educational Publishers, Inc. Reprinted by permission.

Wallbank, T. Walter, and Alastair Taylor et al., from *Civilization Past and Present,* 8th ed., p. 831. Copyright © 1996 by HarperCollins College Publishers. Reprinted by permission of Addison-Wesley Educational Publishers, Inc.

Weaver II, Richard, *Understanding Interpersonal Communication,* 7th ed., p. 220. New York: HarperCollins College Publishers, 1996.

Chapter 7

Appelbaum, Richard, and William J. Chambliss, from *Sociology* pp. 424, 55. Copyright © 1995 by HarperCollins College Publishers. Reprinted by permission of Addison-Wesley Educational Publishers, Inc.

Edwards III, George C., Martin P. Wattenberg, and Robert L. Lineberry, from *Government in America: People, Politics, and Policy ,* 7th ed., pp. 156, 230. Copyright © 1996 by HarperCollins College Publishers. Reprinted

by permission of Addison-Wesley Educational Publishers, Inc.

Ferl, Robert J., Robert A. Wallace, and Gerald P. Sanders, from Biology: *The Realm of Life,* 3rd ed., pp. 870, 252–253. Copyright © 1996 by HarperCollins College Publishers. Reprinted by permission of Addison-Wesley Educational Publishers, Inc.

Glynn, James A., Charles F. Hohm, and Elbert W. Stewart, from *Global Social Problems,* p. 154. Copyright © 1996 by HarperCollins College Publishers. Reprinted by permission of Addison-Wesley Educational Publishers, Inc.

Greenberg, Edward S., and Benjamin I. Page, from *The Struggle for Democracy,* Brief Version, 2nd ed., p. 71. Copyright © 1999 by Addison-Wesley Educational Publishers, Inc. Reprinted by permission.

Harris, C. Leon, from *Concepts in Zoology,* 2nd ed., p. 402. Copyright © 1996 by HarperCollins College Publishers. Reprinted by permission of Addison-Wesley Educational Publishers, Inc.

Hicks, David, and Margaret A. Gwynne, from *Cultural Anthropology,* 2nd ed., p. 304. Copyright © 1996 by HarperCollins College Publishers. Reprinted by permission of Addison-Wesley Educational Publishers, Inc.

Kinnear, Thomas C., Kenneth L. Bernhardt, and Kathleen A. Krentler, from *Principles of Marketing,* 4th ed., pp. 143, 180, 290, 475–476. Copyright © 1995 by HarperCollins Publishers. Reprinted by permission of Addison-Wesley Educational Publishers, Inc.

Laetsch, Watson M., *Plants: Basic Concepts in Botany,* p. 393. Boston: Little, Brown, 1982.

London, Barbara, and John Upton, *Photography,* 6th ed., p. 134. New York: Longman, 1998.

Miller, Roger LeRoy, from *Economics Today,* 8th ed., pp. 112, 147, 335. Copyright © 1994 by HarperCollins College Publishers. Reprinted by permission of Addison-Wesley Educational Publishers, Inc.

Mix, Michael C., Paul Farber, and Keith I. King, from *Biology: The Network of Life,* 2nd ed. Copyright © 1996 by Michael C. Mix, Paul Farber, and Keith I. King. Reprinted by permission of Addison-Wesley Educational Publishers, Inc.

Mosley, Donald C., Paul H. Pietri, and Leon C. Megginson, from *Management: Leadership in*

Action, 5th ed., pp. 289, 333–336. Copyright © 1996 by HarperCollins College Publishers. Reprinted by permission of Addison-Wesley Educational Publishers, Inc.

Preble, Duane et al., from *Art Forms: An Introduction to Visual Arts,* 6th ed., pp. 60, 98–99. Copyright © 1999 by Addison-Wesley Educational Publishers, Inc. Reprinted by permission.

Thompson, William E. and Joseph V. Hickey, from *Society in Focus: An Introduction to Sociology,* 2nd ed., pp. 135–136, 65. Copyright © 1996 by William E. Thompson and Joseph V. Hickey. Reprinted by permission of Addison-Wesley Educational Publishers, Inc.

Tortora, Gerard, *Introduction to the Human Body: The Essentials of Anatomy and Physiology,* 2nd ed., p. 30. New York: HarperCollins, 1991.

Wade, Carole, and Carol Tavris, from *Psychology,* 4th ed., pp. 494, 86. Copyright © 1996 by HarperCollins College Publishers. Reprinted by permission of Addison-Wesley Educational Publishers, Inc.

Wallace, Robert A., from *Biology: The World of Life,* 6th ed., p. 785. Copyright © 1992 by HarperCollins Publishers. Reprinted by permission of Addison-Wesley Educational Publishers, Inc.

Wallbank, T. Walter, and Alastair M. Taylor et al., from *Civilization Past and Present,* 8th ed., p. 671. Copyright © 1996 by HarperCollins College Publishers. Reprinted by permission of Addison-Wesley Educational Publishers, Inc.

Zimbardo, Philip G., and Richard J. Gerrig, from *Psychology and Life,* 14th ed., p. 337. Copyright © 1996 by Philip G. Zimbardo, Inc. and Richard J. Gerrig. Reprinted by permission of Addison-Wesley Educational Publishers, Inc.

Zinn, Maxine, and D. Stanley Eitzen, from *Diversity in Families,* 4th ed., pp. 199, 201. Copyright © 1996 by HarperCollins College Publishers. Reprinted by permission of Addison-Wesley Educational Publishers, Inc.

Chapter 8
[19]Appelbaum, Richard, and William J. Chambliss, from *Sociology,* p. 427. Copyright © 1995 by HarperCollins College Publishers. Reprinted by permission of Addison-Wesley Educational Publishers, Inc.

[22]Compton's Interactive Encyclopedia, "Thrush," in Electronic Resources on Ornithology. Copyright © 1994, 1995, 1996, 1997, 1998, 1999 by the Learning Company, Inc. and its licensors. All rights reserved. Used by permission.

[9]Dunham, Randall B., and Jon L. Pierce, from *Management,* p. 185. Copyright © 1989 by Randall B. Dunham and Jon L. Pierce. Reprinted by permission of Addison-Wesley Educational Publishers, Inc.

[3]Edwards III, George C., Martin P. Wattenberg, and Robert L. Lineberry, from *Government in America: People, Politics, and Policy,* Brief Version, 3rd ed., p. 113. Copyright © 1997 by Addison-Wesley Educational Publishers, Inc. Reprinted by permission.

[18]Edwards III, George C., Martin P. Wattenberg, and Robert L. Lineberry, from *Government in America: People, Politics, and Policy,* 7th ed., p. 47. Copyright © 1996 by HarperCollins College Publishers. Reprinted by permission of Addison-Wesley Educational Publishers, Inc.

[21]Hardy, Thomas, "The Darkling Thrush," 31 December, 1900.

[20]Jewett, Sarah O., "A White Heron," 1886.

[4]Kaufman, Donald G., and Cecilia M. Franz, from *Biosphere 2000: Protecting Our Global Environment,* pp. 143, 257. Copyright © 1993 by HarperCollins College Publishers. Reprinted by permission of Addison-Wesley Educational Publishers, Inc.

[12]Kinnear, Thomas C., Kenneth L. Bernhardt, and Kathleen A. Krentler, from *Principles of Marketing,* 4th ed., p. 634. Original source: Coca-Cola USA, from Marketing Division organizational chart. Reprinted by permission of Coca-Cola USA.

[2]Mix, Michael C., Paul Farber, and Keith I. King, from *Biology: The Network of Life,* 1st ed., p. 165. Copyright © 1992 by Michael C. Mix, Paul Farber, and Keith I. King. Reprinted by permission of HarperCollins Publishers.

[13]Nickerson, Robert C., from *Business and Information Systems,* p. 309. Copyright © 1998 by Addison-Wesley Educational Publishers, Inc. Reprinted by permission.

[5]Pride, William, and O. C. Ferrell, from *Marketing: Concepts and Strategies,* 9th ed., p. 329. Original source. Yankelovich, from

"Preference for Private Brands of Food Products by Age and Sex," *Yankelovich MON-ITOR,* 1989. Reprinted by permission of Yankelovich.

[14]Pride, William, Robert Hughes, and Jack Kapoor, from *Business,* 6th ed., p. 290. Copyright © 1999 by Houghton Mifflin Company. Used with permission.

[10]Rollins, Boyd C., and Harold Feldman, from *Journal of Marriage and the Family,* February 1970, 32:1, pp. 20–28. Copyright © 1970 by the National Council on Family Relations, 3989 Central Ave. NE, Suite 550, Minneapolis, MN 55421. Reprinted by permission.

[11]Schmalleger, Frank, from Criminal Justice Today, 5th ed., p. 239. Original Source. ODMP, from *Officer Down Memorial Page* (http://www.odmp.org). Used by permission.

[6]Skolnick, Arlene S., from The Intimate Environment: *Exploring Marriage and the Family,* 5th cd., p. 443. Copyright © 1992 by Arlene S. Skolnick. Reprinted by permission of Addison-Wesley Educational Publishers, Inc.

[1]Thio, Alex, from *Sociology,* 5th ed., p. 299. Copyright © 1998 by Addison-Wesley Educational Publishers, Inc. Reprinted by permission.

[8]Thompson, William E., and Joseph V. Hickey, from *Society in Focus: An Introduction to Sociology,* 2nd ed. (Inside Cover). Copyright © 1996 by William E. Thompson and Joseph V. Hickey. Reprinted by permission of Addison-Wesley Educational Publishers, Inc.

[17, 23]Wallace, Robert A., from *Biology: The World of Life,* 5th ed., p. 321, 237–238. Copyright © 1987 by Scott, Foresman. Reprinted by permission of Addison-Wesley Educational Publishers, Inc.

[7]Wallace, Robert A., from *Biology: The World of Life,* 6th ed., p. 794. Copyright © 1992 by HarperCollins Publishers. Reprinted by permission of Addison-Wesley Educational Publishers, Inc.

[16]Wallace, Robert A., from *Biology: The World of Life,* 7th ed., p. 568. Copyright © 1997 by Addison-Wesley Educational Publishers, Inc. Reprinted by permission.

Chapter 9
CAREERMagazine, from *CAREERMagazine* home page (www.careermag.com), 8/16/99. Used by permission.

Virginia Tech, "Site Map" from Virginia Tech web page http://www.vt.edu/vt99/third/sitemap. html), 8/30/99. Used by permission.

Chapter 10
Agee, Warren K., Phillip H. Ault, and Edwin Emery, from *Introduction to Mass Communications,* 12th ed., p. 466. Copyright © 1997 by Addison-Wesley Educational Publishers, Inc. Reprinted by permission.

Bayles, Martha, "Rock 'n Roll has Lost Its Soul," *Wilson Quarterly,* Summer 1993.

Bianculli, David, "In Defense of TV" in *Reading Today,* October/November 1993. Reprinted by permission of International Reading Association and the author.

Bolte, Bill, "Jerry's Got to Be Kidding" from *In These Times,* September 16, 1992. Reprinted by permission.

Clarke, Kevin, "Growing Hunger," Salt, March 1993.

Conniff, Dorothy, from "What's Best for the Child," *The Progressive,* November 1988. By permission of The Progressive Magazine.

Courlander, Harold, from *the King's Drum.* Copyright © 1962, 1990 by Harold Courlander. Reprinted by permission of the Estate of Harold Courlander.

Durst, Will, "We Don't Know Squat" as appeared in *Utne Reader,* March/April 1995, originally from The Nose. Reprinted by permission of Will Durst.

Greenberg, Edward S., and Benjamin I. Page, from *The Struggle for Democracy,* Brief Version, 1st ed., p. 186. Copyright © 1996 by HarperCollins College Publishers. Reprinted by permission of Addison-Wesley Educational Publishers, Inc.

Jones, Edwin, and Richard Childers, *Contemporary College Physics,* 2nd ed., p. 188. New York: Addison-Wesley Publishing Co., 1993.

Mander, Jerry, from *In the Absence of the Sacred: The Failure of Technology and the Rise of the Indian Nations.* San Francisco: Sierra Club Books, 1991.

McMiller, "Stiff Laws Nab Deadbeats," *USA Today,* August 16, 1995. Copyright © 1995, USA Today. Reprinted by permission.

Otto, Whitney, *How to Make an American Quilt,* p. 183. New York: Villard, 1991.

Skolnick, Arlene S., from *The Intimate Environment: Exploring Marriage and the Family,* 6th ed., p. 95. Copyright © 1996 by HarperCollins College Publishers. Reprinted by permission of Addison-Wesley Educational Publishers, Inc.

Swardson, Roger, "Greetings from the Electronic Plantation," *City Pages,* October 21, 1992.

Thio, Alex, from *Sociology,* 5th ed., pp. 376–377. Copyright © 1998 by Addison-Wesley Educational Publishers, Inc. Reprinted by permission.

Yuhfill, Ji-Yeon Mary, "Let's Tell the Story of All America's Cultures," *Philadelphia Inquirer,* 1991. Copyright © 1991 by Ji-Yeon Mary Yuhfill.

Chapter 11

Roget, from *Roget's International Thesaurus,* 4th ed., edited by Robert L. Chapman. Copyright © 1997 by Robert Chapman. Reprinted by permission of HarperCollins Publishers.

Chapter 12

[2, 8, 11, 14]Campbell, Bernard G., and James D. Loy, *Humankind Emerging,* 7th ed., pp. 38, 21, 189, 16. New York: HarperCollins College Publishers, 1996.

[9]Gannon, Martin J., *Management: An Organizational Perspective,* p. 20. Boston: Little, Brown, 1977.

Harris, C. Leon, from *Concepts in Zoology,* 2nd ed., pp. 417, 408–409. Copyright © 1996 by HarperCollins College Publishers. Reprinted by permission of Addison-Wesley Educational Publishers.

[10, 16]Macmillan, Donald L., *Mental Retardation in School and Society,* pp. 5, 11. Boston: Little, Brown, 1982.

[1, 5, 7, 13]Newell, Sydney B., *Chemistry,* pp. 17, 43, 45, 388. Boston: Little, Brown, 1977.

[6]Pillitteri, Adele, *Nursing Care of the Growing Family,* p. 280. Boston: Little, Brown, 1976.

Thio, Alex, from *Sociology,* 5th ed., p. 235. Copyright © 1998 by Addison-Wesley Educational Publishers, Inc. Reprinted by permission.

[3, 4, 12, 15]Wasserman, Gary, *The Basics of American Politics,* pp. 25, 8, 33, 87. Boston: Little, Brown, 1985.

Chapter 13

Campbell, Bernard G., and James D. Loy, from *Humankind Emerging,* 7th ed., pp. 22–23, 127–128. Copyright © 1996 by HarperCollins College Publishers. Reprinted by permission of Addison-Wesley Educational Publishers, Inc.

DeVito, Joseph A., from *Messages: Building Interpersonal Communication Skills,* 3rd ed., pp. 161–162. Copyright © 1996 by HarperCollins College Publishers. Reprinted by permission of Addison-Wesley Educational Publishers, Inc.

Gronbeck, Bruce E., et al., from *Principles of Speech Communication,* 11th Brief Instructor's Edition, p. 25. Copyright © 1992 by HarperCollins Publishers. Reprinted by permission of Addison-Wesley Educational Publishers, Inc.

Kinnear, Thomas C., Kenneth L. Bernhardt, and Kathleen A. Krentler, from *Principles of Marketing,* 4th ed., p. 537. Copyright © 1995 by HarperCollins Publishers. Reprinted by permission of Addison-Wesley Educational Publishers, Inc.

McCarty, Marilu Hurt, from *Dollars and Sense: An Introduction to Economics,* 8th ed., pp. 272–273, 213–214. Copyright © 1997 by Addison-Wesley Educational Publishers, Inc. Reprinted by permission.

Thio, Alex, from *Deviant Behavior,* 4th ed., pp. 311–312. Copyright © 1995 by HarperCollins College Publishers. Reprinted by permission of Addison-Wesley Educational Publishers, Inc.

Thio, Alex, from *Sociology,* 4th ed., pp. 100, 232. Copyright © 1996 by HarperCollins College Publishers. Reprinted by permission of Addison-Wesley Educational Publishers, Inc.

Thompson, William E., and Joseph Hickey, from *Society in Focus: An Introduction to Sociology,* 2nd ed., p. 65. Copyright © 1996 William E. Thompson and Joseph V. Hickey. Reprinted by permission of Addison-Wesley Educational Publishers, Inc.

Tortora, Gerard, from *Introduction to the Human Body,* 3rd ed., p. 221. Copyright © 1994 Biological Science Textbooks, Inc. and A&P Textbooks, Inc. Reprinted by permission of Addison-Wesley Educational Publishers, Inc.

Wade, Carole, and Carol Tavris, *Invitation to Psychology,* p. 182. New York: Longman, 1999.

Wallbank, T. Walter, and Alastair Taylor et al., from *Civilization Past and Present,* 8th ed., pp. 1012–1013. Copyright © 1996 by HarperCollins College Publishers. Reprinted by permission of Addison-Wesley Educational Publishers, Inc.

Chapter 14

Berman, Lois, and J. C. Evans, *Exploring the Cosmos,* p. 145. Boston: Little, Brown, 1986.

DeVito, Joseph A., from *The Interpersonal Communication Book,* 8th ed., pp. 266, 268. Copyright © 1998 by Joseph A. DeVito. Reprinted by permission of Addison-Wesley Educational Publishers, Inc.

Chapter 15

Ross, David A., from *Introduction to Oceanography,* p. 239. Copyright © 1995 by David A. Ross. Reprinted by permission of Addison-Wesley Educational Publishers, Inc.

United States Constitution, Section 7.

von Eschenbach, Wolfram, from *Parzival.* Translated and with an introduction by Helen M. Mustard and Charles E. Passage. Copyright © 1961 by Helen M. Mustard and Charles E. Passage. Reprinted by permission of Vintage Books, a division of Random House, Inc.

Wade, Carole, and Carol Tavris, from *Psychology,* 4th ed., pp. 124–125. Copyright © 1996 by HarperCollins College Publishers. Reprinted by permission of Addison-Wesley Educational Publishers, Inc.

Wallace, Robert A., from *Biology: The World of Life,* 5th ed., p. 434, 443. Copyright © 1987 by Scott, Foresman. Reprinted by permission of Addison-Wesley Educational Publishers, Inc.

Chapter 16

Lial, Margaret, et al., *Basic College Mathematics,* 5th ed., p. 689. Reading, MA: Addison Wesley Longman, Inc., 1998.

Chapter 18

Berkeley Wellness Letter, "Aromatherapy: The Nose Knows," from *Berkeley Wellness Letter,* May 1995, Vol. 11, No. 8, p. 4 (I). Reprinted by permission of University of California at Berkeley Health Letter Associates.

Kinnear, Thomas C., Kenneth L. Bernhardt, and Kathleen A. Krentler, from *Principles of Marketing,* 4th ed., pp. 311, 654, 61, 138, 388, 495. Copyright © 1995 by HarperCollins College Publishers. Reprinted by permission of Addison-Wesley Educational Publishers, Inc.

Skolnick, Arlene, from *The Intimate Environment: Exploring Marriage and the Family,* 6th ed., p. 107. Copyright © 1996 by HarperCollins College Publishers. Reprinted by permission of Addison-Wesley Educational Publishers, Inc.

Wade, Carole, and Carol Tavris, from *Psychology,* 4th ed., pp. 284–285. Copyright © 1996 by HarperCollins College Publishers. Reprinted by permission of Addison-Wesley Educational Publishers, Inc.

Wallbank, T. Walter, et al., from *Civilization Past and Present,* 6th ed., Vol. 2, pp. 533, 781. Glenview, IL: Scott, Foresman, 1987.

Part Seven: Thematic Readings

Ash, Barbara, "Communication Between Sexes: A War of the Words?" from *Knight Ridder News Service,* February 13, 1996. Reprinted with permission of Knight Ridder/Tribune Information Services.

Beekman, George, from *Computer Confluence: Exploring Tomorrow's Technology,* 3rd ed., pp. 203–206. Copyright © 1997 by Addison Wesley Longman, Inc. Reprinted by permission.

Borel, France, "The Decorated Body" from *Le Vetement Incarne—Les Metamorphoses du Corps.* © Calmann-Levy, 1992. Reprinted by permission of Calmann-Levy, Paris. English translation © by Ellen Dooling Draper as appeared in Parabola, Fall 1994, V. 19, No. 3, p. 74+. By permission of Ellen Dooling Draper.

Campbell, Neil A., Lawrence G. Mitchell, and Jane B. Reece, from *Biology: Concepts & Connections,* 2nd ed., p. 763. Copyright © 1997 by The Benjamin/Cummings Publishing Company. Reprinted by permission.

INDEX